THE CODES GUIDEBOOK FOR INTERIORS

THE CODES GUIDEBOOK FOR INTERIORS

Third Edition

Sharon Koomen Harmon, IIDA
Katherine E. Kennon, AIA

WILEY
John Wiley & Sons, Inc.

This book is printed on acid-free paper. ∞

Published by John Wiley & Sons, Inc., Hoboken, New Jersey

Published simultaneously in Canada

Library of Congress Cataloging-in-Publication Data:

Harmon, Sharon Koomen, 1964–
The codes guidebook for interiors / Sharon Koomen Harmon, Katherine E. Kennon.— 3rd ed.
p. cm.
ISBN 0-471-64864-7 (cloth : acid-free paper)
1. Building laws—United States. 2. Buildings—Specifications—United States. 3. Interior Architecture—United States. I. Kennon, Katherine E. II. Title.
KF5701.H37 2005

2004014942

Printed in the United States of America

10 9 8 7 6 5 4 3 2 1

To all of the victims who lost their lives
in recent tragedies
and the families they left behind,
including September 11, 2001,
and the various nursing home
and nightclub fires in recent years.

CONTENTS

Note: A more detailed table of contents can be found on the companion Web site www.wiley.com/harmon.

PREFACE

As we have seen in recent years, building codes cannot protect people in every situation. Since September 11, 2001, there has been much talk about creating stricter codes, standards, and federal regulations for the purpose of making buildings safer. But, realistically it is not practical to construct every building to withstand every possible catastrophe. Although the events of September 11 have not yet greatly affected the codes, there may be changes in the future. These changes, from what we have learned, will probably affect some aspects of the codes and standards more than others.

A wide variety of concepts and parameters must be considered in the creation of codes and standards. For example, in addition to September 11, there have been several recent nightclub and nursing home fires that have caused multiple deaths. The similarities and differences in the contributing factors of these tragedies must be considered. Codes will continue to change to address these types of events as well as other historical and social data, new technology in construction, and developments in building materials. All of these contribute to the health, safety, and welfare of the people who live in and use these buildings. This only proves how important it is to know the many aspects of the codes and standards as a designer. Understanding applicable federal regulations is just as critical.

The purpose of this book is to make the codes user-friendly and to provide a good overall understanding of codes, standards, and federal regulations that apply to interior projects. An understanding of the basics makes code research more efficient, which can save both time and money. This book also provides the necessary background required for code research and use of code, standard, and federal publications. The third edition of this book has been totally updated and enhanced. Following is a preview of what is included:

- Describes how to integrate codes, standards, and federal regulations throughout the design process
- Includes the newest information on the International Codes (I-Codes) by the International Code Council (ICC)

- ❑ Focuses on the most current and widely used building code, the *2003 International Building Code (IBC)*
- ❑ Includes information on the new National Fire Protection Association (NFPA) codes, such as their first building code, the *2003 NFPA 5000*
- ❑ Discusses how to use the NFPA's 2003 *Life Safety Code (LSC)* in relation to the building codes
- ❑ Discusses the relationship of the ANSI accessibility standard (*ICC/ANSI 117.1*) and the *ADA Accessibility Guidelines (ADAAG)* and how to use them in conjunction with the codes. Also includes information on the new *ADA-ABA Accessibility Guidelines*
- ❑ Includes information on the fire codes, energy codes, and performance codes as they correspond to the building codes
- ❑ Explains plumbing codes (and plumbing fixtures), mechanical codes, and electrical codes as they pertain to interior projects
- ❑ Mentions various code-related sustainability issues
- ❑ Explains the terms and concepts of the codes, standards, and federal regulations in a simple, organized format
- ❑ Adds multiple new examples and sample floor plans covering a wide variety of building types and occupancy classifications
- ❑ Adds many diagrams combining code- and accessibility-related requirements for items such as means of egress, toilet and bathing rooms, and finish and furniture-related items
- ❑ Includes an updated checklist in each chapter
- ❑ Discusses the newest information on finish and furniture standards and testing with new explanatory diagrams
- ❑ Includes the latest information on working with code officials and documenting your projects
- ❑ Addresses a variety of building and project types both large and small, and includes information on single-family homes as well as historical and existing buildings

Overall, this book focuses on codes, standards, and federal regulations that affect interior projects, and it is designed to be an educational and resource tool. We hope you find this book helpful.

SHARON KOOMEN HARMON, IIDA

KATHERINE E. KENNON, AIA

ACKNOWLEDGMENTS

First and foremost we want to thank our husbands and families for their continued patience and constant support. In addition, we are grateful to the many who made suggestions and comments as we strived to provide the best book possible. We would especially like to thank Hamid Naderi, PE, with the International Code Council, who did a thorough review of the final manuscript.

Numerous others made contributions to the figures in the book. They include Teresa Cox and Danny Roberts with Apco Graphics, Sandi Wake with Viking Group, Rick Carroll with ICC, and Cheryl Langway with NFPA. Thank you also to Amanda Miller, Vice President and Publisher at John Wiley & Sons, Inc., for the continued support, as well as to Paul Drougas, Lauren LaFrance, and Shannon Egan for helping us through the process.

A special thanks goes to our readers who continue to buy and recommend the book and whose praise of the book continues to motivate us. And finally, thank you to all of the various code jurisdictions, educators, and design professionals we have had the pleasure to work with through the years. You continue to give us inspiration.

INTRODUCTION

HOW TO USE THIS BOOK

Codes, standards, and federal regulations are an essential part of designing building interiors. Whether you are space planning the interior of a new building or making some minor changes in an existing building, all of these must be taken into consideration. They should become a natural part of every project you design.

The Codes Guidebook for Interiors is designed to help you as the designer. If you are a design professional, such as an architect, an interior designer, or an engineer, you must know the code. Most of the code publications deal with an entire building—exterior and interior as well as the structure of the building itself. This book concentrates on the codes that pertain to the interior of a building, helping you to minimize your research time. It will make the many interior codes, standards, and federal regulations user-friendly.

In this third edition of the *Codes Guidebook*, each section has been expanded to cover the important code issues more thoroughly as well as updated to inform you of the most current changes in the codes, standards, and federal regulations. The newest changes in the ICC and the NFPA codes and standards are included. Information on performance codes, energy codes, and fire codes has also been added. In addition, the most current accessibility issues are discussed in each chapter.

This book will assist you in your code research, providing you with multiple examples, explanatory diagrams, and checklists to help you to eliminate costly mistakes and time-consuming changes in a project.

Note

This book deals with interior codes only. Unless otherwise noted, it is assumed that the exterior walls—including doors and windows—and the existing shell of the building are either existing or already determined.

DEFINITIONS

Below are some common terms used throughout this book. Additional terms are provided at the beginning of each chapter and defined in the Glossary in the back of the book.

ACCESSIBLE: Unless otherwise noted, it refers to areas, products, or devices usable by persons with disabilities, as required by the codes, federal legislation such as the Americans with Disabilities Act, and accessibility standards.

AUTHORITY HAVING JURISDICTION (AHJ): Used by the code organizations to indicate organizations, offices, or individuals that administer and enforce the codes. In this book we designate these as jurisdictions, code departments, and code officials, respectively.

Note

All codes can be divided into two types. In the past, most codes were considered *prescriptive type* codes. These codes require specific compliance. Today, more *performance type* codes are being developed, which allow more than one solution to achieve the same results.

CODES DEPARTMENT: A local government agency that administers and enforces the codes within a jurisdiction. Some small jurisdictions may have a codes department that consists of only one person or code official, while some large jurisdictions may consist of many different agencies and departments. Also generally referred to as the AHJ by the codes.

CODE OFFICIAL: Also known as a building official, it is an employee of a codes department who has the authority to interpret, administer, and enforce the codes, standards, and regulations within that jurisdiction. A code official can have a number of different titles, including plans examiner, building inspector, and, sometimes, fire marshal. Also generally referred to as the AHJ by the codes.

JURISDICTION: A determined geographical area that uses the same codes, standards, and regulations. Each jurisdiction passes a law specifying which codes and standards are required and how they will be regulated. A jurisdiction could be as small as a township or as large as an entire state. The code jurisdiction of a project is determined by the location of the building. Also generally referred to as the AHJ by the codes.

PERFORMANCE CODE: A code that is more generally described and gives you an objective but not the specifics of how to achieve it. The focus is on the desired outcome, not a single solution, and compliance is based on meeting the criteria established by the performance code. (Engineering tools and methodologies are often used to substantiate the use of the code criteria.)

PRESCRIPTIVE CODE: A code that provides a specific requirement that must be met for the design, construction, and maintenance of a building. The focus is on a specific solution to achieve an objective or outcome based on historical experience and established engineering. Historically, codes have been prescriptive in nature.

USING CODES IN THE DESIGN PROCESS

The best time to research codes and use this book is in the early stages of a design project, preferably in the programming phase while the designs are still preliminary, before construction documents are started and construction costs are estimated. Figure I.1 summarizes how the various phases in the traditional design process relate to the typical steps taken during the code process. Refer to this chart as you work on a project to make sure you are covering the necessary code steps. (A more detailed flow chart of the code process is included in Chapter 10.) The *Codes Guidebook* is organized so that you can follow it while working on a design project from beginning to end—in the order you would typically research the codes.

Design Process	Code Process	Description
Programming/Pre-design	Preliminary Research	• Determine applicable codes, standards, and federal regulations • Preliminary code research to determine important code issues such as occupancy type, occupancy load, etc.
Schematic/Conceptual Design		• Incorporate code compliance into design, keeping in mind means of egress, rated walls, etc.
Design Development	Preliminary Review	• Meet with code official to review conflicting code requirements (optional unless using performance codes but could be helpful) • May also be done during Schematic Design Phase
Construction Documents		• Check specific technical requirements such as aisle widths, stair dimensions, clearances, finish classifications • Compare code and accessibility requirements • Incorporate requirements into final design • Specify and/or detail items as required to meet codes, standards, and federal requirements
Bidding Process	Permitting Process	• Contractor applies for building permit
Purchasing		• As items are ordered confirm compliance to applicable codes and standards
Construction Administration	Inspection Process	• Code officials review work by contractor to confirm work complies with approved construction documents
Client Move-in	Final Inspection	• Final code approval of construction must occur before client can move in
Post-Occupancy Evaluation		• Provide client with documentation necessary for them to maintain building and/or contents as required for codes and standards

Figure I.1 Comparison of Design and Code Process

ORGANIZATION OF THE BOOK

Note

You may have a project that is governed by more than one jurisdiction. For example, both a city and a state municipality may regulate a project.

The first chapter in *The Codes Guidebook for Interiors* gives a brief history of codes and provides some background on each of the main code publications, federal regulations, and standards organizations. Although this edition concentrates on the International Codes® (I-Codes®) by the International Code Council (ICC), Chapter 1 briefly explains the newer NFPA codes as well as including information on the more established National Fire Protection Association (NFPA) codes and standards. (First available in 2003, the newer NFPA codes are currently not as widely adopted as the ICC codes.) Information on performance codes, fire codes, and energy codes has also been added. (All of these codes are discussed throughout this revised edition of the book.) Chapter 1 is helpful in determining which publications are required for a project. Chapter 10, the last chapter in this book, discusses code officials and the code process. It describes how they work and how to work with them as well as how to document the codes you research. If you are new to codes research, you may want to review this chapter to gain a basic understanding before continuing on to the rest of the book.

The remaining chapters have been arranged with each pertaining to a specific code concept, including the related code, standard, and federal requirements for that topic. The chapters have been organized in the order that these issues are typically considered during an interior project. Once you have used Chapter 1 to determine which publications to apply to your project, we suggest you research the codes and standards in the following order:

- Occupancy Classifications and Loads (Chapter 2)
- Construction Types and Building Sizes (Chapter 3)
- Means of Egress (Chapter 4)
- Fire-Resistant Materials and Assemblies (Chapter 5)
- Fire Protection Systems (Chapter 6)
- Plumbing and Mechanical Requirements (Chapter 7)
- Electrical and Communication Requirements (Chapter 8)
- Finish and Furniture Selection (Chapter 9)

Note

When using the code tables, be sure to check all footnotes. They often specify extra conditions that can apply to your project.

Like the code publications, most of the chapters in this book build and add to the preceding ones. For example, occupancy classifications in Chapter 2 are important because many of the other codes are based on the occupancy of a building. Therefore, it is suggested that the first-time user read this book in the order it is written and use it as a guide while referencing the actual codes, standards, and federal publications. Each chapter in the book includes the most current code tables, realistic design examples, summary charts, helpful diagrams, and project checklists. Each chapter in this book also includes relevant accessibility requirements and performance code information.

An index is provided so you can refer to specific topics of interest. As you become familiar with the codes, use the index and the table of contents to direct you to the section of the book that applies to a specific code issue. Then refer to the appropriate code, standard, and federal publication to get the specific details.

Appendix A (which was Appendix E in the last edition) provides more information on the Americans with Disabilities Act (ADA). (See Accessibility Regulations later in this introduction.) Appendix B briefly discusses codes relating to the interior of private residences, referred to by the codes as "one- and two-family dwellings." Compared to the number of codes for commercial and public buildings, there are relatively few interior regulations for private residences. Since they have their own code publication, they have been addressed separately.

The interiors of existing and historical buildings are also discussed separately. Appendix C briefly describes these additional codes and regulations, concentrating on the new ICC code for existing buildings. Special consideration must also be given to historical buildings, since they usually have additional regulations on a local level within the code jurisdiction or within the township of the building.

The last two appendixes are for your reference. Appendix D lists the many abbreviations or acronyms used throughout this book and the code publications. Web site addresses are included as well. The complete list can be found on the companion Web site www.wiley.com/harmon. Appendix E provides the phone numbers and Web sites of many code, federal, standards, and national organizations. The full contact information for these organizations can be found on the companion Web site, so you can obtain your own code books and other reference material. Many bookstores throughout the country are listed as well. The Bibliography in the back of this book has been organized by topic to help you start or add to your own personal reference library.

Note

Appendix D, most of Appendix E, and the Bibliography can now be found on the companion Web site: www.wiley.com/harmon.

AVAILABLE CODES

Since the last edition of this book, the original three main code organizations in the United States have merged into one code organization. This organization, known as the International Code Council (ICC), publishes a comprehensive set of codes known as the *International Codes* (I-Codes). There are many code jurisdictions throughout the United States now using these codes. However, there may still be some jurisdictions that are using one of the older model codes—now known as *legacy* codes. Also new since the last edition of this book is another full set of codes (C3-Codes) published by the National Fire Protection Association (NFPA). Although many of the NFPA codes are relatively new, a code jurisdiction could be using any one of these available codes.

Overall, this third edition of *The Codes Guidebook for Interiors* concentrates on the descriptions and code tables from the *International Building Code*, as well as other code publications from the ICC. However, many jurisdictions also use NFPA publications such as the *Life Safety Code* and the *National Electrical Code*. (See Chapter 1.) These codes, as well as certain sections of the newer NFPA codes, are explained throughout this book in relation to the I-Codes. If you are working in more than one code jurisdiction, it is important for you to know the differences.

Note

Many jurisdictions are using the *International Building Code*. The first official adoption took place in May 2000.

PRESCRIPTIVE AND PERFORMANCE

Performance-based codes have gained more prevalence since the last edition of this book. Both the ICC and the NFPA now include performance criteria in addition to prescriptive requirements. (See previous Definitions.) The NFPA includes the performance-based requirements as a separate chapter within many of their publications. By contrast, the ICC produces a separate performance code publication that can be used in conjunction with their other codes when recognized by the code jurisdiction. (See Chapter 1.)

The performance codes are meant to be used in conjunction with the prescriptive codes. If you have a project with an unusual design that requires the use of a performance code, most often performance-based criteria will be used for a particular part of the project and the standard prescriptive codes will be used for the rest. It would be unusual for an entire project to be designed using only performance codes. When a performance code requirement is used, there is more responsibility on the designer. Not only do the performance-related criteria need to be correctly documented, but you must also prove how you are meeting these criteria (e.g., fire models, testing, etc.).

Note

When discussing prescriptive codes, the term *requirements* is often used. However, performance codes typically set *criteria*, *goals*, or *objectives*.

Various performance codes will be mentioned in each chapter of this book as they relate to the corresponding prescriptive codes. Chapter 10 will discuss how to document the use of performance codes for codes review. Ultimately, the performance codes can be used to explore unique designs and allow for the use of new technology. Yet, since performance-type codes are fairly new, it may take a while for them to be used widely. Even if you do not typically use them, by becoming familiar with the various performance requirements you will gain more insight into the prescriptive codes.

ACCESSIBILITY REGULATIONS

Today, accessible design is required for the majority of interior projects. The most current building codes now include accessibility regulations and reference the ICC/ANSI accessibility standard *ICC/ANSI A117.1*. Many jurisdictions also refer to the ICC/ANSI standard as a stand-alone accessibility document. In addition, federal law has required the use of the *ADA Accessibility Guidelines (ADAAG)* in many projects since the early 1990s. A totally revised ADA guideline has been available from the Access Board since July 2004. However, until it is approved by the appropriate government agencies, it will not be enforceable. (See section titled New ADA Guidelines in Appendix A on page 422.) (Other federal accessibility regulations are discussed in Chapter 1.)

Since accessibility affects all aspects of a design, accessibility standards and the ADA are discussed throughout this book as they relate to each relevant topic. For example, accessible toilet facilities are discussed in the plumbing chapter, and accessible ramps are discussed in the means of egress chapter. Because the new ADA guidelines have been closely associated with the more current editions of the ICC/ANSI standards, many of these requirements are included as well. Appendix A elaborates on the compliance and enforcement issues of the ADA and the ADA guidelines.

Note

Universal design is a term often used with accessibility. However, universal design is more inclusive—making sure a design considers the needs of different age groups as well as persons with disabilities.

Like the codes discussed in this book, not every specific accessibility dimension and requirement has been mentioned. Instead, a general outline of the applicable accessibility regulations is discussed to aid you in your research. Although more accessibility-related information has been added to this book, for the specific requirements and additional information, you must still consult the ADA and its related guidelines, specific chapters within the building codes, and any other accessibility regulations required by a jurisdiction. (When discrepancies are found between the ADA guidelines and the ICC/ANSI standard, the strictest requirements are typically discussed.)

Note

The codes and accessibility publications do not always use the same metric conversion for a particular dimension. When discussing codes in this book, the code-related metric numbers have been used, and when explaining accessibility requirements the metrics from the ADA guidelines and the ICC/ANSI standard have been used.

FIGURES IN THE BOOK

Most of the figures in this book have been updated since the last edition and many new ones have been added. Metrics have been included as well. In the diagrams, these metric numbers are shown in parentheses, similar to other code and accessibility documents, and represent millimeter measurements unless noted otherwise.

Many of the diagrams include both code and accessibility requirements. For example, the means of egress diagrams in Chapter 4 include clearances and minimum dimensions as required in the building codes, the ADA guidelines, and the ICC/ANSI standard. In each case, the most stringent requirements were used. In some instances, notes have been added to clarify conflicting requirements. When working on a project, however, be sure to consult the original document as required by your jurisdiction.

GETTING STARTED

Note

This book is not intended to be a substitute for any code, standard, or federal publication required by a jurisdiction. It should be used as a reference book to gain a better understanding of the codes and to guide you through the code process.

This book should be used as a guide to assist you in researching the codes and to help you organize your projects. It is not a substitute or replacement for the actual code publications. It would be impossible to discuss every specific code, standard, and federal regulation in one book. In addition, each jurisdiction will have slightly different requirements. Therefore, this book must be used in conjunction with the code publications. You must still carry out a thorough investigation of the codes and standards and work closely with code officials, engineers, and other professionals as required by the scope of your project.

Before beginning a project you need to know which code, standards, and federal publications must be referenced. Use Chapter 1 to help you get started. To confirm which codes and standards are required, contact the codes department in the jurisdiction of your project. Ask the codes department to verify the publications that must be referenced and notify you of any required local codes or amendments. Since federal publications are not typically regulated on a local level, you will need to keep abreast of the latest changes in the laws. We will explain how to do this as well. It is important for you to have the actual publications on hand during the project so specific codes and regulations can be referenced and verified.

MINIMUM REQUIREMENTS

Note

Rather than viewing codes as restrictive or as a burden, remember that they allow people to feel safe as they live and work in the buildings you design.

Always remember that codes, standards, and federal regulations have been developed as *minimum* requirements. There may be equivalent solutions, and there are often superior alternatives and solutions available. When designing a space, it is up to you to consider the project as a whole. By working with your client, the building requirements, and the budget of the project, you can make informed design decisions. Through the creative thinking process and by working in conjunction with the code officials and other professionals, you, as the designer, can develop the best design solutions for everyone.

CHAPTER 1

ABOUT THE CODES

A variety of codes regulate the design and construction of buildings and building interiors. In addition, there are a large number of standards and federal regulations that play a major role. The most nationally recognized codes, laws, and standard organizations are described in this chapter. Most of them are referenced and discussed throughout this book as they pertain to the interior of a building.

As you read about each of these codes, standards, and regulations, keep in mind that *not all of them will be enforced by every code jurisdiction.* (See Definitions in Introduction.) The jurisdiction chooses which publications to use and the edition of each publication. For example, a jurisdiction could decide to adopt the 2003 edition of the *NFPA 101, Life Safety Code* as a stand-alone document or to be used in conjunction with a building code. The jurisdiction could also make a variety of local amendments that add or delete clauses from the code. You must know which codes are being enforced in order to do your code research for a particular project. (See Chapter 10.)

Note

There are now two main sets of codes. The ICC codes have been available longer and are used in many jurisdictions. Many of the NFPA codes first became available in 2003.

In addition, each code publication references certain standards; therefore, the standards that need to be used depend on the required code publications. Other standards may not be referenced by a publication. Instead, they may be individually required or may be accepted as industrywide standards. For example, some finish standards are not *required,* but you will want to follow them for safety and liability reasons. The only regulations that are consistent in every jurisdiction are the federal regulations that are made mandatory by law.

A BRIEF HISTORY

The use of regulatory codes can be traced back as far as the eighteenth century BCE to the *Code of Hammurabi,* a collection of laws governing Babylonia. The *Code of Hammurabi* made the builder accountable for the houses he built. If one of his buildings fell down and killed someone, the builder would be put to death.

In the United States, the first codes addressed fire prevention. The first building law on record was in 1625 in what was then called New Amsterdam (now New York). It governed the types and locations of roof coverings to protect the buildings from chimney sparks. Then, in the 1800s, there were a number of large building fires, including the Chicago fire of 1871, which caused many fatalities. As a result, some of the larger U.S. cities developed their own municipal building *codes.* Some of these are still in existence today. In the mid-1800s, the National Board of Fire Underwriters was set up to provide insurance companies with information on which to base their fire damage claims. One of the results was the publication of the 1905 *National Building Code*—a code that helped spark the original three model building codes.

Meanwhile, the federal government was also creating *regulations.* Many of these laws pertained to government-built and -owned buildings. Some were national laws that superseded other required codes. In 1973, in an attempt to control government intervention, Congress passed the *Consumer Product Safety Act* and formed the Consumer Product Safety Commission (CPSC). The goal of the commission is to prevent the necessity of federal regulations by encouraging industry self-regulation and *standardization.* This resulted in the creation of a number of new standards-writing organizations and trade associations. Additional legislation since then has been used to promote this even further.

Note

For a comprehensive list of the code organizations, federal agencies, standards organizations, and trade associations, see Appendix D and Appendix E and the companion Web site: www.wiley.com/harmon.

Today, there are many separate codes in existence in the United States, a wide variety of federal regulations, and hundreds of standards organizations and regulatory and trade associations in almost every industry. Only the most widely recognized have been described below, to provide you with the groundwork as they are discussed throughout this book. (For more information refer to the resources in the Bibliography.)

CODE PUBLICATIONS

Codes are a collection of regulations, ordinances, and other statutory requirements put together by various organizations. Each jurisdiction decides which codes it will follow and enforce. (See more on jurisdictions in Chapter 10.) Once certain codes are adopted, they become law within that jurisdiction. Many changes have occurred in the code industry in the last five to ten years that have affected the codes available for adoption by a jurisdiction. For more than 50 years there had been three main model code organizations that created and published many of the codes used throughout the United States. They included the Building Officials Code Administrators International (BOCA), the Southern Building

CODE AND STANDARDS CHANGES

Each code and standards organization has its own procedures for changing and updating the requirements in its publications. Most of them use a *consensus* process to revise their publications. Each organization has a membership that consists of a wide range of individuals. These could include code officials, design professionals, building users, academics, manufacturers, building owners, consumers, contractors, and others. These members make up the committees that oversee the proposed changes. However, both members and nonmembers can typically propose and comment on changes either in writing or in person at open public hearings.

Many standards organizations as well as the National Fire Protection Association (NFPA) use a consensus process developed by the American National Standards Institute (ANSI). Once a code or standard is ready to be revised, a *call for proposals* is issued. For example, the NFPA will request proposals for changes to a code or standard. As the proposals are received, they are sent to a technical committee made up of NFPA members for review. The committee makes revisions if necessary and then reissues them for public comment. Typically both members and non-members can submit comments. These comments are used to modify the proposal so that it can be presented for recommendation and discussion at one of NFPA's membership meetings. Here, the various change proposals are voted on by the membership for the purpose of making a recommendation to the overseeing Standards Council. This council takes the votes into consideration but makes the final decision.

The International Code Council (ICC) uses what it calls a governmental consensus process—or open process. (This was also used by the legacy model code organizations.) Much of the process is the same as described above. The main difference is that the final decision is made by the "governmental" members of the ICC, rather than a small group or council. These governmental members consist of code officials and employees of the governmental agencies that administer and enforce the codes. Although this does not include all ICC members, it is a large part of their membership base.

Once a proposed code or standard change is voted on and approved, it is adopted by the organization. Usually once a year, or as needed, the organization will publish the most current changes in an addendum or supplement. When the next full edition of the code or standard is published, it incorporates all the changes into one text.

Code Congress International (SBCCI), and the International Conference of Building Officials (ICBO). However, in 1994 these three organizations agreed to form an umbrella organization called the International Code Council (ICC). In 2003, the legacy organizations (BOCA, ICBO, and SBCCI) formally consolidated into the ICC. As they began the integration process, the model code organizations put their effort into one set of codes and eventually stopped producing their own separate code publications. Now, rather than three different sets of codes

Note

The older model codes are now collectively known as the *legacy* codes.

there is one complete set of codes published by the ICC, known as the *International Codes*—or *I-Codes* for short. The first code produced by the ICC was the *International Plumbing Code* in 1995.

However, in the late 1990s the National Fire Protection Association (NFPA) decided to create its own set of codes. Prior to this, NFPA mainly created and published standards and a few codes such as the *Life Safety Code* and the *National Electrical Code*. Now it has a complete set of codes, some of which were created in collaboration with other industry organizations. This series of codes is called the *Comprehensive Consensus Codes*—or *C3-Codes* for short. Currently, the NFPA's collaboration partners include the International Association of Plumbing and Mechanical Officials (IAPMO), the Western Fire Chiefs Association (WFCA), and the American Society of Heating, Refrigeration, and Air-Conditioning Engineers (ASHRAE). The various interior-related code publications from both the ICC and NFPA are summarized in Figure 1.1.

In the past, the model codes catered to certain regions of the country. The newer codes by the ICC and NFPA now take into account the many regional differences that can be found throughout the United States. For example, certain coastal states need more restrictive seismic building code provisions to allow for the many earthquakes in that area, and the northern states need codes to allow for long periods of below-freezing temperatures. All these various requirements are now in the current building codes. In some cases, a code jurisdiction will add amendments to the code they adopt to create requirements unique to their area.

In addition, some states and cities continue to maintain their own set of codes. Until the comprehensive set of I-Codes by the ICC became available, a number of state codes were based on or closely followed the model codes. These codes were usually created in response to unique situations or unique problems that had occurred. Often they set stricter building requirements. Boston, for example, established the *Boston Fire Code* as a result of fatal fires that occurred in the city. A devastating hurricane in the state of Florida prompted them to create their own set of statewide codes. Other states with their own codes include California, New York, and North Carolina.

However, even the differences between these customized codes are becoming less obvious as more states and cities are working closely with the code organizations. For example, many states are working with the ICC to revise the *International Building Code* as required for their state. The ICC then reprints the code specifically for that state as a customized code. Some of these locations have a complete set of unique codes, while others may have just one or two special code publications and use one of the available codes for everything else.

ICC **I-Codes®**		NFPA **C3-Codes**	
IBC®	International Building Code®	**NFPA 5000®**	Building Construction and Safety Code®
ICC PC	ICC Performance Code for Buildings and Facilities		(performance requirements included in each code)
IFC®	International Fire Code®	**NFPA 1®**	Uniform Fire Code® (UFC)
	(similar requirements found in IBC and IFC)	**NFPA 101®**	Life Safety Code® (LSC)
IPC®	International Plumbing Code®	**IAPMOs**	Uniform Plumbing Code® (UPC)
IMC®	International Mechanical Code®	**IAPMOs**	Uniform Mechanical Code® (UMC)
ICC EC™	ICC Electrical Code™ - Administrative Provisions (references NEC)	**NFPA 70®**	National Electrical Code® (NEC)
IECC®	International Energy Conservation Code®	**NFPA 900®**	Building Energy Code® (based on ASHRAE standards 90.1 and 90.2)
IRC®	International Residential Code® for One- and Two-Dwelling Units		(residential requirements included in other codes)
IEBC®	International Existing Building Code®		(existing building requirements included in each code)
IFGC®	International Fuel Gas Code®	**NFPA 54®**	National Fuel Gas Code® also refer to: NFPA 30®, Flammable and Combustible Liquid Code NFPA 30A®, Code for Motor Fuel Dispensing Facilities and Repair Garages NFPA 58®, Liquefied Petroleum Gas Code

NOTE: This chart includes interior related codes. Other codes dealing with overall building or site-related items are not included.

Figure 1.1 Comparison of Code Publications (This chart is a summary of publications from the International Code Council® and the National Fire Protection Association that pertain to interior projects. Neither the ICC® nor the NFPA assume responsibility for the accuracy or the completion of this chart.)

Figure 1.2 is a map that indicates the number of states currently using one or more of the I-Codes. This could include an original I-Code or one that was revised by a city or state. Some of the NFPA codes, such as the *NFPA 5000*, are fairly new and have not been reviewed or adopted by many jurisdictions in their code adoption cycle. This may change in the future. In addition, both the ICC and NFPA work with federal and state agencies for possible adoption. For example, the U.S.

- 44 states plus Washington, D.C. and the Department of Defense use the *International Building Code*
- 44 states plus Washington, D.C. use the *International Residential Code*
- 36 states plus Washington, D.C. use the *International Fire Code*

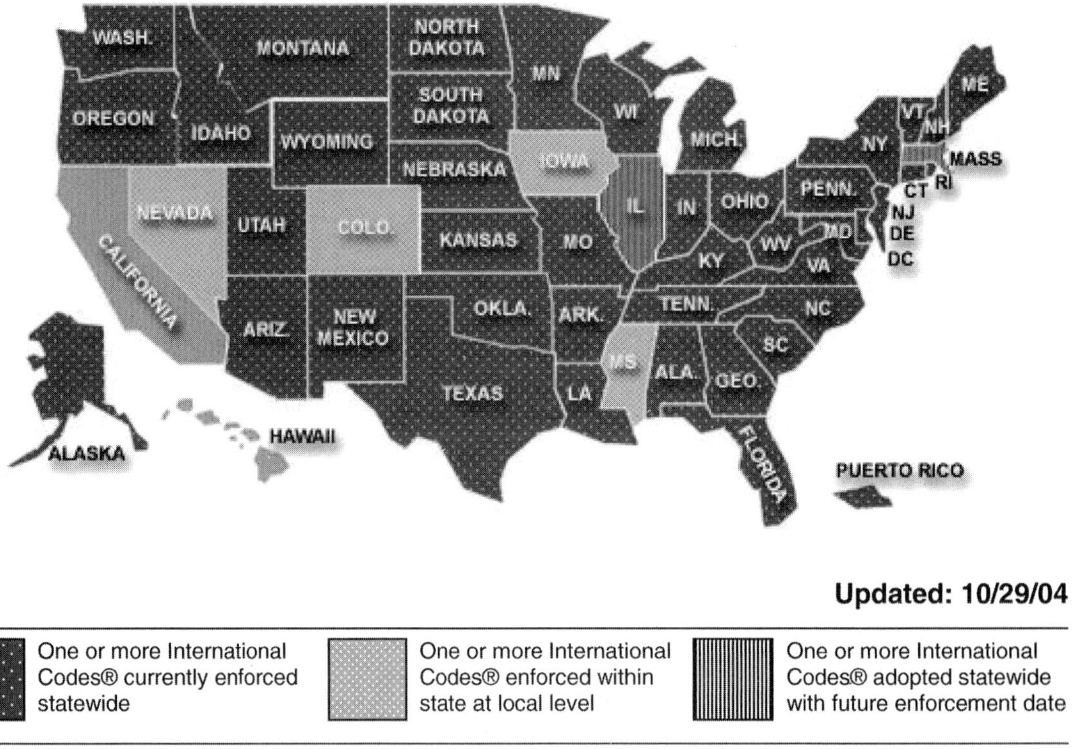

Figure 1.2 International Code Adoptions (Reproduced with permission from the International Code Council, www.iccsafe.org. See Web site for most current edition.)

Department of Defense and the National Park Services currently require the use of some I-Codes in their buildings. The Department of Veterans Affairs and the Centers for Medicare and Medicaid Services utilize the *Life Safety Code*. You can go to both the ICC and the NFPA Web sites to learn about the latest code adoptions. (See Resources in Appendix E.)

It is extremely important to know what codes and standards apply to your project before you start. Each of the codes produced by the ICC and NFPA, as they pertain to interior projects, are described in this section. The various standards are described in the next section. Be sure to contact the local jurisdiction to obtain a list of the approved code publications and any other special requirements or addendums.

Building Codes

Building codes stress the construction requirements of an entire building and place restrictions on hazardous materials or equipment used within a building. The principal purpose is to ensure the public health, safety, and welfare of the people using these buildings. This includes structural, mechanical, electrical, plumbing, life safety (egress), fire safety (detection and suppression), natural light and air, accessibility standards, and energy conservation. Although other codes and standards may be referenced, the building codes cover each of these topics.

In the past, the three model building codes were the most common building codes used throughout the country. They were the *BOCA National Building Code (NBC)* published by BOCA, the *Standard Building Code (SBC)* published by SBCCI, and the *Uniform Building Code (UBC)* published by ICBO. New editions of what are now called *legacy codes* are no longer being created. The older editions will stop being used as jurisdictions update the codes they enforce. Now the option is to adopt the *International Building Code (IBC)* published by ICC or the *Building Construction and Safety Code® (NFPA 5000®)* published by NFPA. The *IBC* was first published in 2000, with the most current edition being 2003 and the next edition due in 2006. *NFPA 5000* was first published in 2003, with the next edition due in 2006. As with the previous model codes, the ICC and the NFPA typically work on a three-year cycle, but this might vary as the NFPA coordinates the development of their publications. Usually, each state or jurisdiction adopts one of these two building codes or is covered by a state building code based on one of these codes (as described above). Since the *IBC* was published before the *NFPA 5000* and is based on the earlier legacy codes which were used extensively throughout the United States, many more states and local jurisdictions are currently using the *IBC* or a code based on the *IBC*. According to Figure 1.2, more than 40 states are using the *IBC*. You can see why it is so important to know which codes are being used in a particular jurisdiction to determine which requirements must be met.

> **Note**
> Since the model code organizations no longer publish their respective codes, they will not be discussed in this book.

> **Note**
> Some jurisdictions mention the "model" codes in their laws. As a result, the ICC has republished some of their codes with an older model code name on them until the laws can be changed.

The organization of the two main building codes is different. The *IBC* is organized by various aspects of a building and continues to use the CABO Common Code Format. This format was started by the model code organizations in 1994. Therefore, all the chapters in the *IBC* are arranged in the same order as the last editions of the model building codes. This allows designers working on projects in different jurisdictions with different codes to find information easily. Specific requirements for each occupancy or building type are referenced within each chapter.

The *NFPA 5000* uses a different format. Instead, it is organized using the new NFPA Manual of Style, where there are several key chapters in the beginning and end of the book and the rest of the chapters are divided by occupancy type. (This

IBC (2003) **International Building Code**		NFPA 5000 (2003) **Building Construction & Safety Code**		LSC (2003) **Life Safety Code***	
Chapter 2	Definitions	**Chapter 3**	Definitions	**Chapter 3**	Definitions
Separate	References separate code: *ICC Performance Code for Buildings and Facilities (ICCPC)*	**Chapter 5**	Performance-Based Option	**Chapter 5**	Performance-Based Option
Chapter 3	Use and Occupancy Classification	**Chapter 6** **Varies**	Classification of Occupancy, Classification of Hazard of Contents, and Special Operations Multiple chapters 16–30 each on a different occupancy classification	**Chapter 6** **Varies**	Classification of Occupancy and Hazard Contents Multiple (even) chapters 12–42 each on a different occupancy classification
Chapter 4	Special Detailed Requirements Based on Use and Occupancy	**Chapter 31** **Chapter 33** **Chapter 34**	Occupancies in Special Structures High-Rise Buildings High Hazard Contents	**Chapter 11**	Special Structures and High-Rise Buildings
Chapter 5	General Building Heights and Areas	**Chapter 7**	Construction Types and Height and Area Requirements		(none)
Chapter 6	Types of Construction	**Chapter 7**	Construction Types and Height and Area Requirements		(none)
Chapter 7	Fire-Resistance-Rated Construction	**Chapter 8**	Fire-Resistive Materials and Construction	**Chapter 8**	Features of Fire Protection
Chapter 8	Interior Finishes	**Chapter 10**	Interior Finish	**Chapter 10**	Interior Finish, Contents, and Furnishings
Chapter 9	Fire Protection Systems	**Chapter 55**	Fire Protection Systems and Equipment	**Chapter 9**	Building Service and Fire Protection Equipment
Chapter 10	Means of Egress	**Chapter 11**	Means of Egress	**Chapter 7**	Means of Egress
Chapter 11	Accessibility	**Chapter 12**	Accessibility		(none)
Chapter 12	Interior Environment	**Chapter 49**	Interior Environment		(none)
Chapter 13	Energy Efficiency	**Chapter 51**	Energy Efficiency		(none)
Chapter 24	Glass and Glazing	**Chapter 46**	Glass and Glazing		(none)
Chapter 26	Plastic	**Chapter 48**	Plastics		(none)
Chapter 27	Electrical	**Chapter 52**	Electrical Systems		(none)
Chapter 28	Mechanical Systems	**Chapter 50**	Mechanical Systems		(none)
Chapter 29	Plumbing Systems	**Chapter 53**	Plumbing Systems		(none)
Chapter 31	Special Construction	**Chapter 32**	Special Construction		(none)
Chapter 34	Existing Structures OR use separate code: *International Existing Building Code (IEBC)*	**Chapter 15**	Building Rehabilitation	**Varies**	Multiple (odd) chapters 13–39 each on a different occupancy classification
Chapter 35	Referenced Standards	**Chapter 2**	Referenced Standards	**Chapter 2**	Referenced Standards

***NOTE:** This chart includes interior-related chapters only. The *Life Safety Code* is not a buildings code so it will not have all the same type of chapters but it is often used in conjunction with a building code.

Figure 1.3 Comparison of Building Codes and Life Safety Code (This chart is a summary of information contained in the *International Building Code® (IBC®),* the *NFPA 5000®*, and the *Life Safety Code® (LSC®)*. Neither the ICC nor the NFPA assume responsibility for the accuracy or the completion of this chart.)

format is being incorporated into all of the NFPA publications.) The occupancy chapters allow you to go directly to the chapter that pertains to your building type to start the code review. The particular occupancy chapter will reference the various other chapters as required. The most important building interior–related chapters in both the *IBC* and the *NFPA 5000* are summarized in the comparative list found in Figure 1.3.

Although there are more than 30 chapters and 10 appendixes in the *IBC* and even more chapters in the *NFPA 5000*, not all of them pertain to the interior of a building. The most common chapters (not including the *NFPA 5000* occupancy chapters) that you will need for working on building interiors are listed as follows and are discussed throughout this book. You should become the most familiar with these, although certain projects may require you to refer to other sections of the building code as well. For example, you may also need to look up information in the chapters on glass and glazing, plastic, or existing structures.

Note

The *IBC* contains appendixes with additional accessibility requirements. However, these are only required when specifically adopted by a jurisdiction.

Use or Occupancy Classification
Special Use or Occupancy Requirements
Types of Construction
Fire-Resistant Materials and Construction
Interior Finishes
Fire Protection Systems
Means of Egress
Accessibility
Interior Environment
Plumbing Systems

Note

A more comprehensive list of code adoptions can be found on the ICC and NFPA Web sites. (See resources in Appendix E.)

To cover as much as possible, the building codes frequently reference other codes and standards within their text. Each code organization publishes a number of other codes and standards that may be referenced. These include a plumbing code, a mechanical code, a fire prevention code, an energy conservation code, and an existing structures code, many of which are described later in this chapter. Many of these same topics are listed as chapters in the *IBC* and *NFPA 5000*. However, these chapters typically refer you to another code or standard. (Refer to Figure 1.1 for a full list of interior-related code publications.) Performance codes (described next) are also referenced within each building code. *NFPA 5000* includes a chapter within the text, while the *IBC* tells you to reference its own separate performance code publication. In addition, other nationally recognized standards organizations and publications are referenced by each of the codes. (See the section on Standards Organizations later in this chapter.)

Performance Codes

Note

The *SFPE Engineering Guide to Performance-Based Fire Analysis and Design of Buildings* is a good resource when working with performance-based codes.

Traditionally, codes have been more prescriptive in nature. A *prescriptive* code gives you a precise requirement so you know exactly what needs to be done to meet the code. A *performance* code, on the other hand, gives you an objective but not the specifics of how to achieve it. Yet, some requirements in the prescriptive codes have also included parameters for the use of alternate methods, materials, and systems that can be considered more performance-like. These alternate methods allowed some flexibility in the past; however, the traditional code does not describe how to show equivalency, which can make it hard to obtain approval from your code official. A performance-based code, instead, provides more structure by stating an objective and providing an administrative process to follow. It shows the designer how to meet these objectives, how to document the results, and how to work with the code official to obtain final approval.

A good example of the difference between a prescriptive code and a performance criterion can be found in the spacing of guardrail elements. In the *International Building Code* the prescriptive requirement specifies that rail elements must be spaced so "that a 4-inch-diameter (102 mm) sphere cannot pass through any opening up to a height of 34 inches (864 mm)." This requirement was developed specifically with children in mind. The *ICC Performance Code* does not mandate this narrow spacing. Instead, it specifies "that the openings shall be of an appropriate size and configuration to keep people from falling through based on upon the anticipated age of the occupants." If it can be shown that children are not expected to frequent the building, then different spacing of the guardrail elements may be allowed. An example might be a manufacturing facility.

Note

The use of performance codes actually started in other countries. Australia was one of the first to use them.

The development of performance-based codes separate from prescriptive codes is fairly recent in the United States. The International Code Council first published the *ICC Performance Code for Building and Facilities (ICCPC)* in 2001. Updated again in 2003, it is now on a three-year revision cycle. The *ICCPC* is meant to be used in conjunction with the *IBC*, as well as most of the other I-Codes. It addresses the overall scope of each of the I-Codes in performance-based language and describes how to use them together. However, the *ICCPC* cannot be used with the other I-Codes unless it is adopted by the code jurisdiction.

The NFPA, on the other hand, does not plan to have a separate text for performance criteria. Instead, the new *NFPA 5000* and the *Life Safety Code* starting with the 2000 edition (which will be discussed later) each include both performance requirements and prescriptive requirements. The information is organized in both publications in similar ways. Each has a Chapter 5 titled "Performance-Based Option." In addition, NFPA recommends that you reference Chapter 4 in each text. This general chapter discusses some of the code's goals, assumptions, and objectives that give you additional insight to using prescriptive type codes. Since a jurisdiction that adopts one of the NFPA codes does have the option to exclude Chapter 5, you need to confirm that you are able to use the performance requirements if you are referring to these codes.

The purpose of performance codes is to allow for more creative design solutions in the use of materials and systems of construction and to allow innovative engineering to solve code requirements in ways that can be specific to each

USING PERFORMANCE CODES

With the introduction of performance requirements within the code publications, using performance codes on an interior project is an option. By using performance codes you may be able to specify innovative materials and develop unique design solutions for your projects. Performance codes can be especially helpful when trying to incorporate sustainable design into a project or when working on an existing building with unusual characteristics. However, it is the designer's responsibility to convince the client and the code official that the proposed situation meets the performance code criteria. You must take additional steps to prove that your design will provide equivalent safety to the same prescriptive requirements. Examples of additional steps that may be required include:

- ❑ *Acquire data.* You can work with an engineer or other consultant to obtain specific data or develop new data through the use of available design guides, calculation methods, and computer models. These are currently used in supporting fire and structural-related scenarios but may have many new applications in the future.
- ❑ *Obtain reports.* You can do your own research on specific materials and assemblies by obtaining reports from product evaluation services (see separate inset in this chapter) and working with the manufacturer of a particular product. Existing products often have already gone through the necessary testing and have available evaluation reports. But, if you develop something new, you may be able to work with a manufacturer to obtain the necessary tests and reports.
- ❑ *Find comparables.* You can look to other buildings and projects with similar situations or a similar use of a product. Contact the designers and contractors involved in those projects for information that could be useful. (This usually cannot be your only supportive documentation.)

In the future more alternatives will become available to help analyze and support your use of performance codes. The best method to support your solution depends on the extent of the performance criteria as well as the uniqueness of your design. No matter which steps you take to provide documentation, the ultimate goal is to show that the safety of the building occupants will be maintained. It is also suggested that you work with the code official early in the design process to establish what criteria will be required for approval.

Note

Other countries that use performance codes include Australia, Canada, Japan, New Zealand, and the United Kingdom.

project. In designing to meet the requirements of a performance code, there are a number of parameters or assumptions that must be determined in the beginning of a project. (See inset titled *Risk Factors and Hazards in Occupancies* on page 45.) These assumptions are used to create performance guidelines that are followed throughout the design process. (Similar assumptions were used by the code organizations in the development of the prescriptive codes.)

When using performance codes, it becomes even more important to start working with the code official in the early stages of a project. An overall team approach is actually encouraged by the code. For the solution to be acceptable, the code official must agree that your design and the supporting documentation meet the intent of the code. Performance codes are intended to allow for creativity in design and engineering while still providing for the necessary safety and welfare concerns of the code. You will need to prove this to the code official. (See Chapter 10 and the inset on page 19, *Using Performance Codes*, for additional information.) Performance codes may be applied to any design project if allowed by the code official. However, they may be most effective in unique situations, including the use of new technology, incorporating sustainable design, and the reuse of existing and historic buildings, which may not easily meet the strict requirement of the prescriptive codes. In most cases, performance codes will only apply to part of a project and will not totally replace the required prescriptive codes.

Fire Codes

Both the ICC and the NFPA now have a fire code as well. The first fire code produced by the ICC was in 2000 and is called the *International Fire Code (IFC)*. Like the other I-Codes it is on a three-year revision cycle with newer editions in 2003 and 2006. In 2003, NFPA came out with a new fire code, which was developed in partnership with the Western Fire Chiefs Association (WFCA). Titled the *Uniform Fire Code® (UFC)* or *NFPA 1®*, it integrates the older *NFPA 1, Fire Prevention Code* with the *Uniform Fire Code* originally developed by the ICBO and WFCA. This new version is organized similarly to the other C3-Codes and includes a chapter on performance-based design. It will be revised again in 2006. Much of the *UFC* is taken from various other codes and standards produced by NFPA, such as the *Life Safety Code*. When a specific requirement comes from another code, the *UFC* refers to the code so that you know where the requirement originated.

When adopted by a jurisdiction, the fire code is typically used in conjunction with the related building code. The fire code addresses building conditions that are hazardous and could cause possible fire and explosions. This could be due to a number of reasons such as the type of occupancy or use of the space, the type of materials stored, and/or the way certain materials are handled.

Although applicable to almost all building types, it becomes more prevalent when you are working with a building type that may not be fully covered by the building code. For example, the fire code gives you specifics for a paint booth in a car shop, a commercial kitchen in a restaurant, and a dry-cleaning facility.

However, there are a few chapters or sections in each of the fire codes that you will reference more frequently. They include the following:

Means of Egress
Fire-Resistant Construction
Fire Protection Systems
Interior Finishes
Furnishings and Decorative Materials

These are similar to the chapters in the building codes. In addition, the fire codes each have a chapter on emergency planning, which addresses such things as evacuation plans and fire drills for each type of occupancy. Although this chapter is geared more toward building owners and fire departments, there are certain occupancy provisions that may also affect an interior project such as signage and keying requirements. Many of the various fire code requirements as they relate to interiors and the chapters listed above will be mentioned throughout this book.

Life Safety Code®

The *Life Safety Code (LSC)* was one of the first codes published by the NFPA. It is also referred to as *NFPA 101®*. Like the building codes, the *LSC* is typically revised every three years. More current editions would include 2003 and 2006, yet a jurisdiction may still be using an older version. The *LSC* is not a building code. It is a life safety code that concentrates on problems involving the removal or evacuation of all persons from a building. As stated in the *LSC*, the purpose of the code is to "establish minimum requirements that will provide a reasonable degree of safety from fire in buildings and structures." The difference between the *LSC* and the building codes can also be seen in Figure 1.3. You will notice that the *LSC* chapters correspond to those found in the *IBC* and the *NFPA 5000*, but since it is not a building code it does not address all the issues required for the construction of a building. For example, it does not include chapters on accessibility, glazing, or plumbing.

Note

The *Life Safety Code (LSC)* does have two corresponding documents: *NFPA 101A, Alternative Approaches to Life Safety* and *NFPA 101B, Means of Egress for Buildings and Structures*. (See Chapter 4.) A jurisdiction has the option of adopting these documents with the *LSC* or in place of the *LSC*.

The *LSC* uses the NFPA's Manual of Style format. The first part of the *LSC* concentrates on the broad topics of occupancies, means of egress, and fire protection. The remainder is divided into chapters by occupancy classification for both new and existing buildings. For example, there is a chapter on new apartment buildings and existing apartment buildings. This distinction is made to provide older buildings with additional safety and protective devices so they are virtually as safe as newly constructed buildings. (This is different from the *NFPA 5000*, which has only one chapter per occupancy and puts all existing requirements into one separate chapter.) Once you know the occupancy classification of your project and whether it is considered new or existing, most of your research will be limited to one chapter of the *LSC*. This occupancy chapter will direct you to other chapters as required. (See Chapter 2 for more detail.)

Note

A proposal has already been approved by the ICC to revise the first six chapters in the 2003 edition of the *IEC*, making it easier to use.

Starting in 2000, the *LSC* also includes a chapter on alternative performance-based options, giving you the ability to select the requirements that best suit your project. (See Performance Codes and the inset titled *Using Performance Codes*, earlier in this chapter.) Like other codes, the *LSC* also references additional standard publications within its text. These are typically other NFPA standards, such as *NFPA 80, Standard for Fire Doors and Windows*, and *NFPA 220, Standard on Types of Building Construction.* (See the section on the NFPA standards later in this chapter.)

The *LSC* is used throughout the United States and in several other countries. It is currently used in at least one jurisdiction in every state and has been adopted statewide by at least 35 states in the United States. (A map of locations can be found on the NFPA Web site. See Appendix E.) When a jurisdiction requires you to use the *LSC* in conjunction with a building code, you must satisfy both sets of requirements in your design. Sometimes a requirement in the *LSC* might conflict with a requirement in the building code. When this occurs you need to use the more restrictive requirement or, if necessary, work with the local code official to determine the best way to meet both requirements.

Plumbing Codes

Note

The *IBC* also includes a chapter on plumbing fixtures. This chapter and other plumbing requirements will be explained in Chapter 7.

The *International Plumbing Code (IPC)* was actually the first I-Code published by the ICC in 1995. The most current version of the *IPC* is 2003, and it will continue to be revised every three years. Also available in 2003 as part of NFPA's set of C3-Codes was the *Uniform Plumbing Code (UPC)*. This code was produced in conjunction with one of their new partners: the International Association of Plumbing and Mechanical Officials (IAPMO). IAPMO originally published this code under the same name for the International Conference of Building Officials (ICBO) before ICBO consolidated with BOCA and SBCCI to form the ICC. In addition, the Plumbing-Heating-Cooling Contractors Association is continuing to publish its *National Standard Plumbing Code (NSPC)*. The newest edition is 2003. Currently, most code jurisdictions use the *IPC*; however, with the reintroduction of the *UPC*, this may change in the future.

Most of the chapters in the plumbing code are geared toward an engineer and the professional plumbing contractor. In a project requiring plumbing work, you will often use the services of a licensed engineer to design the system. You will notice in Figure 1.3 that both building codes have a chapter on plumbing systems as well. These chapters refer you to the respective plumbing code. However, in the *IBC* the plumbing chapter also includes the minimum plumbing facility section of the *IPC* with the related table. It is this plumbing fixture table and its related chapter that will be discussed in this book. (See Chapter 7 for more detail.) When designing interior projects, you will find this plumbing code chapter important in helping you determine the minimum number and type of fixtures required for a particular occupancy classification.

Mechanical Codes

Similar to the plumbing codes, a mechanical code was also published by each of the model code organizations. The first *International Mechanical Code (IMC)* was published by the ICC in 1996. The more current editions include 2003 and 2006. It is widely accepted. However, in 2003 the first edition of the new *Uniform Mechanical Code (UMC)* was published by IAPMO in partnership with NFPA. The *UMC* was originally published by the ICBO but has now been significantly modified to meet the requirements of NFPA's set of C3-Codes. Jurisdictions may now choose between the *IMC* and the *UMC*.

Again, as shown in Figure 1.3, each building code has a chapter on mechanical systems. However, this chapter refers you to the respective mechanical code. The mechanical codes are geared toward mechanical engineers and professional installers. Although you will very rarely have to refer to the mechanical codes, on interior projects you should be familiar with some of the general requirements and the terminology. These are discussed in more detail in Chapter 7.

Electrical Codes

The *National Electrical Code (NEC)*, published by the NFPA, is one of the oldest existing codes. Originally published in the late 1800s, it is now a part of the NFPA C3-Code set. The current edition is 2002 with the next one expected in 2005. Also known as *NFPA 70*, the *NEC* is the most used electrical code, and is the basis for electrical codes in almost all code jurisdictions. Even the ICC references this code. In 2000, the ICC published the first edition of the *ICC Electrical Code—Administrative Provisions (ICCEC)*. The most current edition is 2003. However, rather than creating a new electrical code, the *ICCEC* refers you to the *NEC* and outlines the provisions required for the enforcement of the *NEC* so that enforcement is similar to the other

I-Codes. At this time ICC does not plan to create an electrical code and will continue to refer to the *NEC*.

In addition, each building code has a chapter on electrical systems as shown in Figure 1.3. In the *IBC* this chapter refers you to the *ICCEC* and includes a section on emergency and standby power systems. In the *NFPA 5000*, the electrical chapter refers you to the *NEC*. You will rarely, if ever, refer directly to the electrical code, since it is the responsibility of an engineer to design electrical systems. On the other hand, for an interior project you will often locate electrical outlets and fixtures as well as specify light fixtures and other equipment. Therefore, it is important to have a basic understanding of this code. The most common requirements are explained in Chapter 8.

Note

ASHRAE 90.1 is a standard geared toward energy efficiency in commercial buildings. Although the 1999 edition is required by the DOE, newer editions might be required by a code jurisdiction.

Energy Codes

Both the ICC and the NFPA have an energy conservation code that establishes minimum regulations for energy efficient buildings. The ICC has the *International Energy Conservation Code (IECC)*, which was originally based on the *Model Energy Code* (1992 edition). First published in 1998, the most current edition of the *IECC* is 2003. It includes prescriptive and performance-related provisions. It also covers both residential buildings and commercial buildings. A majority of states in the United States currently require the use of the *IECC*.

In 2004 the NFPA came out with its first energy conservation code, titled *NFPA 900, Building Energy Code (BEC)*. Rather than creating a totally new code, the *NFPA 900* outlines the provisions required for administering and enforcing two ASHRAE standards. The standards are *ASHRAE 90.1, Energy Standard for Buildings Except Low-Rise Residential Buildings* (geared toward commercial buildings) and *ASHRAE 90.2, Energy-Efficient Design of New Low-Rise Residential Buildings* (geared toward residential homes). Both standards were most recently updated in 2004, although an older version might still be referenced by a jurisdiction. The *IECC* also references the *ASHRAE 90.1* for commercial buildings. In addition, the U.S. Department of Energy has established this standard as a requirement under the federal Energy Conservation and Production Act, which requires all states to have energy codes in place that are at least as strict as the 1999 edition of the standard.

Each building code has a chapter on energy efficiency; however, the chapter simply refers you to their respective energy code. Energy conservation codes address many aspects of a building, starting with the energy efficiency of the building envelope, which promotes adequate thermal resistance and low air leakage. For example, in an exterior wall the code will specify how much and what type of glass can be used and the rating of the wall insulation required. If you were to change an interior element that connects to an exterior wall, you may need to confirm that you are not changing the energy efficiency of the original exterior wall.

The energy codes also cover the design, selection, and installation of energy-efficient mechanical systems, water-heating systems, electrical distribution, and illumination systems. Since most of the requirements are geared to either the building shell or mechanical and electrical systems, you will not have to refer to the code often. However, you should be aware of the basic requirements, especially as they relate to illumination and the selection of light fixtures. These requirements will be further explained in Chapter 7 and Chapter 8. Other energy requirements related to the interior of a building will be mentioned throughout the book. (Using energy codes also greatly affects the sustainability of a building or space. See inset titled *Sustainability and LEED* in Chapter 9 on page 374.)

Residential Code

The *International Residential Code (IRC)*, published by the ICC, first became available in 1998 and is based on the former *One- and Two-Family Dwelling Code (OTFDC)*. The more current editions include 2003 and 2006. It is the main code used for the construction of single-family and duplex residences and townhouses. It covers the typical residential home that is not more than three stories in height and has a separate means of egress. All other types of residential uses would be regulated by a building code. For example, if you were working on a house that is over three stories or a small apartment building where the units do not exit directly to the outside, you would need to use the building code instead of the *IRC*. The *IRC* is a stand-alone code meaning that it covers all construction aspects of the building without having to refer to other code documents. In addition to the typical building code chapters, it includes complete chapters on mechanical, electrical, plumbing, and energy requirements.

Note

Refer to Appendix B for more information on codes for single-family homes.

The NFPA currently does not have a separate residential code. Instead, it covers the building aspects of single-family homes in both the *NFPA 5000* and the *Life Safety Code*. Each has an occupancy chapter titled "One- and Two-Family Dwellings." This chapter provides specific requirements and directs you to other chapters in the text that provide exceptions for single-family homes. This chapter also directs you to other NFPA codes as well as multiple NFPA standards that are geared toward one- and two-family dwellings. For example, the *NFPA 5000* refers you to the *UMC, NEC, UPC*, and *ASHRAE 90.2* for residential requirements dealing with mechanical, electrical, plumbing, and energy provisions, respectively. If a jurisdiction requires the *IRC* in addition to an NFPA code, you would need to make sure the most restrictive requirements are followed. (Although this book concentrates more on commercial type projects, codes and standards specifically for residential homes are briefly discussed in Appendix B.)

Existing Building Code

Note

Design and construction projects in existing buildings typically require the use of the building codes. However, a jurisdiction may also have the option of using the *IEBC*. See Appendix C.

In the past, there were two model codes available for use with existing buildings. These included the SBCCI's *Standard Existing Building Code* and the ICBO's *Uniform Code for Building Conservation*. Some code jurisdictions may still be referring to them. The ICC and NFPA building codes both dedicate an entire chapter to existing buildings—Chapter 34 on "Existing Structures" in the *IBC* and Chapter 15 on "Building Rehabilitation" in the *NFPA 5000*. (The *Life Safety Code* includes existing occupancy chapters throughout its text.) However, in 2003 the ICC published the first *International Existing Building Code (IEBC)*. The next one is expected in 2006. It is dedicated entirely to existing buildings, providing requirements for reasonable upgrades and improvements depending on the type and the extent of the work.

PRODUCT EVALUATION SERVICES

In 2003 the International Code Council (ICC) merged the National Evaluation Service (NES) with the evaluation services of the three model code organizations. The new organization, called the ICC Evaluation Service (ICC ES), is a subsidiary of the ICC. Like its predecessors, the ICC ES evaluates new materials, methods of construction, and testing as they become available to make sure they comply with the I-Codes, as well as other codes in the United States. The ICC ES works closely with various accredited testing laboratories and approved inspection agencies in order to accomplish this. These laboratories and agencies are reviewed and approved by the International Accreditation Services (IAS), another independent subsidiary of the ICC.

The request to evaluate a product or system often comes from the manufacturer, but others, such as builders, code officials, engineers, architects, and designers, can do so as well. The ICC ES will evaluate the characteristics of the product, the installation of the product, and the conditions of its use to verify that it meets or exceeds the requirements of the codes and standards. Once a product or system is approved, a report is issued and made available to the industry. (The reports are posted on its Web site, www.icc-es.org.) These reports can then be used to support the use of a building material by code officials and designers. It is especially helpful as part of a performance-based design. The evaluation report also allows manufacturers to gain national recognition of a new product. Other evaluation services are available as well. For example, some states, such as California and Florida, have developed their own uniform requirements to meet their statewide codes. (Reports created by the older model code organizations are still available and are known as ICC-ES "Legacy Reports." As each report is updated, it becomes part of the I-Codes.)

If you are working in an existing building, you will need to confirm that the *IEBC* has been adopted by that jurisdiction. If not, you need to determine if the jurisdiction requires the use of one of the older codes mentioned above or the appropriate chapter in the building code. When using the *IEBC*, the extent of work (i.e., repair, alteration, or addition) will determine the level of code compliance. In some cases the requirements will be more lenient than those in the building code. The *IEBC* also includes both prescriptive and performance-related provisions. All of this is explained in more detail in Appendix C. (Although this book concentrates on codes for new construction, many of the same requirements apply to new work being done in existing buildings. For more detailed information on codes for historic and existing buildings, see Appendix C.)

FEDERAL REGULATIONS

A number of federal agencies and departments work with trade associations, private companies, and the general public to develop federal laws for building construction. These regulations are published in the *Federal Register (FR)* and the *Code of Federal Regulations (CFR)*. The *FR* is published daily and includes the newest updates for each federal agency. However, not all rules published in the *FR* are enforceable laws. Typically, a federal agency must review the regulations published in the *FR* and make a formal ruling. Once the regulations are passed into law, they are published in the *CFR*. The *CFR* is revised annually to include all permanent agency rules.

Note

When using federal regulations, both the *FR* and the *CFR* should be reviewed to determine the most current requirements.

The federal government plays a part in the building process in a number of ways. First, it regulates the building of its own facilities. These include federal buildings, Veterans Administration (VA) hospitals, and military establishments. The construction of a federal building is usually not subject to state and local building codes and regulations. Instead, each federal agency has criteria and regulations that must be met when constructing a new building or renovating an existing one. For example, the Department of Defense or the Department of Transportation might have certain building requirements and regulations that are not required by the Department of Justice.

Note

The Occupational Safety and Health Act (OSHA) is another federal regulation affecting building interiors. It stresses the safe installation of materials and equipment to ensure a safe work environment for construction workers and building occupants. It must be strictly observed by contractors.

More recently, however, the federal government has begun to adopt more of the codes and standards from the private sector rather than create its own. This became more prevalent with the passing of the National Technology Transfer and Advancement Act (NTTAA) of 1995, which establishes the responsibility for federal agencies to use national voluntary consensus standards instead of developing

Note

The NTTAA gives the National Institute of Standards and Technology (NIST) the authority to assist with coordination between federal agencies and the private sector. You can find out more on the NIST Web site. (See resources in Appendix E.)

their own, wherever practical. Many federal agencies have been working with the ICC and the NFPA as well as standards organizations such as the American National Standards Institute (ANSI) to adopt existing codes and standards. (See Standards Organizations later in this chapter.) For example, multiple federal agencies require the use of the *Life Safety Code*, and the Department of Defense requires the use of the *International Building Code*. In some cases, the federal agencies collaborate with the organizations to develop new documents. Some of these are discussed in this chapter. If you are working on a federally owned or funded building, you will need to determine from the federal agency which codes and standards apply. Keep in mind that there could be more than one federal agency involved.

Another way the federal government plays a part in the building process is that it can pass federal legislation creating a law that supersedes all other state and local codes and standards. Each piece of legislation is created by a specific federal agency. When passed into law, it becomes mandatory nationwide. This is typically done to create a uniform level of standards throughout the country. The Americans with Disabilities Act (ADA) is one example. Although there is a wide variety of legislation covering everything from energy to transportation, only a few laws that pertain to the design of interiors are discussed in this section. (Also see Energy Codes on page 24.)

Americans with Disabilities Act

The Americans with Disabilities Act (ADA) is a four-part federal legislation that became law on July 26, 1990, and became enforceable beginning in 1992. Prior to this, only federal buildings and federally funded projects had to comply with similar legislation under the Architectural Barriers Act (ABA) and its related *Uniform Federal Accessibility Standards (UFAS)*. With the passing of the ADA, many other types of projects are required to meet accessibility guidelines as outlined through the various titles of the law.

The ADA is a comprehensive civil rights law that protects individuals with disabilities in the area of employment (Title I), state and local government services and public transportation (Title II), public accommodations and commercial facilities (Title III), and telecommunication services (Title IV). The ADA was developed by the Department of Justice (DOJ) and the Department of Transportation (DOT).

The regulations that will apply most often to interior projects are found in Title III and Title IV. Title IV requires telephone companies to provide telecommunication relay services for the hearing and speech impaired. When you specify a public phone you must be familiar with the requirements. (See inset titled *Public Telephones* on page 329 in Chapter 8.)

Title III covers all public accommodations (any facility that offers food, merchandise, or services to the public) and commercial facilities (nonresidential buildings that do business but are not open to the general public). The intent of Title III is to regulate the design and construction of buildings so that persons with disabilities can use them. These regulations were incorporated into the *Americans with Disabilities Act Accessibility Guidelines (ADAAG)* as developed by the Architectural and Transportation Barriers Compliance Board (ATBCB or Access Board) and first published in 1991. The *ADAAG* deals with architectural concerns, such as accessible routes and restrooms, and communication concerns, such as visible alarm systems and signage.

Note

The Access Board researches accessibility needs and is responsible for updating and adding to the ADA guidelines when necessary. They also offer a toll-free number, a Web site (see Appendix E), and a variety of publications for guidance.

The Access Board continually works with other organizations to conduct research and create new documents. Some of the research is used to create proposed additions to the ADA guidelines, while other research is used to create guidance materials, such as checklists and technical bulletins, which can be used to gain additional insight. Although the Access Board has proposed changes to the *ADAAG*, very few changes have actually been incorporated into the guidelines since it was first published. This is because the Department of Justice (DOJ) must rule on and approve a proposal before it becomes an official part of the ADA guidelines. However, you need to be aware that some of the newer copies of the guidelines might include sections that are still waiting on a DOJ ruling. Until they are approved by the DOJ and become enforceable as part of the ADA law, you are not required to meet these requirements. (See the section on New ADA Guidelines in Appendix A for more detail.) To keep abreast of these latest changes and rulings you should regularly check the Access Board Web site. (See Resources in Appendix E.)

Note

To review other guidance material available from the Access Board, go to their Web site. (See resources in Appendix E.)

Most recently, the Access Board has been working with multiple agencies and organizations to combine the *ADAAG* with the *Uniform Federal Accessibility Standard (UFAS)*, which is used for federal buildings. (See inset titled *Accessibility Requirements—ANSI, ADAAG, UFAS, and FHAG* on page 32.) The new document, released in July 2004, is titled the *ADA and ABA Accessibility Guidelines*, but it will not be required by law until it goes through the proper government approvals. (See Appendix A.) The most comprehensive revision to date, these guidelines are organized to more closely correspond to the accessibility chapters in the building codes and other industry standards. The International Code Council worked closely with the Access Board to assist with its organization as well as reduce the differences in the accessibility provisions in its own 2003 edition of the *IBC*. The newer editions of the ICC/ANSI standard have also been harmonized with the new document. The organization of the new *ADA and ABA Accessibility Guidelines* as compared to the 1998 and 2003 ICC/ANSI standards is shown in Figure 1.4.

Although ADA regulations are mandatory, they may not be the only guidelines for accessibility issues that you follow. Each of the building codes contains an

ANSI (1998 and 2003) **ICC/ANSI 117.1 Accessibility Standard**		ADA Guidelines (2004) **ADA and ABA Accessibility Guidelines**	
		PART I	**ADA APPLICATION AND SCOPING**
Chapter 1	Application and Administration	**Chapter 1**	Application and Administration
Chapter 2	Scoping	**Chapter 2**	Scoping Requirements
		PART II	**ABA APPLICATION AND SCOPING**
		PART III	**TECHNICAL REQUIREMENTS**
Chapter 3	Building Blocks	**Chapter 3**	Building Blocks (basic technical requirements)
Chapter 4	Accessible Routes	**Chapter 1**	Accessible Routes
Chapter 5	General Site and Building Elements	**Chapter 5**	General Site and Building Elements
Chapter 6	Plumbing Elements and Facilities	**Chapter 6**	Plumbing Elements and Facilities
Chapter 7	Communication Elements and Features	**Chapter 7**	Communication Elements and Features
Chapter 8	Special Rooms and Spaces	**Chapter 8**	Special Rooms, Spaces, and Elements
Chapter 9	Built-in Furnishings and Equipment	**Chapter 9**	Built-in Elements
Chapter 10	Dwelling Units*		(distributed throughout other chapters)
	(not included)	**Chapter 10**	Recreation Facilities

*titled Dwelling Units and Sleeping Units in 2003 edition.

Figure 1.4 Comparison of Accessibility Publications (This chart is a summary of information contained in the *ICC/ANSI 117.1* standard and the *ADAAG*. The ICC, ANSI, and the Access Board do not assume responsibility for the accuracy or the completion of this chart.

accessibility chapter that includes specific requirements and references the ICC/ANSI standard *ICC/ANSI A117.1*. (See section on American National Standards Institute on page 34.) The requirements in these documents may differ. For example, the building codes may include accessibility requirements not found in the ADA guidelines. However, these requirements must still be followed. In addition, some states, such as California and North Carolina, have adopted their own accessibility requirements. You must research, compare, and follow the most stringent requirements for that jurisdiction while maintaining the minimum federal requirements. Various accessibility requirements are addressed throughout this book. (Typically, the most restrictive requirements are used.) You will often have to incorporate both a code requirement and a related accessibility requirement together into your design. (Other aspects of ADA, such as the varying levels of compliance and responsibility for compliance, are discussed further in Appendix A.)

> **Note**
>
> The Appendix of the original *ADAAG* provides additional guidelines that enhance and clarify the main text. The new ADA-ABA Accessibility Guidelines inserts these as notes throughout the text. Although they are helpful, they are not binding. The *ADAAG* text is law. The Appendix or additional notes are not.

Fair Housing Act

The Fair Housing Act (FHA) is federal legislation enforced by the Department of Housing and Urban Development (HUD). Originally established in 1968, the FHA regulates fair housing and protects the consumer from discrimination in housing when buying or renting. In 1988, the FHA was expanded to include persons with disabilities. The FHA prohibits discrimination because of race, color, national origin, religion, sex, family status, or disability. Although the FHA is not specifically accessibility legislation, it does incorporate a number of provisions for people with disabilities and families with children.

The FHA regulations may apply to private housing, private housing that receives federal financial assistance, and state and local governmental housing. The FHA typically pertains to residential housing that has four or more dwelling units, such as apartments and condominiums. The ADA generally covers the places of public accommodation in these facilities, such as the related sales and rental offices; the FHA covers additional accessibility requirements. In 1991, HUD developed the final *Fair Housing Accessibility Guidelines (FHAG)* to help clarify these requirements. Many of the interior aspects of a dwelling are regulated, such as the location of thermostats, electrical outlets, light switches, and maneuvering areas in hallways, bathrooms, and kitchens. In addition, at least the ground floor units must be accessible and meet specific construction requirements.

Another document that became available in 2001 is the *Code Requirements for Housing Accessibility (CRHA)*. This code was developed by the International Code Council in conjunction with the National Association of Home Builders (NAHB) and HUD. HUD endorses this document as being equivalent to the most current version of the *FHAG*. Now, a jurisdiction can adopt the *CRHA* as an enforceable code. When you use this code you know that you are meeting, if not exceeding, the requirements of the *FHAG*. Other compliant documents considered equivalent to the *FHAG* include the 2000 *IBC* if used in conjunction with the 2001 *Supplement to the International Codes* and the 1986, 1992, or 1998 editions of the *ICC/ANSI A117.1*.

Some consider the FHA to be the residential version of the ADA. (See Appendix A.) Both were originally based on the same edition of the ANSI standards. However, the FHA does not require total compliance to the ICC/ANSI standards; it uses them only as a reference.

ACCESSIBILITY REQUIREMENTS—ANSI, ADAAG, UFAS, and FHAG

There are four main accessibility documents that are used most frequently for interior projects. In addition, each building code has a chapter dedicated to accessibility requirements. Although in many ways they are similar, none of them match exactly. It is important to know which document applies to your project.

ANSI A117.1 was originally developed by the American National Standards Institute (ANSI). It was one of the first accessibility guidelines used throughout the United States. It has served as the basis for other accessibility documents as well. The 1998 edition, known *as ICC/ANSI A117.1,* was developed in conjunction with the International Code Council (ICC) using the ANSI consensus process. The more current 2003 edition was developed by the ICC with the Access Board to be more consistent with the new *ADA and ABA Accessibility Guidelines*.

The *Americans with Disabilities Act Accessibility Guidelines (ADAAG)* was developed by the Architectural and Transportation Barriers Compliance Board (ATBCB or Access Board) as guidelines for the ADA legislation. It was originally based on the 1986 *ANSI A117.1*. A few minor updates have been made to it since its inception. More recently, the Access Board updated and totally reorganized the *ADAAG* and combined it with the *UFAS* to create the new *ADA and ABA Accessibility Guidelines*.

The *Uniform Federal Accessibility Standards (UFAS)* was developed as guidelines for the Architectural Barriers Act (ABA) legislation and applies to federal government buildings and recipients of federal funding (i.e., schools, hospitals, etc.). Although federal buildings are not currently required to conform to ADA regulations, a project that uses federal funding may be required to meet both the ADA guidelines and the *UFAS*. First issued in 1989, the *UFAS* is based on the 1980 ANSI standard. However, with the combination of the *UFAS* and the *ADAAG*, the requirements between both are becoming more consistent. The new *ADA and ABA Accessibility Guidelines* share the technical requirements. However, there are still separate scoping requirements for each legislation.

The *Fair Housing Accessibility Guidelines (FHAG)* was developed in 1991 as part of the Fair Housing Act (FHA). It provides accessibility requirements specifically for multi-unit housing that consists of four or more dwelling units and can include apartments as well as other building types such as dormitories and assisted living facilities.

Because the various agencies and organizations continue to work together, these separate accessibility documents are becoming more similar in scope and organization. However, each document still has some unique requirements and different characteristics. Although the ICC/ANSI standard is referenced in the building codes, the various federal laws are not. Therefore, all applicable documents must be reviewed for the most stringent accessibility requirements. In some cases more than one federal document will apply to one project. There may also be additional and/or conflicting state or local accessibility codes that need to be considered.

STANDARDS ORGANIZATIONS

A standard is a definition, a recommended practice, a test method, a classification, or a required specification that must be met. Standards are developed by trade associations, government agencies, and standards-writing organizations where members are often allowed to vote on specific issues. The size of these groups can range from a worldwide organization to a small trade association that develops one or two industry-related standards.

By themselves, standards have no legal standing. Instead, they are typically referenced by the codes. The standards become law when the code is adopted by a jurisdiction. In some cases, a jurisdiction will adopt an individual standard. In this way, standards supplement the code. Rather than giving all the details, the code will establish the minimum quality and performance criteria for a particular material or method. The code will then reference a standard, which sets the conditions or requirements for the material or method to meet. This allows the codes to provide specific instructions without going into great detail. For example, instead of setting specific fire extinguisher requirements, the *International Building Code (IBC)* references the *NFPA 10, Portable Fire Extinguishers. NFPA 10* then becomes a part of the enforced building code.

When a standard is referenced, the acronym of the standard organization and a standard number is called out. For example, "*ASTM E152*" is an American Society for Testing and Materials standard known as *E152*. It is a standard method of fire testing for door assemblies. The reference also typically includes the year of the latest revision of the standard. When listed in a code publication, be sure to note the year to make sure you are using and/or referencing the correct edition. Although the year might not be used when mentioned within the text, each code publication includes a separate list of all the standards referenced within the text. This list will include the year or edition of the standard to be used.

The most common standards organizations that pertain to interior projects are described in this section. Each develops a wide variety of standards. Some may need to be examined in detail prior to designing an interior project. Others may only need mentioning in the specifications of the project. The most common standards that pertain to interior projects are discussed throughout this book.

Note

Each of the code publications has a chapter or appendix listing the standards mentioned throughout its text. This list will indicate which edition of the standard is required.

Note

Some smaller standards organizations are specific to an industry. For example, the Business and Institutional Furniture Manufacturers Association (BIFMA) and the Upholstered Furniture Action Council (UFAC) are specific to the finish and furnishings industry. These and other organizations are listed in Appendix D.

National Fire Protection Association

The National Fire Protection Association (NFPA) was originally founded in 1896 to develop standards for the early use of sprinklers. Today it is one of the largest standards organizations. It develops and publishes more than 300 different

TESTING AGENCIES

Many standards affect the way building materials and other products are made. Manufacturers must know these standards and incorporate them into the manufacturing process. Many finished building products must pass one or more specific tests before they can be sold and used.

These tests are developed by the standards organizations. Some of the organizations provide testing services, but many of them do not have the facilities. Instead, a number of independent testing laboratories and testing agencies in the United States and throughout the world are set up to perform these tests. (Many are listed in a database available on the Internet at www.findtesting.com.) A manufacturer will typically send them a finished product, which is then tested and evaluated. (See inset titled *UL Labels* on page 37.)

Tested products are given a permanent label or certificate to prove they pass a required standard. Depending on the test and the specific standard, the manufacturer will either attach a label to the product or keep a certificate on file. For example, a fire-rated door will typically have a label on the edge of the door. Other materials such as carpets or wallcoverings might not be easily labeled. Instead, these labels may be located on samples or be available from the manufacturer upon request. As the designer, you should be specifying tested products when required as well as keeping records of the products you specify. (This is discussed further in Chapter 10 in the section on Documentation and Liability.) The only way to know if they are required is to know the codes and standards and consult with the local code officials.

standards, many of which are used internationally. Each document is available from NFPA in book or booklet form.

As mentioned earlier in this chapter, NFPA also publishes a full set of codes known as the C3-Codes. All of the NFPA codes and many other codes, including those produced by the International Code Council, reference the NFPA standards in their text. Many of the NFPA standards are geared toward fire protection. Generally, they are designed to reduce the extent of injury, loss of life, and destruction of property during a fire. Their testing requirements cover everything from textiles to fire fighting equipment and means of egress design. The standards are developed by committees made up of NFPA members. (See inset titled *Code and Standards Changes* on page 11.) They are reviewed and updated as needed. Similar to the C3-Codes, the newer standards and the most current editions of the existing standards have been formatted to meet NFPA's new Manual of Style format.

Note

When a code requirement varies from that of a standard referenced by the code, the code requirement takes precedence over the standard.

American National Standards Institute

The American National Standards Institute publishes the *American National Standard*. Both are generally referred to as ANSI. ANSI is a private corporation that was originally founded in 1918 as the American Engineering Standards Committee. ANSI is a coordinator of voluntary standards development. Instead of concentrating on developing standards, ANSI generally approves the standards developed by other organizations. It also helps to establish priorities and avoid duplications between different standards.

ANSI undertakes the development of a standard only when commissioned by an industry group or government agency. Representing virtually every facet of trade, commerce, organized labor, and the consumer, ANSI's approval procedures ensure a consensus of interests. They are widely accepted on an international level, and local jurisdictions often require compliance with ANSI's standards. ANSI's standards are published annually, though the actual text is updated only on an as-needed basis.

Note

An *active* standard is the current official standard as required by a jurisdiction, which supersedes any older versions of the same standard.

The most common ANSI designated standard used by designers for interior projects is *ANSI A117.1*. Its full title is *ICC/ANSI A117.1, Standard on Accessible and Usable Building and Facilities* (referred to as the "ICC/ANSI standard" throughout this book). It concentrates on the accessibility features in the design of buildings and their interiors, allowing people with disabilities to achieve independence. It was the first standard written for accessibility and is the most widely known. Various editions of the ANSI standard were used as the basis for the *ADAAG*, the *UFAS*, and the *FHAG*. (See inset titled *Accessibility Requirements—ANSI, ADAAG, UFAS, and FHAG* earlier in this chapter.) The 1998 edition of the ICC/ANSI standard was developed by the International Code Council (ICC) to create consistency with the accessibility chapter in the 2003 *International Building Code*. The *NFPA 5000* references it as well. In addition to the many requirements included in the standard, the ICC/ANSI standard also refers to other industry standards for certain items such as power-operated doors, elevator/escalators, and signaling systems.

Note

Many of the *UBC* standards and tests are similar to those of other standards organizations such as NFPA, ASTM, and UL. The last editions of these standards were published in 1997 and are still used by some jurisdictions.

A 2003 edition of the ICC/ANSI standard, which became available May 2004, was developed in conjunction with the ICC and the Access Board to create consistency between the next edition of the *IBC* and the new *ADA and ABA Accessibility Guidelines*. A comparison of the various sections in the 1998 and 2003 editions of the ICC/ANSI standard and the new ADA guidelines is shown in Figure 1.4. Although the 1998 ICC/ANSI standard is the edition required by the 2003 building codes, the 2003 standard may be adopted separately by a jurisdiction. (Other jurisdictions may have their own accessibility standards.)

Note

The building codes each have a chapter dedicated to accessibility requirements, which references the *ANSI/ICC 117.1* accessibility standard.

American Society for Testing and Materials

The American Society for Testing and Materials (ASTM) is a standards-writing organization formed in 1898 as a nonprofit corporation. In 2002, it changed its name to ASTM International to reflect its global reach and participation. ASTM International does not perform testing or certify products. Instead, it manages

Note

ASTM and UL now offer publications that combine the standards referenced by the *IBC* into one document so that you do not need to purchase their entire catalog to review the standards you need.

the development of standards and the promotion of related technical knowledge received from over 30,000 members around the world.

There are more than 11,000 ASTM standards used to specify materials, assure quality, integrate production processes, promote trade, and enhance safety. They are updated and/or published each year in more than 70 volumes of the *ASTM Annual Book of Standards.* These standards are divided into 15 different categories, two of which include construction and textiles. Many of the ASTM standards are referenced in the codes and other reference materials. Copies of these standards can be obtained from ASTM International. In addition, they publish a special grouping of standards for the building construction industry. In 2003, ASTM International also developed, in conjunction with the International Code Council, a comprehensive volume that contains all the standards that are referenced in the 2003 *International Building Code*. Titled the *2003 International Building Code-ASTM Referenced Standards*, it contains more than 260 ASTM standards representing close to half of all the standards referenced in the *IBC*. The NFPA codes reference some of these standards as well.

ASTM International is currently working on creating some of the first standards for sustainable design. The first two available standards include *E2114, Terminology for Sustainability Relative to the Performance of Buildings* and *E2129, Practice for Data Collection for Sustainability Assessment of Building Products*. Other sustainability standards are in committees being developed.

American Society of Heating, Refrigeration, and Air-Conditioning Engineers

The American Society of Heating, Refrigeration, and Air-Conditioning Engineers (ASHRAE) came into existence in 1959 with the merger of two engineering groups. ASHRAE is a worldwide standards organization. It sponsors research projects and develops standards for performance levels of HVAC (heating, ventilating, and air conditioning) and refrigeration systems. ASHRAE standards include uniform testing methods, design requirements, and recommended standard practices. ASHRAE also distributes technological information to the public.

As a designer you will generally not refer to ASHRAE standards. They are typically used by mechanical engineers and refrigerant specialists and installers. Two of the more widely used standards include *ASHRAE 90.1, Energy Standard for Buildings Except Low-Rise Residential Buildings* and *ASHRAE 90.2, Energy-Efficient Design of New Low-Rise Residential Buildings*. They are referenced by the ICC and the NFPA in their energy codes and are the basis for most of the energy code provisions required in the United States. (See section on Energy Codes earlier in this chapter.)

Underwriters Laboratories

Underwriters Laboratories (UL) is primarily a testing agency that approves products. It has a number of testing laboratories around the world. It tests various devices, systems, and materials to see if they meet specific requirements and to determine their relation to life, fire, casualty hazards, and crime prevention.

UL LABELS

Underwriters Laboratories (UL) tests a wide variety of products all over the world. The UL label is the most widely recognized mark of compliance with safety requirements. These safety requirements are based on UL standards as well as standards from other organizations. Most federal, state, and municipal authorities, as well as architects, designers, contractors, and building owners and users, accept and recognize the UL mark.

UL can test whole products, components, materials, and systems depending on the standard required. The products tested include building materials, finishes, upholstered furniture, electrical products, HVAC equipment, safety devices, and more. Once the initial product passes a test, it is retested at random to make sure it continues to function properly.

There are four common types of labels or UL marks a product can receive. (Other marks are more specific to other industries.) The UL Web site describes them as follows:

1. *Listing Mark:* The most popular, it indicates that samples of the product have been tested and evaluated and comply with UL requirements. It is found on appliances and equipment including alarm systems and light fixtures. The mark generally includes the UL registered name or symbol, the product name, a control number, and the word *listed.*
2. *Classification Mark:* This label may list a product's properties, limited hazards, and/or suitability for certain uses. It is found on building materials such as fire doors as well as industrial equipment. The label includes the UL name or symbol and a statement indicating the extent of the UL evaluation and a control number.
3. *Recognized Component Mark:* This covers the evaluation of a component only. The component is later factory-installed in a complete product or system. The label includes a manufacturer's identification and product model number.
4. *Certificate:* This is used when it is difficult to apply one label to a whole system. The certificate indicates the type of system and the extent of the evaluation. It accompanies the product and is issued to the end user upon installation.

There are other marks specific to other countries, as well. For example, the GS Mark (which stands for German Safety Mark) is used in Europe, the AR-UL Mark is used in Argentina, and the BR-UL Mark is used in Brazil. If there is a capital "C" on the mark it means it is accepted in Canada.

UL develops and performs tests in conjunction with other standards organizations. When testing new products, if a standard exists UL will use it. If no standard exists, UL will use its own existing standard or create a new one. All of the more than 800 different UL safety standards are published in the UL *Catalog of Standards*. In 2000, Underwriters Laboratories also created the first *International Codes UL Referenced Standards—Building Provisions* in conjunction with the International Code Council. It is a single volume that contains the more than 25 UL standards referenced in the *International Building Code* and the building portions (Chapters 1 to 10) of the *International Residential Code*. This allows I-Code users to obtain one volume with all the relevant standards. UL standards are referenced in the NFPA codes as well.

Note

The largest International standards-setting organization is the International Organization for Standardization (ISO) with national standards bodies in more than 140 countries.

UL's findings are recognized worldwide. When a product is approved, it receives a permanent label or classification marking that identifies Underwriter Laboratories, the word *classified*, a class rating, and a UL control number. (See example in Chapter 5, Figure 5.14, page 204 and the inset titled *UL Labels* in this chapter.) UL also lists all approved products and assemblies in a number of product directories. The directories most likely to pertain to interior projects include *Building Materials, Fire Protection Equipment*, and *Fire Resistance*. These directories, which are used to find information about UL certified products, components, and materials, are published yearly. In 2001, the directories were reorganized to make them easier to use with the code publications. An electronic version of the directory, known as the *Online Certification Directory*, is also available on the Internet, where it is updated regularly as new information becomes available. (See resources in Appendix E.)

Note

UL labeled products may also include country-specific identifiers such as US and C (Canada) to show that they comply with that country's product safety standards.

Note

In addition to the standards organizations discussed in this chapter, there are two *national* organizations that can provide valuable information. Although they do not create codes or standards, they play a major role in supporting them. These organizations are the National Conference of States on Building Codes and Standards (NCSBCS) and the National Institute of Building Sciences (NIBS). Both supply a wide variety of helpful publications. (See Appendix E.)

LOCAL CODES

In addition to the codes, standards, and regulations already mentioned, there are more specific codes within each jurisdiction. They can include, but are not limited to, local municipal ordinances, health codes, zoning regulations, historic preservation laws, and neighborhood conservation restrictions. For example, health codes must typically be followed when working on projects that involve food preparation, such as restaurants. In addition, other occupancies (e.g., hospitals) have regulations that must be incorporated into the design in order for the facility to obtain a license to operate. These regulations can control the size, location, and use of a building, and are usually set and controlled at a local level.

This book does not cover these local codes, since they are specific to each jurisdiction. However, it is important to consult the jurisdiction of a project for

Interior Codes and Standards Checklist

Date:____________

Project Name:______________________________

PUBLICATIONS REQUIRED	YEAR OF EDITION	YEAR OF AMENDMENT (if required)	RESEARCH DATE
Codes and Regulations			
BUILDING CODE - Circle One: IBC NFPA 5000 OTHER _______	_______	_______	___/___/___
Structural Engineer Required? _____ YES _____ NO			
PERFORMANCE CODE - Circle One: ICCPC NFPA[1] OTHER _______	_______	_______	___/___/___
FIRE CODE - Circle One: IFC UFC OTHER _______	_______	_______	___/___/___
LIFE SAFETY CODE (NFPA 101)	_______	_______	___/___/___
PLUMBING CODE - Circle One: IPC UPC OTHER _______	_______	_______	___/___/___
Plumbing Engineer Required? _____ YES _____ NO			
MECHANICAL CODE - Circle One: IMC UMC OTHER _______	_______	_______	___/___/___
Mechanical Engineer Required? _____ YES _____ NO			
ELECTRIC CODE - Circle One: ICCEC NEC OTHER _______	_______	_______	___/___/___
Electrical Engineer Required? _____ YES _____ NO			
ENERGY CODE - Circle One: IECC NFPA 900 OTHER _______	_______	_______	___/___/___
Engineer Required? _____ Structural _____ Electrical _____ Mechanical			
RESIDENTIAL CODE - Circle One: IRC OTHER _______	_______	_______	___/___/___
EXISTING BUILDING CODE - Circle One: IEBC OTHER _______	_______	_______	___/___/___
ACCESSIBILITY REGULATIONS/STANDARDS			
ADA Guidelines[2]	_______	_______	___/___/___
ICC/ANSI A117.1 Accessible and Usable Buildings and Facilities	_______	_______	___/___/___
Other: ______________________	_______	_______	___/___/___
OTHER: [3] ______________________	_______	_______	___/___/___
______________________	_______	_______	___/___/___
______________________	_______	_______	___/___/___
Standards [4]			
NATIONAL FIRE PROTECTION ASSOCIATION (NFPA):			
NFPA ____ ______________________	_______	_______	___/___/___
NFPA ____ ______________________	_______	_______	___/___/___
NFPA ____ ______________________	_______	_______	___/___/___
AMERICAN SOCIETY OF TESTING & MATERIALS (ASTM)			
ASTM ____ ______________________	_______	_______	___/___/___
ASTM ____ ______________________	_______	_______	___/___/___
UNDERWRITERS LABORATORIES (UL)			
UL ______ ______________________	_______	_______	___/___/___
UL ______ ______________________	_______	_______	___/___/___
OTHER: ______________________	_______	_______	___/___/___
______________________	_______	_______	___/___/___
______________________	_______	_______	___/___/___

NOTES:

1. Circle NFPA if you are using another NFPA document and plan to use a performance-based requirement listed in that document.
2. All projects should be reviewed for ADA compatibility with few exceptions (i.e., federal buildings, religious facilities, one/two family homes).
3. Be sure to check for other state and local codes. Local codes can include special ordinances, health codes, zoning regulations, and historic preservation laws. List the specific ones.
4. Refer to the codes as well as local requirements to determine which standards are required. List the specific publications.

Figure 1.5 Interior Codes and Standards Checklist

these specific regulations so they can be appropriately researched and referenced. (See Code Enforcement in Chapter 10.)

INTERIOR CODES CHECKLIST

When working on a new project it can be difficult to remember all the applicable code sources that must be referenced. Depending on the type of interior project and the jurisdiction in which it is located, you could be using any number of the codes, regulations, and standards described in this chapter. Figure 1.5 is a checklist that provides a comprehensive list of these codes and standards. Use this list, or develop your own, to be sure you reference the necessary codes and regulations.

Note

If an interior project is somehow affecting the structure of a building, the services of a structural engineer may be required.

Before starting an interior project, refer to this checklist to determine which code, standard, and federal publications must be referenced. Remember that not all of them will apply every time. If you are uncertain, consult the code officials in the jurisdiction of the project. Check off the publications you will need in the "Publications Required" column and enter the edition or year of the required publication in the next column. Remember that not every jurisdiction uses the most current edition of a code, and that a jurisdiction may have made amendments to an existing publication. If there are amendments, make a note of this in the third column.

Note

To further document your research, make copies of any sections of the codes that specifically pertain to your project and attach it to the code checklist. (Refer to Chapter 10.)

Do this for each code, regulation, and standard listed. A reminder for engineering involvement is given under each of the code headings. Blank spaces have been provided for specific state or local codes that must be consulted. Blank spaces have also been provided for you to fill in the specific standards and/or federal regulations to be used. For example, depending on the type of project, you could be required to follow the ADA guidelines, the *UFAS*, or the *FHAG*.

As you work on the project, continue to refer to the checklist to make sure each of the checked codes, standards, and federal regulations is being used. As the research is completed for each publication, enter the date in the "Research Date" column. You will find that as you research the codes, additional standards may be required. Add these to the checklist in the spaces provided or on a separate piece of paper. When the project is complete, keep this form with the project's files for future reference and proof that each of the code sources was reviewed.

CHAPTER 2

OCCUPANCY CLASSIFICATIONS AND LOADS

The occupancy classification of a building or space is generally determined by how that building or space is to be used. Occupancy classifications have been developed by the codes to address the different hazardous situations, often referred to as *risk factors*, associated with each type of use. These risk factors consider the typical characteristics of both the activity that will occur in the space and the occupants using the space. Risk factors may include spatial characteristics (low light levels, fixed seating, and high sound levels), fuel loads (amount of finish materials, upholstered furniture, and other flammable contents), concentration of occupants, characteristics of the occupants (mobility, age, alertness) and sometimes the familiarity of the occupants with the building. In some cases, these unique characteristics call for additional code requirements so that buildings are safe. For example, more exits are required in auditoriums (Assembly) due to the large number of people using the space, and alternate exiting methods are required in hospitals (Institutional) where occupants often are not mobile because of age, health, or security reasons. The different occupancy classifications in the codes are based on these various characteristics. The codes address these conditions for each occupancy classification, so that people can be considered equally safe at work, at a crowded concert, or any other type of use.

In some cases, the projected occupant load will be the most influential component in determining the occupancy classification. The occupant load is basically the number of people that are assumed to safely occupy a space or building. Since occupancy classifications and occupant loads are, in a sense, dependent on each other, both should be considered at the beginning of a project. Once you have determined the occupancy classification, the projected occupant load, or expected number of people, is used to determine a number of other code requirements. The first part of this chapter concentrates on occupancy classifications and their relationships; occupant loads are discussed in the last part of the chapter. A checklist for both is provided at the end.

KEY TERMS

Before continuing, make sure you are familiar with the following terms. They are discussed and used throughout the chapter and this book. They are also defined in the Glossary.

Building Type
Fuel Load
Occupancy
Occupant
Occupant Load
Risk Factors
Use Group or Type

OCCUPANCY CLASSIFICATIONS

Note

The codes often reference the occupancy classifications by letters or a combination of letters and numbers. For example "A" represents Assembly occupancies and "R-2" represents a Residential occupancy subclassification. (See Figure 2.2.)

An occupancy classification must be assigned to every building or space within a building. Determining the occupancy classification is one of the most important steps in the code process. It should be the first thing you determine when designing the interior of a building, since virtually every interior code and regulation is based on the building's occupancy. Figure 2.1 lists the most common code requirements that are affected by an occupancy classification. The occupancy of a space must

Building Areas	Fire Extinguishing Systems
Building Heights	Furniture Selection/Placement
Construction Types	Means of Egress
Egress Capacities	Occupancy Loads
Emergency Lighting	Plumbing Fixtures
Finish Selection/Placement	Smoke Barriers
Fire Barriers	Smoke Detection Systems
Fire Detection Systems	

Figure 2.1. Codes Affected by Occupancy.

also be known in order to effectively use most of the remaining chapters in this book. Once you know the occupancy, it will guide you in your research.

In some buildings, the occupancy classification may have already been determined. But for a new or existing building that is intended to have different types of tenants, the occupancy classification for each tenant must be determined separately. These different tenants may, in turn, affect how the shared public spaces are classified. In existing buildings, determining the occupancy classification may be particularly important if the intended use of the building is changing significantly, such as an old warehouse building being renovated into apartments. The occupancy classification needs to be reexamined whenever changes are made in the use of a building or space. Some of these changes are obvious, such as a change in building type. Other changes may be less noticeable but still require reclassification.

Be sure to consult your code official early in a project whenever there is uncertainty. It is always a good idea to have a code official confirm your choice of occupancy. If you find out later that your choice is incorrect or is not approved by the code official, the rest of your research may be incorrect and your design may not meet the appropriate code requirements.

Understanding Classification Differences

In understanding which occupancy classification(s) or building type(s) apply to your project, it is very important to understand how the occupants will actually be using the space or plan to use the space in the future. For example, if a space will be used for an open office plan now but in the future will be used as a conference room for training, you may need to classify it as an Assembly instead of Business so that the design will address the most stringent code requirements.

The ICC codes divide the occupancy classifications similarly to how the legacy codes did in the past. You will find a slight difference in the way that the NFPA codes define the occupancy types. (See Comparing the Codes, page 45.) However, the 10 most common occupancy classifications used throughout the various building and life safety codes are listed below. Some of the following occupancies also have subclassifications. The occupancy classifications and their subcategories will be discussed in the first part of this chapter.

Assembly occupancies
Business occupancies
Educational occupancies
Factory or Industrial occupancies
Hazardous occupancies

Institutional occupancies
Mercantile occupancies
Residential occupancies
Storage occupancies
Utility or Miscellaneous occupancies

Many of these classifications seem self-explanatory, especially if a building type is straightforward, but remember that you need to know three things before you can accurately determine the occupancy classification: (1) the type of activity occurring, (2) the expected number of occupants, (3) whether any unusual hazards or risk factors are present. These factors can affect the classification of a building type or spaces within a building.

A boutique that sells clothing, for example, has an *activity* that is straightforward. It is a Mercantile occupancy. However, in some cases, small differences in the use can change the occupancy classification. For example, a television studio is a Business occupancy, but if the studio allows audience viewing, it will typically be considered an Assembly occupancy. You need to know specifically what types of activities are occurring.

Many of the classifications allow for a specific *number of people*. For example, for spaces that appear to be an Assembly use, if a small number of people will be using the space it may be allowed to be classified as Business. When using the *IBC*, if a day care has less than five children, it may be considered Residential, but if it has more than five it may be considered Institutional or Educational. So, if the number of occupants increases or decreases, you may need to reexamine the occupancy classification.

Hazards to occupants can include harmful substances and/or potentially harmful situations. (See inset titled *Risk Factors and Hazards in Occupancies* on page 45.) When either is present, different types of requirements are necessary. The storage or use of flammable, explosive, or toxic materials is considered to be hazardous and can either change an occupancy to a stricter classification or require all or part of a building to be classified as a Hazardous occupancy and be subject to tougher codes. Small levels of certain hazardous materials, however, are allowed in almost every occupancy classification. For example, a small amount of paint can be stored in any occupancy. However, in large amounts it would be considered a Hazardous use. Certain situations within a building or the condition of the occupants themselves can create potential risk factors or hazards as well. Low light levels, low awareness or mental capacity, restricted movement due to security, and similar characteristics can create potential hazardous situations. If you are aware that hazardous materials or situations will be present in the building or space, it may affect the appropriate choice of occupancy classification.

RISK FACTORS AND HAZARDS IN OCCUPANCIES

The type of risk factors or hazards found in a building help to determine its occupancy classification. They can vary dramatically from one building type to the next. Each occupancy was created by the code organizations to handle different types of hazards. Some of the risk factors that are typically considered when determining an occupancy classification are:

- ❑ Number of occupants (large group versus a small gathering)
- ❑ If occupants are at rest or sleeping
- ❑ Alertness of the occupants (considers mental capabilities and inherent distractions caused by the activities going on in the space)
- ❑ Mobility of the occupants (considers physical abilities, age, and security measures)
- ❑ Familiarity of occupants with the space or building
- ❑ Typical characteristics of the space used for a particular activity (includes fixed seating and aisles, light levels, noise levels, etc.)
- ❑ Potential for spread of fire (due to airborne flammable particles, storage of hazardous materials, combustible finishes, decoration or contents, etc.)

These risk factors were considered by the code organizations in the development of each occupancy classification and their various subcategories. You may also need to consider if any of these factors are specifically known to exist within the proposed space. You must consider both the occupants in the space and the use of the space, to correctly determine the occupancy classification. Similar risk factors must also be considered when working with performance codes.

COMPARING THE CODES

The *International Building Code (IBC)*, the *NFPA 5000*, and the *Life Safety Code (LSC)* assign occupancy classifications to similar uses of a space or building. When using the building codes and the *LSC*, knowing the appropriate occupancy classification and/or subclassification is the most important step to understanding what code and standard requirements apply to your space or building. Most of the requirements and a majority of the exceptions will be based on occupancy. And, since the NFPA codes are organized largely by individual occupancy chapters, you must know the occupancy to refer to the correct chapter to determine the requirements that apply to your project.

Other codes also use the occupancy classifications to call out particular code requirements. This includes the fire codes. The *International Fire Code (IFC)* provides specific fire-related requirements for each occupancy type within various chapters. For example, if you need to know if the *IFC* requires an Educational facility to have an automatic sprinkler system, you would find it in the "Automatic Sprinkler Systems" section within the chapter titled "Fire Protection Systems." (This is true for most of the I-Code publications.) The *Uniform Fire Code* (*UFC* or *NFPA 1*) has a separate chapter titled "Occupant Fire Safety" listing similar information.

The fire codes provide additional requirements for other special uses as well. This includes unusual buildings and rooms that might not be covered in the building codes. Because these uses have unique activities or hazards associated with them, special requirements are called out by separate chapters or sections within the fire codes. For example, both the *IFC* and the *UFC* have chapters on airports, cleanrooms in laboratories, and rooms used for dry cleaning. If you have a special use in your design, be sure to research the building code and the fire code when required in your jurisdiction.

The assigning of occupancy classifications by the codes allows for some assumptions to be made as to how people will be able to react and move within a space or building in the case of a fire or emergency. The prescriptive requirements then define specifically how safety can be achieved. By contrast, when using performance codes, only general parameters for what should be considered about the activities and the occupants are given by the codes. The design must then describe and/or prove how safety is accomplished. Therefore, if you have an unusual building type or an occupancy with multiple uses, you may want to consider using performance criteria if allowed by the jurisdiction.

The *ICC Performance Code (ICCPC)* has a section titled "Use and Occupancy Classification" within the "Design Performance Levels" chapter. Instead of grouping types of activities into occupancy types, it states that the objective is to identify the primary use of a space or building and the risk factors associated with that use. The risk factors that must be considered include the type of activity, hazards, number of occupants, length of occupancy, alertness (sleeping or awake), familiarity with the space, vulnerability (lack of mobility or cognitive awareness), and whether occupants are related. The NFPA codes discuss similar issues that should be considered by discussing occupant characteristics and assumptions within the "Performance-based Option" chapter in each code. The design must then take into account the unique characteristics of the use and occupants.

Because accessibility requirements apply to almost every occupancy type or building use, be sure to refer to the necessary accessibility documents. The building codes include an accessibility chapter and refer you to the accessibility standard *ICC/ANSI 117.1*. Depending on the building type, you will also need to use the Americans with Disabilities Act (ADA) guidelines or the *FHA Accessibility Guidelines (FHAG)*. Many include requirements for specific building types as well. In addition, the ADA guidelines have requirements that must be met for certain occupancies such as Mercantile and Health Care, although some building uses may be exempt. (See the section on ADA regulations later in this chapter and Appendix A for more information.)

DESCRIPTION OF OCCUPANCIES

Use the following description of each occupancy to help you determine the occupancy classification of a space or building. In addition, an occupancy may be subdivided into smaller, more specific categories. For example, the *IBC* divides its Assembly occupancy into five different subclassifications. These subclassifications are explained as well. A wide range of common building types has been provided to help you get started.

The list is not all-inclusive, and it does not replace the applicable code publications. You must refer to them as well. Each code also classifies its occupancies a little differently. For example, the classifications used in this chapter are based on the ICC's I-Codes. Although many are similar to those used in the NFPA codes, the NFPA may use a different name for a classification or subdivide them differently. You can refer to Figure 2.2 for a comparison of how each occupancy classification differs in the *International Building Code (IBC)*, the *NFPA 5000*, and the *Life Safety Code (LSC)*.

Assembly Occupancy

A building or part of a building is classified as an Assembly occupancy if people gather for political, social, or religious functions, recreation, entertainment, eating, drinking, or awaiting transportation. The most common shared characteristic of an Assembly occupancy is that it holds a large number of people (usually more than 50) who are unfamiliar with the space. Other common characteristics include such aspects as low light levels, the occupant's lack of awareness of surroundings, and the potential for panic because of the number of occupants. Because of these multiple risk factors, there are a number of additional codes that apply strictly to Assembly occupancies.

Note

A restaurant can be classified as a Business occupancy (if the number of occupants is small enough), as an Assembly, or as an accessory to a larger adjacent occupancy.

Typically in Assembly occupancies, there are a large number of occupants. Examples include a theater or large restaurant. However, when a space is used for a small group of people to gather—such as a college classroom, an office conference room, or a small-scale restaurant—the codes often allow these uses to be classified under another occupancy type. The NFPA codes use 50 people as the cutoff point. (Some jurisdictions may use a different limit.) Business is a common reclassification. For example, a small restaurant may be classified as a Business

Occupancy Classification	ICC **International Building Code**	NFPA **Life Safety Code** and **NFPA 5000**
ASSEMBLY	**A-1** Assembly, Theaters (Fixed Seats) **A-2** Assembly, Food and/or Drink Consumption **A-3** Assembly, Worship, Recreation, Amusement **A-4** Assembly, Indoor Sporting Events **A-5** Assembly, Outdoor Activities	**A-A** Assembly, O.L. > 1000 **A-B** Assembly, O.L. > 300 1000 **A-C** Assembly, O.L. ≥ 50 ≤ 300
BUSINESS	**B** Business	**B** Business
EDUCATION	**E** Educational (includes some Day Care)	**E** Educational
FACTORY/INDUSTRIAL	**F-1** Factory Industrial, Moderate Hazard **F-2** Factory Industrial, Low Hazard	**I-A** Industrial, General **I-B** Industrial, Special Purpose **I-C** Industrial, High Hazard
HAZARDOUS	**H-1** Hazardous, Detonation Hazard **H-2** Hazardous, Deflagration Hazard or Accelerated Burning **H-3** Hazardous, Physical or Combustible Hazard **H-4** Hazardous, Health Hazard **H-5** Hazardous, Hazardous Production Materials (HPM)	(included in Group I)
INSTITUTIONAL	**I-1** Institutional, Supervised Personal Care, O.L. > 16 **I-2** Institutional, Health Care **I-3** Institutional, Restrained **I-4** Institutional, Day Care Facilities	**D-I** Detentional/Correctional, Free Egress **D-II** Detentional/Correctional, Zoned Egress **D-III** Detentional/Correctional, Zoned Impeded Egress **D-IV** Detentional/Correctional, Impeded Egress **D-V** Detentional/Correctional, Contained **H** Health Care **DC** Day Care
MERCANTILE	**M** Mercantile	**M-A** Mercantile, > 3 levels or >30,000 sq.ft. **M-B** Mercantile, floor above or below grade level, or > 3,000 ≤ 30,000 sq.ft. **M-C** Mercantile, 1 story and ≤ 3,000
RESIDENTIAL	**R-1** Residential, Transient **R-2** Residential, Multi-Dwelling Unit **R-3** Residential, One- and Two-Dwellings Units **R-4** Residential, Care and Assisted Living Facilities O.L. > 5 ≤ 16	**R-A** Residential, Hotels and Dormitories **R-B** Residential, Apartments **R-C** Residential, Lodging or Rooming Houses **R-D** Residential, One- and Two-Family Dwellings **R-E** Residential, Board and Care
STORAGE	**S-1** Storage, Moderate Hazard **S-2** Storage, Low Hazard	**S** Storage
UTILITY/MISCELLANEOUS	**U** Utility and Miscellaneous	Special Structures and High-rise Buildings

NOTE: The *Life Safety Code* designates between new and existing, the*NFPA 5000* does not.

O.L. = Occupancy Load

Figure 2.2 Comparison of Occupancy Classifications (This chart is a summary of information contained in the *International Building Code (IBC),* the *NFPA 5000*, and the *Life Safety Code (LSC)*. Neither the ICC nor the NFPA assume responsibility for the accuracy or the completion of this chart.)

occupancy if its occupant load is less than 50. In many cases, the codes will also allow any Assembly-type use with an occupant load less than 50 to be considered as the same occupancy type that it serves. For example, a small conference room in an elementary school would be classified as Educational.

Note

A good rule of thumb is that when the occupant load is 50 or more, you should research the requirements for an Assembly occupancy.

Although the NFPA codes rely on the number of people to determine its classification of an Assembly, the *IBC* bases its classifications more on the type of activity and not the density of occupants. As a result, NFPA codes have fewer Assembly subclassifications. (See Figure 2.2.) Each building code also provides specific requirements for unique uses such as malls, theaters with stages, and other building types that may seem to fit the Assembly use. In the *IBC* this information is in a separate special-use chapter; in the NFPA codes it is included in the Assembly occupancy chapters.

The *IBC* designates five subclassifications of Assembly based on the type of activity occurring. They are designated as A-1 through A-5.

A-1

This type is for the viewing of performing arts or movies. The space often includes a stage. (There are many code requirements specifically for stages.) The common characteristics of these types of spaces are low light levels and above normal sound levels. Seating usually consists of fixed seating with well-defined aisles. Occupants are alert but generally unfamiliar with the building.

Sample Building Types

Motion picture theaters
Radio and television studios with audiences
Symphony and concert halls
Theaters for stage production

A-2

This type is for the consumption of food and drink. Often these types of spaces have low light levels, loud music, late operating hours, and ill-defined aisles (e.g., movable tables and chairs). The serving of food and drink is the most defining characteristic.

Sample Building Types

Banquet halls
Dance halls (serving food and drink)
Drinking establishments
Fast-food restaurants
Fellowship halls (serving food and drink)
Night clubs
Restaurants (can also be classified as Business)
Taverns and bars (can also be classified as Business)

A-3

This type is for the gathering of people for worship, recreation, or amusement. Types of activities that are not classified by other types of Assembly are typically included in this subclassification. The common characteristics of this subclassification are clear or defined egress patterns and moderate to low fuel loads. For example, in a church or an auditorium, aisles used for egress are defined by the placement of pews or chairs. Occupants in an A-3 subclassification are also usually alert and are often more familiar with the space than in other assembly uses.

Sample Building Types

- Amusement arcades
- Armories
- Art galleries
- Assembly halls
- Auditoriums
- Bowling lanes
- Churches and religious structures
- Community halls
- Courtrooms
- Dance halls (not including food or drink consumption)
- Exhibition halls
- Fellowship halls
- Funeral homes
- Galleries
- Gymnasiums (without spectator seating)
- Lecture halls (can also be Business)
- Libraries
- Mortuary chapels
- Museums
- Passenger stations, terminals, or depots (waiting areas)
- Pool and billiard rooms
- Public assembly halls
- Recreation halls and piers
- Tents for assembly

A-4

This type is for the viewing of indoor sporting events and other activities with spectator seating. The spectator seating can consist of a defined area for seating or fixed seats such as bleachers. Although A-3 and A-4 can have similar activities, if a defined area for viewing the activities is provided, then it is an A-4. For example, an indoor pool can be classified as an A-3 Assembly, but if the pool area also includes seating for viewing swim competitions, it would be considered an A-4. (Similar activities can also occur between A-4 and A-5 Assemblies.)

Sample Building Types

- Arenas
- Gymnasiums
- Indoor skating rinks
- Indoor swimming pools
- Indoor tennis courts

A-5

This type is for the participation in or viewing of outdoor activities. This would be similar to A-4, except that it is outdoors.

Sample Building Types

- Amusement park structures
- Bleachers
- Grandstands
- Stadiums

Business Occupancy

A building or part of a building is classified as a Business occupancy if it is used for the transaction of business, such as accounting, record keeping, and other similar functions. It also includes the rendering of professional services. Limited areas that are a natural part of a business setting, such as small storage or supply areas and breakrooms, are included as well. The risk factors in a Business occupancy are considered to be relatively low. This is because there is a low concentration of occupants and they are alert and generally familiar with their environment. It is considered one of the lowest-risk occupancies.

Note

A wide variety of building types can fall under the Business occupancy classification.

This classification can become very broad. For example, a smaller Assembly-like occupancy that has a fewer number of occupants can sometimes be classified as a Business occupancy, such as a small restaurant. Conversely, when the function or size of any of the Business building types expands beyond a typical business, the occupancy needs to be reexamined. Examples might include city halls that include assembly areas or doctors' offices that are part of a hospital. These types of buildings may be classified as an Assembly occupancy, an Institutional occupancy, or a mixed occupancy. (See the section on Mixed Occupancies later in this chapter.)

Educational-type occupancies can also be confusing. Colleges and universities (educational facilities after the 12th grade) are considered Business occupancies. Yet, business and vocational schools are often considered as the same occupancy as the trade or vocation that is being taught. For example, general classrooms for a college would be classified as Business, but the classrooms for instruction in automotive repair may be considered Factory/Industrial.

Sample Building Types

- Airport traffic control towers
- Animal hospitals, kennels, and pounds (part of building could be considered Storage)
- Automobile and other motor vehicle showrooms
- Automobile service stations (can also be classified as Hazardous)

- Banks
- Barber shops
- Beauty shops
- Car washes
- City halls
- Civic administration buildings
- Clinics (outpatient)
- College and university classrooms
- Dentist's offices
- Doctor's offices
- Dry-cleaning facilities (can also be classified as Hazardous)
- Educational facilities (above 12th grade)
- Electronic data processing facilities
- Fire stations
- Florists and nurseries
- Government offices
- Greenhouses
- Laboratories (nonhazardous)
- Laboratories (testing and research)
- Laundromats
- Libraries (can also be classified as Assembly or Business)
- Medical offices (separate from Institutional occupancies)
- Motor vehicle showrooms
- Office buildings
- Outpatient clinics, ambulatory
- Police stations
- Post offices
- Print shops
- Professional offices (architect, attorney, dentist, physician, etc.)
- Radio and television stations (without audiences)
- Repair garages (small, nonhazardous)
- Telecommunication equipment buildings
- Telephone exchanges
- Travel agencies

Note

Although it would seem normal for colleges and universities to fall under the Educational occupancy, these building types are typically classified as Business or Assembly occupancies.

Educational Occupancy

A building or part of a building is classified as an Educational occupancy if it is used for educational purposes by a specified number of persons at any one time through the 12th grade. Usually the specified number of persons ranges from six to the minimum number of people required for an Assembly occupancy. (For colleges and universities, see Assembly and Business occupancies.) The NFPA codes also specify a minimum amount of time that a space is used for educational purposes. For example, if there is less than 12 hours of instruction per week, the building type could be governed by a different occupancy classification according to the *LSC*.

It is common for an Educational occupancy to be considered a mixed occupancy due to the auditoriums, cafeterias, and gymnasiums usually built with them. In most cases, these additional uses will be classified separately under an Assembly occupancy. Vocational shops, laboratories, and similar areas within a school will usually be considered Educational, even though they may require additional fire protection. As mentioned in a previous section, if the entire school is considered vocational, some codes may require that it fall into the same classification as the trade or vocation being taught. In addition, a length of stay over 24 hours may require the reclassification of an Educational occupancy to Institutional, such as an adult care facility that provides extended care. Day care centers can also be classified as Institutional, depending on the number of children and their age. You should verify the proper designation with the local code official when necessary.

Sample Building Types

- Academies
- Day care centers (can also be considered Institutional)
- Elementary schools
- High schools
- Junior high schools
- Kindergartens
- Nursery schools
- Preschools
- Secondary schools

Factory or Industrial Occupancy

A building or part of a building is designated as a Factory or Industrial occupancy if it is used for assembling, disassembling, fabricating, finishing, manufacturing, packaging, processing, or repairing. This designation generally refers to a building in which a certain type of product is made. The product that is made or the materials used to make the product can be considered a low or moderate hazard. If it is a more hazardous material or product, the building or space where it is made can be considered a Hazardous occupancy. The sample product types listed below are typically considered low to moderate types of hazards by the building codes. However, each code groups them a little differently under the Factory/Industrial occupancy, and there may be different code requirements, depending on which hazardous group it is in. For example, the *IBC* divides its Factory occupancy into F-1 and F-2. The NFPA uses the term Industrial occupancy and has three subclassifications. (See Figure 2.2. Also see Hazardous Occupancy.) These subclassifications are made for the different levels of hazardous materials or activities that are part of the manufacturing process. Be sure to refer to the specific code to determine if a manufactured product is considered moderate or low hazard; if more hazardous materials are used or created in the space or building, it may need to be classified as a Hazardous occupancy.

Sample Building Types

- Assembly plants
- Factories
- Manufacturing plants
- Mills
- Processing plants

Low and Moderate Hazardous Products

- Aircraft
- Appliances
- Athletic equipment
- Automobiles and other motor vehicles
- Bakeries
- Beverages (alcoholic)
- Beverages (nonalcoholic)
- Bicycles

Boats (building)
Boiler works
Brick and masonry
Brooms or brushes
Business machines
Cameras and photo equipment
Canneries
Canvas or similar fabric
Carpets and rugs (includes cleaning)
Ceramic products
Clothing
Condensed powdered milk manufacturing
Construction and agricultural machinery
Creameries
Disinfectants
Dry cleaning and dyeing
Creameries
Electric light plants and power houses
Electrolytic—reducing works
Electronics
Engines (includes rebuilding)
Film (photographic)
Food processing
Foundries
Furniture
Glass products
Gypsum products
Hemp products
Ice
Jute products
Laboratories (can also be classified as Business)
Laundries
Leather products
Machinery
Metal products (fabrication and assembly)
Millwork (sash and door)
Motion pictures and television filming
Musical instruments
Optical goods
Paper mills or products
Plastic products
Printing or publishing
Recreational vehicles
Refineries
Refuse incineration
Sawmills
Shoes
Smokehouses
Soaps and detergents
Sugar refineries
Textiles
Tobacco
Trailers
Upholstering
Water pumping plants
Wood (distillation of)
Woodworking (cabinetry)

Hazardous Occupancy

A building or part of a building that involves the generation, manufacturing, processing, storage, or other use of hazardous materials is typically classified as a Hazardous occupancy. These materials can include flammable dust, fibers, or liquids, combustible liquids, poisonous gases, explosive agents, corrosive liquids, oxidizing materials, radioactive materials, and carcinogens, among others. In general, this classification is categorized by an unusually high degree of explosive, fire, physical, and/or health hazards.

Note

The NFPA codes do not have a separate Hazardous occupancy. Instead, it is a subclassification under the Industrial occupancy.

Hazardous building types require additional precautions. Each of the codes sets different standards and has special sections dedicated to hazardous uses, which list very specific materials. In most cases, a Hazardous occupancy can be subclassified into a low, medium, or high hazard. Each building code categories the hazards a little differently. Often the lower hazards are made part of the Factory/Industrial or Storage occupancy classification. Each code also has a different number of subclassifications. The *IBC* has five different Hazard classifications (H-1 through H-5). The NFPA codes, however, include high-hazard building types as a subclassification under Industrial. (See Figure 2.2.) They do not have a separate Hazardous occupancy.

Another factor to consider is the amount of hazardous materials. If the amount of hazardous materials is small enough, the space or building may not be considered Hazardous by the codes. A common example is a chemistry lab in a high school. As more performance-type requirements are introduced into code publications, more emphasis will be placed on the types of products or materials used in a space rather than concentrating on the type of building.

If you are designing the interior of a building that you believe contains hazardous materials or conditions, be sure to consult the specific codes and work closely with the local code officials. Some buildings may require only part of the building to be classified as Hazardous. (Hazardous buildings and materials are beyond the scope of this book.)

Note

Sometimes two different buildings with the same building type may have different occupancy classifications if hazardous materials are present in one but not the other. For example, some auto repair shops are considered a Hazardous occupancy. Others are considered a Business occupancy.

Sample Building Types

- Airport hangars or airport repair hangars
- Dry-cleaning plants
- Explosives manufacturers
- Film storage, combustible
- Firearm/ammunition warehouses
- Gas plants
- Laboratories with hazardous chemicals
- Paint and solvent manufacturers
- Paint shops and spray painting rooms
- Pesticide warehouses
- Power plants
- Pumping/service stations
- Tank farms
- Warehouses with hazardous materials

Institutional Occupancy

A building or part of a building is classified as an Institutional occupancy if it includes medical treatment or other type of care or contains occupants detained under security measures. The primary distinction of this classification is that the occupants are either limited in their mobility, immobile, or incapable of mobility due to physical or security restraints. In most cases, the occupants must depend on others to help them evacuate the building in case of an emergency. The *IBC* has four Institutional subclassifications (I-1 through I-4). The NFPA, on the other hand, separates these uses into different occupancy classifications. The NFPA codes refer to them as Detentional/Correctional, Health Care and Day Care occupancies. (See Figure 2.2.)

Note

The *IBC* has four Institutional subclassifications. The NFPA codes divide these into separate Health Care, Detentional/ Correctional, and Day Care occupancies.

Using the *IBC* designations, each subclassification is described as follows. The similar NFPA classification is given as well. Note, however, that the specific definition for each NFPA occupancy may vary from those in the *IBC*. The minimum and maximum quantities of occupants can vary as well. For example, the minimum number for a I-4 classification in the *IBC* is five and the minimum number for a Day Care occupancy in the NFPA is four. You should refer to the applicable code to determine the occupancy classification correctly. (Also see inset titled *Types of Rooms and Spaces* on page 63.)

Because some uses can be determined by subtle differences, you may need to discuss this with a code official to confirm whether the jurisdiction will consider your facility Institutional, Residential, or one of the other NFPA classifications. The applicable code requirements can vary significantly between these occupancies.

I-1

This type is for the housing and care of a certain number of occupants on a 24-hour basis. The codes often use 16 occupants as the limit. (This quantity does not include staff.) These occupants, because of age or mental disability, must be supervised. However, they can typically respond to an emergency without physical assistance from staff. If fewer than 16 people were being cared for with the same characteristics, it would be reclassified as Residential. The NFPA considers this building type a Residential occupancy (Board and Care), which includes a section for larger and smaller types of facilities.

Sample Building Types

- Alcohol and drug centers
- Assisted living facilities (can also be classified as Residential)
- Congregate care facilities
- Convalescent facilities
- Group homes
- Halfway houses
- Social rehabilitation facilities

I-2

This type is for medical, surgical, psychiatric, nursing, or other type of care on a 24-hour basis for more than five persons. These occupants are not capable of self-preservation. If fewer than five people were being cared for, it would typically be reclassified as Residential. The similar NFPA category is under a separate occupancy classification called Health Care.

Sample Building Types

- Day cares (24 hour)
- Detoxification facilities
- Hospitals
- Infirmaries
- Limited care facilities
- Mental hospitals
- Nursing homes (intermediate care and skilled nursing)
- Sanitariums
- Treatment or rehabilitation centers

I-3

This type is for the detention of more than five persons. These occupants are incapable of self-preservation due to security measures. There are additional "conditions" based on the level of security provided and the amount of free movement allowed within the building that need to be considered to accurately determine the specific code requirements for this use. (This is beyond the scope of this book.) The similar NFPA category is the Detention/Correction occupancy classification, which is divided into five separate subclassifications (D-I through D-V) depending on the level of security.

Sample Building Types

- Correctional institutions
- Detention centers
- Jails
- Prerelease centers
- Prisons
- Reformatories
- Work camps

I-4

This type is for the care of more than five persons for less than 24 hours a day. This includes adults and children under 2½ years of age. One typical exception is that if adults in this type of facility are incapable of self-preservation without help from staff, it would be reclassified as an I-3. Another is when the area where children are cared for opens directly to the exterior; it then can be reclassified as Educational. (Also see Residential occupancy R-3.) This is considered as a separate Day Care occupancy in the NFPA codes.

Sample Building Types

- Adult day cares
- Day care centers—caring for infants (can also be classified as Educational)

Mercantile Occupancy

A building or part of a building is classified as a Mercantile occupancy if it is open to the public and used for the display, sale, or rental of merchandise. This classification includes most stores and showrooms, including large malls. The *IBC* groups these into one main occupancy. Mercantile in the NFPA has three subclassifications based on the type and size of the building. (See Figure 2.2.)

You also need to consider the codes when there is a group of retail stores. Each store would be considered a separate Mercantile occupancy. However, as a group it may also be considered a *covered mall.* The codes have special requirements for malls because in addition to the large anchor retail stores and the multiple smaller retail tenants, there can be other uses within the same building as well. Most typically, these can include restaurants and entertainment areas. You may have to determine if the general mercantile requirements apply or if the requirements for a mall will apply to your project. (Usually you will use one or the other.) These mall requirements can be found in the "special occupancy" chapter of the *IBC*. In the NFPA codes, special requirements for malls are called out within the Mercantile chapter. When necessary, review these requirements with the code official in your jurisdiction.

Sample Building Types

- Auction rooms
- Automotive service stations
- Bakeries
- Department stores
- Drug stores
- Grocery stores
- Markets
- Paint stores (without bulk handling)
- Rental stores
- Retail stores
- Salesrooms
- Shopping centers
- Shops
- Show rooms
- Specialty stores
- Supermarkets
- Wholesale stores (other than warehouses)

Note

Certain Residential building types may need to be reclassified as Institutional, depending on the number of occupants and their length of stay. Examples include day cares and nursing homes.

Residential Occupancy

A building or part of a building that acts as a dwelling and provides sleeping accommodations for normal residential purposes is designated as a Residential occupancy. Most of the codes further categorize this classification based on the probable number of occupants and how familiar they are with their surroundings. For example, a person in a hotel would probably not be familiar with the escape routes, making it more hazardous. Such an occupancy will need stricter codes than an apartment complex, where a tenant should be more familiar with his/her surroundings. In some cases, the number of units in the building may also make a difference. (For other occupancies that provide sleeping accommodations but with additional care, see Institutional occupancy.)

The *IBC* has four subclassifications: R-1 through R-4. The NFPA codes separate these into five subclassifications. They include Apartment Buildings, Hotels and Dormitories, Lodging or Rooming Houses, One- and Two-Family Dwellings, and Board and Care. (See Figure 2.2.) Although these categories are similar to those in the *IBC*, there are differences. Be sure to refer to the applicable code to determine the correct occupancy subclassification. (Also see inset titled *Types of Rooms and Spaces* on page 63.)

R-1

This type is for occupants who are transient, or in other words, do not stay for an extended amount of time. If occupants typically stay more than 30 days, a building type may be required to be reclassified to R-2 or other use. In the NFPA, R-1 building types are addressed separately as hotels in the Hotels and Dormitories subclassification and in the Lodging or Rooming Houses subclassification.

Note

The term *dwelling unit* is often associated with Residential and Institutional occupancies. (See inset titled *Types of Rooms and Spaces* for more information).

Sample Building Types

- Boarding houses
- Hotels
- Inns
- Lodging and rooming houses
- Motels
- Rooming houses

R-2

This type is for buildings that contain more than two dwelling units with occupants who are somewhat permanent. The similar NFPA categories include Apartment Buildings, Lodging or Rooming Houses, and Hotels and Dormitories. However, the NFPA sets limits on the number of people allowed to use the space rather than the number of dwelling units in the building.

Sample Building Types

- Apartments
- Boarding houses (depends on length of stay)
- Convents
- Dormitories
- Fraternities/sororities
- Hotels (depends on length of stay)
- Monasteries
- Motels (depends on length of stay)
- Multiple single-family dwellings
- Vacation timeshare properties

R-3

This type is for more permanent residences but, unlike R-2, it is strictly for single or duplex units. The typical single-family home falls into this category. Some residential care facilities (see R-4) may also be allowed under this classification, if the number of occupants is limited to five and the length of stay is less than 24 hours. If using the I-Codes, a jurisdiction will typically require the use of the *International Residential Code (IRC)* for the specific code requirements. The NFPA codes refer you to the chapter on one- and two-family dwellings. (See Appendix B for more information on family residences.) Verify with your code official which code is applicable to your residential project.

R-4

This type is for small to medium-sized residential care facilities. The allowable size of the facility is based on the number of persons receiving care and does not include staff. The typical number of occupants is between 6 and 16 residents. If fewer people are receiving care, it may be considered a R-3. If a higher number of people are receiving care, then it may be considered Institutional. (See I-1.) The similar NFPA category would be Residential Board and Care. It could also be considered a Health Care occupancy by the NFPA, depending on the number of occupants.

Sample Building Types

- Assisted living facilities (can also be classified as Institutional)
- Retirement homes
- Residential board and care facilities
- Halfway houses
- Group homes
- Congregate care facilities
- Social rehabilitation facilities
- Alcohol and drug abuse centers
- Convalescent facilities (can also be classified as Institutional)

Storage Occupancy

A building or a predominant part of a building is classified as a Storage occupancy if it is used for storing or sheltering products, merchandise, vehicles, or animals. Minor storage uses, such as smaller storage rooms and supply closets, are typically treated as part of the predominant occupancy.

Similar to the Factory/Industrial occupancies, low or moderate hazard contents are typically allowed in the Storage occupancy, while the storage of high hazard contents may cause the building or space to be classified under Hazardous.

The classification depends on the type of hazard and the quantity being stored. It is important to check the code to determine the level of hazard of the material being stored. A list of low and moderate hazardous items is shown below, but remember that each code groups them differently and each level will have slightly different requirements. The *IBC* has two storage subclassifications—one for moderate hazards (S-1) and another for low hazards (S-2). The NFPA has only one main storage classification. If you are unsure about the type of hazardous materials being stored, check with the code official in your jurisdiction.

In addition, within Storage building types it is generally understood that relatively few people will occupy the space. If the number of occupants is large or increases substantially in the future, the building occupancy may need to be reclassified.

Sample Building Types

- Aircraft hangars (nonhazardous)
- Creameries
- Cold storage facilities
- Freight terminals and depots
- Grain elevators
- Repair garages (nonhazardous)
- Truck and marine terminals
- Warehouses (nonhazardous)

Sample Low and Moderate Hazard Storage Contents

- Asbestos
- Beer or wine up to 12% alcohol in metal, glass, or ceramic containers
- Cement in bags
- Chalk and crayons
- Cold storage
- Creameries
- Dairy products in non-wax-coated paper containers
- Dry cell batteries
- Dry insecticides
- Electrical coils
- Electrical insulation
- Electrical motors
- Empty cans
- Food products
- Foods in noncombustible containers
- Fresh fruits and vegetables in nonplastic trays or containers
- Frozen foods
- Glass
- Glass bottles, empty or filled with noncombustible liquids
- Gypsum board
- Inert pigments
- Ivory
- Meats
- Metal cabinets
- Metal desks with plastic tops and trim
- Metal parts
- Metals
- Mirrors
- New empty cans
- Oil-filled and other types of distribution transformers
- Open parking structures
- Porcelain and pottery
- Stoves
- Talc and soapstone
- Washers and dryers

Utility or Miscellaneous Occupancy

A building or part of a building that is not typical and/or cannot be properly classified in any of the other occupancy groups is often classified as a Utility or Miscellaneous occupancy. The building codes and *LSC* list different items in this category, and they are usually covered as a group in a separate chapter or in multiple chapters within each of the codes.

If one of the other occupancies is being housed in an unusual structure, additional codes are usually required. Examples include underground and windowless buildings. The size of the space or building should be a consideration as well. (High-rise buildings are sometimes included here because of the many additional code requirements they must meet.) If you are unsure whether a building would be considered a Utility or Miscellaneous occupancy, check with the code official in the building's jurisdiction in the early stages of a project. (Unusual structures are beyond the scope of this book.)

Sample Building Types

- Agricultural buildings (including barns, stables, livestock shelters)
- Carports
- Grain silos
- Greenhouses
- Mobile homes
- Open structures
- Parking garages (can also be classified as Storage)
- Private garages
- Retaining walls
- Sheds
- Tall fences (over 6 feet, or 1829 mm)
- Tanks
- Temporary structures
- Towers
- Underground structures
- Walkways and tunnels (enclosed)
- Water-surrounded structures
- Windowless buildings

OTHER OCCUPANCY CONSIDERATIONS

Since a majority of code requirements are based on the occupancy classification of the space or building, understanding their differences is important. For many projects there will be additional occupancy-related items that must be considered. In some cases, for example, different code requirements may apply depending on whether the project is considered a renovation or a new construction. In other projects, several occupancies may exist in the same space or building. The relationship between these occupancies will affect how the codes must be applied. These various considerations and additional requirements are discussed in this section.

TYPES OF ROOMS AND SPACES

Each building or space must be assigned an occupancy classification so you can determine which codes apply. In addition, certain rooms within an occupancy can affect the requirements. This is especially true in Residential and Institutional occupancies. The codes have very distinct definitions for various types of spaces, depending on how they are utilized. You should be familiar with the following:

- ❑ *Occupiable space.* A room or enclosed space designed for human occupancy that is equipped with means of egress, light, and ventilation, as required by the codes. This can include the spaces and rooms in most occupancies. It excludes such things as mechanical and electrical rooms, crawl spaces, and attics. If a space is not considered occupiable, it usually does not need to meet typical accessibility requirements as specified in the building codes, the ICC/ANSI standard, and the ADA guidelines.
- ❑ *Dwelling unit.* A single unit providing complete independent living facilities for one or more persons, including permanent provisions for living, sleeping, eating, cooking, and sanitation. Building types that fall into this category include single-family homes, apartment units, townhouses, and certain assisted living units. However, a hotel guest room can also be considered a dwelling unit if it has a kitchenette, eating area (i.e., table or bar top), and living area (i.e., upholstered seating area) in addition to the typical sleeping area and bathroom. (The ICC/ANSI standard and the *IBC* divide dwelling units into Type A and Type B types for accessibility reasons. Type B dwellings have requirements similar to the *FHA Accessibility Guidelines (FHAG).* Type A dwellings have additional requirements for accessibility.)
- ❑ *Sleeping room.* A space is considered a sleeping room when it is used primarily for sleeping and does not fit the definition of a dwelling unit. The space often includes a bathroom, but it would not include a cooking area. Examples include typical guestrooms in hotels and boarding houses, jail cells, dorm rooms, and patient rooms in nursing homes or hospitals.
- ❑ *Living area or room.* This is considered any occupiable space in a Residential occupancy, other than sleeping rooms or rooms that are intended for the combination of sleeping and living. It includes spaces such as bathrooms (or toilet compartments), kitchens, closets, halls, and storage/utility spaces, but can also include other rooms such living rooms, dining rooms, family rooms, and dens.
- ❑ *Habitable room.* A room in a Residential occupancy that is used for living, sleeping, cooking, and eating, but excludes such things as bathrooms, storage/utility spaces, and hallways.

New versus Existing Occupancies

Whether an occupancy is new or existing becomes important when using the *Life Safety Code (LSC)*, because the *LSC* separates its regulations into these two different categories for each occupancy classification. An occupancy is considered *new* if it falls into one of the following categories.

1. The occupancy is in a newly constructed building.
2. The occupancy is relocated to an existing building.
3. The occupancy is in a new addition to an existing building.
4. The occupancy is remaining in the same building, but changing its size or use to a different subclassification.

Note

When using the *LSC*, it makes a difference if the project is considered new or existing. You may also be required to use the *IEBC* instead of the *IBC* in some jurisdictions.

This last category is important to remember since it is the least obvious. A change in occupancy classification can affect a number of other code regulations, including those found in the building codes, the *International Existing Building Code (IEBC)* and the *LSC*. (See Appendix C for more information on changes in occupancies in existing buildings.)

More Than One Occupancy Type

Two or more occupancies can occur in the same building. In fact, it is actually more common to see several different occupancies in the same building than to see a single-occupancy building. A common example is a large hotel. Many larger hotels have restaurants and indoor pools with exercise rooms. The hotel itself would be classified as Residential, and the restaurant and pool would each be classified as an Assembly occupancy.

A variety of examples are indicated below to help you begin analyzing different building types and distinguishing between various uses. (There are many other possibilities.) Notice how often the Assembly and the Business occupancies occur together. These are occupancies you especially want to look for in mixed building types.

- Hotels (Residential) with restaurants, ballrooms, or workout rooms (Assembly or Business)
- Grammar and high schools (Educational) with gymnasiums, auditoriums, and cafeterias (Assembly)
- Office buildings (Business) with day care centers (Educational or Institutional)
- Hospitals (Institutional) with cafeterias (Assembly)
- Reformatories (Institutional) with recreational rooms (Assembly) and offices (Business)
- Factories (Industrial) combined with the office headquarters (Business)
- Malls (Mercantile) with small restaurants (Business) or large food courts (Assembly)

It is important to determine if more than one occupancy is occurring in the same building. If so, it can affect a number of other codes, such as those listed earlier in Figure 2.1. For example, you would need to determine whether the occupancies can be designed as one or if they must be separated by rated walls. The *IBC* refers to the relationship of different occupancies as incidental, accessory, or mixed (separated or non-separated). The NFPA codes define the relationship of more than one occupancy as multiple, mixed or separated occupancies. Each of these will be discussed in this section. For all of these, the ultimate goal is to provide the safest building possible.

Incidental Use

Certain uses within a building are determined to be hazardous when they exist within any occupancy type. These uses are called *incidental use* areas. Typically, these spaces are relatively small compared to the rest of the building. For example, the storage room within the preschool facility (Educational) shown in Plan A of Figure 2.3 would be considered an incidental use area within the other "primary-use" areas such as classrooms and office areas.

The types of spaces and rooms that are considered incidental are called out within each code either within a table or the text. These spaces include boiler rooms, furnace rooms, large storage rooms, and other spaces containing hazardous items. For example, the *IBC* lists specific incidental use areas in a table within the general occupancy chapter, as shown in Chapter 5 in Figure 5.8. As indicated in this table, additional fire and smoke protection is required for these areas. (This is discussed further in Chapter 5.) When this additional protection is provided, all other code requirements for the incidental use follows the codes required for the main occupancy. If this protection is not provided, the building must be classified as a mixed occupancy. (See Mixed Occupancies, page 68.) The NFPA codes list incidental use areas within the occupancy chapter in which they are most likely to occur. For example, you will find the requirement to separate soiled linen rooms in the Health Care occupancy chapter.

Accessory Occupancies

Sometimes two or more occupancies exist in a building, but one or more of them is much smaller than the main occupancy type. In this case, the smaller occupancy(s) may be considered an *accessory* occupancy by the codes. For an area to be considered an accessory use, the codes typically require the smaller occupancy classification(s) to be less than 10 percent of the total area. An example would be a furniture store that offers design services, as shown in Plan B of Figure 2.3. The furniture store is Mercantile, but the design center area would be Business (B). However, since the area of the design center is less than 10 percent of the overall area, it can be considered an *accessory* to the main Mercantile occupancy. And, because it can be

Note

When more than one occupancy exists in the same building or space, it will be considered an accessory, a mixed, or a multiple occupancy.

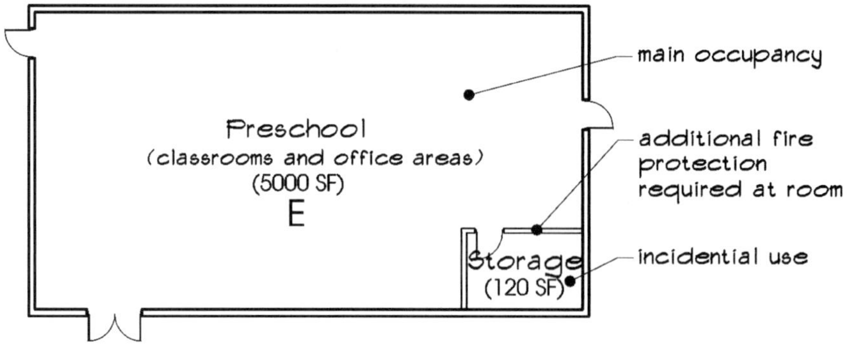

PLAN A - Incidental Use Area

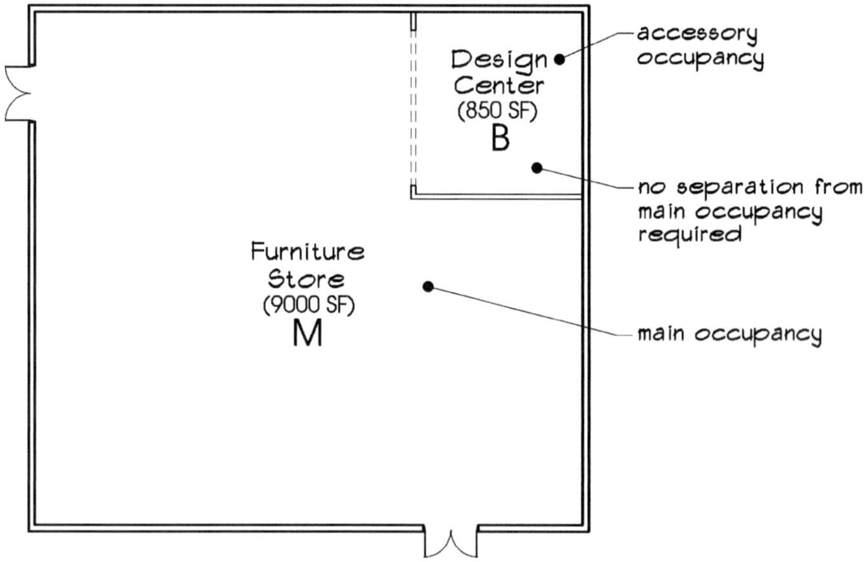

PLAN B - Accessory Occupancy

Figure 2.3 Incidental Use versus Accessory Occupancies (1 square foot = 0.0929 square meter)

considered an accessory use, the two areas will not have to be designed under separate occupancy requirements.

Sometimes there are several smaller uses occurring within a larger occupancy classification, and all are located in the same building. An example would be a large discount store, like the one shown in Plan A of Figure 2.4. This particular store has a bakery, photo shop, hair salon, and snack bar as part of its space. In

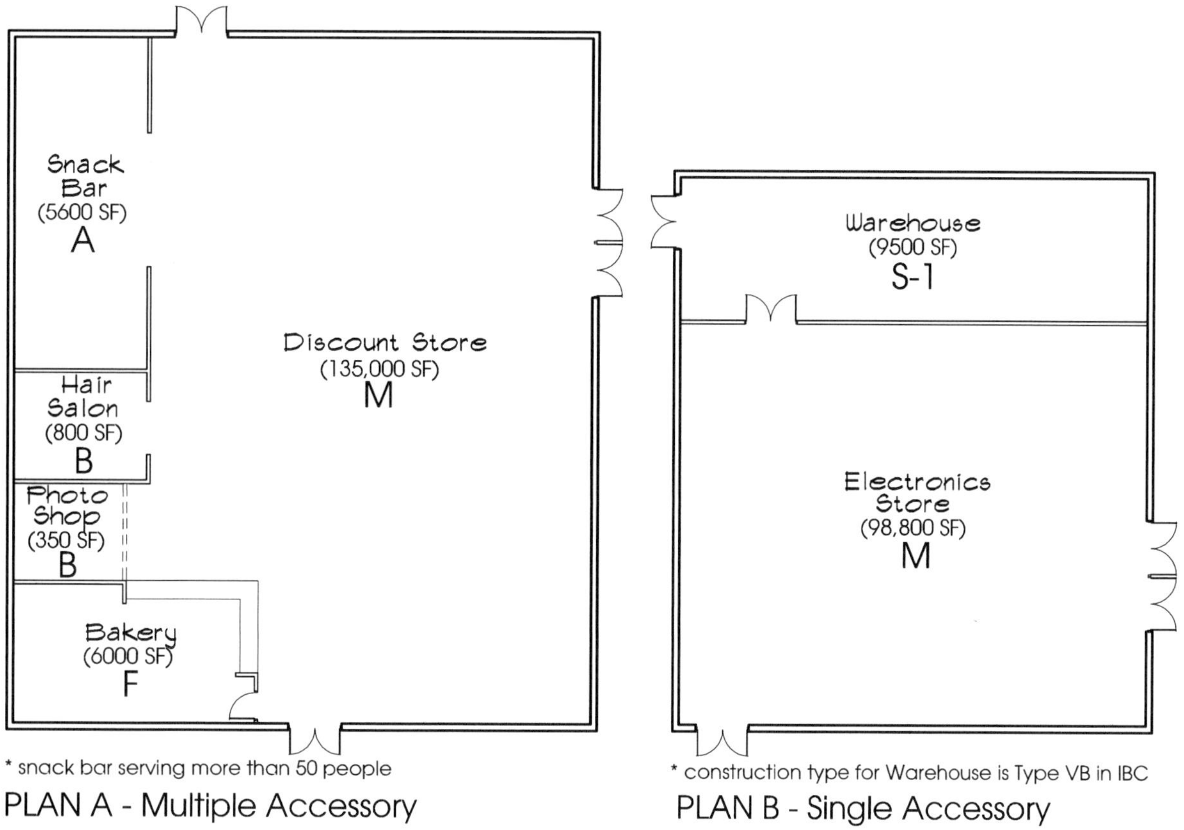

Figure 2.4 Accessory Occupancy Examples (1 square foot = 0.0929 square meter)

this case, all the accessory spaces combined together cannot be more than 10 percent of the total area.

In addition to the 10 percent requirement, an accessory occupancy cannot exceed the allowable area for that occupancy classification in relation to the construction type of the building. For example, Plan B in Figure 2.4 is an electronics store (Mercantile) with its warehouse located in the same building. The warehouse is considered a Storage (S-1) occupancy. It could be considered an accessory occupancy because it does not exceed 10 percent of the total area of the building. However, because the area of the S-1 occupancy exceeds the allowable area for this particular construction type, the S-1 occupancy cannot be considered an accessory to the Mercantile. (Construction types and allowable areas will be discussed in more detail in Chapter 3.) In this case, the storage area would need to meet the code requirements for an S-1 occupancy classification instead of the requirements for a Mercantile occupancy.

If there are approved accessory occupancies within a space or building, most of the code requirements (including the allowable construction type and the automatic sprinkler requirements) are based on the larger occupancy. However, the occupant load and means of egress requirements are based on each individual use. (This is explained later in this chapter.)

In some cases, certain areas are allowed to be accessory regardless of the percentage of area. For example, Assembly areas with an occupant load less than 50, and areas with less than 750 square feet (69.7 s m), are typically considered accessory to the main occupancy. Assembly areas that are accessory to Educational occupancies and in some cases education rooms in religious buildings may be allowed to be accessory as well. It is useful to your design to determine if an area can be considered accessory to the main area, because it simplifies the code requirements and allows areas to be more open. If the smaller occupancy(s) cannot be considered accessory, the space or building would be considered a mixed occupancy. (Hazardous occupancies can never be considered as accessory to another occupancy.)

Mixed Occupancies

When two or more occupancies in a building or space are relatively the same size or do not meet the requirements to be considered accessory, then you have a *mixed occupancy*. A mixed occupancy can exist when different occupancies are adjacent horizontally, as in the Plan in Figure 2.5, or vertically in the case of a multistory building, as shown in the Section in Figure 2.5. Because each occupancy type has different safety risks, special measures are necessary to make the building safe. In general, the codes require that you either separate the occupancies or treat both of them as one using the most stringent requirements. As a result, the *IBC* further divides mixed occupancies into separated mixed occupancies and non-separated mixed occupancies. The NFPA also uses the term *separated* but uses it in relation to multiple occupancies. This is explained in the next section.

When the different occupancies are divided by the required rated assemblies (e.g., walls, floor, and/or ceiling assemblies), these occupancies are considered by the *IBC* to be *separated mixed* occupancies. (The requirements for rated assemblies are discussed further in Chapter 5.) Once separated, each occupancy then must meet the requirements of its own occupancy classification. For example, if you refer to Plan A in Figure 2.6, the Business (B) occupancy and the Mercantile (M) occupancy are separated by a rated wall. Thus, the code requirements for the Business occupancy would apply within the Business occupancy, and vice versa.

Note

Both the *IBC* and the NFPA codes use the term *separated* for when two or more occupancies are divided by rated assemblies—called *separated mixed* by the ICC and *separated multiple* by the NFPA.

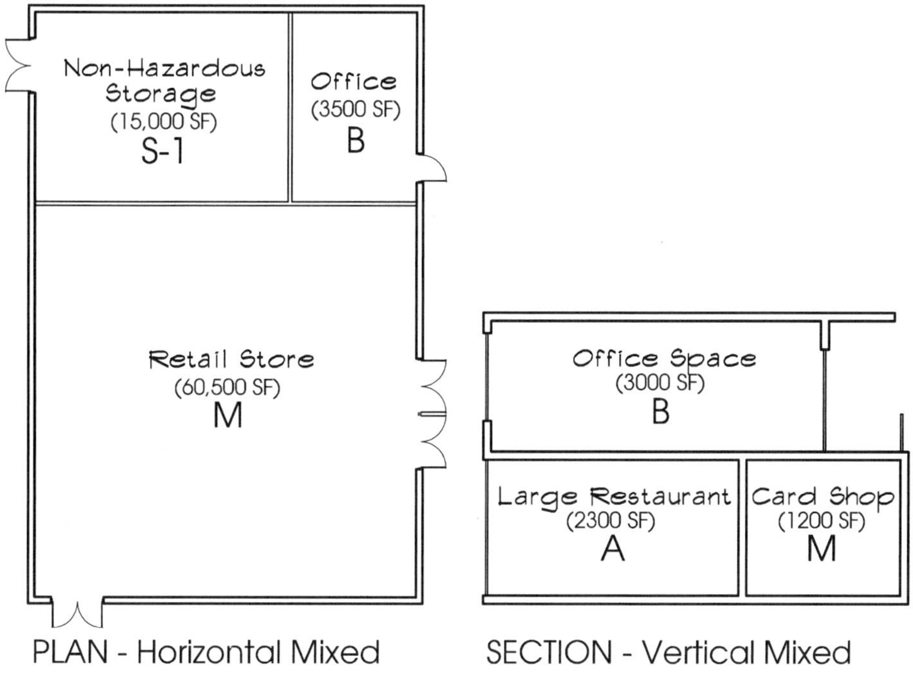

Figure 2.5 Mixed Occupancies: Horizontally and Vertically (1 square foot = 0.0929 square meter)

When there is no rated separation between the occupancies, it is considered by the *IBC* as a *non-separated mixed* occupancy. (This term is not used by the NFPA.) When the occupancies are considered non-separated, both occupancies must then meet the requirements of the most stringent occupancy classification, including construction type, allowable area, finishes, and exiting requirements. For example, in Plan B of Figure 2.6, the Mercantile (M) and the Assembly (A-2) occupancies are separated by a partition only for visual reasons and so are considered non-separated. In this case, the more stringent Assembly requirements would be applied to the entire area of the building, including the gift shop.

Many aspects can influence the choice to treat a mixed occupancy as separated or non-separated. Constructing rated assemblies for separation can be expensive or undesirable to the design, but having to meet the most stringent exiting requirements, construction type, or area limitations for the whole building or space may limit the design unnecessarily. You will have to consider these factors to decide which is the better choice for your project.

Note

The term *mixed multiple* occupancy is unique to the NFPA. Although similar to *non-separated mixed* occupancies in the *IBC*, a mixed multiple occupancy includes a wider variety of building scenarios.

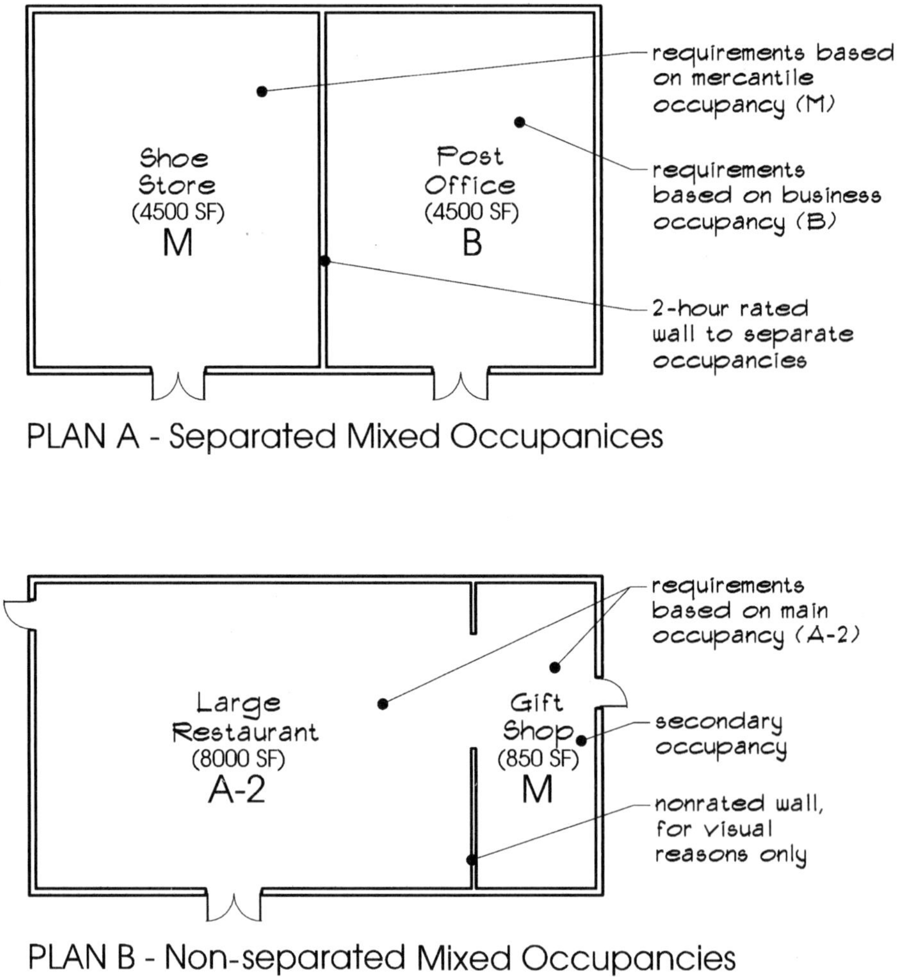

Figure 2.6 Mixed Occupancies in the *IBC*: Separated and Non-separated (1 square foot = 0.0929 square meter)

Multiple Occupancies

Note

If they meet all the code requirements, accessory areas and incidental use areas will not make a building a mixed-use occupancy.

Multiple occupancies is a term used by the NFPA (not the ICC). It occurs when two or more occupancies exist in a building or space either horizontally or vertically. Multiple occupancies are designated more specifically as mixed or separated.

The NFPA codes consider a *mixed multiple* occupancy to be when two or more occupancies exist in a building or space and they are "intermingled." This can occur if (1) there is no rated separation(s) between the occupancies, (2) the different occupancies use the same exiting components (aisle, corridors, stairs, etc.), or (3) both occur at the same time. For example, refer again to Plan B in Figure 2.6; because there is no rated separation between the Assembly and the Mercantile occupancies, it is considered a mixed multiple occupancy. In addition, if a portion of the occupants from the restaurant must exit through the gift store as part of the required exiting, that would also make it a mixed occupancy.

A different type of mixed multiple occupancy is shown Plan A of Figure 2.7. These occupancies are separated by rated walls and may seem to be separated occupancies. However, because the tenants share the corridor when exiting from

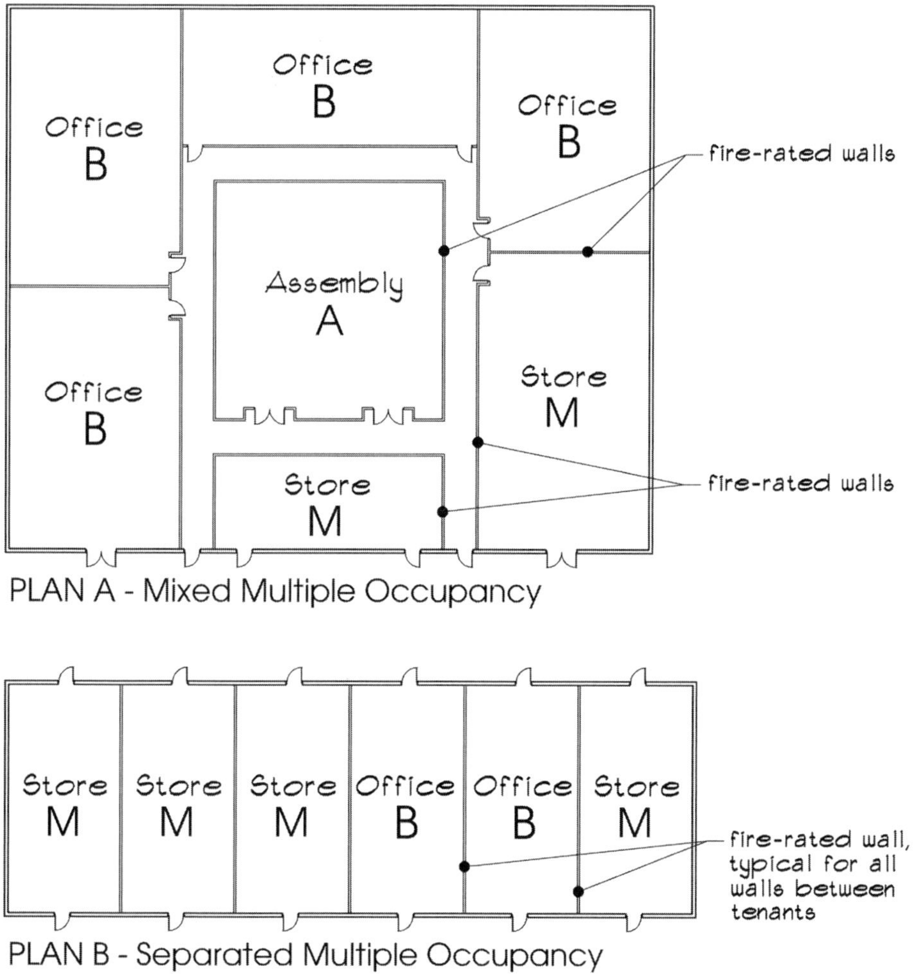

Figure 2.7 Multiple Occupancies in the NFPA: Mixed and Separated

each space, it would be considered a mixed multiple occupancy by the NFPA. If a multiple occupancy is considered mixed, the construction type, fire protection, and means of egress, as well as other requirements, must follow the most restrictive occupancy requirements. (In this way, it is similar to non-separated mixed occupancies in the *IBC*.)

On the other hand, if the occupancies are separated by rated walls but do not share exiting, then the NFPA considers it a *separated multiple* occupancy. Like the separated mixed occupancy in the *IBC*, each space must meet the code requirements for its occupancy classification. An example of separated multiple occupancy can be seen in Plan B of Figure 2.7. In this example, the multiple occupancy classifications are separated from each other by a rated wall. In addition, each has its own separate means of egress so that they do not share a common corridor. All of these factors make it a separated multiple occupancy.

The NFPA codes designate how a mixed or separated multiple occupancy should be handled. More specific information on multiple occupancies may also be found within each occupancy chapter. These requirements supersede the general requirements for mixed or separated occupancy classifications. You must refer to these individual occupancy chapters to know when they apply. In addition, you may need to work with the code official to determine which requirements will apply to the different areas or the whole building. This is especially important if you are working in a jurisdiction that requires both the *IBC* and the *LSC*.

Accessibility Requirements

Almost all occupancy classifications under certain conditions can be considered public accommodations and/or commercial facilities and be regulated by the ADA guidelines under the ADA. However, the original *ADAAG* includes specific requirements for certain building types within various occupancies. The building codes and the *ICC/ANSI 117.1* accessibility standard also include some similar requirements, although not as extensive as the *ADAAG*. The building types that are specifically addressed in the original *ADAAG* and require special regulations include assembly spaces, restaurants and cafeterias (Business or Assembly), libraries (Business or Educational), many businesses and mercantile establishments, medical facilities (Institutional and Health Care), and transient lodging (Residential and Correctional/Detentional). In addition, the Access Board has issued proposed regulations for state and local government buildings (Business and Assembly), Detentional/Correctional facilities, and dwelling units (Residential). Even proposed requirements more appropriate for children will affect certain occupancies such as Educational. Although these proposed regulations have not yet been officially approved by the Department of Justice (DOJ), you should be aware of them. Many of the same requirements are also included in the new *ADA-ABA Accessibility Guidelines* (see Appendix A). Although the building types might not be as easily recognized because of how the new guidelines are organized, they must still be incorporated into your designs once approved. It is important to keep abreast of the new guideline requirements as they are issued and to know when they become required by law. Additional regulations for certain occupancies may be added in the future.

Note

Revisions to the ADA guidelines made by the Access Board are enforceable only when approved by the Department of Justice (DOJ).

Below is a general list of the special accessibility requirements for many of these building types. In addition, there are specific storage requirements for any occupancy that requires accessible storage. When working within these occupancies, your research should include reviewing the current ADA guidelines as well as comparing them to the ICC/ANSI standard and other codes enforced in your area to see if there are contradictory or stricter requirements. For example, some ADA guideline requirements not yet passed and enforced might already be included in a more current code or standards publication. Other federal accessibility regulations may also apply (e.g., *FHAG* and *UFAS*), as explained in Chapter 1. When necessary, consult your local code official or the ADA Access Board for clarification. (See resources in Appendix E.)

Assembly Areas

- ❑ Percentage of accessible wheelchair locations
- ❑ Location/size of wheelchair areas in relation to fixed seats
- ❑ Access to performance areas
- ❑ Types of floor surfaces
- ❑ Possible assistive listening systems
- ❑ Types and placement of listening systems

Businesses and Mercantile

- ❑ Size of checkout counters and worksurfaces
- ❑ Clearance and height of self-service shelves/display units
- ❑ Size of teller windows and information counters
- ❑ Width and quantity of checkout aisles
- ❑ Clearance at security elements
- ❑ Quantity, size, and types of dressing/fitting rooms
- ❑ Type and clearance of automatic teller machines

Libraries

- ❑ Percentage of accessible fixed seating, tables, and study carrels
- ❑ Width of access aisles

- ❏ Number and size of accessible checkout areas
- ❏ Clearance at security elements
- ❏ Height of card catalogs and magazine displays
- ❏ Systems for book retrieval

Medical (and Long-Term Care) Facilities

- ❏ Size of covered entrances for unloading patients
- ❏ Percentage of accessible toilets
- ❏ Percentage of accessible patient bedrooms
- ❏ Size of maneuvering spaces in patient rooms
- ❏ Clearance area at patient beds
- ❏ Width of accessible doors and aisles

Note

Although certain accessibility items in the ADA guidelines might not yet be enforceable, similar requirements may be required by the ICC/ANSI standard, a building code, or a code jurisdiction.

Restaurants and Cafeterias

- ❏ Percentage of accessible fixed tables
- ❏ Access to sunken and raised platforms
- ❏ Width of food service lines
- ❏ Height of counters and self-service shelves
- ❏ Access to controls of vending machines
- ❏ Width of access aisles

Transient Lodgings

- ❏ Percentage of accessible sleeping rooms
- ❏ Specific requirements within accessible rooms
- ❏ Number of hearing impaired rooms
- ❏ Access to rooms and public and common areas
- ❏ Width of door openings
- ❏ Size of maneuvering spaces
- ❏ Percentage of accessible amenities (ice machines, washers and dryers, etc.)
- ❏ Clearance, height, and hardware of storage units

Judicial, Legislative, and Regulatory Facilities (pending incorporation by the DOJ)

- ❏ Access to secured entrances (including accessible security system)
- ❏ Access to courtroom elements (judges bench, jury assembly, and deliberation areas, etc.)
- ❏ Access to holding cells (and amenities)
- ❏ Accessible security systems
- ❏ Percentage of assisted listening systems

Detention and Correctional Facilities (pending incorporation by the DOJ)

- ❑ Access to cells and visiting areas
- ❑ Percentage of holding and housing cells or rooms (and amenities)

Spaces for Children (pending incorporation by the DOJ)

- ❑ Access to drinking fountains
- ❑ Access to toilet facilities (including water closets, toilet stalls, lavatories)
- ❑ Access to fixed or built-in seating and tables
- ❑ Adjusted reach ranges
- ❑ Height of handrails at ramp and stairs
- ❑ Height of mirrors
- ❑ Height of controls

DESIGN LOADS

Occupant loads as described in this chapter are not to be confused with two other types of design loads required by the codes—dead loads and live loads. *Dead loads* include all permanent components of a building's structure, such as the walls, floors and roof. *Live loads*, on the other hand, include any loads that are not the actual weight of the structure itself. They include interior elements such as people, furniture, equipment, appliances, and books. Other loads that are sometimes considered live loads but are separate exterior elements include wind loads, rain and flood loads, snow loads, and earthquake loads. These types of load factors affect the design of the structure of the building.

Specific calculations must be made to determine each type of load. These calculations are typically done by engineers during the initial design and construction of a building. Most of the calculations take into consideration that some of the loads will change during the normal use of a building. For example, in an office building it is common for interior walls to change and be relocated as tenants move. The number of people will vary as well.

Some interior projects may require you to research certain live loads when significant changes are proposed in your design. The most common situations include (1) adding a wall, such as brick or concrete, that is substantially heavier than a standard wall; (2) creating a filing area or library that concentrates the weight at one point; (3) adding a heavy piece of equipment; and (4) adding an assembly seating area in an existing room.

In most cases you will need to work with a structural engineer to determine if the existing structure will hold the added load/weight. If not, the structural engineer will determine how to add additional support, if possible.

OCCUPANT LOADS

Note

Occupant loads are typically determined using the load factors given by the codes. However, sometimes the occupant load can be determined by the "actual number" of occupants expected to be in the space or building when that number exceeds the number set by the codes.

In addition to determining the occupancy classification at the beginning of a project, you also need to determine the occupant load. The *occupant load* is used to determine how many people can safely use the space. It sets the number of occupants for which you must provide adequate exiting from a space or building. Proper exiting allows people to evacuate safely and quickly. Usually, the occupant load is determined for each space or building either by using a load factor given by the code or by establishing a desired number of occupants. If multiple spaces will be exiting into a common area or *converging* into a common path of travel, the codes require that the occupant load for the shared area be determined by adding the number of occupants who will share a common path to an exit. By these methods, you can determine the number of people that you must assume will be using the corridors, stairs, and exits in the event of a fire.

The occupant loads are often based on a relationship between the size and use of the space or building. In most cases, this means a larger space allows more occupants, and the need for more occupants requires a larger space. In some cases, you may be allowed to increase the number of occupants without increasing the size of the space. However, the building codes and the *LSC* do set limits as to the allowable concentration of occupants within a building. In addition, the occupant load may be needed to determine the occupancy classification. An example is a restaurant with an occupancy under 50 (Business) and a restaurant with an occupant load over 50 (Assembly) in the NFPA codes.

Note

The terms *occupancy load* and *occupant load* are often used interchangeably and mean the same thing. However, do not confuse them with occupancy classifications.

An occupant load is important to determine. Not only will it guide you in the correct selection of a building's occupancy, but it affects other codes as well. For example, it is needed to figure means of egress codes. (See the Means of Egress section later in this chapter and in Chapter 4.) The number of required plumbing fixtures also depends on the occupant load. (See Chapter 7.) The remainder of this chapter explains occupant loads.

Occupant Load by Load Factor

Because most means of egress requirements will be based on the occupant load, the code must establish a *minimum* level of safety. To do this, each code assigns a predetermined amount of area or square feet (or square meters) required for each occupant based on the occupancy classification and the specific use of the space. This predetermined figure is called the *load factor*. The load factor is used to help you determine the required minimum occupant load of a space or building. This is almost always the lowest number of occupants for which you must design the space.

Using the Table

Each code discusses occupant load requirements, including load factors and exiting requirements within the means of egress chapter. The NFPA codes, including the *LSC*, have additional occupant load factors and requirements in each separate occupancy chapter as well. Figure 2.8 is the load factor table from the *IBC*, titled Table 1004.1.2, "Maximum Floor Area Allowances per Occupant." The NFPA codes have similar load factor tables.

Notice that the first column in Figure 2.8 is titled "Occupancy." This column lists the different occupancy classifications and use groups. For example, there is not just one load factor for Assembly occupancies—there is "Assembly with fixed seats" and "Assembly without fixed seats." In addition, under that Assembly type, there is the option of "Concentrated (chairs only—not fixed)," "Standing space," or "Unconcentrated (tables and chairs)." You must consider specifically how the space is being used. The load factors are listed in the next column in square feet per person. (A metric conversion is shown at the bottom of the table.) These areas are given for each of the specific uses or building types within the different occupancy classifications. The load factor indicates the amount of space or area it is assumed each person present will require. Although the square foot figures may seem high for one person, they allow for furniture and equipment and, in some cases, corridors, closets, and other miscellaneous areas.

Note

The load factor does not mean that each person is required to receive a particular amount of square feet (square meters) when space planning a project. The figure is used only to determine an occupant load. The placement of furniture, equipment, and walls will affect the size of the final space.

The area in this case refers to the floor area *within* the exterior walls of a building. Notice that the load factors are designated as gross or net area. The *gross* area refers to the building as a whole and includes all miscellaneous spaces within the exterior walls. The *net* area refers to actual occupied spaces and does not include ancillary spaces such as corridors, restrooms, utility closets, or other unoccupied areas.

When net figures are required, it is assumed that the occupants who are using an ancillary area would have left the occupied space to do so and, therefore, would already be taken into account. For example, a person in the corridor of a school would most likely be a student or teacher already accounted for in a classroom. Usually, deductions are also made for fixed items that take up space, such as interior walls, columns, and built-in counters and shelving (areas that are not habitable).

The Formula

The formula that is used with the load factor tables is

$$\text{Occupant load} = \text{Floor area (sq ft or sq m)} \div \text{Occupant factor}$$

Note

The NFPA codes give load factors in square feet and in metric dimensions.

Note

Gross area includes all areas within the exterior walls. *Net area* consists of all areas within the exterior walls minus ancillary spaces such as corridors, restrooms, utility closets, and other unoccupied areas.

TABLE 1004.1.2
MAXIMUM FLOOR AREA ALLOWANCES PER OCCUPANT

OCCUPANCY	FLOOR AREA IN SQ. FT. PER OCCUPANT
Agricultural building	300 gross
Aircraft hangars	500 gross
Airport terminal	
Baggage claim	20 gross
Baggage handling	300 gross
Concourse	100 gross
Waiting areas	15 gross
Assembly	
Gaming floors (keno, slots, etc.)	11 gross
Assembly with fixed seats	See Section 1003.2.2.9
Assembly without fixed seats	
Concentrated (chairs only—not fixed)	7 net
Standing space	5 net
Unconcentrated (tables and chairs)	15 net
Bowling centers, allow 5 persons for each lane including 15 feet of runway, and for additional areas	7 net
Business areas	100 gross
Courtrooms—other than fixed seating areas	40 net
Dormitories	50 gross
Educational	
Classroom area	20 net
Shops and other vocational room areas	50 net
Exercise rooms	50 gross
H-5 Fabrication and manufacturing areas	200 gross
Industrial areas	100 gross
Institutional areas	
Inpatient treatment areas	240 gross
Outpatient areas	100 gross
Sleeping areas	120 gross
Kitchens, commercial	200 gross
Library	
Reading rooms	50 net
Stack area	100 gross
Locker rooms	50 gross
Mercantile	
Areas on other floors	60 gross
Basement and grade floor areas	30 gross
Storage, stock, shipping areas	300 gross
Parking garages	200 gross
Residential	200 gross
Skating rinks, swimming pools	
Rink and pool	50 gross
Decks	15 gross
Stages and platforms	15 net
Accessory storage areas, mechanical equipment room	300 gross
Warehouses	500 gross

For SI: 1 square foot = 0.0929 m^2.

Figure 2.8 *International Building Code (IBC)* Table 1004.1.2 Maximum Floor Area Allowances per Occupant (*International Building Code* 2003. Copyright 2002. Falls Church, Virginia: International Code Council, Inc. Reproduced with permission.

To determine the occupant load for an existing building or layout, you take the area of the interior space and divide it by the load factor for the appropriate occupancy and/or use. If the space or building you are working on has more than one type of use, you do the same for each and add them together. This gives you the number of occupants that are allowed in the space. If your total results in a fraction, round up to the nearest whole number. Depending on the project, you may also need to add together the calculation for separate occupancies. The final occupant load gives you the number of occupants for which you must design the space.

Note

Depending on the project, you may need to determine the load factor for a single space or add together multiple spaces that share an exit.

Example 1

To help you further understand the difference between gross and net area and how to use the load factor table, refer to the example floor plan for a library in Figure 2.9. A library is considered an Assembly (A-3) occupancy. However, when you look at the *IBC* table in Figure 2.8 you will see that libraries are not listed under Assembly use but are listed separately as "Library." This use is further divided into two separate uses: reading rooms and stack areas. The occupant load for each must be determined separately.

The occupant load factor for the reading rooms is set at "50 net square feet (4.6 s m)" meaning the area should not include ancillary spaces. Therefore, the corridor or the utility closet adjacent to the reading rooms on the floor plan should not be included when determining the area of the reading rooms. The load factor for the stack area of the library, however, is set at "100 gross square feet (9.3 s m)." So the area measurement should include the entire stack area with aisles, reference, checkout counter, and so on. (Do not include the corridor since it is enclosed with the reading room area.)

Note

Even if the number of occupants you are planning for in your design is less than the calculated occupant load, you must use the determined load figure as required by the codes.

Using the dimensions of the floor plan and the occupant load formula to determine the area for each space, Figure 2.9 shows you how to determine the occupant load for the entire library. The total occupant load is 266 people.

Example 2

Sometimes, load factors can be used in a slightly different way. If you need to determine the area required for a particular occupancy or use, the load factors may help determine the space requirements. This may be helpful in the programming stage of a project. For example, if you are planning a new office space for a client with 125 employees, you can use the table to look up the occupant load factor for the Business use (100 gross sq ft or 9.3 s m) and multiply it by the number of people you want to occupy the space (125) to determine how large a

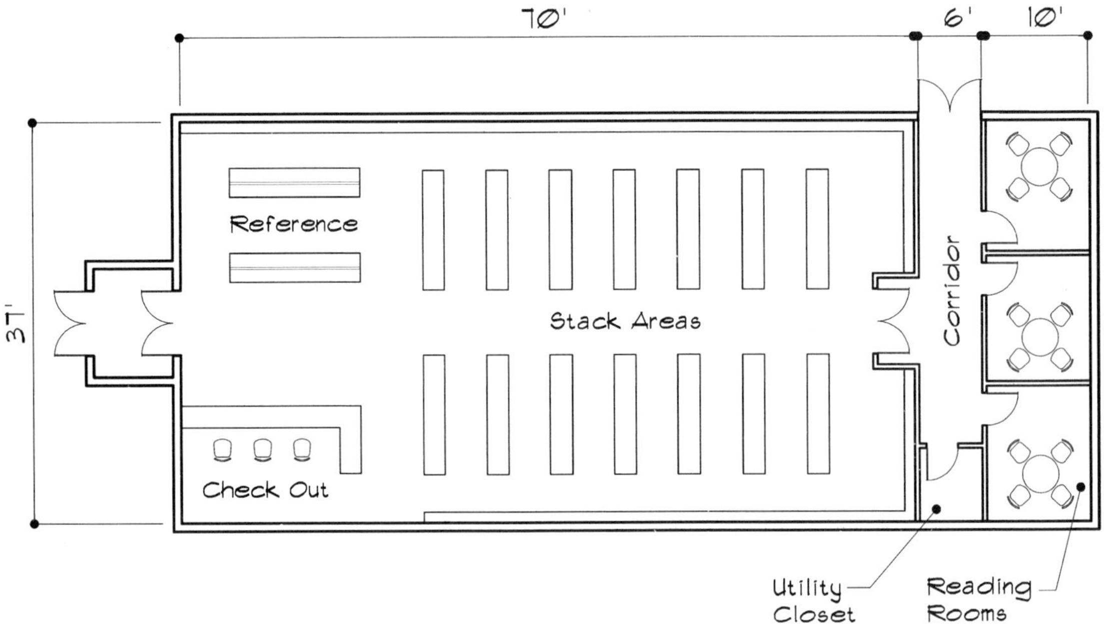

ROOM	LOAD FACTOR	SIZE OF SPACE	FLOOR AREA	OCCUPANCY LOAD
Reading Room	50 net	10 x 37	370 SF	370 ÷ 50 = 7
Stack Area	100 gross	70 x 37	2590 SF	2590 ÷ 100 = 259
				Total Number of Occupants = 266

Figure 2.9 Occupant Load Example: Single Occupancy (Library) (1 square foot = 0.0929 square meter)

space you will need. In this case, you will need at least 12,500 square feet (1161.3 s m) according to the codes. You can do this for a smaller use such as a break room or conference room as well. Although this will give you a good estimate, typically other program requirements must be added to that area to determine the final size of a space or building.

Increasing the Occupant Load

In some cases, it might be desirable to have more people occupy a space than determined by the load factor. You may be allowed to increase the occupant load of a space, but you will typically have to provide additional exiting for the increased number of occupants. The *IBC* uses the term *actual number* because the space is to be designed for the actual number of occupants intended to occupy the space (rather than the number calculated using the load factor). The NFPA codes use the term *increased number* because this option is used when an increased occupant load is desired.

For example, say you have a client who rents a space that is 5000 square feet (464.5 s m) for use as a restaurant (Assembly). Refer to the load factor table in Figure 2.8. The load factor is 15 gross square feet (1.4 s m) gross for an "Assembly without fixed seats, Unconcentrated (tables and chairs)." By dividing 5000 square feet (464.5 s m) by 15 gross square feet (1.4 s m), you get an occupant load of 133 occupants. However, if your client wanted to be able to seat 150, then 150 would be considered the desired occupant load—the actual or increased number. The means of egress (i.e., exits, aisles, corridors, and number of doors) would then be designed for an occupant load of 150. That would also be the maximum number allowed within the space at any one time. You would need to make sure the space or building could handle the increased exiting requirements and other accessible clearances. When you design for an increased occupant load it is advisable to review it with the code official. Typically, you are not allowed to design for a number less than the calculated occupant load.

Occupant Load for Primary and Secondary Spaces

When one or more smaller spaces exits into a larger or primary space before reaching the final exit, the codes usually require that the occupant load of the primary space include the occupant loads of the secondary spaces that exit through it. Two examples are shown in Figure 2.10. The business offices are secondary spaces within the Business occupancy. Occupants must walk through the open office area in order to exit the building. However, the training room would also be considered a secondary space, since it too must empty through the open office area. In this case, the occupant load for the large training room in Figure 2.10 should be calculated separately using an Assembly (A) factor, not the load factor of the main Business (B) occupancy. When these separate calculations are added together, they would provide an occupant load that more accurately addresses the use of the space.

An accessory space can sometimes be considered a secondary space as well. For example, the occupant load for the design center (B) in Figure 2.3B should be added to the occupant load of the Mercantile (M) portion of the furniture store, since the occupants of the design center must walk through the store to exit the building. Each would be calculated separately according to the load factor for its occupancy classification. This total would be used to determine the exiting from the primary space.

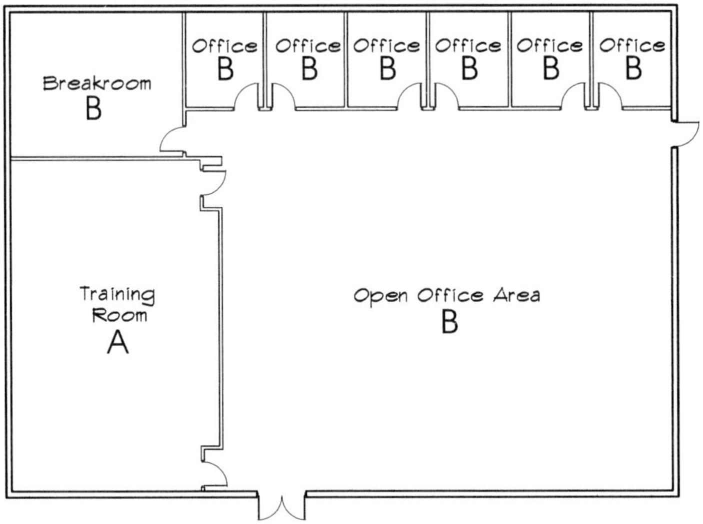

Figure 2.10. Occupant Load Example: Primary and Secondary Spaces.

Occupant Load for More than One Occupancy

Whenever you have more than one occupancy in the same space or building, you will typically need to do additional calculations. For example, if you have two occupancies sharing the same floor you will need to determine the occupant load for each occupancy separately. You will then determine the exiting requirements for each particular space based on each calculated occupant load. However, if these occupancies share common spaces such as exiting corridors or restrooms, you may also need to determine the total occupant load of the floor. This will be used to determine the requirements for the common areas and the exiting requirements for the entire floor. Additional calculations may also be required when you have mixed or multiple occupancies in the same floor or building and when you have a space used for more than one function. Each of these is explained as follows.

Mixed or Multiple Occupancies

When there is more than one occupancy type on the same floor or in the same building, the occupant load for each occupancy must be calculated separately. These occupant loads are added together to determine the occupant load of the floor. Shared common areas must also be considered. The total occupant load is then used to determine other code requirements, such as exiting and plumbing

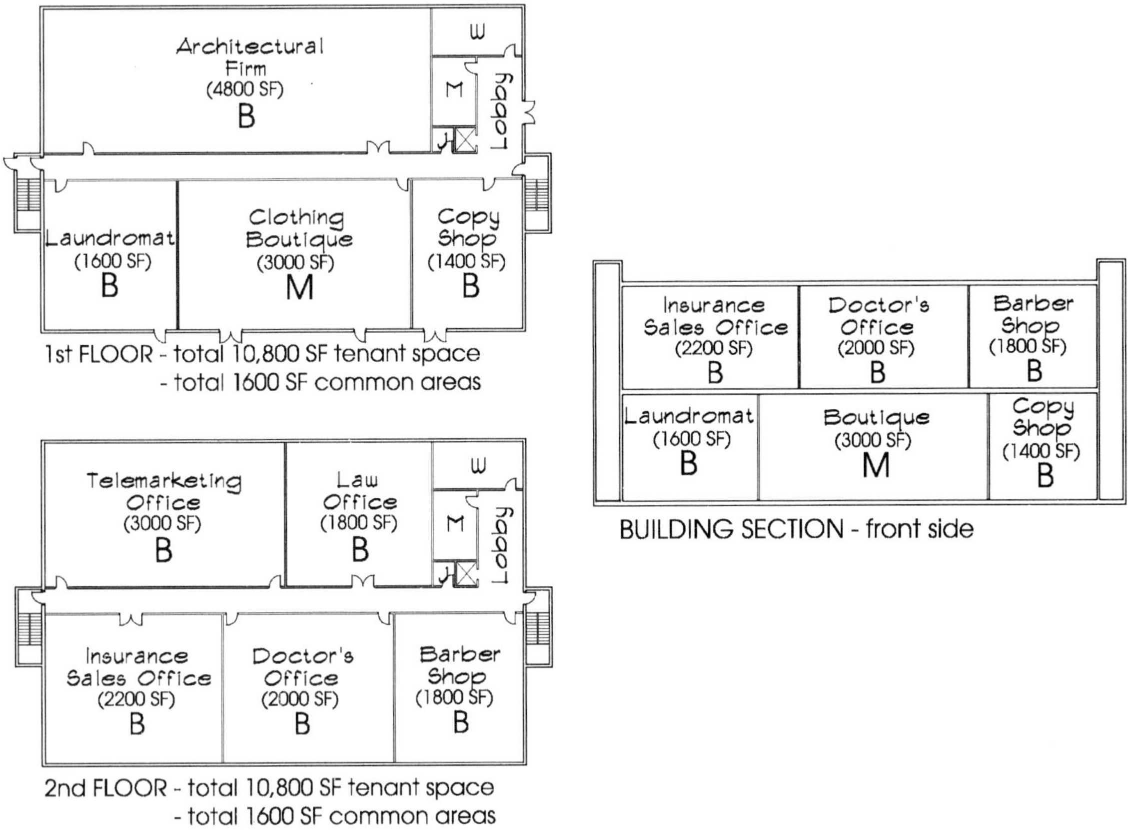

FIRST FLOOR	LOAD FACTOR	FLOOR AREA	OCCUPANCY LOAD
M (Mercantile) Tenants	30 gross	3000 SF	3000 ÷ 30 = 100
M Common Area*	30 gross	448 SF (1600 x 28%)	448 ÷ 30 = 15
B (Business) Tenants	100 gross	7800 SF (10,800 – 3000)	7800 ÷ 100 = 78
B Common Areas*	100 gross	1152 SF (1600 x 72%)	1152 ÷ 100 = 12
		Total Number of Occupants @ 1st FLOOR =	205
SECOND FLOOR			
B (Business) Tenants	100 gross	10,800 SF	10,800 ÷ 100 = 108
B Common Areas	100 gross	1600 SF	1600 ÷ 100 = 16
		Total Number of Occupants @ 2nd FLOOR =	124
		TOTAL OCCUPANT LOAD FOR BUILDING =	329

*NOTE: Of the total tenant square footage for the 1st floor, the Business tenants occupy 72% of the space (7800 divided by 10,800) and the Mercantile tenant occupies the remaining 28%.

Figure 2.11. Occupant Load Example: Mixed/Multiple Occupancy Building (1 square foot = 0.0929 square meter).

fixtures. An example is shown in Figure 2.11. In this example, there is a mixture of Mercantile (M) and Business (B) spaces on the first floor and multiple Business (B) spaces on the second floor.

One way to figure the occupant load for the first floor is to calculate the occupant load separately for each tenant space and required common areas and then add them together. Another way (as shown in Figure 2.11) is to combine the area for all the occupancy classifications that are the same (i.e., all the Business occupancies) and then use the load factor for that use. You would then do the same for Mercantile. In this case, because a gross load factor is required you will also have to include the public areas within your calculations (i.e., lobby, restrooms, main corridor). Typically, this would be proportionally divided among the different occupancy types as shown in Figure 2.11. (See note at bottom of figure.) Once you have figured the occupant load for each occupancy or each tenant, add them together with the common areas to get the total occupant load for the whole floor. The total occupant load on the first floor is 205.

The same process is used for the second floor, as shown in Figure 2.11. However, in this case there is only one occupancy type. The total occupant load for the second floor is 124. The occupant load for each floor (including common areas) will be used for code requirements such as exiting, which affect the entire floor and the stairs. (See Chapter 4.) It will also be used to determine the number of plumbing fixtures in the common toilet facilities on each floor. (See Chapter 7.)

Areas with Multiple Uses

Note

When reading code tables it is important to read all the footnotes at the bottom of the tables for additional information and possible exceptions.

Some buildings or building areas are used for different uses at different times. For example, a church fellowship hall might be used for a large assembly one night and as a cafeteria the next. The following weekend it might be used as a gymnasium or exercise room. In other words, any area of a building that has more than one type of function is considered to have multiple uses. The occupant load is determined by the use that indicates the largest concentration of people. You might need to do several calculations to determine which occupancy will provide the largest number.

Occupant Load for Fixed Seats

Fixed seating arrangements are common in some building types, especially in Assembly occupancies. The seats are considered fixed if they are not easily moved and/or if they are used on a more permanent basis. Instead of using the standard formula for calculating the occupant load when separate fixed seats are present, the actual seats are counted. For example, the occupant load in an movie theater as shown in Plan A of Figure 2.12 would be determined by the number of seats used in the space (including spaces specifically created for wheelchair users).

Counting seats with arms is self-explanatory. However, fixed seating may also consist of continuous seating such as benches, bleachers, and pews. Each of

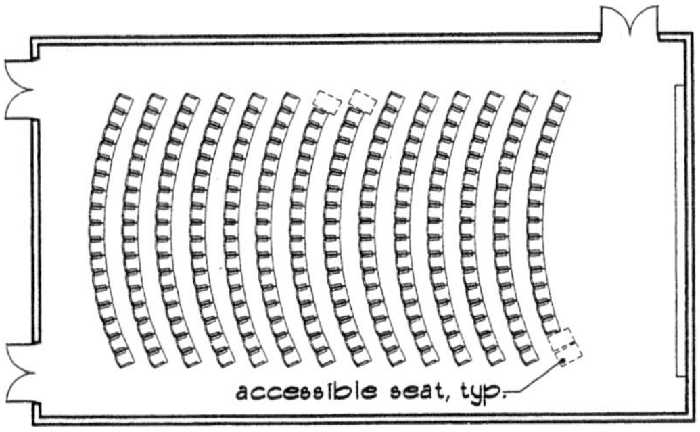

PLAN A - Movie Theater (total 238 seats)

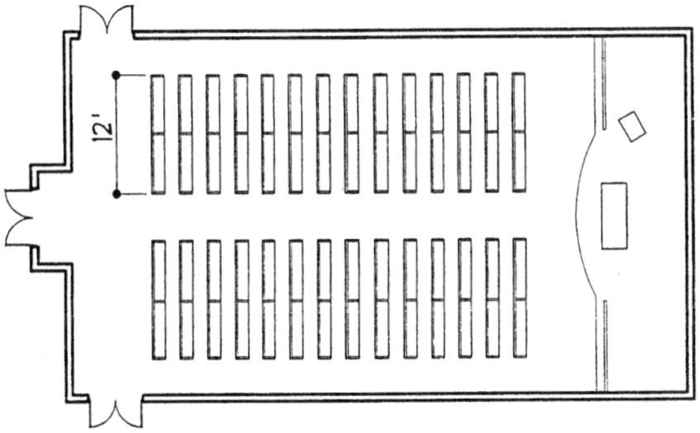

PLAN B - Church (28 pews - 8 people each)

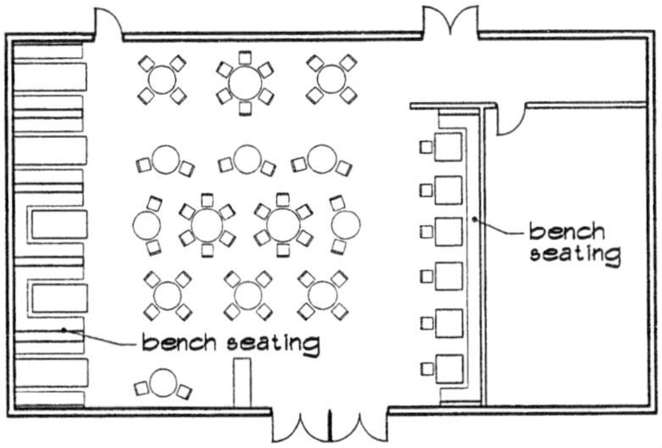

PLAN C - Restaurant (includes bench seating)

Figure 2.12. Occupant Load Example: Occupancy with Fixed Seats

Note

The continuous seating variable will not always evenly divide into the length of the seating. Usually, if the remaining fraction is one-half or greater, you round up to include another occupant. Consult your code official when there is uncertainty.

Note

Buildings with fixed seats may require additional occupant load calculations depending on the amount of adjacent open area. Check with the code official.

the codes provides a variable (either in the occupant load table or the text) to be used for continuous seating. They typically allow 18 linear inches (457 mm) of seating for each occupant.

If, for example, you are working on a church that has 28 pews and each pew is 12 feet long, as shown in Plan B of Figure 2.12, you would use the 18-inch (457 mm) variable. A 12-foot pew equals 144 inches (3658 mm). Divide the 144 (3658 mm) by the 18-inch (457 mm) variable to get 8 people per pew. Since there are a total of 28 pews, this church has an occupant load of 224 people (28 pews × 8 people/pew).

Booth seating is another type of continuous fixed seating. Booth seating usually has a separate variable provided by the codes. The typical increment is 24 inches (609.6 mm). For example, Plan C in Figure 2.12 shows several types of booth seating. Each should be calculated separately. Measure the length of the bench along the front edge (especially at corners) and divide by 24 inches (609.6 mm). Add all the calculations together to determine the occupant load for the bench areas. This would be added to the occupant loads of the other seating areas within the space to determine the total occupant load of the restaurant.

Depending on the type of building and how much space the fixed seating takes up in relation to the rest of the space, you may need to do additional calculations as well. For example, you may be working on a nightclub that has fixed seating in one area and a dance floor in another. In this case, you would calculate the occupant load for both areas separately, and add them together to get the final count.

Occupant Load for Unusual Uses

There may also be occasions when the building type or the use of a space is not typical. The occupant load factors given in the tables may not be appropriate for a unique use. Or, a specific occupancy use may not be listed on the table. On other occasions, you may have a space that does not clearly fit one of the use categories. When this occurs you should meet with a code official for guidance. Only the code official can approve the final decision. Another option is to obtain an appeal. (See Chapter 10.) It is important for this decision to be made at the beginning of a project, because occupancy classifications and many of the codes depend on the determined occupant load.

Occupant Load and Means of Egress

The occupant loads you determine in the beginning of a project will be used again later in your code research to determine the means of egress, such as the number of exits and the width of the exits. (See Chapter 4.) You should check to make sure that the layout of the space and the occupancy classification will allow the occupant load you need. If, after figuring the occupant load, you find that the code will not allow the number of occupants you are planning for in your design, you may have to increase the size of the space. (This, in turn, may change the occupancy classification.) In some cases, however, the codes may allow you to plan your design within the same area and occupancy classification based on an increased occupant load, as previously discussed.

In all cases, adequate means of egress must be provided for the number of people who will be occupying a space or building. Once the occupant load is set and the means of egress has been designed for that number, the quantity of people allowed within a space cannot exceed that number. For Assembly uses, the approved occupant load is required to be posted for each space. Exceeding the posted allowable occupant load is unsafe and unlawful.

Note

Every assembly room or Assembly occupancy usually requires the approved occupant load to be permanently posted near the main exit from the space. A typical sign might read: "Occupancy by more than 100 persons is dangerous and unlawful."

CHECKLIST

Figure 2.13 is designed to help you determine the occupancy classification(s) and occupant load(s) for a particular project. It is a basic checklist that is set up to make sure you address the same typical occupancy questions for each project. The top of the checklist provides spaces to include project information and indicate the codes sources used.

The first part of the checklist is used to identify the risk factors and unique conditions that exist within your space or building. For some projects the occupancy classification may be straightforward or already determined. You can also use the multiple lists in this chapter in conjunction with the codes to help you determine the use of your building or space. However, if special conditions exist, or if you are using performance codes, identifying these unique conditions within your project can be important. Check the risk factors you know exist within your space, then compare that to the definitions of each occupancy classification and/or subclassification. From what you know about the activities within the space and these risk factors, you should be able to determine the correct occupancy. If hazards are present, note them as well. Each of the code publications lists the types of hazards to look for and whether they are explosive, fire, physical, or health hazards.

Keep in mind that you may have more than one type of occupancy within your space or building. In the next section of the checklist, indicate whether you will need to consider the requirements for incidental uses, accessory uses, mixed occupancies (separated or non-separated), multiple uses (mixed or separated),

Note

Not only can a building have more than one occupancy, but also each occupancy can have more than one use for the purpose of determining the occupant load. Therefore, one building can have a number of calculations.

or fixed seats. Check the ones that apply to your project and use the notes provided in parenthesis to assist you in determining the types of occupant load calculations you will require. For example, if you are working on a department store that includes a photography studio as an incidental use, you know that you would have to calculate each area separately. Or, you may need to calculate a fixed seating area separate from an open area. (Refer to this chapter for additional information as required.)

The next part of the checklist is to help you determine the occupant load of the entire space, floor, or building, as necessary for your project. Depending on the type of occupancy considerations you checked, it allows you up to three separate occupant load calculations. You can calculate different parts of the space or building separately and then add them together at the bottom or use one of the calculations to determine the occupant load for any shared common areas. Starting with the first calculation, indicate the occupancy classification and/or subclassification (i.e., Business or Assembly/A-3) and then the building use (i.e., Doctor's Office or Library). Also check if space is new or existing. This will be important if you are using the *Life Safety Code*. (You may also be required to use the *International Existing Building Code*.)

Continuing with "Calculation 1," the rest of the calculation will depend on if it is a space with or without fixed seating. More commonly, you will need to use the load factor provided by the codes, so you would check "Load Factor" on the next line and write in the load factor from the code table. Also indicate if it is a gross or net load factor. If, on the other hand, this building use has fixed seats or benches, check "Fixed Seat Variable" on the next line instead, indicate the type of fixed seat and write in the fixed seat variable provided by the codes. (If they are fixed seats with arms, no variable is required.)

The next line is to record the actual floor area to be used for the calculations of the building use or space. Note whether you determined net or gross square feet (s m). Which one you use depends on whether the load factor is net or gross. Remember that when net area is required, you do not include the ancillary spaces. (See the definition of net area in the Glossary if necessary.) If you indicated the space has fixed seats, then write in the total number of fixed seats with arms or the overall length of the continuous seats instead (i.e., linear length of each bench).

The last part of "Calculation 1" asks you to calculate and record the occupant load for that particular use. Remember, if you are using load factors, you divide the actual measured floor area by the load factor you wrote down. If using fixed seats, calculate the number of seats using the overall length of fixed seats divided by the fixed seat variable. (Or, write in the total number of seats with fixed arms.)

Because you may often have more than one building type or use in the same space, there is a place for you to figure the occupant load for a second and third

Occupancy Checklist

Date:____________

Project Name: ____ Space: ____________________

Code Source Used (check all that apply): __ IBC __ LSC __ NFPA 5000 __ OTHER: ________________________

Occupancy Risk Factors/Hazards (check those that apply):

__ High number of occupants
__ Occupants resting or sleeping
__ Alertness of occupants
__ Mobility of occupants
__ Age of occupants
__ Security measures
__ Occupant generally unfamiliar with space
__ Unusual characteristics of building/space
__ Potential for spread of fire
__ Hazardous materials stored or used
Type of hazard: ______________________________
__ Other: ______________________________

Occupancy Considerations (check those that apply): [1]

__ Single Occupancy (may require more than one calculation based on types of use and/or load factors)
__ Incidental Use (if separated according to code, include in main occupancy; if not, may need to calculate separately)
__ Accessory Use (occupant load calculated separately from main occupancy; may need to include with main for exiting)
__ Separated - Mixed or Multiple Occupancy (calculate occupant load for each occupancy)
__ Non-Separated Mixed Occupancy (IBC only) (use strictest occupancy requirements)
__ Mixed Multiple Occupancy (NFPA only) (calculate occupant load for each occupancy)
__ Occupancy with Fixed Seats (may need to calculate fixed seats and surrounding open areas)

Occupancy Loads [1]

Calculation 1 - Occupancy Classification: ______________________________
Building Use (__ NEW __EXISTING): ______________________________
__ Load Factor [2] (__ GROSS __NET): ____________
__ Fixed Seat Variable (__ WITH ARMS __CONTINUOUS __ BENCH): ____________
Actual Floor Area (__ GROSS __NET):__________ **OR** Number/Length of Fixed Seats: ____________
Occupant Load 1 (__ USING LOAD FACTOR FORMULA __ BASED ON FIXED SEATS): ____________

Calculation 2 - Occupancy Classification: ______________________________
Building Use (__ NEW __EXISTING): ______________________________
__ Load Factor [2] (__ GROSS __NET): ____________
__ Fixed Seat Variable (__ WITH ARMS __CONTINUOUS __ BENCH): ____________
Actual Floor Area (__ GROSS __NET):__________ **OR** Number/Length of Fixed Seats: ____________
Occupant Load 2 (__ USING LOAD FACTOR FORMULA __ BASED ON FIXED SEATS): ____________

Calculation 3 - Occupancy Classification: ______________________________
Building Use (__ NEW __EXISTING): ______________________________
__ Load Factor [2] (__ GROSS __NET): ____________
__ Fixed Seat Variable (__ WITH ARMS __CONTINUOUS __ BENCH): ____________
Actual Floor Area (__ GROSS __NET):__________ **OR** Number/Length of Fixed Seats: ____________
Occupant Load 3 (__ USING LOAD FACTOR FORMULA __ BASED ON FIXED SEATS): ____________

Total Calculated Occupant Load: _________ (__ SPACE __FLOOR __ BUILDING)

Adjusted Occupant Load - Based on Actual Needs: _________

Local Code Approval (when required)

__ NO __YES NAME: ______________________________ DATE: ________________

NOTES:

1. If there is more than one main occupancy in the same space or building, you may want to use a separate checklist for each.
2. If you are using a gross load factor you may need to include shared common spaces in addition to the ancillary spaces.

Figure 2.13 Occupancy Checklist

occupancy or use, if necessary, or the common areas. Repeat the process for each one. If there are several occupancies, however, you may want to complete a separate checklist for each occupancy or parts of a building.

After you have calculated the occupant load for each use, add them together to determine the "Total Calculated Occupant Load" and write this in the space provided. Indicate also the part of the building that was calculated. An additional line is provided in case you have chosen to design the space by using an actual number for the occupant load. For example, a special Assembly space may need a slightly higher occupant load because of the anticipated use of the space. Note this adjusted number in the "Adjusted Occupant Load" space. Use the back of the checklist to write down the reason for the adjustment.

A code approval section has been provided at the bottom of the checklist. It may not always be necessary to get approval from your code official at this point in a project, but each situation is different. (See the section on Preliminary Approval in Chapter 10.) If you have an unusual occupancy or building type or you need approval on an adjusted occupant load, you may want to discuss these with the code official early within the programming and design process. Remember, it is important to accurately determine both the occupancy classification(s) and the occupant load(s) in the beginning of a project, since a number of the other codes depend on them. Record the name and the date of your discussion in this section.

This checklist allows you to document essential information that will be used in the rest of your code research. As mentioned, most of the code requirements and allowable exceptions will be based on the occupancy classification and the occupant load. Having this information clearly documented may be useful if questions come up during your research.

CHAPTER 3

CONSTRUCTION TYPES AND BUILDING SIZES

Construction types are very important at the time a building is being constructed. Structural engineers and architects must be thoroughly familiar with them to determine the type of construction materials that can be used throughout a building—both exterior and interior.

Construction types become a factor on interior projects as well. When working on an interior project that requires the reconfiguring of building elements, such as relocating walls, making changes to floor or ceiling conditions, or adding a stairway, you must be familiar with the different types of construction to determine if and when specific regulations must be followed. Some construction types are stricter than others. Each code will also list minimum construction type requirements for specific types of occupancy classifications.

In addition, construction types are used in conjunction with occupancy classifications to determine the building's maximum height and floor area. You should be aware of the codes that apply to a building's size and when they would affect a project. For example, you may need to research the maximum size of a building allowed by the codes for a specific occupancy.

This chapter familiarizes you with construction types, building heights, and floor areas as required by the codes. It includes how they are typically used for new construction and how they can affect an interior project. The first part of this chapter concentrates on construction types. The second half discusses how they relate to occupancy classifications and building sizes.

KEY TERMS

Below is a list of terms used when discussing construction types and building sizes. They are defined and discussed in this chapter. They are also defined in the Glossary.

Building height
Combustible
Fire resistive
Floor area
Limited combustible
Noncombustible
Protected
Story height
Unprotected

CONSTRUCTION TYPES

Note

On interior projects you must make sure you do not affect the fire rating of existing structural or building elements. For example, removing the gypsum board from a structural column can reduce the rating of the column.

Every building is made up of a variety of what the codes define as *building elements* and *structural elements*. They can be as simple as four exterior walls and a roof or as complicated as the many parts that make up a high-rise building. For example, columns, floor/ceiling systems, interior walls, and vertical shafts are all considered building elements. Structural elements are building elements that actually support the weight of the building and its contents. For example, a column is a structural element and a building element, but a vertical shaft is only a building element. Some of these elements are covered in the construction type chapters of the code. These requirements will be explained in this chapter. Additional elements are discussed in other sections of the code. (See Chapter 5.)

The codes define the differences in construction types by governing the kinds of materials allowed for construction of each of the structural elements in a building and by establishing minimum hourly fire resistance ratings for each essential building element. The materials that are allowed in each construction type are most often described as noncombustible, limited combustible, and combustible. Depending on the level of fire resistance required, the codes will specify the type of material allowed. For example, Type I construction, which requires the highest level of fire resistance, must consist almost completely of noncombustible materials, and combustible materials are only allowed in limited amounts and locations.

Each construction type also assigns a minimum fire rating to building elements. These ratings are based on the number of hours the building element must be fire resistant, meaning it will not be adversely affected by flame, heat, or hot gases. Note, though, that fire resistant does not mean fireproof. Instead, it is an hourly *fire endurance rating*. By controlling each element, the codes are able to regulate the fire resistance of a whole building. On an interior project, the most critical building element will be interior walls, but you could be working with a number of the other elements as well.

The Table

The building codes and the *Life Safety Code (LSC)* have a similar table that lists the requirements for each type of construction. Figure 3.1 is the *International Building Code (IBC)* construction type table, Table 601, "Fire-Resistance Rating Requirements for Building Elements (hours)." Similar tables can be found in the NFPA codes.

TABLE 601
FIRE-RESISTANCE RATING REQUIREMENTS FOR BUILDING ELEMENTS (hours)

BUILDING ELEMENT	TYPE I		TYPE II		TYPE III		TYPE IV	TYPE V	
	A	B	A[d]	B	A[d]	B	HT	A[d]	B
Structural frame[a] Including columns, girders, trusses	3[b]	2[b]	1	0	1	0	HT	1	0
Bearing walls Exterior[f] Interior	 3 3[b]	 2 2[b]	 1 1	 0 0	 2 1	 2 0	 2 1/HT	 1 1	 0 0
Nonbearing walls and partitions Exterior	See Table 602								
Nonbearing walls and partitions Interior[e]	0	0	0	0	0	0	See Section 602.4.6	0	0
Floor construction Including supporting beams and joists	2	2	1	0	1	0	HT	1	0
Roof construction Including supporting beams and joists	$1^1/_2$[c]	1[c]	1[c]	0	1[c]	0	HT	1[c]	0

For SI: 1 foot = 304.8 mm.

a. The structural frame shall be considered to be the columns and the girders, beams, trusses and spandrels having direct connections to the columns and bracing members designed to carry gravity loads. The members of floor or roof panels which have no connection to the columns shall be considered secondary members and not a part of the structural frame.

b. Roof supports: Fire-resistance ratings of structural frame and bearing walls are permitted to be reduced by 1 hour where supporting a roof only.

c. 1. Except in Factory-Industrial (F-1), Hazardous (H), Mercantile (M) and Moderate-Hazard Storage (S-1) occupancies, fire protection of structural members shall not be required, including protection of roof framing and decking where every part of the roof construction is 20 feet or more above any floor immediately below. Fire-retardant-treated wood members shall be allowed to be used for such unprotected members.
   2. In all occupancies, heavy timber shall be allowed where a 1-hour or less fire-resistance rating is required.
   3. In Type I and II construction, fire-retardant-treated wood shall be allowed in buildings including girders and trusses as part of the roof construction when the building is:
      i. Two stories or less in height;
      ii. Type II construction over two stories; or
      iii. Type I construction over two stories and the vertical distance from the upper floor to the roof is 20 feet or more.

d. An approved automatic sprinkler system in accordance with Section 903.3.1.1 shall be allowed to be substituted for 1-hour fire-resistance-rated construction, provided such system is not otherwise required by other provisions of the code or used for an allowable area increase in accordance with Section 506.3 or an allowable height increase in accordance with Section 504.2. The 1-hour substitution for the fire resistance of exterior walls shall not be permitted.

e. Not less than the fire-resistance rating required by other sections of this code.

f. Not less than the fire-resistance rating based on fire separation distance (see Table 602).

Figure 3.1 *International Building Code (IBC)* Table 601 Fire-Resistance Rating Requirements for Building Elements (*International Building Code* 2003. Copyright 2002. Falls Church, Virginia: International Code Council, Inc. Reproduced with permission. All rights reserved.)

In the *IBC* table in Figure 3.1, the construction types are listed across the top of the table in descending order from the most fire resistive (Type I) to the least fire resistive (Type V). The various structural or building elements are listed down the side to the left. The hourly fire endurance ratings are listed under the construction types for each structural element in the body of the table.

Most of the construction types are further divided into subcategories. These subcategories indicate whether the structural elements are required to be *protected* or remain *unprotected*. In a construction type where the structure is allowed to be *unprotected*, no additional treatment or materials are required to be added to the natural fire-resistant characteristics of the structural system. In a construction type that is required to be *protected*, structural components have been enclosed or covered in materials that add to the fire resistance of the system. This allows for a wide variety of construction systems and components. (Also see inset titled *Protected or Unprotected* on page 104.) The *IBC* table generally uses the "A" and "B" designation to indicate protected (A) and unprotected (B). For example, in Figure 3.1, you can tell the difference between a protected and an unprotected structural frame. Type IIIA has a 1-hour rating and Type IIIB has no rating. In the case of a Type I construction, IA is considered highly protected and IB is considered protected. (This is shown in Figure 3.2.) The *NFPA* documents use a different numbering system to indicate the various hourly ratings. (This can be seen in the comparison in Figure 3.2 and will be discussed below.)

Every building, whether new or existing, must fall under one of the construction types. To be classified it must meet the minimum requirements for every structure or building element in that type. If it fails to meet even one of the criteria, it will be classified in the next less restrictive type of construction. For example, if a building meets all the requirements of a construction Type I in Figure 3.1 except that the floor construction is rated only one hour, the whole building will be classified as a Type IIA.

This becomes important on interior projects. When adding new or modifying existing interior building elements, you need to know the construction type of the building. You need to be consistent with the existing building materials and maintain the required minimum hourly rating of each building element. If you do not specify the correct rated materials or assemblies or if you affect the hourly rating of a building element required by the building's construction type, you could reduce the whole building's classification. For example, if part of an existing concrete floor is chipped away to create a slope to the drain for a new tiled shower, you could be reducing the fire resistance rating of the floor/ceiling assembly. Not only would you be ignoring the building codes, but also you would be reducing the safety of the building and affecting such things as building insurance and liability.

ICC **International Building Code** (2003)	NFPA **NFPA 220 Standard** (1999)
TYPE IA **Highly Protected**	**I (443)**
TYPE IB **Protected**	**I (332)**
TYPE IIA **Protected**	**II (222)**
TYPE IIB **Unprotected**	**II (111)**
	II (000)
TYPE IIIA **Protected**	**III (211)**
TYPE IIIB **Unprotected**	**III (200)**
TYPE IV **Heavy Timber**	**IV (2HH)** **Heavy Timber**
TYPE VA **Protected**	**V (111)**
TYPE VB **Unprotected**	**V (000)**

NOTE: The NFPA 220 table is repeated in the *Life Safety Code* and the *NFPA 5000*. In the 2003 edition of *NFPA 5000*, the first Type I category is slightly different.

Figure 3.2 Comparison of Construction Types. (This chart is a summary of information contained in the *International Building Code (IBC)* and the *NFPA 220*. Neither the ICC nor the NFPA assume responsibility for the accuracy or the completion of this chart.)

Comparing the Codes

The *IBC* and the NFPA codes refer to the Type I through Type V. The *IBC* uses a written description and Table 601 to describe the different construction types. The *NFPA 5000* and the *LSC* define the construction types based on another standard, *NFPA 220, Standard on Types of Building Construction.* A comparison of the construction types in the *IBC* and the *NFPA 220* can be seen in Figure 3.2. (If a jurisdiction requires the use of the *IBC* and the *NFPA 220* standard, the strictest requirements will apply.)

Note

The construction type tables used by the NFPA may be slightly different, depending on the edition of the NFPA 220 standard and other NFPA codes.

The *NFPA 220* assigns a three-digit code to describe the fire resistance rating of each construction type instead of using words such as *protected* or *one-hour*. For example, if you refer to Figure 3.2 under the *NFPA 220* column, the second item in the column is Type 1 (332). The three digits in the parentheses represent the hourly fire ratings for three structure elements: 3-hour, 3-hour, and 2-hour ratings. As a standard, the first digit pertains to exterior load-bearing walls, the second digit includes the frame, columns, and girders, and the third digit represents floor construction. These three digits are a helpful quick reference, but they do not provide all the necessary information. You must refer to the rest of the *NFPA 220* table to obtain the ratings for the remaining structural elements. A similar table is also included in the *NFPA 5000*. The table is essentially the same as the *NFPA 220* table except that it adds a category for interior nonload-bearing walls.

Note

Even when a construction type is considered noncombustible, some combustible materials can be used. You must refer to the codes for specifics.

Unlike the building codes, the *LSC* does not have a chapter dedicated to construction types. Instead, it refers you to the *NFPA 220* and lists the allowable construction type for each occupancy within the text. In each occupancy chapter, it will list the "minimum construction requirements" indicating which construction types are allowed, but you must reference the *NFPA 220* to get the specifics. Note that the construction type table found in the *NFPA 220* is repeated in the Appendix of the *LSC* for easy reference. Be aware that the tables in the *NFPA 220*, *NFPA 5000*, and *LSC* may differ slightly depending on the edition of the publication.

In some aspects the way that the various codes define construction types is very similar. For example, a Type I construction would be considered to be noncombustible in both the *IBC* and the NFPA documents. However, the required ratings for specific structural elements may vary between codes. For example, the fire resistance ratings for columns in a Type I in the *IBC* may be different than required in the *NFPA 220*. (See Chapter 5 for more information on fire-rated interior building elements and assemblies.) Because the rating of the structural elements is one of the main ways that construction types are defined, this may mean that a building's structure may be considered a Type I for one code but would be considered a Type II if the building was reviewed under a different code.

In certain cases, the use of performance codes may also be required. Both the *ICC Performance Code (ICCPC)* and the *NFPA 5000* provide alternate performance criteria that can be used when dealing with the construction elements of a building. For interior projects, these may be useful when dealing with an older existing building that is not easily classified within the current construction types or that includes materials or assemblies not addressed by the codes. In the *ICCPC*, for example, the criteria for fire resistance of structural members within a building are not given in hourly ratings, but are required to be "appropriate" for the particular use of the structural member, its potential exposure to fire, the height of the building, and the use of the building. In the "Performance-Based Option" chapter of the *NFPA 5000*, the code requires that the building be designed and constructed to "reasonably prevent" the spread of fire or structural failure to allow sufficient time for occupant evacuation and for firefighters to begin suppression of the fire.

In an older building, it may be difficult to determine if all the components within the structure consist of noncombustible materials. Or, the rating of a particular building element or assemblies may be impossible to determine. Without this clear information, it may be difficult or impossible to classify the construction type of an older building. Similarly, when changes occur to the interiors, matching existing construction methods may not meet current code standards. In these cases, using performance-based codes may allow you to provide the best design for your project. But, as always with performance codes, you will have to prove to the code official that the design and specifications meet the criteria set by the performance requirement.

Note

Nearly all materials are eventually affected by flame and heat. Even materials that have been treated to become fire retardant will still burn or char when exposed to a continuous flame.

Combustible versus Noncombustible

The hourly ratings on a construction type table such as the *IBC* table in Figure 3.1 indicate how fire resistant a material or an assembly of materials must be. The ratings represent the length of time a material or a combination of materials must resist fire. The resistance of these materials is based on how easily they ignite, how long they burn once ignited, how quickly the flames spread, and how much heat the material generates. Most products are differentiated as either noncombustible, fire resistant, limited combustible, or combustible. The higher hourly fire ratings typically tell you that noncombustible materials are required, and the lower ratings indicate that fire-resistant materials or limited combustible materials are allowed. For example, Type I and Type II are usually designated to be constructed of noncombustible materials; Type III is a combination of combustible and noncombustible materials; and Type IV and V are typically allowed to be constructed of fire-resistant and combustible materials. Combustible materials are usually allowed by the codes when no ratings are specified and in limited amounts in construction types considered to be noncombustible.

Note

After a fire occurs in a building, the exposed building elements may be altered. Many noncombustible materials may appear to have endured the fire unchanged, but flame and heat can change the strength and structural makeup of noncombustible materials. Unseen damage can occur.

Noncombustible materials are defined as materials that will not ignite, burn, or release flammable vapors when subject to fire. These materials are required to pass *ASTM E 136, Standard Test Method for Behavior of Materials in a Vertical Tube Furnace at 750 degrees C.* They are used to prevent substantial fire spread, since they do not contribute fuel to a fire. (See inset titled *High-Rise Buildings* on page 108.) Four basic materials are generally considered noncombustible: steel, iron, concrete, and masonry. Their actual performance in the event of a fire, however, depends on how they are used. Occasionally they may require additional fire treatment or protection for extra strength and stability. For example, steel has a rapid loss of strength at high temperatures and must be given extra protection if used on its own. To avoid this, steel is often encased in concrete or covered in a protective coating.

On the other side of the spectrum are *combustible materials.* These are materials that will ignite and continue to burn when the flame source is removed. Wood is a common combustible item. However, wood and other construction materials can be chemically treated to gain some amount of fire resistance. For example, chemically treated wood is called "fire-retardant treated wood" (also commonly known as FRTW). These are considered *fire-resistant materials;* once treated they will delay the spread of a fire by a designated time period and can prevent or retard the passage of heat, hot gases, and flames. The fire retardant treatment allows the material to be used in more places throughout a building. It can even be substituted for materials required to be noncombustible where specified in the code. For example, some fire-treated wood can be used in most rated walls. (See inset titled *Use of Combustible Materials* on page 99.)

Note

Some fire-retardant chemicals may cause wood to absorb more moisture. This can cause loss of strength, rot, decay, corrosion of fasteners, poor paint adhesion, staining, and even loss of the fire retardant chemical. Therefore, in high moisture areas be sure to specify the correct type of fire-treated wood.

Wood can also be considered fire resistant if it is large enough in diameter. *Heavy timber* is considered to be fairly fire resistant because of its size. Typically, columns are required to be at least 8 × 8 inches (203 × 203 mm) and beams a minimum of 6 × 10 inches (152 × 254 mm). The bigger the timber, the longer it takes to burn. Heavy timber builds up a layer of char during a fire that helps to protect the rest of the timber.

The NFPA uses an additional term to define certain types of fire-resistant materials. *Limited combustible materials* are defined as materials that do not meet the requirements of noncombustible material because they do have some capacity to burn. Although treated materials typically fall into this category, the material is considered limited combustible only if it passes a specific standard test. This test is used to determine if a material or assembly is considered limited combustible is *NFPA 259, Standard Test Method for Potential Heat of Building Materials.*

These fire-resistant and limited combustible materials can also be used in conjunction with other materials to create rated assemblies. The materials work together as an assembly to create a higher fire resistance. (See Chapter 5.) For example, wood studs used with gypsum board on both sides can create a one-hour-rated wall. Other common fire-resistant materials include gypsum concrete, gypsum board, plaster, and mineral fiber products.

When the construction type tables specify a rated structure or building element, it means the element must be composed of the appropriate rated building materials. You must be sure you are specifying fire-rated products or fire-rated

USE OF COMBUSTIBLE MATERIALS

Combustible, limited combustible, or treated materials are allowed in all construction types, even in noncombustible Type I and Type II in limited amounts and uses. The following are some of the allowable uses of combustible materials:

- ❑ Fire-retardant treated wood (FRTW) in nonload-bearing walls less than 2 hours
- ❑ Thermal or acoustical insulation with a flame spread not greater than 25
- ❑ Interior finishes, trim, and millwork for doors, door frames, and window sashes
- ❑ Blocking required for mounting handrails, millwork, and cabinets
- ❑ Construction of certain platforms for worship, music, and other entertainment
- ❑ Foam plastics and other plastics installed according to the code
- ❑ Plastic glazing and decorative veneers
- ❑ Nail strips and furring strips (fire blocking may be required)

Some of these items will be described in more detail in Chapter 5 and Chapter 9. In each case, there are requirements for the proper installation of these materials and exceptions for when the materials may not be allowed. For example, if a hardwood floor is installed with sleepers (i.e., furring strips) on a noncombustible floor slab, the code specifies how to fire block the space created by the sleepers. You must refer to the code for more information.

assemblies when required. All fire-rated products are tested to obtain an hourly fire rating. Manufacturers must label their tested products to ensure that they have passed the tests. Chapter 5 elaborates on fire ratings and how to specify rated materials and assemblies.

Note

Construction types of some existing buildings are difficult to differentiate. Some types are very similar. When necessary, be sure to consult an engineer, an architect, a codes official, or the original contractor of the building to accurately determine the type of construction.

Using the Table

The building codes and the *NFPA 220* each give a detailed description of the construction types within their text. The construction type tables, such as the one shown in Figure 3.1, need to be used in conjunction with these descriptions as well as those in the *LSC*. Since each code is slightly different, it is difficult to specifically summarize all the construction types. Instead, some generalities have been made here and are shown in Figure 3.3.

Types I and II

These are the strictest construction types. These buildings are typically constructed with steel and concrete and are considered noncombustible. The main

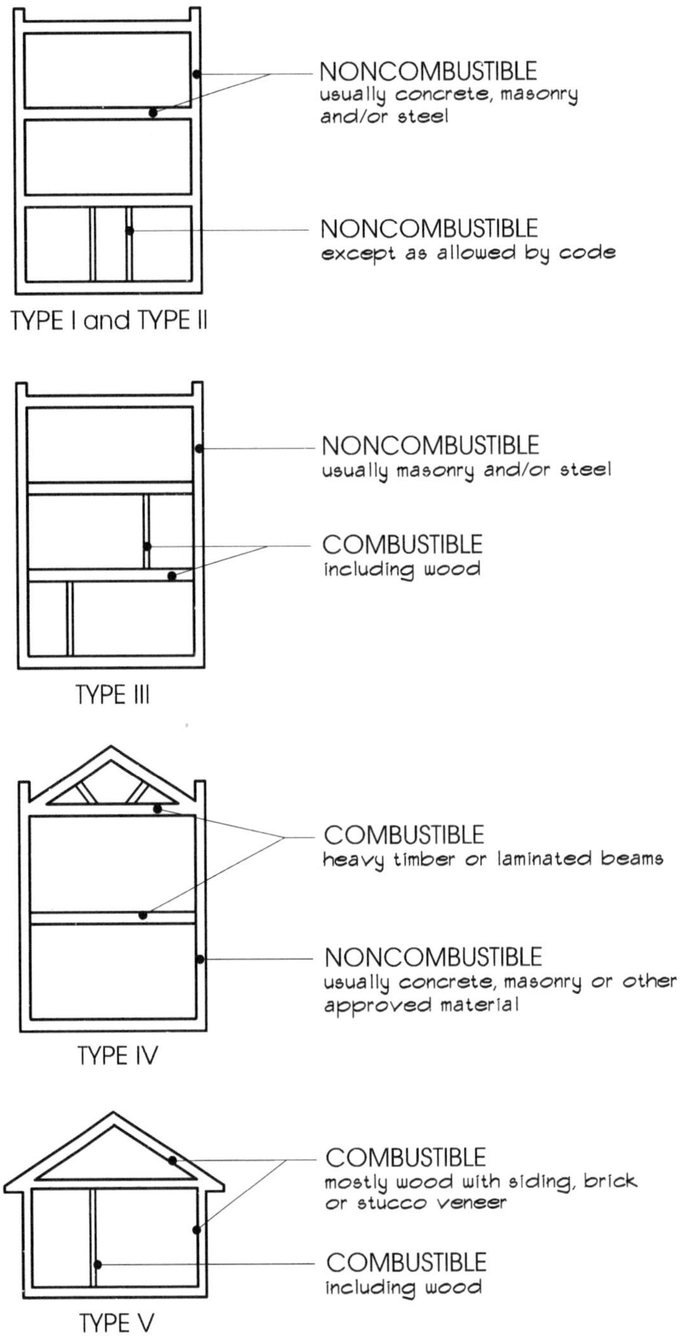

Figure 3.3 Typical Construction Type Characteristics

difference between these two types is the required hourly ratings of the structural elements as shown in the *IBC* Table 601. The types of combustible and limited combustible materials and allowable locations are indicated specifically in the text of the code. Wood, for example, is very rarely used, and is highly fire retardant if used at all. High-rise buildings and many large buildings fall into this category.

Type III

This construction type is considered combustible because it is a mix of noncombustible and combustible elements. The exterior is usually composed of noncombustible materials such as masonry, but the interior structural elements may be wholly or partially constructed with wood. This construction type is typical of small office buildings with wood or metal stud interior partitions and urban buildings where spread of fire from building to building is a concern.

Type IV

This construction type is sometimes referred to as *mill construction* or *heavy timber*. This type is typically composed of heavy-timber structural members and heavy wood floors. Although these buildings are predominantly wood, the char created during a fire results in a natural fire resistance to the structure. Modern heavy-timber construction is usually made of wood veneer laminated beams and trusses. Because of the large timber members, these buildings are relatively easy to identify. It is important to note that for interior projects in this type of construction, there can be no concealed spaces such as soffits, plenums, or suspended ceilings.

Type V

This is the most combustible construction type and is basically an all-wood structure. These buildings are usually characterized by wood framed exterior walls and interior walls. The exterior may have a veneer of brick, siding, or stucco. These buildings are typically small in size. Common examples include a residential house, a small dentist's office, or a convenience store.

In determining the construction type of a building that seems to have a combination of noncombustible and combustible components, you need to examine almost every building element using a process of elimination. You need to determine what materials have been used to construct the building, as well as what materials have not been used. The building will be classified by the lowest rated element or by the use of the most combustible material. For example, if a building does not meet the bearing wall rating for Type I even though the other structure elements meet the requirements, it will still be considered a Type II. Or, if combustible materials are predominantly used, then it cannot be classified as a noncombustible construction type.

Example

When working on interior projects where reconfiguration or addition of building elements is required, you will need to determine the construction type(s) of the building. Although you will be dealing mostly with nonload-bearing walls, other building elements become a factor as well. The ratings of some *interior* building elements will be found in the construction type table, such as the one in Figure 3.1. These elements include load-bearing walls, party walls, and demising walls, as well as shaft enclosures and other building elements. Although the building codes also include a nonload-bearing wall category in the table, additional information is typically included within the text.

Note

The main difference between Type I and Type II construction is the fire-resistance ratings of the structural members.

As you will see in Chapter 5, these elements become important when you are adding such things as walls, ceilings, doors, and windows. They will also be a factor when you are penetrating them with items such as sprinkler pipes and ducts. Remember, it is important to specify the correct building material for interior partitions, because if the rating is too low, a whole building might be reclassified into a lower category.

Let's say, for example, that you are asked to design office spaces on the first floor of an existing three-story building. Before you can specify the correct rating and materials for the interior walls and ceilings, you need to determine the building's type of construction. To do this, you need to know what materials were used to construct the building's existing structure. Ask yourself: Is the frame wood, steel, concrete block, or other masonry? What are the exterior walls? Are the floors wood or concrete? Go through the process of elimination described in the previous section.

As you examine the building and answer these questions, you will be able to pinpoint the materials used and determine which construction type fits the structure of the building. When necessary, try to obtain the original construction documents, consult the original building architect, or review the building with a structural engineer. Once you know the construction type, you will use the construction type table and other information in the codes to design the interior elements of a space such as walls, ceilings and column wraps. Other examples are given in Chapter 5.

ATRIUMS AND MEZZANINES

Atriums and mezzanines are common design elements used on the interior of a building. The codes set a number of additional requirements for them, some of which are described here. However, be sure to check the codes for the specifics and work closely with the local code officials. (Typically, engineers are required as well.)

Atriums

An atrium is commonly found in building lobbies and shopping malls. It is basically a multi-story space contained within a building, often surrounded by glass or open balconies. Atriums are required to be separated from all adjacent spaces by fire-resistance rated walls. When glass is used as part of the enclosure, additional requirements may be necessary. The codes also usually limit the number of floors that can open directly into the atrium to three floors. New atriums are allowed only in a fully sprinklered building. In addition, a mechanical smoke exhaust system is usually required at the ceiling and is typically tied into other fire-protection systems that would activate the exhaust system should a fire occur.

Mezzanines

A mezzanine is an intermediate floor level placed between the floor and the ceiling of a room or space. It is usually allowed only if it does not exceed more than one-third of the room or area in which it is located. There can be more than one mezzanine in a space, and even some at different levels, but the one-third rule would still apply. The appropriate headroom must also be provided at each level. The construction of a mezzanine is required to be the same as the construction type of the building in which it is located, and it is usually not counted as a story when determining the building height. Typically the mezzanine must be open to the room in which it is located and requires one or two exits to the room or space below.

Mixed Construction Types

It is unusual for multiple construction types to be located in a single building structure; however, they do occur. One example would be a medical office building adjacent to or on top of a parking garage. Typically, different construction types must be separated from each other by a separation wall. This separation wall is called a *fire wall* or *party wall*. It creates, in effect, two or more separate buildings.

In most cases, a fire wall must extend from the foundation of a building through the roof to a parapet wall and must be constructed so that it will remain stable even if one side of the wall or building collapses during a fire. In some cases, a fire wall separation can be created horizontally—for example, between a parking garage and an office building above. A fire wall is considered a building element and its rating is specified by the codes in the construction type tables such as the one in Figure 3.1. (See Chapter 5 for additional information on fire walls.)

Note

It could become a costly endeavor if you were to try to section off a part of an existing building by using a firewall. The wall must be continuous and would have to cut through vertical and horizontal elements. Be sure to consult an engineer.

Occupancy Requirements

Construction types set minimum building requirements. This, in turn, may set certain occupancy requirements. These requirements determine the structural integrity of a building for a required time period in case of a fire. For example, Type I is the strictest and will result in the most fire-resistant building and allow the most evacuation time. This evacuation time is critical for each occupancy classification.

Because some occupancies will require more evacuation time than others, they will require a stricter construction type. Assembly, Hazardous, and Institutional occupancies are the strictest. In a few cases, the code will not allow an occupancy to be in a certain construction type. For example, according to the *IBC*, certain Hazardous (H-1) and Institutional (I-2) occupancies cannot exist in a Type VB construction type. (Occupancy classifications are described in more detail in Chapter 2.)

Specific sections of the building code and each occupancy chapter in the *LSC* will specify the minimum construction type requirements for each occupancy. This becomes especially important when the occupancy classification of an existing building is being changed. Since many jurisdictions use both a building code and the *LSC*, it is important to consult both codes and use the strictest construction type requirements. When there are discrepancies, consult the code official in your jurisdiction for clarification. (Additional fire restrictive requirements are described in Chapter 5 and Chapter 6.)

PROTECTED OR UNPROTECTED

When discussing building limitations in the building code, the issue of *protected* and *unprotected* is often a source of confusion. Whether the construction of a building is considered protected or unprotected does not have anything to do with the use of an automatic sprinkler system. Instead, *unprotected* indicates that the structure or building elements of a building have not been treated in any additional way to increase their fire resistance beyond the natural characteristics of the materials. *Protected* indicates that the structural elements of a building have been treated to increase their fire resistance. This may include the use of noncombustible or limited combustible materials or fire-proofing materials to enclose or cover the elements of the structural assembly. Ultimately, a protected construction type provides more resistance to fire than the same construction type that is unprotected.

Note, however, that the inclusion of a sprinkler system within a building does affect the building limitation in a similar way. A building that has an approved automatic sprinkler system is allowed greater area and often more stories than the same construction that is not sprinklered. Sprinklering a building will often double the allowable area for a particular construction type. (See Chapter 6 for additional sprinkler trade-offs.)

BUILDING HEIGHT AND AREA

Building height and area are directly related to construction types. Building height and floor area control the overall size of a building. Similar to construction types, a building's size is usually determined at the time the building is originally constructed. Even when additions are made, the overall size of the building must remain within the appropriate height and area limitation.

Although code limitations on building size will not play a major role on interior projects, it is important to be aware of them and know when they apply. Many interior projects will not require you to analyze the size requirements. In most instances, the height and area of a building will be predetermined and will not need to be considered. In other situations it will be your responsibility to make sure an occupancy is appropriate for the selected building. (See Example on page 107.)

Note

If your project entails enlarging a building either horizontally or vertically, be sure to consult the codes as well as the appropriate experts—engineers, architects, contractors, and local code officials. Such a project is beyond the scope of this book.

Comparing the Codes

Building codes set limitations for the height and area of a building. These limitations are based on occupancy type, construction type, whether the building is sprinklered, and whether there are adjacent buildings. Once the building size is determined, all other code requirements work together to make the building safe for the occupants within it. Performance codes, such as the *ICCPC*, do not specifically have criteria for limiting the size of the building. Rather they set goals and objectives for the structural stability, fire safety, means of egress, and the acceptable level of damage or impact caused by a fire within the building's size and use.

The fire codes do not set limitations on the overall size or height of a building either. They will, however, designate when a building must be divided into separate fire areas (either within a floor or between stories) to control the amount of area that can be directly affected by a fire. (This is discussed in Chapters 5 and 6.) The fire codes will also determine when large areas must be sprinklered. Therefore, the fire codes deal with the fire safety of a building regardless of size or height. They also set limitations to large spaces and potentially hazardous uses within a building. If a fire code is required in your jurisdiction, you will have to refer to it to determine when the requirements apply.

The Table

The building codes control a building's height and area, and each has a chart that sets specific parameters. Figure 3.4 is a table taken from the *IBC*, titled Table 503, "Allowable Height and Building Areas." The *LSC* does not include a similar table, because it does not regulate a building's size.

TABLE 503
ALLOWABLE HEIGHT AND BUILDING AREAS
Height limitations shown as stories and feet above grade plane.
Area limitations as determined by the definition of "Area, building," per floor.

		TYPE OF CONSTRUCTION								
		TYPE I		TYPE II		TYPE III		TYPE IV	TYPE V	
		A	B	A	B	A	B	HT	A	B
GROUP	Hgt(feet) / Hgt(S)	UL	160	65	55	65	55	65	50	40
A-1	S	UL	5	3	2	3	2	3	2	1
	A	UL	UL	15,500	8,500	14,000	8,500	15,000	11,500	5,500
A-2	S	UL	11	3	2	3	2	3	2	1
	A	UL	UL	15,500	9,500	14,000	9,500	15,000	11,500	6,000
A-3	S	UL	11	3	2	3	2	3	2	1
	A	UL	UL	15,500	9,500	14,000	9,500	15,000	11,500	6,000
A-4	S	UL	11	3	2	3	2	3	2	1
	A	UL	UL	15,500	9,500	14,000	9,500	15,000	11,500	6,000
A-5	S	UL	UL	UL	UL	UL	UL	UL	UL	UL
	A	UL	UL	UL	UL	UL	UL	UL	UL	UL
B	S	UL	11	5	4	5	4	5	3	2
	A	UL	UL	37,500	23,000	28,500	19,000	36,000	18,000	9,000
E	S	UL	5	3	2	3	2	3	1	1
	A	UL	UL	26,500	14,500	23,500	14,500	25,500	18,500	9,500
F-1	S	UL	11	4	2	3	2	4	2	1
	A	UL	UL	25,000	15,500	19,000	12,000	33,500	14,000	8,500
F-2	S	UL	11	5	3	4	3	5	3	2
	A	UL	UL	37,500	23,000	28,500	18,000	50,500	21,000	13,000
H-1	S	1	1	1	1	1	1	1	1	NP
	A	21,000	16,500	11,000	7,000	9,500	7,000	10,500	7,500	NP
H-2	S	UL	3	2	1	2	1	2	1	1
	A	21,000	16,500	11,000	7,000	9,500	7,000	10,500	7,500	3,000
H-3	S	UL	6	4	2	4	2	4	2	1
	A	UL	60,000	26,500	14,000	17,500	13,000	25,500	10,000	5,000
H-4	S	UL	7	5	3	5	3	5	3	2
	A	UL	UL	37,500	17,500	28,500	17,500	36,000	18,000	6,500
H-5	S	3	3	3	3	3	3	3	3	2
	A	UL	UL	37,500	23,000	28,500	19,000	36,000	18,000	9,000
I-1	S	UL	9	4	3	4	3	4	3	2
	A	UL	55,000	19,000	10,000	16,500	10,000	18,000	10,500	4,500
I-2	S	UL	4	2	1	1	NP	1	1	NP
	A	UL	UL	15,000	11,000	12,000	NP	12,000	9,500	NP
I-3	S	UL	4	2	1	2	1	2	2	1
	A	UL	UL	15,000	11,000	10,500	7,500	12,000	7,500	5,000
I-4	S	UL	5	3	2	3	2	3	1	1
	A	UL	60,500	26,500	13,000	23,500	13,000	25,500	18,500	9,000
M	S	UL	11	4	4	4	4	4	3	1
	A	UL	UL	21,500	12,500	18,500	12,500	20,500	14,000	9,000
R-1	S	UL	11	4	4	4	4	4	3	2
	A	UL	UL	24,000	16,000	24,000	16,000	20,500	12,000	7,000
R-2[a]	S	UL	11	4	4	4	4	4	3	2
	A	UL	UL	24,000	16,000	24,000	16,000	20,500	12,000	7,000
R-3[a]	S	UL	11	4	4	4	4	4	3	3
	A	UL	UL	UL	UL	UL	UL	UL	UL	UL
R-4	S	UL	11	4	4	4	4	4	3	2
	A	UL	UL	24,000	16,000	24,000	16,000	20,500	12,000	7,000
S-1	S	UL	11	4	3	3	3	4	3	1
	A	UL	48,000	26,000	17,500	26,000	17,500	25,500	14,000	9,000
S-2[b, c]	S	UL	11	5	4	4	4	5	4	2
	A	UL	79,000	39,000	26,000	39,000	26,000	38,500	21,000	13,500
U[c]	S	UL	5	4	2	3	2	4	2	1
	A	UL	35,500	19,000	8,500	14,000	8,500	18,000	9,000	5,500

For SI: 1 foot = 304.8 mm, 1 square foot = 0.0929 m^2.
UL = Unlimited, NP = Not permitted.
a. As applicable in Section 101.2.
b. For open parking structures, see Section 406.3.
c. For private garages, see Section 406.1.

Figure 3.4 *International Building Code (IBC)* Table 503 Allowable Height and Building Areas (*International Building Code* 2003. Copyright 2002. Falls Church, Virginia: International Code Council, Inc. Reproduced with permission.)

These tables govern the size of a building by setting height and floor area limits by occupancy classification within each type of construction. In Figure 3.4, each of the occupancy classifications used by the *IBC* are listed down the left side of the table. Along the top are the construction types (Type I to Type V). Under each construction type there is the letter "A" to designate a *protected* construction type and the letter "B" to designate an *unprotected* construction type. (See the discussion of protected and unprotected earlier in this chapter.) The remainder of the table provides the height and area limitations for these categories.

When the type of construction is cross-referenced with the occupancy classification, the table will indicate two sets of figures. The top figure indicates the maximum allowable number of stories. The bottom figure in the corresponding box indicates the maximum allowable area per floor. (The areas are indicated in square feet; a metric conversion factor is given at the bottom of the chart.) You will also notice that some classifications allow unlimited (UL) size or number of stories depending on the occupancy and the construction type. Others are not permitted (NP), especially for more Hazardous occupancies. (Additional notes are given at the bottom of the table.)

Example

If you are hired to do a design for a particular occupancy that is moving into a new building not originally built for that occupancy classification, you may be required to determine if it is allowed by codes. The requirements for the same use may have changed as well. It is important to make sure that the occupancy or use can occupy a building with a particular construction type and that it does not exceed the area or height limitations. It is important to determine this early in the design because you may find that a project is not feasible.

You may be helping a client select a space or building or helping a client who owns a building look for a particular tenant. If you are doing the former, you will need to determine the occupancy classification of the proposed use, calculate the approximate number of occupants (to determine the approximate area required), and determine the construction type restrictions for that occupancy. The code will either (1) give you restrictions for a specific occupancy to help limit the choice of buildings to the stricter construction types or (2) give you no restriction so you know any type of building is allowed.

For example, a client has located an existing two-story building that he wants to renovate into a hotel. It has 12,000 square feet (1115 s m) per floor. The construction type of the building has been determined to be a Type VB. You need to confirm that a hotel use can be located in the building according to the building code and that it has the area required by the code for that use. According to the *IBC*, hotels are an R-1 occupancy classification. (See Chapter 2.) You have also determined with your client that the total number of occupants (including guests and employees) will be 100 people. Next, you need to use the occupant load table and formula found in Chapter 2 to determine how much square footage (or square meters) is required for a 100-person hotel. The occupant load table in Figure 2.8 indicates that the load factor for Residential uses is 200 gross square feet (GSF) (18.58 g s m). By adjusting the formula Occupant Load = Floor Area ÷ Load Factor, to Floor Area Required = Load Factor × Occupant Load, the total would be 100 people × 200 GSF = 20,000 square feet (1858 s m) of floor area. Since the building is a total of 24,000 square feet (2230 s m), the required area is provided in the existing building. However, you still need to see if the occupancy is allowed in this construction type.

With this minimum area of 20,000 square feet (1858 s m), go back to the allowable area table in Figure 3.4. You can see that this use cannot be located within this existing building, according to the table. A Type VB construction type for a R-1 allows only 7000 square feet (650 s m) per floor on two floors, for a total of 14,000 square feet (1301 s m). However, if the various elements in the structure can be protected and the building can be reclassified as a Type VA, a hotel of this size could be located in this building, because the allowable area per

HIGH-RISE BUILDINGS

The most common definition of a high-rise building is any building that exceeds 75 feet (23 m) in height. This dimension is based on the fact that the ladders on fire department vehicles typically do not reach past this point. Therefore, the building height is typically measured from the lowest ground level a fire truck can access outside the building to the floor of the highest occupiable story.

The codes apply stricter requirements to high-rise buildings because of additional dangers posed by the increased height and characteristics of a tall building in the event of a fire. One of the particular dangers that is created by a tall building is that it is often impractical to evacuate all the occupants within a reasonable time. Also, because the fires are often beyond the reach of the fire department equipment, fires must be fought in place within the building. Compartmentation (including protected stairwells and areas of refuge), means of egress, and active fire protection systems (including detection and suppression) become very important. (See Chapters 4, 5, and 6.) Smoke control is also critical because tall buildings are affected by the stack effect of smoke during a fire. Additional safeguards include the mandatory use of automatic sprinkler systems and an overlapping of detection and suppression systems.

Note: Some local jurisdictions may use a shorter dimension to define the height of a high-rise building, based on the local conditions and the fire department equipment.

floor is increased to 36,000 square feet (12,000 square feet × 3 floors = 36,000 total square feet, or 1115 s m × 3 floors = 3345 s m). However, adding protection to the structure might not be feasible. Instead, you may have to consider additional area increases allowed by the codes, which may allow this building to be used for this occupancy classification. For example, if an automatic sprinkler system is installed, the allowable area could be increased significantly. The existing building could then be renovated into a hotel.

Height and Area Limitations

A building's maximum size is limited by many factors, such as construction type, occupancy classification, and location. In other cases the regulated size may be exceeded if the building is equipped with features such as automatic sprinklers and fire walls.

Some of the typical rules and most common exceptions when evaluating allowable building heights and floor areas are listed here as reference points to help guide you in your research. If you ever need to determine or analyze a building's allowed height and area, be sure to consult the building code in the jurisdiction of your project and reference the correct tables. Each building code will vary slightly.

1. *Construction type.* Generally, the stricter the construction type and the more noncombustible a building, the larger the allowed building. For example, Type I construction, which is noncombustible and the most protected, usually has no height limitations and few area limitations.
2. *Occupancy classification.* Certain occupancy classifications will restrict the size of a building as well as the type of construction. For example, in the *IBC* an Assembly (A-1) occupancy in a Type VB construction cannot exceed one story or 5500 square feet (511 s m). Other occupancies need to meet specific requirements to allow an increase in area and/or height. These requirements are stated in other sections of the code, usually by occupancy. For example, an Educational building that has at least two exits per classroom with one opening directly outdoors can increase in size.
3. *Number of occupants.* As the number of occupants increases and the occupants become more immobile, there will be more restrictions on the height and area. Assembly and Institutional occupancies are especially affected. (See Chapter 2 for occupant loads.)
4. *Location.* The location or distance of adjacent buildings, as well as the amount of street frontage, can affect the allowed area. For example, buildings with permanent surrounding open spaces can increase the amount of

floor area as indicated in the tables. This exterior space prevents fire spread to or from adjacent buildings.

5. *Sprinklers.* The use of approved automatic sprinkler systems can increase the allowable number of stories or the floor area allowed. In some cases, the use of a sprinkler system can be counted as added protection to the structure and thus allow the construction type to be reclassified to a different construction subclassification. For example, in the *IBC* a Type IIIB building may be reclassified to a Type IIIA building, which may, in turn, allow greater height, area, or use. Some occupancies require sprinklers in buildings of every size. Other occupancies may limit this option. (See Chapter 6 for additional sprinkler trade-offs.)
6. *Fire walls.* Fire walls can subdivide a building so that each created space is treated as a separate entity. Each created fire area or compartment must stay within its own size limitation, allowing the overall building to become larger. (See Chapter 5 for more information.)
7. *Hazardous.* Hazardous occupancies have a number of specific requirements. Refer to the codes.
8. *Single stories.* Single-story buildings are usually allowed greater flexibility in size of floor area. Each code sets a limit on the height of the story.
9. *Mezzanines.* Each code treats mezzanines differently. They can be considered part of the story in which they are located or they can be treated as a separate story. There are a number of other limitations as well. (See inset titled *Atriums and Mezzanines* on page 103.)
10. *Basements.* Area and height requirements for basements are specific to each code. Whether a basement is counted as a story depends on how much of it is above ground level and the occupancy of the building.

Determining construction types and building sizes may not be a part of every interior project. These variables are usually determined at the initial construction of the building. However, if the occupancy of a building changes, it will be important to be able to analyze an existing building and determine its construction type and building size. You need to do this in the early stages of the design. You may determine that the project is not feasible, or you may need to include certain things (e.g., sprinklers) in your design to make it comply with the codes. Be sure to work closely with the appropriate professionals when necessary. These include architects, engineers, contractors, and code officials.

CHAPTER 4

MEANS OF EGRESS

A means of egress is most commonly described as a continuous and unobstructed path of travel from any point in a building to its exterior or a public way. It can also be the path of travel an occupant uses to get to a safe area of refuge within a building. A means of egress is comprised of both vertical and horizontal passageways, including such components as doorways, corridors, stairs, ramps, enclosures, and intervening rooms. The design of these components is crucial to the safety of the building occupants in normal use of a building and especially during emergencies.

This chapter explains the various means of egress. The first half of the chapter concentrates on explaining the different types and components of the means of egress. The rest of the chapter discusses how to determine the required quantities, sizes, and locations of the parts of the means of egress. Accessibility requirements are also discussed. Although the codes usually separate means of egress codes and accessibility requirements, they should be considered together. In most cases, the means of egress will be required to be accessible or special conditions will have to be provided. And, since many of the means of egress and accessibility requirements overlap, you must compare them to make sure you are using the strictest ones. This chapter has combined the discussion of these topics wherever possible. (The figures typically show the strictest requirements as well.)

Note

Elevators, escalators, and moving walks are typically *not* considered a means of egress, since the codes do not usually allow them to be used as an exit during an emergency. However, this is changing as more elevators are required as an accessible means of egress. (See Elevators, page 144.)

Remember that not every type of means of egress mentioned in this chapter will be used in every interior project. In addition, many existing buildings will already have the required number of exits. You may be working with just one occupant or tenant in the building and will only need to consider the exiting within and from that tenant space. Some projects may require you to reevaluate the existing exit requirements and make alterations. Other projects will require new calculations. Either way, every interior project must meet specific means of egress requirements.

In this chapter you will learn how and when to use a wide variety of codes, standards, and federal regulations that pertain to the various means of egress.

Some of the requirements are based on occupant loads as discussed in Chapter 2. Specific fire ratings are also required for each means of egress. Chapter 5 explains the fire-rating requirements for building materials and assemblies. Chapter 9 explains the different types of finishes allowed in each area of a means of egress.

KEY TERMS

Below is a list of key terms used when discussing means of egress. These terms are defined and discussed in this chapter. They can also be found in the Glossary. Before continuing, be sure you are familiar with some of the common means of egress terms:

Building core
Common path of travel
Corridor
Means of egress
Means of escape
Natural path of travel
Occupant load
Passageway
Stairway
Story
Tenant

COMPARING THE CODES

Although the various codes define the parts of the means of egress in similar ways, the specific requirements can vary. For instance, all the codes agree that the means of egress includes exit accesses, exits, and exit discharges. However, the required width of exits, allowable length of corridors, and the hourly fire-resistance rating of the components and similar requirements may differ between codes.

Note

The means of egress chapter in the *IBC* went from nine sections in 2000 to 25 different sections in the 2003 edition. However, most of the information is generally in the same order.

The building codes and the *Life Safety Code (LSC)* set most of the requirements for the various parts of the means of egress. Each of these code publications has a whole chapter dedicated to means of egress. In the NFPA codes, specific requirements are also included in the individual occupancy chapters. In the *LSC*, these requirements can be different for new or existing buildings or spaces. If your jurisdiction enforces a building code as well as the *LSC*, you will have to compare their requirements to be sure you are using the most restrictive ones. Other code publications may need to be referenced as well, depending on those required by the jurisdiction.

The NFPA also publishes the *NFPA 101B, Code for Means of Egress for Buildings and Structures*. The most current edition of this standard is 2002. This document is similar to the means of egress chapter in the *LSC*, but it also has its own administrative, definition, and general requirements section. The *NFPA 101B* is not intended to be a stand-alone document. Rather, it can be adopted by a jurisdiction to be used with a building code in place of the means of egress chapter in the required building code. Unlike the *LSC*, the *NFPA 101B* requirements are mostly directed toward new construction, with only specific exemptions given for alterations, repairs, and changes in occupancies within existing buildings or spaces. The *NFPA 101B* also addresses means of escape within the various types of residential uses.

Note

Many accessibility requirements are similar in the ICC/ANSI standards and the ADA guidelines, but they are not the same. If a jurisdiction requires you to use the ICC/ANSI standard, you should check both the ADA guidelines and the ICC/ANSI to make sure you are using the most stringent requirements.

The fire codes include requirements that affect the means of egress as well. In the *International Fire Code (IFC)*, the chapter titled "Means of Egress" includes several sections that repeat the information found in the means of egress chapter in the *IBC*. These sections include requirements for exit accesses, exits, exit discharges, and emergency exits. However, the means of egress chapter in the *IFC* also includes maintenance requirements so that the means of egress remain usable. This includes limitations on the use of decorations, mirrors, and other objects that may obstruct the egress path. In addition, it includes special requirements for existing buildings that may allow exceptions to the requirements for new buildings. In the "Emergency Planning and Preparedness" chapter of the *IFC*, the code requires that occupants be made aware of evacuation procedures. This typically includes announcing the location of exits at assembly events and practice fire drills for schools. Although these requirements may not directly affect the design of a space, in some cases you may assist in developing diagrams that indicate the egress patterns that are required to be posted by the fire code. The *Uniform Fire Code (UFC)* contains similar means of egress information.

The *ICC Performance Code (ICCPC)* also has an entire chapter dedicated to means of egress. Additional information is included in the chapter titled "Pedestrian Circulation." This chapter includes accessibility criteria as well. For performance criteria in the NFPA codes, you should refer to the performance chapter included in each code. Although this chapter does not set specific requirements for the means of egress, it does require that a building and its design allow occupants sufficient time to evacuate, relocate, or have a "defend in place" location. Obviously, this could be achieved in several ways. The chapter also sets several objectives for safety during an emergency that, in turn, affects the means of egress.

Although all the same concepts of a means of egress as discussed by the prescriptive codes—such as area of refuge, travel distance, and unobstructed path—can be part of a performance design, those specific terms are usually not used by performance codes. Instead the phrases are more generic, like "safe place," "appropriate to the travel distance" and "adequate lighting." In that way, it may not matter if a particular area is a corridor or a passageway according to the definition of the prescriptive code. Instead, what matters is how it works within the path to safety.

In addition, performance codes require the designer to consider the characteristics of the occupants, characteristics of the design, and the hazards that may exist to determine and to identify the specific challenges in evacuating a particular space or building. For example, you should consider if the occupants are capable of moving to an exit by themselves, are limited in physical mobility, or are confined by certain security measures. Understanding the special conditions that exist within a building and using the performance criteria may allow you, when necessary, to develop a unique system of evacuation for the particular occupants and building configuration. Prescriptive codes may then be used to define other specific elements of the means of egress, such as the location of exit signs and emergency lighting. (It will be rare when only performance codes are used for the design of the entire means of egress.) As always, when using performance criteria, you must establish the appropriate criteria of the design and then provide supporting evaluations and information to the code official for approval.

Because the means of egress in most cases is required to be accessible, you must also review the requirements in conjunction with the appropriate federal regulation, such as the Americans with Disabilities Act (ADA) guidelines. The building codes also reference the *ICC/ANSI 117.1* accessibility standard. As discussed throughout this chapter, accessibility requirements will affect the size of many of the means of egress elements, as well as the shapes and mounting heights of the various elements that occupants must use as part of the means of egress. Both the ADA guidelines and the ICC/ANSI standard set minimum requirements that are, in many cases, stricter than the codes. You should compare the ADA guidelines with the ICC/ANSI standard as well as the accessibility chapter in the building codes to confirm the strictest requirements. Some of these differences are explained in this chapter. You will find others as you do your research for particular projects. Remember, if there is a conflict in the requirements, you must meet the strictest requirement—in other words, you must satisfy the need for both accessibility and safety.

In addition, be sure to review the particular occupancy classification(s) of your project. Although most of the regulations are fairly consistent, some occupancies allow certain exceptions or have additional requirements. Some of the exceptions are given within the means of egress chapters, and others are grouped by occupancy classification in different sections of the codes. Assembly occupancies especially must be reviewed, since the use of fixed seats can create unusual egress paths. (See the section on Aisles and Aisle Accessways later in this chapter.)

TYPES OF MEANS OF EGRESS

A *means of egress* is a broad term that covers a variety of building components. Each of the codes divides a means of egress into three main categories: exit access, exit, and exit discharge. In most cases, a public way is the final destination of a means of egress. In some cases, an area of refuge is the final destination. All of the means of egress components are defined as follows:

- **Exit access:** The portion of a means of egress that leads to the entrance of an exit. It includes any room or space occupied by a person and any doorway, aisle, corridor, stair, or ramp traveled on the way to the exit.
- **Exit:** The portion of a means of egress that is protected and fully enclosed and is between the exit access and the exit discharge or public way. It can be as basic as the exterior exit door or it can include enclosed stairwells and ramps. In some special cases, it can include certain corridors or passageways. The components of an exit are distinguished from the exit accesses by higher fire ratings.
- **Exit discharge:** The portion of a means of egress between the termination of an exit and the public way. It can be inside a building such as the main lobby, or outside a building such as an egress court, courtyard, patio, small alley, or other safe passageway.
- **Public way:** The area outside a building between the exit discharge and a public street. Examples would include an alley or a sidewalk. The area must have a minimum clear width and height of not less than 10 feet (3048 mm) to be considered a public way.
- **Area of refuge:** A space or area providing protection from fire and/or smoke where persons who are unable to use a stairway (or elevator) can remain temporarily to await instruction or assistance during an emergency evacuation.

Note

An exterior space outside a building can be either an exterior exit discharge or a public way. To be a public way, the space must be at least 10 feet (3048 mm) wide and 10 feet (3048 mm) high and be considered a public space.

It is important to understand the relationship of these components and when each exists. The simplest relationship is when the exit access leads directly to an exit that takes occupants out of the building. This is shown conceptually in Figure 4.1A and 4.1B. In the first diagram, the exit may simply be an exterior door.

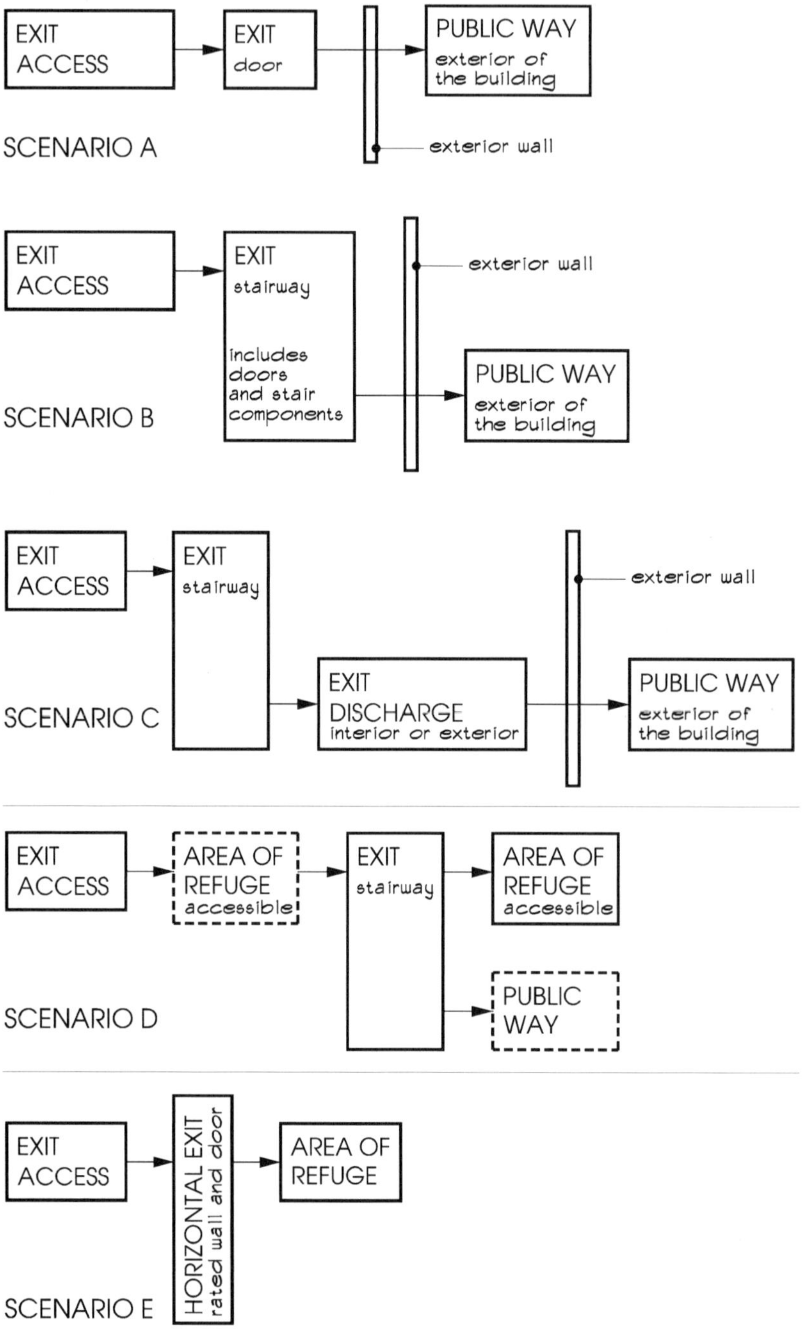

Figure 4.1 Means of Egress Components

In the second diagram, the exit may be an exit stair that opens at the bottom to the exterior of the building.

In some cases, an exit does not end at the exterior of the building or public way but leads into an exit discharge. As shown in Figure 4.1C, the exit discharge connects the exit to the public way. The exit discharge can be inside the building or outside the building. In each case, the code will have specific requirements for its use.

The other basic relationship is when the means of egress ends in an area of refuge instead of a public way. This can happen in two basic ways: vertically and horizontally. For example, Figure 4.1D indicates the use of a stair as an exit to lead down and out of a building. The exit access can lead to an area of refuge adjacent to but outside the stairwell or directly inside the stairwell for disabled persons who cannot use the stair. In this case, the means of egress ends at the area of refuge on that particular floor instead of the public way at the bottom of the stairwell. Emergency personnel will then assist them in getting out of the building as soon as possible or when safe. An area of refuge can also be used to keep people safe on the same floor. As shown in Figure 4.1E, the exit access leads through a horizontal exit to an area of refuge. (This will be described in more detail later in the chapter.)

In order to know what requirements apply to a particular space, you need to know whether it is part of the exit access, exit, or exit discharge. For example, different finish classifications will be required for an area that is an exit access than for one that is part of an exit. (See Chapter 9.) Some means of egress components within a space may be easy to identify. For others, you may have to consider the path of the occupants to identify the relationship of a component and its role within the means of egress. This is shown on the floor plan in Figure 4.2.

In this floor plan, different shading patterns indicate whether the space is considered an exit access, an exit, an exit discharge, or a public way. In some cases, a space may be considered to be more than one part of the means of egress. For example, in all cases, the exit stair is considered an exit. However, the location of an occupant can determine what part of the means of egress a particular room or space would be considered, and ultimately, what requirements must be applied to it. For example, if a person were standing in the lobby of this diagram, the distance from the person to the exterior door would be the exit access and the exterior door would be the exit. Once through the exterior door, the person would be in an exterior exit discharge (egress court), because, in this case, the sidewalk is the public way. However, for a person coming down the stairway at the left of the plan and emptying into the lobby, the stairway is the initial exit component, the lobby is then part of the exit discharge, and the exterior door is the end of the interior exit discharge because it leads to the exterior of the

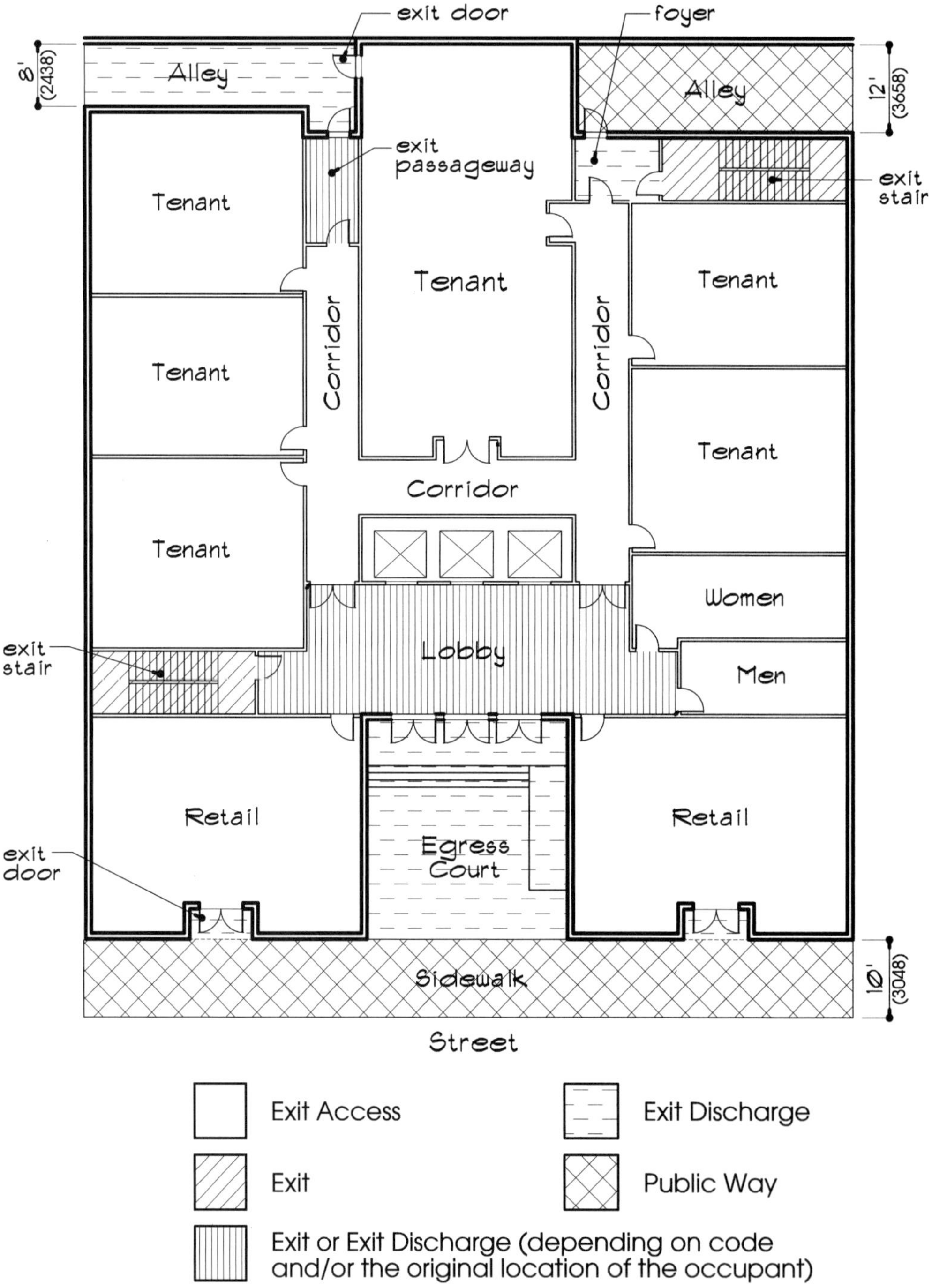

Figure 4.2 Means of Egress in a Typical Building

building. From that point, the egress court continues as an exterior exit discharge until it reaches the sidewalk as previously discussed. When a space can be considered more than one part of the means of egress, it must meet the requirements of the most restrictive component.

Although the parts of an exit can be defined somewhat differently among the various codes, they all assume that a means of egress will be continuous. This path provides protection to the occupant from the floor of origin to an area of refuge or to the ground level and public way. And, because an exit has a higher fire rating and provides a better level of protection, the codes also assume that an occupant is relatively safe once he or she reaches an exit. The requirements for the types of means of egress and its components are to assure that the level of protection is maintained until the occupant is in the public way.

What follows is a description of the types of means of egress and the various components of each. Exit accesses are described first. These components are elaborated in more detail, since similar components in the other means of egress categories have many of the same requirements. For example, *exit access* stairs and *exit* stairs are used for different purposes and require different fire protection, but they both use the same tread and riser dimensions, landing widths, handrail requirements, and so on.

Exit Accesses

An exit access is that portion of a means of egress that leads to an exit. It leads an occupant from a room or space to an exit and can include doors, stairs, ramps, corridors, aisles, and intervening rooms. Exit accesses do not necessarily require a fire-resistance rating or need to be fully enclosed. For example, a corridor in a tenant space usually does not need to be rated; however, a main building corridor connecting the tenants and the public spaces may be required to be rated. (See Chapter 5 for information on fire ratings.)

The type and location of an exit access depends on the layout of the building or space and the location of the occupants in the area. For example, in a large, open space or room that has a door as the exit, the exit access is the path of travel to that exit door. In a multi-story building where an enclosed stair is the exit, the exit access can include the enclosed corridor leading to the exit and the rooms and doors leading into the corridor. (See Figure 4.2.)

Each component of an exit access is described in this section. The descriptions include the basic code requirements, as well as many of the necessary accessibility requirements. (The various diagrams typically include the most restrictive code and accessibility requirements.) The second half of this chapter discusses how to determine the quantity, width, and location of an exit access.

Note

When determining the location of means of egress remember that, except for doors, the typical headroom required from floor to ceiling is 90 inches (2286 mm).

Doors

The codes regulate each component of a doorway. First, the door itself must be of a particular type, size, and swing, depending on where it is located. The most common exit access door is used along a corridor and connects the adjacent rooms or spaces to the exit access corridor. When the walls in these corridors are rated, the doors must be rated as well. (See the section on Rated Door Assemblies, page 202.) Other exit access doors, such as those within a tenant space, are not typically required to be rated.

Note

Exit access doors typically have a lower rating than exit doors.

Determining the required size and number of doors is described in the section on Exit Width later in this chapter, but the codes set minimum dimensions and other requirements that must be followed as well. Most doors in the means of egress cannot be less than 80 inches (2032 mm) high. The building codes, the ICC/ANSI standard, and the ADA guidelines specify that when in an open position, a door must provide 32 inches (815 mm) of clear width. Since this must be the clear inside dimension, as shown in the Plan in Figure 4.3, typically a door that is at least 36 inches (915 mm) in width must be used. Other clearance dimensions are required as well, depending on the type of door, its location within the space, and the occupancy classification. This includes minimum clearances on the jamb side of the door and allowable projections (including hardware and closers), as indicated in Figure 4.3.

Note

Most doors are side hinged and swinging. However, certain occupancies are allowed to use other types of doors under separate code provisions. These include sliding doors, balanced doors, overhead doors, revolving doors, security grilles, and turnstiles. Check the codes for specific requirements.

Usually, the codes require an egress door to be side-hinged and swinging. The direction of the swing depends on its location. In most cases, means of egress doors must swing in the direction of exit travel. However, the door cannot reduce any required stair landing dimensions or corridor width by more than 7 inches (118 mm) when the door is fully open. (This includes the door hardware as shown in Plan B of Figure 4.4.) It also cannot impede on more than half of the required corridor width at any open position. There are additional accessibility maneuvering clearances required as well. Depending on whether the approach to the door is from the push or pull side and hinge or latch side, you will typically need to include a minimum clearance of 12, 18, or 24 inches (305, 445, or 610 mm). (See Figure 4.4.) If you have an existing condition that makes it virtually impossible to obtain the required accessible clearances, an automatic door may be an option.

To avoid obstructing the required widths, the codes allow some smaller occupancies or rooms to have doors that swing into a space. An example would be an office or small conference room. (Usually the limit is 50 occupants.) However, if an interior project requires a door to swing out toward the path of exit travel, there are several options that can be used to meet the minimum code requirements. The most common are listed next. Figure 4.4 indicates these options and highlights the critical dimensions required by the codes, the ADA guidelines, and the ICC/ANSI standard.

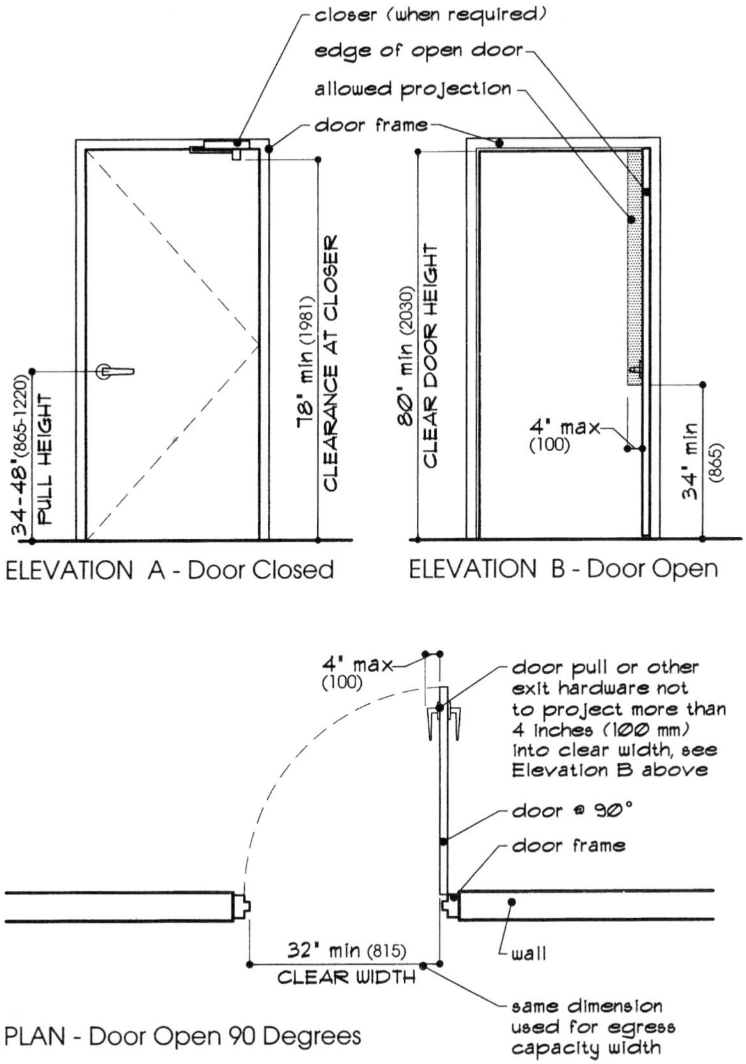

Figure 4.3 Required Door Clearances

1. *Increase swing of door.* Use a 180-degree swing door instead of a 90-degree door to allow it to fully open against the wall. This can be done only if a corridor is wide enough, as shown in Plan B of Figure 4.4.
2. *Create alcove.* Recess the door into the room, as shown in Plan E of Figure 4.4, so that the walls create an alcove that the door can swing into. (The alcove must allow maneuvering room.)

3. *Enlarge landing.* Enlarge the landing at the door, such as widening a corridor or lengthening a vestibule, to allow enough maneuvering space. Typical vestibule dimensions are shown in Plan A of Figure 4.4.
4. *Possible use of sliding door.* Use a sliding door in low traffic areas and when allowed by the codes. (See Plan C and D in Figure 4.4.)

Other types of doors are allowed to be part of the means of egress in certain situations. These types include revolving doors, power-operated swinging doors, and power-operated horizontal sliding doors. Because they work differently than swinging door types, the codes impose additional requirements for their use in the case of an emergency. For example, revolving doors are required to collapse to provide the minimum clear width, and power-operated doors are required to be capable of opening manually in case of an emergency or loss of electricity. Automatic sliding doors can also be used in some cases, but when pushed with a certain force must be capable of swinging into the direction of exit travel. In most cases, the codes limit the number of these special door types in a means of egress. The occupancy type can also determine if these door types can be used in a project. For example, many of these special doors are limited to use in occupancies such as Institutional and Mercantile.

Note

Where doors are subject to two-way travel, it is suggested that a vision panel be used in the door to avoid collisions.

The threshold is another part of a doorway regulated by the codes. Each code states that the finished floor surface or landing on either side of an interior door must be at the same elevation as the threshold or within ½ inch (13 mm) of the threshold. In addition, if the transition is greater than ¼ inch (6.4 mm), the ADA guidelines and the ICC/ANSI standard require both sides of the threshold to be beveled. (Refer to Figure 9.19 in Chapter 9.)

Hardware on means of egress doors is also regulated for safety and for accessibility. The codes require that the hardware on exit access doors be easily used by occupants. This is so that occupants are not delayed in evacuating a building because of difficulty in opening a door in their path. In most cases, locks that would hinder an egress are not allowed. (See codes for exceptions.) The building codes, the ADA guidelines, and the ICC/ANSI standard also require that all door pulls consist of accessible operating devices. They must be a certain shape and be installed at a specific height. (See Elevation A in Figure 4.3.) Any operating device must be capable of operation with one hand and without much effort. For example, lever, push-type, and U-shaped pulls are accessible.

For each type of door, the building codes set a maximum allowable force that is required to manually open the door. For typical swinging doors, the allowable force is typically between 5 and 15 pounds (22 to 67 N). However, for other special types of doors such as revolving, automatic, or sliding, the allowable force may vary from 30 to 180 pounds (133 to 801 N), depending on its use and location.

The ADA guidelines and the ICC/ANSI standard also set maximum force allowances for doors that are along the accessible route or are part of an accessible exit. You must compare these requirements and determine which ones apply to the door and its intended use.

Closers may also be required by the codes or accessibility standards so that the door is self-closing. For example, doors within rated walls are required to be

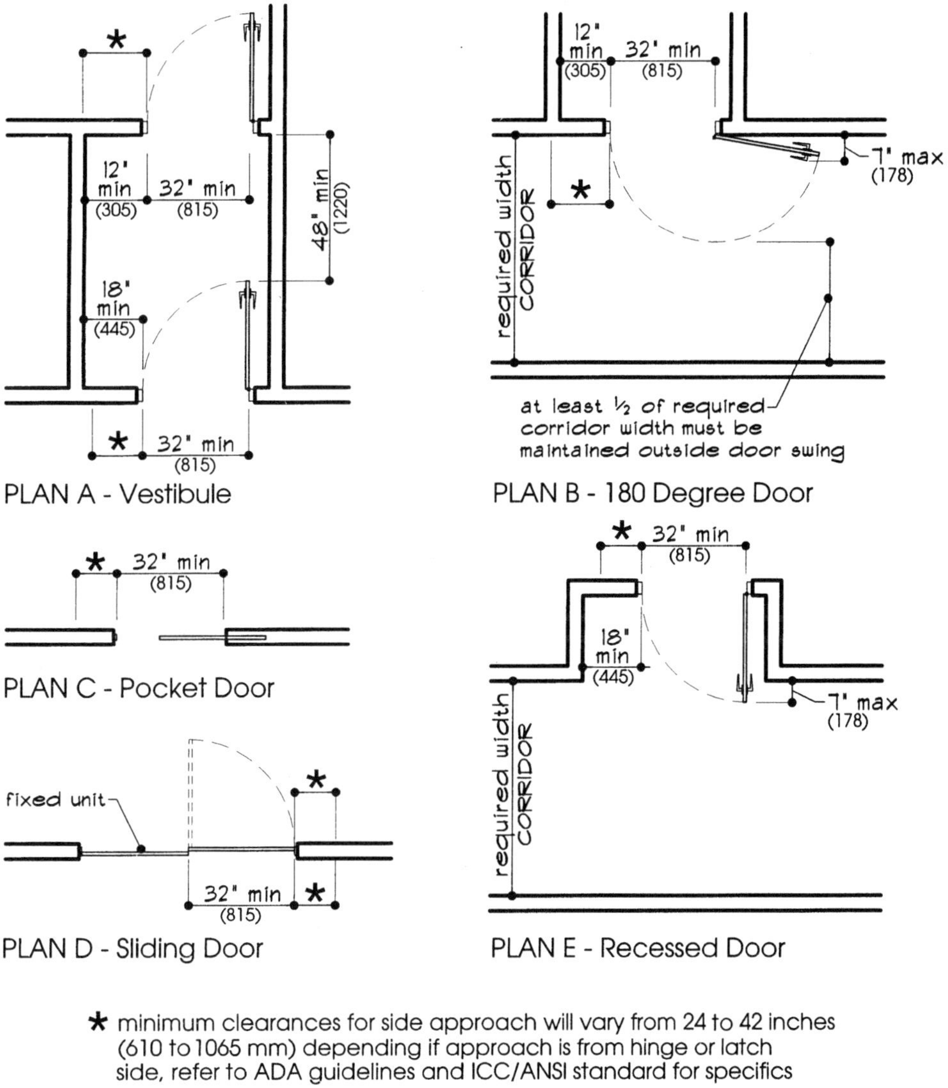

Figure 4.4 Typical Clearances at Doorways

self-closing to maintain the fire separation. In some cases, restroom doors are required to be self-closing for privacy and accessibility. Or, for convenience, it may be desirable to have a door to a particular room close after every use. In all cases, maximum allowable force required to open the door still applies. The closer must also be located on the door and frame so that it does not interfere with head clearance requirements as indicated in Figure 4.3. In some cases, the time it takes the door to close is also regulated by the codes and the accessibility standards. (For additional information, see section on Security in Chapter 8.)

ELEVATORS

Elevators are not typically considered a means of egress, especially during an emergency. However, since they are used on a daily basis during normal operation, elevators must meet specific accessibility requirements as defined in the codes, the ADA guidelines, and the ICC/ANSI standard. The following list includes some of the more common requirements. (Diagrams are available in the ADA guidelines and the ICC/ANSI standard.)

1. Automatic operation with self-leveling within a certain range
2. Power-operated sliding doors that open to a minimum width
3. Door delay and automatic reopening device effective for a specific time period
4. Certain size car, depending on the location and size of the sliding door (longer cabs allow for the transport of beds and gurneys should it be required)
5. Hall call buttons and car controls with specific arrangement, location, and height (including Braille and raised lettering)
6. Minimum distances from hall call button to elevator door
7. Hall lanterns and car position indicators that are visual and audible
8. Specific two-way emergency communication system
9. Handrail on at least one wall of the car
10. Floor surfaces that are firm, stable, and slip resistant
11. Minimum lighting levels
12. Specific door jamb signage at hoistway entrance on each floor
13. Emergency exit signs located near elevator doors

Although many of the requirements are consistent between the codes and accessibility publications, there are some variations. The requirements listed above may also vary based on if the elevators are intended for general use, for travel to designated floors only, or for a more limited use. In addition, in buildings of a certain height the codes may require at least one of the passenger elevators to be larger for use with an ambulance stretcher. Refer to the building codes, the ADA guidelines, and the ICC/ANSI standard for specifics.

Stairs

Exit access stairs are not as common as exit stairs. They are typically found within a space when one tenant occupies more than one floor of a building or where there is a mezzanine within a space. For example, a flight of stairs between the 16th and 17th floors within a tenant space will allow the occupant to move between the two floors without leaving the tenant space. Usually these exit access stairs do not need to be enclosed with rated walls unless the same stair connects more than two floors. Most of the requirements for an exit access stair are the same as for exit stairs. (See Exit Stairs on page 138.)

Note

The *LSC* permits new stairs in existing buildings to comply with previous stair requirements when alterations are made. However, other codes may not. In addition, depending on the location of the stairs be sure you follow any necessary ADA regulations.

There are a number of different stair types in addition to the straight run stair. These include curved, winder, spiral, scissor, switchback, and alternating tread stairs. Most of these are allowed by the codes as part of the exit access on a limited basis, depending on the occupancy classification, the number of occupants, the use of the stair, and the dimension of the treads. However, some of them may not be allowed as a means of egress. In addition, the materials used to build the stairway must be consistent with the construction type of the building. (See Chapter 3.)

All stairs are required to meet specific code and accessibility requirements. The most important are the tread and riser dimensions. The most common dimensions are shown in Figure 4.5, with a minimum tread depth of 11 inches (280 mm) and a range of 4 to 7 inches (100 to 178 mm) for riser height. The actual size of the riser will be determined by the overall vertical height of the stairway. Once the riser size is determined, it is not allowed to fluctuate more than a small fraction from step to step. The shape and the size of the nosings in relation to the riser are defined as well. Various nosing examples are shown in Figure 4.5.

Note

When determining stair dimensions you should know what floor covering will ultimately be used on the construction. Some floor coverings may change the final dimension of the treads or risers and, therefore, the effectiveness of the stair. The required dimensions are based on much research and are critical for ease of use.

Each run of stairs must have a landing at the top and the bottom. In addition, the codes do not usually allow a stairway to rise more than 12 feet (3658 mm) without an intermediate platform or landing. The width of the stair (as determined later in this chapter) determines the minimum dimensions of these required landings or platforms. Other variables must also be considered. For example, when fully open the door cannot project into the clear exit width more than 7 inches (178 mm), and the door cannot impede on more than half of the required exit width at any open position similar to the door shown in Plan B of Figure 4.4. Additional stair requirements are shown on the Plan in Figure 4.6. Any required areas of refuge may also increase the size of a landing. (See Areas of Refuge section later in the chapter.)

The ceiling above a stair and its landing must also meet certain requirements. Both a minimum ceiling height and minimum headroom are set by the codes. As shown in Elevation in Figure 4.6, the minimum ceiling height is typically 90 inches

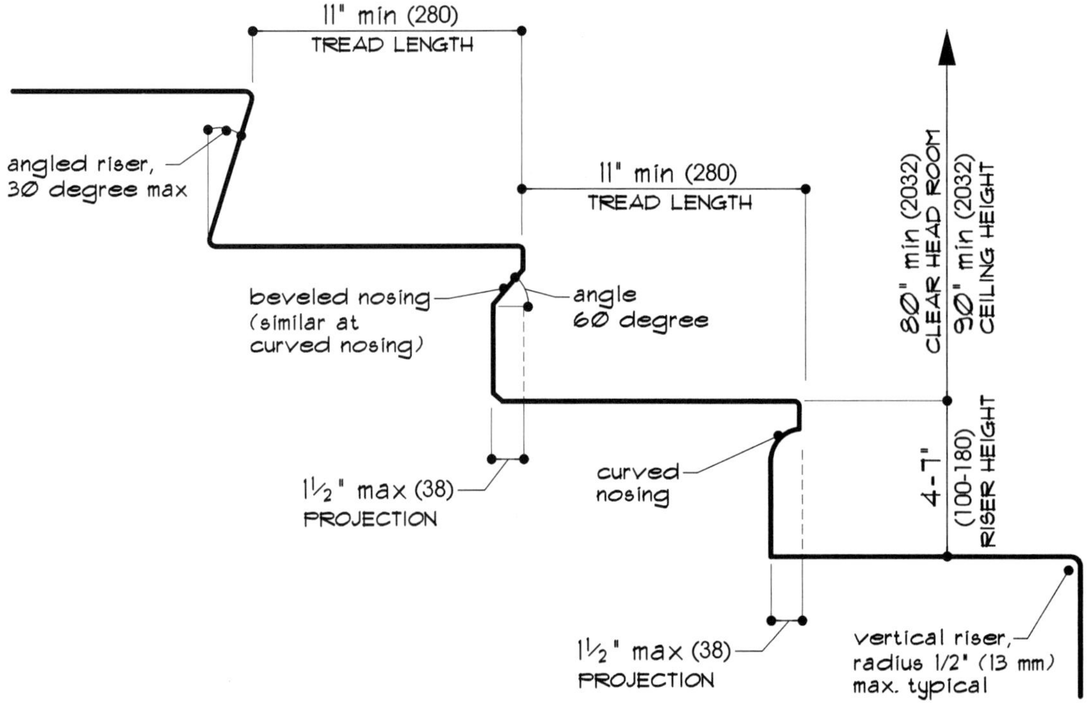

Figure 4.5 Typical Stair Requirements: Treads and Risers

(2286 mm). It is measured vertically from the landing and the front edge of the tread of the stair to the ceiling directly above. Some projections below that height are allowed. These may include structural elements, light fixtures, exit signs, or similar ceiling-mounted items. However, a minimum headroom of 80 inches (2032 mm) is required. This height is measured in the same way.

> **Note**
>
> The width of a *stair* is measured to the outside edges of the steps. The width of a *ramp* is measured to the inside face of the handrails.

Handrails and guards are regulated as well. Most stairs require a handrail on both sides. (See the codes for exceptions.) When wide stairs are used, additional intermediate handrails may be required. Building codes and accessibility standards require handrails to be certain styles and sizes, to be installed at specific heights and distances from the wall, and to be continuous wherever possible. Figure 4.7 and Figure 4.8 indicate some of these typical handrail dimensions and locations. Handrails must also extend a certain distance beyond the top and bottom of the stairway and have an uninterrupted grip. (Note that the bottom extension requirement is different in the newer editions of the ICC/ANSI standard and the ADA guidelines.)

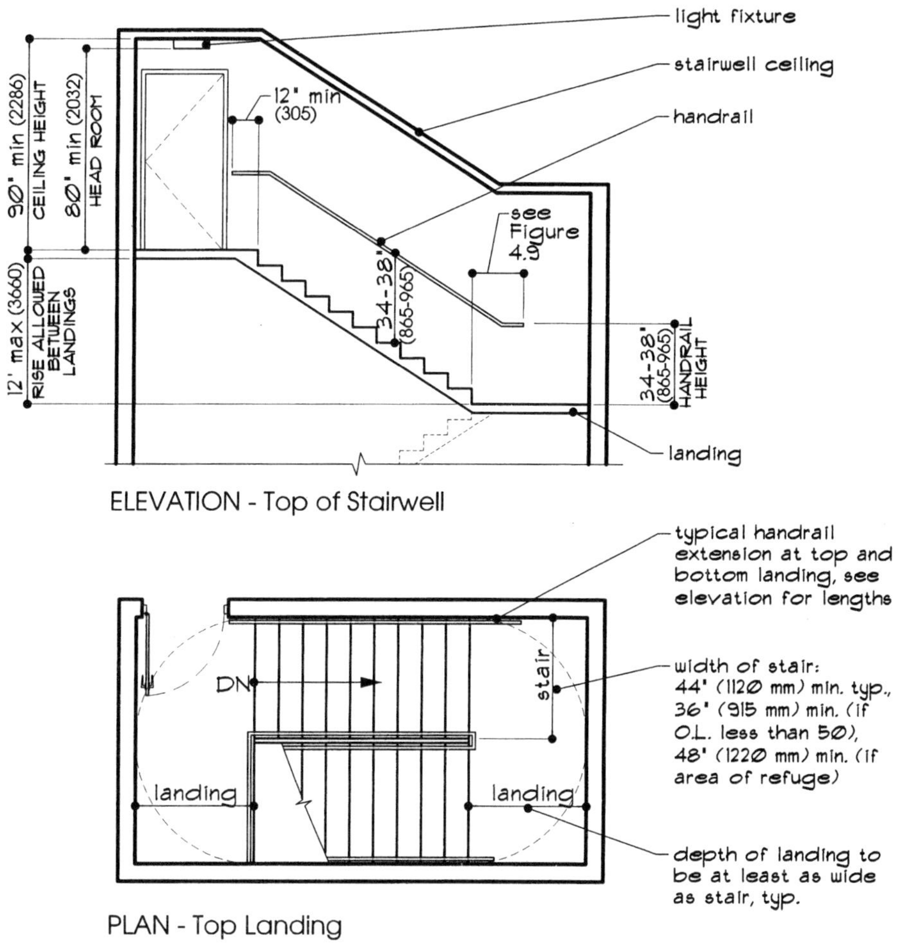

NOTE: If an open stairway, guards at a minimum height of 42 inches (1067 mm) would be required in addition to handrails.

Figure 4.6 Typical Stair Requirements: Clearances

Guards may also be required in certain locations. Guards are railings that are required by the code to keep people from falling off changes in elevations. They are typically necessary whenever there is a drop over 30 inches (762 mm) where occupants are walking and there is no adjacent wall. (Guards were known as *guardrails* in some of the legacy codes, but that term is not used by the newer codes.) The most common example of a guard is at a balcony or a stair when any side of the stair is exposed and not enclosed by a wall, as shown in Figure 4.8. In

Note

Current codes use the term *guard*. Many of the legacy codes referred to them as guardrails.

Note

Handrails are critical during an emergency. When stairs are full of smoke, handrails often are the only guide to an exit.

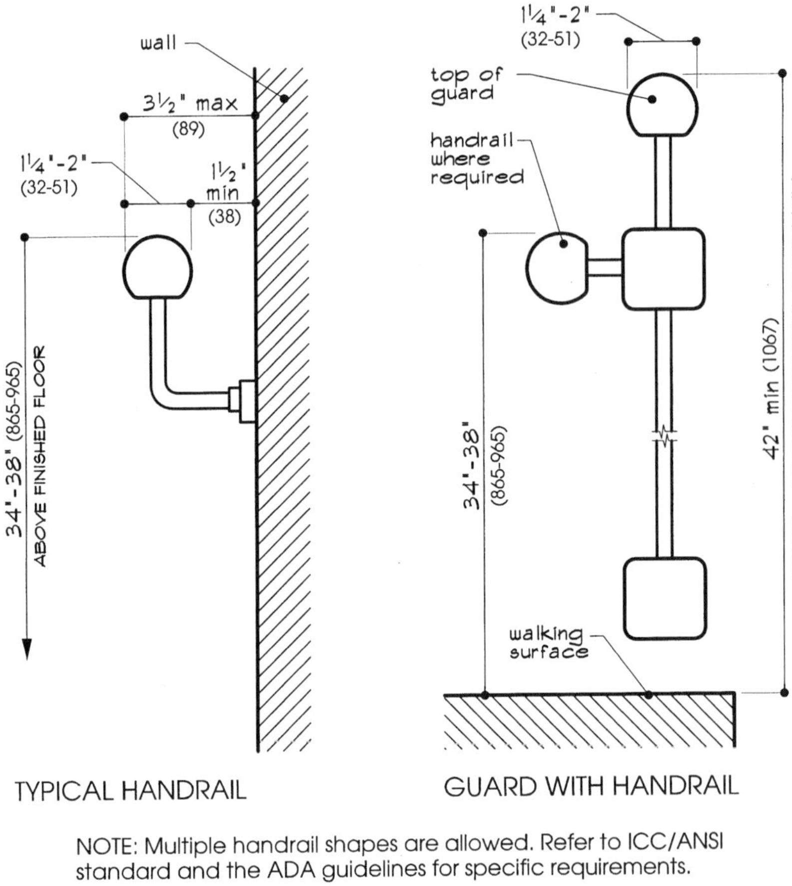

Figure 4.7 Typical Handrail and Guard Sections

most instances, the guards must be at least 42 inches high (1067 mm). If a handrail is also required, such as at the stair, it must be mounted at the required height for a handrail, as shown in Figure 4.7.

The guard must be constructed so that nothing with a diameter of 4 inches (100 mm) can pass through any opening created by the rail configuration. This is shown at the top of Figure 4.8. In addition, 6 inches (152 mm) is allowed between the bottom rail and the steps and 8 inches (203 mm) is allowed above 34 inches (865 mm). There are some exceptions for particular occupancy types. You should refer to the codes to determine if the exceptions apply. These requirements must be met whether you are specifying a prefabricated rail system or designing your own.

Note

In certain building types where children are not expected to be present, handrails and guards can allow up to a 21-inch (533 mm) sphere to pass through the rail configuration.

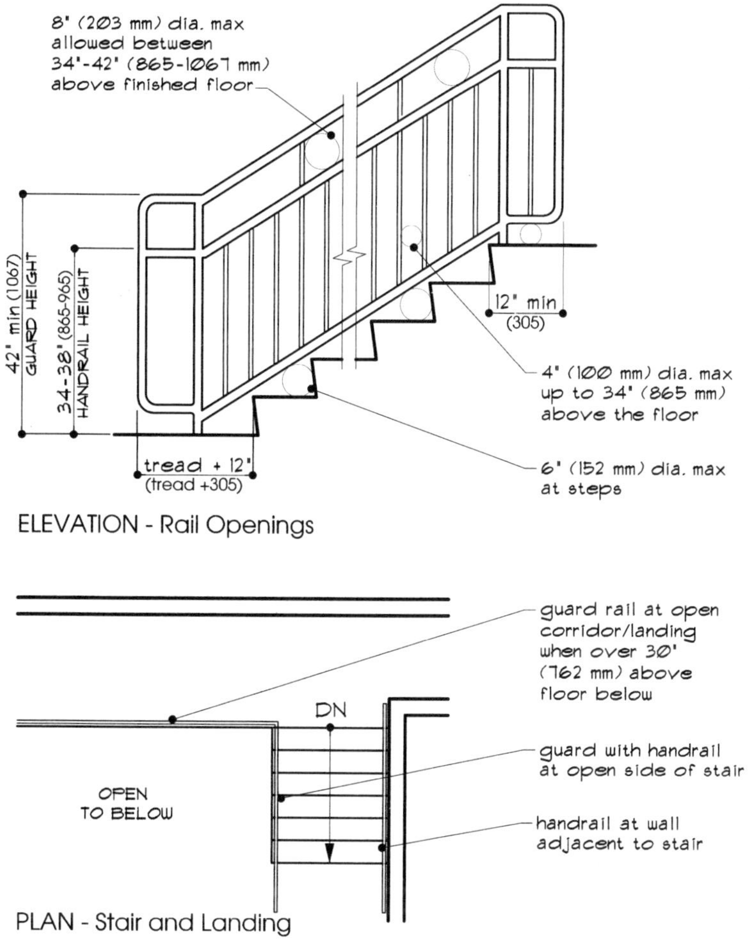

NOTE: New editions of the ICC/ANSI standard and the ADA guidelines allow the bottom rail extension at stairs to equal the depth of one tread in lieu of a tread plus 12 inches (305 mm).

Figure 4.8 Typical Handrail and Guard Requirements

Note

If glass is used as part of a handrail or guard, it must pass safety glass requirements as required by the codes.

Note

Handrails are critical during an emergency. When stairs are full of smoke, handrails are often the only guide to an exit.

Escalators and Moving Walks

Escalators and moving walks are not typically allowed as a means of egress. However, there are some exceptions in existing buildings. Existing escalators may be allowed only if they are fully enclosed within fire-rated walls and doors. Some may also require specific sprinkler requirements.

Newer escalators and moving walks are usually installed as an additional path of travel or as a convenience to the occupants of a building. Some of the more common occupancy classifications that use escalators and moving walks are Assemblies, large Mercantile, and certain Residential occupancies. When the escalators or moving walks are used, they are typically *not counted as a means of egress.* In most cases, each space or building must still have the required number of enclosed stairs as specified by the codes.

Ramps

Note

A ramp with a lower slope ratio should be used whenever possible. For example, a 1 to 16 ratio is more manageable and safer for persons with disabilities than the minimum required 1 to 12.

In general, ramps are used anywhere there is a change in elevation and accessibility is required. Although you should try to avoid changes in elevation on a single floor, if steps are provided, then a ramp must be provided as well. The most important requirement of a ramp is the slope ratio. Most codes and accessibility standards set the *maximum* ratio at 1 unit vertical to 12 units horizontal. That means for every vertical rise of 1 inch, the horizontal run of the ramp must extend 12 inches. The same proportion would be required in centimeters: 1 centimeter to 12 centimeters. This is shown at the top of Figure 4.9.

Typically, a ramp must be at least 36 inches (915 mm) wide (measured to the inside of the handrail). The other important requirement is the use of landings. The codes, the ADA guidelines, and the ICC/ANSI standard require landings at certain intervals and of certain dimensions. In most cases, the width of the landing must be the same as the width of the ramp, although a minimum length of 60 inches (1525 mm) is usually required, as shown in Landing A on the Plan in Figure 4.9. When changes in direction are required, the landing must allow a 60-inch (1525 mm) turnaround, as shown on Landing B in Figure 4.9. To limit the length of a ramp, a landing is usually required for every rise of 30 inches (760 mm) or a run of 30 feet (9144 mm). Landings are also required at the top and bottom of every ramp and must take into account any adjacent doors. Both the landings and the ramps require specific edge details and a rough type of nonslip surface. (Refer to ADA guidelines and ICC/ANSI standard for specifics.)

Note

Ramps not specifically designed or intended for the disabled can usually have a slightly steeper slope, as allowed by the codes. Please note that you should verify this with your code official. However, it is advisable to use an accessible slope whenever possible.

The construction of the ramp and its handrails is similar to that of stairs. Handrails are typically required when the ramp exceeds a certain length or rise. Similar to stairs, the handrails are required to extend a certain distance beyond the landing. (See Elevation in Figure 4.9.) Guards are also required when there is no adjacent wall and the overall rise of the ramp is greater than 30 inches (760 mm). Width and clearance requirements for ramps are similar to those for corridors.

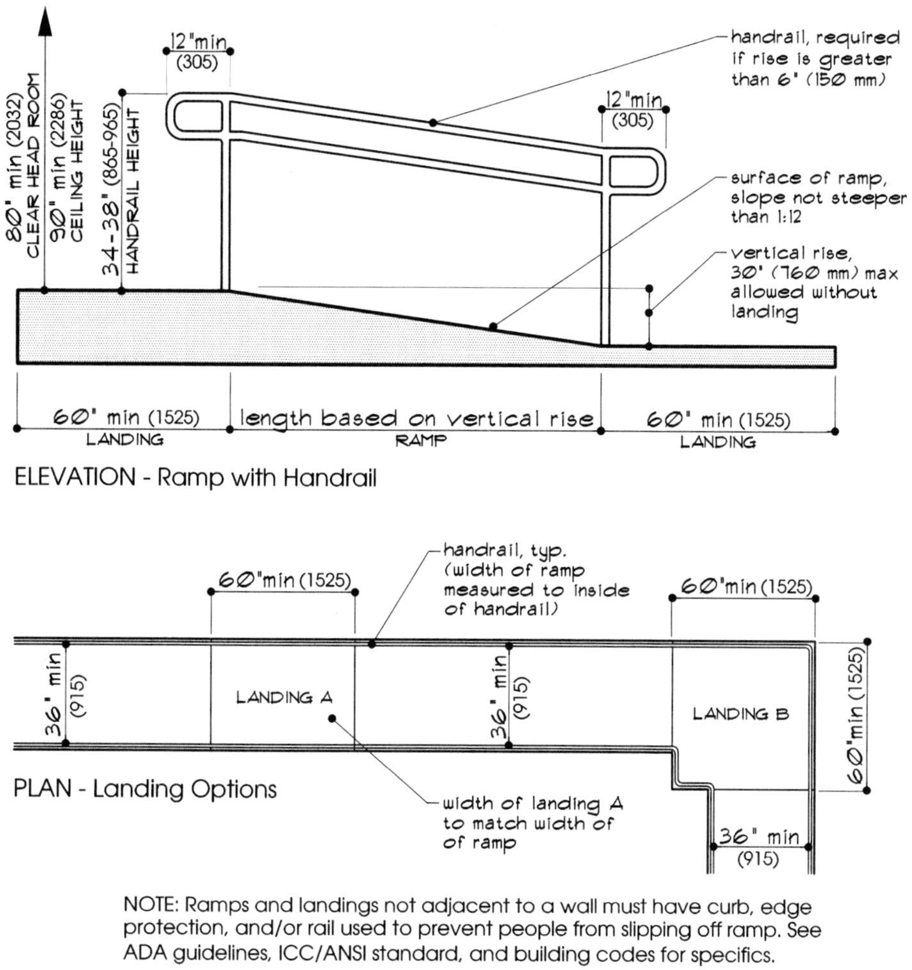

Figure 4.9 Typical Ramp Requirements

Note

There is a distinction between ramps and curb ramps. Curb ramps are typically exterior ramps cut through or leading to a curb. Other ramps can be interior or exterior.

Corridors

A corridor consists of the surrounding walls, the floor below and the ceiling above. An exit access corridor is any corridor leading to the exit in a building. Typically, these corridors are either nonrated or have a one-hour fire rating, depending on their location, the occupant load that they are serving, and if the building is sprinklered. For example, the corridor in a small tenant space leading to a door that empties into the main exit access corridor for the building is not

Note

A jurisdiction may place limitations on file cabinets used along an exit access. In some cases, an open drawer cannot protrude into the required width of the corridor or aisle. Confirm with the code official when necessary.

typically required to be rated. By contrast, the main exit access corridor that connects each of these tenant spaces and leads to the exit stairs will typically be required to be rated one hour. (In some cases, if sprinklers are used, a rating may not be required.) This rating also determines the fire rating of the doors entering the exit access corridor. (See section on Means of Egress Components in Chapter 5, page 195.)

The codes have minimum and maximum requirements for the width and the length (travel distance) of a corridor. The codes require minimum widths for corridors to assure that there is adequate room for the number of people using the corridor to get to the nearest exit. The travel distance is limited so that occupants will reach an exit within a reasonable amount of time. (Travel distances are described later in this chapter.) The typical corridor widths required by the codes are indicated in Figure 4.10A. The type of use and the occupant load usually determine the corridor width. For example, although 44 inches (1118 mm) is typically the minimum required width of a corridor, in some occupancies a wider corridor may be required for the moving of beds or to accommodate the movement of people between spaces. Smaller widths may be allowed in smaller spaces and many Residential building types.

In addition, specific accessibility clearances must be met. These are shown in Figure 4.10 B through F. These include (B) passing room for two wheelchairs in extra long corridors, (C) minimum clearances for corridors that change direction, (D) turning space in narrow corridors, (E) maximum depth of objects protruding into the corridor, and (F) maneuvering space in a switch-back configuration. Although a 60-inch (1525 mm) wide corridor as shown in 4.10B is not specifically required by the codes or the accessibility standards, an area along the accessible path that allows a wheelchair to turn around is required. Typically at least one turning space, as shown in Figure 4.10D, is required if the corridor is not 60 inches (1525 mm) wide. Additional ones might be needed in longer corridors. When doors are recessed or used at the end of a corridor, additional clearances must be added to the width of the corridor to make sure the access to the door is wide enough. (See clearances in Figure 4.4 and the example given in the section on Exit Widths, page 151.)

Note

The required dimensions for stairs and ramps used in Assembly aisleways are different than those for other standard ramps and stairs. Typically, the riser of the stair is shorter and the slope of the ramp is smaller to accommodate the large number of people.

Aisles and Aisle Accessways

An exit access *aisle* is similar to an exit access corridor in that it is a passageway required to reach an exit. The difference is that a corridor is enclosed by full-height walls, while an aisle is a pathway created by furniture or equipment. A short portion of aisle that leads to another aisle is called an *aisle accessway*. The

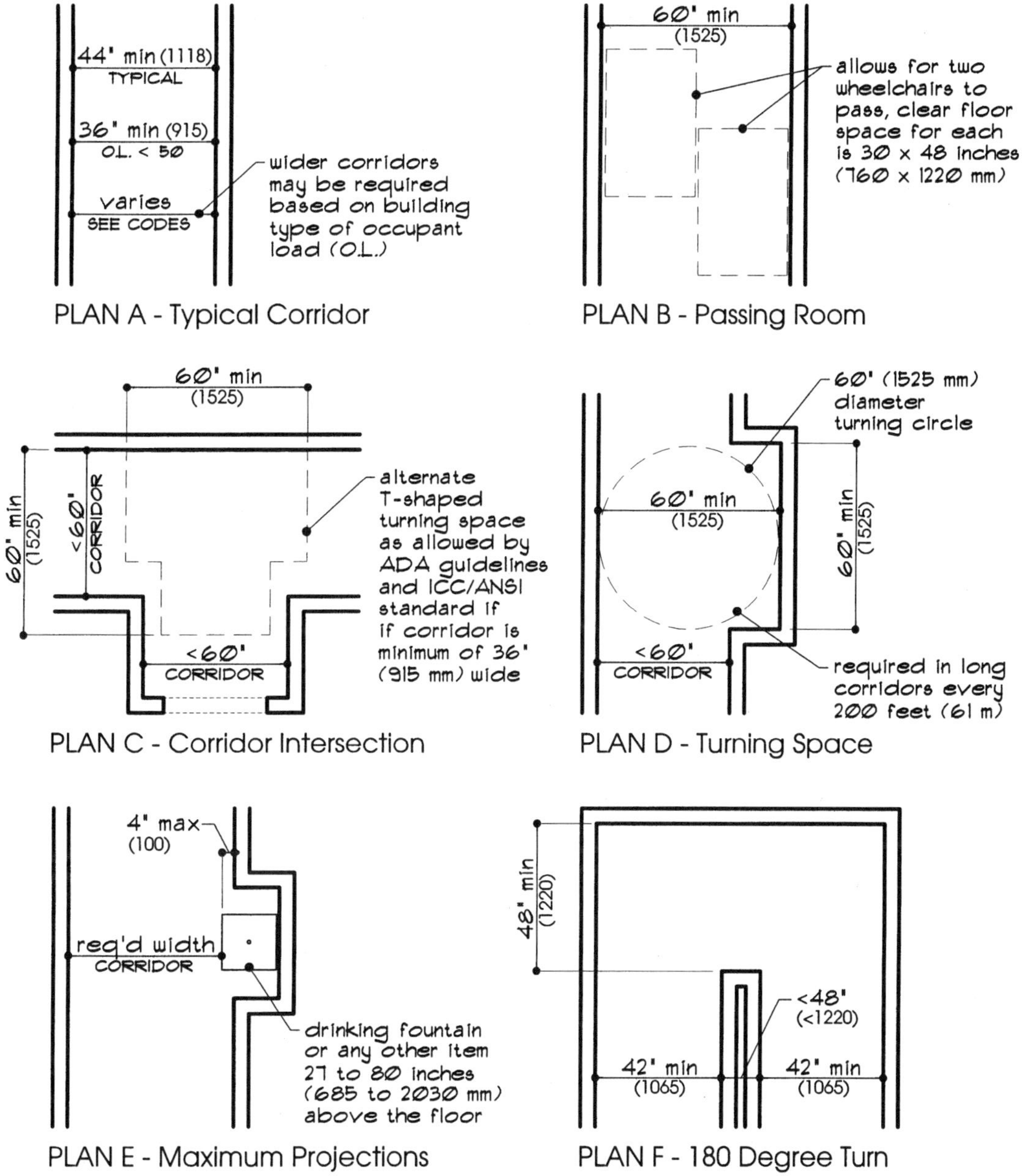

Figure 4.10 Typical Corridor Requirements

Note

The widths of aisles and corridors are calculated similarly. Each is based on the occupant load of the space or set by the code minimums.

Note

Aisle accessways have special width requirements and can usually be less than the width of an aisle.

Note

Aisles assume travel in two directions. Aisle accessways assume travel in only one direction.

codes and the ADA guidelines set minimum widths for both aisles and aisle accessways.

Aisles can be created by movable furniture or fixed seats. When there are no fixed seats, aisles can be created by tables, counters, furnishings, equipment, merchandise, and other similar obstructions. For example, aisles are created between movable panel systems in offices, between tables and chairs in restaurants, and between display racks in retail stores. The codes and the ADA guidelines give specific width requirements in each of these situations.

Aisles, like corridors and other parts of the exit access, must be sized for the number of people using them. So in many cases, the width of the aisle will be determined by the same calculation using the occupant load as are other parts of the means of egress. (See the section on Exit Widths later in this chapter.) However, the codes set minimum widths of aisles as well. This is different for aisles with fixed seats and moveable seating or furnishings.

Aisles and aisle accessways created by *fixed seats* are typically found in Assembly occupancies such as theaters and auditoriums. Because of the large number of occupants, the codes set strict requirements on the width of these aisles and aisle accessways, depending on the size of the occupancy, the number of seats they are serving, and whether it is a ramp or a stair. The minimum distances between the seats and where the aisles terminate are also regulated. The requirements for these aisles and aisle accessways are located in separate sections of the code that cover Assembly uses. In the NFPA codes, this information is included in the separate Assembly chapters. Because there are several factors that influence these widths, you will need to refer to the specific requirements in the codes to correctly determine the required width for aisles at fixed seats.

For *movable seating or furnishings*, such as between tables and chairs in a restaurant, the minimum aisle width is typically 36 inches (914 mm). This is shown in Figure 4.11. However, you must also consider accessibility requirements for aisle width and the placement of seating. Although the codes allow some nonpublic aisles to be less than 36 inches (914 mm) wide, you must consider when accessibility to those areas is necessary according to the ADA. The ADA guidelines include various width requirements where accessible routes are necessary and have additional requirements for specific uses such as restaurants, cafeterias, and libraries. (Refer to the ADA guidelines for specifics.) The most common width requirement, however, is a minimum of 36 inches (914 mm).

The codes provide additional width requirements at moveable seating for aisle accessways. These are shown in Figure 4.11 as well. These dimensions are much narrower than aisles because they are not used by as many occupants and are limited in length. These minimum widths are often determined by the length of the accessway. The length is measured to the centerline of the farthest seat

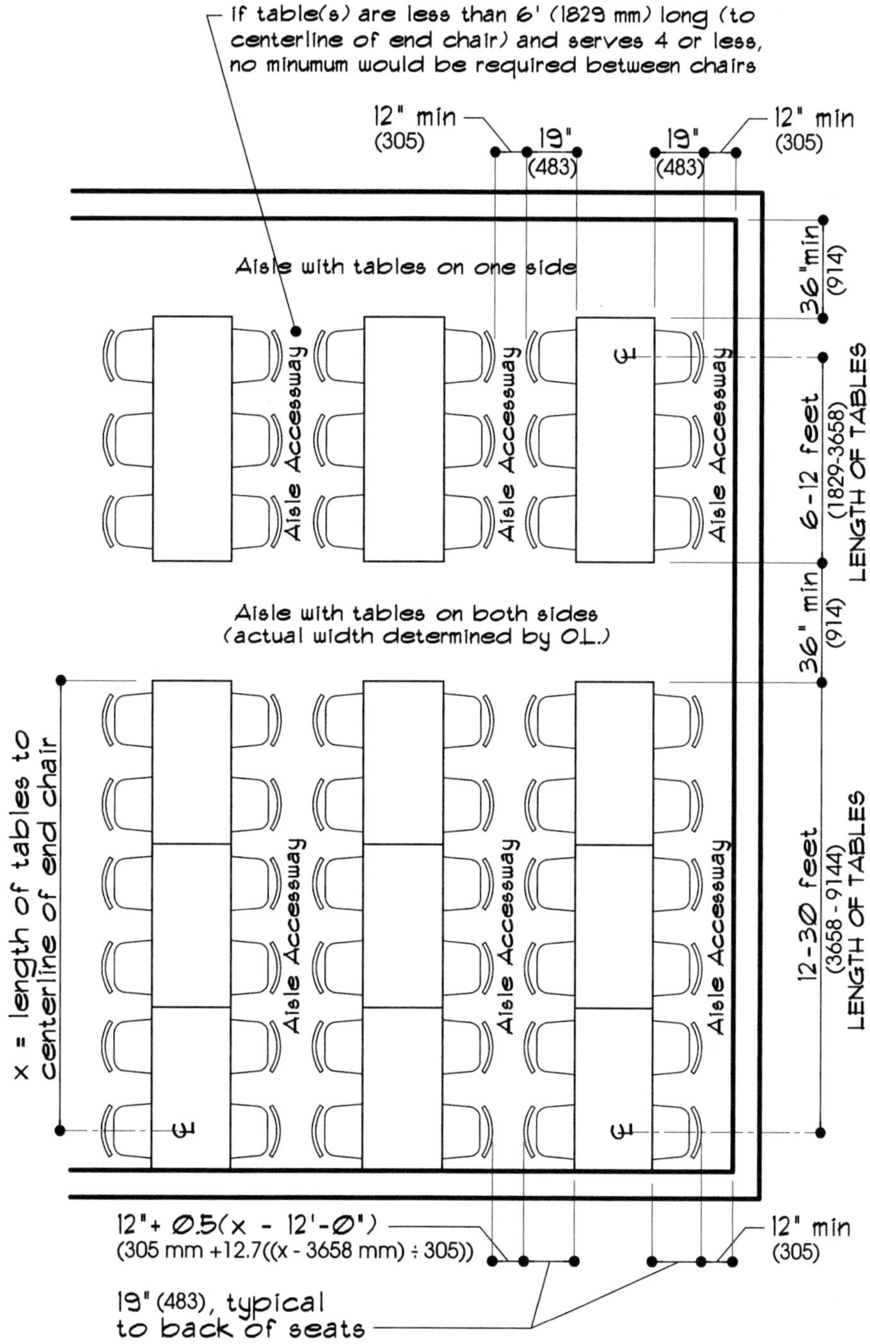

Figure 4.11 Typical Aisle and Aisle Accessway Requirements: Tables and Chairs

according to the code. If an aisle accessway at a row of tables or chairs is less than 6 feet (1829 mm) and is used by four or less people, the codes do not set a minimum width. However, for an aisle accessway that is between 6 and 12 feet (1829 to 3658 mm) in length, the accessway must be at least 12 inches (305 mm) wide. For a longer aisle accessway between 12 and 30 feet (3658 to 9144 mm) long, a separate calculation is required. This required formula is shown at the bottom of Figure 4.11. (Also see the Example 2: Aisle Exit Width later in this chapter.) When tables and movable chairs are used in an aisle accessway, the minimum width is measured from a point 19 inches (483 mm) from the edge of the table to allow for the chair, as indicated in Figure 4.11. If the seat is a fixed stool, however, the width would be measured from the actual back of the seat.

Aisle accessways as defined by the code will not usually meet the clearance requirements of the accessibility standards. Additional clearance is usually required to maneuver a wheelchair. For this reason, accessible seating is typically provided along the main aisles. (This is shown in a restaurant in Figure 4.19 and in a theater in Figure 2.12.A.) However, you must determine if the appropriate amount of accessible seating is provided. The area served by an aisle accessway may also need to be accessible. Therefore, in some cases, you may need to provide additional width for accessibility.

Remember that aisles and aisle accessways can be created by a variety of interior furnishings and elements including banks of filing cabinets, kiosks, chairs, copiers, and similar elements. In older editions of the *IBC*, aisles for Business and Mercantile uses were determined by whether furniture or display items were on one or both sides of the aisle. A *double-loaded* aisle was required to be wider than a *single-loaded* aisle. However, the more current codes typically require a minimum aisle width of 36 inches (914 mm) in both cases. Some of these elements may be movable by the occupants. Although as the designer, you may not have control after the client occupies the space, you must arrange the space and the furniture in a way that provides the required egress patterns.

Adjoining or Intervening Rooms

Although an exit access should be as direct as possible, some projects may require an access path to pass through an adjoining room or space before reaching a corridor or exit. Most of the codes will allow this as long as the path provides a direct, unobstructed, and obvious means of travel toward an exit. Such a path may be as simple as a route from a doctor's office that requires passing through the waiting room to reach the corridor.

It is this requirement that allows smaller rooms adjoining larger spaces to exit through the large room to access a corridor. For example, a number of private offices might surround an open office area. Some other common adjoining or intervening rooms that are not restricted by the codes include reception areas, lobbies, and foyers. Exit accessways are allowed to pass through these rooms or spaces as long as they meet the specified code requirements.

The codes do place some restrictions on this rule, especially on rooms that tend to be locked some or all of the time. Storage rooms, restrooms, closets, bedrooms, and other similar spaces subject to locking are not allowed to be a part of an exit access unless the occupancy is considered a dwelling unit or has a minimum number of occupants. Rooms that are more susceptible to fire hazards, such as kitchens and file rooms, are also restricted. (See inset titled *Types of Rooms and Spaces* in Chapter 2 on page 63. Also refer to the building codes and the *LSC* in your jurisdiction for additional requirements.)

Exits

At the end of the exit access is an exit. An exit is a portion of the means of egress that is separated from all other spaces of the building. Unlike an exit access, all exits must be *fully enclosed* and *rated* with minimal penetrations. A typical example of an enclosed and rated exit is a stairway. Fire-rated walls, rated doors, and other rated through-penetrations are used to make an exit a *protected way of travel* from the exit access to the exit discharge or public way. The typical fire rating for an exit is one or two hours. Some stairwells and other exits must be smoke protected as well. (See Chapter 5 for additional fire rating information.)

There are four main types of exits: exterior exit doors, enclosed exit stairways, horizontal exits, and exit passageways. In addition, an exit may include an area of refuge. An elevator is also sometimes used as an exit. These are explained throughout this section. Each must exit into another exit type, into an exit discharge, or directly onto a public way. Keep in mind that the codes have specific quantity, location, and size requirements for all exits. These are explained later in this chapter. Everything that composes the exit must have the same hourly rating. For example, if an exit passageway is used to extend an exit, then the exit passageway must have the same rating as the exit. Other basic code requirements and accessibility standards are similar to those for exit accesses as described in the previous section.

Exterior Exit Doors

An exterior exit door is an exit that simply consists of a doorway. It is located in the exterior wall of the building and typically leads from the ground floor of the building to the open air of an exit discharge or a public way. For example, it might

Note

The exterior exit door is the only type of exit door that consists of the doorway alone. Other exit doors are found in exit stairs, exit passageways and horizontal exits, but they are a part of the whole exit enclosure. (See the section on Fire Doors in Chapter 5 for additional door requirements.)

Note

When exit stairs continue past the exit discharge at grade level, an approved barrier must be used. Typically a gate (e.g., metal gate) is installed at the grade level landing of the stair to prevent occupants from continuing to the basement or sublevels during an emergency.

be a door at the bottom of an exit stair, at the end of an exit access corridor, or out of a building lobby on the ground floor. In older buildings there may be an exterior door on each floor that leads to a fire escape attached to the exterior of the building. An exterior door is not typically required to be rated unless the exterior wall is rated because of the potential exposure to fire from an adjacent building. (See Figure 4.3 for typical clearance requirements.)

Exit Stairs

An exit stair is the most common type of exit and is composed of a protected enclosure. It includes the stair enclosure, any doors opening into or exiting out of the stairway enclosure, and the stairs and landings inside the enclosure. What makes an exit stair different from other stairs is that its enclosure must be constructed of rated assemblies. (See Chapter 5.)

Exit stair widths are determined in the same manner as the widths of other exits, as explained later in this chapter. The doors of an exit stair must swing in the direction of the exit discharge. In other words, all the doors swing into the stairway except at the ground level, where the door swings toward the exit discharge or public way. (The basic stair requirements are described earlier under Stairs in the section on Exit Accesses. Also see Figures 4.5 through 4.8.) Exit stairs may also include an area of refuge if required by the codes. This is explained below.

Area of Refuge

An area of refuge is an area where one or more people can wait safely for assistance during an emergency. It is considered an alternative exit to leaving the building or using the exit stairwells. It is also considered an accessible exit. These areas provide safety because they are typically required to be enclosed by fire and/or smoke partitions. Areas of refuge are usually provided adjacent to exit stairwells, in exit stairwells, or at elevator lobbies, as indicated in Figure 4.12.

An area of refuge located adjacent to an exit stair provides room for wheelchairs while maintaining the required exit width to the exit stairway as shown in Plan A of Figure 4.12. When an area of refuge is located within an exit stairwell, the landings at the doors entering the stair are enlarged so that one or more wheelchairs can comfortably wait for assistance without blocking the means of egress at the landing and stair. This is shown in Plan B of Figure 4.12. The number of wheelchair spaces that must be provided is determined by the occupant load of the floor. The most common requirement is one space for every 200 occupants. (Remember, you can consider other accessible means of egress on the same floor

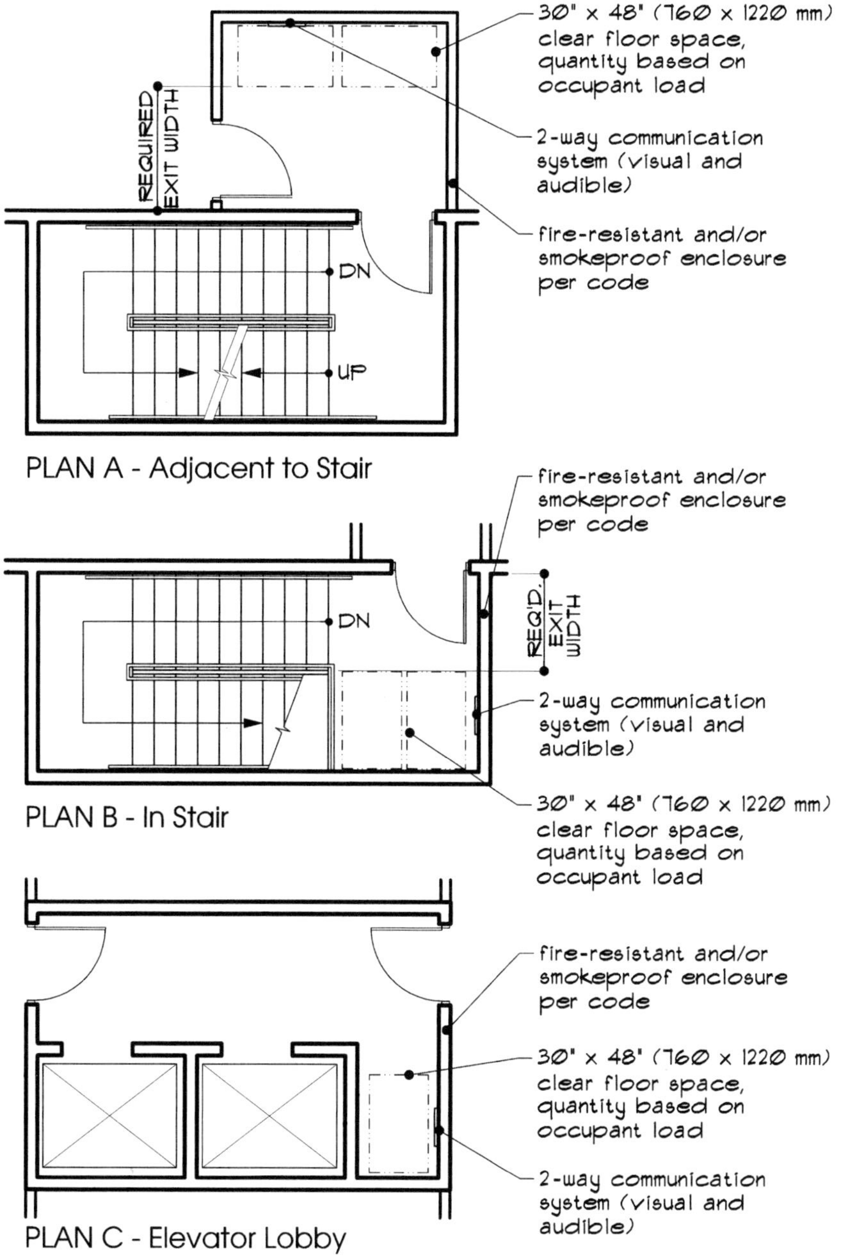

Figure 4.12 Area of Refuge Examples

Note

When an area of refuge is used in conjunction with an exit stair, the minimum stair width as required by the codes will usually increase.

level, too.) Although the egress width of an exit stair is usually determined by the occupant load, a stair with an area of refuge may be required to have a minimum width of 48 inches (1220 mm) to allow for the disabled person to be carried down the stair by emergency personnel.

An area of refuge can also be located adjacent to the elevator as shown in Plan C of Figure 4.12. An area of refuge is required if the elevator is serving as an exit. (See the section on Elevators on page 144.) In some cases, a portion of an exit access corridor located immediately adjacent to an exit enclosure (i.e., stairwell) can have an alcove created for one or more wheelchairs to wait. Usually this is only allowed when the exit access corridor is rated or the building is sprinklered.

A horizontal exit provides another type of area of refuge. It is different in that it does not provide a small separated area but, instead, divides an entire floor of a building into separate areas using a rated wall. When you pass through the door the whole space beyond the door becomes an area of refuge. You can either wait for assistance or use the available exit stairs. (See next section on Horizontal Exits.)

The codes typically use the term *area of refuge*; the ADA guidelines and accessibility standards use the term *area of rescue assistance*. In either case, an area of refuge must meet specific accessibility requirements. These include minimum space dimensions for wheelchairs. (The typical clear floor space for wheelchairs is 30 inches (760 mm) wide by 48 inches (1220 mm) long.) In addition, the area of refuge is required to be clearly identified and have a two-way emergency communication system. In some cases, both visual and audible communication must be provided. However, in existing buildings and in buildings with an automatic sprinkler system, the requirements for the area of refuge may be exempted. You must check the codes for the specific exceptions.

Horizontal Exits

Note

The codes place certain limitations on a horizontal exit, such as the size and the number of occupants it can serve. Some are mentioned in this chapter. Refer to the codes for the specific limitations.

A horizontal exit is different from the other exits because it does not lead a person to the exterior of a building. Instead it provides a protected exit to a safe area of refuge. This area of refuge may be another part of the same building or an adjoining building. As the name implies, there is no change in level. This allows the occupants to move into a safe zone where they can either wait for help or use another exit to safely leave the building.

The components of a horizontal exit consist of the walls that create the enclosure around the areas of refuge and the doors through these walls. Plan A of Figure 4.13 shows an example of a horizontal exit in a one-story building. In this case, a horizontal exit is used for one of the two required exits from Area A and one of the three required exits from Area B. Plan B of Figure 4.13 indicates the horizontal exits between the rated walls of a building core and the exterior wall. In this example, occupants from Area A can exit into area B and vice versa, because there are doors that swing in both directions of travel. Thus, each area serves as the area of refuge for the other area. When the horizontal exit leads to another building, such as in Plan C of Figure 4.13, structural features such as balconies and bridges can also be used. In this example, a horizontal exit is used for Building A

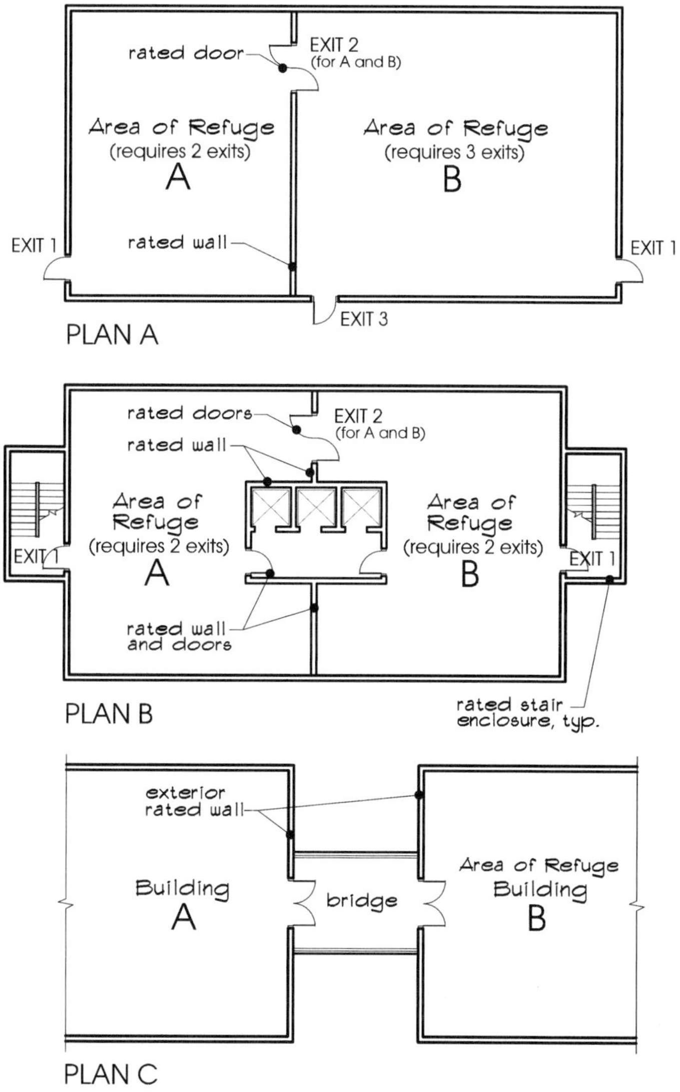

Figure 4.13 Horizontal Exit Examples

into Building B, but Building B is not using the horizontal exit into Building A. You can tell because the doors swing only in the direction of Building B. (Building B, therefore, must have the required number of exits without using the horizontal exit).

The codes specify the additional area that must be provided in the area of refuge to hold the occupants that come through the horizontal exit. This additional area varies, depending on the occupancy classification. For example, the typical factor is 3 square feet (0.28 s m) per person for most occupancies, but for occupancies where occupants are confined to beds, 30 square feet (2.8 s m) may be required.

Note

When determining the width for doors, as described later in this chapter, only the doors swinging in the direction of egress may be counted.

The codes also place strict requirements on the horizontal exit components. Since they are part of an exit, the walls and doors used to make the enclosures must be fire rated. The walls must either be continuous through every floor to the ground or be surrounded by a floor and ceiling that are equally rated. This rated wall usually has a rating of 2 hours. The doors must also be rated (usually 1½ hours) and swing in the direction of an exit. If the horizontal exit has an area of refuge on either side, two doors must be used together, each swinging in the opposite direction, to serve the occupants on either side. (See Figure 4.13A and B.) In most cases, horizontal exits can be used for only a portion of the total number of required exits. The number allowed varies according to the occupancy classification. A horizontal exit cannot serve as the only exit in any case.

Horizontal exits can typically be used in any occupancy classification. The most common use is in Institutional occupancies. Hospitals use horizontal exits to divide a floor into two or more areas of refuge. This allows the employees to roll patients' beds into safe areas should a fire occur. Prisons also use horizontal exits so that a fire can be contained and the entire prison will not have to be evacuated in an emergency. Other common types of buildings that use horizontal exits are large factories, storage facilities, and high-rise buildings.

Exit Passageways

Note

The length of an exit passageway cannot exceed the maximum dead-end corridor length specified by the code. (See the section on Dead-End Corridors in this chapter.)

An exit passageway is a type of horizontal passage or corridor that provides the same level of protection as an exit stair. An exit passageway must be a fully enclosed, fire-rated corridor or hallway that consists of the surrounding walls, the floor, the ceiling, and the doors leading into the passageway. It is most commonly used to extend an exit and must typically be the same width as the adjacent exit. For example, an exit passageway can be used to extend an exit to the exterior of the building, as indicated in Plan A of Figure 4.14. In this example, the exit stair empties into a corridor instead of directly to the exterior of the building. The exit passageway is used to extend the exit to the exterior of the building.

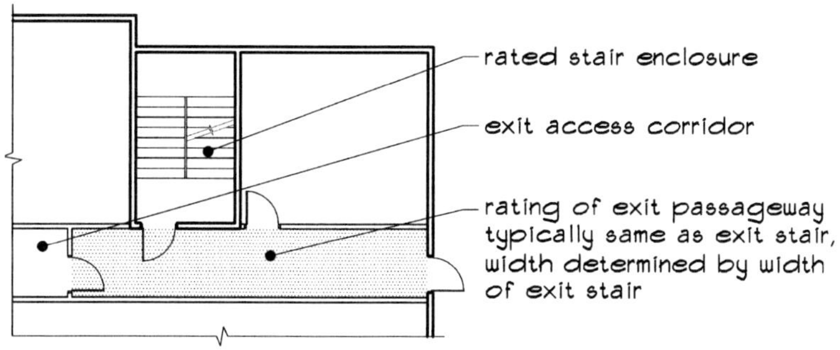

PLAN A - Connecting Exit Stair to Exterior Exit

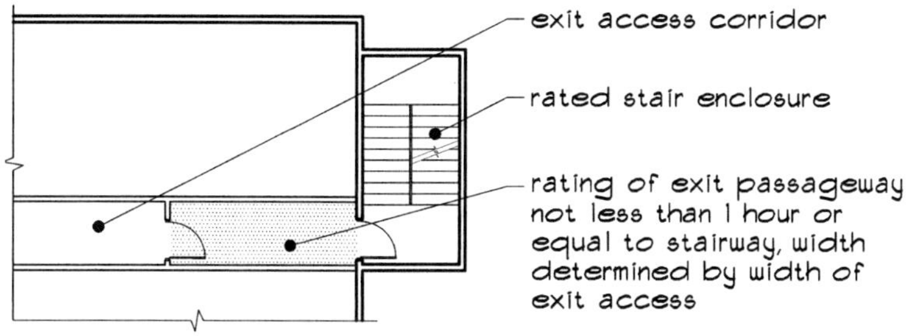

PLAN B - Extending Exit Stair

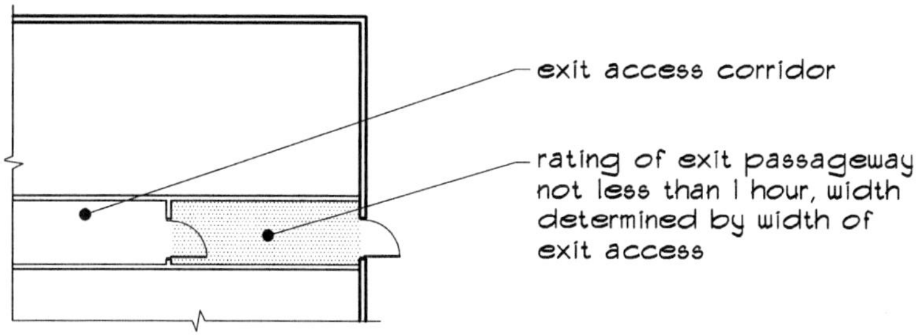

PLAN C - Extending Exterior Exit

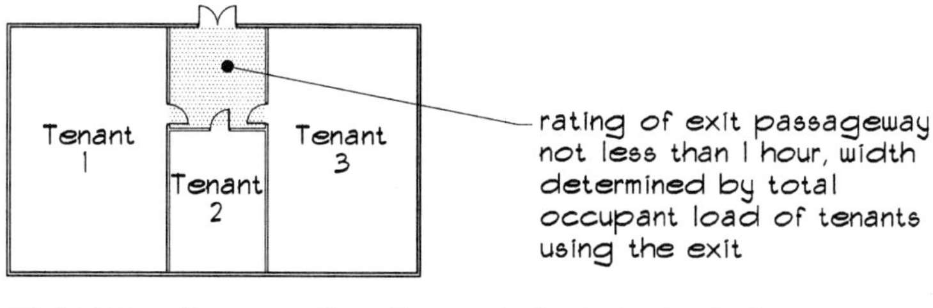

PLAN D - Connecting Tenants to Exterior Exit

Figure 4.14 Exit Passageway Examples

Note

In some instances, an exit passageway can have an occupied room or rooms enter directly into it; however, since it is a rated corridor, the codes limit the type of rooms and require rated doors into the rooms. Be sure to refer to the codes for specific requirements.

Since it has the same rating as the stair, occupants leaving the exit stair are still in a protected enclosure until they reach the exterior of the building.

Another way to use an exit passageway is to bring an exit closer to the occupants in the building, as shown in Plan B and C of Figure 4.14. This is especially useful when you need to shorten a travel distance. (Travel distance is explained later in this chapter.) For example, if the travel distance to the door of an exit stair is 10 feet (3048 mm) longer than allowed, instead of relocating the exit stair you can add an exit passageway leading to the door of the exit stair as shown in Plan B. The door of this newly created exit passageway is now the end point for measuring the travel distance. This can also be used to bring an exterior exit door closer into the building, as shown in Plan C of Figure 4.14. In both cases, the travel distance to the exit is reduced.

An exit access such as a door leading out of a tenant space can also exit into an exit passageway, as indicated in Plan D of Figure 4.14. This typically occurs on the ground floor of a building when secondary exits are required. In addition, when the tenants occupy the perimeter of the building, an exit passageway may be created between two of the tenants so that an exterior door can be reached off the common corridor. This is often seen in malls and office buildings with center building cores.

Elevators

Note

Accessible elevator requirements are different for private dwelling units and other buildings. Be sure to check the ADA guidelines, the *FHAG*, and the ICC/ANSI standards for specifics.

Note

The new *ADA-ABA Accessibility Guidelines* includes many additional requirements for elevators to allow for a greater range of designs and more types of elevators.

There are two main types of elevators: freight and passenger elevators. In most cases, elevators are not used as part of the required means of egress for a space or building. That means that typically *they are not counted* when determining the total exits provided in a building. Instead, elevators are typically used for convenience by occupants of the building. However, in the event of a fire, firefighters can use the elevators. Since elevators are linked to a building's smoke alarm system, when a smoke detector is activated during a fire, the elevators are automatically recalled to an approved location (usually the ground floor). They can then be activated manually with a key by the firefighters. The firefighters can use them for access to the upper floors or for rescue. When the elevator is not being used as a means of egress for the occupants, you must have directional signage in the elevator lobby as well as a diagram that identifies the direction to the nearest exit.

On the other hand, since both the codes and the ADA guidelines require that an accessible means of egress be provided, an elevator can be used as part of the means of egress in certain situations. For example, elevators are most commonly used in high-rise buildings. However, for an elevator to be considered part of the means of egress, additional code provisions must be met. These requirements affect its location within the building, the construction of the elevator shaft, the type of elevator cab and the controls of the elevator. The elevator itself must comply with emergency operation and signaling device requirements, as specified in *ANSI/ASME A17.1, Safety Code for Elevators and Escalators,* and be provided with standby power. Other special mechanical and electrical requirements are necessary as well. It also typically requires an adjacent area of refuge and an enclosed fire-rated lobby, as shown in Plan C of Figure 4.12.

Because of all the specific requirements, the decision to include an elevator as an exit is often made as part of the initial design of the building and is not part of a typical interior project or renovation. Retrofitting an existing elevator and shaft in most cases would be costly. Currently, using elevators as an exit even in new buildings is not as common as providing areas of refuge in stairways and at elevator lobbies. However, in the future, this may become more prevalent.

Even if an elevator is not to be used as an exit, when they are included in a building typically at least one is required to be accessible for use by persons with disabilities. (There is an exception for some two-story buildings.) Many new buildings are required to make all passenger elevators accessible. If you are working with existing elevators, you must make them as accessible as possible. (See inset titled *Elevators* on page 124.) New elevators are usually designed in conjunction with an engineer or an elevator consultant.

Note

Platform lifts are a form of elevator. They are usually used in existing buildings when short vertical distances must be covered for accessibility reasons and a ramp is not feasible. Most are not allowed as a means of egress, but the ADA guidelines do provide exceptions.

Note

Elevators can sometimes be used as a means of egress, especially in high-rise buildings, but many additional code requirements must be met that may make the cost prohibitive.

Exit Discharges

An exit discharge is that part of a means of egress that connects an exit with a public way. It is typically found on the ground floor of a building; however, in older buildings a fire escape is sometimes described as an exit discharge—connecting the exterior exit door(s) on each level to the sidewalk or alley. The required fire rating of an exit discharge will vary, depending on the type and where it is located. In some types of exit discharge, the enclosure may be allowed to have a lower rating than the exit it serves.

The first three exit discharges described in this section are used on the interior of a building. Others are exterior exit discharges. The width of an exit discharge is typically dictated by the width of the exit it is supporting, but accessibility requirements must be taken into consideration as well. Usually, when more than one exit leads into the exit discharge, the width of the exit discharge is a sum of these exit widths. In existing buildings an existing exit discharge may dictate the maximum size of an interior means of egress. The key to determining if an exit discharge exists is that it occurs after a protected exit. A few common examples are explained below. Many of these are also shown in Figure 4.2 earlier in this chapter.

Note

The lobby or main entrance of a building often serves as a means of egress. It might act as the exit if it is fully enclosed and has the appropriate fire rating. If it is an extension of the corridors on that floor, it can be considered an exit access with the exterior door(s) acting as the exit. The lobby can also be an exit discharge if an exit stair empties into the space. (See Figure 4.2.)

Note

All means of egress are intended to take occupants to a safe place. If it is not possible to get occupants to a safe public way, a *safe dispersal area* may be required. (Refer to the codes.)

Note

The codes allow some exceptions for interior exit discharges in certain occupancies, especially Detentional/Correctional. Check the specific occupancies in the codes for details.

Main Lobby

One of the most common interior exit discharges is the ground floor lobby of a building. For example, an exit stair may empty out into the lobby. The distance between the door of the exit stair and the exterior exit door is the exit discharge. An example is shown in Figure 4.2. However, a lobby is not always considered an exit discharge. For example, the lobby shown in Figure 4.14D is not an exit discharge because it connects exit accesses, not exits. Remember, an exit discharge occurs after a protected exit.

Foyer or Vestibule

An interior exit discharge can include an enclosed foyer or vestibule. These are small enclosures on the ground floor of a building between the end of a corridor and an exterior exit door as labeled and shown in Figure 4.2. If the size of the enclosure is kept to a minimum, the codes may not require it to have a high fire rating. Therefore, it would be considered an exit discharge instead of an exit passageway. Remember that the ADA guidelines and the ICC/ANSI standard require the size to be large enough to allow adequate maneuvering clearance within the vestibule or foyer and the swing of the doors. (See Plan A in Figure 4.4.)

Discharge Corridor

Occasionally, a corridor is considered an exit discharge. Usually this occurs in older buildings where an exit stair empties into a ground floor corridor. If there is not a fire-rated exit passageway connecting the exit stairs to the exterior exit door, the corridor becomes an exit discharge. Usually this is not recommended and is allowed only if the entire corridor is protected by automatic sprinklers. (See the codes for specifics.)

Egress Court

An egress court is an exterior exit discharge as shown in Figure 4.2. It can be in the form of a courtyard, patio, or other type of partially enclosed exterior area. It is the portion of the exit that connects the exterior exit door to the public way.

Small Alley or Sidewalk

If the width of an alley or sidewalk is less than 10 feet (3048 mm), it is no longer considered a public way. Instead, it becomes an exterior exit discharge that connects the exterior exit door to a larger alley, sidewalk, or street. An example includes the alley shown in Figure 4.2. The sidewalk in this figure would also be considered an exit discharge if it was under 10 feet (3048 mm) wide.

MEANS OF EGRESS CAPACITY

The capacity of the means of egress reflects the number of people that can safely exit a building in an emergency. This part of the chapter concentrates on determining means of egress capacities. It answers the questions: How many? How large? and In what locations? There are four specifics to be determined: number of exits, exit width, arrangement of exits, and travel distance. These must be determined on any interior project, whether you are changing a room, a tenant space, one floor, or an entire building. Dead-end corridors and common paths of travel must also be considered. Each is explained in this section.

Note

When an interior project involves only part of a building or floor, you need to determine the exit capacity for this new area. However, it is also your responsibility to make sure the other existing building exits can accommodate this new area. In some cases you may need to increase the existing exits or decrease the size of the new space or occupant load.

In most cases you will not need to change the exiting capacity of the building itself. Exits for an entire building are determined during the initial building design, and they usually allow for future changes within the building. However, there may be instances in which you are redesigning an entire floor and need to add or enlarge an exit. For example, a new occupant may require the exits to be updated to meet a more current code, or a different occupant type or greater occupant load may require additional exits. Since adding an exit or increasing the size of an exit above the ground floor in a building is not typically feasible, you may need to change the scope of the project to make the project work in a particular building.

Each aspect of exit capacity is dependent on the others. So, in many cases you may have to work back and forth in your calculations to determine the final number and widths of exits. For example, exit widths will depend on the required number of exits. But the number and location of required exits depends on the occupant load and maximum travel distances. If any of these change or exceed the maximum requirements, the calculations have to be adjusted. Another point to remember as you are determining exit capacities is that the requirements must be determined using the building codes and the *LSC* as well as any accessibility requirements, such as those found in the ADA guidelines or the ICC/ANSI standard. When necessary, have a code official review and approve your calculations early in the design of your project. (See Chapter 10.)

Number of Exits

Typically, you should determine the number of exits required by the codes before determining the total width required for each exit. Most of the codes require a minimum of two exits, whether they are for an entire building or a space within the building. However, in each occupancy a single exit from a space or building is sometimes allowed when specific requirements are met.

Note

None of the codes specifically requires more than four exits in a building, yet additional exits are typically required in larger spaces or buildings.

The number of exits is based on the occupant load of the space or building. Use the occupant load tables in the codes (such as the one shown in Figure 2.8 in Chapter 2) to determine the occupant load of the area requiring exits. If you are determining the required number of exits for an entire building, you must calculate the occupant load of each floor or story. Each floor is considered separately.

When a floor has mixed occupancies or more than one tenant, you must calculate the occupant load of each occupant or tenant and add them together to get the total occupant load for the floor. If you are determining the number of exits for a particular room, space, or tenant within the building, you only need to figure the occupant load for that area. (Refer to Chapter 2 for a more detailed explanation of occupant loads and how to calculate them.)

Once you know the occupant load for the space or entire floor, refer to the building codes and/or the *LSC* to calculate the required number of exit locations. Each code has the same basic breakdown, as shown below. Although some of the codes go into more detail by occupancy, we will use these quantities to determine the number of exits for the purpose of this book.

Occupant Load per Story or Area	Minimum No. of Exits
1–500	2
500–1000	3
over 1000	4

Note

In some projects, you may be able to increase the occupant load by providing additional exits. This usually means increasing the provisions of every exit requirement.

The important factor to remember when confirming the required exits for a multi-story building is that the number of exits cannot decrease as one proceeds along the egress path toward the public way. Therefore, the floor with the largest occupant load determines the number of required exits for all lower floors. For example, if the floor with the highest occupant load is in the middle of the building, all the floors below it must have the same number of exits. This is easily accomplished by one or more continuous exit stairwells, each counting as an exit on each floor that opens into it. (See the Example that follows.)

Each of the codes allows exceptions to the total number of exits. The most typical exception allows only one exit in smaller buildings or spaces. This is generally allowed in an occupancy that has a minimum number of occupants and a minimum travel distance to the exit. Figure 4.15 shows two tables from the *International Building Code (IBC)*. Table 1018.2, titled "Buildings with One Exit," lists the one-exit

TABLE 1018.2
BUILDINGS WITH ONE EXIT

OCCUPANCY	MAXIMUM HEIGHT OF BUILDING ABOVE GRADE PLANE	MAXIMUM OCCUPANTS (OR DWELLING UNITS) PER FLOOR AND TRAVEL DISTANCE
A, B[d], E, F, M, U	1 Story	50 occupants and 75 feet travel distance
H-2, H-3	1 Story	3 occupants and 25 feet travel distance
H-4, H-5, I, R	1 Story	10 occupants and 75 feet travel distance
S[a]	1 Story	30 occupants and 100 feet travel distance
B[b], F, M, S[a]	2 Stories	30 occupants and 75 feet travel distance
R-2	2 Stories[c]	4 dwelling units and 50 feet travel distance

For SI: 1 foot = 304.8 mm.

a. For the required number of exits for open parking structures, see Section 1018.1.1.

b. For the required number of exits for air traffic control towers, see Section 412.1.

c. Buildings classified as Group R-2 equipped throughout with an automatic sprinkler system in accordance with Section 903.3.1.1 or 903.3.1.2 and provided with emergency escape and rescue openings in accordance with Section 1025 shall have a maximum height of three stories above grade.

d. Buildings equipped throughout with an automatic sprinkler system in accordance with Section 903.3.1.1 with an occupancy in Group B shall have a maximum travel distance of 100 feet.

TABLE 1014.1
SPACES WITH ONE MEANS OF EGRESS

OCCUPANCY	MAXIMUM OCCUPANT LOAD
A, B, E, F, M, U	50
H-1, H-2, H-3	3
H-4, H-5, I-1, I-3, I-4, R	10
S	30

Figure 4.15 *International Building Code (IBC)* Table 1018.2, Buildings with One Exit, and Table 1014.1, Spaces with One Means of Egress (*International Building Code* 2003. Copyright 2002. Falls Church, Virginia: International Code Council, Inc. Reproduced with permission. All rights reserved.)

requirements for buildings, and Table 1014.1, titled "Spaces with One Means of Egress," lists the one-exit requirements for separate tenant spaces or areas. In both of these tables, you can see that the primary deciding factor for allowing one exit is the number of occupants. Other factors such as travel distance also affect when a single exit is allowed. (This will be discussed more later.) In both tables the information is listed by occupancy classification (or use group). The NFPA codes provide similar information within their texts.

Each code has additional exceptions as well. You must check the specific occupancy section of the required code publications to determine the exceptions, since each occupancy classification addresses unique means of egress issues. Some occupancies may require additional exits, while others may reduce the number of exits, depending on the situation. The occupancy classifications with the most exceptions and special requirements are Assembly, Institutional, and Residential occupancies. The following example, which describes how to determine exits for an entire building, provides you with an overall concept for determining exit quantities. (See the next section for additional examples.)

Note

Occupant load and travel distance can both affect the required number of exits.

Note

If a lower floor requires fewer exit stairs than the floor above, you may be able to leave one of the stairs inaccessible or blocked off on that lower floor. Although it is not recommended, check with your local code officials if it becomes necessary.

Example

> **Note**
>
> It is not uncommon for a multi-story building to have a large Assembly occupancy on the top floor. If it has the largest occupant load it could dictate the exit requirements for the whole building.

Figure 4.16 indicates the outlined section of a multi-story building. It calls out the occupant load for each floor and the number of exits based on these occupant loads (using the code breakdown shown earlier). As you can see, the fourth floor has the largest occupant load, with a total of 1020, and, therefore, requires the largest number of exits. The code specifies four exits for any occupant load over 1000. As a result, every floor below it must also have four exits, even though their occupant loads specify fewer exits. Four separate exit stairs that are continuous from the fourth to the first floor would meet the requirement. The first floor would require the exit doors to be located in four separate locations.

Notice the floors above the fourth floor. Each of these floors has a lower occupant load than the fourth floor. Since these floors are above the fourth floor, fewer exits can be used. The seventh floor has the largest occupant load (above the

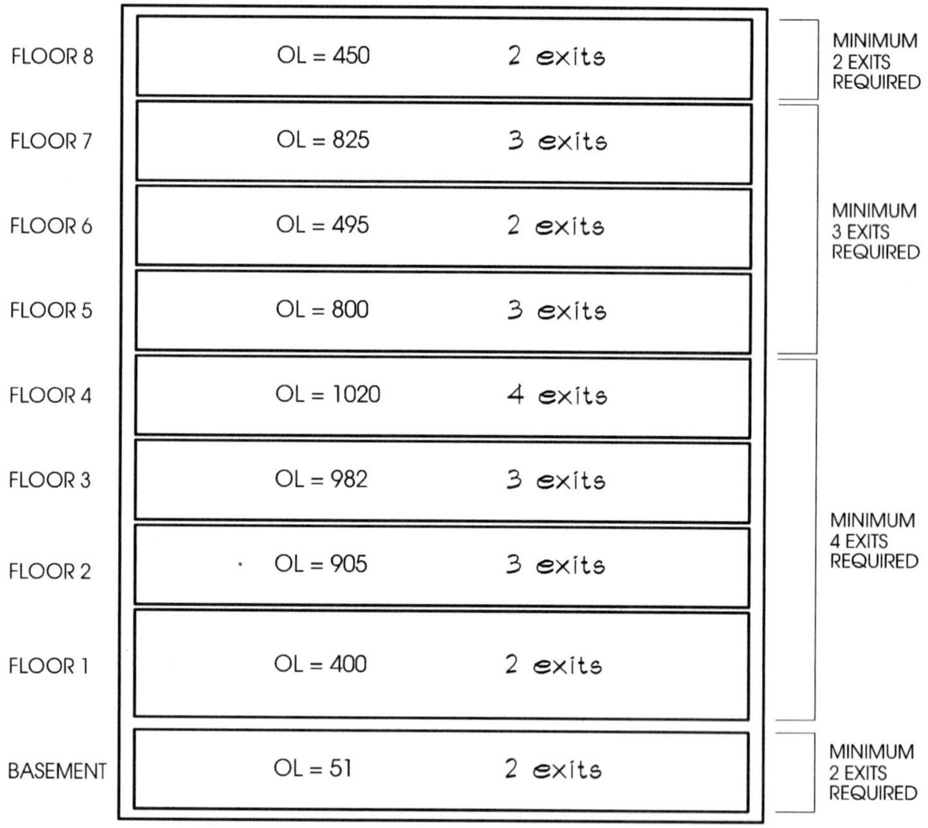

Figure 4.16 Number of Exits Example (Multi-Story Building)

fourth floor), so it controls the exit quantity for the seventh, sixth, and fifth floors. Three exits must be provided for these floors. However, the eighth floor has an even lower occupant load, requiring only two exits. So in this example, at the eighth floor, only two exit stairs are required; at the seventh floor a third stair is required; and beginning at the fourth floor, a fourth exit stair is required.

In most cases, these decisions will be made at the initial design and construction of a building. However, in some cases, when the use of an existing building changes significantly, an additional exit stairway may be required.

Exit Widths

The building codes and the *LSC* set minimum width requirements for each part of the means of egress. These include exit access and exit doors and the various corridors, aisles, stairs, and ramps that connect these doors. Different components will require different exit widths. Remember, in general, this minimum width must be maintained throughout the means of egress. It cannot be reduced anywhere along the path of travel as it moves toward the exit discharge and/or public way. (The exception is at some door locations, which is explained later in this chapter.) Therefore, it is important to determine the exit width of each exit component in question so that the minimum exit width can be obtained.

Like the number of exits, exit widths are based on the occupant load of an area or floor. Each is calculated separately to accommodate a specific area. If you are determining the exit widths for a multi-story building, the exit sizes are determined by the floor with the largest occupant load. Usually that means figuring the occupant load of every floor to find the one with the largest occupant load. That floor will require the largest exit widths and dictate the exit widths of every floor below it. For example, in Figure 4.16, the fourth floor would determine the width of the exit stairs from the fourth floor down to the first floor.

Exit widths must also be determined for every enclosed area and separate tenant space. The same basic principles apply. Instead of using the occupant load of the entire floor, use the occupant load for that particular space. If it is a room, the calculation will determine the width of the door. If it is a tenant space, the exit door(s) and any corridor(s) leading up to the door(s) will be determined. On the other hand, the width of the shared exit access corridor leading from each tenant space to the exit stairs is based on the total occupant load for that floor. If there is more than one tenant on a floor, the occupant loads of each must be added together to determine the required exit width for that floor.

Once you know the occupant load for the floor or space, it is multiplied by specific width variables supplied by the codes. This results in the total exit width that is required. As shown in Figure 4.17, the *IBC* Table 1005.1, "Egress Width Per

Note

Many smaller enclosed rooms, such as offices and apartment dwelling units, are small enough that they will not require calculating the exit width. The calculation will be required on larger rooms, such as the ones found in open office spaces, factories, malls, and assembly buildings.

Note

The required width of a corridor will typically be less than the required width of a stair.

Note

Aisle accessways and horizontal exits have additional variables and specific requirements that must be met. Refer to the codes.

Occupant Served," provides separate multipliers for the width of "stairways" and for "other egress components." These other components would include exit access corridors, aisles, ramps, and exit door widths, as well as other exit components. Some of the other codes use the term *level components* to indicate that it does not include exit stairways. The difference in the width variables for exit stairs and other level exits is based on the fact that stairs cause a person to decrease speed and, therefore, could result in more people using the stairwell at one time during an emergency. The larger stair variable allows for stairs to be wider than level exits such as corridors and ramps. Therefore, if you are calculating exit widths for an exit stair and the exit passageway or corridors leading from the stairs, you should calculate the stairs first, since an exit width must be maintained as it moves toward the public way.

The NFPA codes have similar tables. However, these width variables vary slightly from code to code. They also vary depending on whether a building is equipped with an approved automatic sprinkler system, as shown in the *IBC* table in Figure 4.17. (The multipliers for buildings with automatic sprinkler systems will result in narrower widths.) Different occupancies may also require other variables—either listed in the table or under special occupancy sections of the code. These additional variables in each code allow for the difference in occupancy classifications where wider exit widths are needed for faster egress times in more hazardous occupancies.

TABLE 1005.1
EGRESS WIDTH PER OCCUPANT SERVED

OCCUPANCY	WITHOUT SPRINKLER SYSTEM		WITH SPRINKLER SYSTEM[a]	
	Stairways (inches per occupant)	Other egress components (inches per occupant)	Stairways (inches per occupant)	Other egress components (inches per occupant)
Occupancies other than those listed below	0.3	0.2	0.2	0.15
Hazardous: H-1, H-2, H-3 and H-4	0.7	0.4	0.3	0.2
Institutional: I-2	NA	NA	0.3	0.2

For SI: 1 inch = 25.4 mm. NA = Not applicable.

a. Buildings equipped throughout with an automatic sprinkler system in accordance with Section 903.3.1.1 or 903.3.1.2.

Figure 4.17 *International Building Code (IBC)* Table 1005.1, Egress Width per Occupant Served (*International Building Code* 2003. Copyright 2002. Falls Church, Virginia: International Code Council, Inc. Reproduced with permission. All rights reserved.)

After determining the total exit width required by the code, it must be compared to the total number of exits already determined for that space or floor. (See previous section.) The total width must be equally distributed between the total number of exits serving the area. For example, if you are calculating the width for an entire floor, the determined width must be divided among all exits leaving the floor. If the determined width is for a room or tenant space, it is divided among the exits leaving the calculated area. If it is a space that contains aisles or aisle accessways, additional calculations may be required. (See the Examples that follow.)

As you are determining exit widths, make note of the following additional requirements. All of them can affect the final width. (Additional ones may be required for specific occupancies.)

1. **Minimum door widths:** Building codes and accessibility standards require all means of egress doors to provide a *minimum* clear width of 32 inches (815 mm). In practical terms, a standard 36-inch (915 mm) wide door when open will provide 32 inches (815 mm) of the clear width. (See Figure 4.3 for a diagram of clear width dimension.) Therefore, if you calculate a 30-inch (760 mm) exit width, you will still need to specify a 36-inch (915 mm) door.
2. **Maximum door widths:** The building codes do not allow any leaf of a door used as part of the means of egress to be more than 4 feet (1220 mm) wide. Therefore, if you need 60 inches (1525 mm) of exit width, you will need to provide more than one door. If two separate 36-inch (915 mm) doors are used, this will provide 64 inches (1630 mm) of clear width. This exceeds the required width but is the closest increment. (Remember, each single 36-inch (915 mm) wide door must be considered in increments of 32 inches (815 mm) of clear width, which is the minimum for the codes and the accessibility requirements.) If 40 inches (1015 mm) of exit width are required, a 48-inch (1220 mm) door would provide adequate width where a 36-inch (915 mm) door would not and two 36-inch (915 mm) doors might seem excessive.
3. **More than one exit:** The required width of an exit access (e.g., corridor) can be affected if it leads to more than one exit on the floor that it serves. In that case, you may be able to reduce its width. This is determined by dividing the total occupant load of the floor by the number of exits to which the exit access connects. This is done before making any calculations. (See Example 1, explained next.)
4. **Minimum exit discharge width:** When an exit discharge, such as a corridor, leads from an exit enclosure, its width cannot be less than that of the exit.

5. **Minimum corridor widths:** In no case can a corridor width or stair width be less than 36 inches (915 mm); however, the typical code minimum is 44 inches (1118 mm), and some codes require accessible stairs to be a minimum of 48 inches (1220 mm) wide. The building codes set additional minimums for certain occupancy classifications. The ADA guidelines and the ICC/ANSI standard also specify certain accessibility and clearance requirements that may affect the width of a means of egress. (See Figures 4.4, 4.6, 4.9, and 4.10, as well as the Example that follows.)
6. **Exiting from basement:** If a building has a basement that is occupied, some codes require the occupant load of the level of discharge to be increased. The exit discharge on the ground floor would need to allow for the exiting of the basement level(s) in addition to the upper floors. (Not all of the codes require this cumulative effect.)
7. **Minimum horizontal exit sizes:** Horizontal exits are allowed only if the area of refuge created is large enough to accommodate its own occupants and those from the "fire side." For most occupancies, the codes allow 3 square feet (0.28 s m) of floor space per occupant. Increased area for the area of refuge is required for Institutional occupancies. (See Horizontal Exits on page 140.)
8. **Unobstructed paths:** The exit path must be clear and unobstructed. Unless the codes or accessibility requirements specifically state that a projection is permitted, nothing may reduce the determined exit width. The most common exceptions include handrails that meet accessibility requirements, nonstructural trim or wall application less than ½ inch (13 mm) thick, wall sconces and other devices not deeper than 4 inches (100 mm) in addition to doors that do not project more than 7 inches (178 mm) when open. (See Figures 4.4 and 4.10E.)
9. **50 percent rule:** In some occupancies, the expected loss of any one exit location cannot reduce the total capacity of the exit width by more than 50 percent. For example, in an Assembly occupancy, if multiple exit doors are required at the main entrance/exit and that location becomes blocked by a fire, the total exit width may be reduced significantly. If additional exit locations do not provide for at least 50 percent of the total exit width required, additional exit locations or additional doors at the other exits must be added. (If you are designing an Assembly occupancy, you need to refer to the required codes.)
10. **Aisles and aisle accessways:** The codes set additional requirements for aisles and aisle accessways. Different aisle widths are required, depending on whether the aisles are created by fixed seats or movable furniture. The typical minimum width for an aisle between tables and chairs is 36 inches (914 mm).

Note

The total width of the exits will usually be more than that required by the codes, because of all the additional code and accessibility requirements.

Although the occupant load determines the actual width, some jurisdictions may require at least 44 inches (1118 mm). Aisle accessways have additional code requirements. (See Aisles and Aisle Accessways earlier in the chapter and Example 2 below.)

The goal of these and other exit requirements is to balance the flow of the occupants during an emergency. You want to make sure an occupant can reach an exit and then get through it without any delay.

Example 1—Corridor and Doors

Figure 4.18 is the floor plan of the second floor in a two-story, mixed-use building that is unsprinklered. Imagine that this floor is vacant and you are asked to design three tenant spaces. As you are laying it out, you need to make sure you have the

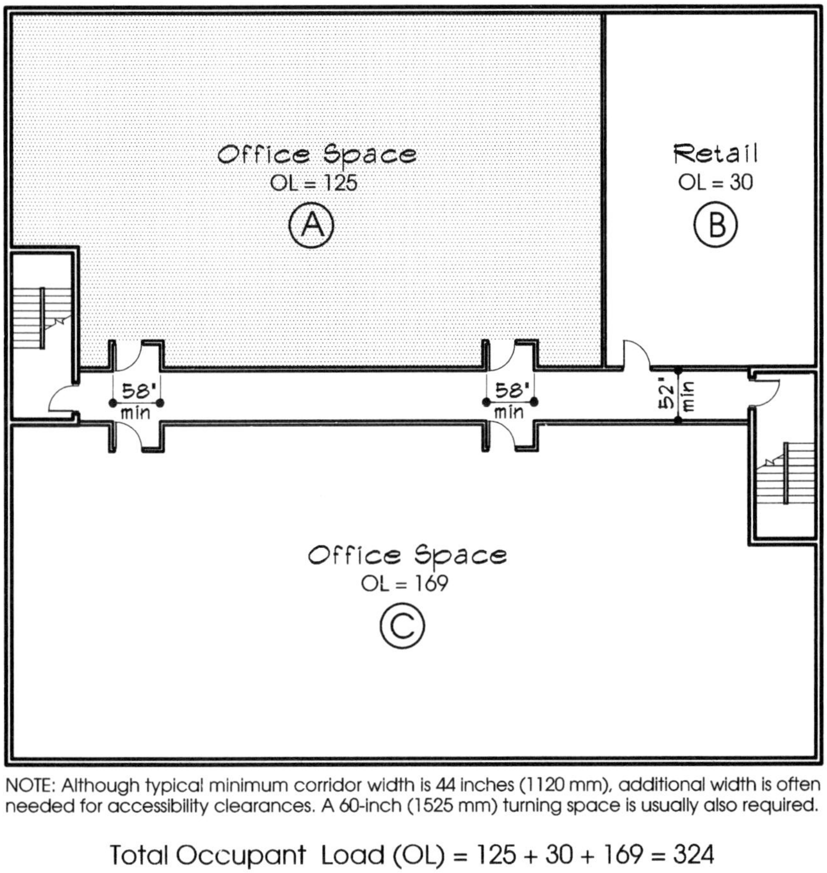

Figure 4.18 Egress Width for a Mixed Occupancy Building (unsprinklered building)

correct number and width of exits. Spaces A and C (Business) are typical tenant office spaces, and Space B is a wholesale retail store (Mercantile). You would use the following process:

Space A

From the occupant load, you have already determined that two means of egress leading out of Space A are required. (Referring to the chart shown earlier in the Number of Exits section, the occupant load of 125 is under 500.) You now need to determine the required width of the exits for Space A to make sure two 36-inch (915 mm) doors are enough.

This space is considered a Business occupancy. Using the *IBC* Table 1005.1 in Figure 4.17, the exit width variable for "other egress components" is 0.2 inches (5 mm) for an unsprinklered building. To determine the width of the exit doors, take the occupant load of 125 and multiply it by the level exit variable of 0.2 inches (5 mm). (The bottom of the table tells you how to convert to metric, if necessary.) This equals 25 inches (635 mm). This is the total required width that must be divided between the two doors. Hence, each door must be at least 12.5 inches (317.5 mm) wide. However, since the code requires all means of egress doors to provide a minimum clear width of 32 inches (815 mm), each door must be specified as a 36-inch (915 mm) wide door. (Note that the 25 inches (635 mm) seems to indicate that only one door or exit is required instead of two. That is why the number of exits required should be determined first.)

The size of the doors will also determine the minimum door alcove into the space and corridor width within the tenant space. In this case, the corridors must work with a 36-inch (915 mm) door. However, the codes typically specify that a corridor cannot be less than 44 inches (1118 mm). Additional accessibility standards require at least 18 inches (445 mm) to be clear on the latch and pull side of the door. (Refer to Figure 4.4 and the ADA guidelines and the ICC/ANSI standard.) Therefore, you will need a minimum of 54 inches (36 + 18) (that is, 1360 mm (915 + 445)) for the door and pull clearance. On the hinge side of the door you will also need a minimum of 4 inches (100 mm) to allow for a hollow metal door frame and the framing around the door. Adding these together, you will require a minimum 58-inch (1460 mm) wide alcove on the pull side of the door.

Inside the tenant space on the push side of the door, accessibility standards require a clearance of 12 inches (305 mm) (instead of 18 inches (445 mm)). Therefore, you can reduce the required width on the tenant side to 52 inches (1320 mm). (See note at side.)

Note

The accessibility clearance required at the latch side of a door can include the width of the doorframe adjacent to the latch.

Floor

This is a mixed occupancy floor. That means that before you determine the exit widths for the entire floor you must first make sure the egress width variables are the same for both Group B and Group M occupancies. If you go back to the IBC Table 1005.1 in Figure 4.17 both require 0.3 inches (7.5 mm) for stairs and 0.2 inches (5 mm) for other types of exits. (If they were different for the different occupancies, you would use the higher of the two variables.) You must also add up the occupant loads for each tenant to obtain the total for the floor. This total is 324 occupants.

Since the width variable for the stairs will result in a larger width, it should be determined first. The occupant load of 324 multiplied by the 0.3 (7.5 mm) *stair variable* equals 97.2 or 97 inches (2464 mm). (Typically if it is less than 0.5, you can round down; if it is 0.5 or more you should round up.) This total is divided between the two exit stairs, leaving 48.5 inches or 49 inches (1245 mm). Therefore, each run of both stairs must be at least 49 inches (1245 mm) wide to meet the code requirements. (Note that this 49-inch (1245 mm) width cannot be reduced as the exit moves toward the public way. If the exit stairs empty into a corridor or exit passageway at the ground level, it must be at least 49 inches (1245 mm) wide as well.)

> **Note**
>
> As you can see from these examples, all the means of egress requirements must be determined and compared together. Each affects the other.

To figure the width of the corridor leading to the exit stairs, you must first examine the layout of the floor. Since there are two exit stairs, each stair needs to serve only one-half of the total occupant load for the floor. Therefore, the corridor width can be reduced as well. Take the total occupant load of 324 and divide it in half to obtain 162 occupants. When you multiply 162 by the level variable of 0.2 inches (5 mm), you obtain a minimum corridor width of 32.4 or 33 inches (838 mm). That means that the doors entering the exit stairs can each be the minimum 36-inch (915 mm) width. However, most codes specify a 44-inch (1118 mm) minimum for the corridor. If you use the same 36-inch (915 mm) door, allow 4 inches (100 mm) on the hinge side of the door (for door frame and wall construction), and allow the 12-inch (305 mm) accessibility requirement on the push side of the door, the total exit width of the corridor for the floor is 52 inches (1320 mm). (See previous note.) An additional consideration is that it takes 60 inches (1525 mm) for a person in a wheelchair to turn around. If the corridor is not 60 inches wide (1525 mm), you will either need to make sure the alcoves provide enough turnaround space or add a turnaround space like the one shown in Plan D in Figure 4.10.

Example 2—Aisles and Aisle Accessways

Figure 4.19 shows the floor plan of a restaurant in a sprinklered building. It has an occupant load of 100. In this example, there are aisles and aisle accessways of different lengths and capacities. Each aisle and aisle accessway width must be determined separately. Some widths will be determined by the minimums set by the codes, others will require calculations. To determine the main aisle widths (W), you must know the occupant load of the space and the number of exits in order to compare the calculated exit width to the required minimum width. The

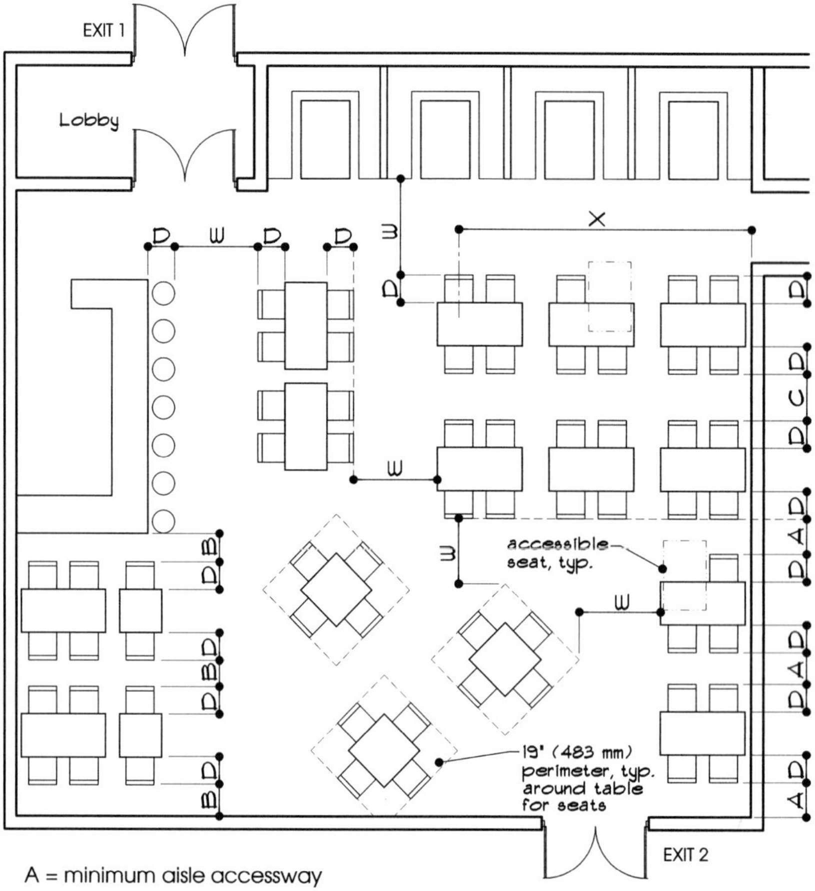

A = minimum aisle accessway for <6' (1829 mm) or <5 people (no minimum width required)

B = minimum aisle accessway for 6' - 12' (1829 - 3658 mm) (12" (305 mm) min. width required)

C = minimum aisle accessway for 12' - 30' (3658 - 9144 mm) (use width formula 12" + 0.5(x - 12'-0") or 305 mm + 12.7((x - 3658 mm) ÷ 305))

D = 19" (483 mm) allowance for movable chairs, typ.

W = 36" (914 mm) minimum aisle width allowed by code

X = length of tables measured to centerline of seat furthest from the aisle

Figure 4.19 Egress and Aisle Widths for Movable Tables and Chairs (sprinklered building)

larger width will be required. If you refer back to *IBC* Table 1005.1 in Figure 4.17 and use the process described in Example 1, you can calculate the required exit access width. First, multiply the occupant load of 100 by 0.15 inches (3.81 mm) (for a sprinklered building) to get a total exit width of 15 inches (381 mm). Then, because there are two exits, the total exit access width is divided between the two exits. So, the calculated exit width is 7.5 inches (190.5 mm). However, the codes set a minimum width for aisles of 36 inches (914 mm). The main aisles (shown as "W" in Figure 4.19) are therefore required to be at least 36 inches (914 mm) wide.

If the occupant load is much greater, however, the calculated aisle width may be larger than the required minimum aisle width. For example, if the occupant load was 300, the calculated width would be 45 inches (1143 mm). The main aisles (W) would then be 45 inches (1143 mm) wide instead of the minimum 36 inches (914 mm).

Note

The formula for calculating the width of accessways translates slightly differently when the formula is converted to metrics.

Next, you need to determine the widths of the aisle accessways. Some are determined by standard widths given by the codes as discussed earlier in the chapter. (See Figure 4.11.) For example, the codes do not require a minimum width for the aisle accessway A at the lower right of the plan because of its limited length and capacity. The minimum width at the aisle accessway B at the left of the plan is 12 inches (305 mm). This is added to the 19 inches (483 mm) required for the chair (D) to obtain the overall distance between tables. (See the section on Aisles and Aisle Accessways earlier in this chapter.) However, since aisle accessway C is longer than 12 feet (3658 mm), the required width must be calculated. The building codes and the *LSC* use a similar formula to obtain this calculation. The formula is 12 inches + 0.5 (x − 12 feet), or when using metrics the formula is 305 mm + 12.7((x − 3658 mm) ÷ 305). By using this formula, the calculated width of an aisle accessway will be wider for longer aisle accessways. As shown in Figure 4.19, the variable "x" is the length of the aisle, measured from the end of the last table to the centerline of the seat furthest from the aisle. In this case, the length of aisle accessway C is 17 feet (5182 mm); therefore, 12 inches + 0.5 (17 − 12 feet) = 12 inches + 0.5(5) = 12 + 2.5 = 14.5. So a width of 15 inches (381 mm) must be provided in addition to the 19 inches (483 mm) required for the chairs.

Arrangement of Exits

The arrangement of exits is also specified by the codes. Each of the building codes and the *LSC* require exits to be located as remotely from each other as possible so that if one becomes blocked during an emergency, the other(s) may still be reached. When two or more exits are required, at least two of the exits must be a certain distance apart. This is referred to as the *half-diagonal rule.*

The half-diagonal rule requires that the distance between two exits be at least one-half of the longest diagonal distance within the building or the building area the exits are serving. The easiest way to understand this rule is to review Figure 4.20. These diagrams are representative of open building plans or separate tenant spaces within a building. In a tenant space, the measurement is unaffected by the presence of other surrounding spaces. Notice that the shape or size of the area or the building does not matter. You must find the longest possible diagonal in that space. Measure the length of that diagonal in a straight line from one corner of the floor plan to the other corner (as represented by "D" in each case). Then take one-half of that length. The result indicates how far apart the exits must be. This is the *minimum* distance allowed between the two exits. The *IBC* requires the distance to be measured to the centerline of each door; the NFPA codes allow it to be measured to the edge of the door.

Note

When there are two or more exits, two of the exits must be located a distance equal to at least half of the longest diagonal within the space or building. This is referred to as the *half-diagonal rule*.

When a building has exit enclosures, such as exit stairs that are interconnected by a fire-rated corridor, some of the codes, including the *IBC*, require the exit distance to be measured differently. Figure 4.21 illustrates this point for an entire floor in relation to a tenant space. Notice that the overall diagonal length (D2) is also measured using a straight line across the top of the floor plan. On the other hand, when you are placing the two exits at the stairwells, the half-diagonal distance between the exits ($\frac{1}{2}$ D2) is measured along the path of travel within the rated corridor. (The tenant space exit access doors are located using a straight line.)

When more than two exits are required, at least two of the exits must be placed using the half-diagonal rule. The remaining exits should be placed as remotely as possible so that if one exit becomes blocked in an emergency, the others would still be usable. Most of the codes also allow an exception to the half-diagonal rule if the entire building is equipped with an automatic sprinkler system. Usually the one-half measurement can be reduced to one-third. (Refer to the codes.)

Note

Typically, when a building is sprinklered, the two exits can be located at a distance equal to at least one-third of the overall diagonal of the space or building.

The overall objective of each of the codes is to make the exits as far apart as possible—for example, at opposite ends of a corridor or tenant space. The best scenario is to allow every occupant the choice of two exit paths no matter where he or she is located within a space. Although this is not always possible, especially in older buildings, as the designer you need to use your space planning skills as well as your common sense to arrive at the best solution.

Travel Distance

In general, travel distance is the measurement of an exit access. It is the measurement of the distance between the most remote, occupiable point of an area, room,

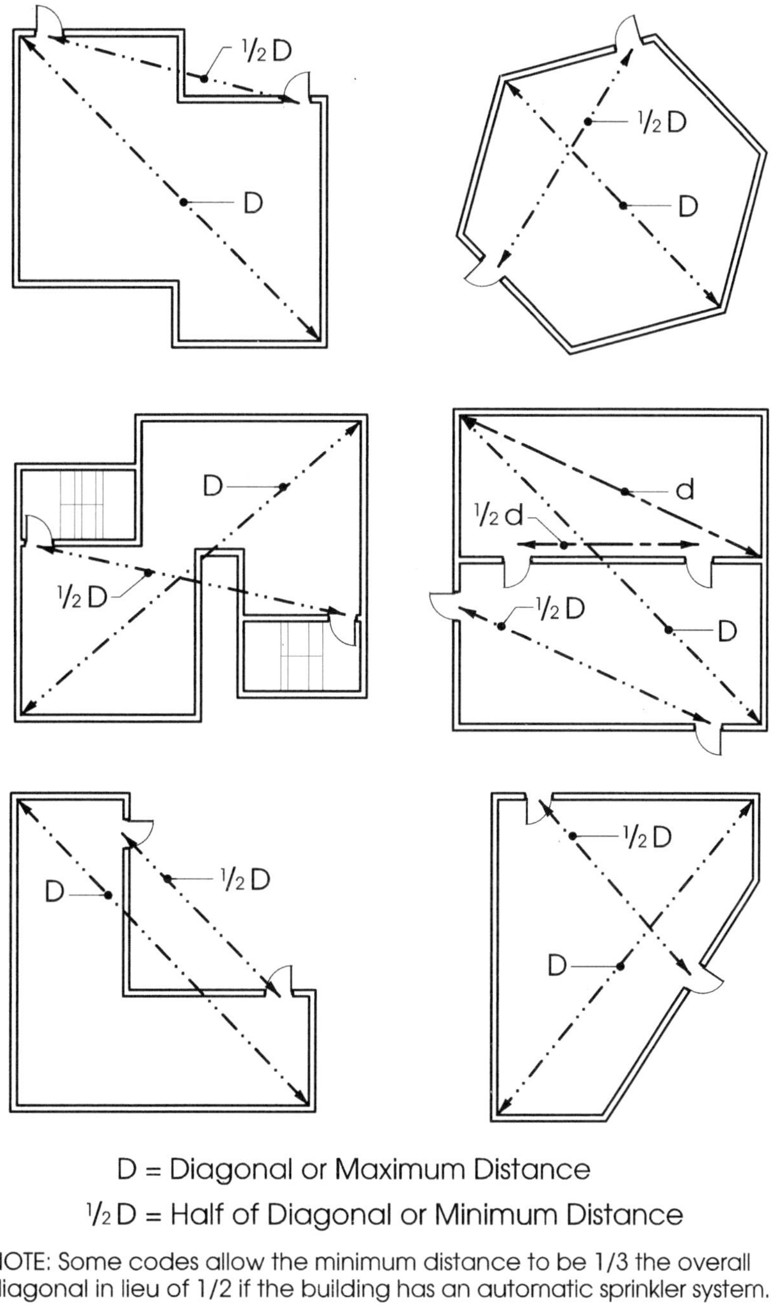

Figure 4.20 Half Diagonal Rule Example: Building

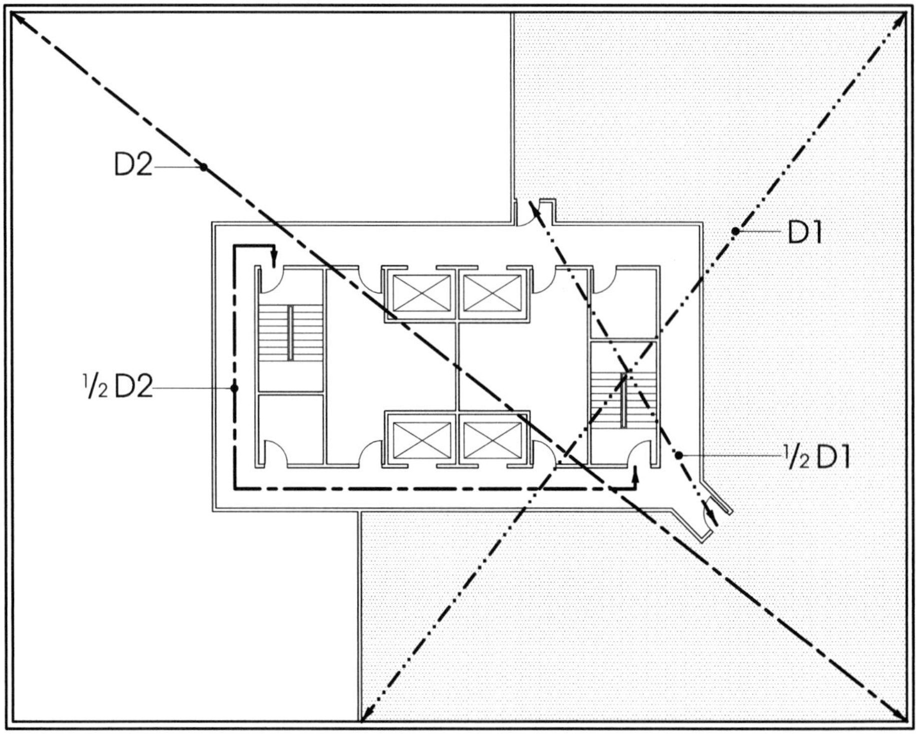

D1 = Diagonal Distance for Tenant Space
D2 = Diagonal Distance for Entire Floor

NOTE: Some codes allow the minimum distance to be 1/3 the overall diagonal in lieu of 1/2 if the building has an automatic sprinkler system.

Figure 4.21 Half Diagonal Rule Example: Tenant and Floor

or space to the exit that serves it. Two types of travel distance are regulated by the codes. First, the codes limit the length of travel distance from within a single space to the exit access corridor. This is known as a common path of travel, because all the occupants of that space will have to travel approximately the same direction before they come to two options for exiting. (See the section on Common Path of Travel on page 169.) The codes also regulate the length of travel distance from anywhere in a building to the exit of the building or floor. These are separate travel distance calculations and the information is located in different areas of the codes.

Travel distance from within a *single space* is basically determined the same way by the building codes and the *LSC*. Travel distance within a single space is especially important when the occupant load requires only one exit. Typically, if the travel distance within a tenant space exceeds 75 feet (22,860 mm), then an additional exit is necessary even if the occupant load does not require it. There are exceptions. The most obvious is the addition of an automatic sprinkler system. For example, if there is an automatic sprinkler system within the building, the travel distance usually can be increased to 100 feet (30,480 mm). Other exceptions may require shorter travel distances, such as in some Hazardous occupancies. (Refer to the specific codes for more information.)

Likewise, travel distance to the exit for the *entire building* or *individual floor* is basically determined the same way by the building codes and the *LSC*. The difference in each code is the standard distance allowed and the format of the information. The *IBC* uses Table 1015.1, "Exit Access Travel Distance," as shown in Figure 4.22. The *NFPA 5000* includes the regulations in each occupancy chapter.

TABLE 1015.1
EXIT ACCESS TRAVEL DISTANCE[a]

OCCUPANCY	WITHOUT SPRINKLER SYSTEM (feet)	WITH SPRINKLER SYSTEM (feet)
A, E, F-1, I-1, M, R, S-1	200	250[b]
B	200	300[c]
F-2, S-2, U	300	400[b]
H-1	Not Permitted	75[c]
H-2	Not Permitted	100[c]
H-3	Not Permitted	150[c]
H-4	Not Permitted	175[c]
H-5	Not Permitted	200[c]
I-2, I-3, I-4	150	200[c]

For SI: 1 foot = 304.8 mm.

a. See the following sections for modifications to exit access travel distance requirements:
Section 402: For the distance limitation in malls.
Section 404: For the distance limitation through an atrium space.
Section 1015.2: For increased limitation in Groups F-1 and S-1.
Section 1024.7: For increased limitation in assembly seating.
Section 1024.7: For increased limitation for assembly open-air seating.
Section 1018.2: For buildings with one exit.
Chapter 31: For the limitation in temporary structures.

b. Buildings equipped throughout with an automatic sprinkler system in accordance with Section 903.3.1.1 or 903.3.1.2. See Section 903 for occupancies where sprinkler systems according to Section 903.3.1.2 are permitted.

c. Buildings equipped throughout with an automatic sprinkler system in accordance with Section 903.3.1.1.

Figure 4.22 *International Building Code (IBC)* Table 1015.1, Exit Access Travel Distance (*International Building Code* 2003. Copyright 2002. Falls Church, Virginia: International Code Council, Inc. Reproduced with permission. All rights reserved.)

However, the *LSC* has a chart in its appendix that includes all common path limits, dead-end corridor limits, and travel distance limits.

Travel distance is *not* measured in a straight line; instead it is measured on the floor along the centerline of the natural path of travel. You start one foot from the wall at the most remote point (usually the corner of a room) and move in a direct path toward the nearest exit, curving around any obstructions such as walls, furniture and equipment, or corners with a clearance of one foot. The measurement ends at the exit. Typically this will be a door. Common examples include the following:

1. The exterior exit door
2. The door to an enclosed exit stair
3. The door of a horizontal exit
4. The door to an enclosed exit passageway
5. The door to an enclosed area of refuge
6. The door to the exit access corridor (for common path of travel)

Note

Whenever a jurisdiction requires both a building code and the *LSC*, be sure to compare the maximum travel distances. In most cases, the shortest required distance applies. Also be sure to check the sprinkler requirements and individual occupancies for any exceptions to the allowable travel distances.

Maximum travel distances can increase in length in certain occupancies when additional requirements are met. (Refer to the specific codes.) For example, as shown in the *IBC* table in Figure 4.22, the use of an automatic sprinkler system will increase the allowed travel distance. In addition, some codes allow the use of exit passageways to extend the location of an exit and thus reduce the actual travel distance. (See the Exit Passageway section earlier in the chapter.) For example, if the last portion of the travel distance is entirely within a rated exit passageway, or sometimes even with a fire-rated corridor, the *IBC* will allow it to be extended up to 100 feet (30,480 mm). That means, in effect, the 200-foot (60,960 mm) travel distance for a sprinklered building can be increased to 300 feet (91,440 mm).

Note

If an occupancy has an open stairway within its space that is part of an exit access, it must be included in the travel distance. You measure up to the centerline of the nosing of the top tread. Then the measurement of the stair is taken on the angle of the stairway in the plane of the tread nosing plane. You measure from the top tread nosing to the bottom tread nosing to get the stair travel length. To continue the overall travel distance, start at the bottom edge of the last riser to the exit.

Example

The floor plan in Figure 4.23 gives an example of measuring travel distances in a space that requires only one means of egress. The floor plan is that of an accounting firm that occupies part of one floor in a four-story sprinklered building. It is considered a Business occupancy. Since it is a new occupancy and separate from the other tenants in the building, it must have a travel distance acceptable to the current code requirements.

The dashed line on the floor plan indicates the path of travel distance. The travel distance measurement starts at the most remote point, in other words, the farthest point from the exit. It is indicated by the "X" on the floor plan. The first calculation is to determine if this tenant space will require a second exit. (Only

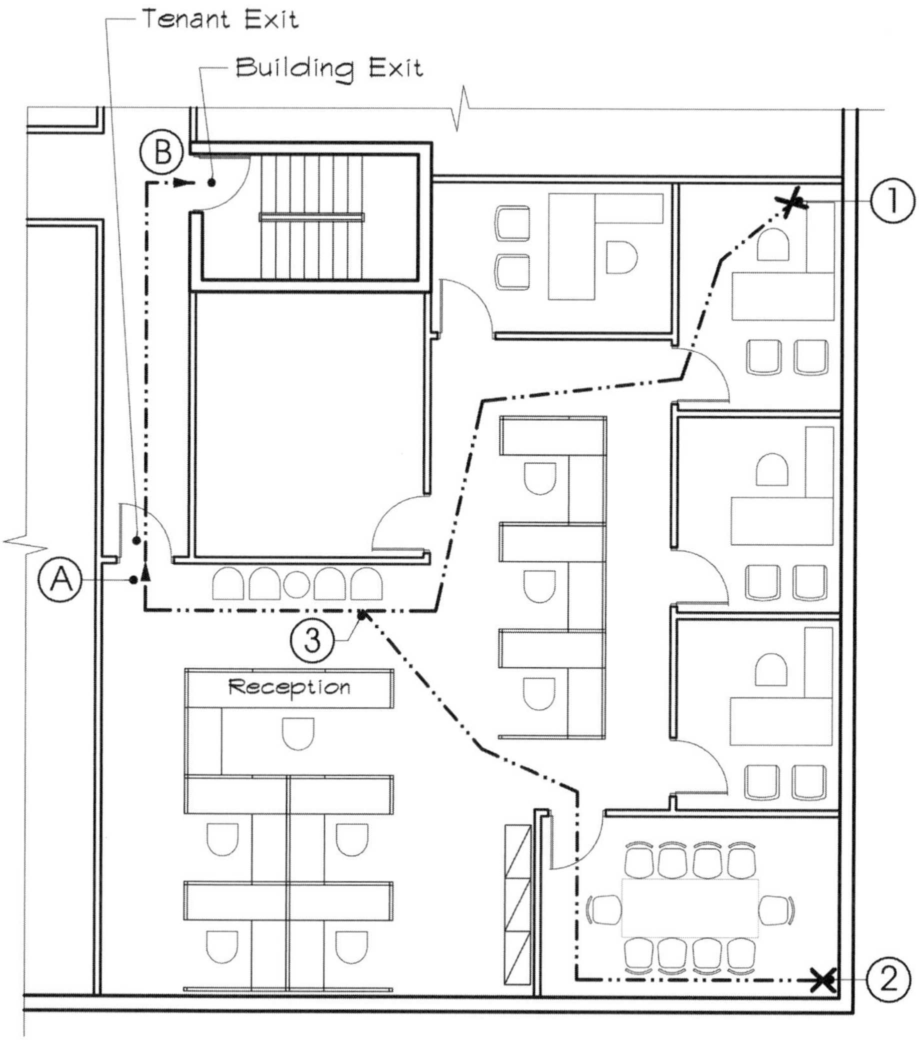

A1 = 56 feet (17,069 mm) B1 = 80 feet (24,384 mm)
A2 = 57 feet (17,374 mm) B2 = 81 feet (24,689 mm)

Figure 4.23 Travel Distance Example: Tenant Space (sprinklered building)

one is required by the occupant load.) In this case the exit is the door leading from the tenant space to the exit access corridor as indicated by "A". Therefore, the travel distance measurement ends at the center of this door. Since the tenant has two points that seem to be about the same distance from the exit, both must be measured. You start one foot from the wall at the farthest corner and move

Note

Typically, if the longest travel distance within a space to the entry door exceeds 75 feet (22,680 mm), the space would require two exits.

Note

If you are designing a number of different tenant spaces in the same building, the travel distance must be measured for each tenant. It does not matter if the tenants are all the same occupancy. If they are separated from each other by a demising wall, they must be treated separately.

toward the exit using the most direct path and staying one foot away from any obstacles. Obstacles can include walls, corners, furniture, fixtures, equipment, and machinery.

Once the travel distance line is drawn as directly as possible, measure the line to get the travel distance measurement. In the example in Figure 4.23, the longest travel distance to "A" is 57 feet (17,374 mm). Since it does not exceed the minimum 75 feet (22,860 mm) required by the code, a second exit is not required.

The next calculation is to determine the travel distance to the exit for the building floor. In this case the exit is the door leading to the exit stair as shown by "B." Therefore, the travel distance measurement begins at the same point as before, but ends at the center of this exit stair door. The distance is measured along the longest path and extends to the stairwell. In this example, the longest travel distance to "B" is 81 feet (24,689 mm). You then compare this to the maximum travel distances allowed by the codes. Using Figure 4.22, the *IBC* table indicates that for Business occupancies the travel distance limit is 300 feet (91,440 mm) for sprinklered buildings. The design of the accounting firm meets the codes, since both measurements are below the maximum travel distance allowed. (Note that if this had been an unsprinklered building, the travel distance would have still met the code.)

TRAVEL DISTANCE FACTORS

Travel distance measurement is not based on a code formula. Rather, it is based on the space or building as a whole. *The Life Safety Code Handbook (2003)* lists the factors on which the required code travel distances are based:

- ❑ The estimated number, age, and physical condition of building occupants and the rate at which they can be expected to move.
- ❑ The type and number of expected obstructions such as display cases, seating, and heavy machinery that must be negotiated.
- ❑ The estimated number of people in any room or space and the distance from the farthest point in that room to the door.
- ❑ The amount and nature of combustibles expected in a particular occupancy.
- ❑ The rapidity with which a fire might spread, which is a function of the type of construction, the materials used, the degree of compartmentation, and the presence or absence of automatic fire detection and extinguishing systems.

Obviously, travel distance will vary with the type and size of an occupancy and the degree of hazards present.

Dead-End Corridors

A dead-end corridor is a corridor with only one direction of exit. In other words, if a person turns down a corridor with a dead end, there is no way out except to retrace his or her path. An example of a dead-end corridor has been indicated on the floor plan in Figure 4.24.

> **Note**
>
> In some jurisdictions, the placement of freestanding furniture and panel systems does not create dead-end corridors. It is assumed that in an emergency this furniture can be moved or climbed over.

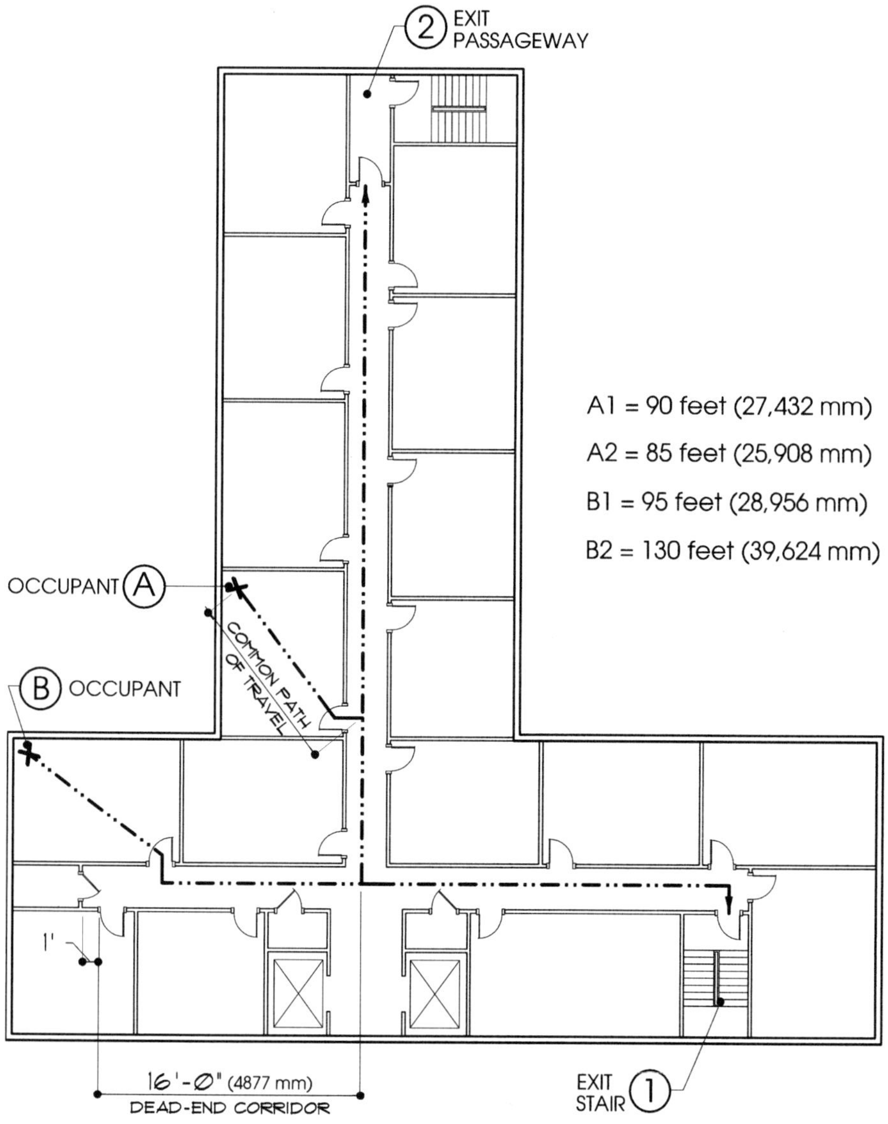

Figure 4.24 Travel Distance Example: Building (Hotel) (sprinklered building)

The codes set maximum lengths for dead-end corridors because they can be deadly in an emergency. When a corridor is filled with smoke it is difficult to read exit signs. Occupants could waste valuable time going down a dead-end corridor only to find out they have gone the wrong way and must turn back. If a dead-end corridor is long, a person can easily get trapped by fire and/or smoke.

Note

Some of the codes allow a dead-end corridor longer than 20 feet (6096 mm) when sprinklers are present. It depends on the type of occupancy.

The building codes and the *LSC* describe the limits of a dead end within the text. (In the *LSC*, they are also listed in a table within its appendix.) The most common dead-end length is a maximum of 20 feet (6096 mm). It is measured one foot from the end of a corridor, following the natural path of travel, to the centerline of the corridor that provides the choice of two means of egress. In some codes, when an automatic sprinkler system is installed, a dead-end corridor can be longer. For example, in the *IBC*, a dead-end corridor in a sprinklered building in Business and Factory occupancies is allowed to be up to 50 feet (15,240 mm) in length. There may be other conditions that would allow longer dead-end corridors. (Refer to the codes for specifics.)

Although it would be best to eliminate dead-end corridors altogether, it is not always possible—especially in older, existing buildings. If one becomes necessary, locate the rooms or spaces that are the least used at the end of the corridor. When a dead-end corridor longer than 20 feet (6096 mm) is unavoidable, which can sometimes happen in older buildings, be sure to contact the code officials in that jurisdiction.

Example

Note

For most occupancies, one exit is allowed if the occupant load is 50 or less and the travel distance to the exit is less than 75 feet (22,860 mm). Check the codes for specific requirements.

A second travel distance example is an entire third floor of a hotel in a sprinklered building. The floor plan in Figure 4.24 indicates that there are two exits. Both are enclosed stairways. (In this example it is assumed that the elevators do not constitute an exit in an emergency.) Refer back to the *IBC* table in Figure 4.22. Under the Residential (R) occupancy for hotels, the maximum travel distance allowed is 250 feet (76,200 mm) for a sprinklered building. (The bottom of the table gives the metric conversion unit.) This means that an occupant located anywhere on the floor of this hotel cannot travel more than 250 feet (76,200 mm) to reach the closest exit.

In this example several measurements must be made. Point A as indicated on the floor plan is midway between the two exits. An occupant in this location must be able to reach at least one exit within 250 feet (76,200 mm). In both cases (A1 and A2) the total distance is less than this.

Point B must also be within 250 feet (76,200 mm) from the enclosed exit stairs. Note, however, that the point is located in a dead-end corridor. You must first check to make sure the dead end is not longer than 20 feet (6096 mm). Since the dead-end length is 16 feet (4877 mm), you can proceed to measure the travel distance. As shown in Figure 4.24, the travel distance to both exits (B1 and B2) falls under the 250-foot (76,200 mm) maximum distance.

Common Path of Travel

Some of the codes set maximum lengths for common paths of travel. The specified length depends on the occupancy and can apply to either of the following types of common paths of travel. The first type occurs when a person can travel in only *one direction* to reach the point where there is a choice of two exits. For example, a dead-end corridor can be considered a common path of travel. Both paths B1 and B2 in Figure 4.23 are also common paths of travel. In addition, any room that has only one exit door also has a common path of travel, as indicated at "A" in Figure 4.24. The common path is measured similarly to travel distance, starting one foot from the wall at the most remote location. It is the distance from this point measured along the natural path of travel to the centerline of the first corridor or aisle that provides a choice of two paths of travel to remote exits.

Note

If a floor plan exceeds the maximum travel distance, you need to change the floor plan to meet the requirements. Often, moving a wall or relocating equipment is all it takes. Adding or increasing an exit passageway is another solution. If all else fails, work closely with the local code officials.

The second definition of a common path of travel is an exit access where two paths merge to become one. The *merged* path becomes the common path of travel. For example, a reception area in a tenant space typically becomes a common path of travel. Two corridors or aisles accessing the various rooms and/or offices would merge together at the reception area to arrive at the door exiting the space. This is shown in Figure 4.23 beginning at point "3" and leading to "B." Most exit discharges can be considered a common path of travel, such as a lobby or vestibule, where other means of egress must converge to leave the building.

SIGNAGE

A variety of signs are required by the codes in a means of egress. These include exit signs and other exiting and location related signs. Some signs will be required by the codes; others may be requested by the client. Various types of signs are discussed below. (Restroom signs are discussed in Chapter 7.) As the designer, it is your responsibility to specify the signage products that meet the requirements for your jurisdiction as well as accessibility standards, including the ADA guidelines.

Note

Some exterior exit doors, such as those found in main lobbies or vestibules, may not require an exit sign if they are clearly identifiable. However, this must be approved by a code official.

Note

Some code jurisdictions are beginning to require *floor-level exit signs* in addition to regular exit signs in some occupancies. These are typically placed 8 inches (203 mm) above the floor near the exit door so that they are easy to read in emergencies with heavy smoke. Look for additional uses in the future.

Note

The requirements for signage are strict in the ADA guidelines and the ICC/ANSI standard, whether it is for exit signs or other required signage. Be sure to use the most rigid regulations.

Note

Although not currently required by the codes, photo-luminescent marking devices like signage and tape can be added to exit corridors and stairs to provide additional direction.

Exit Signs

Exit signs are typically required whenever a floor or space has two or more exits. (Some smaller occupancies may not require exit signs.) They must be installed at the doors of all stair enclosures, exit passageways, and horizontal exits on every floor. They must also be installed at all exterior exit doors and any door exiting a space or area when the direction of egress is unclear. For example, a sign is often required when a corridor changes direction. The purpose of the exit sign is to lead occupants to the nearest exit or to an alternate exit if necessary. Although codes provide some specific requirements about the placement of exit signs, additional signs may be necessary to clearly designate a path or location within a space or series of corridors. (See Other Signs below.)

The building codes and the *LSC* specify the placement, graphics, and illumination of exit signs. They may also refer to *NFPA 170, Standard for Fire Safety Symbols*. The ADA guidelines and the ICC/ANSI standard have specific regulations as well. Exit signs located directly over an exit door are usually required only to say "EXIT." Signs that lead occupants to the exit doors often are required to have directional arrows. (Some jurisdictions may allow the use of other languages where a majority of the occupants may speak a language other than English. And in some cases, graphic signs without words may be used.) Be sure to confirm the specific requirements with the jurisdiction. For example, contrast letters on exit signs are usually available in green and red; some jurisdictions, however, allow only red.

When placing exit signs, the most common requirement is that no point within the exit access can be more than 100 feet (30,480 mm) from the nearest visible sign. Therefore, if you have a long corridor or a large space, additional exit signs are often required. Figure 4.25 indicates typical locations of exit signs within a building and within a tenant space. The general rule is to use a regular exit sign at an exit or exit access door and directional exit signs at all other locations (i.e., corridors, open areas). Although exit signs are usually ceiling mounted or wall mounted, some jurisdictions may also require exit signs to be located near the ground so that they can be seen when smoke gathers at the ceiling.

Other Signs

In addition to exit signs, other exit-related signs may be required, especially when a means of egress is confusing. For example, if a regular door or stairway can be mistaken for an exit, the codes typically require a "NO EXIT" sign be posted on the door. (Supplemental lettering such as "STOREROOM" or "TO BASEMENT" can be used to indicate the name of the area as well.) Exiting sign-

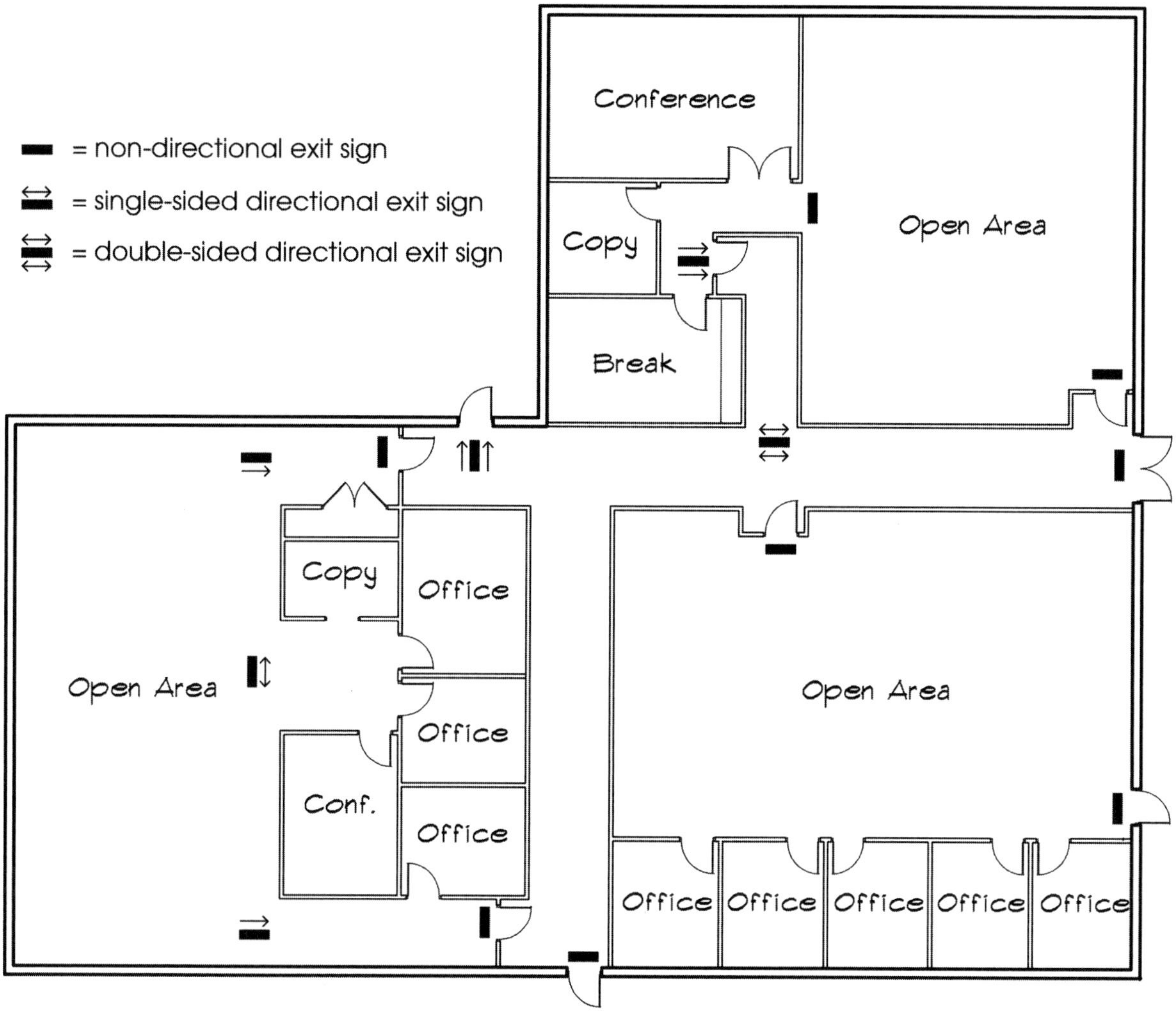

Figure 4.25 Exit Sign Location Example

age can also include signs that help orient the occupants to where they are in the building (e.g., floor levels, stair numbers, and floor numbers at stairs and elevator banks). Other code-required signage typically includes locating areas of refuge, labeling entrance and exit doors, indicating locked doors, and so on. An example would include a fire exit sign mounted on the corridor side of a stairwell door that also says "KEEP DOOR CLOSED." (Other signs may be requested by the client, such as room names and/or room numbers.)

When a sign is required by codes, the codes refer you to the ICC/ANSI accessibility standard for specific sign requirements. Similar regulations are required by the ADA guidelines whenever a sign is permanent and must be followed even when the sign is not required by codes. For example, a room number sign would need to meet accessibility requirements. Specifics include lettering heights, mounting locations, lettering contrast, and, in certain cases, the use of Braille. Mounting locations in relation to the door are specified as well. Most commonly, a sign must be mounted from 48 to 60 inches (1220 to 1525 mm) above the floor. Typically this height is measured to the baselines of the lettering on the sign. The sign must also be mounted on the latch side of the door. If it is a double door, the sign should be mounted to the right of the door. Clear floor space in front of the sign may also be required. (See Figure 7.11 in Chapter 7 for other information.)

Note

When double doors are used as an entry into a space, the sign is required on the wall to the right of the door.

EMERGENCY LIGHTING

Like exit signage, emergency lighting is typically required whenever two or more exits are present. Sometimes referred to as exit lighting, emergency lighting must be connected to a backup system in case of power failure during an emergency. This could mean connection to a backup generator in the building or battery packs located within the light fixture. Generally, the codes require emergency lighting to be provided at all exits and any aisles, corridors, passageways, ramps, and lobbies leading to an exit. Both general exit lighting and exit and area of refuge signs must be lit at all times a building is in use. The codes specify minimum lighting illumination levels. Lower levels might be allowed for certain building types, such as theaters, concert halls, and auditoriums. (Chapter 8 describes emergency lighting in more detail.)

CHECKLIST

Although a means of egress is made up of a number of components, the ultimate goal is to provide a direct route or exit to the exterior of a building. The checklist in Figure 4.26 has been designed to help you design the means of egress for your project. It helps you to determine which components must be researched, reminds you of the required calculations, and provides a form for documentation of your research.

The top of the checklist is used to distinguish the use and size of the project. You should indicate the name of the project and/or the space that you are currently researching. The checklist also asks for the occupancy classification of that

Means of Egress Checklist

Date:____________

Project Name:__________________________________ Space: __________________________

Main Occupancy (new or existing):___________________________Occupant Load: _______________

Type of Space (check one): ______ Building ______ Floor ______ Space/Tenant ______ Room

Exit Access Requirements (if more than 2 attach additional calculations)

Exit Access 1 (check/research those that apply and fill in the corresponding information)

Type of Component(s): __ DOOR __STAIR __ RAMP __CORRIDOR __ AISLE __ INTERVENING ROOMS

Required Width: ____________________ Using: __ LEVEL VARIABLE __STAIR VARIABLE __OTHER VARIABLE

Exit Access 2 (check/research those that apply and fill in the corresponding information)

Type of Component(s): __ DOOR __STAIR __ RAMP __CORRIDOR __ AISLE __ INTERVENING ROOMS

Required Width: ____________________ Using: __ LEVEL VARIABLE __STAIR VARIABLE __OTHER VARIABLE

Travel Distance (check those that apply and indicate lengths where required)

__ Common Path of Travel: _________ __ Max. allowed travel distance for space: __________

__ Dead-End Corridor: __________ __ Max. allowed travel distance for floor/building: __________

Exit Requirements (may require up to 4 exits, if more than 2 attach additional calculations)

Required Number of Exits (check those that apply and indicate quantity where shown)

__ One Exit Exception __ Required Number of Exits: ________________

__ Minimum of Two Exits __ Number of Exits Provided: ________________

Location of Exits Determined By (check one)

__ 1/2 Diagonal Rule __ Other Remoteness Requirement

__ 1/3 Diagonal Rule Explain: ___________________________

Exit 1 (Check/research those that apply and fill in the corresponding information)

Type: __ EXTERIOR DOOR __EXIT STAIR __ EXIT PASSAGEWAY __HORIZONTAL EXIT __ AREA OF REFUGE

Required Width: ____________________ Using: __ LEVEL VARIABLE __STAIR VARIABLE __MINIMUM REQUIRED

Number of Doors: ________________ Distributed: __ EVENLY AMONG EXITS __ASSEMBLY EXCEPTION

Exit 2 (Check/research those that apply and fill in the corresponding information)

Type: __ EXTERIOR DOOR __EXIT STAIR __ EXIT PASSAGEWAY __HORIZONTAL EXIT __ AREA OF REFUGE

Required Width: ____________________ Using: __ LEVEL VARIABLE __STAIR VARIABLE __MINIMUM REQUIRED

Number of Doors: ________________ Distributed: __ EVENLY AMONG EXITS __ASSEMBLY EXCEPTION

Exit Discharge Components (check those that apply and research if required)

__ MAIN LOBBY __ FOYER __VESTIBULE(S) __DISCHARGE CORRIDOR(S) __EXIT COURT(S)

Other Code and Accessibility Requirements to Consider (check/research those that apply)

__ Doors: Type, Swing, Size, Hardware, Threshold, Clearances, Fire Rating

__ Stairs: Type, Riser Height, Tread Depth, Nosing, Width, Handrail, Guard, Fire Rating

__ Ramps: Slope, Rise, Landings, Width, Edge Detail, Finish, Handrail, Guard

__ Corridors: Length, Width, Protruding Objects, Fire Rating

__ Aisles: Fixed Seats, No Fixed Seats, Ramp(s), Steps, Handrails

__ Intervening Rooms: Type, Size, Obstructions, Fire Rating

NOTES:

1. Refer to codes and standards for specific information as well as ADA guidelines and ICC/ANSI standards for additional requirements.
2. Attach any floor plans indicating locations of components and other paperwork required for calculations.
3. Check specific occupancy classifications and/or building types for special requirements that may apply.

Figure 4.26 Means of Egress Checklist

Note

Particular attention should be given to the type of occupancy when determining means of egress requirements, since the codes may allow exceptions or require more severe regulations, depending on the occupancy.

project as well as the occupant load. (See Chapter 2.) Next, you are asked to indicate the scope of the project. For example, if you check "Floor," that means you are designing an entire floor of a building. You must calculate the egress capacities for everything on that floor, including the exit stairs leaving the floor. If you are designing a portion of a floor, such as a "Space/Tenant" space on a multitenant floor, your main concern will be that tenant.

The first section addresses requirements for exit access portions of the means of egress. First, you are asked to identify components of the exit access that will be included in your project. For example, if you are laying out a single tenant with an open office plan, you may need to research aisle requirements. However, if you are laying out an entire floor area, you may have to consider corridor requirements as well as aisle requirements. By checking which ones apply to your project, you will know which codes and accessibility requirements must be researched. You can then concentrate on only those you need. Use the section called Exit Access 1 for the first component and Exit Access 2 for the second component. For example, Exit Access 1 may be used to document the corridor requirements and Exit Access 2 may be used to document the door requirements. If you have multiple exit access components, you may need additional sheets.

You will need to determine the required width for each component and note it in these sections. Note also which variable and method you used. (See the section on Exit Widths to help you with this calculation). As you lay out your design, it is important for you to know the maximum travel distance allowed by the code. You must research this early in the process. The checklist includes a place to record the allowable dead-end corridors as well as the overall maximum travel distance. There are separate places for you to indicate the allowable travel distances for a space or for the entire floor. You should also research and note the limitations for common paths of travel. These may affect the location of exits as well as the most appropriate layout of various rooms and furniture.

Next, you must determine how many exits are required from each space, the overall space, or the entire floor. Although two exits are almost always required, in some cases you may be allowed to have only one exit. In other cases, you will be required to have multiple exits. Note which requirement applies to your project. If you are working with an existing space, note how many exits are already provided. You can check this against how many are required.

If two or more exits are required, the codes set various requirements so that all of the exits are not easily blocked by a single fire. Note in the next section which requirement you used to locate the exits. For example, did you verify that two exits meet the half-diagonal rule, or is the building sprinklered and you are allowed to use the one-third diagonal rule? If you are evaluating an existing layout and location of exits, note which rule the existing exits meet. You may want to attach a reduced copy of the floor plan to show your measurements.

Once you know the number of exits and the location of the exits, you must determine the required width for the exits. The following section of the checklist gives you a place to document two separate exit locations. (Attach additional calculations as required.) First, indicate what type of exit is used. For example, one exit may be a door and the second exit may be a horizontal exit. These different exit types will require separate calculations. Then research the requirements for each exit and record the calculated or minimum width required. Depending on the type of exit, also note the variable that was used in your calculations or note that you used the minimum width required by the codes. Finally, indicate the number of actual doors that will be or are provided at each exit location. Remember, that although exit width is typically distributed equally between exits, a large Assembly use may require a different distribution. (See Exit Widths earlier in the chapter for help with this section, if necessary.)

If your project includes an exit discharge, indicate in the next section which type and research the requirements for that particular situation. You may need to attach documentation of your research to this checklist for your records.

The last section of the checklist indicates the main means of egress components and typical characteristics that must be researched. Many of these will require additional calculations. Check any that apply and use the codes and the accessibility standards as well as this book to determine what is required for your project. Many of the calculations can be scaled off and completed right on the project's actual floor plans. All of the required calculations and special code information should be attached to the checklist and kept with the project records. Be sure to check the building code and/or the *LSC*, the ADA guidelines, and the ICC/ANSI standard. In addition, pay particular attention to any exceptions that are allowed.

Note

Once a building occupant is brought into the protected portion of a means of egress, the level of protection cannot be reduced or eliminated unless an exception is allowed by your jurisdiction.

CHAPTER 5

FIRE-RESISTANT MATERIALS AND ASSEMBLIES

Approximately 75 percent of all codes deal with fire and life safety. Their enforcement affects virtually every part of a building, focusing first on prevention and then on early detection and suppression as the primary means of providing safe buildings. Interior fire-related codes focus on protecting the occupants of the building, allowing time to evacuate during a fire as well as access for firefighters and equipment. The ultimate goal of fire-related codes is to confine a fire to the room of origin, and therefore limit the spread of the fire and prevent flashover.

The codes include provisions for both fire protection and smoke protection. In the past, most regulations were directed to controlling fire within a building. Yet smoke can be just as deadly as fire, if not more so, because of how fast it can travel. The toxicity of the smoke is a large factor as well. Whether a fire is full blown or just smoldering, the smoke it produces can travel quickly and cause harm to the occupants of the building before the fire ever reaches them. The smoke causes asphyxiation and obstruction of sight, making evacuation difficult.

Note

More people die from asphyxiation due to smoke than from burns due to fire. Toxicity from burning or smoldering items also causes a large number of deaths.

Because the control of fire and smoke is such a serious life safety issue, the prevention of fire and smoke spread is addressed in the codes in several ways. The codes and standards place strict requirements on the materials that are used to construct a building. The construction type of a building as discussed in Chapter 3 assigns an hourly fire-resistance rating to almost every structural element in a building, including walls and floor assemblies. Other parts of the codes place restrictions on the building materials used inside the building. These materials include everything from interior walls, windows, and doors to ductwork, wiring, and plumbing pipes. Interior finishes and furniture, as discussed in Chapter 9, are regulated by codes and standards as well. All of these materials and components are considered combustible materials that can feed and sustain a fire within a building. Also known as *fuel loads*, they are restricted and managed by the codes of the different types of fire-protection systems.

In addition to regulating the materials that go into a building or space, the codes require various *systems* that are intended to aid in fire safety. Generally, the systems can be defined as passive fire-protection systems, active fire-protection systems, and exiting systems. The specific issues of each category are listed below.

Note

A balance of active and passive fire protection systems is necessary for a safe building.

Passive Systems

Passive systems focus on prohibiting and containing fires. They are sometimes referred to as *prevention systems*. These elements are considered *passive* because, once in place, nothing else has to occur for them to be part of the control of a fire. Most parts of a passive or prevention system are discussed in this chapter:

Note

Passive fire protection systems may also be referred to as prevention systems.

- ❑ Fire and smoke barriers and partitions (e.g., walls, floors, ceilings)
- ❑ Opening protectives (e.g., windows, doors)
- ❑ Through-penetration protectives (e.g., firestops, draftstops, dampers)
- ❑ Finishes and furniture (e.g., wall coverings, finish floor materials, upholstered pieces, mattresses, and similar elements) (These are discussed in Chapter 9.)

Active Systems

These systems are considered *active* because they have to be *activated* in order to work against the fire.

- ❑ Detection systems (e.g., detectors, fire alarms, and communication systems) (Detection systems are discussed in Chapter 6.)
- ❑ Extinguishing and suppression systems (e.g., fire extinguishers, fire hoses, and sprinkler systems) (These systems are discussed in Chapter 6.)
- ❑ Emergency lighting (These systems are discussed in Chapter 4 and in Chapter 8.)

Exiting Systems

Exiting systems are the elements of a space or building that assist and direct occupants to a place of safety.

- ❑ Means of egress (e.g., corridors, exits, stairs, ramps, and similar components) (These components are discussed in Chapter 4.)
- ❑ Exit communication systems (e.g., signage, audible and visual communication) (These are discussed in Chapter 4 and Chapter 6.)

Each system plays an important part in making a building safe. In recent code developments, emphasis on the use of active systems such as automatic sprinkler systems has changed many requirements. However, most experts agree that a balance of active and passive systems is necessary for the safest building. In other words, components of each system should be included in the overall fire protection design.

This chapter will discuss how compartmentation in interior projects works as part of the passive fire protection system by the use of assemblies that resist the spread of fire or smoke. These assemblies include fire walls, fire barriers and partitions, smoke barriers and partitions, opening protectives, and through-penetration protectives. Each type is explained in this chapter. Detection and suppression systems will be discussed in the following chapter.

KEY TERMS

Below is a list of terms used when discussing fire and smoke separation. These terms are defined and discussed in this chapter. They are also defined in the Glossary.

Assembly
Automatic closing
Compartmentation
Fire area
Fire barrier
Fireblocking
Fire partition
Fire resistant
Fire protection rating
Fire resistance rating
Fuel load
Membrane penetration
Opening protective
Self closing
Smoke barrier
Smoke partition
Through-penetration
Through-penetration protective

COMPARING THE CODES

The building codes typically have several chapters pertaining to passive and active fire protection systems within a building. In most cases, the codes discuss passive and active systems separately. For example, each building code has a chapter on fire-resistance-rated materials and assemblies, which make up the majority of a passive fire-protection system. The *Life Safety Code (LSC)* has two chapters on fire protection, as well. (The NFPA codes have additional information in their individual occupancy chapters.) A number of requirements for fire-resistance-rated partitions can also be found in the means of egress chapter within each code. Together these chapters define the use of compartmentation for a space or building. Other chapters and sections within the codes contain the information on the active fire protection systems. (These systems are discussed in more detail in the Chapter 6.)

Note

A number of cities and some states have adopted their own fire codes. Some of the strictest include those of California, Boston, Florida, Massachusetts, New Jersey, New York City, and New York State. Be sure to check the jurisdiction of your project and use the strictest codes.

The building codes also set additional regulations by specifying the types of materials and assemblies and where they should be used. These requirements are included in the building codes in the chapters on construction types, as well as in the fire-resistance-rated chapters. When specific testing and installation methods are required, the building codes and the *LSC* refer you to various standards. Many of these are NFPA standards. The NFPA standards that are geared more to the interior of a building are listed in Figure 5.1. These and other standards are discussed throughout the chapter.

The fire codes also give requirements for the different types of fire-resistance-rated partitions and materials. The *International Fire Code (IFC)* has separate chapters titled "Fire Resistance Rated Construction" and "Interior Finish, Decorative Materials and Furnishings." In the *Uniform Fire Code (UFC)* or *NFPA 1*, the "Features of Fire Protection" chapter has separate sections for various types of fire-resistance-rated partitions, furnishing, and finishes. In some cases, the requirements of the fire code are repeated within the building codes so that the related documents are consistent. When a fire code is required in your jurisdiction, you should compare the applicable building code and fire code to know all the requirements that apply to your project.

In addition, performance codes and criteria may be very useful when designing a passive fire-protection system, especially in an existing building. Sometimes the best balance for a particular building may require innovative engineering, not represented in the prescriptive codes. And because even new buildings or spaces do not always fit the configurations assumed by the codes, broader ideas about compartmentation sometimes need to be explored.

Although the *ICC Performance Code (ICCPC)* does not have a specific section or chapter on the use of rated walls, it does set objectives for overall building safety

NFPA 80	Fire Doors and Fire Windows
NFPA 92A	Smoke Control Systems
NFPA 92B	Smoke Management Systems in Malls, Atria, and Large Areas
NFPA 105	Installation of Smoke Door Assemblies
NFPA 204	Smoke and Heat Venting
NFPA 221	Fire Walls and Fire Barrier Walls
NFPA 251	Methods of Tests of Fire Endurance of Building Construction and Materials
NFPA 252	Methods of Fire Test of Door Assemblies
NPFA 255	Method of Test of Surface Burning Characteristics of Burning Materials
NFPA 257	Fire Test for Window and Glass Block Assemblies
NFPA 258	Determining Smoke Generation of Solid Materials
NFPA 259	Test Method for Potential Heat of Building Materials
NFPA 270	Test Method for Measurement of Smoke Obscuration Using a Conical Radiant Source in a Single Closed Chamber
NFPA 271	Method of Test for Heat and Visible Smoke Release Rates for Materials and Products Using an Oxygen Consumption Calorimeter
NFPA 288	Methods of Fire Tests of Floor Fire Door Assemblies Installed Horizontally in Fire Resistance-Rated Floor Systems
NFPA 555	Methods for Evaluating Potential for Room Flashover
NFPA 703	Fire Retardant Impregnated Wood and Fire Retardant Coatings for Building Materials

NOTE: There are other standards organizations with similar standards as those shown above. These include ASTM and UL standards. See other figures in this chapter for more detail.

Figure 5.1 Common NFPA Standards for Building Materials and Assemblies

during a fire, including the protection of occupants. The *ICCPC* also sets criteria for limiting the impact of a fire, the exposure to hazards because of burning materials, and the overall fuel load. This information can be found in various *ICCPC* chapters. The performance-based chapters in the NFPA codes include a section on "safety from fire." This section sets objectives that the building should be able to "reasonably" limit the spread of fire to the compartment in which the fire originates. This, in a way, suggests that compartmentation is expected to be a part of a building's fire protection plan even when using performance codes. Various sample fire scenarios are also included in the performance chapter of the NFPA codes.

The performance codes and alternate methods criteria within each building and fire code may also allow the use of new materials and assemblies. You will have to confirm if these methods will be allowed in your jurisdiction. As in most cases, even when using performance codes to design an overall fire protection plan, many of the related prescriptive requirements would be used as part of the design as well.

The Americans with Disabilities Act (ADA) guidelines and other accessibility standards such as the *ICC/ANSI 117.1* do not play a major role in passive fire-prevention requirements. However, many of the fire-resistant components such as fire doors and enclosed stairwell are still required to meet the accessibility requirements. Since Chapter 4 has already discussed the accessibility requirements related to doors, stairs, and other means of egress, this chapter will only mention the ADA guidelines and the ICC/ANSI standard a few times.

COMPARTMENTATION IN A BUILDING

The overall concept of a passive fire-protection system is *compartmentation*. Compartmentation is the separation of areas in a building to control fire and smoke by the use of wall, floor, and ceiling assemblies. The codes specify when certain areas must be separated from another area and when the spread of fire or smoke must be limited. Some of these assemblies will be required to be fire rated; others will need to be smoke rated or a combination of both. (These are discussed later in this chapter.)

Compartments are created by fire-resistance-rated assemblies, which include fire walls, fire barriers, and fire partitions. These assemblies create separate, self-contained areas within a building, or separate "buildings" in a single structure. As a result, the fire can spread to only a limited area before meeting resistance from the rated assemblies. These areas are required by the code at certain intervals, between different uses and where different levels of hazard may exist. In some cases, as the designer, you may also choose to create separate fire areas for better fire protection. (The requirements for the doors, windows, and other penetrations within the fire-rated walls are discussed later in the chapter.)

In some cases, the control of smoke is as important or more important than the control of fire. And because assemblies that have fire-resistance ratings do not necessarily resist the spread of smoke, the codes also require the use of smoke barriers and smoke partitions in some cases. When required, these assemblies become part of the compartmentation of the space or building. When assemblies are required to be both fire resistant and smoke resistant, they are referred to as fire and smoke barriers.

In many cases, the use of automatic sprinkler systems within a building will affect the requirements for compartmentation. For example, if a building is equipped with a fully automatic sprinkler system, some fire rating requirements may be reduced. This will be discussed in more detail in the next chapter. (See the section on Sprinkler Systems in Chapter 6 starting on page 240.) However, during a project, it is important for you to know if an automatic sprinkler system will be provided or an approved one exists within the building, so that you can correctly research the requirements for compartmentation.

Each type of separation wall or assembly used to create a rated compartment has specific requirements depending on its use and location. The various uses of fire-resistance-rated walls and smoke-tight walls as part of compartmentation are discussed in the next several sections.

FIRE WALLS

Fire walls are used by the codes either within a building structure or between buildings to create two or more separate buildings according to the code. Sometimes called a *party wall*, the main purpose of a fire wall is to provide complete vertical separation of areas in a building. A fire wall has a separate foundation from the rest of the building structure and extends to the roof. Within a building, it must extend at least from exterior wall to exterior wall. In some cases, the wall is required to extend beyond the exterior walls and project through the roof (i.e., parapet wall).

Fire walls can be used to subdivide a building with two separate types of construction or to create building divisions within the same construction type for the purpose of allowing larger building areas. (See Chapter 3.) For example, if a medical office building and a hospital were built of different construction types but were built so that they were connected, a fire wall may be necessary to separate the different uses and construction types. Another example would be if the design for a factory exceeded its allowable area; fire walls could be used to divide the total area into two or more smaller areas that fall within the allowable area limitations.

Fire walls are built so that if the construction on one side of the wall fell during an emergency, the fire wall and the construction on the other side would remain standing. A fire wall can be rated a minimum of 2 hours, but the most common required rating is 3 hours or 4 hours. The rating of a fire wall is usually determined by the occupancy classification within the building, as shown in the *IBC* Table 705.4, "Fire Wall Fire-Resistance Ratings" in Figure 5.2. You can see

Note

When an exterior wall becomes part of a required fire-rated enclosure, the interior wall rating requirements do not typically apply to the exterior wall.

Note

In some cases, a fire wall can be used to create a horizontal separation. For example, a fire wall can be used to separate one floor from another when construction types are different.

TABLE 705.4
FIRE WALL FIRE-RESISTANCE RATINGS

GROUP	FIRE-RESISTANCE RATING (hours)
A, B, E, H-4, I, R-1, R-2, U	3[a]
F-1, H-3[b], H-5, M, S-1	3
H-1, H-2	4[b]
F-2, S-2, R-3, R-4	2

a. Walls shall be not less than 2-hour fire-resistance rated where separating buildings of Type II or V construction.
b. For Group H-1, H-2 or H-3 buildings, also see Sections 415.4 and 415.5.

Figure 5.2 *International Building Code (IBC)* Table 705.4 Fire Wall Fire-Resistance Ratings (*International Building Code* 2003. Copyright 2002. Falls Church, Virginia: International Code Council, Inc. Reproduced with permission. All rights reserved.)

Note

Firewalls are not usually added to existing buildings. They are very costly because the wall must extend continuously from the foundation of the building up to or through the roof.

that the rating of the fire wall is listed by the occupancy classification. If the two areas of the building were different occupancies, the highest rating would be required. Although the NFPA codes set a minimum rating of 2 hours for a fire wall, other specific requirements are listed within the text and in the occupancy chapters. Within a fire wall, openings and penetrations are very limited. In some cases, certain penetrations are not allowed. You must check the codes for the specific requirements for each fire wall location.

Because fire walls are usually planned and built during the initial construction of the building, they may not be part of a typical interior project. However, if you are penetrating the fire wall for any reason (e.g., adding a door), you will have to research the requirements for the wall to make sure you maintain the fire-resistance rating. To determine the fire-resistance rating of an existing fire wall, it may be necessary to refer to the original construction documents or contact the original architect to obtain the actual rating.

FIRE BARRIERS AND FIRE PARTITIONS

Fire barriers and fire partitions are required by the codes to separate different areas of a building. However, they are different. *Fire barriers* are building elements that have a fire-resistance rating and are used to separate specific areas into compartments within a building. Fire barriers can be *vertical or horizontal.* They include wall, ceiling, or floor assemblies that prevent the spread of flame and heat from one compartment to another. In most cases, walls that are fire barriers must be continuous and extend vertically from the top of a floor assembly to the bottom of a roof/ceiling assembly. For example, a vertical fire barrier would extend through a suspended ceiling to the slab above. Floor/ceiling assemblies that are fire barriers must extend horizontally from one rated wall or exterior wall to another. Whenever a fire barrier ends at another assembly, additional fireblocking is

Note

A fire barrier provides more protection than a fire partition.

required at the joint. In addition, the amount of openings in a fire barrier, including doors and windows, is limited. The doors, windows, and other penetrations in the rated assemblies must be rated as well. (Opening protectives and through protectives are discussed later in this chapter.)

In most cases, when the codes require the separation of a specific area by fire barriers, it means that the walls, floors, and ceiling assemblies surrounding the area must have the same fire-resistance rating. Often the ceiling/roof assembly may be required to have the same rating as well. This creates a complete compartmentation or *enclosure* both vertically and horizontally—like a four-sided box with a top and bottom. An example would be the enclosure of an exit stairway where all four walls, the floor, and the ceiling have a 2-hour rating. However, there are exceptions to this, and you will have to confirm the requirements in each case.

Keep in mind that an assembly may need to meet more than one code requirement. This is especially true for structural components such as a floor/ceiling assembly that must also meet construction type requirements. (See Chapter 3.) For example, if a space or room requires a 1-hour rated floor fire barrier, but the construction type requires the floor assembly be rated 2 hours for that construction type, the floor assembly must provide the 2-hour rating. The highest required rating must be provided. If you determine that a horizontal separation is required and the existing floor/ceiling assembly does not provide adequate fire resistance rating, then you may have to install a rated ceiling assembly below the existing ceiling structure.

Fire partitions are similar to fire barriers, but in most cases have less restrictive requirements than a fire barrier. In the *IBC*, the term fire partition is used in addition to fire barrier to mean a *vertical* rated partition that separates certain uses within a building. (This term is not used by the NFPA.) Fire partitions are most often used to separate exit access corridors, dwelling units and/or sleeping rooms. (Refer to inset titled *Types of Rooms and Spaces* in Chapter 2 on page 63.) However, according to the *IBC*, fire partitions do not provide the same level of protection as fire barriers. For example, although fire partitions can extend from structure to structure of a building, they are also allowed to stop at a rated ceiling system; fire barriers cannot. This difference is shown in Figure 5.3.

A fire partition provides a separation from one area to another but is not required to be a full enclosure. In other words, the floor and ceiling assemblies do not have to have the same rating. Yet, like a fire barrier, the amount of openings in a fire partition is limited and requires protection by rated components. The NFPA codes do not differentiate between fire barriers and fire partitions. However, by allowing exceptions to the requirements for fire barriers in cases where the *IBC* calls for the use of fire partitions and by adding requirements where a

Note

Keep in mind that fire and smoke barriers are an important component of a means of egress. A safe means of egress as required by the codes is a combination of the requirements discussed in Chapters 4, 5, 6, and 9 of this book.

Note

Fire barriers and partitions are given fire-*resistant* ratings and through-penetrations are given fire-*protection* ratings.

Note

Fire and smoke *barriers* are typically used to create full enclosures with wall, ceiling, and floor assemblies. Fire and smoke *partitions* are used to separate spaces on the same floor rather than to create compartments.

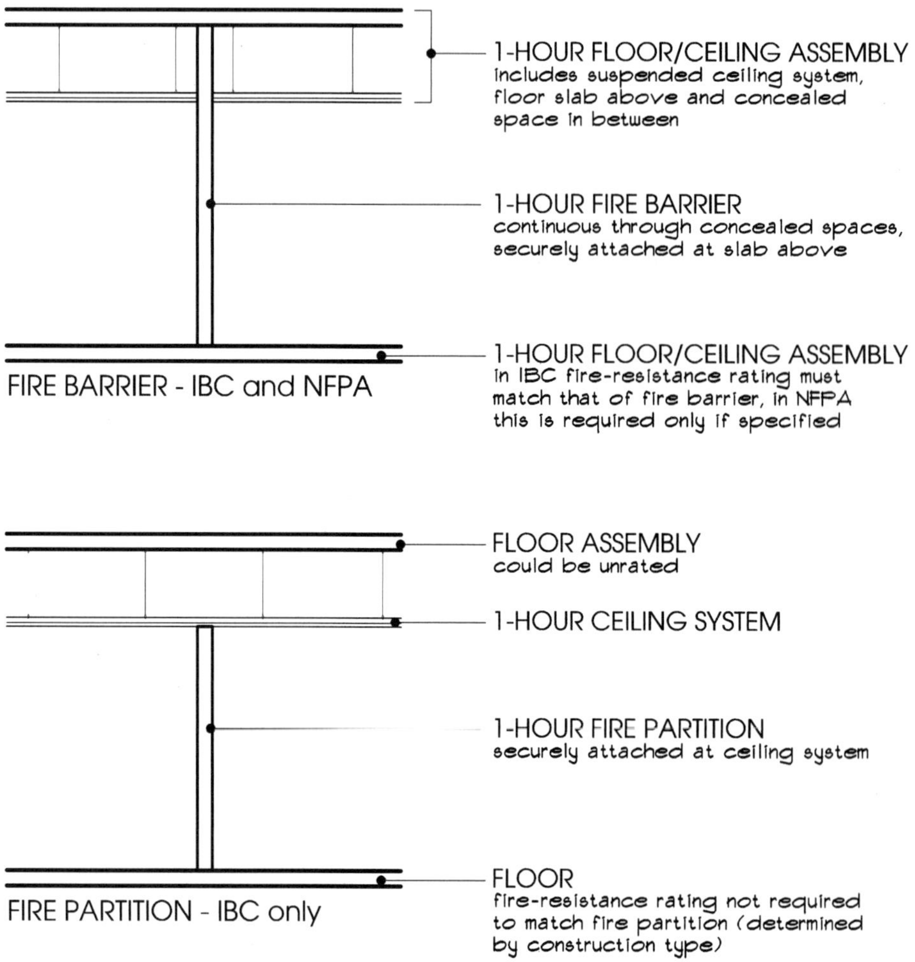

Figure 5.3 Fire Barriers and Fire Partitions

higher level of separation is necessary, the fire-rating requirements are similar between the codes.

It is very common for a rated wall to be added or modified during an interior project. Whether the project includes a new layout, new finishes, or the addition of wiring and cabling, work done may affect a rated wall. Therefore, you must be able to determine the correct use and rating of the fire barrier or partition if you are planning to add a new one or make any changes to an existing one. Also, keep in mind that for both fire barriers and fire partitions, the presence of an automatic sprinkler system may allow for lower fire-resistance ratings. Therefore, the rating depends on the purpose of the fire barrier or partition, the occupancy classifica-

Note

When walls are added to an existing structure it may be necessary to determine if the existing design load of the building will support these walls. See inset titled *Design Loads*, p. 75.

tion, and if the space or building has sprinklers. (The sprinkler system must meet the current code requirements.) The most common uses of fire barriers and partitions for compartmentation are described next.

Fire Areas

Fire barriers and exterior walls are used within a building to separate one area from another, creating two or more *fire areas*. (When a fire wall is used to create separate buildings, the buildings are considered separate fire areas, as well). Fire areas are most often required within a single occupancy type to provide compartmentation. For example, fire areas can be used to divide a large factory building into separate areas. The separate fire areas may allow one area of a building to be sprinklered and another to remain unsprinklered, as shown in the Plan at the top of Figure 5.4. (This is different than the example of using a fire wall to

Note

Some jurisdictions require the rating for a wall assembly to be indicated on the wall somewhere above the finished ceiling.

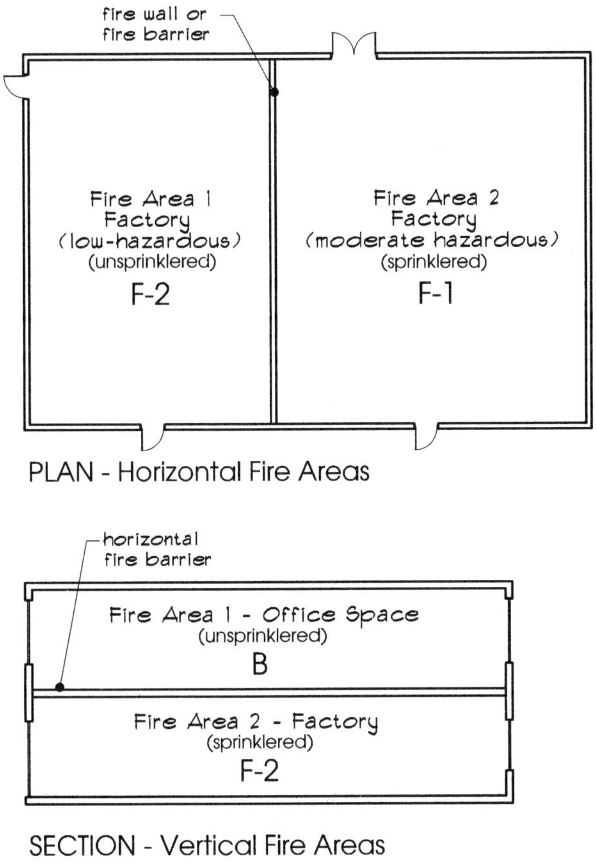

Figure 5.4 Fire Areas: Horizontally and Vertically

divide a large factory into separate buildings, as explained in the Fire Wall section.) In some cases, the codes require separate fire areas within a building. For example, a fire area is almost always required to separate a Hazardous use from another occupancy type. An example would be a small area of hazardous materials being stored within a large Storage occupancy. (This is different from incidental use areas, as described later.) It may also be desirable to split a large floor into more than one fire area if sprinklers are required in one area to manage fire protection and because of hazardous conditions.

Note

Fire ratings for floor/ceiling assemblies are first controlled by the construction type of the building. However, other sections of the codes will affect the rating of these assemblies as well.

In addition, a horizontal fire barrier can be used to create individual fire areas between each floor of a multi-story building. For example, in the building shown in the Section in Figure 5.4, the Business and Factory uses are separate fire areas. As in the previous example, this may allow one floor to be sprinklered and another to be unsprinklered. A fire area can also include more than one floor. This is determined by the codes. For example, high-rise buildings are usually divided into separate fire areas every couple of floor levels.

The required fire-resistance rating of the fire barrier separating each fire area is determined by the code. Each building code has a table similar to the *IBC* Table 706.3.7, "Fire-Resistance Rating Requirements for Fire Barrier Assemblies between Fire Areas," as shown in Figure 5.5. Other sections of the code will tell you when a fire area is required and then refer you to the table to obtain the appropriate hourly rating. The Plan in Figure 5.4 is an example of separate fire areas being created within a Factory occupancy. One area of the factory is considered F-2 because it contains materials that are considered low hazard. The other part of the factory contains more hazardous materials and is considered an F-1. Knowing this and using the *IBC* table in Figure 5.5, you can determine that the rating of the fire barrier between the fire areas is 3 hours. (The strictest requirement applies.) This may allow one area to be sprinklered and the other to be unsprinklered. You can also see from the table that certain occupancies such as Hazardous can require separation as high as 4 hours.

TABLE 706.3.7
FIRE-RESISTANCE RATING REQUIREMENTS FOR FIRE BARRIER ASSEMBLIES BETWEEN FIRE AREAS

OCCUPANCY GROUP	FIRE-RESISTANCE RATING (hours)
H-1, H-2	4
F-1, H-3, S-1	3
A, B, E, F-2, H-4, H-5, I, M, R, S-2	2
U	1

Figure 5.5 *International Building Code (IBC)* Table 706.3.7 Fire-Resistance Rating Requirements for Fire Barrier Assemblies Between Fire Areas (*International Building Code* 2003. Copyright 2002. Falls Church, Virginia: International Code Council, Inc. Reproduced with permission. All rights reserved.)

Occupancy Separation

When more than one type of occupancy exists within a building or space, it is considered a mixed occupancy or a multiple occupancy, depending on which code you are using. It can be treated as a separated or non-separated mixed occupancy or as a separated or mixed multiple occupancy. (See the discussion of mixed and multiple occupancies in Chapter 2.) In order for it to be considered separated, each occupancy must be separated from the other by a fire barrier. Occupancy separation can be used in two distinct ways: (1) separation may occur between separate tenants of different occupancy classifications, such as a restaurant (A or B) located next to a retail store (M); or (2) separation may occur within a single tenant that includes two or more different occupancies, such as a furniture store (M) that has an attached warehouse (S). (If one occupancy type is considered an accessory occupancy to the other, separation by rated walls may not be required. See Accessory Occupancies in Chapter 2.)

Note

Compartmentation is an important concept in the fire codes. It is used to prevent the spread of fire and is especially important in high-rise and Institutional buildings.

Typically, fire barriers for occupancy separation must a have a 1-hour or a 2-hour fire rating. Each building code and the *LSC* use a table similar to the *IBC* Table 302.3.2, "Required Separation of Occupancies (hours)," shown in Figure 5.6. You compare the occupancy classification of the adjacent tenants to determine which hourly rating to use. For example, in Plan A of Figure 5.7, there is a Mercantile occupancy adjacent to a Business occupancy. To determine the rating of the wall between these occupancies, you must refer to the table in Figure 5.6. Using the table, locate Mercantile (M) along the top row and Business (B) in the left column. When you find where the Mercantile row and the Business column meet, a rating of 2 hours is indicated. Therefore, the wall that separates these two occupancy classifications must be rated a minimum of 2 hours. (You may have to look up the occupancies in both directions to find the rating.) The table also leads you to some notes at the bottom that offers exceptions based on the specific circumstance.

Note

The top of a fire *partition* as required by the *IBC* is allowed to terminate at a nonrated floor/ceiling assembly. This is typical of an exit access corridor.

Occupancy separation can be required vertically as well. For example, if a Storage (S-1) use was located below the Business (B) or Mercantile (M) use, you could use the table again to determine that a 3-hour fire-resistance separation is required between these occupancies. The floor assembly then would need to provide the required rating. Since floor/ceiling assemblies can also be regulated by construction types, you should check this rating as well and use the strictest requirement. For example, if you are working on a project in an existing building requiring a 3-hour-rated floor assembly, you would need to check the rating of the floor assembly based on the construction type of the building. If the existing floor assembly provides only a 1-hour rating, for example, additional rated materials would be necessary to increase the fire resistance to 3 hours as required by the codes. If the floor assembly meets or exceeds the required occupancy separation requirement, no additional materials are necessary.

Note

The top of a fire *barrier* is typically not allowed to terminate at a floor/ceiling assembly unless the rating of the assembly is equal to that of the fire barrier.

TABLE 302.3.2
REQUIRED SEPARATION OF OCCUPANCIES (HOURS)[a]

USE	A-1	A-2	A-3	A-4	A-5	B[b]	E	F-1	F-2	H-1	H-2	H-3	H-4	H-5	I-1	I-2	I-3	I-4	M[b]	R-1	R-2	R-3, R-4	S-1	S-2[c]	U
A-1	—	2	2	2	2	2	2	3	2	NP	4	3	2	4	2	2	2	2	2	2	2	2	3	2	1
A-2[e]	—	—	2	2	2	2	2	3	2	NP	4	3	2	4	2	2	2	2	2	2	2	2	3	2	1
A-3	—	—	—	2	2	2	2	3	2	NP	4	3	2	4	2	2	2	2	2	2	2	2	3	2	1
A-4	—	—	—	—	2	2	2	3	2	NP	4	3	2	4	2	2	2	2	2	2	2	2	3	2	1
A-5	—	—	—	—	—	2	2	3	2	NP	4	3	2	4	2	2	2	2	2	2	2	2	3	2	1
B[b]	—	—	—	—	—	—	2	3	2	NP	2	1	1	1	2	2	2	2	2	2	2	2	3	2	1
E	—	—	—	—	—	—	—	3	2	NP	4	3	2	3	2	2	2	2	2	2	2	2	3	2	1
F-1	—	—	—	—	—	—	—	—	3	NP	2	1	1	1	3	3	3	3	3	3	3	3	3	3	3
F-2	—	—	—	—	—	—	—	—	—	NP	2	1	1	1	2	2	2	2	2	2	2	2	3	2	1
H-1	—	—	—	—	—	—	—	—	—	—	NP	NP	NP	NP	NP	NP	NP	NP	NP	NP	NP	NP	NP	NP	NP
H-2	—	—	—	—	—	—	—	—	—	—	—	1	2	2	4	4	4	4	2	4	4	4	2	2	1
H-3	—	—	—	—	—	—	—	—	—	—	—	—	1	1	4	3	3	3	1	3	3	3	1	1	1
H-4	—	—	—	—	—	—	—	—	—	—	—	—	—	1	4	4	4	4	1	4	4	4	1	1	1
H-5	—	—	—	—	—	—	—	—	—	—	—	—	—	—	4	4	4	3	1	4	4	4	1	1	3
I-1	—	—	—	—	—	—	—	—	—	—	—	—	—	—	—	2	2	2	2	2	2	2	4	3	2
I-2	—	—	—	—	—	—	—	—	—	—	—	—	—	—	—	—	2	2	2	2	2	2	3	2	1
I-3	—	—	—	—	—	—	—	—	—	—	—	—	—	—	—	—	—	2	2	2	2	2	3	2	1
I-4	—	—	—	—	—	—	—	—	—	—	—	—	—	—	—	—	—	—	2	2	2	2	3	2	1
M[b]	—	—	—	—	—	—	—	—	—	—	—	—	—	—	—	—	—	—	—	2	2	2	3	2	1
R-1	—	—	—	—	—	—	—	—	—	—	—	—	—	—	—	—	—	—	—	—	2	2	3	2	1
R-2	—	—	—	—	—	—	—	—	—	—	—	—	—	—	—	—	—	—	—	—	—	2	3	2	1
R-3, R-4	—	—	—	—	—	—	—	—	—	—	—	—	—	—	—	—	—	—	—	—	—	—	3	2[d]	1[d]
S-1	—	—	—	—	—	—	—	—	—	—	—	—	—	—	—	—	—	—	—	—	—	—	—	3	3
S-2[c]	—	—	—	—	—	—	—	—	—	—	—	—	—	—	—	—	—	—	—	—	—	—	—	—	1
U	—	—	—	—	—	—	—	—	—	—	—	—	—	—	—	—	—	—	—	—	—	—	—	—	—

For SI: 1 square foot = 0.0929 m^2.
NP = Not permitted.
a. See Exception 1 to Section 302.3.2 for reductions permitted.
b. Occupancy separation need not be provided for storage areas within Groups B and M if the:
1. Area is less than 10 percent of the floor area;
2. Area is provided with an automatic fire-extinguishing system and is less than 3,000 square feet; or
3. Area is less than 1,000 square feet.
c. Areas used only for private or pleasure vehicles shall be allowed to reduce separation by 1 hour.
d. See exception to Section 302.3.2.
e. Commercial kitchens need not be separated from the restaurant seating areas that they serve.

Figure 5.6 *International Building Code (IBC)* Table 302.3.2, Required Separation of Occupancies (Hours) (*International Building Code* 2003.

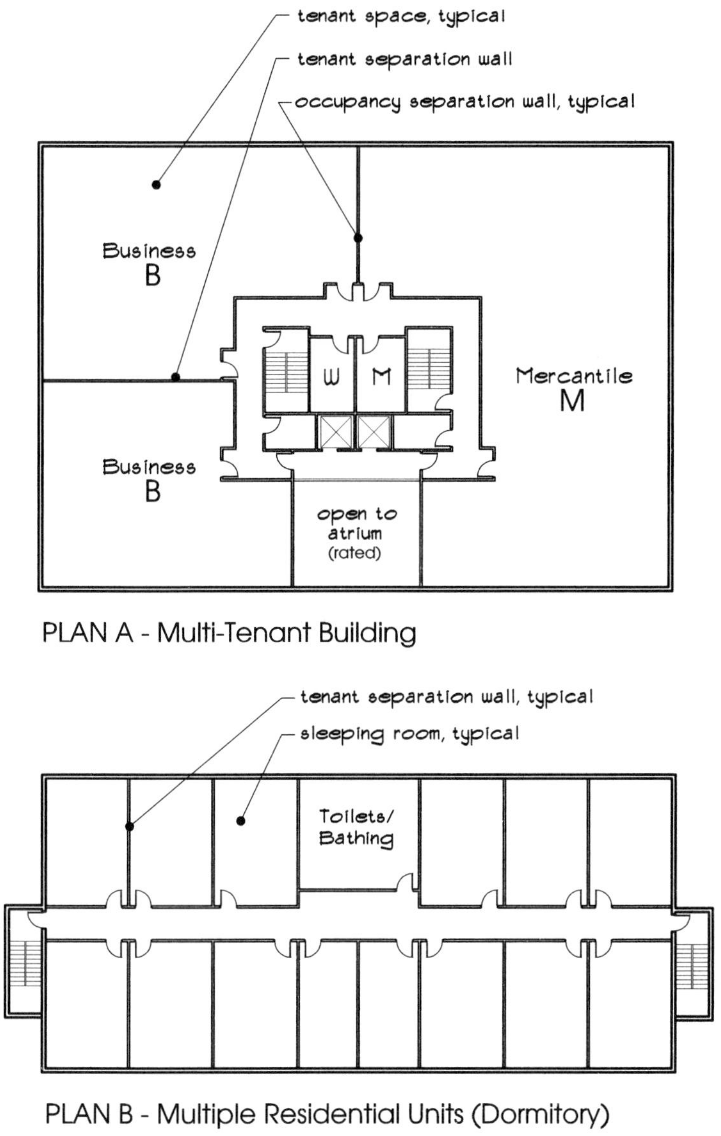

Figure 5.7 Tenant and Occupancy Separation

Tenant Separation

In most cases, individual tenants of the same occupancy within a multi-tenant building and each sleeping room or dwelling unit within a Residential occupancy are required by the codes to be separated. Examples would include the different businesses in an office building and a covered mall or different units in a hotel and an apartment building. Depending on the code, fire barriers or fire partition walls

Note

Tenant separation walls are typically less restrictive than occupancy separation walls.

Note

Walls that divide living units, such as sleeping rooms in hotels and dormitories and dwelling units in apartment buildings, must also meet sound transition code requirements. (See environmental chapter in building codes.)

can be used. These walls are also known as *demising walls*. Their most common fire rating is one hour. However, the exact rating required depends on the occupancy involved. For example, the adjacent Business (B) occupancies in Plan A of Figure 5.7 would require a tenant separation wall rather than an occupancy separation wall as described in the last section. The walls between each sleeping room or dwelling unit in the dormitory in Plan B of Figure 5.7 would also need to be tenant separation walls.

Separation requirements between tenants, however, do not apply to tenants from floor to floor as they do with occupancy separation. In other words, the floor assemblies do not have to meet the tenant separation requirements. For example, even if a 1-hour separation is required between sleeping units in the dormitory, as shown in Plan B of Figure 5.7, the floor/ceiling assembly between the first and second floor would not be required to have a rating of 1 hour. Another example would be the walls between dwelling units in an apartment building. In this case, the rating of the floor/ceiling assembly would be determined only by the construction type, meaning it may have a higher rating or no rating at all.

Each code lists the demising wall requirements in different areas of the text. You may have to compare several tables and written requirements to determine the highest rating to use. Sprinkler systems will also affect the required rating.

Incidental Use Areas or Rooms

Note

The quantity and cost of fire-resistance-rated walls are reduced by designing rooms with like fire ratings adjacent to each other; for example, an employee locker room next to the kitchen.

The codes require that certain rooms, such as machine rooms and storage rooms within a building be separated from the other parts of the building. These are called *incidental uses*. (See the discussion of incidental use areas in Chapter 2.) The codes require these rooms to be enclosed by fire barriers. The required ratings are given in the text and by tables within the codes. The *IBC* Table 302.1.1, "Incidental Use Areas," in Figure 5.8, lists the types of uses or rooms that are considered incidental within the *IBC*.

If one of these rooms is located in a building or particular occupancy, you might need to provide additional fire protection. For example, the storage room shown in the unsprinklered building in Figure 5.9 is 180 square feet (16.7 s m). If you go to the *IBC* table in Figure 5.8, you can see that storage rooms over 100 square feet (9.3 s m) are required to be separated by a fire barrier with a rating of 1 hour or be sprinklered. Because this building is unsprinklered, this room would require fire protection to keep it separate from the rest of the space. Notice in the table that for many of the incidental use areas, an automatic sprinkler system can be provided instead of the fire barrier, and in some cases both a fire barrier and an automatic sprinkler system are required. The NFPA codes list similar information within each occupancy chapter.

TABLE 302.1.1
INCIDENTAL USE AREAS

ROOM OR AREA	SEPARATION[a]
Furnace room where any piece of equipment is over 400,000 Btu per hour input	1 hour or provide automatic fire-extinguishing system
Rooms with any boiler over 15 psi and 10 horsepower	1 hour or provide automatic fire-extinguishing system
Refrigerant machinery rooms	1 hour or provide automatic sprinkler system
Parking garage (Section 406.2)	2 hours; or 1 hour and provide automatic fire-extinguishing system
Hydrogen cut-off rooms	1-hour fire barriers and floor/ceiling assemblies in Group B, F, H, M, S and U occupancies. 2-hour fire barriers and floor/ceiling assemblies in Group A, E, I and R occupancies.
Incinerator rooms	2 hours and automatic sprinkler system
Paint shops, not classified as Group H, located in occupancies other than Group F	2 hours; or 1 hour and provide automatic fire-extinguishing system
Laboratories and vocational shops, not classified as Group H, located in Group E or I-2 occupancies	1 hour or provide automatic fire-extinguishing system
Laundry rooms over 100 square feet	1 hour or provide automatic fire-extinguishing system
Storage rooms over 100 square feet	1 hour or provide automatic fire-extinguishing system
Group I-3 cells equipped with padded surfaces	1 hour
Group I-2 waste and linen collection rooms	1 hour
Waste and linen collection rooms over 100 square feet	1 hour or provide automatic fire-extinguishing system
Stationary lead-acid battery systems having a liquid capacity of more than 100 gallons used for facility standby power, emergency power or uninterrupted power supplies	1-hour fire barriers and floor/ceiling assemblies in Group B, F, H, M, S and U occupancies. 2-hour fire barriers and floor/ceiling assemblies in Group A, E, I and R occupancies

For SI: 1 square foot = 0.0929 m^2, 1 pound per square inch = 6.9 kPa, 1 British thermal unit = 0.293 watts, 1 horsepower = 746 watts, 1 gallon = 3.785 L.

a. Where an automatic fire-extinguishing system is provided, it need only be provided in the incidental use room or area.

Figure 5.8 *International Building Code (IBC)* Table 302.1.1, Incidental Use Areas (*International Building Code* 2003. Copyright 2002. Falls Church, Virginia: International Code Council, Inc. Reproduced with permission. All rights reserved.)

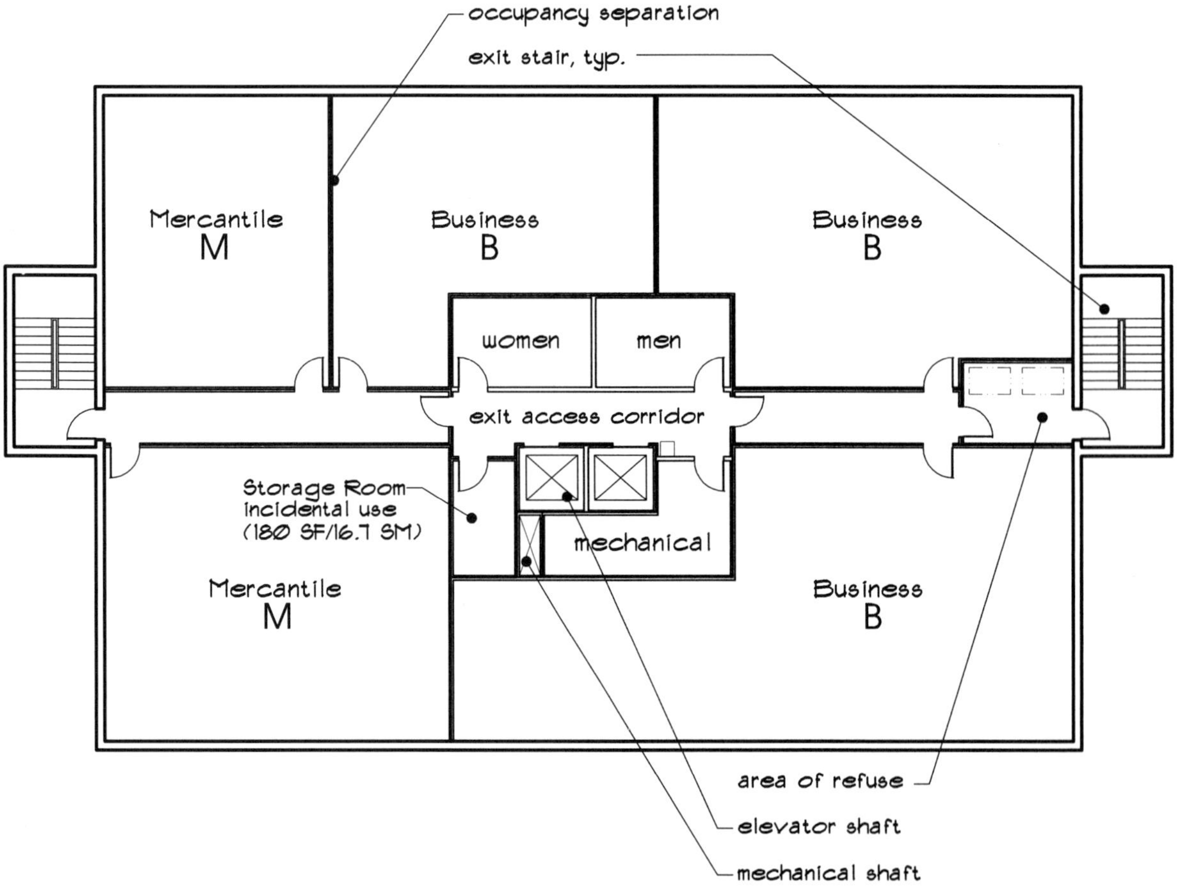

Figure 5.9 Rated Building Components (nonsprinklered building)

Vertical Shaft Enclosures

Fire barriers are used to create vertical shaft enclosures for such things as elevators, dumbwaiters, and building systems such as mechanical chases. Examples of these are shown in Figure 5.9. A stairwell can be considered a vertical shaft as well. The fire ratings for vertical shaft enclosures are primarily determined by the number of floors that they penetrate. Typically a 1-hour or 2-hour separation is required. These walls are usually continuous from the bottom of the building to the underside of the roof deck. When a shaft terminates at a floor level, the top and bottom of the shaft may also be required to be rated.

> **Note**
> Shafts used for refuse and laundry chutes have additional requirements. Refer to the building codes.

For elevators, the codes limit the number of elevator cars in a single shaft or hoistway enclosure to usually no more than two to four elevators. If more elevators are used, additional rated walls will be required to separate them. In addition, each shaft often requires specific venting, smoke detection, and standby power. (See section on Elevators in Chapter 4 on page 144.) The rating of an elevator shaft is also determined by the number of floors that it penetrates. (Also see Smokeproof Vertical Shafts and Stairs later in this chapter.)

Note

Atriums also have additional fire protection requirements. See the inset titled *Atriums and Mezzanines* on p. 103 and the codes for specifics.

Means of Egress Components

In many cases, parts of the means of egress as discussed in Chapter 4 are required to be separated by fire barriers. These may include stairwells, exit passageways, horizontal exits, and other exit enclosures. In most cases, the fire-resistance rating must be provided both vertically and horizontally. The ratings typically get stricter as you move toward the exit. For example, an exit access may require a 1-hour rating, and the exit may require a 2-hour rating. As the different means of egress are discussed, refer to Figure 5.10 for examples of the components that require fire-resistance ratings. Within the building codes and the *LSC*, these requirements are given in tables and within the chapters that discuss fire-resistance ratings and occupancy requirements.

Stairs

Typically, the walls that enclose *exit stairs* must meet the same requirements as a vertical shaft. Usually these stairs must have a 1-hour rating if the stairs are three stories or less and a 2-hour rating if they are four or more stories. Protection from smoke may also be required. (See Chapter 4 for additional information on stairs.) An *exit access stair* may also require a fire-rated enclosure if it connects more than two floors.

The walls surrounding a rated stairwell must be vertically continuous through each floor and fully enclose the stair. In most cases, the floor and ceiling of an exit access stair must also be rated. To protect the fire ratings of the walls, only limited penetrations are allowed. In addition, when a large building has more than one enclosed exit stairway, one may be required to be smokeproof to serve as an area of refuge. (See the next section on Smoke Barriers.)

Note

When dead space below a fire-rated stairway is used for storage, it cannot block the means of egress in any way. That means the door into the storage must be outside the stair enclosure. And the storage compartment must be totally surrounded by fire-rated assemblies that have the same rating as the stair enclosure.

Horizontal Exits

A horizontal exit is used to provide an alternate exiting method within a building. It uses a fire barrier to provide an exit from one space into another on the same floor of a building. (This is discussed in more detail in Chapter 4.) Although a horizontal exit in effect creates separate areas within a building in a similar

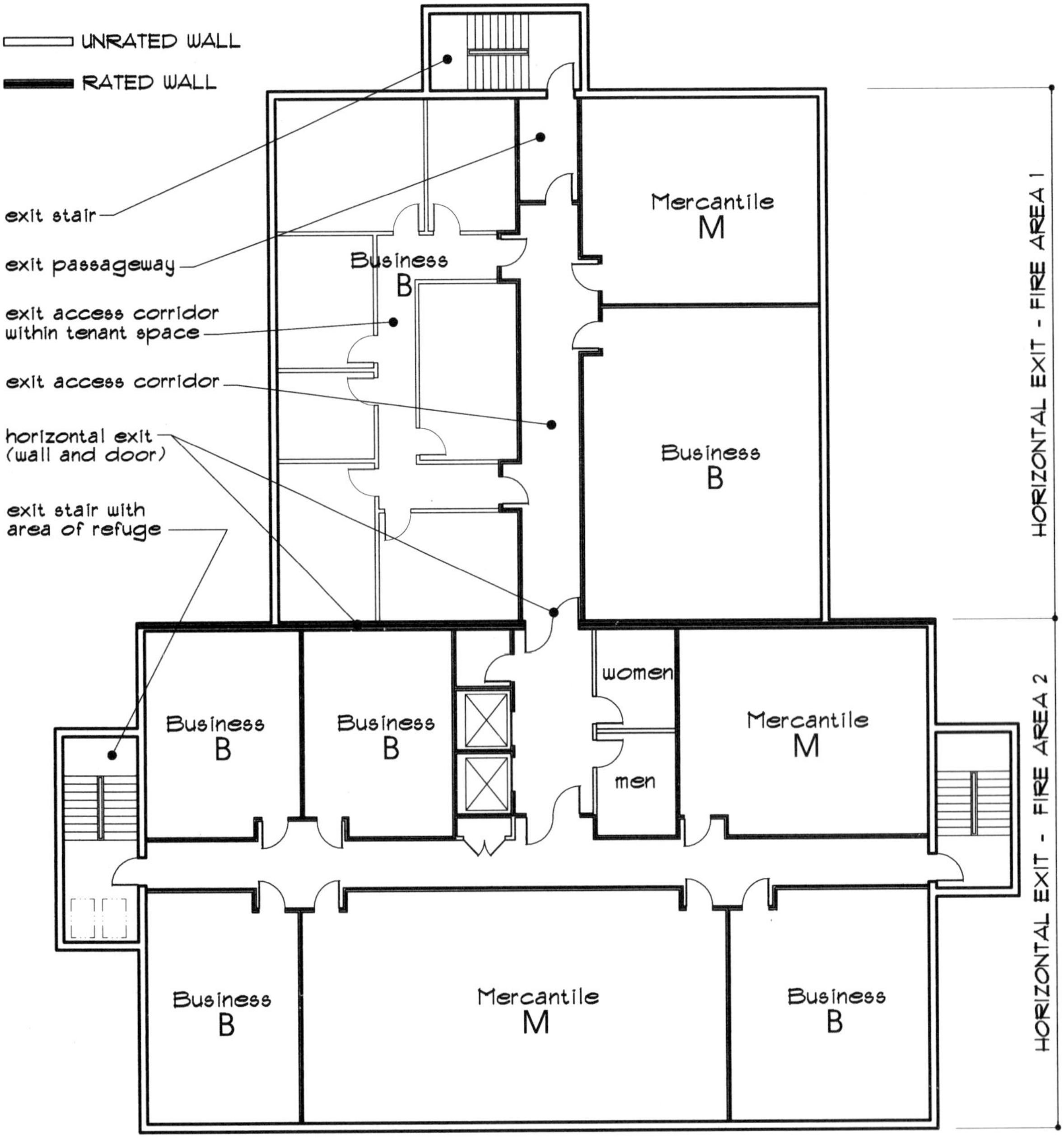

Figure 5.10 Rated Means of Egress Components (nonsprinklered building)

manner to fire areas, the intent of the separation is different. A fire area is created to limit the spread of fire. A horizontal exit, on the other hand, provides an exit away from the fire. A horizontal exit also usually includes smoke protection. Typically, the required rating of the wall is 2 hours and the wall must extend to the exterior walls.

Corridors

Exit access corridors are corridors that lead to an exit or an exit stairwell. The rating of exit access corridors ranges from ½ hour to 1 hour. Refer to the *IBC* Table 1016.1, "Corridor Fire-Resistance Rating" in Figure 5.11. You can see that based on the occupancy type, the occupant load served by the corridor, and whether the building is sprinklered, you can determine the rating of the corridor. (See Chapter 2 for occupant load information.) For example, an exit access corridor for a Business (B) occupancy that has an occupant load greater than 30 and is unsprinklered, a rating of 1 hour is required. If the building was sprinklered, then the corridor would not be required to be rated. If the same Business occupancy had an occupant load less than 30, the exit access corridor would not be required to be rated. Typically, corridors within a small tenant space do not require a rating. However, exit access corridors that serve an entire floor are usually required to be rated, especially in nonsprinklered buildings.

Note

Within a single tenant space, rated corridors are often not required. The rating of a corridor within a building depends on whether the building is sprinklered.

The *IBC* considers the walls in an exit access corridor to be a type of fire partition. Therefore, if the exit access corridor is required to have a fire-resistance rating, it does not apply to the floor assembly or ceiling assembly above the

TABLE 1016.1
CORRIDOR FIRE-RESISTANCE RATING

OCCUPANCY	OCCUPANT LOAD SERVED BY CORRIDOR	REQUIRED FIRE-RESISTANCE RATING (hours)	
		Without sprinkler system	With sprinkler system[c]
H-1, H-2, H-3	All	Not Permitted	1
H-4, H-5	Greater than 30	Not Permitted	1
A, B, E, F, M, S, U	Greater than 30	1	0
R	Greater than 10	1	0.5
I-2[a], I-4	All	Not Permitted	0
I-1, I-3	All	Not Permitted	1[b]

a. For requirements for occupancies in Group I-2, see Section 407.3.
b. For a reduction in the fire-resistance rating for occupancies in Group I-3, see Section 408.7.
c. Buildings equipped throughout with an automatic sprinkler system in accordance with Section 903.3.1.1 or 903.3.1.2 where allowed.

Figure 5.11 *International Building Code (IBC)* Table 1016.1 Corridor Fire-Resistance Rating (*International Building Code* 2003. Copyright 2002. Falls Church, Virginia: International Code Council, Inc. Reproduced with permission. All rights reserved.)

partition. Instead, these ratings would be based on the construction type of the building.

Corridors used as exits, however, such as *exit passageways*, usually must have a 2-hour fire rating. In this case, both the *IBC* and the NFPA codes require that a fire barrier be used and that the floor and ceiling assemblies provide the same fire resistance rating as the walls. For example, if a stairwell with a rating of 2 hours emptied into a lobby, then the lobby would be considered an exit discharge component and would have to maintain the 2-hour rating. You must refer to the specific requirements of each exit component to determine the required rating.

Note

Suspended acoustical ceilings alone do not typically possess a fire-resistance rating, but they could possibly be used as part of a rated floor/ceiling assembly.

SMOKE BARRIERS AND SMOKE PARTITIONS

Smoke barriers and smoke partitions are another part of the passive fire-protection system. Smoke barriers typically provide a higher level of protection than smoke partitions and are often used to create compartments. Smoke barriers *restrict* the movement or passage of smoke and fire gases and are often required to have a fire-resistance rating. Smoke partitions only *limit* the passage of smoke and fire gases and are typically not required to have a fire resistance rating. The idea of smoke partitions was developed by the ICC and the NFPA to take the place of numerous exceptions that had allowed smoke barriers to be nonrated.

Smoke barriers must be continuous and sealed completely where there are joints and where they meet other smoke barriers, smoke/fire barriers, and exterior walls. A smoke barrier can consist of either a *wall assembly* or a *full enclosure*. A full enclosure consists of walls, ceilings, and floor assemblies that create a continuous smokeproof compartment. Vertically, smoke barriers must extend from the floor below to the ceiling assembly above. When used horizontally as a floor/ceiling assembly, they must extend to a smoke barrier wall or an exterior wall.

Smoke barriers are required by the code to separate and protect different types of situations. Although they often require a fire-resistance rating, walls with a rating do not necessarily resist smoke. Therefore, the codes also limit the penetrations allowed in the smoke barrier. If a penetration is allowed, additional requirement, are specified. For example, the building codes include requirements for the use of doors including the type of door, the use of automatic release door closers, and the operation of the door. Smoke dampers are often required at mechanical ducts.

Note

Smoke barriers typically provide a higher level of protection than smoke partitions.

A *smoke partition*, on the other hand, may be allowed by the codes when a lesser degree of protection from smoke is acceptable for life safety. Unlike smoke barriers, smoke partitions can terminate at suspended ceilings systems and some solid ceilings as described by the codes. (Similar to fire partitions, as shown in

Figure 5.3.) The ceilings are also allowed to be penetrated by certain items such as speakers, recessed lighting, diffusers, and similar ceiling elements not typically allowed in smoke barriers. Other requirements also tend to be less restrictive. For example, in some cases a duct passing through a smoke partition may not require a smoke damper. However, other penetrations are regulated. These will be discussed in the section on Opening Protectives later in this chapter.

Other requirements for smoke barriers and smoke partitions may depend on their specific use. Many of these requirements are specified in the building codes, the fire codes, and the *LSC*. The mechanical codes include requirements as well. Be sure to consult a mechanical engineer when required. (See Chapter 7.) Additional requirements are specified in NFPA standards such as such as *NFPA 92A, Smoke Control Systems* and *NFPA 92B, Smoke Management Systems in Malls, Atria, and Large Assemblies*.

The various uses of smoke barriers and smoke partitions as walls and full enclosures are discussed next.

SMOKE AND HOW IT TRAVELS

To gain a better understanding of smoke control systems and how they work, it is important to know how smoke moves. The Council on Tall Buildings and Urban Habitat, in the book *Fire Safety in Tall Buildings,* describes five major driving forces that cause smoke movement:

1. *Buoyancy:* As the temperature of smoke increases during a fire, it becomes buoyant, due to its reduced density. As the buoyancy increases, a pressure builds and the smoke is forced up through any available leakage paths to the floor above and to adjacent areas.
2. *Expansion:* As a fire develops it emits gases. These gases expand and create pressure, causing smoke to be forced out of an enclosed fire compartment.
3. *HVAC:* As a fire progresses, the HVAC system can transport smoke to every area it serves. The system can also supply air to a fire, increasing its intensity.
4. *Stack effect:* Stack effect is a result of exterior air temperature. Generally, if it is cold outside there is usually an upward movement of air within the building shafts, such as stairwells, elevators, and mechanical shafts. When the outside air is warmer than the building air, the airflow moves downward. This air movement can move smoke a considerable distance from a fire.
5. *Wind*: Windows frequently break during a fire, causing outside wind to force smoke through doors into adjacent spaces and other floors.

In a fire situation, smoke movement can be caused by one or more of these driving forces. That is why the correct use and placement of smoke barriers can be critical. (The three stages of a fire are explained in the inset titled *Stages of Fire Development* in Chapter 9.)

Smoke Compartments

Smoke compartments are sometimes created within a building where protection from smoke is required. These compartments are created by smoke barriers. Although smoke barrier walls extend from outside wall to outside wall and from floor slab to floor slab, they do not necessarily have a fire-resistance rating. To create a smoke compartment, wall, floor, and ceiling assemblies are used to construct the full smoke enclosure. An example would be a stairwell with an area of refuge.

To make them smoke resistant, only limited openings are allowed in the smoke barrier. In full enclosures additional mechanical functions are required for ventilation and air circulation. A smoke detector typically activates the ventilation system and automatically closes all doors with a closing device.

Smoke compartments are also used in Institutional occupancies to subdivide floors used by patients for sleeping or treatment for greater safety. Each compartment created by the smoke barrier provides a temporary area of refuge from the adjacent compartment. These are different from horizontal exits and are not usually considered exits. Horizontal exits require a fire barrier and a smoke barrier, which provides another way to protect the occupants in the event of a fire. (See the section titled Horizontal Exits in this chapter and Chapter 4.) In most cases, occupancies that call for smoke compartments are required to be sprinklered.

Smokeproof Vertical Shafts

Vertical shaft enclosures for stairs, elevators, and waste and linen chutes in some cases must be smokeproof, especially if a building is over a certain height. As mentioned earlier, the walls and openings of all vertical shafts must be fire rated. To make them smokeproof, all openings into the shaft must automatically close upon detection of smoke. A *smokestop door* is usually also required. This is a door specially designed to close tightly and inhibit the passage of smoke. (See section on Rated Door Assemblies later in the chapter.) This door is typically connected to the smoke detection and standby power system in the building.

To create the necessary smoke protection, smokeproof shafts also typically need to be pressurized. Certain mechanical components are used so that, should a fire occur, the smoke does not get sucked into the vertical shaft.

Vestibules

Any vestibule adjacent to a smokeproof stairwell or elevator hoistway that is located between the shaft and the exterior exit door must also be smokeproof.

The codes require the vestibule to be a certain size. The doors must also be fire rated, have self-closing devices, and have a drop sill to minimize air leakage.

The ceiling of the vestibule must be high enough so that it serves as a smoke and heat trap and allows an upward-moving airflow. Ventilation is required as well. It might be as simple as an opening in an exterior wall for *natural* ventilation. The most common is *mechanical* ventilation with vents opening to the outside air. The codes regulate a number of items such as the type of system used, the amount of supply and exhaust air, and the location of duct openings. (See Chapter 7.)

Note

The type of vestibule used in conjunction with a stair shaft or elevator hoistway and the presence of an automatic sprinkler system can affect the codes required for smokeproof enclosures.

OPENING PROTECTIVES

An opening protective is a rated assembly that prevents the spread of fire or smoke through an opening in a rated wall. An opening protective is usually a door or a view window. Unlike wall and floor/ceiling assemblies that are assigned a fire-resistance rating, door assemblies are assigned a *fire-protection rating*. The required rating of the opening protective component is determined by the rating of the wall in which it is located. Not only are the ratings important to the integrity of the entire wall during a fire to stop the spread of fire and smoke, but they are also crucial for the evacuation of the occupants during a fire. Opening protectives can also be considered a type of through-penetration system, which is discussed later in the chapter. Through-penetration components control openings required by wiring, ducts, pipes, and similar penetrations in a building. Both are components that are intended to maintain the integrity of a rated wall or floor/ceiling assembly.

Note

Membrane penetrations are not the same as through-penetrations. Instead of piercing the entire thickness of the assembly, membrane penetrations penetrate only one side, or "membrane." Examples include electrical outlets in drywall and HVAC ducts that pierce suspended ceilings. (See Chapter 8 and Figure 8.3.)

The fire-protection ratings for opening protectives are determined by the building codes, the same codes that determine construction assemblies. The *IBC* has two tables that must be referenced. These are shown in Figure 5.12. They include Table 715.3, "Fire Door and Fire Shutter Fire Protection Ratings," and Table 715.4, "Fire Window Assembly Fire Protection Ratings." These tables indicate which rated opening protective is required for each type of rated construction assembly. Based on the fire-resistance rating of the wall or partition, you can determine the fire-protection rating of the fire door assembly or fire window assembly. You need to know the type of construction assembly and its required rating. For example, if you plan to add a door in an existing 2-hour fire barrier, the first table tells you it would require a 1½-hour-rated fire door assembly. However, if you wanted to add a window, the second table indicates that it would not be allowed—or not permitted (NP). (Note how the rating of the opening protective is typically lower than the construction assembly.) The *NFPA 5000* combines the information for fire doors and fire windows into one table and the *LSC* includes

TABLE 715.3
FIRE DOOR AND FIRE SHUTTER FIRE PROTECTION RATINGS

TYPE OF ASSEMBLY	REQUIRED ASSEMBLY RATING (hours)	MINIMUM FIRE DOOR AND FIRE SHUTTER ASSEMBLY RATING (hours)
Fire walls and fire barriers having a required fire-resistance rating greater than 1 hour	4 3 2 $1^1/_2$	3 3[a] $1^1/_2$ $1^1/_2$
Fire barriers having a required fire-resistance rating of 1 hour: Shaft exit enclosure and exit passageway walls Other fire barriers	 1 1	 1 $^3/_4$
Fire partitions: Corridor walls Other fire partitions	 1 0.5 1	 $^1/_3$[b] $^1/_3$[b] $^3/_4$
Exterior walls	3 2 1	$1^1/_2$ $1^1/_2$ $^3/_4$

a. Two doors, each with a fire protection rating of $1^1/_2$ hours, installed on opposite sides of the same opening in a fire wall, shall be deemed equivalent in fire protection rating to one 3-hour fire door.
b. For testing requirements, see Section 715.3.3.

TABLE 715.4
FIRE WINDOW ASSEMBLY FIRE PROTECTION RATINGS

TYPE OF ASSEMBLY	REQUIRED ASSEMBLY RATING (hours)	MINIMUM FIRE WINDOW ASSEMBLY RATING (hours)
Interior walls: Fire walls Fire barriers and fire partitions Smoke barriers	 All > 1 1 1	 NP[a] NP[a] $^3/_4$ $^3/_4$
Exterior walls	>1 1	$1^1/_2$ $^3/_4$
Party walls	All	NP[a]

a. Not permitted except as specified in Section 715.2.

Figure 5.12 *International Building Code (IBC)* Table 715.3, Fire Door and Fire Shutter Fire Protection Ratings, and Table 715.4, Fire Window Assembly Fire Protection Ratings (*International Building Code* 2003. Copyright 2002. Falls Church, Virginia: International Code Council, Inc. Reproduced with permission. All rights reserved.)

Note

Fire-rated doors and windows are designed to protect the opening under normal conditions with clear space on both sides. When combustible materials are stored against them, the protection is not guaranteed.

this information within its text. The building codes and the *LSC* also direct you to a number of NFPA publications and standards for additional information. For example, *NFPA 80, Standard for Fire Doors and Windows* is specified for the installation of fire doors and windows. Others, as explained later, are specifically for fire and smoke testing.

The intent of the codes and other standards is to regulate openings in rated walls, floors, and ceilings so that the required rated construction does not lose its effectiveness. The most common opening protectives are described next.

Rated Door Assemblies

As mentioned in Chapter 4, the codes actually describe doors as door assemblies. A typical door assembly consists of three main components: door, frame, and hardware. The doorway (or wall opening) can also be considered part of the door assembly—including the lintel above and the threshold below. Other doors, such as the rated doors listed in Figure 5.13, may consist of even more parts. If the door is a fire door, the whole assembly must be tested and rated as one unit. Each of the following door components has certain characteristics that make it fire rated.

RATED DOORS	RATED WINDOWS	RATED GLAZING
Access Doors	Casement Windows	Clear Ceramics
Accordion/Folding Doors	Double Hung Windows	Insulated Glass
Bi-Parting Doors	Glass Block	Laminated Glass
Conveying System Doors	Hinged Windows	Light Diffusing Plastic
Chute Doors	Pivot Windows	Light Transmitting Plastic
Dutch Doors	Side Lights	Fire-Rated Glazing
Floor Fire Door	Stationary Windows	Tempered Glass
Hoistway Doors	Tilting Windows	Transparent Ceramics
Horizontal Doors	Transom Windows	Wire Glass
Rolling Steel Doors	View Panels	
Service Counter Doors		
Swinging Doors		
Vertical Sliding Doors		

Figure 5.13 Types of Regulated Opening Protectives

Door and Frame

If the wall is fire rated, the door and frame must be rated as well. Because a protection rating is assigned to the entire door assembly, fire doors are typically specified and sold by the manufacturer as a whole unit. To obtain a rating, the door and frame must undergo a fire test as specified in *NFPA 252, Standard Method of Fire Test of Door Assemblies.* A similar test is *ASTM 2074, Standard Test Method for Fire Tests of Door Assemblies, Including Positive Pressure Testing of Side-Hinged and Pivoted Swinging Door Assemblies.* (This test replaced *ASTM E152.*) Rated doors used in fire-resistance-rated floor/ceiling assemblies may also need to pass NFPA 288, *Standard Method of Fire Tests of Floor Fire Door Assemblies Installed Horizontally in Fire Resistance-Rated Floor Systems.* Both the *IBC* and the NFPA codes require fire-rated doors to be tested by a positive pressure test that better resembles actual fire conditions than previous tests. When smokestop doors are used in smoke barriers, they must undergo additional testing as required in *NFPA 105, Installation of Smoke-Control Door Assemblies* or *UL 1784, Air Leakage Tests of Door Assemblies.* Any door that passes the required tests is assigned a fire protection rating, varying from 3 hours to ⅓ hour (20 minutes), and receives a permanent label. An example of this label is shown in Figure 5.14.

Certain doors may also require a rated sill as part of the frame. For example, smokestop doors usually require a sill to maintain a continuous seal around the door. The construction of the sill can vary, depending on the type of door and the

Note

Typically, no openings except for a limited number of doors are allowed in firewalls that require a 3- to 4-hour rating.

Note

Most codes currently require positive-pressure testing of fire-rated doors. This test better represents the conditions of a fire that would cause flames to penetrate through cracks and openings in a fire door.

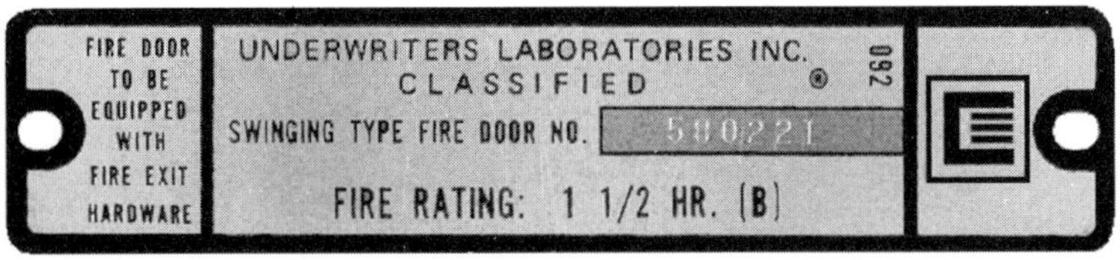

Figure 5.14 Typical Label for a Fire-Rated Assembly (Reprinted with permission from Ceco Door Products.)

construction of the floor on either side of the door. If a door requires a sill, you will need to consider the profile of the threshold. In most cases, it must meet accessibility requirements based on the ADA guidelines and the ICC/ANSI standard. (See Figure 9.19 in Chapter 9.) (Chapter 4 discusses doors in relation to size, swing, accessibility, and the means of egress concerns.)

Note

Oversize doors cannot be labeled because of their size. Instead, their approval is based on a certificate of inspection furnished by an approved testing agency.

Since doors usually undergo more stringent testing, make up only a portion of an entire wall, and are not generally exposed to the same level of fire as walls, their ratings are not as strict as those of the walls in which they are located. However, properly specified door assemblies maintain the integrity of the fire barrier. In the past, doors that had a fire-protection rating were typically flush and either solid core wood or hollow metal. And even currently very few panel doors meet the fire-protection requirements, although some are available. Recent developments in materials, including glazing, are allowing more options in configurations and finishes for rated doors. Fire-rated frames can be wood, steel (i.e., hollow metal), or aluminum depending on the rating required. The most commonly specified rated frame is hollow metal. The glazing used in fire-rated doors must also meet certain requirements. (This is discussed later in this chapter.)

Door Hardware

The most common *hardware* includes hinges, latches and locksets, pulls, and closers. Hinges, latch sets, and closing devices are the most stringently regulated on fire-rated doors. For example, fire-rated hinges must be steel or stainless steel and a specific quantity are required for each door. Both the hinges and the latch set are important to hold a fire door securely closed during a fire. To be effective they must be able to withstand the pressure and heat that are generated during a fire.

Note

When selecting fire-rated door hardware, be sure you are meeting the additional requirements set in the ADA guidelines and the ICC/ANSI standard, such as the shape of the item and height of installation. (See Chapter 4.)

Fire-rated exit doors also require a specific type of latch or pull. The most common is called fire exit hardware. Fire exit hardware is tested and rated. A similar type of hardware is called panic hardware. Both consist of a panel or bar that must be pushed to release the door latch. However, panic hardware is not tested and should not be used on fire-rated doors. The most common occupancy classifications that require fire exit hardware are Assembly and Educational. Although the codes do not require it in every occupancy, it is often used on exit doors. In occupancies that are not required to use fire exit hardware, approved lever hardware can be used.

Other issues can affect the choice of hardware on a door, including locking methods for security. (See section on Security in Chapter 8.) In addition, the *NFPA 80, Standard for Fire Doors and Fire Windows* places restrictions on the height that kickplates or other protection devices can be installed on fire doors. The requirements of the ADA guidelines and other accessibility standards should also be considered in the final selection of hardware. (See Chapter 4.) However, providing the proper means of egress and maintaining the fire rating of the doors is most important for the safety of the occupants.

The codes also require that fire-rated doors be *self-closing*. This means that the door must have a device called a closer that closes the door after each use. Closers, in general, can be surface mounted or concealed within the door, frame, or floor. You should verify that the closer application does not violate the rating of the door assembly in each case. If it is desirable that certain rated doors be open all the time, an electromagnetic or pneumatic hold-open device can be used. This device holds the door in an open position until an emergency occurs. Either a fusible link is triggered by heat or the activation of a smoke detector causes the door to close. This type of door is considered *automatic-closing* and is allowed in many occupancies within the code.

Note

The legacy codes used a letter designation of A, B, C, D, and E to indicate the type of use for a door. This system is no longer used by the ICC or the NFPA.

Note

If a building is fully sprinklered, the codes may allow an exit door to have an automatic closure with a longer than standard time delay.

Fire Window Assemblies

Windows can be a part of a door assembly, such as a transom, sidelight, or vision panel, or can be a completely separate entity. These and other types of rated windows are listed in Figure 5.13. A fire window is considered an opening protective. It is an assembly that typically consists of a frame, approved rated glazing material, and hardware. The most common interior applications for a fire-rated window are openings in corridor walls, room partitions, and smoke barriers.

Fire window assemblies are given a fire-protection rating similar to doors and are usually classified by hourly designations. Like doors, they must be tested as a complete assembly. The established testing requirements are typically specified in *NFPA 257, Standards on Fire Test of Window and Glass Block. ASTM E 2010, Standard Test Method for Positive Pressure Fire Tests of Window Assemblies* is also used. (This test replaced *ASTM E163*.) The required rating of a window depends on the location within the building. Generally, such fire-protection ratings are not greater

Note

One reason the allowed door rating is usually lower than the wall rating is because it is expected that walls will typically have combustible material such as furniture and paperwork against them. This material would contribute to the fuel should a fire occur, requiring the wall to have a higher rating. Doors are usually kept clear of such fire loads.

than one hour. However, if you refer back to the code Table 715.4 in Figure 5.12, you can see also that in some fire barriers, fire windows are not permitted at all (as indicated by NP). When the codes require a rated window assembly, the assembly must have a permanent label applied by the manufacturer guaranteeing its fire-protection rating. On the other hand, when a window is used in a smoke partition that is not fire rated, the codes do not typically require the window to have a fire-protection rating. Instead, it must be sealed to prevent the passage of smoke.

Note

If an interior window is operable and it is located in an accessible area, the operable parts should be within accessible reach ranges and have controls that are easy to operate.

Rated Glazing and Frames

Note

If a window is large enough to be mistaken for a door, the codes require a rail to be installed across the window at a specific height.

The codes set specific requirements for the size, thickness, location, and types of glazing materials that can be used in opening protectives such as fire doors and fire windows. This information is found in the building codes and the *LSC* in tables or within the text. For example, the *IBC* uses the table shown in Figure 5.15, Table 715.4.3, "Limiting Sizes of Wired Glass Panels." This is for wire glass used in rated doors or as fire windows in rated walls. In the left column, the table lists the various "Opening Fire Protection Ratings" that are allowed. The first five ratings listed on the table are specifically for rated doors. The table indicates the maximum square inches, height, and width of the glazing that can be used in the assembly based on the rating of the door. Glass lites in a door can then be any shape or configuration as long as the glazing does not exceed the sizes. Fire windows are indicated separately at the bottom of the table. (Note that the higher ratings do not allow any glazing.) Other sections of the code, including the chapter on glazing, will provide additional information.

TABLE 715.4.3
LIMITING SIZES OF WIRED GLASS PANELS

OPENING FIRE PROTECTION RATING	MAXIMUM AREA (square inches)	MAXIMUM HEIGHT (inches)	MAXIMUM WIDTH (inches)
3 hours	0	0	0
$1^1/_2$-hour doors in exterior walls	0	0	0
1 and $1^1/_2$ hours	100	33	10
$^3/_4$ hour	1,296	54	54
20 minutes	Not Limited	Not Limited	Not Limited
Fire window assemblies	1,296	54	54

For SI: 1 inch = 25.4 mm, 1 square inch = 645.2 mm^2.

Figure 5.15 *International Building Code (IBC)* Table 715.4.3, Limiting Sizes of Wired Glass Panels (*International Building Code* 2003. Copyright 2002. Falls Church, Virginia: International Code Council, Inc. Reproduced with permission. All rights reserved.)

Glazing products used in fire-rated assemblies are assessed by their ability to stay in place in the event of a fire, resistance to thermal shock in a hose stream test, strength against human contact, and resistance to heat transfer to the unexposed side. When glass products are used in a rated assembly, they must meet the requirements of *NFPA 257*. Based on the results of the test, they are given a fire-protection rating. When it is necessary that glazing products meet safety requirements, *ANSI Z97.1, Glazing Materials used in Building Safety Performance Specification and Method of Test* is used to determine the resistance to impact. This test results in a Category I and II glazing. Category I represents glazing that will resist the equivalent of the impact of a small child. Category II represents glazing that will resist the equivalent impact of a full-grown adult. Therefore a Category II is a more impact-resistant glazing.

Note

In addition to fire resistance, heat transfer must be considered when using large amounts of glass.

The basic types of rated glazing are specially tempered glass, wired glass, glass block, ceramics, laminated, and transparent wall units. Each has unique attributes based on fire protection, resistance to impact, design options, and cost-effectiveness.

Specially Tempered Glass

Not all tempered glass can be used in a rated wall. Only tempered glass that has been specially tempered can receive a 20-minute fire rating. It also meets the requirements for a Category II for impact loads. However, because it cannot withstand the hose stream test, it should not be used near sprinklers.

Wire Glass

Wire glass consists of wire mesh sandwiched between two layers of glass. The steel wire helps to distribute heat and increase the strength of the glass should a fire occur. Wired glass is rated for up to 45 minutes. Each of the codes sets requirements on the sizes allowed in rated assemblies specific to the use of wired glass. (See Figure 5.15.) Until recently, wire glass was the only acceptable glazing for a rated opening protective. It still is an affordable and dependable material for a rated window. However, wired glass does not resist impact well. It is classified only as a Category I and may not be suitable or allowed in high traffic locations in certain occupancy classifications, such as Educational.

Note

Standard fire-rated glass, such as wire glass and glass block, are given fire-*protection* ratings, while other types of glass block and fire-rated glass are typically given fire-*resistance* ratings. (Refer to the section on Test Ratings in this chapter.)

Glass Block

Glass block is typically given a rating of 45 minutes or less and is typically allowed in a wall with a maximum of a 1-hour rating. There are new types of glass block that have ratings of 60 to 90 minutes, but glass block with this type of fire-resistance rating may not be addressed in the codes. Where glass block is allowed, there are often restrictions on the area of glass block used as an interior wall. The codes also set limits when glass block is used as a view panel in a rated wall and may require the block to be installed in steel channels.

Clear Ceramics

Clear ceramics, also known as transparent ceramics, have a very high resistance to heat and can resist the thermal shock of the hose stream test. Because of this, they can be rated from 20 minutes to 3 hours. In addition, they also resist high-impact loads, usually achieving a Category II classification. These characteristics make them desirable for use in areas such as lobbies and offices where the aesthetics and safety are key.

Note

Be sure to check with the codes and standards and the jurisdiction for the specifics on these new types of glazing. They may not be allowed in every situation.

Insulated and Multilayer Laminated Glass

These products typically consist of two pieces of glass laminated together and can have various types of materials sandwiched between the glass. They are often available in ratings of 60 and 90 minutes. Some manufacturers have developed a glazing assembly that meets the requirements of a 2-hour rated wall assembly. Other products can provide only a 20-minute rating but allow greater resistance to impact.

Transparent Wall Units

Unlike laminated glass, which is used in smaller window applications, transparent wall units can be used in larger openings. They are an assembly of different materials, including glazing products, to create a unit which is transparent, fire resistant and in some cases self supporting. As part of their fire resistance, these products often use an inert material that turns into foam during a fire. Because these units are meant to take the place of conventional wall construction, they are actually tested as walls, not glazing within a wall assembly. They can be rated up to 2 hours and pass the fire-hose stream test. They also pass high-impact safety tests. A unique characteristic of these units is that they do not allow the transfer of heat from the fire side of the "wall" to the opposite side. This allows them to be used as a "full glass" barrier wall, such as at a stairwell, when approved by a code official.

Frames

All glazing materials must be fixed within a frame. Similar to door frames, fire window frames must be rated as well, to create the required fire-protection rating. Most rated glazing is installed in hollow steel frames. The rating of the frame typically matches the rating of the glazing. Rated frames are also used around the windows put into fire-rated doors and other fire-window assemblies. Even glass block is required to be installed in a steel frame in certain applications.

Like the newer glazing products, new framing products are becoming available. These framing systems are much thinner than traditional rated frames. Although some systems can be rated for only 20 to 45 minutes, others may reach a rating of 1 to 2 hours. Some products also have a resistance to the transfer of heat. The characteristics of the frame and the requirements of the codes will determine which glazing products or systems they can be used with. You will have to determine the design and performance requirements of your specific installation to correctly choose a framing system.

New glazing materials and frames continue to be developed and provide the designer with a number of design options. Because of their higher ratings, larger sheets of glass can be used. However, some of these sizes may exceed the current maximum listings of fire-rated glazing found in the building codes. The *IBC*, for example, requires glazing other than wired glass to comply with the size limitations in *NFPA 80* and the requirements of *NFPA 257*. Some jurisdictions may also require rated glazing to pass *ASTM E119, Standard Test Methods for Fire Tests of Building Construction and Materials* in order for it to be used as a fire-resistant rated wall assembly. (Other jurisdictions may not yet allow the use of glazing as a rated wall.) Performance-based requirements, however, will give more opportunity to use these materials in ways that vary from the set limitations. (See inset titled *Using Performance Codes* on page 19.)

You should work closely with the code official and manufacturers to determine which glazing product is best for your project and to assure that the glazing material you choose will provide the fire and safety protection required. All fire-rated glazing must pass the appropriate tests and standards and have a permanent label etched into the glass.

THROUGH-PENETRATION PROTECTIVES

A through-penetration is defined as an opening that pierces the entire thickness of a construction assembly, such as a wall or floor/ceiling assembly. When these construction assemblies are fire rated, the codes require the penetrations to be protected with rated assemblies such as firestops, draftstops, fireblocking, and fire dampers. (The codes also include shutters as a common opening protective.) These rated assemblies act as prevention systems and are referred to as through-penetration protection systems. Through-penetration protection systems are required to have a fire-protection rating. Not only are the ratings important to the integrity of the entire fire barrier during a fire to stop the spread of fire and smoke, they are also crucial for the evacuation of the occupants. The most common through-penetration protectives are described in this section.

Firestops

Firestops are a type of through-penetration protection system that is required in fire and smoke barriers. Their purpose is to restrict the movement of fire and hot gases through openings made in the fire-resistance rated walls and floor/ceiling or roof/ceiling assemblies. In some cases they are required to limit the transfer of heat as well. They seal and protect any opening created by penetrations, such as plumbing pipes, electrical conduit and wire, HVAC ducts, communication cables, and similar building service equipment that pass through walls, floors, and ceilings. They may also be required at the intersection of walls and ceilings and at seams in gypsum board in rated walls.

The building codes, the *NEC*, and the *LSC* require the use of listed and approved firestops in fire and smoke barriers. They are rated under *ASTM E814, Standard Test Method for Fire Tests of Through-Penetration Fire Stops* or *UL 1479, Fire Tests of Through Penetration Firestops*. (Prior to these standards being issued, they were tested under *ASTM E119*.) These tests established two ratings. An *F-rating* is based on the number of hours the firestop resists flame and hot gases, its hose stream performance, and whether it remains in the opening. The *T-rating* is stricter and includes the F-rating criteria plus a maximum temperature riser. When specifying a firestop, you need to either list one of these ratings or list the specific devices or system. Each code has slightly different criteria.

A number of noncombustible materials can be used to create firestops. These include fire-rated caulk, silicone foam, mortar, mineral wool, fire-resistive board, wire mesh, collars, and clamp bands. They can be divided into two groups: systems and devices. A *firestop system* is typically constructed in the field and added after the through-penetration has been installed. The most common way to create a firestop is to fill the open space between the penetrating item and the fire barrier with fire-rated material and finish it with an approved sealant. Or, when the openings are close to the size of the item penetrating the assembly, only the rated caulk or other sealant is required. This can be seen in Figure 8.3 in Chapter 8. The amount of damming materials and/or noncombustible sealant are specific to the location of the penetration, the dimension of the opening, the type of smoke or fire barrier, and the type and size of the penetrating item.

A *firestop device* is factory built and is typically installed as part of the through-penetration. For example, it may be a sleeve installed within the wall or floor assembly to allow a pipe to pass through, such as the one shown at the plumbing pipe in Figure 7.12 in Chapter 7. There are two types of devices that prevent the spread of flame and smoke while retarding the rise in temperature as required by a T-rating. Endothermic firestops release water when exposed to heat. This causes a cooling effect that enables the installation to meet the fire rating required by the code. An intumescent firestop expands in volume under fire conditions, forming a strong char. This expansive caulk seals the gaps created as the penetrating items melt away.

Some devices and construction elements penetrate only one side of a wall such as an electrical outlet or sprinkler head. These are called membrane penetrations. (Refer again to Figure 8.3 in Chapter 8.) Although similar, they are not technically a through-penetration. However, in a rated wall, these too must be protected. The codes define the allowable placement and size of these items within a rated wall. For example, the codes limit the size of an opening cut for an outlet box. They also require adequate filling of the area around the penetration and may require additional fireblocking depending on the location. (See Electrical Boxes in Chapter 8 for more information.)

Fireblocks and Draftstops

Fireblocks (or fireblocking) and draftstops are used as a means of restricting the spread of smoke and fire through concealed spaces should a fire occur. *Fireblocking* uses building materials to prevent the movement of air, flame, and gases through *small* concealed areas. In interior projects these could occur in several conditions, such as:

- **Dropped or coved ceilings:** If a wall stops at the underside edge of a dropped or coved ceiling, fireblocking may be required at the top of the wall to break the continuous air space.
- **Double stud walls:** When a deeper wall assembly is necessary to accommodate large pipes and mechanical ducts or for acoustical separation, a double stud wall system may be used. In a long double stud wall, fireblocking may be required at certain intervals to limit the continuous air space.
- **Stairs:** Blocking may be required at the openings at the top and bottom of a run of stairs to block the open space created between the steps and the ceiling below.
- **Concealed floor spaces:** When hardwood floors or other finishes are installed on furring strips (i.e., sleepers), fireblocking may be required at certain intervals to limit the continuous space between the sleepers.

Note

Firestops and draftstops are similar, but not the same. Firestops are used in all types of buildings to close off small spaces. Draftstops are required in combustible construction to close off large concealed spaces.

Draftstops use building materials to prevent the movement of air, smoke, gases, and flame through *large* concealed spaces. Typically these spaces include certain floor/ceiling spaces, attics, and concealed roof spaces in Residential type uses. The codes specify where draftstops are required and the allowable size of the spaces they divide. For example, the attic space in a row of townhouses might require a draftstop to be constructed above each tenant separation wall. Typically required in combustible construction types, draftstops can be required in noncombustible construction as well. However, in either type of construction, draftstopping may not be required if the building has an automatic sprinkler system.

Although there are no specific tests for materials that can be used as fireblocks and draftstops, each code lists acceptable materials within its text. They tend to be noncombustible types of materials. Some examples include gypsum board and certain sheathing and plywood materials. The material must be properly supported so that it remains in place during an initial fire.

Damper Systems

A damper is another type of opening protective. (See inset titled *Smoke and How It Travels* on page 199.) It is used specifically in HVAC systems, either where a duct passes through a rated assembly or an air transfer opening is cut into a rated assembly. It is typically specified by the mechanical engineer. It is a device arranged to automatically interrupt the flow of air during an emergency so that it restricts the passage of smoke, fire, and heat.

There are two kinds of fire or smoke damper systems: static and dynamic. A static damper automatically shuts down during a fire, whereas a dynamic damper system remains in operation even during a fire. Dynamic dampers can be used in either static or dynamic HVAC systems, but static dampers can be used only in static systems. Depending on their installation, fire and smoke dampers may also be used to control the volume of air for the heating and cooling system during normal use. When a fire occurs, the dampers stop or regulate the potential flow of heated air, smoke, or flame through the duct system. There are three main types of dampers used in HVAC systems: fire dampers, smoke dampers, and ceiling dampers. If required, combination fire and smoke dampers also are available. (There is another type of damper called a corridor damper, but since it is used primarily in California, it is not discussed in this book.) Installation of fire dampers in HVAC systems is regulated by *NFPA 90A, Standard for Installation of Air Conditioning and Ventilating Systems* and *NFPA 90B, Standard for Installation of Warm Air Heating and Air Conditioning Systems.* Each type of damper also has a specific test standard it must meet. These are mentioned as the various dampers are explained next.

Fire Dampers

Fire dampers are required by the codes in several locations. They are typically required in ducts that penetrate rated wall assemblies, at air transfer openings in rated partitions, and similar penetrations in rated floor assemblies. One can be installed within the duct or on the outside as a collar fastened to the wall or ceiling. The most common fire damper includes a fusible link on either side of the assembly the duct is penetrating. This fusible link melts during a fire when the area reaches a certain temperature, causing the fire damper to close and seal the duct. A similar system would be used on either side of an air transfer opening.

The rating of a fire damper can range from 1½ hours to 3 hours. The length of the rating is determined by the codes and depends on the rating of the fire-rated construction assembly that the duct passes through. Each building code has a table similar to the *IBC* Table 716.3.1, "Fire Damper Rating," as shown in Figure 5.16. This table indicates the required fire damper ratings based on the type of penetration. Once you know the rating of the assembly, it is easy to determine the required fire damper rating. The required fire test for fire dampers is *UL 555, Standard for Fire Dampers*. It is used to determine the hourly fire rating of a fire damper.

Smoke Dampers

Smoke dampers are similar to fire dampers, but they are activated specifically by smoke rather than heat. They are typically required when ducts penetrate a smoke barrier. Since smoke barriers are not required by the codes as often as fire-rated partitions and assemblies are, smoke dampers are not used as often as fire dampers. When the smoke damper is required, it is installed with a smoke detector. The smoke detector is typically located inside the duct, so that when it detects smoke it causes the smoke damper to close off the duct. Sometimes a smoke damper will be part of a smoke evacuation system. In the event of a fire, the action of the smoke dampers would be controlled by the system. *UL 555S, Standard for Smoke Dampers* is the test standard for smoke dampers. They are designated by four classes (Class I, Class II, Class III, and Class IV), with Class I being the most effective.

TABLE 716.3.1
FIRE DAMPER RATING

TYPE OF PENETRATION	MINIMUM DAMPER RATING (hour)
Less than 3-hour fire-resistance-rated assemblies	1.5
3-hour or greater fire-resistance-rated assemblies	3

Figure 5.16 *International Building Code (IBC)* Table 716.3.1 Fire Damper Rating (*International Building Code* 2003. Copyright 2002. Falls Church, Virginia: International Code Council, Inc. Reproduced with permission. All rights reserved.)

Ceiling Dampers

Ceiling dampers, typically referred to as ceiling radiation dampers, are used in suspended ceilings that are part of the rated floor/ceiling or roof/ceiling assembly. The damper can be located in the duct or be part of the air diffuser that supplies air to the space. In case of fire, they prevent heat from entering the space between the ceiling and the floor or roof above. They also prevent the heat from traveling through the duct system. The ceiling damper closes when the heated air tries to move up through the damper. Ceiling dampers are regulated by *UL 555C, Standard for Ceiling Dampers.*

TEST RATINGS

Note

The International Conference of Building Officials (ICBO) developed a number of its own standards for use in jurisdictions using the *UBC*. Some jurisdictions may still require their use.

Various standard tests have been mentioned throughout this chapter. The American Society for Testing and Materials (ASTM), the National Fire Protection Association (NFPA), and Underwriters Laboratories (UL), in conjunction with the American National Standards Institute (ANSI), have established a wide variety of standard fire tests. These tests are performed by testing agencies. (Some of the more common testing agencies are listed in Figure 5.17.) Manufacturers use these agencies to confirm that their products meet specific requirements.

Note

Other testing agencies can be found by searching Web sites, such as www.astm.org and www.findtesting.com.

Building Research Establishment
Commercial Testing Company
Factory Mutual Research Corporation
Guardian Fire Testing Laboratories
Intertek Testing Services
National Institute of Standards and Technology
The Ohio State University
Omega Point Laboratores
Pacific Fire Laboratory
Portland Cement Association
Radco, Inc.
Standard Fire Test, Fire Prevention Research Institute
Southwest Research Institute
University of California
Underwriters Laboratories, Inc.
Underwriters Laboratories of Canada
United States Testing Company
Warnock Hersey International, Inc.
Western Fire Center

Figure 5.17 Sample of Fire Testing Agencies

Different tests are used for wall, ceiling, and floor assemblies and the items that penetrate these assemblies. These are explained below and summarized in Figure 5.18.

Tests for Wall and Floor/Ceiling Assemblies

Standardized tests are developed to determine the reaction of materials and assemblies to fire in specific uses within a building. There are two basic groups of

RATED ASSEMBLIES AND MATERIALS	REQUIRED TESTS [1]
WALL ASSEMBLIES CEILING ASSEMBLIES FLOOR ASSEMBLIES	ASTM E119 UL 263 NFPA 251
RATED DOORS [2]	
(fire doors)	ASTM E2074 (previously E152) UL 10 (or UL 14) NFPA 252
(smoke doors)	NFPA 105 UL 1784
FLOOR FIRE DOORS CEILING ACCESS DOORS	NFPA 288 (or ASTM E119)
FIRE WINDOWS AND SHUTTERS WIRE GLASS GLASS BLOCK [3]	ASTM E2010 (previously E163) UL 9 NFPA 257
FIRESTOPS	ASTM E814 UL 1479
FIRE RATED GLAZING [3]	NFPA 257
RATED DAMPERS	
(fire damper)	UL 555
(smoke damper)	UL 555S
(ceiling damper)	UL 555C

NOTES:

1 NFPA 80 is not a fire test but should also be referenced since it regulates the installation of an assembly and therefore can affect the final rating.

2. A 20-minute (1/3 hour) door does not require a hose-stream test.

3. If large amounts of glass are used, it could be considered a fire barrier rather than a window and the radiant heat should be tested using NFPA 251.

Figure 5.18 Summary of Tests for Rated Assemblies and Materials

tests for wall and floor/ceiling assemblies. One group of tests evaluates the fire resistance of a material or assembly; the other evaluates how a material reacts to fire. These tests apply to the rated wall, floor, and ceiling assemblies required by the codes as well as the building and structural elements used in the various construction types required by the codes.

The fire-resistance tests generally evaluate how long an assembly will contain a fire, retain its own structural integrity, or both. The test measures the performance of construction assemblies in three areas: (1) the temperature rise on the protected side of the assembly, (2) the smoke, gas, or flames that pass through the assembly, and (3) the structural performance during exposure to the fire. If the assembly being tested is a load-bearing assembly, the test measures the load-carrying ability during exposure to fire. In addition, if a wall or partition obtains a rating of one hour or more, it is subject to a hose stream test to see if it will resist disintegration. (Other components, such as certain doors, may have to pass a pressure test as well.)

Note

In the past, fire-door tests were conducted in furnaces under a neutral pressure. Now, most tests require a positive pressure test.

Based on their performance in these tests, the assemblies are assigned fire-resistance ratings according to the time lapsed when the test is terminated, based on hourly increments. The standard tests used for these types of building materials and assemblies include:

- *ASTM E119, Test Methods for Fire Tests of Building Construction and Materials*
- *UL 263, Fire Tests of Building Construction and Materials*
- *NFPA 251, Standard Methods of Tests of Fire Endurance of Building Construction and Materials*

The other group of tests evaluate how a material or product reacts to fire. These tests specifically measure the extent to which a material contributes to the dangerous elements of a fire, including heat, smoke and combustion products, and flame spread. Whether a material is considered combustible, limited combustible, or noncombustible is also determine by this type of test. Some of these tests were discussed in Chapter 3. Others by NFPA are shown in Figure 5.1. (ASTM has a number of comparable tests.) The codes will specify when they are required. Others may be required by a jurisdiction.

Tests for Opening and Through-Penetration Protectives

Opening protectives and through-penetration protective systems must also pass specific tests. These tests were mentioned earlier as each system was explained. For example, fire doors must conform to the test requirements of *ASTM E2074* and fire windows and shutters must meet the requirements of *ASTM 2010*. The various fire tests are summarized in the chart shown in Figure 5.18. The standard *NFPA*

80, *Standard for Fire Doors and Fire Windows* is also important for opening protective requirements and is listed as a note on the bottom of the chart. Although not technically a fire test, it regulates the installation of fire-door assemblies and fire-window assemblies. The installation can be just a critical as the fire test. For example, if a proper seal is not made between the perimeter of a rated door frame and the adjacent wall, it will not matter how good the assemblies are—fire and smoke can still penetrate.

Any assembly that passes the required tests shown in Figure 5.18 must have a permanent label attached to it to prove it is fire rated. Similar to the label in Figure 5.14, any such label must indicate the manufacturer, the test rating, and, in some cases, the maximum transmitted temperature. The label often indicates the seal of the testing agency as well. When a required assembly such as a fire door is not sold as an assembly or is only partially complete, it is up to you to make sure that each of the additional required components has the proper rating and that each is appropriately labeled.

Note

Fire-rated labels are either permanently affixed to the product or directly etched into the fire assembly.

USING RATED MATERIALS AND ASSEMBLIES

Several organizations in the United States publish lists of tested assemblies. These organizations have a wide variety of assemblies that have been tested and assigned the appropriate hourly fire rating. Included assemblies are walls and partitions, floor/ceiling systems, roof/ceiling systems, beams, girders, and truss protection systems, column protection systems, door and window assemblies, and various opening protectives. The following are three of the most widely used publications:

Note

ISO 834, the standard used by European countries, is similar to *NFPA 251*.

- ❑ Underwriters Laboratories (UL): *Fire Resistance Directory, Vol. I* for beams, columns, floors, roofs, and partitions and *Fire Resistance Directory, Vol. II* for through-penetration firestop systems
- ❑ Gypsum Association (GA): *Fire Resistance Design Manual*
- ❑ Factory Mutual (FM): *Specification Tested Products Guide*

These publications use line drawings and detailed descriptions for the rated assemblies. They indicate specific materials, workmanship, and detailed sizes and dimensions. An example of a common one-hour wall assembly from the *UL Fire Resistance Directory* is shown in Figure 5.19. Each rated assembly is assigned a file or design number specific to that assembly and organization and an hourly rating. For example, Figure 5.19 is "UL Design No U495" for a nonbearing wall. Since this can be a 1-hour wall or a 2-hour wall, depending on which of the materials are used, you would also need to specify the rating required for your application.

Design No. U495
Nonbearing Wall Rating — 1 or 2 HR.
(See Items 5 and 7)

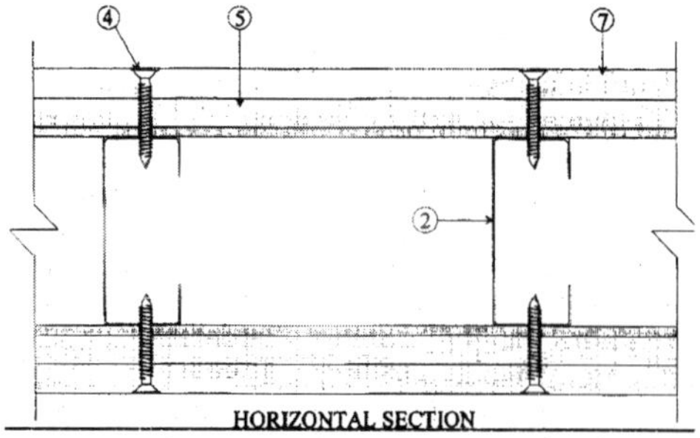

1. **Floor and Ceiling Runners** — (Not Shown) — Channel-shaped runners, 3-5/8 in. wide (min), 1-1/4 in. legs, formed from No. 25 MSG (min) galv steel, attached to floor and ceiling with fasteners spaced 24 in. OC, max.
2. **Steel Studs** — Channel-shaped 3-5/8 in. wide (min), 1-1/4 in. legs, 3/8 in. folded back returns, formed from No. 25 MSG (min) galv steel, spaced 24 in. OC max.
3. **Batts and Blankets*** — (Optional, not shown) — Mineral wool or glass fiber batts partially or completely filling stud cavity.
   See Batts and Blankets (BZJZ) category for names of Classified companies.
4. **Screws** — Type S self-tapping screws, 1-1/4 or 2 in. long, (1 Hr) and 2-1/2 in. long (2 Hr).
5. **Building Units*** — For 1 Hr Rating — Nom 5/8 or 3/4 in. thick, 4 ft wide, faced gypsum wallboard panels with the faced side on the interior wall cavity. Panels attached to studs and floor and ceiling runners with screws spaced 8 in. OC along the edges of the panel and 12 in. OC in the field of the panel. Joints oriented vertically and staggered on opposite sides of the assembly.
   GENERAL ELECTRIC CO
   SILICONE PRODUCTS DIV —Type CoreGuard.
   NATIONAL GYPSUM CO —Type Gold Bond Fire-Shield Type X Hi-Impact Wallboard or Gold Bond Fire-Shield Type X Kal-Kore Hi-Impact Plaster Base.
6. **Joint Tape and Compound** — (not shown) — Vinyl, dry or premixed joint compound, applied in two coats to joints and screw heads; paper tape, 2 in. wide, embedded in first layer of compound over all joints.
7. **Wallboard, Gypsum*** — For 2 Hr Rating — any Classified 5/8 in. thick (minimum), 4 ft wide, wallboard applied over exterior face of Building Unit (Item 5). Wallboard to be applied vertically with joints staggered 24 in. from Building Unit (Item 5) and attached to studs and floor and ceiling runners with screws spaced 8 in. OC.
   See Wallboard, Gypsum (CKNX) Category for names of manufacturers.

*Bearing the UL Classification Marking

Figure 5.19 UL Fire Resistant Assembly Example (Reprinted from the 2000 *Fire Resistance Directory* with permission from Underwriters Laboratories Inc. Copyright 2000 Underwriters Laboratories Inc.)

It is your responsibility to refer to the correct file number when specifying a fire-rated assembly as required by the code. For example, if you were asked to replace some existing steps in an exit access corridor with a ramp, the codes would require that the new elements be consistent with the construction type. It would become part of the existing floor/ceiling assembly. Depending on the occupancy classification and the type of construction of the building, the assembly could require a 1-hour to a 4-hour rating. Once you determined the fire rating required by the building code, you would use one of the publications listed above to find the detail of the rated assembly most similar to the existing construction conditions. Use the file number of this assembly in your specifications of the new ramp.

It is important to note, however, that the test results and ratings of materials and assemblies can become invalid if the materials and assemblies are not used and maintained properly. Keep the following factors in mind when specifying rated assemblies:

1. *If you do not use a product the way a manufacturer specifies or the contractor does not use the correct materials, its rating becomes void.* You must either have it retested the way it is built or add fire protection to create the rating.
2. *If the construction of the joints between the assemblies, such as wall-to-wall, wall-to-ceiling, or wall-to-floor, are substandard, fire and smoke can penetrate no matter how good each assembly is.* Specifying the correct installation standard is just as important as specifying the right assembly.
3. *Conventional openings, such as electrical switches and outlets in wall assemblies and electrical raceways and pull boxes in floor/ceiling assemblies, can affect the fire endurance of an assembly.* Some assemblies are tested with these penetrations; others are not. (See more in Chapter 8.)
4. *A fire can impair the stability of a structural assembly or building element.* If a fire occurs and the assembly is exposed to flame and heat, this exposure can affect the strength and structural integrity of the building materials. After a fire, the original fire rating may no longer be valid.

Note

Performance-based criteria can be helpful when designing the passive fire protection system for a new or existing building.

When a rated assembly is required, the building codes will often refer you to one or more of the earlier mentioned standards within their text. Some jurisdictions may prefer you to use one publication over another. However, the codes may also allow other ways to determine the appropriate construction assembly. For example, some codes specify construction assemblies, and their ratings in their text. The *IBC* includes a table that lists and describes the installation of various structural elements, walls and partitions, and floors and roofs, and their ratings. Depending on the jurisdiction, you may be able to reference these *IBC* details rather than using one of the three publications previously mentioned.

The codes already have provisions for allowing calculations or an engineering analysis of a proposed or existing construction assembly to determine the rating of the assembly. These calculations may be based on information given by the codes as to the fire resistance of certain materials or they may be performance based. For most projects, referring to the tested assemblies represented by the publications listed above will be appropriate. For existing construction or for innovative design elements that are required to be rated, the calculated or performance criteria may be required. If you are using special calculations or criteria in the performance codes, you must meet with the code official to discuss the design early and then be prepared to provide the requested documentation to support your design. In many cases, this will require the assistance of other design professionals and engineers.

In either case, it is important to accurately document the rated assemblies and the compartmentation created by these assemblies. You should indicate which walls or partitions are required to be rated and their required fire-resistance rating. You should supply adequate details for their construction, reference required testing and installation standards, and refer to the assigned number of the tested assembly if possible. All rated opening protectives and through-penetration protectives must be properly noted, as well. In addition, you should verify during the construction that they are installed correctly. If they are not, they will not provide the required compartmentation and may fail in the event of a fire.

CHECKLIST

Figure 5.20 is a fire-resistance checklist that can be used on your interior projects or as a guideline to make your own checklist. It indicates each type of fire barrier, smoke barrier, opening protective, and through-penetration protective typically regulated by the codes. The checklist can be used to remind you of what to look for and research on a project, as well as to give you a place to record the necessary code information for future reference. Not every type of fire-resistant component is included in every project. Remember, however, that it must be used in conjunction with the codes and standards based on the occupancy classification of the project and the construction type of the building.

The checklist begins with the standard blanks for the project and space name, the occupancy classification of the project, and the construction type of the building. (If necessary, refer to Chapters 2 and 3 to determine these.) The remainder of the checklist indicates the various types of interior assemblies and protectives. To the left of each component is a blank space so you can check off each of the components used in your project.

Then for each assembly that you checked off, fill in the necessary information. If the assembly or component already exists in the building, make a note in the "Existing" column. This will be helpful when you need to match existing conditions. Use the next column to indicate the location of the system. For example,

Fire Resistance Checklist

Date:____________

Project Name:______________________________ Space: ______________

Occupancy (new or existing):______________________________

Type of Construction: ______________________________

REQUIRED FIRE PROTECTION (check those that apply)	EXT'G (yes/no)	LOCATION IN BUILDING	TYPE OF MATERIAL OR ASSEMBLY REQUIRED (list information)	HOURLY RATING OR FIRE TEST REQUIRED (list type)

Fire Barriers and Partitions [1]
__ Fire Wall(s)
__ Fire Area(s)
__ Occupancy Separation(s)
__ Tenant Separation(s)
__ Incidental Use Area/Room(s)
__ Vertical Shaft Enclosure(s)
__ Means of Egress Component(s)
    __ Exit Stairway(s)
    __ Exit Access Stairway(s)
    __ Horizontal Exit(s)
    __ Exit Corridor/Passageway(s)
    __ Exit Access Corridor(s)
__ Floor/Ceiling Assembly(ies)
__ Other:______________				

Smoke Barriers and Partitions [1] __ Smoke Compartment(s) __ Vertical Shaft(s) __ Vestibule(s) __ Other:______________				

Opening Protectives
__ Rated Door Assembly(ies)
    __ Fire Door(s)
    __ Smoke Door(s)
__ Fire Window Assembly(ies)
__ Rated Glazing and Frame(s)
__ Special Hardware
__ Other:______________				

Through-Penetration Protectives
Engineer Required? ___YES ___ NO
__ Firestop(s)
__ Fireblock(s)
__ Draftstop(s)
__ Damper System(s)
    __ Fire Damper(s)
    __ Smoke Damper(s)
__ Other:______________				

NOTES:

1 Remember that fire and smoke barriers need to be considered both vertically and horizontally.

2. Refer to codes and standards for specific information. Also check the ADA guidelines and ICC/ANSI standard for accessibility-related requirement

3. Attach all testing verification, including copies of manufacturer labels and/or copies of rated assembly details.

Figure 5.20 Fire-Resistance Checklist

indicate where vertical shafts are located on the floor plan. It may be helpful to attach a reduced-scale floor plan and locate these components graphically.

The next two columns are used to indicate the specific types of systems or material used and the types of tests and/or ratings required by the codes and standards. This information will help you to select the correct products as you are specifying for the project and/or when you are working with an engineer. For example, you can indicate the type of firestop to be used and the rating it must provide, or indicate the size and type of rated glazing that will be used and the specific tests it must pass. For each wall, floor, and ceiling assembly you may want to indicate whether you are required to use a barrier or partition.

As you are filling out the checklist, you may have to consult engineers or other professionals to determine exact requirements. Use this form throughout the project as a guideline and a reminder of the items to be researched and completed. When the checklist is completed, be sure to file it and any other pertinent testing and code information required with the project paperwork for future reference. (See Chapter 10.)

CHAPTER 6

FIRE PROTECTION SYSTEMS

As mentioned in the previous chapter, fire and smoke are the primary threats to the safety of the occupants in a building. Fire and smoke can travel quickly both horizontally and vertically unless special efforts are made to prevent this from happening. Compartmentation of fire areas was discussed in Chapter 5. The use of rated assemblies in this *passive* system of fire protection is considered the first step for controlling the spread of smoke and fire. In addition to compartmentation, an *active* system that reacts when a fire is detected within a building or space can be used to provide another level of fire protection. This chapter will discuss the active fire protection system and its components, which include detection, alarm, and extinguishing systems.

Note

In the past, fire protection systems such as fire extinguishers and sprinkler systems were known as *suppression systems*. The codes now refer to these as *extinguishing systems.*

The overall aim of the fire protection system is to detect a fire in a building or space, warn the occupants, and suppress the fire until the fire department arrives. (In some cases, the system will extinguish the fire.) If that fire can be detected quickly, occupants have more time to exit the building safely and with less panic. Also, if the fire can be suppressed or extinguished early in its development, less damage to the building and its contents may occur. Although the main concern of the codes is occupant safety and not necessarily the actual contents of the building, a fire that is allowed to develop uncontrolled can cause severe structural damage to the building. This can lead to loss of life of the occupants who have not yet exited the building or the firefighters attempting to deal with the fire.

In some cases, the owner's concerns for the contents of a building or space may make fire protection desirable even when not required by the codes. For example, it may be important for a small museum area that contains valuable historic letters to be protected. In most cases, these systems should be installed using the same standards as those required by the code.

Although a complete fire protection system includes detectors, alarms, and suppression or extinguishing systems, not all of these will be required in all buildings or spaces. The codes determine the level of fire protection required according to the type of occupancy, the use of the space, and the size and height of the building. For example, for a mixed occupancy, a detection and fire alarm system may only be required in one fire area of the building.

Depending on the system and the specific code requirements, the fire protection system may be completely automatic, manual, or a combination. The codes determine which aspects of the system must be automatic and which are allowed to be under the control of the occupants. For example, some occupancies do not require automatic detection and notification of fire and instead rely on manual fire alarms. In a fully automatic system, however, once a detector indicates that there is a fire, it sets off the fire alarm to warn the occupants to evacuate and then initiates the extinguishing system. In addition, some occupancies allow the use of portable extinguishers instead of automatic sprinkler systems. (When automatic sprinkler systems are used in a building, other passive fire protection elements may be reduced.)

All of the systems discussed in this chapter are directly tied to the plumbing, mechanical, or electrical system of a building. For this reason, an engineer is typically involved in this portion of a project. (This was also the case with dampers, as discussed in Chapter 5.) However, as the designer you will often need to designate preferred locations of devices, coordinate the location of various design elements, and be involved in other decisions that may affect your project. Some examples may include locating fire extinguishers and fire alarms, selecting the type of sprinkler heads, and coordinating the location of sprinkler heads with the location of the light fixtures.

KEY TERMS

Below are some common terms used when discussing detection and suppression systems. These terms are defined and discussed in this chapter. They are also defined in the Glossary.

Alarm notification appliance
Alarm system
Automatic fire-extinguishing system
Automatic sprinkler system
Backdraft
Detector
Emergency alarm system
Fire area

Fire protection system
Flashover
Fusible link
Initiating device
Radiant heat
Zone

COMPARING THE CODES

With the use of fire protection systems, such as an automatic sprinkler system within a building, the building codes and the *Life Safety Code (LSC)* allow for greater flexibility in construction types, rating of interior walls, and overall area and building heights, as discussed in previous chapters. In addition, the building codes specifically address requirements for the use of fire dampers, fire alarm systems, and automatic sprinkler systems within a building as part of the total fire protection system of a building. Many jurisdictions also require the use of a fire code, which provides additional requirements for approved automatic sprinkler systems and other types of active fire protection components.

The fire codes have several chapters that address the use of fire protection systems within a building. They indicate when specific active fire protection systems are required beyond their requirement in the building codes, the proper installation of automatic sprinkler systems, and additional requirements including maintenance for the use of active systems. (The fire codes typically include prescriptive requirements as well as performance criteria for the development of active protection systems.)

When specific testing and installation methods are required, the building codes, the fire codes, and the *LSC* refer to a number of the standards published by the National Fire Protection Association (NFPA). The NFPA standards specify locations, design details, and installation requirements, as well as testing standards that must be followed. Some of the standards deal with fire prevention. Others concentrate on detection and suppression systems. The standards most used for interior projects have been listed in Figure 6.1 for your reference. Although these codes and standards are most often used by a mechanical or electrical engineer, understanding the scope of these codes is important in the development of the design. They will be included in the discussion of each type of system.

In the past, almost all fire protection systems were designed based on the prescriptive code requirements of the building codes and fire codes. These technical

NFPA 10	Portable Fire Extinguishers
NFPA 11	Standard for Low-, Medium-, and High-Expansion Foam Systems
NFPA 12	Carbon Dioxide Extinguishing Systems
NFPA 12A	Halon 1301 Fire Extinguishing Systems
NFPA 13	Installation of Sprinkler Systems
NFPA 13D	Installation of Sprinkler Systems in One- and Two-Family Dwellings and Manufactured Homes
NFPA 13R	Installation of Sprinkler Systems in Residential Occupancies up to and Including Four Stories in Height
NFPA 14	Installation of Standpipe and Hose Systems
NFPA 15	Water Spray Fixed Systems for Fire Protection
NFPA 16	Installation of Foam-Water Sprinkler and Foam-Water Spray Systems
NFPA 17	Dry Chemical Extinguishing Systems
NFPA 17A	Wet Chemical Extinguishing Systems
NFPA 20	Installation of Stationary Pumps for Fire Protection
NFPA 70	National Electric Code
NFPA 72	National Fire Alarm Code
NFPA 110	Emergency and Standby Power Systems
NFPA 111	Stored Electrical Energy Emergency and Standby Power Systems
NFPA 170	Fire Safety Symbols
NFPA 750	Water Mist Fire Protection Systems
NFPA 2001	Standard on Clean Agent Fire Extinguishing Systems

NOTE: There may be other NFPA standards not listed above that are specific to an occupancy, especially certain hazardous occupancies. Other standards may pertain to the inspection and maintenance of a system.

Figure 6.1 Common NFPA Standards for Fire-Protection Systems

requirements were based on criteria established by the industry (often as a result of a devastating fire) and were determined by typical engineering calculations. Now, the use of performance design is an increasingly acceptable way to design a fire protection system that can address special needs of a design or building. This can be especially helpful for buildings that do not meet the current codes, such as an historic building with an open stairwell, or unusual designs, such as a unique ceiling pattern. In other cases, special needs of the occupants or unique kinds of fire hazards may need to be considered.

With performance design, the design team defines the level of safety that must be provided. This can include how quickly a fire needs to be detected, how soon the suppression system activates, who will be notified of the fire, the safest egress patterns, and other criteria. The unique characteristics of the space or building are also considered. Then, specific engineering calculations and computer fire modeling are used to analyze and create a system that responds best for that design. In most cases, the design will use the performance criteria for selected parts of the building, but the rest of the fire protection system will be specified according to the prescriptive code requirements.

The American with Disabilities Act (ADA) guidelines and other accessibility standards such as *ICC/ANSI 117.1* do not play heavily in the development of fire protection systems. The main accessibility requirement for fire prevention has to do with fire alarms and accessible warning systems. Also keep in mind that any device that is part of the fire protection system and meant for occupant use must be placed at accessible reaching heights and locations and cannot be located so that it becomes a projection into the accessible path. Signage, as well as the type and location of the operational mechanisms, is also important. These items will be discussed throughout the chapter.

DETECTION SYSTEMS

The best way to protect the occupants in a building from the dangers of a fire is to know that there is a fire as early as possible. This, of course, allows more time to contain the fire and remove the occupants, if necessary, before the danger escalates. Detection systems, then, are meant to recognize the first signs of a fire. For this reason detectors are also known as initiating devices because their activation initiates the rest of the fire protection system. Although there are several different types of detection systems, the most common systems rely on the detection of heat or smoke. (See inset titled *Carbon Monoxide Detection* on page 228.)

In most cases, the requirements in the codes will determine if a detection system is required throughout the building or in certain fire areas. These specific fire areas can be large areas of a building or selected rooms. If more protection is not required by the codes, the owner may ask that you supplement the fire protection of certain areas. In all cases, the type of detection should be appropriate for the anticipated type of fire. For example, most fires will release heat and smoke, but a liquid fire causes a drop in temperature instead. In addition, smoke detectors are better for a smoldering fire but heat detectors are better for large flaming fires in large spaces.

Note

New detectors can recognize various fire *signatures.* Examples include the amount of smoke and change in temperature.

Note

Never paint over smoke detectors or other fire safety equipment. It can hamper their effectiveness. Many operate by fusible links. Paint may keep the fusible links from melting.

Fire protection systems have changed dramatically over the last several decades due to technological advances. Today, these systems can employ everything from programmable computers to remote controls. Detectors can be programmed to require that more than one aspect of a fire be detected before signaling the alarm system to prevent unnecessary false alarms. Other programs will require additional types of alarm verification. (See inset titled *Fire Technology* on page 230.)

These modern advances in detection systems have resulted in better-protected buildings. They have also resulted in a multitude of new codes, regulations, and standards. Most of the building codes, the fire codes, and the *LSC* require detection systems to conform to *NFPA 72, National Fire Alarm Code* for minimum performance, location, installation, and maintenance requirements. The codes typically specify the use of smoke detectors. In some cases, a heat detection device may also be required. Both of these detectors, as well as fire alarm pull boxes, are discussed next.

Note

Some jurisdictions may already require carbon-monoxide detectors in certain Residential occupancies. Be sure to check with the jurisdiction.

Most of the time, you will have to work with an electrical engineer or fire protection designer to coordinate these systems with the rest of your design. Detection systems must also be integrated into other systems within the building, including the electrical system. Detection systems rely on electricity as their main power source, and in most cases require an emergency source of power as well. (See Chapter 8.)

CARBON MONOXIDE DETECTION

Carbon monoxide is produced by incomplete combustion of organic materials. Prolonged exposure to carbon monoxide can be fatal. The first sign of a problem is often occupants experiencing flu-like symptoms. Continued and prolonged exposure will cause drowsiness to the point of unconsciousness and ultimately death.

Exposure to this gas occurs most frequently from appliances or engines powered by gas, such as automobiles, lawnmowers, stoves, and hot water heaters. These items are often used in and around Residential occupancies. However, carbon dioxide detection is not yet required by any of the building codes. Even if detection systems were required, the standards for the manufacture and installation of CO_2 detectors are still emerging, such as *UL 2034, Standard for Safety, Single and Multiple Station Carbon Monoxide Detectors*. It is unclear what level of exposure to the gas should be considered dangerous.

Carbon monoxide detectors are available to the public for use in residential settings. They rely on the occupants to report to authorities, usually the fire department, when alarms indicate a high level of carbon monoxide. As detection systems develop and additional standards are set, carbon monoxide detection will be required in Residential occupancies and others. You should continue to be aware of current requirements that may affect your project.

Smoke Detectors

Since smoke and toxic gases are the main killers in a building fire, smoke detectors are important in every design. Smoke detectors are especially effective in detecting smoldering fires that do not produce enough heat for sprinkler activation. For this reason, smoke detectors are the most widely used initiating device.

Smoke detectors can be used in two ways. They can be wired to act individually (e.g., single-station) or as a group (e.g., multi-station). Based on the type of detector, the type of alarm it has, and how it is wired, it can signal one area or a whole building. (See Alarm Systems, later in the chapter.) They are often used in conjunction with a smoke damper. (See Chapter 5.) Other smoke detectors may be required to activate automatic doors. They act as releasing devices in the presence of smoke so that the door will automatically close. Both multiple- and single-station detectors must be tied into the building's power source.

Although the codes specify which occupancies require smoke detectors, they do not always specifically state where to locate them within a space or building. You need to determine the best placement. For example, in a cooking area you do not want to place the smoke detector where standard cooking procedures may activate the alarm. In addition, do not place detectors too close to the intersection of a wall and ceiling or too close to a doorway, because air currents may cause smoke and heat to bypass the unit. When mounted on a wall, smoke detectors should typically be between 6 and 12 inches (152 to 305 mm) from the ceiling. When unusual design situations occur or include unique elements, such as coffered ceilings, work with the manufacturer as well as the code officials in your jurisdiction to locate the detectors.

Note

Smoke detectors will increase in importance as more finishes and furnishings become flame resistant. (See Chapter 9.) Such materials will be more likely to smolder for long periods of time without a flame at temperatures too low for sprinklers to respond.

Note

Battery-operated smoke detectors are typically not allowed by the codes unless they are an added precaution not required by the codes.

Heat Detectors

Next to smoke, heat is the most common type of fire detector. Heat detectors are sensitive to any change in temperature. This can be especially important in liquid fires where an actual drop in temperature occurs. Heat detectors can monitor temperatures at a specific spot or monitor the temperature range within a designated area. For example, they might be placed along an assembly line in a factory. Often, heat detectors are used with smoke detectors to avoid false alarms. In these systems, more than one sign of fire is needed before an alarm is signaled. A combination may also be used in highly sensitive areas so that the detection of either smoke or heat will activate the fire protection system.

FIRE TECHNOLOGY

For more complex or larger projects, expanding technology is allowing for additional ways to recognize the presence of fire because fire creates more than just smoke and heat. Fire actually produces various types of symptoms. These include molecular gases (smoke that includes carbon dioxide), aerosols, heat conduction, thermal radiation (heat), and acoustic waves. New technology allows for the detection of these multiple symptoms to determine if a fire really exists. This allows for better detection of a fire and also reduces the number of false alarms.

For example, just because there is smoke does not necessarily mean that there is a fire. Someone with a cigarette standing directly below a smoke detector could cause it to alarm. More sophisticated detection systems will then compare that input with the presence of other symptoms of fire or whether another smoke detector nearby indicates that there is smoke. If no other symptoms of fire exist, the detection system may delay setting off the fire alarm until another symptom is present or the smoke continues.

Technology, especially the use of computers, has allowed advancements not only in the individual detectors but in the detection systems as well. Now, systems can check each detector individually to see if it is working properly, and in the event of a fire to determine the exact location of the fire, not just the floor on which the fire originated. The sensitivity of particular zones of detectors can also be modified to allow for different levels of heat or smoke that might be present in normal conditions.

Manual Fire Alarms

Note

The traditional manual fire alarm box is a pull device. New accessible types of boxes are available. Instead of pulling a handle to activate the alarm, the devices require pushing with minimal effort. Both types must be red.

The codes consider a manual fire alarm to be part of the detection system. This is because the occupant who uses the manual alarm has actually detected the fire. He or she then sets off the alarm system by the use of a *pull* station. If an automatic smoke detection system or sprinkler system is not provided in a building, manual fire alarms are typically required. However, in certain occupancies, a manual fire alarm may additionally be required to be available to the occupants of the building. This is common in Educational occupancies. Although the alarm does not usually activate the extinguishing system, it will notify the occupants of a problem.

When manual fire alarms are provided, the codes typically require them to be located adjacent the entrance of each required exit. It should be located on the latch side of the door so that it is easily seen no farther than 5 feet (1525 mm) from the door. Some occupancies may require a more unique location. For example, pull stations in hospitals are typically located at control rooms or nurses' stations for use by staff. Manual alarms are usually required to be no more than 200 feet (60 m) travel distance to a station. The codes also specify their color, signage, and power supply. Since the device is meant to be used by building occupants, accessibility requirements for the mounting height of a pull device will apply. In most cases, they must be within the accessible reach range and typically have a clear floor space of 30 inches (760 mm) by 48 inches (1220 mm) in front of the device. In addition, new types of manual alarms have been developed to be more easily used by persons with disabilities. These include devices that are more easily grasped and do not require complex movement to activate. Figure 6.2 indicates the typical location of a manual fire alarm according to code and accessibility requirements.

Note

Instead of listing all the alarm requirements within its text, the new *ADA-ABA Accessibility Guidelines* reference the *NFPA 72, National Fire Alarm Code.*

ALARM SYSTEMS

Note

In the future, *NFPA 72* will also include more information on building security, especially as it relates to mass notification.

Alarm systems within a building or space make occupants aware that something unusual is occurring. In most cases, they are used to warn occupants that a fire has been detected and that they should evacuate. Alarm systems also can be used to notify occupants of other types of emergencies, such as toxic spills or severe weather conditions. (See Emergency Alarm Systems below.) In either case, the type of alarm system and how it works depends on the type of emergency, who needs to be aware of it, and what actions are expected to be taken.

The devices that make up the different types of alarm systems are sometimes referred to as notification appliances. An alarm system can be activated

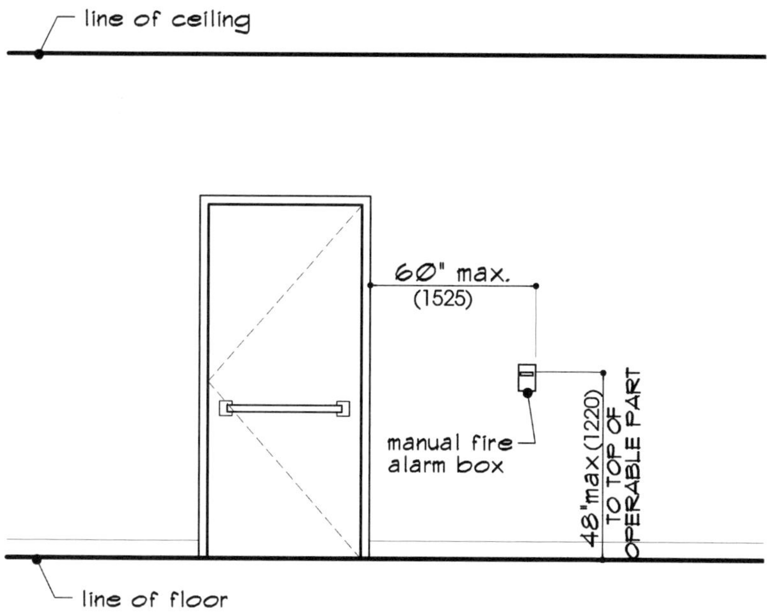

Figure 6.2 Typical Manual Alarm Mounting Requirements

either *manually* by the use of a pull device or *automatically* by a smoke detector, fire detector, or automatic sprinkler system. (Refer back to Detection Systems earlier in this chapter.) The codes will specify which type of system is required for a particular occupancy classification. Some occupancies may require both types of activation.

There is also a difference between single-station and multiple-station alarms. A *single-station* alarm will sound only within the area where the fire is detected. A *multiple-station* alarm system is a system of fire alarms that is interconnected so that the indication of fire anywhere in the building will sound all the alarms within the building. So, typically, the activation of the fire alarm will immediately warn the occupants within the area of the fire or throughout the building so that they can begin evacuating the building. However, in some occupancies, such as hospitals or nursing homes, the signal will only annunciate at a controlled station, such as a nurses' station, so that only staff is alerted. The alarm can also go to a remote control room where someone decides what action should be taken. Often, the fire alarm will notify the local fire department as well.

Like the detection system described in the last section, the alarm system is tied to the electrical system of a building and may be tied to other similar systems. For example, a building may be required to have a control panel at the fire department entrance to the building so they can quickly determine the location of the problem. An electrical engineer usually needs to be involved in projects requiring an alarm system. Typically, the engineer will design the system and reference the appropriate codes. As the designer, you will want to coordinate the location of devices and confirm that the system meets the intent of the design. The various types of alarm systems, as described next, include visual and audible alarms, voice communication, accessible warnings, and emergency alarms. (See also inset titled *Integrated Alarms* on page 235.)

Visual and Audible Alarm Systems

Note

Visual alarms can be referred to in a number of ways. Depending on the publication and the manufacturer, they can be called visual alarm signals, visible signal devices, visual signaling appliances, or visual notification appliances.

Alarms are required to use both audible and visual signals. This assures that the majority of people within a building will be notified that a fire or emergency is occurring. An *audible* alarm signals an emergency by a loud sound. The sound can be a steady hornlike sound, a pattern of sound, or bell sounds. A *visual* alarm signals by the use of a strobe light. The strobe usually emits a pulsing light that cannot easily be ignored or is intended to actually awaken occupants who are sleeping. Where different types of warnings are required, each would have a different pattern or intensity. For example, the fire alarm may make a single loud blast, but the emergency alarm may be a pattern of short blasts. There are also alarm devices that have both audible and visible notification in one unit. When a combination device is used, it must be located according to the requirements for visual alarms. The fire codes and fire protection chapters of the building codes specify the type of alarm, its location, and the wiring required. For installation of the fire alarm the codes refer to the standard *NFPA 72, National Fire Alarm Code.* Certain accessibility requirements also apply.

An *audible* alarm must be set within a certain decibel and pressure range so that it exceeds the prevailing sound level in the room or space where it is used. For example, an audible alarm in a factory where machines are working may require a louder sound than in an office building. In most cases, the alarm must be able to be heard throughout the building and must be located accordingly. The alarms must also be placed in a natural path of escape and at each required exit from a building (within approximately five feet of the exit) because the noise from the alarm helps the occupants to locate the exits during a fire. Audible alarms must meet certain accessibility requirements that affect the type, sound quality, and pulse rate. Although locations for audible alarms are not specified, if they are more than 4 inches (100 mm) deep, they must be mounted high enough on the wall not to create a protrusion.

Note

A *public mode* alarm notifies all occupants. A *private mode* alarm notifies only control staff.

Visual alarms are basically white or clear flashing lights used as an alarm signal and are sometimes referred to as *strobes.* Visual alarms were first required because of the ADA. Similar requirements are now included in the codes and the ICC/ANSI standard as well as the ADA guidelines. The color, intensity, flash rate, and pulse duration of a visual alarm is regulated by the codes and standards. In addition, they also must be placed in specific locations—certain heights above the floor and certain distances apart. (See ADA guidelines and the ICC/ANSI standards for details.) When required, they must be provided in at least each restroom, hallway, and lobby of a building in addition to other common use areas such as meeting rooms, break rooms, examination rooms, and classrooms. In occupancies with multiple sleeping units, a certain percentage of the units must be equipped with a visual alarm as well. (Devices located in sleeping units have additional mounting requirements.)

Note

Visual alarms must typically be installed in more locations than audible alarms, since a visual alarm can be observed only in the space in which it is installed.

As the designer, you may need to coordinate the placement of the audible and visual alarm systems with an engineer based on the design of the space to assure that the alarms can be seen and heard. In particular, the distance of occupied spaces from the origin of the alarm and any doors that would reduce the level of sound should be considered. In addition, you must coordinate the placement of the devices to meet the accessibility requirements.

Voice Communication Systems

Some occupancies and building types are required by the codes to have a voice communication system tied into the fire alarm system. These include factories, some Institutional occupancies such as hospitals and assisted living facilities, large storage facilities, occupancies in high-rise buildings, and other Assembly and Hazardous occupancies. Also sometimes referred to as an audio system, a voice communication system is basically an intercom system that directs the occupants out of the building during an emergency. The emergency could be a fire or other event that threatens the occupants of the building. Some systems may also indicate the location of the emergency. *NFPA 72* includes standards that regulate the message so that it is clear and easily understood by the occupants. If you are working in these types of occupancies, be sure to check for specific code requirements.

Note

A voice communication system can be automatically transmitted or can use live voice transmission. A jurisdiction may require one over another.

Accessible Warning Systems

As already mentioned, visual alarms were first required by the ADA for accessibility. Now, both audible and visual alarms are required by the building codes, the fire codes, and the *LSC*, as well as the ADA guidelines. Although not currently required by code, additional accessible warning systems are available. The ADA does not specifically require these other types either; however, it does require that an appropriate system be provided for occupants with disabilities. And as a designer, you must provide safety for the occupants of your design. You may need to provide a special type of system. For example, tactile notification appliances that producc a vibrating sensation could be specified where a large number of occupants may be seeing impaired and hearing impaired, such as a special school or dormitory. A visible text messaging system could also be used to assist other types of disabilities. In these cases, you would refer to the ADA guidelines for the placement and visual characteristics based on the standard audible and visual alarms. In some building types, such as hotels, the ADA guidelines will specify the percentage of rooms or units that require these systems.

With the continued influence of ADA on safety and accessibility concerns for the disabled, new types of accessible warning systems will continue to be developed. Note that there can sometimes be conflicts within the technical requirements between the accessibility standards and the codes. You must provide the greatest extent of accessibility when possible. And, you should keep up to date on the development of accessible products so that you can incorporate them into your designs as necessary.

Emergency Alarm Systems

Emergency alarm systems typically indicate that an emergency other than a fire has occurred. These systems are not required in all buildings. They are most commonly required in high-rise buildings and Hazardous occupancies. An emer-

INTEGRATED ALARMS

Alarm systems can be integrated with other building controls, such as mechanical and security. When alarm systems are connected to a mechanical system, they can shut down the air distribution system that would spread smoke to other parts of the building. When they are connected to the security system, they can signal the unlocking of doors that are normally required for security. With the use of new technology, computers, motion detectors, and closed-circuit cameras can be used to tie multiple systems together to monitor and control evacuation and monitor a fire in a more comprehensive way.

The development of software and products to work within an integrated system is ongoing. However, this type of system is complex and most suitable for complex projects. If you are designing an extensive project, you may need to involve a fire-protection system designer and other engineers. (See inset titled *Building Automation Systems* in Chapter 8 for more information.)

gency alarm system may include emergency, security, trouble, or evacuation alarms. Similar to fire alarms, they may signal the need to evacuate the area or building or signal to a control system. The control system may be computer controlled or may be manually observed by a person who will decide the appropriate action to take. A voice communication system is most often used for general emergency situations. The voice message instructs the occupants what to do. Where a voice message may not easily be understood, a trouble or evacuation signal may be used. This signal must be distinct from the fire alarm signal so that occupants can distinguish between the two types of alarms. Another example is a sprinkler alarm that may sound on the exterior of a building when the sprinklers have activated, to tell the public that a fire emergency is occurring inside the building.

EXTINGUISHING SYSTEMS

Extinguishing systems were also referred to as suppression systems in older editions of the codes. These systems provide for the control and extinguishment of fires once they occur. Like detection and alarm systems, their installation often needs to be coordinated with other trades and professionals. Since most of them use water, a mechanical engineer usually needs to be involved. Typically, a fire protection designer or an engineer will design the system and reference the appropriate codes. (See Chapter 7.)

The most common extinguishing systems include fire extinguishers, standpipes, fire hoses, and sprinkler systems. These are explained in more detail throughout this section.

Fire Extinguishers

Portable fire extinguishers are one means of fire suppression meant for use by the building occupant. Since they are movable and do not require access to plumbing lines, they are often specified by the designer on interior projects. They can be surface mounted where space allows or recessed within a wall using a special cabinet. The cabinet must either have a vision panel or be clearly marked with a sign because the fire extinguisher must be visible at all times. The fire extinguisher must also be tested and have an approved label.

Note

When surface mounting a fire extinguisher, be sure you note both code and accessibility heights and projection requirements.

Both the building codes and the fire codes specify the occupancies and types of building uses that require fire extinguishers. The codes also refer to *NFPA 10, Standard for Portable Fire Extinguishers,* which indicates more detailed information including specific numbers, sizes, and extinguisher types. Most occupancies require an extinguisher. Specific areas or rooms within a building require them as well. For example, most commercial kitchens as well as smaller kitchens and break rooms require a fire extinguisher. (Other NFPA publications provide fire extinguisher requirements for special occupancies.) Some specific location requirements include the following:

- Within 30 feet (9145 mm) of commercial cooking equipment
- In areas with flammable or combustible liquids
- In buildings under construction
- Where open flames are present
- In laboratories, or computer and generator rooms

Fire extinguishers are available in various sizes and contain an array of substances. The type of extinguisher required will depend on the occupancy and/or contents of the space. The fire codes will classify a space or building as either a Class A, B, or C fire hazard. Class A is the least hazardous and the most common. In a Class A space, no occupant can be more than 75 feet (22,860 mm) from a fire extinguisher when fire extinguishers are required. (Other classes require shorter distances.) Figure 6.3 is an example of a large office space, indicating typical fire extinguisher locations in the overall space as well as in the breakroom.

Note

Depending on the occupancy and type of hazards present, different types of fire extinguishers may be required.

The codes typically specify the maximum height of the extinguisher based on its weight, as shown in Figure 6.4. However, because a fire extinguisher is meant to be used by an occupant, it must also be accessible. It must be mounted at an

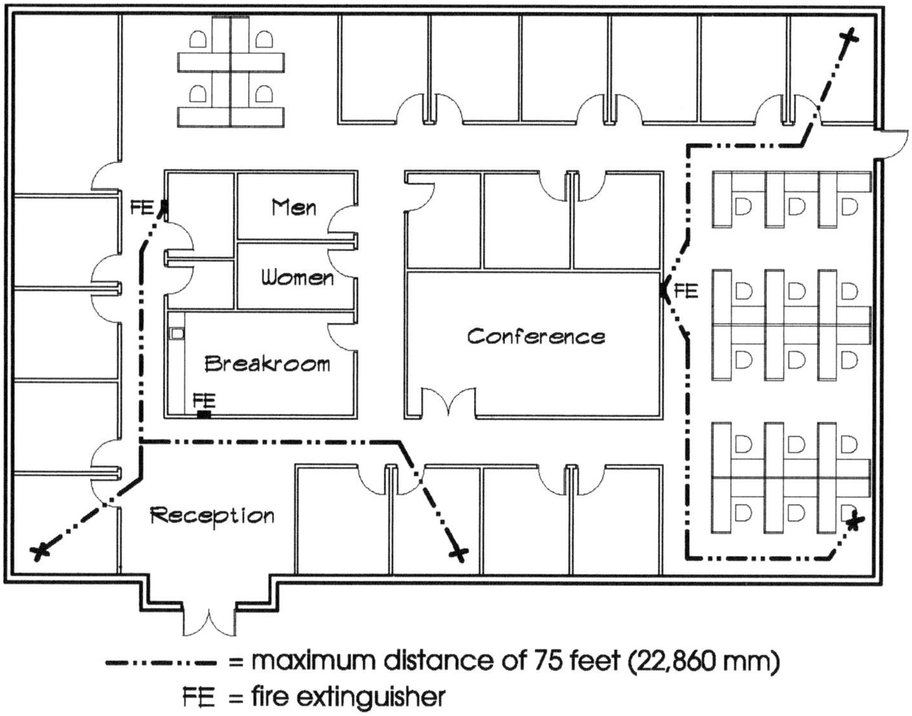

Figure 6.3 Travel Distance to Fire Extinguishers Example

accessible height and be located within accessible reach from a front or side approach as required by the ADA guidelines and the ICC/ANSI standard. The top of Figure 6.4 indicates the required code and accessibility heights in relation to the fire extinguisher cabinet. In addition, the extinguisher cannot protrude more than 4 inches (100 mm) into a path of travel. This may eliminate bracket-mounted fire extinguishers in certain areas. Often a fire extinguisher cabinet is recessed either partially or fully into a wall. The bottom of Figure 6.4 shows two types of partially recessed cabinets. Even the pull on the cabinet needs to be within the 4 inches (100 mm).

Standpipes and Fire Hoses

Standpipes and fire hoses are typically installed during the initial construction of a building. However, they may also need to be upgraded when new work is done in an existing building. They are a manual, fixed fire system. Some are easily recognized by the glass-enclosed cabinet and the folded fire hose. Others are simply large-diameter pipes that extend vertically through a building with connections

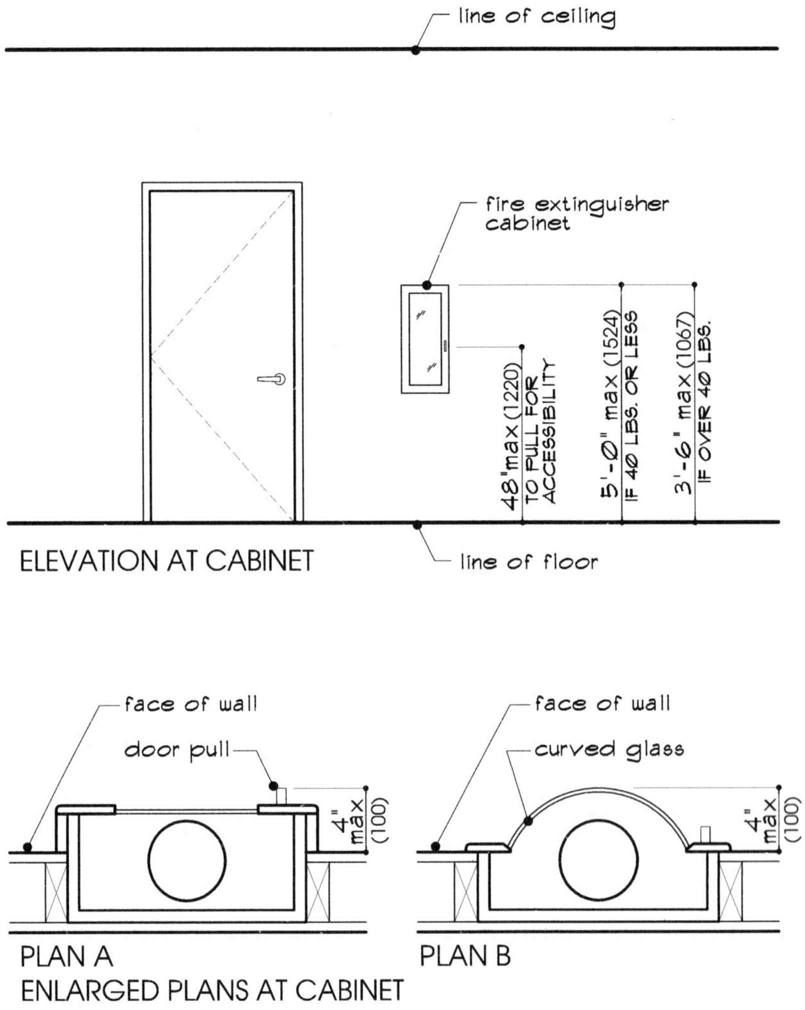

Figure 6.4 Typical Fire Extinguisher and Cabinet Mounting Requirements

for fire hose hookup. The system supplies water for extinguishing fires and can be used by firefighters or building occupants, depending on the class and type of system.

Class of Standpipes

Three classes of standpipes are classified by the codes. The classes are based on the purpose and intended use of the system.

1. *Class I:* Designed for fire department use or use by limited building personnel trained in its operation, Class I standpipes consist of pipes with high-pressure 2½-inch (63 mm) outlets for hookup to fire department hoses.
2. *Class II:* Primarily designed for building occupants, Class II standpipes have hoses attached that are usually limited to 1½ inches (38 mm) in diameter or smaller. They are designed for small-scale fire protection and are mostly used in buildings that do not have a sprinkler system.
3. *Class III:* Class III is a combination of Class I and Class II standpipes. It is designed for use by the building occupants or the fire department. It includes both a 2½-inch (63 mm) outlet for fire department hookup and a 1½-inch (38 mm) outlet with 1½-inch (38 mm) hose and nozzle.

Note

A standpipe riser (e.g., pipe) may also serve as a sprinkler system riser if specific codes requirements are met.

Types of Standpipes

There are also five different types of standpipe systems.

1. *Automatic wet system.* An automatic wet system has a water supply within the piping system that is ready upon demand. It is considered the most effective and most reliable system.
2. *Automatic dry system.* An automatic dry system is normally filled with pressured air. The use of a hose valve is required to admit water into the system.
3. *Manual wet system.* A manual wet system does not have water in the pipes themselves, but is connected to a water supply that must be pumped into the pipes by the fire department.
4. *Manual dry system.* A manual dry system does not have water within the pipes or in an attached supply. The water must be pumped in from the fire department.
5. *Semiautomatic dry system.* A semiautomatic dry system is similar to an automatic dry system, but a remote control located at the hose connection is required to activate the valve to admit water into the system.

The type and class of a required standpipe depends on the code, the type of occupancy, the height of the building, and the presence of a sprinkler system. The types of buildings that may require standpipes include multi-story buildings with or without sprinklers, high-rise buildings (see inset titled *High-Rise Buildings* on page 108), storage buildings, and certain other spaces. Also, large stages within any building type must have a standpipe.

Each code sets slightly different requirements for standpipes. These requirements are included in the building codes, and the fire codes. The codes also refer to the standard *NFPA 14, Installation of Standpipes, Private Hydrants and Hose Systems.* This standard specifies the number, type, and locations for standpipes. Most standpipes are located on each landing in the building's exit stair enclosure or smokeproof vestibule. Not only does this provide easy access, it also provides fire protection for one to two hours. Class II standpipes may require additional locations for accurate coverage with the fire hose. Since Class II standpipes are meant for use by building occupants, placing the fire hose cabinet so that it is accessible also becomes important. Both the pull to the cabinet and the operable parts in the cabinet should be at accessible height and reach ranges.

Sprinkler Systems

Note

Since automatic sprinklers have been in use since the beginning of the century, some older buildings may have systems that are considered antiquated. Ultimately, a code official must decide whether an old system needs to be replaced to meet the codes.

Automatic sprinkler systems are invaluable in the containment of a fire. Research shows that the number of lives lost during a fire is greatly reduced when automatic sprinklers are present. As a result, more occupancies and use groups are required to install automatic sprinkler systems where previously these systems were optional. In addition, when an automatic sprinkler system is installed, the codes allow trade-offs in other aspects of a design. For example, when an automatic sprinkler system is provided within a incidental use room, the one-hour separation is often not required. (Refer to Sprinkler Design Issues section for additional trade-offs.)

Automatic sprinklers are devices that are sensitive to heat. When exposed to a certain amount of heat, the sprinkler heads will release the water. Typically, only the sprinkler heads exposed to the heat will be activated, although this might not always be the case, especially with older systems. In addition, most are required to be tied into an alarm system so that the occupants, the appropriate building personnel, and the fire department are notified in an emergency. Although water damage may occur from the release of water by the sprinkler system (5 to 25 gallons/minute, depending on the type of sprinkler), it will be considerably less than the damage that would occur if the fire department had to extinguish the fire with a fire hose (200 to 250 gallons/minute).

The NFPA is the main source for sprinkler requirements. *NFPA 13, Standard for Installation of Sprinkler Systems* is the standard most referenced by the codes, and is used throughout the country. It lists detailed design and installation requirements, and references a number of other NFPA standards. (Other sprinkler standards are shown in Figure 6.1.) However, it is the building codes, the fire codes, and *LSC* that specify when an automatic sprinkler system is required. Each code specifies the types of occupancies, types of buildings, and special rooms that generally require sprinklers. The type of construction may also make a difference.

Uses and Occupancies Requiring Sprinkler Systems

Almost all occupancies are required by codes to have automatic sprinkler systems when certain conditions exist. However, each occupancy also has exceptions for when an automatic sprinkler system is not required. The size of the space, the number of occupants, the mobility of the occupants, height and area of the overall building, types of hazards present, and sometimes the capacity of the local fire department all factor into when the fire and building codes require sprinklers. In addition, incidental use rooms, as discussed in Chapter 5 (see Figure 5.8), are often allowed to use an automatic sprinkler system in place of fire-resistant rated construction. You should refer to the code for the specific requirements. The most common areas where sprinkler systems are required are listed here.

Note

Depending on the occupancy, the amount of hazards, and the type of system, most sprinkler systems require each sprinkler head to cover and protect 90 to 200 square feet (8.4 to 18.6 s m). The typical distance between the sprinkler heads ranges from 12 to 15 feet (3658 to 4572 mm). It is usually up to the sprinkler designer or engineer to determine the exact requirements.

Buildings

- ❑ Aircraft hangars
- ❑ Amusement buildings
- ❑ Parking garages
- ❑ Covered malls
- ❑ High-rise buildings
- ❑ Underground structures
- ❑ Unlimited area buildings
- ❑ Windowless story

Note

Sprinkler requirements for some occupancies may result in a partial system or a "limited area" sprinkler system, where only a part of a building is covered by sprinklers to meet minimum code requirements. However, this is usually not recommended, and it must be approved by the jurisdictions.

Special Rooms and Areas

- ❑ Atriums
- ❑ Drying rooms
- ❑ Duct systems exhausting hazardous materials
- ❑ Furnace and boiler rooms
- ❑ Hazardous materials
- ❑ Incinerators
- ❑ Kitchen exhaust systems
- ❑ Rubbish and linen chutes
- ❑ Spray-painting shops or booths
- ❑ Stages
- ❑ Tops of chutes
- ❑ Unenclosed vertical openings

Other common locations for sprinklers depend on your design. Unique situations often call for additional sprinkler locations. For example, if you use a continuous glass wall as a rated wall, you may need to add a number of sprinkler heads to both sides of the wall. Even using some finishes such as light-transmitting plastic may require the use of additional sprinkler heads.

Types of Sprinkler Systems

An engineer typically determines which type of sprinkler system to use. Using the codes and the NFPA standards, the engineer also determines the size and number of pipes and the spacing of the sprinkler heads. Most systems are one of these four types:

1. **Wet pipe system:** A wet pipe system is the most common system. It uses water to extinguish a fire and consists of pipes that are water filled at all times. When a fire occurs, the heat from the fire activates the sprinkler. The heat melts the fuse link, causing water to discharge immediately. This type is typically considered the most effective and is used most often.

> **Note**
> The typical wet pipe sprinkler system is usually equipped with a fire department connection as a secondary source of water supply when 20 or more sprinklers are present.

2. **Dry pipe system:** A dry pipe system is used in unheated building types such as storage facilities to prevent freezing. Instead of water, the pipes are filled with pressurized air or nitrogen. When activated by the heat of a fire, the air is released and water floods the pipes to extinguish the fire.
3. **Deluge system:** A deluge system is an open-head water system. It is usually activated by a separate detection system (sometimes a controlled system) and is used in hazardous situations. The deluge system discharges large quantities of water to control severe fires. In areas where large quantities of water are not desirable (e.g., electrical situations), it can be used in conjunction with other agents.
4. **Preaction system:** A preaction system is a combination of wet and dry systems to allow delayed reaction and warning signals. Like the deluge system, it is activated by a detection system. The delayed reaction allows the system to be manually intercepted and turned off if the sprinklers are not necessary. It is used primarily in areas where property is susceptible to water damage (e.g., museums) or where sprinkler pipes are likely to get damaged.

> **Note**
> Some jurisdictions will have additional sprinkler requirements for certain occupancies or building types, such as schools or nursing homes. Be sure to check with the jurisdiction.

Both wet and dry systems require the same piping. The risers supply the water from the building's incoming water supply to the cross mains at each floor. The cross mains supply the branch lines. Sprinkler heads are at the end of each branch line.

Types of Sprinkler Heads

The most common types of sprinkler heads are described in this section. The different types are determined by how quickly they respond to a fire, the size of the orifice, and the distribution of water, as well as other special features. The orientation of the head also makes a difference in its effect. The most common orientations include pendant, upright, sidewall, recessed, and concealed. Figure 6.5 explains these orientation styles and their uses. The orientation of the head is typically determined by the design or construction requirements, the location of the head, and the area it is meant to cover. For example, a finished ceiling will require a sprinkler head with a different orientation than an exposed or open ceiling. A wall-mounted head will be different, also. These various sprinkler orientations are noted for each of the following types of sprinkler heads:

1. *Standard spray head:* This is the most common type of sprinkler head. It can be used in most occupancies and building uses. It can be used as an upright, pendant, or sidewall type. Recessed pendant or sidewall heads, as well as concealed heads, are also options. Each head can typically cover approximately 225 square feet (20.9 s m). The standard for their use and installation is *UL 199, Standard for Automatic Sprinklers for Fire Protection Service* or *FM Class 2000, Approval Standard for Automatic Sprinklers for Fire Protection.*

2. *Fast-response sprinkler head:* This type is activated by a low level of heat. The name is somewhat misleading in that it does not mean that this system will respond quicker than other systems. Response time is affected by ceiling height, spacing, ambient room temperature, and distance below the ceiling. However, it may activate earlier because it requires less heat. Sprinkler systems described as early suppression and quick response typically use fast-response sprinkler heads.

3. *Residential sprinkler head:* This type is not typically intended to extinguish the fire but to minimize the heat buildup and the production of carbon monoxide in order to provide an acceptable environment within the space while occupants are exiting. These sprinkler heads are considered a type of fast-response sprinkler. They have a unique spray pattern that is different from standard or quick-response sprinklers. They can be pendant or sidewall type heads and are often recessed when used in Residential occupancies. Although designed for *NFPA 13D* systems, they can be used in *NFPA 13R* and *NFPA 13* systems as allowed by code. (See Figure 6.1.) The standard for their use and installation is *UL 1626, Standard for Residential Sprinklers* and *FM Class 2030, Approval Standard for Residential Automatic Sprinklers.*

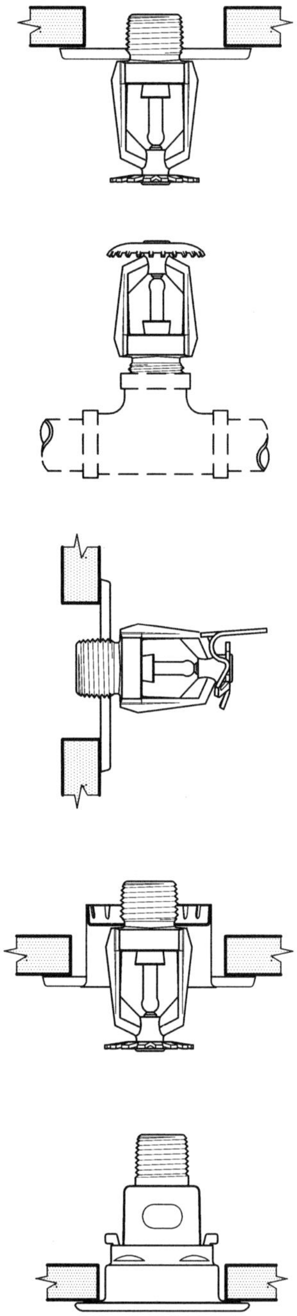

PENDANT
the head is surface mounted and extends below the finished ceiling, most commonly used in finished ceilings and suspended ceiling tiles

UPRIGHT
the head is fully exposed and sits above the branch "feed lines" which supply the water, typically used in spaces with high or unfinished ceilings

SIDEWALL
the head is surface mounted to a finished wall, commonly used in corridors and small rooms where one head or one row will adequately cover the area (also available to be mounted recessed)

RECESSED
the head is partially recessed into the ceiling, the depth of the recess can vary but the lower portion of the head is always exposed, often used in residential occupancies

CONCEALED
the head is fully recessed and includes a cover that hides the fusible element so that you cannot see it, the cover falls off when a fire occurs to allow the head to activate and disperse water, often used in decorative ceilings

Figure 6.5 Orientation of Sprinkler Heads (Line drawings reprinted with permission from Viking Group, www.vikingcorp.com.)

4. *Quick-response sprinkler head:* Sometimes residential and quick-response sprinklers are thought to be the same type. However, they have different uses, spray patterns, and designs. Quick-response heads can be upright, pendant, or sidewall. They can be used in residential and commercial occupancies as allowed by the codes. The standard for their use and installation is *UL 199* and *FM Class 2000.*
5. *Extended coverage sprinkler head:* These heads have a spray pattern that can cover up to 400 square feet (37.2 s m), requiring fewer heads but higher water pressure and water flow rate. These are often used in large open areas and can be upright, pendant, or sidewall. Also, some can be considered quick response.
6. *Large drop sprinkler head:* These heads deliver water in large droplets and are often used in occupancies where a fire may be difficult to suppress, such as a large fire that could occur in a storage facility.
7. *Open sprinkler head:* These heads are used in deluge systems. The heads remain open and are not activated by their own heat detector but by a separate detector. These systems are often monitored or controlled. When activated, the heads release large amounts of water. They are used in areas where severe fire could occur.
8. *Specialty sprinkler head:* Specialty sprinklers are available for other needs of a space, such as tamper-resistant or corrosion-resistant sprinklers. In addition, many new types of sprinkler heads are available for specific design criteria to meet both functional requirements and aesthetic needs. Decorative sprinkler heads in custom colors, flush or low profiles, and with other similar features are available. Different types of cover plates can also be used to conceal recessed sprinkler heads. These may be especially desirable in lobbies, conference rooms, and living areas where other types would distract from the design of the space.

New types of sprinklers are constantly being developed to address the specific needs of building uses and design ideas. You should keep up to date so that you can assist in the choice of the best type for your project and your client's needs.

Sprinkler Design Issues

Although adding a sprinkler system is expensive, it usually saves money in other areas of construction. The codes allow automatic sprinkler systems as a trade-off for other code requirements. It may be a major trade-off, such as constructing a larger building, or a smaller trade-off, such as not having to rate a wall. For example, in some occupancies, the corridor walls are not required to be rated if the building is sprinklered. Other common sprinkler trade-offs have been listed for you in Figure 6.6. Be sure to refer to the specific codes if any of them pertain to an interior project and make sure it is allowed by your jurisdiction. Also, remember that an existing sprinkler system must typically meet the current code require-

Note

Before using any of the allowed sprinkler trade-offs, be sure the building or space has an approved automatic sprinkler system, as defined by the most current code.

BUILDING AREA

May allow some buildings to increase in size horizontally resulting in more square feet per building.

BUILDING HEIGHT

May allow one story to be added to the height of a building.

CONSTRUCTION TYPES

May allow a less fire-resistant construction type.

MEANS OF EGRESS

May allow an increase in the distance of travel from the most remote point to the exit, certain escalators are permitted without enclosure, exit stairs and accessible elevators may not need an area of refuge, possibly longer dead-end corridors.

FIRE AND SMOKE SEPARATION

May allow up to three floor levels of stairways and other openings between floors not to be fully enclosed, may eliminate separate means of venting smoke in elevators, omit fire dampers, reduce number of draftstops, larger areas of glazing, lower fire ratings of assemblies, lower rating of opening protectives, less compartmentation in high-rise buildings.

FIRE PROTECTION

May reduce number of fire alarms, reduce number of fire extinguishers, eliminate or reduce number of standpipes.

INTERIOR FINISHES AND FURNISHING

May allow a lower class rating of a finish, eliminate firestops behind raised finishes, additional foam plastic insulation, additional decorative trim, lower furniture ratings.

NOTE: An existing sprinkler system must typically meet the most current code requirements of an automatic sprinkler system in order for you to use any of the sprinkler trade-offs listed above. Be sure to consult with a code official when necessary.

Figure 6.6 Common Sprinkler Trade-Offs

ments of an automatic sprinkler system in order for you to use any of the sprinkler trade-offs.

For interior projects, the most significant design issues include the selection of the type(s) of sprinkler system and sprinkler heads and the layout of the sprinkler heads. These decisions are based on the actual situation, as well as the code requirements. For instance, the configuration of the space and the desired coverage determine the layout of the sprinkler heads. The ceiling height and type of ceiling may also affect the layout, as will the type of desired head and head orientation. For example, different types will be used if the ceiling is sloped, horizontal, smooth, or coffered. An exposed ceiling versus a finish ceiling also makes a difference. For many projects these will be determined in conjunction with an engineer or fire protection (sprinkler) designer as they design the overall sprinkler system based on the layout and design of the space. You may also want to direct the use of specialty sprinkler heads in certain areas such as lobbies or conference rooms for aesthetic reasons.

Note

In a multi-story building, it is possible to have a sprinkler system installed in one story and not another.

Note

A project may have more than one type of sprinkler head. For example, you might want to use a concealed head in a decorative ceiling and an exposed pendant in less public areas.

As the designer, you should be familiar with common layout parameters so you can coordinate other aspects of the design, such as lighting, ceiling grids, decorative ceiling elements, furr downs, and other design elements. It is a good idea to coordinate these items with the sprinkler designer early in a project. The location of partial height walls, tall furniture, shelving, or cabinetry can block the coverage of some sprinkler heads. Although 18 inches (457 mm) of clearance below the sprinkler deflector is a rule of thumb, the use of specialty sprinklers may require additional clearances. Clearances and spacing dimensions are beyond the scope of this book but are found within standards such as *NFPA 13*.

Changes to an existing space can also affect the proper layout of the sprinkler heads. If the occupancy type in a space has changed, the existing layout of sprinklers may not be adequate. Also, the addition or removal of walls may affect the required sprinkler head locations as needed for proper coverage, or the addition of a suspended ceiling may require a change in the type of sprinkler head. In addition, if you are making changes to an existing space, the existing sprinkler system or layout may not be compliant with the most current codes for that occupancy classification or space. The effect of modifications to a sprinklered space should always be considered in the design. You will want to coordinate these issues with the system designer, or for small projects refer to the codes for the specific requirements.

Note

In some locations, drapes and blinds on windows and glass walls may affect the performance of a sprinkler system.

Alternative Extinguishing Systems

Sprinklers may not be appropriate in every situation. Fires can begin in enclosed spaces or in locations where they are shielded from the sprinkler head. Other fires ignite and travel too quickly. Some types of fires should not be extinguished with water. For example, sprinklers typically should not be used close to large electrical equipment such as the computer and telephone equipment found in telecommunication rooms. Restaurant kitchens and other rooms with the potential for a grease fire should also limit water as an extinguisher. When a sprinkler system does not use water, the system is often referred to as non-water-based fire extinguishing. Alternate systems include wet-chemical, dry-chemical, foam, carbon dioxide, halon, and clean-agent extinguishing materials. Each agent may have a separate standard it must meet. Many of these are listed in Figure 6.1.

Note

If you are working on a project in which a sprinkler system may be inappropriate, be sure to research other fire-extinguishing systems, as well as automatic fire-detection systems.

The codes generally allow the code official to approve the appropriate alternative agent. This allows you, the system designer, and the client to propose the best agent for the situation. Other buildings that contain extremely valuable items, such as libraries and museums, may eliminate sprinklers, limit their use, or use delayed reaction sprinklers.

In the past, systems that discharged halon were widely used in situations where a water-based system was not desirable. But since halon has been determined to contribute to the erosion of the ozone layer, it is no longer produced. However, systems that use halon may still be in place in existing buildings. Recycled halon is still available for use in these systems, since replacing existing systems with alternatives can require redesign of the entire system.

CHECKLIST

Figure 6.7 is a fire protection checklist that can be used on your interior projects or as a guideline to make your own checklist. It indicates each main type of detection, alarm, and extinguishing system required by the codes. The checklist can be used to remind you of what to look for and research on a project, as well as to give you a place to record the necessary code information for future reference. Remember, however, that it must be used in conjunction with the codes and standards required in your jurisdiction as well as the ADA guidelines and other accessibility requirements.

The checklist begins with the standard blanks for the project and space name, the occupancy classification, and the construction type of the building. (If necessary, refer to Chapters 2 and 3 to determine these.) The remainder of the checklist lists the types of detection, alarm, and extinguishing systems. To the left of each component is a blank space so you can check off the systems required in your project. For example, if you are using alarms, some may need to be both visual and audible. Others may need to be only visual. Check only those that apply.

Fire Protection Checklist

Date:____________

Project Name:____________________________________ Space: ______________

Occupancy (new or existing):____________________________________

Type of Construction:____________________________________

REQUIRED FIRE PROTECTION (check those that apply)	EXT'G (yes/no)	LOCATION(S) IN BUILDING	TYPE OF SYSTEM/ ITEM REQUIRED (list information)	QUANTITIES REQUIRED (new or add'l)
Detection Systems Engineer Required? ___YES ___ NO __ Smoke Detector(s) __ Heat Detector(s) __ Manual Fire Alarm(s) __ Other:_______________				
Alarm Systems Engineer Required? ___YES ___ NO __ Visual/Audible Alarm(s) __ Audible only __ Visual only __ Voice Communication System(s) __ Accessible Warning System(s) __ Emergency Alarm(s) __ Other:_______________				
Extinguishing Systems Engineer Required? ___YES ___ NO __ Fire Extinguisher(s) __ Fire Extinguisher Cabinet(s) __ Standpipe(s) __ Fire Hose(s) __ Sprinkler System(s) __ Types of Head(s) __ Orientation of Head(s) __ Alternate System(s) __ Other:_______________				

NOTES:

1. Refer to codes and standards for specific information as well as ADA guidelines and ICC/ANSI standard for additional requirements.
2. If automatic sprinkler systems are used, make sure they are approved and check for possible code trade-offs.
3. Consult and coordinate detection/alarm systems with electrical engineers and extinguishing systems with mechanical engineers.
4. Be sure to note on floor plans the location of fire-rated walls and floor/ceilings for placement of required fire dampers and fire stops.

Figure 6.7 Fire Protection Checklist

Then for each component that is required, fill in the necessary information. If the system or component already exists in the building, make a note in the "Existing" column. This will be helpful when you need to match existing conditions. Use the next column to indicate the location of the system. For example, indicate which areas of the building or space require a sprinkler system. You may want to use a separate checklist for different areas of a building or attach a copy of a floor plan locating the devices.

The next two columns are for you to indicate the specific types of systems or components and quantities that may be required. Use the lists and figures in the text to help you. For example, for sprinkler systems you might list a wet pipe system. Then list standard spray as the type of head and pendant/concealed as the orientation of the head. As you are filling out the checklist, be sure to consult with the appropriate engineer or other experts to determine the exact requirements necessary for your project.

CHAPTER 7

PLUMBING AND MECHANICAL REQUIREMENTS

This chapter covers two separate code items—plumbing codes and mechanical codes. Unlike most of the codes already discussed in the previous chapters, the mechanical and plumbing codes address issues that concentrate on health and welfare concerns instead of life safety. Although there were originally separate plumbing and mechanical codes for each model code organization, these were replaced by the I-Codes. The International Code Council (ICC) published the first *International Plumbing Code (IPC)* in 1995 and the first *International Mechanical Code (IMC)* in 1996. Each is updated every three years. However, in 2003 the National Fire Protection Association (NFPA) published their first version of the plumbing and mechanical codes as part of their set of C3-Codes. (See Comparing the Codes sections later in the chapter.) Although most jurisdictions are currently using the I-Codes, this might change in the future. You may also find some jurisdictions are still requiring one of the older model codes instead.

Note

Requirements for other plumbing-related items such as sprinklers and standpipes (as discussed in Chapter 6) are found in the building codes and other standards.

On interior projects that include major plumbing or mechanical work, you will usually require the services of a professional engineer who will know and incorporate these codes. (Whether an engineer is required will depend on the amount of work that needs to be done and the code jurisdiction's rules regarding the use of a licensed engineer.) Even on smaller projects that do not require the services of an engineer, a licensed plumbing or mechanical contractor will know the codes. Yet, as the designer, you need to know certain requirements in each code. For example, you will need to be able to determine the quantity of plumbing fixtures required in your projects. You will also need to be aware of how your design affects various components of a mechanical system. In addition to the requirements in the plumbing and mechanical codes, further related requirements are found in other code publications, such as the building codes and energy codes. The key terms and requirements in each of the codes will be discussed throughout this chapter.

The first part of this chapter is dedicated to the plumbing codes required for interior projects. It covers the quantities and types of plumbing fixtures and plumbing facilities required by the codes and discusses the accessibility standards for each. The second part of the chapter discusses the main types of mechanical systems and the codes that affect the various components. The last part of the chapter discusses related sustainability issues and then introduces a checklist that incorporates the various plumbing and mechanical requirements discussed throughout the chapter.

PLUMBING REQUIREMENTS

As the designer, you will need to know certain plumbing code requirements. However, when an interior project requires a substantial amount of plumbing work, you will generally use the services of a licensed engineer. Typically, you will design the space and place the fixtures, and the engineer will design the corresponding plumbing system. (See inset titled *The Basic Plumbing System* on page 255.) Smaller design projects, like adding a breakroom or a small toilet facility, or relocating a few sprinkler heads, may not require the services of an engineer. Instead a licensed plumbing contractor will do the work directly from your drawings or, if required, supply plumbing "shop" drawings.

Note

Whether an engineer is required depends on the jurisdiction of the project. Each jurisdiction has specific requirements for professional services and stamped drawings. (See Chapter 10.)

In each case, you should be familiar with various plumbing code requirements, especially as they apply to plumbing fixtures. These will be explained below. After reviewing the various codes and standards that affect plumbing systems, the rest of this section will concentrate on how to determine which plumbing fixtures are required in a project and the specific requirements for each fixture. It discusses the codes and accessibility requirements that apply to each fixture. The last part of this section will discuss how to incorporate these fixtures, along with the necessary accessories, finishes, and signage, into toilet and bathing facilities.

Key Terms

Below is a list of terms relating to plumbing codes and plumbing fixtures that will be defined and discussed in this chapter. They are also defined in the glossary.

Accessory
Bathing facility

Family toilet room
Plumbing fixture
Restroom
Toilet facility
Unisex toilet facility

Comparing the Codes

As mentioned earlier in the chapter, there are two main plumbing codes. The *International Plumbing Code (IPC)*, as published by the International Code Council (ICC), has been in existence since 1995 and is now on a three-year publication cycle. This is the most widely used plumbing code. The more current editions include 2003 and 2006. More recently, the National Fire Protection Association (NFPA) collaborated with the International Association of Plumbing and Mechanical Officials (IAPMO) to publish the first edition of the *Uniform Plumbing Code (UPC)* in 2003. (This is not to be confused with the older model code with the same title.) In addition, the Plumbing-Heating-Cooling Contractors Association continues to publish its *National Standard Plumbing Code (NSPC)*, and older editions of the model plumbing codes may still be in use in some jurisdictions. You should verify which plumbing code your jurisdiction enforces.

The plumbing codes cover all parts of a plumbing system and include requirements on such things as water supply and distribution, water heaters, and sanitary and storm drainage, as well as vent, trap, and interceptor requirements. The codes also reference multiple industry standards. The part of the plumbing code that you need to know as the designer can basically be narrowed down to one chapter in each code. It is the chapter on plumbing fixtures. In the *IPC* this chapter is titled "Fixtures, Faucets and Fixture Fittings"; in the *UPC* it is called "Plumbing Fixtures and Fixture Fittings." Each code describes the types of fixtures and supplies a table that indicates the number and type of plumbing fixtures required for each occupancy classification or building type. This table is discussed later in this chapter.

However, the plumbing codes are not the only resource for plumbing requirements. Both the *International Building Code (IBC)* and the *NFPA 5000* have a chapter titled "Plumbing Systems." For the most part, these short chapters refer you to their respective plumbing codes and other standards for additional requirements. In addition, the *IBC* chapter discusses minimum toilet facility requirements and duplicates the plumbing fixture table found in the *IPC*. It also includes a short section on materials for toilet and bathing facilities in its "Interior Environment" chapter. Other plumbing-related items such as sprinkler systems, standpipes, fire hoses, and fire extinguishers can be found in other sections of the building codes dealing with fire protection. These sections often refer you to various standards as well. (These are explained in more detail in Chapter 6.) Additional plumbing requirements will be found in the energy codes. (This is described in more detail in the section on Energy Efficiency and Water Conservation at the end of this chapter.)

Note

When determining clearances and specific dimension requirements for accessible toilet facilities, pay particular attention to whether they are minimum, maximum, or absolute dimensions. Many of these dimensions are critical.

Depending on your project, you may also need to reference the performance codes. When using the *IPC* and other corresponding I-Codes, plumbing-related performance criteria will be found in the *ICC Performance Code (ICCPC)*, which has a chapter dedicated to plumbing. Its sections include personal hygiene, laundering, domestic water supplies, and wastewater. The *UPC*, on the other hand, has some alternate materials and methods provisions within the code but does not include a performance chapter like other publications by the NFPA. Instead, you will need to refer to the performance chapter in the *NFPA 5000* for related performance criteria.

Specific accessibility requirements must also be followed when selecting and locating plumbing fixtures. Both the Americans with Disabilities Act (ADA) guidelines and the ICC/ANSI accessibility standard *ICC/ANSI 117.1* provide similar requirements. Accessibility requirements are also found in the accessibility chapter of the building codes. The building codes then reference the ICC/ANSI standard for specifics. When used together they include such things as minimum clearances, location requirements, ease of control use, and other accessibility standards. These accessibility requirements are discussed in this chapter as they apply to various plumbing fixtures, plumbing facilities, and other related items. Note, however, that the accessibility requirements in each document are not always the same. (Some of the differences will be described throughout this chapter with the most stringent requirements used in each diagram. Be sure to consult original sources when required.)

Quantity of Plumbing Fixtures

Determining the quantity of plumbing fixtures is the first step when designing an interior project that requires them. The number of plumbing fixtures required by the codes must be calculated when there is new construction, when a building addition is made, and when an occupancy classification changes. The number of water closets, urinals, lavatories, sinks, drinking fountains, bathtubs, showers, and other required plumbing fixtures will affect the type of toileting and/or bathing facilities required in each project. Typically, you need to know the number of *fixtures* before you can determine the type or number of *facilities* you need. The total quantity of fixtures will also affect the number that are required to be accessible. All these factors will affect your design. For example, the number of stan-

THE BASIC PLUMBING SYSTEM

All plumbing systems can be broken down into three main components:

1. *Drainage system:* This part of the plumbing system is usually referred to as the DWV or *drain-waste-vent* system. It consists of wide pipes, since it operates on gravity, starting at the plumbing fixture and ending at the public sewage system. It consists of three parts. *Traps* are used at the discharge of each fixture to prevent odors, gases, and insects from entering the building. Branch and stack *pipes* are required to transport the used water from the trap to the sewer. (It is a *soil stack* if it carries solid human waste and a *waste stack* if it carries other wastes.) And, vertical stack *vents* penetrate the roof of a building and allow harmful gases to escape as water is discharged.
2. *Water supply system:* This system consists of small-diameter pipes that use pressure to convey hot and cold water. First is the *main water line*, which brings water into the building from the public water system. Once in the building, it splits into two *distribution lines*. One leads cold water directly to the plumbing fixtures, and the other leads to the hot water heater for the water to be heated before it is distributed to a fixture. This system is controlled by valves located both at the entry into the building and at each fixture.
3. *Plumbing fixtures:* The fixtures are the beginning of the drainage system and the end source for the water supply system. They consist of water closets, lavatories, urinals, sinks, drinking fountains, bathtubs, showers, dishwashers, clothes washers, and other miscellaneous fixtures.

dard and accessible water closets will affect the size of a restroom or toilet facility, and the type of drinking fountain may affect the width or shape of a corridor. The plumbing code table is explained first, followed by a discussion of other code and accessibility requirements. Requirements for each fixture and how to use them together for the necessary toileting and bathing facilities will be discussed in the next sections.

Note

Unlike the other plumbing codes, the older *Standard Plumbing Code* by the SBCCI requires a separate calculation to determine the *occupant content* before the number of plumbing fixtures can be determined.

The Table

The number and type of fixtures required are determined by a table in the plumbing code. Each plumbing code has a table similar to the *IPC* Table 403.1, "Minimum Number of Required Plumbing Fixtures" shown in Figure 7.1. (The same table is also repeated in the *IBC* as Table 2902.1.) For each occupancy classification, the table lists the number of water closets, lavatories, bathtubs or showers, drinking fountains, and other miscellaneous fixtures, such as service sinks and washing machines, required by the codes. The number of required fixtures per person is based on the occupant load within the building or space. Typically,

TABLE 403.1
MINIMUM NUMBER OF REQUIRED PLUMBING FIXTURES
(See Sections 403.2 and 403.3)

NO.	CLASSIFICATION	USE GROUP	DESCRIPTION	WATER CLOSETS (URINALS SEE SECTION 419.2)		LAVATORIES		BATHTUBS/ SHOWERS	DRINKING FOUNTAIN (SEE SECTION 410.1)	OTHER
				MALE	FEMALE	MALE	FEMALE			
1	Assembly (see Sections 403.2, 403.5 and 403.6)	A-1	Theaters usually with fixed seats and other buildings for the performing arts and motion pictures	1 per 125	1 per 65	1 per 200		—	1 per 500	1 service sink
		A-2	Nightclubs, bars, taverns, dance halls and buildings for similar purposes	1 per 40	1 per 40	1 per 75		—	1 per 500	1 service sink
			Restaurants, banquet halls and food courts	1 per 75	1 pe r 75	1 per 200		—	1 per 500	1 service sink
		A-3	Auditoriums without permanent seating, art galleries, exhibition halls, museums, lecture halls, libraries, arcades and gymnasiums	1 per 125	1 per 65	1 per 200		—	1 per 500	1 service sink
			Passenger terminals and transportation facilities	1 per 500	1 per 500	1 per 750		—	1 per 1,000	1 service sink
			Places of worship and other religious services. Churches without assembly halls	1 per 150	1 per 75	1 per 200		—	1 per 1,000	1 service sink
		A-4	Coliseums, arenas, skating rinks, pools and tennis courts for indoor sporting events and activities	1 per 75 for the first 1,500 and 1 per 120 for the remainder exceeding 1,500	1 per 40 for the first 1,500 and 1 per 60 for the remainer exceeding 1,500	1 per 200	1 per 150	—	1 per 1,000	1 service sink
		A-5	Stadiums, amusement parks, bleachers and grandstands for outdoor sporting events and activities	1 per 75 for the first 1,500 and 1 per 120 for the remainder exceeding 1,500	1 per 40 for the first 1,500 and 1 per 60 for the remainder exceeding 1,500	1 per 200	1 per 150	—	1 per 1,000	1 service sink
2	Business (see Sections 403.2, 403.4 and 403.6)	B	Buildings for the transaction of business, professional services, other services involving merchandise, office buildings, banks, light industrial and similar uses	1 per 25 for the first 50 and 1 per 50 for the remainder exceeding 50		1 per 40 for the first 50 and 1 per 80 for the remainder exceeding 50		—	1 per 100	1 service sink
3	Educational	E	Educational facilities	1 per 50		1 per 50		—	1 per 100	1 service sink
4	Factory and industrial	F-1 and F-2	Structures in which occupants are engaged in work fabricating, assembly or processing of products or materials	1 per 100		1 per 100		(see Section 411)	1 per 400	1 service sink

Figure 7.1 *International Plumbing Code® (IPC®)* Table 403.1 Minimum Number of Required Plumbing Fixtures (*International Plumbing Code* 2003. Copyright 2003. Falls Church, Virginia: International Code Council, Inc. Reproduced with permission. All rights reserved.)

NO.	CLASSIFICATION	USE GROUP	DESCRIPTION	WATER CLOSETS (URINALS SEE SECTION 419.2		LAVATORIES		BATHTUBS/ SHOWERS	DRINKING FOUNTAIN (SEE SECTION 410.1)	OTHER
				MALE	FEMALE	MALE	FEMALE			
5	Institutional	I-1	Residential care	1 per 10		1 per 10		1 per 8	1 per 100	1 service sink
		I-2	Hospitals, ambulatory nursing home patients [b]	1 per room [c]		1 per room [c]		1 per 15	1 per 100	1 service sink per floor
			Employees, other than residential care [b]	1 per 25		1 per 35		—	1 per 100	—
			Visitors, other than residential care	1 per 75		1 per 100		—	1 per 500	—
		I-3	Prisons [b]	1 per cell		1 per cell		1 per 15	1 per 100	1 service sink
		I-3	Reformitories, detention centers, and correctional centers [b]	1 per 15		1 per 15		1 per 15	1 per 100	1 service sink
		I-4	Adult daycare and childcare [b]	1 per 15		1 per 15		1 per 15 [d]	1 per 100	1 service sink
6	Mercantile (see Sections 403.2, 403.5 and 403.6)	M	Retail stores, service stations, shops, salesrooms, markets and shopping centers	1 per 500		1 per 750		—	1 per 1,000	1 service sink
7	Residential	R-1	Hotels, motels, boarding houses (transient)	1 per guestroom		1 per guestroom		1 per guestroom	—	1 service sink
		R-2	Dormitories, fraternities, sororities and boarding houses (not transient)	1 per 10		1 per 10		1 per 8	1 per 100	1 service sink
		R-2	Apartment house	1 per dwelling unit		1 per dwelling unit		1 per dwelling unit	—	1 kitchen sink per dwelling unit; 1 automatic clothes washer connection per 20 dwelling units [e]
		R-3	One- and two-family dwellings	1 per dwelling unit		1 per dwelling unit		1 per dwelling unit	—	1 kitchen sink per dwelling unit; 1 automatic clothes washer connector per dwelling unit [e]
		R-4	Residential care/assisted living facilities	1 per 10		1 per 10		1 per 8	1 per 100	1 service sink
8	Storage (see Sections 403.2 and 403.4)	S-1 S-2	Structures for the storage of goods, warehouses, storehouse and freight depots. Low and Moderate Hazard.	1 per 100		1 per 100		1 per 1,000	See Section 411	1 service sink

a. The fixtures shown are based on one fixture being the minimum required for the number of persons indicated or any fraction of the number of persons indicated. The number of occupants shall be determined by the *International Building Code*.

b. Toilet facilities for employees shall be separate from facilities for inmates or patients.

c. A single-occupant toilet room with one water closet and one lavatory serving not more than two adjacent patient rooms shall be permitted where such room is provided with direct access from each patient room and with provisions for privacy.

d. For day nurseries, a maximum of one bathtub shall be required.

e. For attached one- and two-family dwellings, one automatic clothes washer connection shall be required per 20 dwelling units.

every floor in a building will require at least one toilet or restroom, but the actual number of fixtures and facilities depends on the type of occupancy and the number of occupants. In addition, some tenant spaces may want their own toilet facilities even if they are not required by the code. For example, an executive might want a private bathroom. In other cases, the code may require an additional facility to be added if a tenant or occupant does not have access to the common building facilities. For example, a guard station separate from the main building may need its own restroom.

The plumbing codes base the number of fixtures on the calculated occupant load. This depends on the occupancy classification of the space or building and is determined using the building code. (See Chapter 2 for more information on occupant loads.) Once you know the occupant load for the space or building, you can use the plumbing fixture table to determine the quantity and type of plumbing fixtures required. If any fixture total results in a fraction, *round up* to the nearest whole number. For example, if you are working on a school that will have 680 occupants, you would refer to the Educational occupancy section of the table in Figure 7.1. It requires one water closet for every 50 people. By dividing 680 by 50 and rounding up, you know that you will require a minimum of 14 water closets. Continuing across the *IPC* table, the school in this example would require the same number of lavatories, seven drinking fountains, and one service sink. The quantities would then be used to design the appropriate plumbing facilities for the school.

The plumbing fixture table should be used in conjunction with the other plumbing and fixture requirements specified in the plumbing code chapter. For example, the text will specify when urinals are allowed. Each table also has multiple footnotes. When determining plumbing fixture quantities and how to arrange them within a project, you should be aware of the following important aspects of the code:

1. *Male/female ratios:* You will notice in the plumbing fixture table that some water closets and lavatories are divided into male and female categories. When the code does not specify a fixture as male or female, the total number of fixtures should be distributed equally between the sexes. In the previous example, the 14 lavatories and water closets would be equally divided between male and female facilities. If the resulting quantity had been an odd number such as 15, you would typically round this up to allow for equal fixtures for each gender. (Also see item 7.)
2. *Grouping fixtures:* The required number of plumbing fixtures for toilet facilities can be combined into one common restroom (separate for males and females) if all applicable building occupants have access to them. For exam-

ple, if five female water closets are required on a floor, they can be combined into one women's restroom. However, in a large building, maximum travel distances might limit the number of fixtures that can be grouped together. Typically, no path of travel to a facility can be longer than 500 feet (152 m). (Also see item 5.) In addition, a certain percentage of the fixtures on each floor will need to be accessible.

3. *Private facilities:* A separate toilet facility provided for private use by a tenant or individual cannot be deducted from the total common facilities required for general use on the floor or in the building. For example, an executive suite might have a private toilet within the suite. (In addition, if it is for private use only, as in the case of an executive toilet room, accessibility requirements will typically not apply, but you may want to make it adaptable so that it could easily be converted to an accessible room should it become necessary.)

4. *Unisex facilities:* Typically, separate facilities are required for each sex. However, certain circumstances allow or require the use of a unisex or shared facility. First, some smaller occupancies with limited square footage and minimal occupants will sometimes *allow* a single facility with one lavatory and one water closet. Common examples include small office spaces and restaurants, individual retail stores, laundries, and beauty shops. In these cases, the plumbing codes give some parameters, but the final decision is usually made by the code official. Other occupancies may be *required* to have a separate unisex toilet or bathing facility in addition to the main facilities. They are intended to allow someone who is elderly or disabled, or even a child, to be assisted by someone of the opposite sex. Depending on the publication you are using, this requirement is located either within the accessibility chapter of the building code or in the plumbing code. These unisex toilet facilities are usually required by the codes when six or more water closets are provided. This includes many Assemblies and large Mercantile occupancies (e.g., malls). In addition, recreational facilities (e.g., gyms or health spas) that provide separate-sex bathing facilities will also require a unisex bathing room. These unisex facilities are counted in the total number of plumbing fixtures required, not in addition to the required amount, and are usually noted by a sign such as "Family" or "Unisex." In each case, the shared or unisex facility must be fully accessible. (See Single-Toilet Facilities on page 271.)

5. *Employee and customer facilities:* Typically, toilet facilities must be provided for both the employees in the space and the customers who visit the space. In most occupancies you have the choice to provide separate employee

Note

Remember that the plumbing fixture tables specify *minimum* requirements. You may want to include more fixtures, especially in Assembly occupancies, where it is normal for large groups of people to use the restrooms all at the same time, such as during intermissions.

and public facilities or combine them into one facility. Typically, a combined facility must be located within the employee working area. However, if the location is not accessible to customers, you may need to provide separate toilet facilities for them. An example may be a toilet facility located in a manufacturing area that might not be safe for a customer to walk through. Toilet facilities in Mercantile and Assembly occupancies such as restaurants, nightclubs, retail stores, and malls are allowed to be shared as well, but they are not required to be within the employee work area. Instead, the plumbing code specifies maximum travel distances from the employee area to the toilet facility. These are usually required within 500 feet (152 m) or 300 feet (91.4 m), depending on the building type. Some jurisdictions may require larger restaurants to have separate employee and customer facilities. In addition, Detentional/Correctional and Health Care occupancies must typically keep their employee toilet facilities separate from the inmates and patients.

6. *Unusual use group:* If a particular occupancy or use group is not covered by the plumbing fixture table, you must consult a local code official for the specific requirements. (If you want to get an estimate, use the type of occupancy most similar to your project; however, remember that the code official makes the final decision.)
7. *Unusual male/female ratios:* An adjustment may be made to the total number of fixtures or to the ratio of male to female facilities in certain cases. The codes typically allow you to work with your code official in special circumstances. The performance codes also allow for flexibility based on the intended use of the space or building. In addition, some jurisdictions have *potty parity* regulations that allow modification to the values provided within the code tables. These regulations often apply to Assembly occupancies. Modifications take into account factors like the probable division of the male and female population using the facilities, the frequency of use by each gender, and the difference in time it takes each gender to utilize the facilities. An example would be a sports stadium. With approval from the code official, you may also be able to modify the allocation of fixtures in facilities that are used predominantly by one gender, such as an all-female health club or an all-male dorm. In each case, you must provide satisfactory data to the code officials.

Accessibility Percentages

After determining the number and type of plumbing fixtures required by the codes, you need to determine which ones are required to be accessible. These requirements are found in the accessibility chapter of the building codes, the ADA guidelines, and the ICC/ANSI standard. Typically, all the fixtures used in a unisex or single-toilet facility must be accessible. Other requirements will be based on the number of fixtures within each facility. For example, when multi-toilet facilities are explained below, you will see that the number of water closets used in one room will determine the quantity of stalls that need to be accessible in that room. Other accessible facilities are based on the type of occupancy. For example, when an occupancy has a number of individual dwelling or sleeping units, such as hotels and apartment buildings in Residential occupancies and hospitals in Institutional occupancies, the percentage of units that are required to be fully accessible is also given. (See Chapter 2 for more information on occupancy classifications.)

Note

If an elevator does not service the floors above the ground floor of a building, the toilet facilities on these floors may not have to be accessible.

In some existing buildings it may be necessary to add a single-toilet or single-bathing facility that is accessible when it is not possible to adapt an existing facility. For example, more than one existing water closet may need to be removed to make room for an accessible one requiring a larger stall; this in turn may reduce the total number of fixtures to below what is required by the plumbing code. In some cases, adding a separate accessible single-toilet facility instead may satisfy the requirement for an accessible toilet when allowed in a jurisdiction. In addition, it may also be possible for it to be unisex so that it covers male and female requirements. Also note, as mentioned earlier, that the plumbing code requires some building types to have a separate unisex toilet facility in addition to and separate from the other required accessible facilities. This facility should follow the ADA guidelines and other accessibility requirements, since its primary intention is for elderly or disabled individuals. (See the Toileting and Bathing Facilities section starting on page 270.)

Note

Some accessibility standards may require different floor clearances for wall-mounted and floor-mounted water closets. This is not distinguished in the newer editions of the ADA guidelines and the ICC/ANSI standard.

Plumbing Fixture Requirements

Once you know the quantity and the type of fixtures required by the plumbing code table and the number of fixtures that have to be accessible, you need to research the specific requirements for each fixture. The most common plumbing fixtures are listed on the plumbing code table and are discussed here. These include water closets, urinals, lavatories, sinks, drinking fountains, bathtubs, and showers. Requirements for other types of fixtures are discussed in the plumbing code as well. Examples include bidets, food waste grinders, and laundry trays. In most cases, the codes simply reference industry standards for the installation of these fixtures, so they will not be discussed. However, if you are using more specialized fixtures such as baptisteries, aquariums, ornamental and lily ponds, ornamental fountain basins, and swimming pools, be sure to check for other code requirements. Fixtures in certain building types such as restaurants and hospitals may need to meet local health code requirements as well. In addition, you need to see if a jurisdiction has special requirements. For example, New York City requires the use of automatic faucets in many public toilet facilities.

Note

The local Health Department might also place requirements on certain plumbing fixtures in some occupancies.

The one code requirement that all plumbing fixtures have in common is that each fixture must be durable and finished with a smooth, nonabsorbent material. Although most fixtures are fabricated by the manufacturer this way, it might become an issue when specifying or designing custom plumbing fixtures. (See Finish Requirements in the next section.) Many fixtures must also meet certain water consumption standards as required for water conservation. (This will be discussed in more detail at the end of the chapter.)

Note

Except for waterclosets, the clear floor space required for accessibility at most plumbing fixtures is 30 by 48 inches (760 by 1220 mm).

Typically, the ADA guidelines and the accessibility chapter in the building codes will specify when a fixture is required to be accessible. If a fixture is to be accessible, the codes refer you to the ICC/ANSI standard. Specific dimension and location requirements are located in both the ADA guidelines and the ICC/ANSI standard. Although all fixtures must meet the basic code requirements, if a fixture is required to be accessible, different dimension and clearance criteria must usually be met. This section will discuss the various code and accessibility requirements for each fixture. The next section will explain additional requirements necessary when using these fixtures together in a toilet or bathing facility. (Be sure to refer to the plumbing and building codes, the ADA guidelines, and the ICC/ANSI standard for the specific requirements.)

Water Closets

Note

Additional plumbing fixtures that are not as common include spas, hot tubs, whirlpools, baptisteries, ornamental and lily pools, aquaria, and fountains. They have specific code requirements, as well. Consult an engineer or plumbing contractor when required.

The codes typically require every floor in a building to have at least one water closet (i.e., toilet). The plumbing code requirements for water closets include the types allowed and the clearances for installation. The most common requirement is that all water closets specified for public use must have an elongated bowl and a hinged seat with an open front. The codes also specify the maximum amount of water allowed per flush. Clearances for installation include specific dimensions at each side and in front of the bowl. For example, the *IPC* requires a typical water closet to have a minimum of 15 inches (381 mm) from the center of the bowl to the adjacent side wall and at least 21 inches (533 mm) clear in front of the bowl.

Accessible water closets must meet other requirements. For example, instead of a 15-inch (381 mm) minimum to the centerline of the bowl, 18 inches (455 mm) is typically required. (Some code and accessibility publications may allow a range of 16 to 18 inches (405 to 455 mm), but be sure to use the most restrictive requirements.) The height of the toilet seat must be between 17 and 19 inches (430 to 485 mm), as shown in Figure 7.2. Additional requirements are specified in the ADA guidelines and the ICC/ANSI standard. These include a variety of required floor clearances, depending on how the water closet is used. It depends on whether the water closet is the only one in the room or in a toilet stall. It can also depend on if the water closet is wall hung or floor mounted, or if it will have a front approach or side approach. (See Toilet and Bathing Facilities later in this chapter for additional options.) The most common clear floor space for a single water closet is 60 inches by 56 inches (1525 mm by 1420 mm). This extra clearance allows for the maneuverability of a wheelchair and access to grab bars.

Accessible water closets can have an automatic flushing mechanism or a manual control. If a manual flush control is used, it must be located on the "open side" of the toilet at a certain height (reach range) above the floor (see Figure 7.2) and must meet certain operable conditions. For example, it must be operable with one hand and it cannot take more than 5 pounds (22.2 N) of force to operate. Additional requirements for accessories such as grab bars and toilet paper dispensers are described later in the chapter.

Note

When designing spaces for children under the age of 6 such as nursery schools, a jurisdiction may allow some plumbing fixtures to be the size and height suitable for children.

Urinals

Urinals are not required by the plumbing codes in every occupancy. They are typically found in the male restrooms of schools, restaurants, clubs, lounges, transportation terminals, auditoriums, theaters, and churches. If they are required, they are usually substituted for one or more of the required water closets but only up to a certain quantity. The codes typically do not allow the number of urinals to be substituted for more than two-thirds (or 67 percent) of the required number of male water closets. (The *UPC* includes urinals as a category on its plumbing

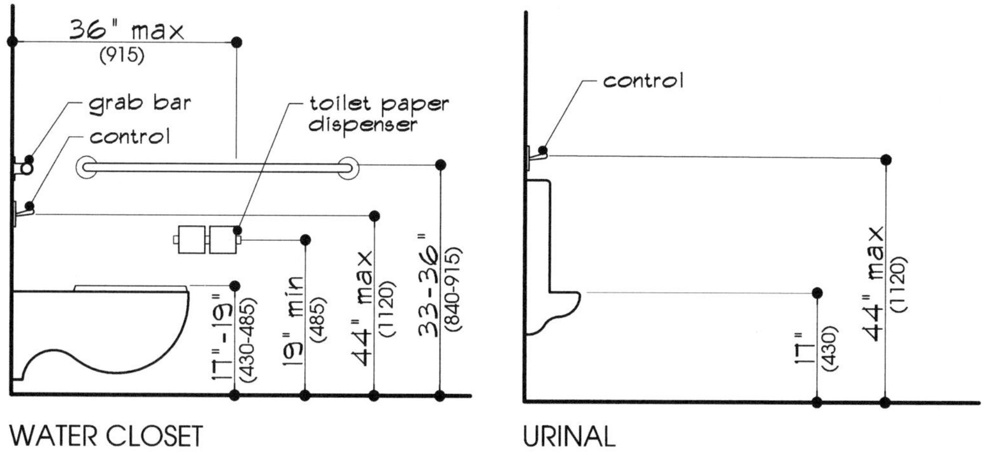

Figure 7.2 Typical Accessible Plumbing Fixture Dimensions: Water Closets and Urinals

fixture table.) Like water closets, urinals must meet a maximum water consumption requirement when flushed. In addition, the codes specify the type and location of the finish material surrounding the urinal for ease of cleaning and sanitation. (See section on Finish Requirements on page 278.)

When urinals are provided, the plumbing codes require minimum clearances for installation similar to those for water closets. In addition, at least one must comply with accessibility requirements. It must be either a stall type or a wall-hung fixture with an elongated rim at a maximum height above the floor, as shown in Figure 7.2. Clear floor space allowing front approach must be provided as well. This is typically 30 inches by 48 inches (760 mm by 1220 mm). If a privacy screen is used to the side of the urinal, it can be located either inside the clear floor space or outside the clear floor space. If it is located inside the required clear floor space, it cannot extend past the front edge of the urinal rim. The flush control requirements are similar to those on water closets.

Note

Although not required by the ADA guidelines, the use of automatic water and flushing controls that activate upon movement are also considered accessible, and are becoming more popular, especially in Assembly occupancies. Some jurisdictions may require them.

Lavatories

Anywhere a water closet is used, a lavatory (i.e., hand-washing sink) must also be installed. However, the same ratio is not always used by the codes. Typically the codes require fewer lavatories than water closets/urinals. The plumbing codes set few requirements for the location of a lavatory in a room. However, when locating the lavatory it must allow for the required clearance at the water closet and/or other fixtures in the room. The codes concentrate more on the faucet supplying the water. The codes typically limit the amount of hot water delivered by the faucet in the lavatory, especially in public facilities, to prevent scalding. Some jurisdictions may also set limits on the amount of water it dispenses and require that the faucet be automatic (i.e., sensor-operated) or metered so that it is self closing. This is more common in transient public facilities such as service stations, train stations, airports, restaurants, and convention halls, but could be required in other occupancies as well.

When the lavatory is required to be accessible, the faucet must meet additional requirements. The faucet must be within accessible reach ranges and have controls that are easy to operate. Lever handles, push types, and automatic faucets are often used.

Accessibility requirements call for at least one lavatory on each floor to be fully accessible. This includes the depth and height of the fixture. This is shown in Figure 7.3. In many restrooms where a continuous counter or vanity is provided, the entire run of lavatories is often made accessible for consistency of design. A washfountain that has multiple sprayheads and can accommodate multiple users at once is another option. These are found in building types such as

Note

There are at least three different ways to prevent contacts with hot water and drain pipes under a lavatory: (1) wrap them with insulated materials, (2) create an enclosure around the pipes, or (3) reconfigure the location of the pipes.

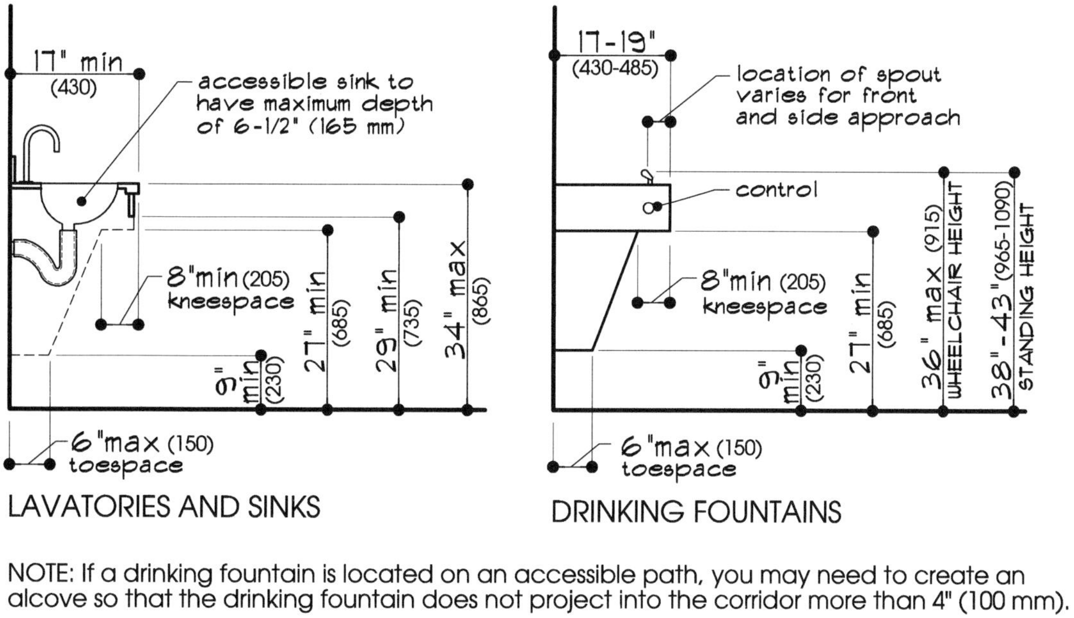

Figure 7.3 Typical Accessible Plumbing Fixture Dimensions: Lavatories, Sinks, and Drinking Fountains

schools, athletic facilities, industrial plants, movie theaters, and shopping malls. An accessible lavatory or washfountain must meet specific clearances and heights. (See Figure 7.3.) Most important is the clear floor space leading up to the lavatory and the kneespace and toespace underneath. The typical clear floor space required is 30 inches by 48 inches (760 mm by 1220 mm) that extends 19 inches (485 mm) under the sink to allow for a forward approach.

Because kneespace is required, all hot water and drain pipes must be covered to prevent contact. A cover can be as simple as insulated pipe wrapping, or it can be part of the countertop design, as shown by the dotted outline in Figure 7.3; however, the cover must be removable to allow access to the pipes when necessary. (Insulated covers must meet necessary finish requirements. See Chapter 9.)

Note

Installing lavatories and sinks with drains located toward the rear of the bowl can help save kneespace. Some pipes can be installed inside the wall if planned in advance.

Sinks

Sinks required by the codes are usually considered miscellaneous fixtures on the plumbing fixture table. They can include service sinks, utility sinks, kitchen sinks, and laundry basins. Some are required by the code, depending on the occupancy. For example, most occupancies require a utility sink (i.e., janitor or mop sink), although certain Residential occupancies are exempt. Other sinks are installed even when they are not required by the plumbing code. For example, kitchen or bar sinks in breakrooms are fairly common additions to an interior project. Utility sinks are not generally required to be accessible. However, in most nonresidential occupancies, at least one sink (and up to 5 percent when multiple sinks are used) is usually required by the codes to be accessible. For example, a sink in a breakroom must be accessible.

Note

Additional sink requirements for some occupancies or building types, such as restaurants and hospitals, are set by the local health department within a jurisdiction.

Most of the accessibility requirements are for kitchen-type sinks. The mounting requirements are similar to lavatories, as shown in Figure 7.3. The height is especially important when designing pantry areas in a breakroom or kitchenettes in a hotel room, where the counter height is typically 36 inches (915 mm) above the floor. An accessible counter has a maximum height of 34 inches (865 mm) at the sink, which means you need to either use a bi-level counter or lower the entire counter to 34 inches (865 mm) above the floor. You should also limit the depth of a kitchen counter to 25 inches (635 mm) so that you do not obstruct any reach ranges for items that may be installed above the sink.

Note

When plumbing pipes under an accessible sink are wrapped with insulation, the insulation must meet Class A requirements of the *Steiner Tunnel Test*. (See Chapter 9.)

The design of the counter with the sink must allow for a front approach. Similar to a lavatory, the typical clear floor space is 30 inches by 48 inches (760 mm by 1220 mm) that extends 19 inches (485 mm) under the sink. This can be done by leaving it open below the sink and covering the pipes accordingly or by installing specially designed doors that, when open, provide full clearance below. Another requirement sets the maximum depth of an accessible sink to 6½ inches (165 mm).

Drinking Fountains

Drinking fountains are required in most occupancies except certain Residential occupancies. If a building has more than one floor, the codes require that each floor have its own drinking fountain. However, restaurants that serve water are typically exempt from supplying a drinking fountain. More recently, the plumbing codes and some local code jurisdictions have also started to make allowances for spaces that provide bottled water dispensers and/or purified tap water in common areas. If these are supplied, a drinking fountain may not be required, but the final decision is still up to the code official.

Note

Some jurisdictions allow an alternate source of water in lieu of a drinking fountain (e.g., water cooler, accessible sink).

The codes restrict the location of drinking fountains. They cannot be installed in public toilet rooms or the vestibules leading to the toilet room. One of the most common locations for a drinking fountain is the corridor outside the restroom area. This typically provides a central location for the user and easy access to the plumbing pipes. If the drinking fountain is located in a corridor or other accessible path of travel, you must locate it so that it will not be considered a "protruding object." In many cases, this will require you to create an alcove or recessed area along the corridor. (An example is shown in Figure 7.6.) A protruding object is considered to be any object between 27 inches (685 mm) and 80 inches (2030 mm) above the floor that protrudes more than 4 inches (100 mm) into an accessible path.

At least one drinking fountain on every floor of a building must be accessible. If there is only one located on the floor, you typically have the option of using a "hi-low" fountain with water spouts at wheelchair and standing heights or an accessible drinking fountain with an adjacent water cooler. The "hi-low" drinking fountain provides a lower accessible spout for wheelchair users and a higher spout for people who find it difficult to bend low. If there is more than one drinking fountain on the same floor, the two types (one high, one low) can be located in different places. When there are multiple fixtures, usually 50 percent of them must be at the lower accessible height.

Note

When locating a drinking fountain in a corridor or other path of travel, remember that it cannot project more than 4 inches (100 mm) into the path according to the ADA guidlines and the ICC/ANSI standards.

The wheelchair accessible drinking fountain, like the one shown in Figure 7.3, requires the spout to be no higher than 36 inches (915 mm) above the floor and a front or side control that is easy to operate. The drinking fountain for standing persons should be located so that the spout outlet is located between 38 and 43 inches (965–1090 mm) above the floor. In addition, specific amounts of clear floor space must be provided. Cantilever drinking fountains for wheelchair access must allow a front approach and minimum knee and toe space, as shown in Figure 7.3. These units must typically have a clear floor space of 30 inches by 48 inches (760 mm by 1220 mm); but if the unit is built into an alcove, the alcove must be minimum of 36 inches (915 mm) wide to allow for the forward approach. (See Figure 7.6.) If a unit is free-standing or built in without clear space underneath, you must provide the clear floor space perpendicular to the unit to allow a parallel approach. (Note that a parallel approach for wheelchair accessible drinking fountains is not allowed by the new ADA guidelines in most occupancies.)

Bathtubs

Bathtubs are rarely required by the plumbing codes. When bathing facilities are required, typically a shower can be used in its place. (Local codes in certain jurisdictions may require at least one bathtub in some occupancies.) Bathtubs are most commonly found in Residential occupancies such as hotels, dormitories, and apartment buildings as well as single-family homes. (Many Institutional occupancies require a tub or shower as well, but showers are typically used.)

Note

One of the best types of accessible bathtub seats is one that extends from outside the tub into the head of the tub. It allows a person to do the maneuvering outside the tub before sliding in.

Although the plumbing codes do not regulate the size or type of bathtub, they do have requirements for certain accessory components, including the faucet, enclosure, and mechanical equipment. The faucet must be able to regulate the mix of hot and cold water to prevent scalding. If the tub is enclosed by glass and/or glass doors, safety glass must be used as specified in the building codes. In addition, if a whirlpool or spa type bathtub that includes a motor is used, the codes require that access be provided to the pump. Often this requires preplanning in the arrangement of the room and/or how certain finishes, such as ceramic tile, are being used.

If a bathtub is required in an accessible bathing room, it must meet specific requirements. As shown in Figure 7.4, there are certain height and location requirements for the tub itself as well as the faucet controls. In addition, the shower spray unit must be able to convert from a fixed to a hand-held unit and have a hose that is at least 60 inches (1525 mm) long. If there is a tub enclosure, it cannot hinder any of the accessible requirements and no tracks can be mounted to the top of the tub rim. (Glass doors are not recommended at accessible bathtubs.) All accessible tubs must also have a seat. This can include either a removable in-tub seat that spans the width of the bathtub or a permanent fixed seat a minimum of 15 inches (380 mm) deep at the head of the tub. The grab bar locations at the walls and the clear floor space required at the side of the tub will depend on the type of seat being used. For example, the typical floor clearance at the entrance side of a tub with an in-tub seat is 30 inches by 60 inches (760 mm by 1525 mm), but if a parallel approach is not possible you may need to allow for a 48-inch by 60-inch (1220 mm by 1525 mm) clear floor space. On the other hand, if the bathtub has a fixed seat, it will require a minimum clear floor space of 30 inches by 75 inches (760 mm by 1905 mm) and in some cases a longer clear space. (Also refer to section on Bathing Facilities later in this chapter.)

Note

The building codes typically allow light-transmitting plastics to be used as shower and tub enclosures as long as safety glass is used. (See Chapter 9.)

Showers

Like bathtubs, showers are typically required by the plumbing code in Residential and Institutional occupancies. (In many cases they are allowed to replace the bathtub.) Some Assembly occupancies, such as gymnasiums and health clubs, require showers as well. In addition, manufacturing plants, warehouses, foundries, and other similar establishments may require showers if employees are apt to be exposed to excessive heat or skin contamination. The plumbing fixture table as shown in Figure 7.1 will indicate when they are required.

The plumbing code specifies the type of shower pan and drain that must be used. In addition, it restricts water flow (for greater water conservation) and sets the maximum hot water temperature of the faucet. When prefabricated shower and shower compartments are not used, the codes specify the types of finish materials allowed. (See Finish Requirements in next section.) The size of a typical shower is regulated by the code as well. Overall, the shower cannot be less than 900 square inches (0.58 s m) with at least one direction being a minimum of 30 inches (762 mm) wide. The minimum shower wall height is 70 inches (1778

Note

When safety showers are required, you must also refer to *ANSI Z58.1, Emergency Eyewash and Shower Equipment.*

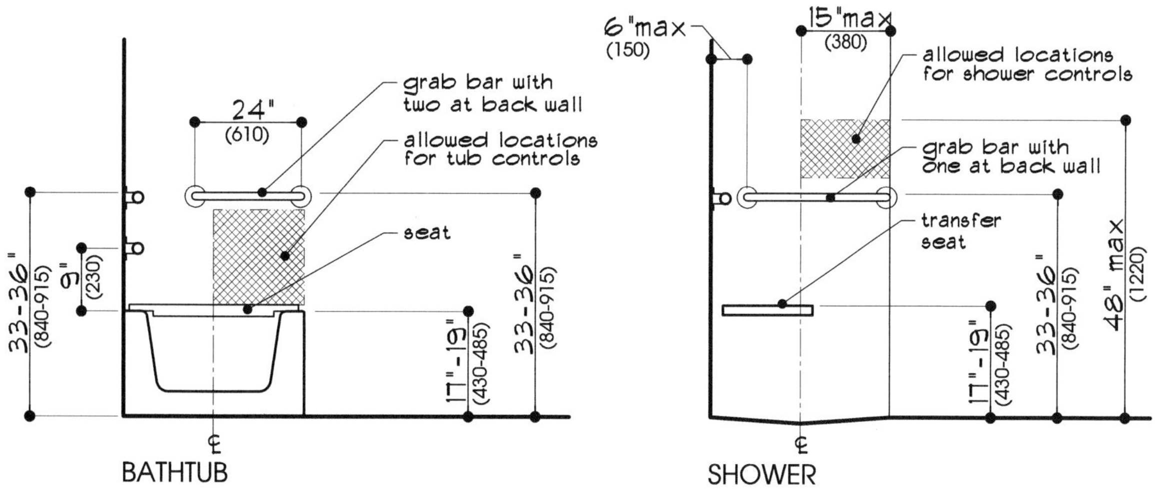

NOTE: An accessible shower head must be able to convert from a handheld to a fixed with a hose at least 60" (1525 mm) long.

Figure 7.4 Typical Accessible Plumbing Fixture Dimensions: Bathtubs and Showers

mm) above the shower drain. If a glass shower door is used, you must refer to the building codes for safety glass requirements.

If a shower is required to be accessible, two types of showers are typically allowed: transfer showers and roll-in showers. *Transfer showers* are smaller and are typically required to have an inside clear dimension of 36 inches by 36 inches (915 mm by 915 mm) and a clear floor space in front of the shower of 36 inches by 48 inches (915 mm by 1220 mm). They must also include a fixed or folding seat of a specific size and shape. *Roll-in showers* are more elongated and are typically 30 inches by 60 inches (760 mm by 1525 mm) in size with a larger adjacent clear floor space of 36 inches by 60 inches (915 mm by 1525 mm). Grab bar sizes and locations are also different for each type of shower.

The controls and shower spray unit requirements are similar to those of an accessible bathtub. Allowed locations are shown in Figure 7.4. If a curb or threshold is used, it can only be 0.5 inches (13 mm) high. (If it is more than 0.25 inches (6.4 mm), the edges must be beveled. See Figure 9.19 and the section on Floor Finishes in Chapter 9.) This is especially important in roll-in showers so that the curb does not hinder the wheelchair user. In addition, if an enclosure is used (i.e., shower stall or door), it cannot obstruct the transfer of the person into the shower or any use of the controls in the shower. (Also see section on Bathing Facilities later in this chapter.)

Dishwashers and Clothes Washers

There are very few requirements for dishwashers and clothes washers. Dishwashers are typically not required. Clothes washers are required only in certain Residential occupancies. For example, a clothes washer connection is typically required in a one- or two-family dwelling. In buildings with multiple Residential units, one clothes washer is usually required for every 20 units. These are usually combined together in a shared laundry room. The plumbing codes will tell you when they are required and provide installation standards. However, if multiple clothes washers are used in a laundry-type facility, a floor drain is usually required as well.

Note

Accessible requirements for washers and dryers are included in newer editions of the ICC/ANSI standard and the new *ADA-ABA Accessibility Guidelines.*

If multiple clothes washers are provided in a laundry facility, typically at least one of the units needs to be accessible. If it is top loading, the top of the unit should be no higher than 34 inches (865 mm) above the floor. If it is a front-loading washer, the door and all operable parts should be within accessible reach ranges. Typical accessible floor clearances and turning space should also be provided to allow approach to and use of the appliance.

Toilet and Bathing Facilities

After you have determined the quantity and type of plumbing fixtures required in a project, you need to place them in the space or building. The requirements for each plumbing fixture were discussed in the previous section. Individually, each fixture must meet certain code and accessibility requirements. However, most plumbing fixtures are usually used in a group to create a toilet facility or a bathing facility. Not only must you know how to group these fixtures together so that the individual requirements of each fixture are still met, but when the fixtures are grouped together, additional code and accessibility requirements must also be met in the construction and layout of these facilities.

Note

When a turning space of 60 inches (1525 mm) is not possible, a T-shaped space is sometimes allowed, especially in existing spaces. See the ADA guidelines and the ICC/ANSI standard for specific requirements.

The codes require that all toilet and bathing rooms have privacy. This includes privacy at the entrance to the restroom and within the room when there are multiple water closets and bathing fixtures. When a restroom is connected to a public area or passageway, it must be screened so that no one can look directly into the toilet or bathing facility. This is usually accomplished with either a vestibule leading into the room or a deliberate arrangement of walls either in front or beyond the doorway. When a door is used at the entrance, the codes typically require a closer on the door so that it self-closes with each use.

In addition, the ADA guidelines and ICC/ANSI standard require all restrooms, whether they are fully or partially accessible, to be directly accessible to the public. This includes minimum door clearance into the room and an unobstructed turning space within the room, as well as accessible corridors leading to the facility. The ADA guidelines and the accessibility chapter in the building codes typically indicate when an accessible facility is required. You should then refer to ADA guidelines and the ICC/ANSI standard for the specific requirements such as the use of stalls, grab bars, and accessories. (See Chapter 4 for additional information on corridor and door clearances.)

Various types of toilet and bathing facilities and their requirements are described next, followed by a discussion of the appropriate use of finishes, accessories, grab bars, and signage.

Note

Toilet facilities with only one water closet and one lavatory do not normally require additional partitions inside the space.

Single-Toilet Facilities

Single-toilet facilities consist of one lavatory and one water closet. They are used in a building or space for a number of reasons. Most commonly, they are used in smaller spaces or occupancies where only one female and one male single-toilet facility is required. Single-toilet facilities are also used as unisex toilet rooms. As described earlier in this chapter, these may be allowed as a shared facility in a smaller occupancy or required as a "family toilet room" in an Assembly and Mercantile occupancy. A unisex toilet facility may also have to be added because you need to add accessible fixtures in a renovation and you cannot increase the size of an existing multi-toilet facility to do so.

Most single-toilet facilities must be accessible. If they are added as a private facility (e.g., executive toilet), they should at least be adaptable. (For example, additional blocking should be added in the walls so that grab bars can be added and fixtures may be adjusted for later conversion when required.) In a fully accessible single-toilet facility, all fixtures, accessories, and grab bars must be mounted at accessible heights and specific floor clearances must be provided. Figure 7.5 indicates the requirements of a typical accessible single-toilet facility. (Two floor plan options are provided.) A similar facility could be used for a unisex toilet room. However, if you are designing a "family toilet room" such as those required in certain Mercantile or Assembly occupancies, you may want to add additional space to allow for someone to assist in the room. Often these types of rooms also have other amenities not typically required by the codes, such as a fold-up changing table or a wall-mounted baby seat.

Note

Doors swinging into accessible restrooms or toilet stalls cannot reduce the clear floor space required for each fixture. However, depending on the standard and the jurisdiction, the door is sometimes permitted to swing into the 60 inch (1525 mm) turning space.

In most cases, the fixtures in single-toilet facilities must be arranged so that the required clear floor space for each fixture is unobstructed. The dimensions of the clear area will depend on which accessibility publication applies to your project. For example, the original *ADAAG* allows the lavatory to overlap the

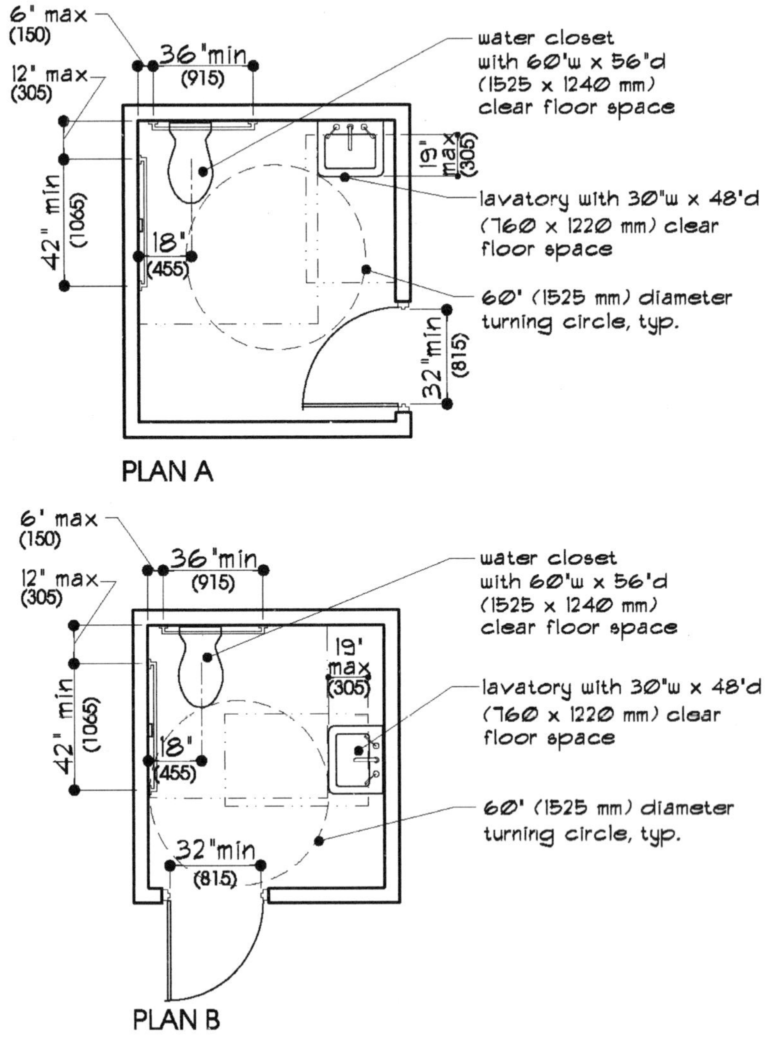

Figure 7.5 Accessible Single-Toilet Facility Examples (See also Figures 7.2, 7.3, and 7.9 for accessible fixture and accessory heights.)

NOTE: Required clear floor space at each fixture can overlap, but door cannot impede on clear floor space. 16"–18" (405–455 mm) to centerline of toilet may be allowed by some publications.

clear floor space at the toilet; the new ADA guideline does not. The clear floor spaces for different fixtures, however, can overlap each other. In addition, all accessible toilet facilities require an unobstructed turning space that is 60 inches (1525 mm) in diameter. This circle can overlap the clear floor space and the space under the fixtures where toe space is provided. It should be drawn directly on the floor plan to indicate compliance. The door into the room is not allowed to open over the clear floor space required at any fixture. (The ADA guidelines and ICC/ANSI standard do allow the door to swing over the required turning space, but not every jurisdiction allows this, so you need to confirm what is allowed.)

Note

The clear floor spaces required at each plumbing fixture can overlap each other.

Multiple-Toilet Facilities

When multiple plumbing fixtures are required for males and/or females in the same space or floor, a multiple-toilet facility is used—one for males and one for females. In a multiple-toilet facility, the water closets must be separated from each other and from the rest of the room by toilet stalls. There are many ways to design the layout of a multi-toilet facility. Figure 7.6 shows one type of layout. When using stalls, the codes require minimum clearance dimensions around the water closet as described earlier and require doors with privacy locks. Urinals must also be separated by a partial screen, but no doors are required. (See section on Urinals earlier in the chapter.)

If the stalls are required to be accessible, additional regulations must be met. When there are multiple fixtures located in a toilet facility, typically at least one of each is required to be accessible. For example, at least one water closet in each multi-toilet facility must be accessible. However, if there are six or more water closets in a toilet facility, two of them must be accessible. When one accessible stall is required, it must allow for use by a person in a wheelchair, often called a *wheelchair-accessible* stall or compartment as shown by "A" in Figure 7.6. If the door swings out, the typical size of this stall is 56 inches by 60 inches (1420 mm by 1525 mm) if it is a wall-hung water closet and 59 inches by 60 inches (1500 mm by 1525 mm) if it is a floor-mounted water closet. If the door swings in, it cannot overlap these clear floor spaces. Toe clearances and specific grab bar locations are important as well. If a second accessible stall is required, the "alternate stall" as described in the ADA guidelines and the ICC/ANSI standard can be provided. This alternate stall is also called an *ambulatory-accessible* stall or compartment. Shown as stall "B" in Figure 7.6, it is not as wide and the arrangement of grab bars is different. The alternate stall configuration provides for a person with a mobility disability but who does not necessarily use a wheelchair.

Note

The 60-inch (1525 mm) turning circle can overlap the clear floor space required at each plumbing fixture. It can overlap part of the fixture too, but only if there is appropriate knee and toe clearance.

In addition to the clear floor space required in each accessible stall, a clear floor space must be provided at each accessible urinal, lavatory, and accessory in the facility. At least one area in the room must also allow a 60-inch (1525 mm) diameter turning space. (See Accessories and Grab Bars later in this chapter.)

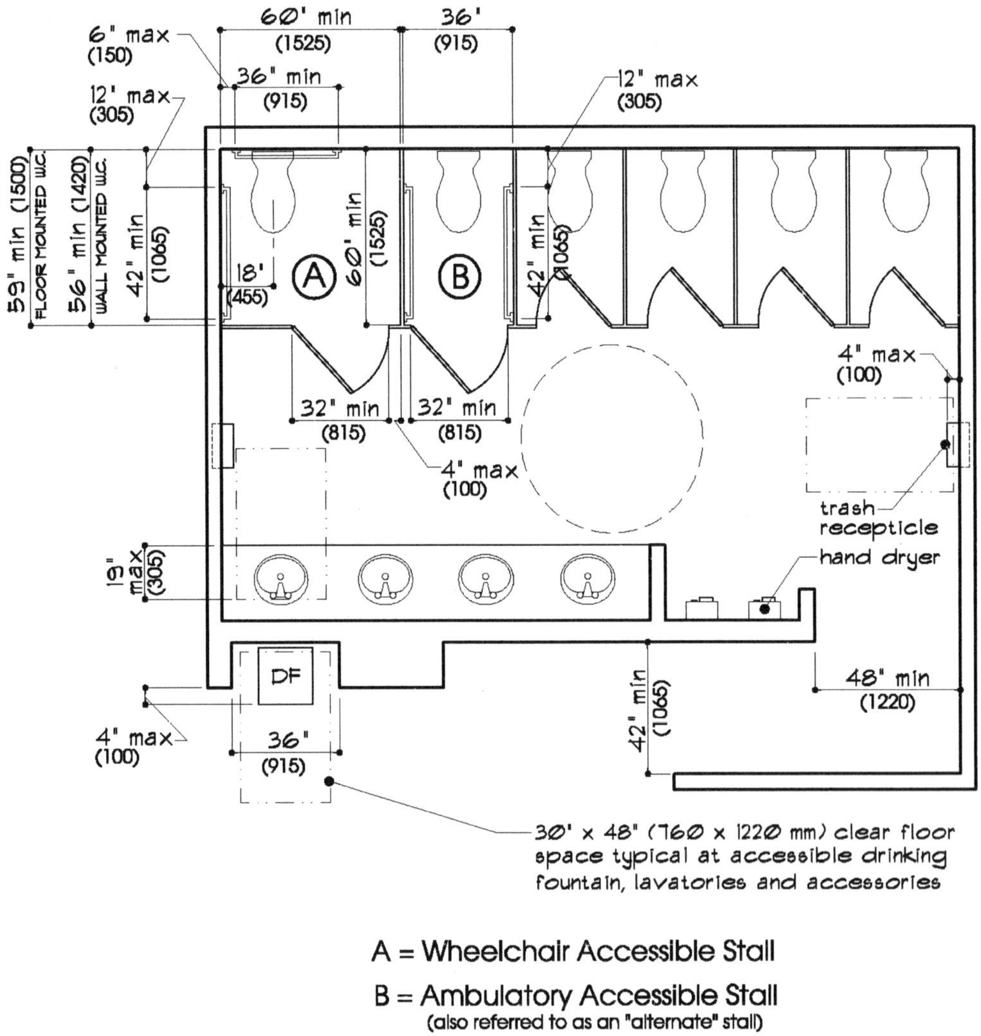

Figure 7.6 Accessible Multi-Toilet Facility Example (See also Figures 7.2, 7.3, and 7.9 for accessible fixture and accessory heights.)

Bathing Facilities

Unlike toilet facilities, bathing facilities include a shower or bathtub. The shower or tub can be used either in conjunction with the lavatory and water closet or separately in its own room. Most Residential occupancies and dwelling units will require a bathroom that includes a water closet, lavatory, and bathtub or shower.

Sleeping rooms in some occupancies might require this as well. (See inset titled *Types of Rooms and Spaces* in Chapter 2 on page 63.) Examples include residential houses, apartments, hotel guest rooms, and guest rooms in assisted living facilities. Other building types, including many Institutional occupancies, will have either separate bathing rooms or group bathing facilities. For example, a nursing home room may have toilet facilities in the patient rooms, but have a separate bathing room on each floor that is shared by the patients and allows the staff to assist with the bathing. Other building types, such as schools, dormitories, health spas, and even prisons, are more likely to have group bathing facilities where there are multiple showers in one room.

Note

In certain Institutional building types, such as rehabilitation centers, all bathing facilities are required to be accessible. Other Health Care facilities may only require a percentage of them to be accessible.

When a building has multiple bathing fixtures or facilities, a percentage of the units will be required to be accessible. (Specific requirements are found in the codes, ADA guidelines, and the ICC/ANSI standard.) For example, a certain number of guest rooms in a hotel must be accessible. That means the room and the adjoining bathroom must be accessible. If multiple bathing fixtures are used in the same room (e.g., shower stalls), at least one of them must be accessible. In some cases, a separate accessible unisex bathing facility may be allowed instead. The unisex bathing facility would then include a lavatory and a water closet in addition to the bathtub or shower. The purpose of the accessible bathing or bathroom is to allow someone in a wheelchair or other disability to have full access to all fixtures. It also allows that person to be assisted by another person.

At each accessible plumbing fixture, the grab bars and controls must be mounted at accessible heights and specific floor clearances must be provided. Figures 7.7 and 7.8 give several examples of single-bathing facilities. Specific floor clearances are designated for each type of bathing fixture. For example, as shown in Figure 7.7 bathtubs with a removable seat in the tub will require less floor space than one with a fixed seat at the end of the tub. In Figure 7.8, roll-in showers are larger and will require more clear floor space than a transfer-type shower. In addition, the 60-inch (1525 mm) diameter turning space must be included in each accessible facility. Also, notice that lavatories are typically allowed to overlap the larger clear floor spaces required at tubs and roll-in showers (not transfer showers). A variety of layouts are possible, depending on the type of bathing fixture. However, when designing the space you should also know how the space is to be used. You may want to include more space than required to allow for assisted help. Additional grab bars might also be useful or be required by a jurisdiction. If it is a multi-fixture bathing facility, at least one of each type of accessory (i.e., soap dispenser, paper towel dispenser, etc.) in the space must be accessible as well. (See Accessories and Grab Bars later in this chapter.)

Note

The codes often require floor drains in multiple-toilet facilities.

Note

A standard accessible stall and the "alternate" stall are shown in Figure 7.6. However, the use of the alternate stall is not typically required unless six or more stalls are provided.

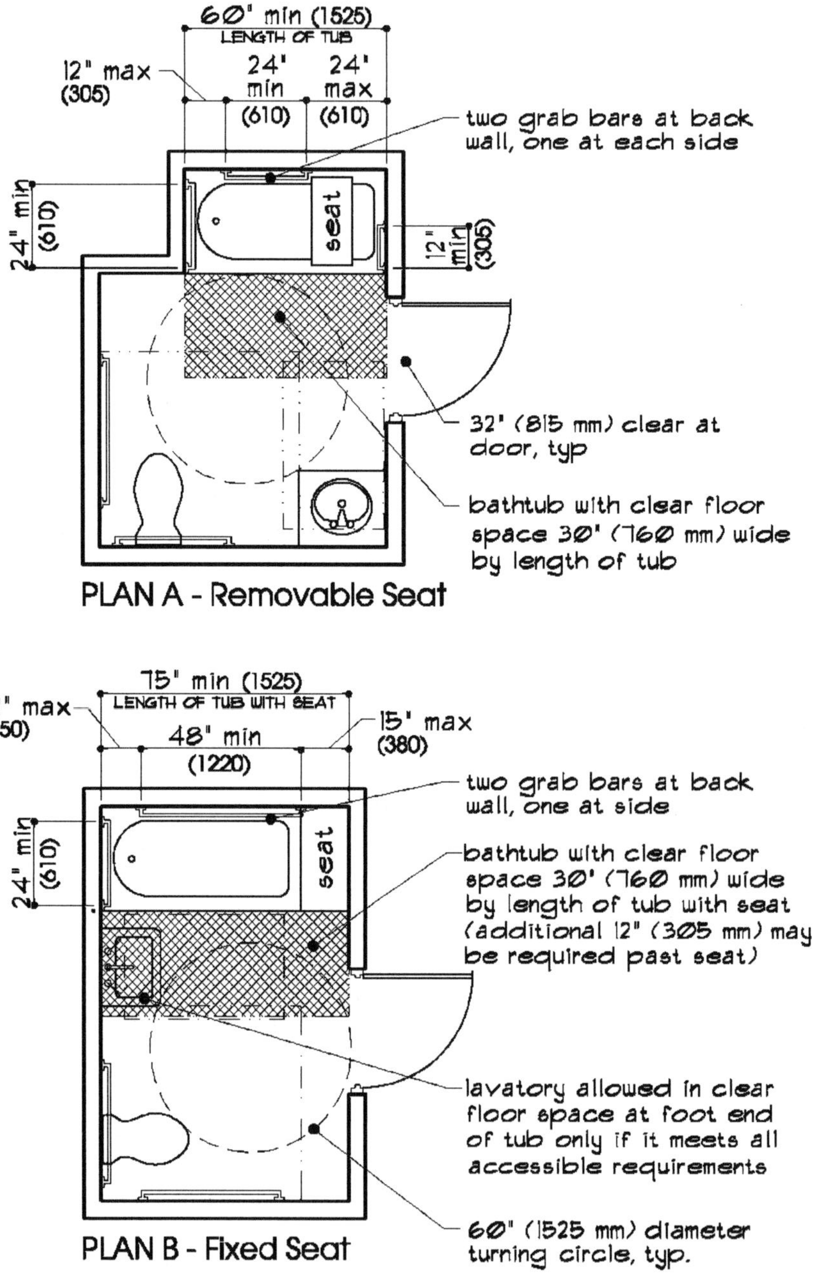

Figure 7.7 Accessible Bathing Facility Examples: Bathtubs (See also Figures 7.2, 7.3, 7.4, and 7.9 for accessible fixture and accessory heights. See Figure 7.5 for additional information at water closets and lavatories.)

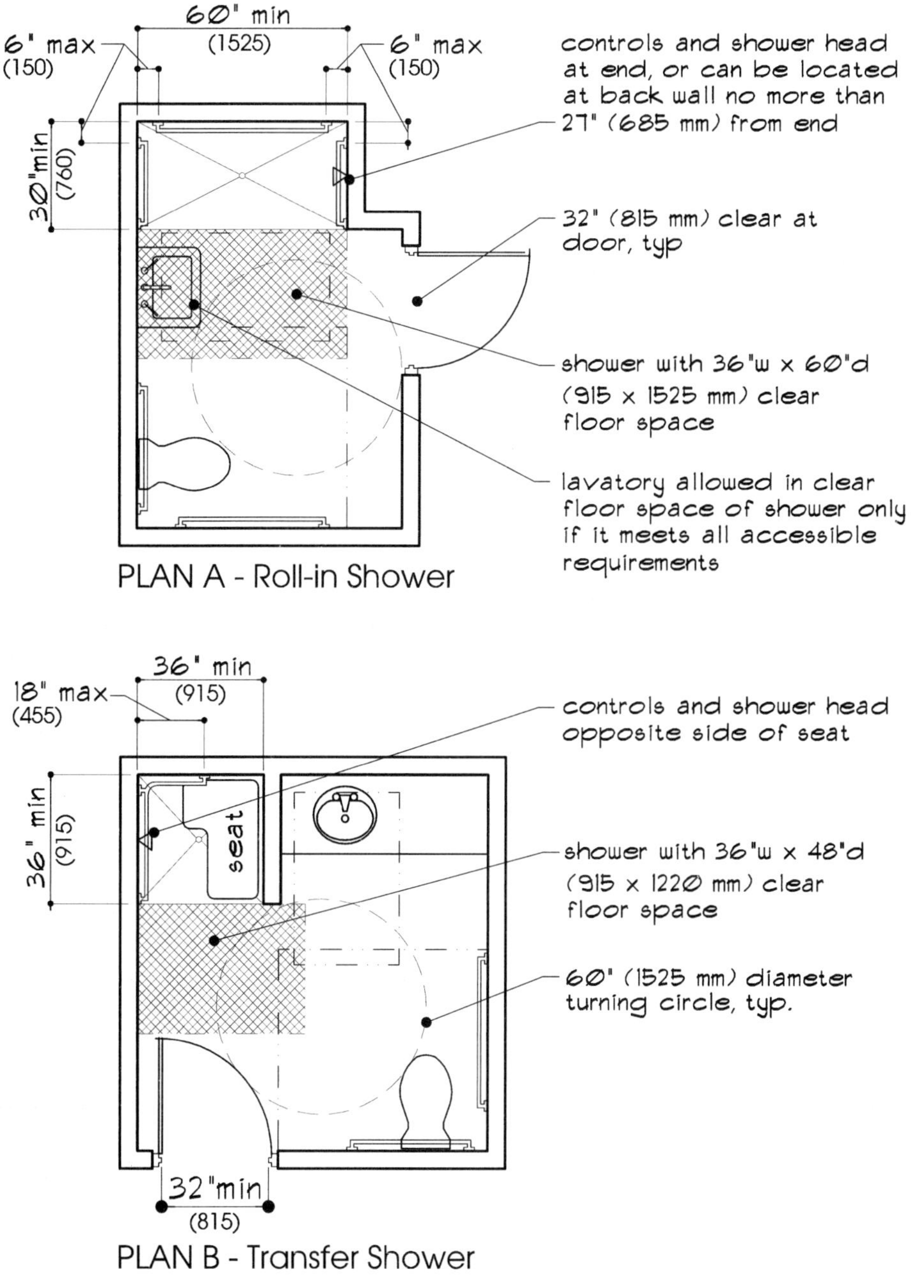

Figure 7.8 Accessible Bathing Facility Examples: Showers (See also Figures 7.2, 7.3, 7.4, and 7.9 for accessible fixture and accessory heights. See Figure 7.5 for additional information at water closets and lavatories.)

Finish Requirements

Both the plumbing codes and the interior environment chapter of the *IBC* specify that toilet and bathing rooms must have smooth, hard, and nonabsorbent surfaces. This limits the spread of germs and allows for easy cleaning. It applies to all floor finishes and includes wall finishes in locations that are close to a water source and/or may become wet. For example, the floor finish throughout the room must typically extend upward onto the wall at least 6 inches (152 mm) to allow for wet mopping without damaging the wall. Ceramic tile is often used to meet these requirements. Walls must also have smooth, hard, nonabsorbent finishes at certain distances around urinals and water closets and surrounding shower and tub compartments. This can be accomplished with ceramic tile as well as other applied vinyl or plastic coverings. Some jurisdictions will also allow epoxy paint. In addition, any accessories such as grab bars and soap dishes installed in the walls must be properly sealed to protect the wall beyond. (See also the Accessibility Requirements for Finishes in Chapter 9 on page 380.)

The codes require that stall panels and privacy screens be made of impervious materials as well. A variety of materials can be used including laminate, stainless steel, solid surface, and painted metal. Finish requirements are also important when custom fixtures are designed and used. For example, a custom counter with an integral sink must be impervious and free of unnecessary concealed spaces. Both the *IPC* and the *UPC* list allowable alternate fixture materials that include such things as soapstone, chemical stoneware or plastic, and stainless steel and other corrosion-resistant metals. In addition, the plumbing chapter in the *ICC Performance Code* more generally states that all plumbing fixtures shall be constructed "to avoid food contamination and accumulation of dirt or bacteria and permit effective cleaning." This may allow finishes such as wood and concrete to be used as long as they are sealed properly. Many options are possible, but ultimately the code official in the jurisdiction of the project will have the final approval.

Accessories and Grab Bars

Note

It is becoming more common for baby-changing tables to be installed in men's toilet rooms as well as women's toilet rooms. They should be installed to meet accessibility requirements.

Restroom accessories and grab bars are also regulated by the ADA guidelines and the ICC/ANSI standards. Accessories include but are not limited to mirrors and medicine cabinets, dispensers, receptacles, disposal units, air hand dryers, and vending machines. The type or quantity of accessories is not typically specified by the codes. However, a certain number of the accessories are required to be accessible. In single-toilet and bathing facilities, all accessories must be accessible. In multi-fixture facilities, only a percentage of the accessories must be accessible; however, many new facilities provide all accessories at accessible heights for consistency of design.

A wide variety of accessory styles are available. For example, both a hand dryer and a paper towel dispenser are available in accessible styles. However, the appropriate choice is usually dependent on the type of space or the client's preference. A client may prefer a hand dryer instead of a paper towel dispenser to limit the amount of trash and maintenance of the facility. (In some cases, a jurisdiction will require specific accessories for certain building types.)

Note

When specifying and locating restroom accessories, remember the maximum 4-inch (100 mm) projection allowance.

When selecting an accessible accessory, you must make sure the controls on the device are easy to operate with minimal turning and pressure required. Devices that are automatic or use levers or push buttons are typical choices. In addition, it is important that the locations of the devices do not create projections of more than 4 inches (100 mm) into the accessible circulation path. In order to accommodate this, many accessories are available that mount fully or partially into a wall. To allow for floor clearances and to avoid projections into accessible paths within a toilet or bathing facility, it is a good idea to recess fixtures whenever possible. When a recessed fixture cannot be used, walls can be built to provide an alcove so that the fixture is not in a direct path. For example, in Figure 7.6 an alcove was created to allow for the deeper hand dryers to be surface mounted on the wall. (The trash receptacles are shown partially recessed into the wall in the same figure.)

Note

Although the original *ADAAG* may allow a reach range up to 54 inches (1370 mm), the newer ADA guidelines and ICC/ANSI standard no longer allow this.

In addition, accessories that are accessible must be installed so that they are within certain reach ranges. Typically they are required to be installed so that the operating part of the device is between 15 inches (380 mm) and 48 inches (1220 mm) above the floor. For example, a fold-down changing table, an amenity often supplied in public restrooms, must be installed so that when folded down the top is no higher than 34 inches (865 mm) above the floor—similar to an accessible counter height. Other accessories such as toilet paper holders have minimum and maximum placement, but you must also allow for the use of the adjacent grab bar. (See the ADA guidelines and the ICC/ANSI standard for specific requirements.) For most of the accessories, a maximum of 48 inches (1220 mm) above the floor is required, as shown in Figure 7.9. The actual height will usually be lower than this and depends on the accessory, how it operates, and the design of the space. You must also make sure you allow for clear floor space in front of the accessory. Typically, at each accessible accessory you should allow for a 30-inch by 48-inch (760 mm by 1220 mm) clearance. This does not include the accessories located within a toilet stall. (See Figure 7.6.)

Note

Additional grab bars may be required by certain code jurisdictions over and above what is required by the ADA guidelines and the ICC/ANSI standard.

Grab bars are required at accessible water closets, showers, and tubs. They must be located beside and/or behind the water closet and within various reach ranges for bathing fixtures. Grab bars must also be mounted at specific heights. Most commonly, a grab bar must be mounted at 33 to 36 inches (840 to 915 mm) above the finished floor at water closets, bathtubs, and showers. This height is shown in Figures 7.2 and 7.4. The specific length, spacing, and orientation

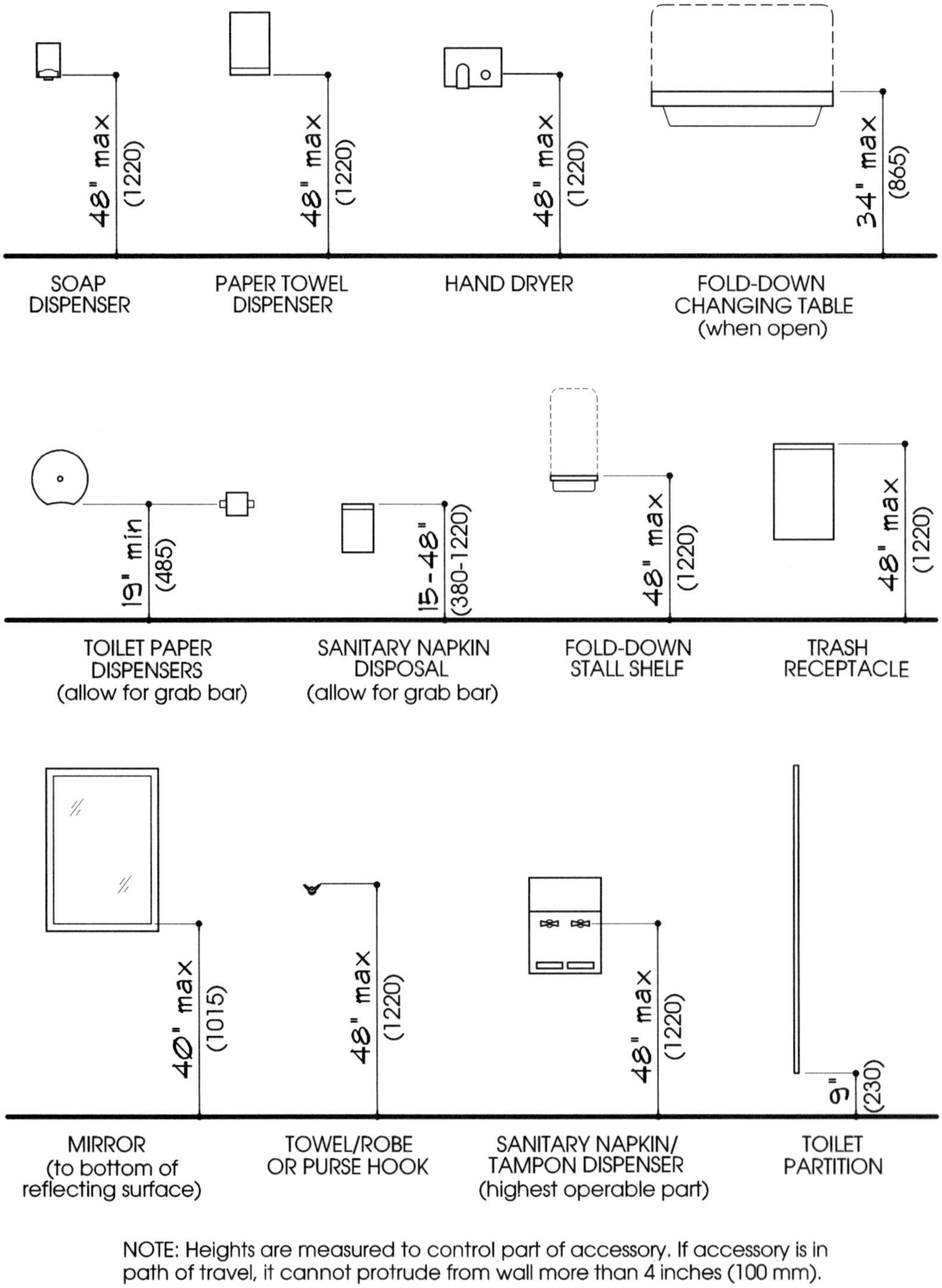

Figure 7.9 Typical Accessible Toilet Accessory Heights

(horizontally or vertically) depends on the location of the grab bar in relation to the fixture. Locations have been shown in the various toilet and bathing facility floor plans used in this chapter. The size and strength requirements of the grab bar are also regulated. The typical diameter allowed is 1¼ inches to 1½ inches (32 mm to 38 mm), which must be mounted with a 1½-inch (38 mm) clearance between the grab bar and the wall. In addition, some jurisdictions or licensing requirements may require grab bars in locations other than those specified by the ADA guidelines or the ICC/ANSI standard. For example, a diagonal bar may be required over a tub to assist in getting in and out of the tub. You may also want to consider a *swing-away* grab bar at certain toilet locations. It can be used as support by a disabled person when in position, or it can be moved out of the way to allow another person to assist. (Be sure to refer to the ADA guidelines and the ICC/ANSI standard for specifics. Newer editions may provide additional grab bar options.)

Note

Although the diameter of a grab bar can vary slightly, the 1½-inch (38 mm) distance from the wall cannot. This distance is a safety clearance that prevents arms from slipping through when a person braces for support.

Note

The height of a grab bar is measured to the top of the gripping surface, not the centerline.

Signage

Most toilet and bathing facilities will require a sign that meets certain accessibility requirements. The type of sign will depend on the type of facility and the types of other facilities located in the same building. For example, if a building contains both accessible facilities and nonaccessible facilities, the nonaccessible facilities must have a sign indicating the location of the accessible ones. Then each accessible facility must have a sign that includes the International Symbol of Accessibility (the wheelchair symbol). These signs would be similar to the women's toilet facility sign, the unisex toilet facility sign, and the unisex bathing sign shown in Figure 7.10. However, if all the facilities in the building are fully accessible, you may not need to include the International Symbol of Accessibility on any of the facility signs. In addition, all multi-toilet or multi-bathing facilities must post a sign of the International Symbol of Accessibility on the accessible stall door. This is also shown in Figure 7.10.

Typically, signage for toilet and bathing facilities must be accessible. The signs must be both visual and tactile and allow for lettering and symbols in a specified size and proportion. Contrast between the sign and the lettering as well as raised lettering and the use of Braille is also important. (See the ADA guidelines and the ICC/ANSI standard for specifics.) Accessible signs must also meet certain mounting requirements. As shown in Figure 7.11, the sign must be located on the latch side of the door entering the facility (not the hinged side). In most cases, it must also be located between 48 and 60 inches (1220 to 1525 mm) above the floor. This height is typically measured to the baseline of the lettering on the sign. (The original *ADAAG* measures this to the centerline of the sign.) If a vestibule is

Note

The required clear floor space at accessible signs is a requirement new to the 1998 ICC/ANSI standard. It is also included in the new ADA guidelines.

Figure 7.10 Types of Accessible Signs for Toilet and Bathing Facilities. (Illustrations by APCO GRAPHICS, INC., www.apcosigns.com.)

used and there is no door, the sign should be located on the right side of the opening. If there is no wall space on the correct side of the door, it should be located on the nearest adjacent wall. Although the sign is not required to be a certain distance from the door frame or opening, it must be located far enough from the door so that the door swing does not overlap the required clear floor space of 18 inches by 18 inches (455 mm by 455 mm) below the sign. This is shown in Figure 7.11. The overall goal is to allow a person to get close enough to the sign to allow them to read the raised letter or Braille without any obstructions.

Note

Some jurisdictions, such as the state of California, may have additional signage requirements.

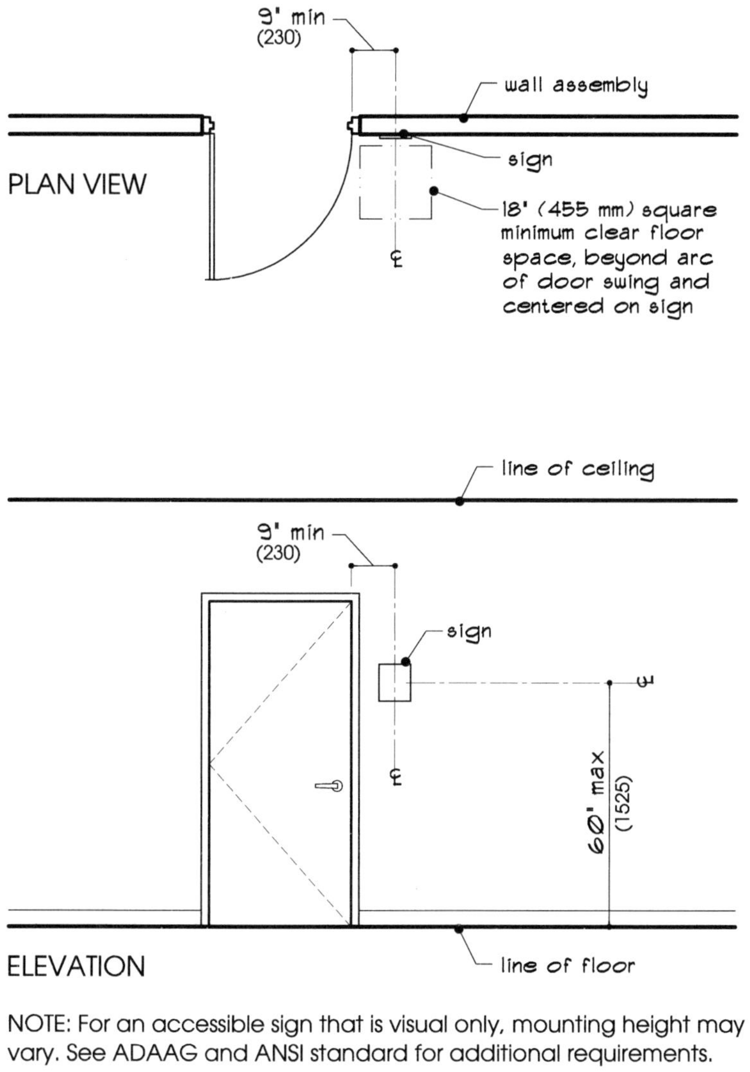

Figure 7.11 Typical Accessible Tactile Sign Location

MECHANICAL REQUIREMENTS

As the designer, it is unlikely that you will need to refer to the mechanical code. However, whether you are working on a large interior project that requires the services of a mechanical engineer or a smaller project with minimal mechanical requirements, you need to know some mechanical code basics. For example, when collaborating with an engineer, you may need to coordinate the location of supply diffusers and return grilles as part of your design, and the engineer will design the corresponding mechanical system. Other parts of your design will also affect the mechanical system, including location of walls and selection of light fixtures and other electrical equipment. In addition, it may also be necessary to coordinate your preliminary design with the engineer to make sure you allow enough clearance for mechanical equipment, especially as it affects ducts and ceiling heights. On projects that require minimal mechanical work, such as adding or relocating a few supply diffusers and return grilles to an existing system, the mechanical contractor may be able to work directly from your drawings or supply the required "shop" drawings.

Note

Although the ADA guidelines do not specify requirements for mechanical systems, the ADA in general may require parts of the mechanical system, such as the controls or registers, to be adjusted to accommodate an individual person.

The rest of this section will discuss the basic mechanical requirements. First, the various code publications as they apply to mechanical systems will be compared. This will be followed by a brief explanation of various mechanical code requirements as they affect the interior of a space. (Also see inset titled *Types of Mechanical Systems* on page 286.)

Key Terms

The following mechanical terms will be discussed and defined in this section. They can also be found in the Glossary.

Damper
Duct
Exhaust air
Plenum
Return air
Supply air
Thermostat
Ventilation
Ventilation air
Zone

Comparing the Codes

Although each of the building codes has a chapter on mechanical systems, they simply refer you to the mechanical codes and other standards where most of the actual requirements are found. The three model mechanical codes were phased out when the International Code Council (ICC) first published the *International Mechanical Code (IMC)* in 1996. It is now on a three-year cycle, with the more current editions being 2003 and 2006. It is the most widely used mechanical code.

The National Fire Protection Association (NFPA) published its first mechanical code in collaboration with the International Association of Plumbing and Mechanical Officials (IAPMO) in 2003. It is known as the *Uniform Mechanical Code (UMC)*. (This is not to be confused with the older model code with the same name.) Some of the older model mechanical codes may also still be in circulation, so be sure to check with the jurisdiction to see which code is enforced.

The mechanical codes contain the requirements for the installation and maintenance of heating, ventilation, cooling, and refrigeration systems. Chapters in the mechanical code include requirements for ventilation and exhaust systems, duct systems, chimneys and vents, boilers and water heaters, refrigeration, hydronic piping, and solar systems, among others. Numerous standards are referenced as well. These include those from the NFPA, the American National Standards Institute (ANSI), and the American Society of Heating, Refrigeration, and Air Conditioning Engineers (ASHRAE). These and other standards are listed in the back of each code publication. Often the corresponding energy code will be referenced as well. (See the section on Energy Efficiency and Water Conservation at the end of the chapter.) Depending on the project, the ICC or NFPA fuel gas code may also be required, as well as some requirements from the corresponding fire code.

The allowable performance criteria for the *IMC* are found in a mechanical chapter of the *ICC Performance Code (ICCPC)*. The *ICCPC* generally states that the installation of mechanical equipment must "safeguard maintenance personnel and building occupants from injury and deliver air at the appropriate temperature for health and comfort." This allows flexibility for the engineer if a building requires a custom mechanical system to be designed. Other performance requirements are given in the *ICCPC* for refrigeration and piped services. If you were using the *UMC*, you would need to refer to the *NFPA 5000* performance chapter for performance criteria. The energy codes have some performance-based criteria as well.

Very few accessibility issues affect mechanical code requirements. However, the codes do become important when locating devices, such as thermostats, that are used by the occupants of the building. These accessibility-related items are mentioned in the sections that follow.

General Code Requirements

All types of mechanical systems will need to meet certain code requirements. Some of these are a part of the building codes. For example, Chapter 5 and Chapter 6 of this book discussed ventilation of vertical shafts and fire/smoke dampers. Each building code also has a chapter on interior environments that includes

TYPES OF MECHANICAL SYSTEMS

Mechanical systems are often referred to as HVAC systems. (This acronym stands for heating, ventilation, and air conditioning.) They can be separate or combined into one system. A wide variety of HVAC systems are available. Various components can be used to customize a system as well. The system that is selected and used in a particular building depends on a number of factors, including the size and use of the building, the number of occupants, the cost, and the maintenance. The three main types of mechanical systems are described as follows:

1. *All-air systems:* This system uses centrally located fans to circulate hot and cold air to and from a space through long runs of ductwork. All-air systems are the most widely used mechanical systems in large buildings. They include the variable air volume system (VAV), which is more popular, and the constant air volume system (CAV).
2. *All-water systems:* This system uses pipes to transport hot and cold water to and from each space where the air is locally circulated by a convector or fan to create the hot and cold air. The most common all-water system is the electric baseboard convector system found in private residences. Other systems include fan-coil terminals, closed loop heat pumps, and hydronic convectors.
3. *Air and water systems:* This is a combination system that uses a central fan to circulate fresh air to a space where it is heated or cooled by water before entering the space. The most common combination system is the air-water induction system.

Most mechanical systems will require some type of ductwork to supply the air, registers to distribute the air, and/or grills to retrieve the return air. Some buildings use ductwork to return air as well. This is called a *duct system*. Other buildings use a *plenum system*, whereby the open space above the suspended ceiling and/or the enclosed vertical shafts are used to collect the return air.

mechanical-related items such as ventilation and temperature control. Other provisions are found in the mechanical codes and the standards they reference. The main mechanical related requirements you should be aware of as a designer are discussed below. (Other specific mechanical code items are more specific to an engineer and are not discussed.)

Mechanical Rooms

Mechanical rooms can include furnace or boiler rooms, fan rooms, and refrigeration rooms. (They are also sometimes called appliance rooms.) Depending on the size of the building and the type of mechanical system used, these rooms can be separate or combined into one. It is the size and location of the mechanical room(s) that are important. The codes specify that each room must have a minimum door width so equipment can be easily replaced. In addition, minimum working space along the control side of the equipment is required. If you need to locate a mechanical room on an interior project, be sure to work closely with the mechanical engineer to size the room correctly. In addition, these rooms often need to have fire-rated walls. (See Chapter 5 for fire rating requirements.) Mechanical rooms are not typically required to be handicap accessible.

Note

Not all buildings require a mechanical room. Many smaller buildings have their HVAC units either on the roof or on the ground adjacent to the building. Consult an engineer for options.

Cooling Loads

The cooling load refers to how much energy is required to cool a space. It is one of the main factors in determining the size and type of a mechanical system. Although the number and size of exterior windows and the type of glazing are typically already determined on an interior project, many other interior aspects affect the cooling load. This includes the overall size of the space, how the space is divided, and the number of people expected to use the space. The quantity of light fixtures and other equipment are also a large contributing factor. The location of equipment such as computers, printer, copiers, fax machines, and various appliances in specific areas of the design may affect the necessary distribution of cooling. In addition, audio/visual, communication, security, and other special systems must be considered. Any concentration of lighting or equipment is also important. Therefore, it is important to work closely with the client, the engineers, and other consultants to accurately determine all the requirements for the space or building.

Note

Existing ductwork can hinder the placement of fire separation walls. You may have to work with a mechanical engineer or contractor to reroute the ducts or add dampers.

The mechanical engineer will need the specification of each light fixture and every electronic piece of equipment to determine how much heat will be generated within the space. This is measured in BTUs (British thermal units). The total expected number of electrical BTUs is factored in with the other loads of the space to correctly determine the required load of the HVAC system. All of these factors are used by the mechanical engineer in conjunction with the codes to determine the size of the main unit, the size of the ducts, and the number of supply diffusers and return grilles required. These loads are also critical to determine efficient energy utilization as required by the energy codes.

Note

Every electrical fixture and piece of equipment has a BTU calculation. The total BTUs in a space are factored in by the mechanical engineer when determining cooling loads and the size of the cooling system.

Zoning and Thermostat Locations

Different areas of a building may be zoned separately to provide different levels of comfort. Typically, parts of a floor or building with similar temperature requirements are grouped into the same zone. For example, perimeter rooms that have exterior windows are typically zoned separately from interior spaces. Other rooms may have particular requirements and need to have a separate zone. Some may even have a separate supplemental system because of their special needs.

Note

It is often required that spaces adjacent to exterior walls and windows be zoned separately from interior spaces. Solar heat and outside temperatures typically cause different temperatures in perimeter rooms.

Note

The energy codes specify minimum and maximum temperature control ranges for thermostats.

Examples include a kitchen in a restaurant, a locker room in a sports complex, a computer room in a school, and a conference room in an office space.

Each mechanical zone has a separate thermostat. The codes do not specify the location of a thermostat. Instead, the environmental chapter in the building codes and the energy codes give a few general guidelines. Ultimately, the quantity of zones and location of each thermostat are determined by the engineer and depends on the surrounding heat sources. Certain thermostat sensors can even be located above the ceiling. The ADA guidelines and other accessibility standards do not specifically regulate the location of a thermostat either. However, when it is placed in general areas where changing the temperature is common, the thermostat should be located within accessible reaching heights similar to an electrical switch. (See Figure 8.5 in Chapter 8.) Clear floor space in front of the thermostat that allows either a size or front approach may also be required.

Exhaust Requirements

Whenever air is removed from a building or space, the process is considered exhaust. An exhaust system is usually required by the code in specific types of rooms and in certain occupancies. An exhaust system can remove air that contains smoke, germs, chemicals, odors, or other unhealthy or contaminated components. This is especially important in more hazardous types of occupancies. Exhaust systems are typically required in toilet and bathing facilities, designated smoking areas, and kitchens with cooking appliances. Clothes dryers are also required to be exhausted. Some Hazardous occupancies require larger exhaust systems that change the air in the space a certain number of times per hour and/or create a specified air flow.

The rate at which air must be removed from an area is generally based on the activity or type of air that is being exhausted. When a pipe or duct is connected to the exhaust fan, it must typically be routed to the exterior of a building. Consideration must be given for its route and how it affects other elements in the building, such as floor/ceiling assemblies or vertical shafts. The codes also may limit the length of the exhaust pipe or duct, including the number of 45- or 90-degree bends it can make. In some cases, locating rooms that require exhaust close to an exterior wall may be required.

Ventilation Requirements

Whenever air from the outside is added to a building or space, the process is considered ventilation. It can be brought in by natural air flow through operable windows, vents, or louvers (known as natural ventilation) or by a mechanical system (known as mechanical ventilation). The mechanical codes regulate both. The code regulates the size of the window, vent, or louver and the amount of required outside air according to the floor area of the space that is being ventilated and the estimated maximum occupant load. If natural ventilation is not possible, then the space is typically required to be ventilated mechanically.

The requirements are generally based on the use or occupancy of the space. Each mechanical code has a table that lists various occupancy classifications and types of occupied rooms within each classification that require outdoor air. The amount of outside air required is measured in cubic feet per minute (CFM) per person. Other specialty rooms, such as a computer or telephone room, may require ventilation that operates only when the room is occupied. It may be advisable to locate these rooms at or near an exterior wall for easier ventilation. Other examples of areas requiring ventilation include atriums and vestibules.

Note

Good ventilation also is important for the control of radon, especially in underground levels of a building.

Plenum Requirements

Most air type HVAC systems use either a duct or a plenum for return air. (See inset titled *Types of Mechanical Systems* on page 286.) When there are no ducts attached to the return grilles, the open space between the ceiling and the floor above creates a ceiling plenum that acts as the duct and collects the return air. When this plenum system is used, it must be limited to specific fire areas within the building. For example, a plenum cannot pass through a stairwell. In addition, the plenum must typically be limited to a particular tenant in a multi-tenant building. This could be accomplished by using a separate HVAC system for each tenant. The other option would be to provide rated dampers where openings allow air to pass through the tenant's demising wall. The important thing to remember is that if an opening is cut in a rated assembly to allow the return air to continue across the ceiling cavity (i.e., air transfer opening), a rated damper must be added to that opening. This includes fire-resistance rated partitions or barriers and smoke barriers. (See Chapter 5.) The building codes also prohibit the use of combustible materials in the plenum space. For example, only certain types of rated electrical and communication cables are allowed in a plenum space. (See Chapter 8.)

Note

Plenum ceiling returns can continue down structurally created vertical shaft enclosures. Both of these spaces must be isolated from other spaces so that debris in these areas will not be drawn into the return air intake.

Duct Requirements

If the mechanical system uses ducts to retrieve the air as well as to supply conditioned air to a space, the codes place fewer restrictions on the types of materials allowed in the ceiling space. Instead, the codes place restrictions on the ducts themselves. The building codes set some requirements, such as the use of firestops and fire dampers when ducts pass through rated walls and other assemblies.

Smoke dampers may also be required when a wall is considered a smoke barrier. (See Chapter 5.) Figure 7.12 indicates the use of a fire damper on a duct that is passing through a fire-resistance-rated wall assembly. The firestop in this case is fire-rated caulk or sealant used continuously around the fire damper on each side where it passes through the wall. The building codes also specify when a damper or shaft enclosure is required around a duct that penetrates a floor/ceiling assembly. (Note that performance codes may allow the use of some of the newer fire-rated duct wrap as an alternative if proper testing and installation can be shown.)

The mechanical codes specify such things as the size of the ducts, types of rated materials allowed, and mounting and clearance requirements. For example,

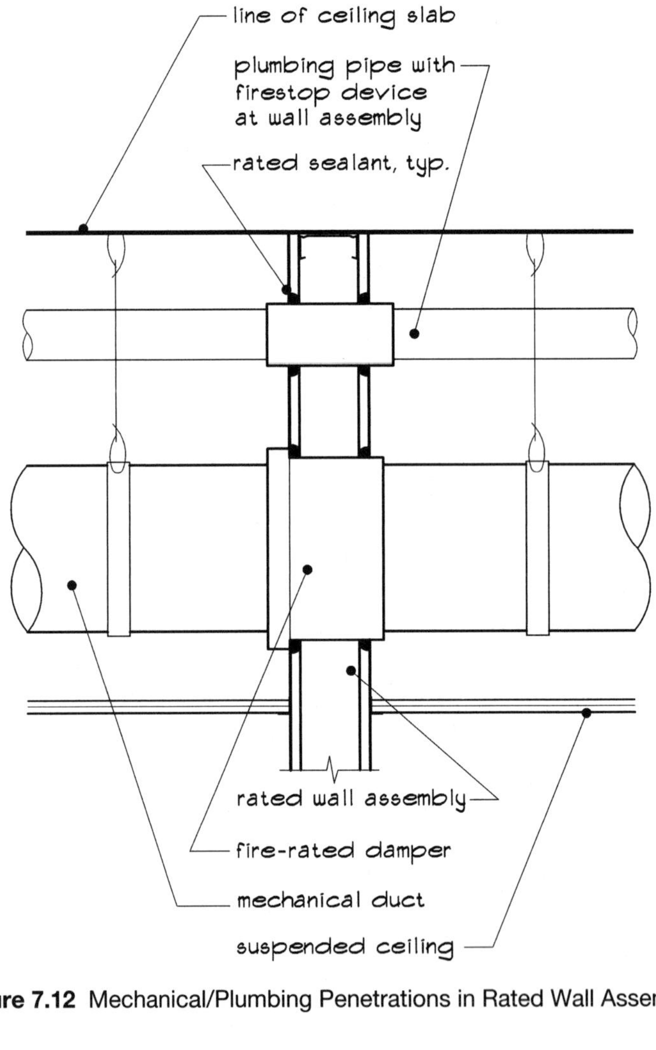

Figure 7.12 Mechanical/Plumbing Penetrations in Rated Wall Assembly

flexible ducts are typically not allowed to penetrate a rated wall; only rigid ducts are allowed. The codes also prohibit the use of mechanical ducts in certain locations and specify when smoke detectors are required in a duct system. (Also see the Energy Efficiency and Water Conservation section below.)

Access Requirements

Certain components of a mechanical system, including ductwork and specific duct connections, must allow adequate access for maintenance. Replacement of major components must be permitted without substantial damage to existing building materials. Suspended ceiling grids, for example, allow easy access to ductwork. When solid ceilings such as gypsum board are used, an access door may be required at specific locations. For example, access must usually be provided at all fire dampers located in the ductwork, at air volume boxes located in the ceiling, and at any shut-off valves used on water type systems. Some of these accesses might also be required in walls.

ENERGY EFFICIENCY AND WATER CONSERVATION

Various codes, standards, and federal laws continue to be created and passed in an effort to make buildings more energy efficient. Water conservation is a part of this as well, because when less water is used, less energy is used by the utility companies supplying the water and less energy is used inside the building to heat and distribute the water. These requirements affect the building's plumbing system and mechanical system.

As mentioned earlier in the chapter, various plumbing fixtures must meet minimum water consumption requirements. These requirements are found in the plumbing codes and the standards they reference. Most plumbing fixtures and faucets currently made in the United States are built to meet or exceed the standards required by the codes. However, since older fixtures may not meet the most current water consumption standard, this may limit the reuse of existing fixtures in renovation projects. In addition, if you specify fixtures manufactured in other countries, you may need to confirm that they will meet the necessary requirements. These requirements must also be considered when custom fixtures are designed and used.

> **Note**
>
> The newest technology in efficient plumbing fixtures includes water-free urinals and solar powered faucets.

The energy codes and standards provide additional requirements for mechanical equipment and systems as well as water-heating related items. For example, to maintain the temperature of the air in ducts or water in pipes, the codes specify the R-value of the insulation required around ductwork and pipes. The energy codes also regulate such things as the use of certified equipment that meet minimum efficiency requirements, in addition to provisions for sealing of ducts, types and location of temperature and humidity control devices (including thermostats), automatic shutdown requirements, and types of balancing devices. Water-heating systems such as water heaters, storage tanks, boilers, and those used in swimming pools are included as well. Although many of these items are covered in the mechanical codes, the energy codes provide additional efficiency parameters that must be followed. The performance codes might also allow the use of other energy-efficient systems not yet allowed by the prescriptive codes. For example, in Europe they have found that radiant cooling and under-floor air systems provide better efficiency in some buildings. (The energy codes also provide allowances for renewable energy sources such as solar radiation, wind, plant byproducts, and geothermal sources.)

Note

Both the building codes and the mechanical codes cover specific requirements for solar-powered systems.

Most of these energy-efficiency items are incorporated into the plumbing and mechanical system design by an engineer. However, you should be aware of the basic requirements as described above. These requirements make for a more sustainable building and are part of many sustainable programs and/or government regulations. (See also inset titled *Sustainability and LEED* in Chapter 9 on page 374.)

CHECKLIST

The checklist in Figure 7.13 combines a number of plumbing and mechanical code requirements. The checklist begins by asking you the project and space name, the occupancy classification, building type, and occupant load of the space or building you are designing. (These are all explained in Chapter 2.)

The first part of the checklist concentrates on plumbing requirements. It asks you if an engineer is required. This will depend on the size of the project, the amount of plumbing work, and the jurisdiction of the project. (See Chapter 10.) After that, the initial two plumbing sections need to be used together. Sometimes you will already know the type of toileting and/or bathing facilities required in your project. In other cases, you will first need to determine the quantity of fixtures. For example, the number of required water closets will determine whether you can use "Single (Separate M/F)" toilet facilities or if you need to use "Multi-Toilet" facilities.

The main types of plumbing fixtures are listed in the first column. Use the plumbing code table and the occupant load of the space or building to determine

Plumbing and Mechanical Checklist

Date:____________

Project Name:______________________________________ Space: ______________

Occupancy (new or existing):______________________________Occupant Load: ____________

Building Type:____

Plumbing Requirements [2] Engineer Required? ___ YES ___ NO

Type and Quantity of Plumbing Fixtures (check those that apply and insert quantities)

Fixture	TOTAL FIXTURES Required	ACCESSIBLE FIXTURES New	ACCESSIBLE FIXTURES Existing	STANDARD FIXTURES New	STANDARD FIXTURES Existing
__ Water Closet	M___/F ___	M___/F ___	M___/F ___	M___/F ___	M___/F ___
__ Urinal	M___/F ___	M___/F ___	M___/F ___	M___/F ___	M___/F ___
__ Lavatory	M___/F ___	M___/F ___	M___/F ___	M___/F ___	M___/F ___
__ Sink	M___/F ___	M___/F ___	M___/F ___	M___/F ___	M___/F ___
__ Drinking Fountain	M___/F ___	M___/F ___	M___/F ___	M___/F ___	M___/F ___
__ Bathtub	M___/F ___	M___/F ___	M___/F ___	M___/F ___	M___/F ___
__ Shower	M___/F ___	M___/F ___	M___/F ___	M___/F ___	M___/F ___
__ Other ____________	M___/F ___	M___/F ___	M___/F ___	M___/F ___	M___/F ___
__ Other ____________	M___/F ___	M___/F ___	M___/F ___	M___/F ___	M___/F ___

Type of Facility Required (check those that apply)

Toilet Facilities: __ Single (Separate M/F) __ Single (Shared Unisex) __ Single (Family Style)
__ Multi-Toilet: quantity (if more than one each M/F) __________

Bathing Facilities: __ Single (Separate M/F) __Single (Shared Unisex) __Single (Family Style)
__ Multi-Toilet: quantity (if more than one each M/F) __________

Other Plumbing Code and Accessibility Requirements to Consider (Check/research those that apply)

__ Fixtures: Mounting Heights, Clear Floor Space, Faucet/Control Location, Projections, Water Consumption

__ Faucet/Controls: Ease of Operation (i.e., lever, automatic, etc.), Water Consumption, Water Temperature

__ Grab Bars: Location, Lengths, Heights, Orientation, Additional for Special Situation

__ Accessories: Mounting Heights, Control Locations, Projections, Clear Floor Space

__ Finishes: Smooth/Nonabsorbent, Slip Resistant, Thresholds, Special Locations

__ Room: Turning Space, Overlapping Clear Floor Space, Privacy, Signage, Stall Size, Door Swing

Mechanical Requirements [2] Engineer Required? ___ YES ___ NO

Type of Mechanical System: ______________________________

Location of Mechanical Room: ____________________Size: ____________

Type of Air Circulation (Duct or Plenum): ________________________

Ventilation Required (Type and Locations): ________________________

Exhaust System Required (Type and Location): ______________________

Ceiling Heights Required (Minimums and Clearances): __________________

Location and Type of Supply Diffusers (Ceiling, Wall, Floor): ______________

Location and Type of Return Grills (Ceiling, Wall, Floor): _______________

Number and Location of Thermostats/Zones: ________________________

NOTES:

1. Refer to codes and standards for specific information. Also check the ADA guidelines and ICC/ANSI standard for accessible mounting locations.
2. See Chapter 6 checklist for additional plumbing and mechanical related requirements such as automatic sprinkler systems, dampers, etc.
3. Be sure to note on floor plans the location of fire-rated walls/ceilings for placement of required supply diffusers and return grills.

Figure 7.13 Plumbing and Mechanical Checklist

what fixtures are required and mark these on the list. (See Chapter 2 for information on occupant loads.) You may need to refer to other sections of the code as well. If a fixture is required, write in the total quantity of male (M) and female (F) fixtures in the next column. This total will be used to fill in the "Standard Fixtures" column and the "Accessible Fixtures" column. Refer to the ADA guidelines, the ICC/ANSI standard, and the codes to determine the quantities that must be accessible. List these required quantities in the "Accessible Fixtures" columns on the checklist, indicating the totals for male and female and whether they are new or existing. Deduct these accessible fixtures from the total to obtain the quantity of each standard fixture required. Indicate in the "Standard Fixtures" column how many will be male or female and whether they will be new or existing. Refer to these quantities as you are locating the fixtures in your design and to determine the types of plumbing facilities.

The next section of the checklist gets into the specifics of toilet and bathing facilities. It provides options to check. Certain types of facilities will be required by the code. For example, a large Assembly occupancy would require a "Single (Shared Unisex)" toilet facility in addition to one or more multi-toilet facilities. You may need to determine the quantity of required fixtures in order to decide what types of facilities are required. If you are designing a smaller space that requires two single toilet rooms, one for males and one for females, you would check the item "Single (Separate M/F)." If you are designing an occupancy that requires both a multi-toilet facility and a separate unisex facility, you would check both of these. If this single toilet facility will be used mostly as a family toilet room and you plan to provide extra features or space in the room, you may want to check off "Single (Family Style)" instead. Similar categories are provided for bathing facilities.

The third section under plumbing requirements is a checklist of the various components that are included in a typical toilet and bathing facility. The various requirements that should be researched are listed for each component. You can use this list to verify that you have included the necessary components in each facility and as a reminder to check both the codes and accessibility requirements for each.

Note

It is often necessary to meet with an engineer in the preliminary stages of a design project, so that your design can be coordinated with new and existing plumbing, mechanical, and electrical systems.

The last section of the checklist concentrates on the mechanical system of a project. Again, it asks you whether an engineer is required. It then lists the main mechanical items you should look for in an existing building or be aware of if a new building or space is being designed. Fill in the information as required and refer to it as you plan your design. If necessary, work with an engineer to determine these items. You may also want to attach a reduced copy of the floor plan indicating the location of rated walls and other assemblies so that the location of dampers and other items can be noted.

CHAPTER 8

ELECTRICAL AND COMMUNICATION REQUIREMENTS

> **Note**
>
> The *NFPA 70, National Electrical Code* is the most commonly used electric code in the United States.

This chapter covers electrical and communication code and standard requirements. Although some of these requirements are found in the building codes, most of them are found in the *National Electrical Code (NEC)*. The *NEC* is also referred to as *NPFA 70* and is published by the National Fire Protection Association (NFPA). It is the main electrical code used in the United States. It also references a variety of standards within its text. Most jurisdictions have either adopted the *NEC* or are enforcing a part of the *NEC* in addition to local code requirements. Even the *ICC Electrical Code—Administrative Provisions (ICCEC)*, developed by the ICC, refers you to the *NEC*. The *ICCEC* is not a separate code; rather, it acts as an administrative supplement that can be used in conjunction with the *NEC* and the other I-Codes.

As the designer you will rarely refer to the *NEC* or the electrical standards. On interior projects you will generally be responsible for determining the location and types of outlets, fixtures, equipment, and appliances used in a project. In some cases, you will also need to coordinate the location of equipment rooms. However, when a project requires substantial electrical work, an electrical engineer is required to design the electrical system. On smaller electrical projects, such as some residential homes or minimal changes to a tenant space, that do not require the services of an engineer, a licensed electrical contractor will know the codes.

The electrical and communication requirements are discussed separately in this chapter. The first part of the chapter concentrates on electrical requirements. It begins with a discussion of the various codes and standards that affect electrical systems and then discusses the requirements for the various components of the electrical systems. It also includes a section on energy efficiency in relation to the codes and sustainable buildings. The second half of the chapter discusses different communication systems and how they are affected by the codes and standards. These systems include telephones, computers, security, background music, and television systems, among others.

Throughout the chapter, accessibility related requirements are mentioned as well. These include relevant regulations in the Americans with Disabilities Act (ADA) guidelines and comparable *ICC/ANSI 117.1* accessibility standard requirements. The last part of the chapter contains an electrical and communication checklist.

KEY TERMS

Below is a list of electrical and communication terms that are discussed and defined in this chapter. They are also defined in the Glossary.

Bandwidth
Cable
Circuit
Circuit breaker
Concealed
Conductor
Conduit
Device
Electrical box
Fuse
Grounded
Light diffusing system
Light fixture
Outlet
Raceway
Receptacle
Telephone bank

ELECTRICAL REQUIREMENTS

The codes and standards that apply to electrical systems are discussed in this section. It begins with a comparison of the relevant code publications. This is followed by an explanation of the various components of an electrical system in relation to the codes and standards that apply to them. Energy efficiency is

ELECTRICAL SYSTEMS

An electrical system consists of a distribution system (also known as a transmission system) and a premises wiring system. The *distribution system* is controlled by the electrical utility company and originates in huge generators. From these generators, high-voltage wires transport the electricity to transformers. The utility transformers convert the electricity to lower voltages before it enters a building. The utility distribution system ends at the service entrance connection point to the building and usually includes the utility meter.

The *premises wiring system* is the electrical system within the building. Premises wiring begins where the utility service connection is made and extends to the building's main electrical panel and to the outlets used throughout the building for fixtures, appliances, and equipment. In larger buildings, where the utility company provides higher voltages, additional interior transformers may be used before or after the electricity reaches the panel board. This panel board is typically contained in an electrical room and may consist of a main disconnect switch, secondary switches, fuses, and circuit breakers.

Cables and wires run from this electrical panel to various locations throughout a building. In smaller buildings, these cables or branch circuits are directly connected to the electrical outlets. In larger buildings, feeder conductors are used to distribute the electricity horizontally and vertically to a number of smaller panel boards. These panel boards supply electricity to separate areas within the building. Branch circuits are then used to connect the smaller panel boards to the various electrical outlets.

The *National Electrical Code (NEC)* regulates only the portion of the electrical system that is controlled by the building. It does not include any part controlled by the electrical utility company.

explained as well. The *NEC* applies to all types of occupancies and building types. However, as you read through each section, you will notice that there are often separate or additional electrical requirements for Residential occupancies, dwelling units, and/or sleeping units. Dwelling and sleeping units can be found in most Residential occupancies as well as in some Institutional building types. To better understand the definition of a dwelling and sleeping unit, you may want to refer to the inset titled *Types of Rooms and Spaces* in Chapter 2 on page 63.

In addition to the various requirements described below, you should be aware that all parts and devices of an electrical system must be tested and approved in order for it to be used. (See inset titled *Testing Agencies* in Chapter 1 on page 34.) This includes the electrical panel, cabling, and other components used to create the system as well as the receptacles, switches, and other devices used by the occupants of the building. Light fixtures, as explained below, must also pass certain tests.

Comparing the Codes

The building codes include a chapter on electrical systems, but these chapters typically reference the *National Electrical Code (NEC or NFPA 70)*. The *International Building Code (IBC)* refers you to the *ICC Electrical Code-Administrative Provisions (ICCEC)*, which, in turn, references the *NEC*. The *IBC* chapter also refers you to various other parts of the *IBC* that relate to electrical requirements. For example, emergency power for exit signs is discussed in the "Means of Egress" chapter and standby power requirements for smoke control systems, as well as alarm and detection systems, are discussed in the "Fire Protection Systems" chapter in the *IBC*. These and other requirements need to be coordinated with those found in the *NEC*. The electrical chapter in the *NFPA 5000* directly references the *NEC*. The *Life Safety Code (LSC)* also references the *NEC*.

The *NEC* references a number of standards throughout its text. Many of them are NFPA standards, such as those found in Figure 8.1. Other standards organizations have electrical standards as well. These include the American National Standards Institute (ANSI), the National Electrical Manufacturers Association (NEMA), and Underwriters Laboratories (UL). In addition to providing supplemental design and installation procedures, these standards organizations develop

NFPA 70	National Electric Code
NFPA 70B	Electrical Equipment Maintenance
NFPA 70E	Electrical Safety Requirements for Employee Workplaces
NFPA 72	National Fire Alarm Code
NFPA 75	Protection of Information Technology Equipment
NFPA 76	Fire Protection of Telecommunication Facilities
NFPA 77	Static Electricity
NFPA 110	Emergency and Standby Power Systems
NFPA 111	Stored Electrical Energy Emergency and Standby Power Systems
NFPA 262	Method of Test for Flame Travel and Smoke of Wires and Cables for Use in Air-Handling Spaces
NFPA 269	Test Method for Developing Toxic Potency Data for Use in Fire Hazard Modeling

NOTE: There may be other NFPA standards not listed above that are specific to an occupancy, especially hazardous occupancies. Additional standards are available from UL and ASTM as well as ISA and IEEE.

Figure 8.1 Common NFPA Standards for Electrical and Communication Systems

standards for the fixtures themselves, as well as provide specific testing and labeling procedures for electrical and communication equipment.

Other codes also affect the installation and design of electrical items. The energy codes, for example, include requirements that affect electrical components. The ICC has the *International Energy Conservation Code (IECC)* and the NFPA has the *NFPA 900, Building Energy Code (BEC)*. Both establish minimum regulations for the design of energy-efficient buildings. (Some of the same requirements have also been made mandatory by the federal government. See Energy Codes on page 24 in Chapter 1.) A large part of the energy codes deals with the thermal design of the building envelope, which is critical in containing the conditioned air in the building. However, this is usually incorporated into the building during its initial construction and does not typically apply to the interior building elements. The rest of the energy codes concentrate on electrical systems, as they affect the overall electrical power and lighting as well as mechanical systems and water-heating plumbing systems. Many of these items are integrated during the design of the interiors. (See Chapter 6 for mechanical and water-heating energy requirements.) Additional energy-related requirements will be discussed later in the section titled Energy Efficiency.

The *NEC* does not include performance code requirements for electrical systems, although some performance-related codes are mentioned in the *ICCEC*. If using other NFPA codes, you can refer to their performance-related chapters for certain performance criteria. In addition, if the *ICC Performance Code (ICCPC)* is allowed in your jurisdiction, it includes electrical related performance criteria. For example, it includes a chapter on electricity as well as a few electrical related items in the fire safety chapter. Most of the criteria concentrate on the safe isolation of electrical equipment, devices, and appliances, as well as protection of the building occupants from live parts.

Accessibility issues that relate to electrical systems mostly apply to the mounting height of the outlets and fixtures. In some cases, the projection of light fixtures must also be considered. These and other accessibility requirements as they apply to electrical systems will be discussed throughout the chapter.

Electrical Panels/Rooms

Three types of electrical panels can be used in a building. The first and largest is the service entrance *switchboard*. It is the main electrical panel that distributes the electricity from the utility service connection to the rest of the building. The *NEC* regulates the size of the room that contains this panel. For example, one of the most typical requirements is that there must be at least a 3-foot (900 mm) deep by 30-inch (750 mm) wide clear floor space in front of the panel. (Larger panels

Note

An electrical panel is a common place for a fire to start. When designing interiors, be careful not to locate electrical panels next to stairwells or other main means of egress.

may need more clearance.) When the switching panel is two-sided, the code requires enough working room on both sides of the panel. Other equipment in the room, including transformers, will require similar clearances. (See inset titled *Electrical Systems* on page 297.) These rooms are typically required to be fire rated. (See Chapter 5.) The switchboard room must also be ventilated to control heat buildup from the equipment. If it is located on an outside wall, ventilation can be done directly to the outside. If not, ducts and fans must be used to provide outside air ventilation. (Refer to *NEC* for duct location restrictions.)

Note

There is often a conflict between sprinklers required in an electrical equipment room and/or a telecommunication room and the safety of the equipment due to water damage. You may need to consider a dry sprinkler system or an alternate sprinkler system.

Power panel boards are used throughout a building to distribute electricity to each floor and/or tenant or dwelling space. They are one-sided electrical panels that are typically housed in electrical closets or in cabinets that are placed in or against a wall. In multi-story buildings the electrical closets should be stacked directly above each other on each floor so that the electrical systems can be vertically distributed. Each floor may also have one or more smaller *branch panel boards* that supply electricity to a particular area or tenant. Typically, closets that contain only panel boards do not have to be rated. Closets that contain large transformers and panel boards are required to be rated.

All these requirements are important to know, especially if you are creating a layout for a new space or building and one or more electrical closets must be located. You would work closely with an engineer to make sure the closets are located as required for distribution. You will also need to confirm that room sizes allow for electrical panels and other equipment to have the correct clearances. In addition, these rooms typically require a visible sign clearly stating "Electrical Room" or similar approved wording.

Electrical Cabling and Conduit

To distribute electricity to all areas where it is needed, electrical wiring must pass through many building elements. When electrical wiring is installed, the diameter of any hole created for the passage of the cable cannot be more than $\frac{1}{8}$ inch (3 mm) larger than the diameter of the cable, conduit, or other device passing through the hole. When these wires pass through a rated floor, ceiling, or wall assembly, the building codes require the use of a rated firestop. (See Chapter 5 for more information on firestops.)

Note

If a cable is run continuously from the electrical panel to the device, without any intermediate connections, it is considered a *home run.*

In some cases, an electrical cable may be allowed to run on its own, while others will require the use of a protected enclosure such as a conduit or raceway. It typically depends on the type of cable and the construction type of the building (see Chapter 3), but it can also depend on the location of the cable within a building. For example, if a cable is run within a rated assembly, it typically must be within a conduit. Certain jurisdictions have special requirements or restrictions as well. Various cables, conduit, and raceways are explained next.

ELECTRICAL CABLES		METAL CONDUIT	
TYPE AC	Armored Cable (BX)	TYPE EMT	Electrical Metallic Tubing
TYPE ALS	Aluminum Sheath Metal-Clad Cable	TYPE FMC	Flexible Metal Conduit
TYPE CS	Copper Sheath Metal-Clad Cable	TYPE FMT	Flexible Metallic Tubing
TYPE FC	Flat Cable Assemblies	TYPE IMC	Intermediate Metal Conduit
TYPE FCC	Flat Conductor Cable (FLAT WIRE)	TYPE LFML	Liquidtight Flexible Metal Conduit
TYPE IGS	Integrated Gas Spacer Cable	TYPE RMC	Rigid Metal Conduit
TYPE MC	Metal-Clad Cable		
TYPE MI	Mineral-Insulated, Metal-Sheathed Cable	NON-METAL CONDUIT	
TYPE MV	Medium-Voltage Cable	TYPE ENT	Electrical Nonmetallic Tubing
TYPE NM or NMC	Nonmetallic-Sheathed Cable (ROMEX)	TYPE LFNC	Liquidtight Flexible Nonmetallic Conduit
TYPE PLTC	Power-Limited Tray Cable	TYPE RNC	Rigid Nonmetallic (PVC) Conduit
TYPE SE or USE	Service-Entrance Cable		
TYPE SNM	Shielded Nonmetallic-Sheathed Cable		
TYPE TC	Power and Control Tray Cable		
TYPE UF	Underground Feeder		

NOTE: Other types and/or subcategories of cables and conduit may also be available.

Figure 8.2 Common Types of Electrical Cables and Conduit

Cabling

The *NEC* specifies the types of electrical wiring or cables that can be used. Figure 8.2 gives you an idea of how many different types of cables there are. (Many of these cable types also have subcategories.) Each cable must go through testing in order to be classified for its specific use. A variety of testing standards are used in order to determine performance and safety. Other tests are used to evaluate the flammability of the cable and determine its flame spread and smoke density (similar to the *Steiner Tunnel Test* described in Chapter 9). Since the protective sleeve of the cable can be highly toxic when exposed to a fire, certain cables must also undergo a toxicity test. (See Toxicity Test section in Chapter 9.) Once tested, the cable is labeled with its appropriate classification.

The types of electrical cables used on a project are typically specified by the electrical engineer or contractor using the requirements of the *NEC*. Although noncombustible cable is required in many occupancies and most building conditions, certain areas within a building may require other types of cables. For example, special rules apply for wiring in ducts, plenums, and other air handling spaces in order to limit the use of materials that would contribute smoke and products of combustion during a fire. (See Chapter 6.) You should be familiar with the most common cables. They are listed here by their more common trade names:

- *Romex:* Romex is the trade name for nonmetallic-sheathed cable (Type NM or NMC). It consists of two or more insulated conductors and should include a ground wire surrounded by a moisture-resistant plastic material. The *NEC* limits this cable mostly to Residential one- and two-family dwellings and multi-unit dwellings not exceeding three floors. Typically these are wood frame buildings.
- *BX or Flex:* BX is a type of armor cable (Type AC). It is a flexible cable that consists of two or more conductors wrapped in heavy paper or plastic and encased in a continuous spiral-wound metal jacket. It is commonly used in commercial applications. In new installations, the *NEC* requires BX to be secured in intervals, but in existing installations you may find that the cable was just fished through walls, floors, and ceilings. In addition, BX is often used to connect light fixtures in suspended ceiling grids to allow relocation flexibility. In most instances, the *NEC* will limit length of an unsecured flex cable to 6 feet (1.8 m) in length; however, other jurisdictions may be stricter.

Note

Some jurisdictions restrict the use of BX cable in buildings, even if the *NEC* allows it.

- *Metal-clad cable:* Metal-clad cable (Type MC) is often used when BX cable is restricted. It looks similar to BX cable, but MC cable has an additional green ground wire that provides extra grounding. As a result, it can be used in more applications than BX cable.
- *Flat wire:* Flat wire is the common name for flat conductor cable (Type FCC). It is a small cable in a flat housing that allows it to be used under carpet tiles without protruding. Flat wire can be used in many applications, and it is often used to rework obsolete wiring systems in existing buildings. The *NEC* prohibits the use of flat wire in wet and hazardous areas and in residential, hospital, and school buildings.
- *Fiber optic cable:* In the past, fiber optic cable was used mostly in low-voltage applications. However, it can also be used as a conductor for electrical components such as lighting. In addition, an optical fiber can be run in a cable that contains an electrical wire. When this occurs it is called a composite cable and classified as an electrical cable according to the type of electrical conductor or wire used with it. (More information on fiber optic and composite cables can be found in the Communication Requirements section of this chapter.)

Conduit

Another option often used when wiring large residential and most commercial buildings is *conduit.* Also known as *tubing* in the *NEC*, conduit is a fire-rated metal piping used to house and protect plastic conductors or cables. It is available in nonmetallic or plastic, too, but these are typically allowed only in nonrated applications. More than one wire or cable can be fished through the conduit; however, the code may limit the types of cables that can be used together. For example, electrical cables often are not allowed to be used in the same conduit as communication cables. The conduit may also act as a system ground (see the section on Grounding and Circuit Interrupters on page 311) and may protect surrounding building materials should a wire overheat.

Note

Empty flexible metal conduit is also known as *green field.*

As shown in Figure 8.2, there are a number of different types of conduits, including rigid and flexible metal conduit and rigid and flexible nonmetallic conduit. (Nonmetallic conduit can be made of plastic, PVC, or fiberglass.) Conduits can also be referred to as *conduit bodies*. This term is used to describe larger raceways that have removable covers for access to the wires inside them. (See Raceways, below.) The type of conduit required depends on where it will be used and the types of hazards present. For example, nonmetallic conduit is often used underground to bring the power into a building; however, its use inside a building is usually restricted, especially in fire-rated assemblies. Instead, rigid and flexible metal conduits are most often used in a building interior. Rigid metal conduit is allowed by the *NEC* in all occupancies and in almost any condition. Flexible metal conduit has some limitations. For example, it cannot be used in certain hazardous areas and its length may be limited. Other code requirements apply more to the installation of the conduit. This includes the requirements for the diameter of the conduit allowed as well as the types of connections and the number of bends allowed in each run. In addition, the building codes will require a firestop or smokestop when conduit is installed in a rated wall or ceiling assembly. This is shown as sealant in Figure 8.3. Additional restrictions might be enforced on a local level by a code jurisdiction.

Raceways

Like conduit, *raceways* and *wireways* can also be used to house and protect electrical cables. The *NEC* may limit their use in some applications, but most of the code requirements are geared instead toward the cable connections made within the raceways. Raceways may be used in place of a conduit or in conjunction with other conduits. For example, some types of buildings are constructed with concrete or metal floor raceways that are part of the structural floor system. Often referred to as cells, these raceways come in different shapes and sizes and are often laid out in a grid-type system, allowing cables to be run from one area of a building to another. As a building's needs change, the cabling can be changed and

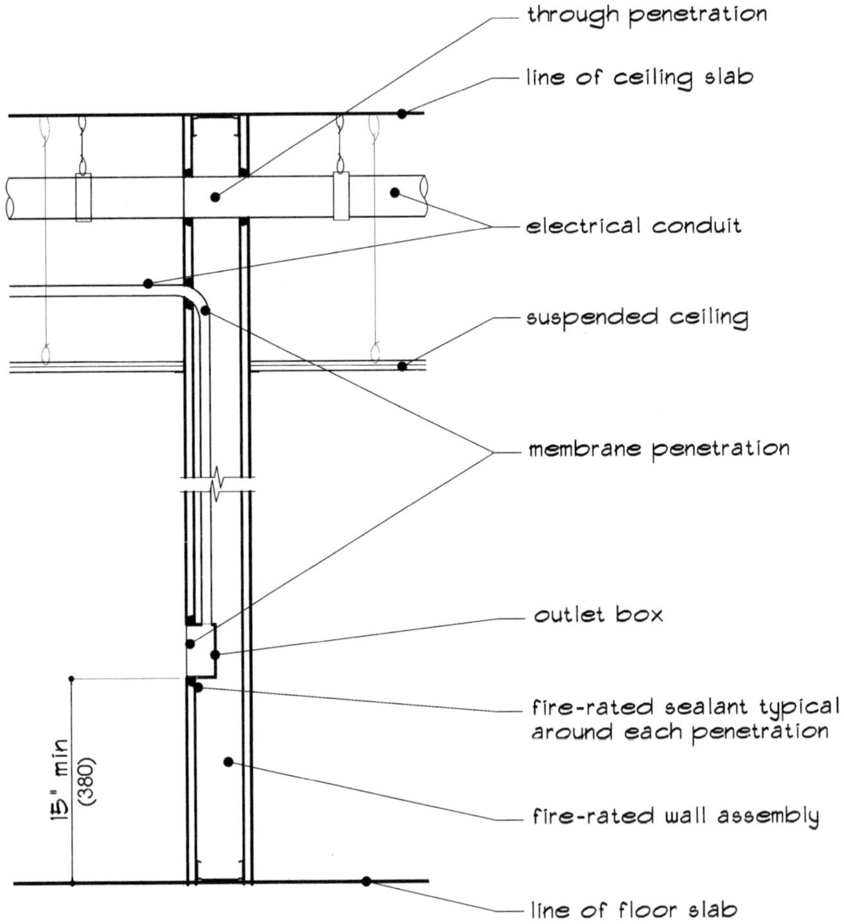

Figure 8.3 Electrical Penetrations in Rated Wall Assembly

redirected. Other under-floor raceways may be added after the initial construction of a building as part of the finished floor assembly.

Raceways may also be mounted on walls for easy access. For example, wireways that are enclosed with removable covers can be installed around the perimeter of a factory to allow access to the cables as locations of equipment change. Openings (e.g., knockouts) in the wireways allow the cabling to be directed to different locations when needed. Other types of raceways can be used to cover a cable run on the surface of the wall. (Certain codes may restrict the use of raceways when used with fire-rated assemblies.)

Circuitry

The distribution of electricity is managed and organized by creating different circuits. Separate circuits are created by wiring (or cable) that branches from the main electrical source to different areas of the building or space. Each circuit feeds electricity to a series of light fixtures, outlets, equipment, and/or appliances before it returns to the branch panel or power panel board. Each circuit may be carrying a different voltage and amperage of power. For example, a washing machine will require a 220-voltage circuit, which must be separate from the 120-voltage circuit required for the lights in the room.

The *NEC* limits the number of volts or amperage that are allowed on a single circuit. Therefore, it is important to supply an engineer with the correct quantity and types of equipment, lighting, and appliances that will be used in a space or building so that the circuitry can be designed correctly. The engineer uses the specifications of the items to determine the electrical loads of the space and how many circuits are needed to meet the requirements of the code. This can affect the number of light fixtures that can be switched together and how many fixtures can be controlled by dimmers. In addition, certain pieces of equipment that require more power may need a circuit that serves only a single outlet. This is called a *dedicated circuit*. It is also known as *clean power*. The outlet that it serves is referred to as a dedicated outlet. For example, dedicated circuits are often used for large equipment such as copiers and many appliances such as refrigerators, electric ranges, and clothes dryers. Most mechanical equipment and the main equipment for many communication systems will require a dedicated outlet as well.

Note

If an outlet has special power requirements, you may want to specify a dedicated circuit so that it will be wired separately. This will prevent electrical disturbances from other nearby electrical equipment.

Electrical Boxes

There are three main types of electrical boxes: outlet boxes, switch boxes, and junction boxes. As the designer, you will often locate outlet and switch boxes but not always the junction box. Unlike electrical conduit that often penetrates the entire wall or ceiling assembly, electrical boxes usually penetrate only the outer membrane of the wall, as shown in Figure 8.3. (See Chapter 5 for more information on membranes.)

When electrical boxes are located in fire-resistance-rated walls, floors, or floor/ceiling assemblies, the building codes set additional requirements. These requirements include the following:

- *Type:* The box must be metal. If not, it must be tested for use in fire-resistance rated assemblies. In addition, one box typically cannot exceed 16 square inches (10,300 sq mm).

Note

If an existing electrical box is not being used, it must either (1) have a cover plate or (2) be totally removed (including box and all wiring) with the wall opening properly patched.

Note

Since the installation of electrical boxes creates a membrane penetration rather than a through-penetration as described in Chapter 5, firestopping is usually not required.

- *Quantity:* The total number of boxes in one wall or ceiling is limited. The total number of openings in a rated wall or ceiling surface measuring 100 square feet (9.3 s m) cannot exceed 100 square inches (64,500 sq mm).
- *Location:* When boxes are used on opposite sides of the same wall, the boxes must be separated horizontally by 24 inches (610 mm) or have some type of barrier or fireblocking between the two boxes. (See section on Fireblocking in Chapter 5.)
- *Firestopping:* Fire-rated caulking or other type of firestop must be used around the box where it penetrates the membrane to seal the space between the box and the wall. (See Figure 8.3 and section on Firestops in Chapter 5.)

This will apply to any type of electrical box (or communication box) that penetrates a rated assembly or membrane and might affect the design of a room or space. For example, if a breakroom is adjacent to a fire-rated wall, you may not want to locate the counter with all its required electrical appliances along that wall, due to the many outlets you will need. You should also be aware of accessibility requirements as they apply to electrical outlets. Similar requirements are given in the ADA guidelines and the ICC/ANSI standard, as well as in the accessibility section of the building codes. The *NEC* and accessibility requirements are described here for each type of box.

Outlet Boxes

Note

A *pull box* is another type of electrical box that is used during installation as an intermediate box for pulling through long runs of cable.

Outlet boxes can be wall- and/or floor-mounted for electrical receptacles or wall- and/or ceiling-mounted for light fixtures. If the box allows for the connection of a plug-in appliance or equipment, it is typically called a *receptacle outlet*. When used for a light fixture, the box is often referred to as a *fixture outlet* or a *lighting outlet*. Most outlet boxes are either 2 × 4 inches (50 × 100 mm), such as those used for duplex receptacle outlets or wall sconces, or 4 × 4 inches (100 × 100 mm) for quadraplex outlets. However, other sizes are also available and will depend on the type or number of devices wired to the one box. Boxes used at a ceiling for hanging light fixtures are often round or octagonal.

Outlet boxes are usually mounted within a wall by fastening the box to a stud. For example, in a metal stud and gypsum board wall, the outlet box is mounted to the metal stud and a hole is cut around the gypsum board to allow access to the box. (Surface-mounted boxes are typically used on masonry walls.) In the ceiling, the box can be mounted to a joist or directly to the underside of the ceiling slab. The *NEC* specifies that the opening in the wall or ceiling cannot exceed ⅛ inch (3 mm) clearance between the box and the gypsum board. In a rated wall, this gap must be fire caulked to create a firestop. (See Light Fixtures on page 313 for additional box requirements.)

Because the needs of residences are somewhat consistent, the codes provide more specific outlet requirements for Residential occupancies such as homes, apartments, and even certain guest rooms in hotels. (They may also include some Institutional building types. See inset titled *Types of Rooms and Spaces* in Chapter 2 on page 63.) If a building or space is considered a dwelling unit, the *NEC* specifies the minimum number of electrical boxes to be provided. In each room of the dwelling unit, receptacle outlet boxes must be installed so that no point measured horizontally along the floor line in any wall space is more than 6 feet (1.8 m) from an outlet. (A wall space is generally defined as any fixed wall that is at least 2 feet (600 mm) wide.) An example of how to place the outlets is shown in Figure 8.4. Hallways that connect the rooms within the dwelling unit that are more than 10 feet (3 m) in length also require at least one receptacle

Note

In Residential occupancies when a wall is broken by a doorway, fireplace, or similar opening, each continuous wall space of two or more feet (600 mm) must be considered separately for the placement of a receptacle outlet.

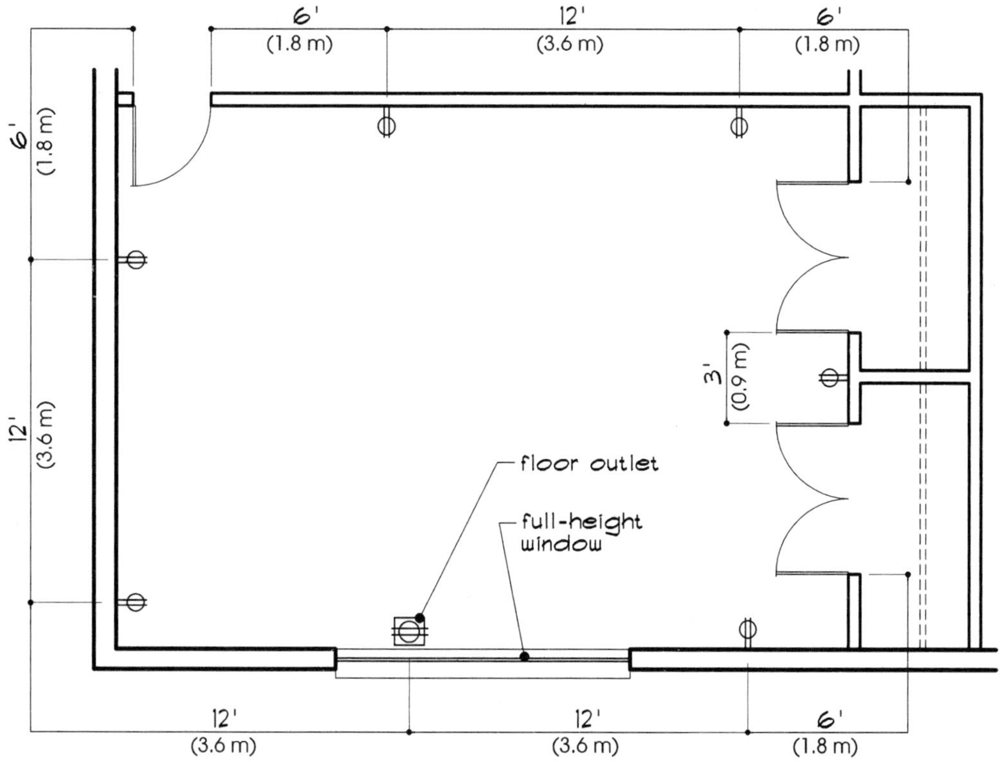

Figure 8.4 Dwelling Unit Electrical Receptacle Location Example

outlet. (This does not apply to common hallways or corridors that connect the dwelling units to each other.) Of course, additional outlets can always be added, but the minimums need to be met. In addition, the *NEC* (and the *IRC*) requires specific location of outlets in bathrooms, kitchens, laundry areas, basements, and garages. (Also see the section on Grounding and Circuit Interrupters later in this chapter.)

Since the needs and requirements in non-Residential facilities vary with the activities and equipment needs of a particular tenant or user, the codes do not provide as many specific requirements as for dwelling units. The *NEC* does not specify the frequency of receptacle or lighting outlet boxes in these occupancies. Instead, their placement is determined by specific equipment requirements and convenience considerations. For example, the location of a copier or fax machine will determine the location of the receptacle, or the typical length of a cord on a vacuum cleaner may be a good guideline for placement of receptacle outlets within a long corridor.

Certain outlet boxes are required to be accessible. It will depend on the location and use of the outlet, the type of equipment connected to it, and if it is meant for use by employees and/or visitors. An example of a nonaccessible outlet may be an outlet in a janitor's closet or an outlet behind a permanent copier where it serves a dedicated use. You need to consider if there is a possibility that the employee who would use the outlet could be disabled and need the outlet within the accessible reach ranges. Other outlets that are meant to be used by clients, visitors, or the general public should be accessible as well. You may need to discuss this issue with the owner to decide. However, when specifying the typical location of wall outlets in a project, it is a good idea to use a height that meets accessibility requirements whenever possible. Should the function of a room or space change in the future, the outlets will already be accessible.

When the outlet box is mounted on a wall, the typical accessible requirement is that it be located at least 15 inches (380 mm) above the floor, as shown in Figures 8.3 and 8.5. In addition, when designing accessible work areas, such as study carrels in public libraries and workstations in offices, the outlet must be located within the appropriate reach ranges. Whenever possible, locate the outlets directly above the worksurface or counter. For example, many workstation panel systems now come with electrical raceways at counter height rather than the traditional floor location. You may also be able to mount a special outlet toward the front edge under the worksurface. (Floor outlets are not typically considered accessible; but if used, be sure they are not located within the clear floor space necessary at an accessible counter, table, or desk.)

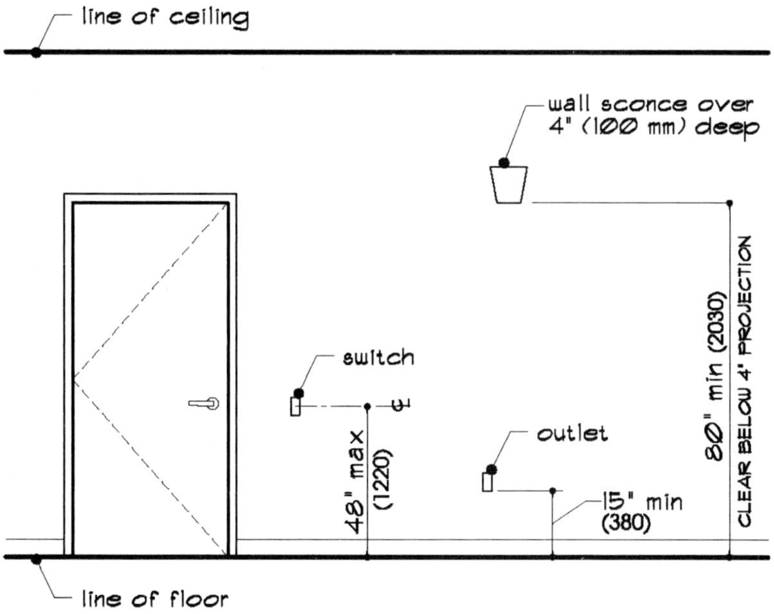

Figure 8.5 Typical Accessible Electrical Device and Fixture Locations

Switch Boxes

Switch boxes are typically wall-mounted and control the lighting outlet. (They can also sometimes be referred to as a *fixture outlet*.) The cable connection between the light fixture and the switch device or control is made at the switch box. This control can be in the form of a toggle, dimmer, or remote. Many of the code requirements for switch boxes are similar to those for outlet boxes. For example, the switch box must be mounted to a stud or other blocking and the hole cut for the box cannot be larger than ⅛ inch (3 mm) around the box.

The *NEC* has requirements specifically for dwelling units. The main requirement is that each habitable room, as well as hallways and stairs that lead up to these rooms, must have a switch outlet that controls the lighting in that room. In addition, a stairway must typically have lighting that is controlled at both the top and bottom of the stair. In other occupancies and building types that do not include dwelling units, the *NEC* does not specify the frequency of a switch outlet. This allows multiple switches to be ganged together and conveniently located in larger open areas. However, the *NEC* does limit the number of light fixtures that can be circuited to one switch. This quantity is based on the voltage of the fixtures used. The total voltages are determined by the electrical engineer based on the cut sheets of the selected light fixtures. (See the Circuitry section earlier in this chapter.) In addition, if an automatic switch sensor is used, the *NES* requires that the switch sensor include a manual switch as part of the device. (Some local jurisdictions may have separate requirements for automatic switch sensors.)

Switch boxes must also be located within the accessible reaching height above the floor. They must be between 15 and 48 inches (380 and 1220 mm) above the floor, as shown in Figure 8.5, measured to the centerline of the box. This allows both a front approach and a side approach. Switches that are not required to be accessible are those in areas used only by service or maintenance personnel, such as janitor closets and mechanical rooms. There is also an exception if there are multiple switches to the same fixture, but it is recommended that you locate switch boxes at accessible heights whenever possible.

Junction Boxes

Unlike the other electrical boxes already explained, a junction box is not used to connect an outlet or fixture. Instead, it is used to tie several wires together. For example, a main cable run that leaves the electrical panel will, at some point, need to branch off to electrify several light fixtures. At the point where these wires come together, a junction box is typically used to protect the various cable connections and to allow for future access. It is also used as an intermediary *pull box* when there are long conduit runs. The size of the box will vary, depending on the number of connections that need to be made, but often a standard 4 × 4 inch (100 × 100 mm) metal box is used.

Note

All electrical junction boxes must be easily accessible, whether they are located in the floor, wall, or ceiling. You must plan your design accordingly.

Although junction boxes are usually specified by an electrical engineer as part of the design and installation of the electrical wiring, there may be times that you specify the location of a junction box. For example, you may know that a client plans to add a future light fixture in a certain location, so you specify a junction box to be wired for future use.

Unless you specify a junction box for a specific future use, junction boxes do not need to meet accessibility requirements. However, the *NEC* does require that a junction box be accessible to the electrician at all times. For example, junction boxes are often located on or near the ceiling slab. If you are using a suspended ceiling grid with removable tiles, access becomes very easy. However, if a junction box is located in an area where you are planning to use a drywall ceiling, an access panel must be added. The size of the panel depends on how easily the box can be reached from the underside of the ceiling. If the junction box is located flush with the surface of a wall or ceiling, a blank cover plate can be used as the access panel. If you have a number of decorative ceilings in your project, you may want to coordinate the locations of any necessary junction boxes with the electrical engineer.

Grounding and Circuit Interrupters

The electrical code requires that all electrical systems be *grounded.* This is accomplished by a third wire that always accompanies an electrical cable. In general, this ground wire redirects live currents into the ground to prevent a person from getting shocked when there is a short circuit. Because a grounding wire is not always 100 percent effective, in certain cases additional measures must be taken to protect the electrical outlet and the person using the outlet. There are two types of *circuit interrupters* that the *NEC* requires, depending on the location of a receptacle outlet. Both are described below.

Ground Fault Circuit Interrupters (GFCI)

The presence of water makes it easier for an electrical current to flow. If the circuit or outlet is wet or if the person touching the outlet or adjacent appliance is wet or standing in water, there is a much higher chance of getting shocked despite the fact that the circuit is already grounded. As a result, the *NEC* requires special grounded circuits in rooms where water will be present.

These circuits are called *ground fault circuit interrupters,* also commonly known as GFCI (or sometimes GFI). The GFCI is a device that is able to detect small current leaks. If a current leak occurs, the GFCI disconnects the power to the circuit or appliance and thus prevents an electrical shock from occurring. The GFCI can be installed in the electrical panel as part of a circuit breaker, or it can be installed as a special type of receptacle at the electrical outlet.

The *NEC* requires that exterior receptacle outlets be GFCIs. On interior projects, typically all standard 125-volt, 15-amp, and 20-amp receptacle outlets located in areas where there is water should be specified as GFCIs. These areas include restrooms, bathrooms, kitchens, breakrooms, bar areas, laundry rooms, and even pools or spas. (Residential garages and unfinished basements usually require them, as well.) The *NEC* divides these requirements into those for dwelling units and those for more commercial applications. (See inset titled *Types of Rooms and Spaces* on page 63.) Some of the more common *NEC* requirements for GFCIs in building interiors include the following:

- *Bathrooms in dwelling units:* The *NEC* requires a receptacle outlet to be located at each bathroom lavatory used in a dwelling unit such as private homes, apartments, and hotels. These outlets must be GFCI. An example of a hotel bathroom with a typical outlet is shown in Plan A of Figure 8.6.
- *Kitchens in dwelling units:* All receptacle outlets that serve the countertop of a kitchen in a dwelling unit, no matter where the sink is located, must be GFCI. This includes outlets in the walls above the counter, outlets in the

Note

A GFCI outlet is not typically required at water coolers unless the water cooler is located in an area where GFCIs are already required.

Note

A GFCI is also available as a device that plugs into an existing outlet. It should be used only on a temporary basis and is often used on a construction site before the permanent wiring has been installed.

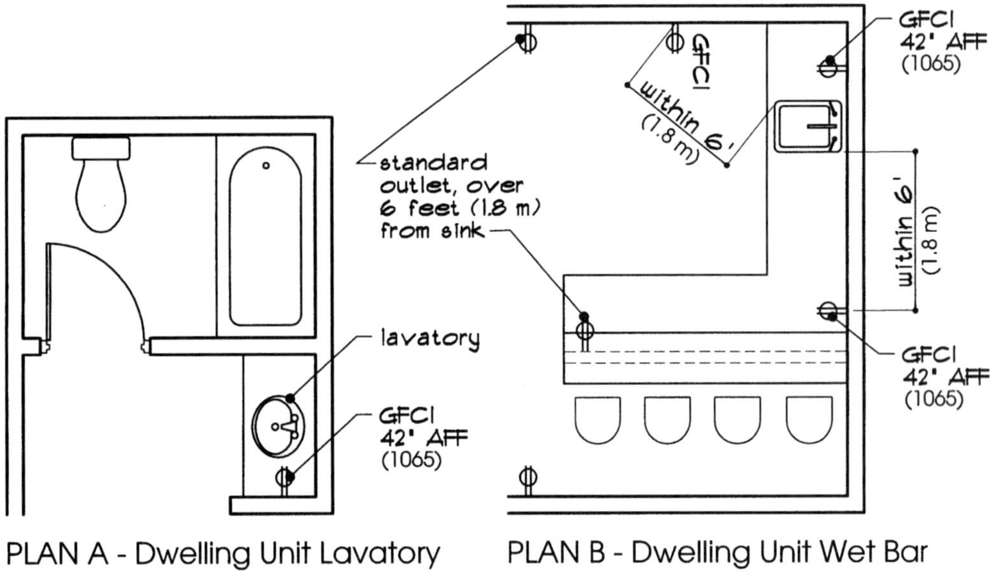

Figure 8.6 Required GFCI Outlets Location Examples

side of a base cabinet, and outlets required at island and peninsular counters. It does not include standard-height wall outlets (e.g., 15 inches or 380 mm above the floor) adjacent to the counter or outlets installed for larger appliances such as a garbage disposal, refrigerator, or stove top.

❑ *Wet bar sinks in dwelling units:* If there is a wet bar in a dwelling unit, any receptacle outlet within 6 feet (1.8 m) of the edge of the sink (or water source) must be a GFCI. This is measured by the shortest distance as shown in Plan B of Figure 8.6, not by the distance along the wall line. Any outlet outside the 6-foot (1.8 m) perimeter of the sink is not required to be a GFCI.

❑ *Public restrooms:* All receptacle outlets provided in public restrooms found in nondwelling building types must be GFCI. This includes any outlet near the lavatory as well as any other outlet in the room. Examples include restrooms in commercial buildings, airports, and train stations.

❑ *Breakrooms and kitchens:* All receptacle outlets located in nondwelling unit kitchens, including breakrooms, must be GFCI. This includes all outlets in the room or area, not just at the counter, but excludes major appliances.

Additional GFCIs may be required by the *NEC* or a jurisdiction in certain building types. For example, additional GFCI outlets are required by the *NEC* in certain Health Care occupancies. In addition, certain nondwelling unit buildings may be required to have ground-fault protection at the main service equipment. When protection is provided at the main equipment, these buildings may not require each outlet to be GFCI as well.

Arc Fault Circuit Interrupters (AFCI)

Sometimes an electrical wire will discharge an unexpected electrical current across the insulation meant to protect it, causing what is known as an *arc fault*. There are a number of reasons this can happen, but it is usually due to a defect in the cable that shows up after extended use or as a result of unseen damage during installation or renovation. An arc fault gets very hot. When it occurs, it creates pressure that will spread hot gases and molten metal to surrounding areas. It has the potential to ignite surrounding combustibles such as wall insulation and start a fire. As a safety precaution, the *NEC* requires protection of certain outlets.

Since 1999, the *NEC* has required the use of *arc fault circuit interrupters*, or AFCIs, in the sleeping rooms of all dwelling units. This includes each bedroom in a residential home or apartment building as well as sleeping rooms in other building types such as hotels and nursing homes that are classified as dwelling units. Every 125-volt, 15-amp, and 20-amp outlet in the sleeping room must be connected to a circuit that is AFCI protected. This includes receptacles, light fixture and ceiling fan connections, switches, and even smoke detectors located in the room. The AFCI essentially disconnects the power to (i.e., de-energizes) the circuit whenever an arc fault is detected, thereby making the arc harmless. Although special AFCI outlets are available, the *NEC* states that the entire circuit supplying the sleeping room must be protected.

Light Fixtures

Light fixtures, also called *luminaires* by the *NEC*, have some additional code and standard requirements. The *NEC* requirements are based on the type of light fixture and where it is installed. The building codes also specify minimum light levels allowed. In addition, the location of the fixture may be affected by accessibility standards and the ADA guidelines. Many of these requirements are discussed in this section.

Note

UL standards for light fixtures also specify the maximum wattage of the lamp to be used in the fixture. Using a higher wattage can result in overheating and damage to the wiring.

Types of Light Fixtures

Only fire tested and labeled light fixtures should be used on interior projects. The most widely accepted standards are created by Underwriters Laboratories (UL). Each light fixture manufactured in the United States is tested to be used in a specific environment or location and is then assigned a UL rating or seal of approval. (See inset titled *UL Labels* in Chapter 1 on page 37.) For example, a fixture installed in a damp location, like the ceiling of an enclosed shower unit, must be marked "Suitable for Damp Locations." (Other bathroom fixtures typically do not need this rating.) Other light fixtures are specifically marked for wall mounting, undercabinet mounting, ceiling mounting, and suspended ceiling mounting. Certain fixtures will also note when they are allowed in noncombustible, nonfire-rated, or fire-resistant construction. You must choose the fixture appropriate to the location in which it will be used.

Note

A light fixture listed for a wet location can also be used in a damp location.

As the designer, it is important to specify UL-approved light fixtures. UL tested and labeled fixtures have undergone rigorous testing. Many jurisdictions allow only UL-approved fixtures on a project. However, even if they are not required, you should be specifying them for safety and liability reasons. You cannot assume every light fixture is UL approved. You need to look carefully when specifying fixtures supplied by countries outside the United States and fixtures made by custom fabricators. This may also limit the use of antique fixtures in many occupancies.

Note

Within their catalogs, manufacturers usually market their accessible wall sconces separate from other light fixtures.

The type of light fixture will affect how it is attached to an outlet box. The *NEC* allows light fixtures weighing less than 50 pounds (23 kg) to be supported by the outlet box that serves the fixture. This usually works for most wall sconces and lighter-weight ceiling fixtures. Heavier fixtures, such as ceiling fans and larger pendants or chandeliers, must either be supported independently of the box or be attached to a box made specifically for heavier fixtures. UL standards for light fixtures also specify the maximum wattage of the lamp to be used in the fixture. Using a higher wattage can result in overheating and damage to the wiring.

Location of Light Fixtures

The *NEC* places strict requirements on the access to the various electrical components that are part of the light fixture. In addition to the electrical box being accessible, all light fixtures must be placed so that both the lamp (i.e., light bulb) and the fixture can be replaced when needed. This becomes especially important when light fixtures are used within architectural elements such as ceiling coves, custom light boxes, and specially designed millwork. The custom unit must be designed so that access is provided to the fixture. Fixtures used in special applications must also be carefully located so that they do not cause the fixture or other adjacent materials to overheat. The performance codes are also very clear on this. For example, the *ICCPC* specifically states that "building elements shall be protected from thermal damage due to heat transfer or electrical arc from electrical power installations." If the light fixture is used in an enclosed space, you may need to provide ventilation to prevent access heat build up, especially when using low-voltage fixtures that tend to get very hot. In addition, if the fixture is used in conjunction with light-transmitting plastics, the "Plastics" chapter of the building codes has additional restrictions and may even require additional sprinkler heads to be provided. (Also see inset titled *Plastic Finishes* in Chapter 9 on page 388.)

In rated ceiling and wall assemblies, only certain types of light fixtures are allowed. For example, when light fixtures (i.e., recessed cans) are recessed into a ceiling that has a one-hour fire rating, the mechanical part of the fixture must be rated. If not, a fully enclosed rated box must be built around the housing to maintain the one-hour rating of the ceiling assembly. In other instances, non-combustible material must also be sandwiched between the fixture and the finished surface. In all cases, you need to be sure to specify a fixture meant for the application so that the appropriate air circulation is maintained.

The *NEC* also places restrictions on certain light fixtures installed over bathtubs and shower areas (in any occupancy). It includes all light fixtures except surface-mounted and recessed fixtures. For example, no part of a hanging luminaire, pendant fixture, track fixture, or ceiling fan can be within 8 feet (2.5 m) above the top of the bathtub rim or within 8 feet (2.5 m) above a shower threshold up to 3 feet (900 mm) away from the plumbing fixture. (This is to make sure they stay out of the reach of a person standing on the tub rim.) This is shown in Figure 8.7. (If the shower has no threshold, the measurement is taken from the floor.) This same requirement applies to hot tubs and similar types of bathing fixtures. Other specific dimensions are given by the *NEC* for light fixtures installed in clothes closets, in show windows, and over combustible materials. For example, a light fixture in a clothes closet must typically be installed so there is a minimum clearance of 12 inches (300 mm) between the fixture and the nearest storage item (e.g., edge of shelf or hanging rod). Similar clearances, although not specified, should be considered in other types of storage spaces where tall shelving may become an issue.

Earlier in the chapter it was mentioned that the *NEC* requires lighting outlets in certain locations within a dwelling unit. Although it does not restrict quantities or locations of light fixtures in most non-Residential occupancies, the building codes do set minimum light levels that must be met in all habitable spaces. (See inset titled *Types of Rooms and Spaces* on page 63.) This is found in the "Interior

Note

Light fixtures that include air handling as part of the mechanical system can typically be used as long as provisions are made to stop the movement of air through the fixtures at the start of a fire.

Note

Although light fixtures placed over tubs and showers may require luminaries "suitable for damp locations," other fixtures in a bathing facility typically do not require this rating. It will depend on the jurisdiction.

Note

Neon lighting has many special code and standard requirements.

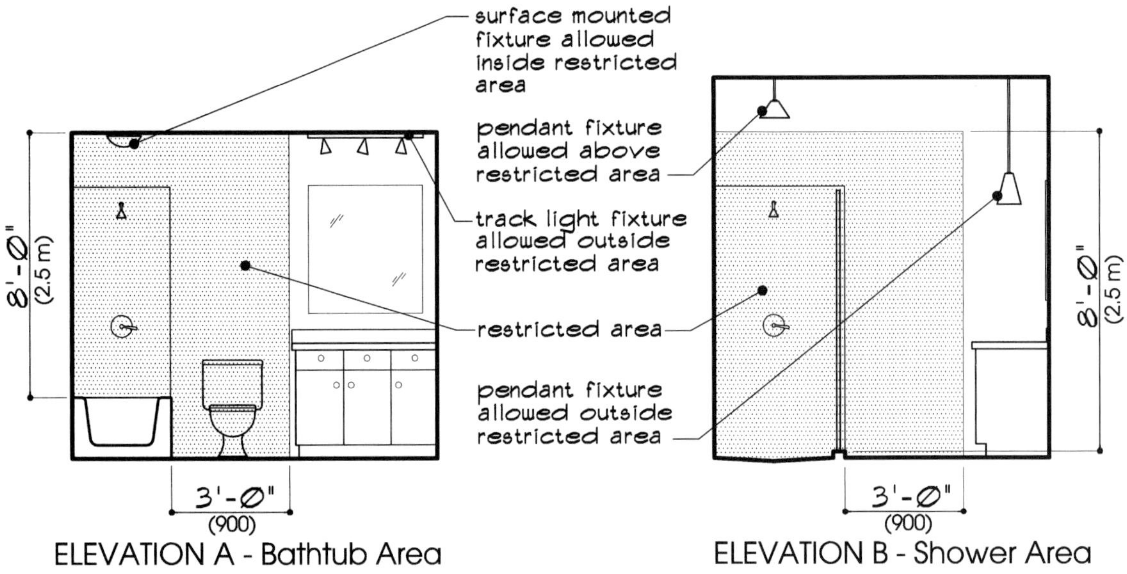

Figure 8.7 Lighting Restrictions at Bathtub and Shower Example

Environment" chapter in each building code. This chapter specifies the amount of glazing that must be used during the construction of a building to provide natural light into a habitable space. It also specifies the amount of artificial light that must be used in a habitable space when enough natural light is not provided. This often applies to interior rooms and spaces that are not along the perimeter of the building and includes stairways in dwelling units. In these spaces, the lighting must typically provide an average illumination of 10 footcandles (107 lux) over the area of the room at a height of 30 inches (762 mm) above the floor. (Certain occupancies, such as Educational occupancies, may have additional requirements.) As long as you meet these minimum light levels, the quantities, types, and locations of the light fixtures do not matter, according to the *NEC*. (See next section for light levels in means of egress.)

Note

If only part of a wall sconce is more than 4 inches (100 mm) deep, only that part needs to be more than 80 inches (2030 mm) above the floor as required for accessibility.

However, if the space is required to meet accessibility regulations, then light fixtures must meet certain height requirements. These are found in the ADA guidelines and the ICC/ANSI standard. Fixtures used as wall sconces must be mounted at least 80 inches (2030 mm) above the floor if they protrude from the wall more than 4 inches (100 mm). This is measured to the bottom of the fixture, as shown in Figure 8.5. This becomes especially important in *circulation paths* such as corridors and other spaces used by the public. If a light fixture is less than 4 inches (100 mm) deep, then it can be mounted at any height. If the sconce is used in a private room or office, you do not necessarily need to meet this requirement. In addition, if the fixture is mounted above a permanently fixed counter or other millwork, you typically do not need to meet the requirement. This minimum height applies to pendant fixtures as well. When hung from the ceiling, it cannot hang any lower than 80 inches (2030 mm) above the floor unless it is mounted directly over a piece of furniture. (The furniture will prevent anyone from knocking into the light fixture; and if the furniture is moved, the height of the pendant can be changed more easily than that of a wall sconce.)

Note

The codes may restrict the minimum height of a ceiling fan above the floor.

Required Electrical Systems

The building codes, the fire codes, and the *Life Safety Code (LSC)* have additional requirements for electrical systems. These include emergency electrical systems and standby power systems. When they are required and to what extent they are required typically depend on the type of occupancy and building type. (A building owner may want to add these types of systems for other reasons as well.) The building codes and/or the *LSC* will specify when a system is required and refer to the *NEC* for the specifics of the system and how it is installed. The *NEC* also references the standards *NFPA 110, Standard for Emergency and Standby Power Systems* and *NFPA 111, Stored Electrical Energy Emergency and Standby Power Systems*. Typically, an electrical engineer would design this type of system, but you need to be aware of both systems because they affect the selection of fixtures and other interior elements.

Emergency Electrical Systems

Emergency electrical systems are required in most buildings to maintain a specific degree of illumination. They are also required in certain building types to provide power for essential equipment, such as fire pumps in high-rise buildings and life-support equipment in hospitals. They are used to back up the normal electrical system in case of an emergency. The goal is to allow the occupants of a building to stay safe or to safely evacuate. The typical emergency electrical system must have the capacity to operate such equipment as means of egress lighting, exit signs, automatic door locks, certain fire protection systems, and other emergency equipment.

Note

An important source for emergency and standby power systems is *NFPA 110, Emergency and Standby Power Systems.*

The building codes and the *LSC* each specify emergency lighting requirements. The requirements are found in the "Means of Egress" chapters of the codes. (See the section on Emergency Lighting in Chapter 4 on page 172.) Each code specifically states the following basic requirements:

❑ *Artificial lighting:* Artificial lighting must be present in the means of egress when a building is in use. (There are exceptions for Residential occupancies.) The intensity of the emergency lighting cannot be less than an average of 1 footcandle (11 lux) at any point and not less than 0.1 footcandle (1 lux) measured at the floor level on the path of egress. (These numbers can be reduced at times of performance in some Assembly occupancies.) The newest NFPA codes additionally specify that new stairways be illuminated at least 10 footcandles (108 lux).

Note

Standby power must initiate within 60 seconds of a power failure. Emergency power must initiate within 10 seconds.

❑ *Exit signs:* Exit signs must be located and illuminated in a way that they can direct occupants safely out of the building. (See section on Signage in Chapter 4.) Exit signs can be externally illuminated, internally lit, or self-luminous. Exit signs must be illuminated by not less than 5 footcandles (54 lux) at the illuminated surface. Typically, a contrast level of not less than 0.5 must be provided as well. (Some jurisdictions may require similar light levels for area of refuge signs.)

❑ *Emergency power:* Provisions must be made so that in case of power loss, emergency or exit lighting will be available for a certain time. Most codes require that exit lighting be connected to an emergency power source that will assure illumination for at least 1½ hours in case of power failure. For example, in Business occupancies, a battery pack can usually be used as the emergency source of power. In some occupancies, such as in Assembly, Institutional, or Hazardous occupancies, a separate source of emergency power (e.g., emergency generator) must be provided for the exit signs. In all cases, the codes also specify how to periodically test emergency lighting equipment to make sure it will work in an emergency.

When allowed, the easiest method of creating emergency lighting in a design project is to add the typical twin-headed emergency light with a battery pack in the appropriate locations. An alternate solution would be to include some of the general lighting fixtures on a separate circuit designated for emergency lighting. This allows the separate circuit to be connected to the main power source as well as the backup power source. You must also make sure that if one light fixture burns out it will not leave an area in darkness. Some ways to ensure this are to use dual-lamp light fixtures or to design an overlapping light pattern. In addition, if there are switches connected to the emergency light fixtures, the *NEC* specifies that the switch be located so that it is convenient to authorized persons who will be responsible for their activation. Automatic, motion sensor–type light switches may also be allowed.

The *NEC* provides other requirements for emergency electrical systems as well. The main requirement specifies that when the power changes from the main power source to the emergency system, the delay cannot be longer than 10 seconds. It also gives the specifics for the types of backup systems that can be used. These usually include a generator, a storage battery system, or a total separate (or redundant) electrical service into the building. Uninterruptible power supplies (UPS) are also sometimes used. Which system to use is typically determined by the electrical engineer and the code official.

Standby Power Systems

Standby power systems are similar to emergency electrical systems. They are used to supply power when the normal power source fails in an emergency. However, instead of operating the emergency systems essential for life safety, standby power is used for other building systems such as the mechanical system, fire pumps, general lighting, communication systems, elevators, and other standby equipment. The *NEC* divides these into two categories: legally required standby systems and optional standby systems.

Legally required standby systems are those that are required by the building codes, the fire codes, the *LSC*, or a code jurisdiction. For example, standby power systems are typically required in some building types, such as certain Assembly, Institutional, and Hazardous occupancies, as well as high-rise buildings. These are systems that are intended to provide electrical power to aid in firefighting, rescue operations, control of health hazards, and similar operations. They are also mandatory when a building has a smoke control system and may be required for other parts of a building's mechanical ventilation system. (See Chapters 5 and 7.)

In other cases, the building owner or tenant may decide to include certain systems on standby power. These would be considered *optional standby systems*. The decision to provide an optional standby system is usually based on the concern for physical discomfort, serious interruption to a business, or damage to certain equipment. Examples would include telecommunication systems, refrigeration equipment, elevators not required on emergency systems, and building automation systems.

The specifics of both types of standby power systems are found in the *NEC* and the standard *NFPA 110*. Often the same system supplying the emergency electrical system will also be used for the standby power system, but it could be a totally separate system. When a standby power system is installed, it must operate 60 seconds after the failure of the normal power supply rather than the 10 seconds required for emergency electrical systems.

Note

In some occupancies, such as hospitals and businesses with critical computer systems, the 10-second power delay may not be acceptable. It may be necessary to add an uninterrupted power supply (UPS) that keeps the electricity flowing during the 10-second transition time.

Energy Efficiency

The energy codes and standards provide additional requirements that need to be met for electrical systems. As mentioned in Chapter 1, the energy requirements first concentrate on the building envelope. Not only is the exterior shell of a building important in controlling how much electricity is required to condition the air in the building, but also it determines how much natural light is available inside the building. The more natural light available, the less electricity it will take to light the space over time.

Note

Requirements for solar power systems are included in the building codes and the mechanical codes.

Inside the building, the energy codes concentrate on efficiency of the equipment. Some of the energy requirements of mechanical and water heating systems were explained in Chapter 7. The goal of many of these requirements is to limit the amount of electricity required to run the systems. Lighting is also a large part of a building's electrical load. The energy codes and required standards can affect the selections of light fixtures as well as their controls (e.g., switches). (Other equipment and appliances, such as copiers, dishwashers, and clothes dryers, are typically not regulated by the codes since they already must meet certain government energy requirements in order to be sold in the United States.)

Note

Energy codes require combination light, fan, and/or heating bathroom fixtures to have separate controls—one for each function of the fixture.

Although most energy codes and standards required for electrical systems will typically be incorporated into the design by the electrical engineer, some of the decisions you make as the designer of the interior space will also affect the building's efficiency. The overall goal is to reduce the electrical load required in a building. You can help by selecting more efficient fixtures and equipment that require less wattage to operate and/or reducing the quantity of fixtures. For instance, you can specify certain light fixtures that use less energy (e.g., the newer T8 electronic fluorescent fixtures over older T12 magnetic systems), specify high-output (HO) lamps over standard lamps, or select fixtures with lower-wattage HID lamps. The lighting layout makes a difference as well. For example, using more indirect lighting combined with task lighting can often help to reduce the overall number of light fixtures. The energy codes and standards will specify certain requirements, such as dual switching so that some lights can be turned off while others remain in use. Some jurisdictions may also require certain buildings to have automatic lighting shut-off devices. In addition, specifying dimmers can help reduce the power used for a fixture as well as lengthen the life of the lamp in the fixture. (Facility-wide dimming could make a huge impact.)

Note

According to the New Building Institute, automatic lighting controls can reduce energy use by as much as 50 percent in existing buildings and 35 percent in new construction.

These requirements provide energy-efficient buildings and spaces, and as a result, these buildings are also considered more sustainable. However, as the designer, it is important to help balance the requirements of energy efficiency with the occupant's safety and visual needs, as well as the aesthetics of the space.

LOW-VOLTAGE CABLING SYSTEMS

The type of cabling system used within a building to support such things as voice, data, video, and security systems is called *structured cabling.* It is also known as integrated cabling or universal cabling. The system is made up of backbone cabling and horizontal cabling. *Backbone cabling* carries the signals to the main distribution areas of the building or space. It begins where the public utility enters the building. This location, where the utility wiring is connected to the building wiring, is called the demark. From there it goes to the main equipment room and then to the local communication closet(s). In large commercial projects, fiber cabling is often used for backbone cabling.

The cables that are pulled to each workstation or outlet are known as *horizontal cabling*. Connections to the individual desktops or outlets can be made through the horizontal cabling system using fiber optic or copper cabling. Because copper is less expensive for individual connections, it is more widely used in horizontal cabling. However, in cases that support complex systems, fiber optics should be considered. A wireless system is another option, but interference might be a problem in buildings that are close to other buildings or have multiple tenants. (See the section titled Low-Voltage Cabling on page 325.)

Both upfront and long-term costs need to be considered as well. For example, facility-wide dimming, although more costly on the front end, can save money long term because of the longer lamp life at each fixture. (Also refer to the inset titled *Sustainability and LEED* in Chapter 9 on page 374.)

COMMUNICATION REQUIREMENTS

A building's communication system can consist of a number of different systems. These include intercoms, telephones, computers, security, background music, and television systems such as surveillance equipment, cable services, and satellite hookups. A communication system can also include an assistive listening system, which is required in some building types. In some cases, fire alarms are integrated into the building's communication system as well.

Note

In the future, as computers continue to change and grow more powerful, additional code provisions will probably be added for the use and wiring of computers and other communication systems.

Computers and advanced electronics have become an essential part of a project in both residential and commercial spaces and can affect each type of communication system. (See the inset titled *Building Automation Systems* on page 324.) Many projects now require one or more communication consultants to adequately plan the overall system. Depending on your role in the design of the various communication systems, it is important to understand the current and future needs of the client and to coordinate your design with the consultants and the vendors doing the installation of the system(s). For example, if you are working on an auditorium project, you may need to coordinate the interior aspects with the audiovisual system. Or, if you are specifying workstations for an open office, you may need to coordinate the power and voice/data needs. In addition, some projects and certain jurisdictions may require the involvement of an electrical engineer during the design of the system and/or a licensed electrician to install the system. You should also know that various communication associations are creating certification programs, and it is becoming more common for designers and installers of communication systems to become certified or licensed.

The related codes and standards for communication systems will be discussed in this section. Specific requirements for communication rooms and low-voltage wiring will be reviewed first. The remainder of this section concentrates on the various types of communication systems as they are affected by the codes and standards. Keep in mind, however, that since the technology is constantly changing, you must closely coordinate communication systems with local vendors and/or consultants.

Comparing the Codes

The *NEC* sets some requirements for communication systems, but not as many compared to those for electrical systems. This is partially due to the fact that the wiring for communication systems is so low in voltage that it poses fewer safety problems. In addition, it is difficult to create codes for systems that tend to change rapidly. As a result, the communication industry has relied more on industry standards to meet certain performance and safety criteria, and even these have gone through many changes in the last few years as technology continues to evolve. There are several standards organizations specific to the communication industry. These include the Telecommunications Industries Association (TIA) and the Electronics Industries Alliance (EIA). Even the Builders Hardware Manufacturers Association (BHMA) is involved in creating standards for security devices. Many of the standards have been created in conjunction with ANSI. Several will be described below. (In the future, more of these standards might be referenced in the *NEC*.)

The communication systems that are covered by the *NEC* include network-powered communication systems and fire alarm systems as well as certain radio and television equipment. Similar to the electrical system, the *NEC* does not regulate the transmission of signals or the connection of communication services to the building. It regulates only the parts of these systems that are inside the building or controlled by the building. The primary concern is the fire hazard caused by the spread of fire along the cables or circuits. Many of the rules for these systems include the type of cable or wiring used, the clearance for power conductors, and the proper grounding procedures. Other codes may also affect certain communication systems. For example, the means of egress requirements in the building codes and the *Life Safety Code* must be consulted when a security system is added, because of how the system affects the building's exits.

Accessibility requirements that affect communication systems mostly control the mounting height of the outlets. Certain operable equipment can also be a factor. For example, the location of devices such as phones and computer terminals provided for use by the public will typically need to be accessible. Other requirements may be more specific to an occupancy or building type. For example, in some Assembly occupancies, the building codes and the ADA guidelines require the use of an assistive listening system. This and other accessibility requirements will be mentioned throughout the rest of the chapter.

Communication Rooms

Every building requires a central area where the incoming communication services are connected to the building's communication systems. In the past, this was primarily the telephone service, and the space was referred to as the telephone switching room. Because advances in technology and communication have expanded the area of communication, the incoming communication service may now include telephone, computer data, cable TV, and similar electronic information relay. Now these rooms can have a variety of names. This room or area is typically located in the basement or on the ground floor as close as possible to the entrance of communication services. In small buildings, only a small panel located in the electrical room or a closet may be required. In larger buildings, a central room is required. The size of the room depends on the quantity and size of the equipment required and the communication connections that must be serviced. When determining the size of the room, you should consult the various consultants and venders installing the communication systems (e.g., telephone, computer, security).

Note

Various communication systems now operate by computer. These computers may be separate or part of the building's main computer system. If separate, they are often also located in the communication room.

Most of these rooms will contain computer equipment. In addition to the computer system itself, many other communication systems, such as telephone and security systems, are run by computers. The *NEC* has specific requirements for the communication rooms that house this equipment, also referred to as information technology equipment. For example, the room must be separated from the rest of the building by fire-rated walls, floor and ceiling assemblies, and fire-rated doors. The *NEC* also includes requirements on how to condition the space and how to penetrate the rated assemblies enclosing the room. If a raised floor is used, special cable and ventilation requirements must be followed. For the remaining requirements, the *NEC* refers you to the standard *NFPA 75, Protection of Information Technology Equipment.* (Also see section on Telecommunication Systems later in this chapter.)

BUILDING AUTOMATION SYSTEMS

A building automation system (BAS) is sometimes referred to as an integrated building system, a building information network, or an intelligent building system. It consists of connecting various building systems into one automated system so that they can communicate with each other and be managed through one source.

The building systems and the various components that can be supported by a BAS include but are not limited to the following:

- ❑ Mechanical systems: HVAC equipment, dampers, zone/thermostat control, etc.
- ❑ Electrical systems: Equipment, lighting systems, energy loads, zone/switch controls, etc.
- ❑ Plumbing systems: Water usages, leak detection, sprinkler activation, etc.
- ❑ Security systems: Surveillance, card access devices, paging systems, etc.
- ❑ Voice/data systems: Local area networks, cable/satellite TV, telephone systems, wireless devices, etc.
- ❑ Fire safety systems: Alarms, smoke detectors, voice notification systems, sprinklers, etc.

In a BAS, the various systems are tied together with low-voltage cabling and connected to one computer workstation. There are a number of propriety software packages that can be used to run the BAS. Custom programs can also be used in place of these or as a means of enhancing them. Since each system becomes interconnected to the others, the key is to make sure that various components are correctly prioritized. For example, a fire detection system usually has a higher priority than a security program. The facility manager can then monitor the various systems from one point and use the software to operate and maintain the equipment. The BAS can also be used to identify performance criteria, such as energy use and reliability, and identify potential problems when they arise.

Many new buildings today are incorporating a BAS in the initial design and construction. Adding one to an existing building can be a little more difficult because of the new wiring that must be installed. As a designer you should be aware of these systems and be involved in the planning process, since it may affect your design. Once connected, each of the systems must individually meet the necessary code requirements. The interconnected systems can also be used to help meet performance code criteria. For example, a BAS can be used to add life safety features to a building by programming office lights to flash when a fire alarm is activated. Many other combinations of system components can be created, as well. (Note that a code jurisdiction may restrict the connection of some systems to a BAS.)

In buildings with multiple floors, each floor typically has its own *communications closet* that feeds off the main communication room. There may be separate closets such as those for telephone and computer equipment or one room that combines the equipment. Like electrical closets, these communication closets or rooms are usually stacked on top of each other to allow for continuous vertical wiring. The closet provides a central location to distribute cabling throughout the floor or space, either directly to equipment such as telephones and computers or to one or more satellite closets. These intermediate closets also help to limit the length of a cable, since some cables are limited to maximum lengths. When there are multiple tenants on the same floor, another closet, known as a *satellite closet*, is often used for each tenant space to allow the separation of utilities. It also allows easier distribution of cables in large buildings. These more-remote closets typically do not need to meet the requirements of the main communication room. However, if it becomes more than just a remote data terminal or personal computer station, it may need to meet some of the requirements already described.

Note

In the past, all communication rooms were required to have sprinkler heads. Newer standards that provide alternate options for protection are now available and may be allowed by a jurisdiction.

Low-Voltage Cabling

Cables used for communication systems are different from electrical cables, because of the lower voltages required for communication systems. They are typically referred to as low-voltage cabling. Many are listed in the *NEC*, and the more common types are shown in Figure 8.8. (Many have subcategories as well.) You will notice that there are different cables for different applications. Each type of cable is divided into plenum, riser, general-purpose, and limited-use categories for use in different parts of a building. For example, if a cable is used horizontally in a mechanical plenum space (see Chapter 7), it must be marked as a plenum cable. A riser cable would be used in vertical shafts. Similar to electrical wiring,

Note

If a low-voltage cable is run continuously in conduit through a fire-rated area or assembly, the cable may not need to be rated.

COMMUNICATION CABLES	
TYPE CMP	Communications Plenum Cable
TYPE CMR	Communications Riser Cable
TYPE CM or **CMG**	Communications General-Purpose Cable
TYPE CMX	Communications Cable, Limited Use
TYPE CMUC	Undercarpet Communications Wire and Cable
FIBER OPTIC CABLES	
TYPE OFNP	Nonconductive Optical Fiber Plenum Cable
TYPE OFCP	Conductive Optical Fiber Plenum Cable
TYPE OFNR	Nonconductive Optical Fiber Riser Cable
TYPE OFCR	Conductive Optical Fiber Riser Cable
TYPE OFN or **OFNG**	Nonconductive Optical Fiber General-Purpose Cable
TYPE OFC or **OFCG**	Conductive Optical Fiber General-Purpose Cable
MULTIPURPOSE CABLES	
TYPE MPP	Multipurpose Plenum Cable
TYPE MPR	Multipurpose Riser Cable
TYPE MP or **MPG**	Multipurpose General-Purpose Cable
COAXIAL CABLE	
TYPE CATVP	Coaxial Plenum Cable
TYPE CATVR	Coaxial Riser Cable
TYPE CATV	Coaxial General-Purpose Cable
TYPE CATVX	Coaxial Cable, Limited Use
FIRE ALARM CABLES	
TYPE FPLP	Power-Limited Fire Alarm Plenum Cable
TYPE FPLR	Power-Limited Fire Alarm Riser Cable
TYPE FPL	Power-Limited Fire Alarm Cable

NOTE: Other types and/or subcategories of cables may also be available.

Figure 8.8 Common Types of Communication Cables

each of these communication cables must go through various industry standard tests before it can be labeled for its appropriate use. These tests include the fire, smoke, and toxicity tests mentioned earlier in the Electrical Cabling and Conduit section. Since the speed at which information travels is such a factor, communication cables also go through additional performance testing to determine their bandwidth and capacity levels.

As the designer, you will rarely specify the exact type of cable, but rather will work closely with the client and their communication consultants or vendors. You should at least know some basic information. Below are the main types of cables and/or connections used today.

Note

When using copper cabling for telecommunication systems, the industry standards often limit the length of the cable run to 300 feet (91 m).

- *Fiber optic cable:* A fiber optic cable transmits light along ultra-thin glass or plastic strands. Each strand is composed of layers of fibers protected by a cabling jacket and a plastic coating. Fiber optic cables provide higher bandwidth than other types of cable, which yields higher speed and capacity. And, because they are smaller and lighter and can withstand greater pulling tension, they are easier to use than copper. In addition, since optical fibers use light waves instead of an electrical current to transmit information, they are not affected by electromagnetic and radio frequency interference. Fiber can also be used in much longer distances before the signal must be amplified, plus additional fibers can easily be included in the initial installation for future expansion of a data or communication system. (See also Composite Cable below.)
- *Twisted-pair cable:* Twisted-pair cabling, sometimes referred to as copper cabling, uses a copper conductor to transmit data using an electrical current. It provides less capacity and speed than fiber optics, but it is still the most common type of low-voltage cabling used today. It is less expensive than fiber optics. The copper wire is twisted into pairs and encased in a protective sheathing. The twisting helps reduce the amount of outside interference. Typically used for voice (i.e., telephones) and data (i.e., computer) connections, it is rated by *category,* which indicates its bandwidth performance. Manufacturers are continually developing copper cabling with more capacity. Although Category 3 (CAT 3) cabling is still used in some instances for telephone cabling, most installations now use at least Category 5 (CAT 5) and often Category 5e (CAT 5e) cables, especially for data installation. Category 6 (CAT 6) cables are also an option. As technology improves, higher categories will become available, but be sure the cable has gone through the appropriate testing before it is used in a building.
- *Coaxial cable:* Coaxial cable (or coax for short) is the standard cable used for video and cable-based transmissions. For example, it is used for cable-TV

and cable-based Internet connections, closed-circuit television connections, and TV antenna connections. Like twisted-pair cable, it uses conductive metal to transmit data using an electrical current, but instead it has a single central conductor. It has the capacity to carry great quantities of information. There are also different types. For example, Series 6 coax cable is often used for cable TV connections.

- *Composite (or hybrid) cable:* Composite cabling, also known as hybrid cabling, bundles various types of cables into one jacket or sleeve. For example, one composite cable containing CAT5, coaxial, and audio cables could be run so that multiple communication connections to various systems can be made. This is often used in Residential type occupancies to eliminate the need to run multiple cables to the same location. A multimedia conference room might also use a cable like this. A variety of composite cables are available—and a variety of qualities. If they consist strictly of communication cables, they are not regulated by the *NEC*. (However, their use might be limited by the manufacturer of the equipment being connected to the cable.) A composite cable can also consist of a combination of optical fibers and current-carrying electrical wires. Because this type can also carry electricity, the *NEC* has separate requirements for these types of composite cables, and they may not always be allowed.

Note

Since cables like CAT5 and composite cables have multiple pairs, one cable can be used to connect multiple devices (i.e., phone, computer, etc.). However, you need to make sure this does not void the warranty of a particular system.

- *Wireless:* Wireless systems use cable to connect the main transmitter to the communication service. Receivers are then used instead of cabling to allow individuals to connect to the system. They use infrared or radio transmission. Sometime microwave and laser signals are used between facilities. For example, microwave signals are used to provide communication links to cell phones. In-house wireless systems work well in situations where reorganization occurs frequently. However, wireless systems can be much slower and are more expensive (although you may save in wiring costs). Other problems can occur as well. For example, wireless computer systems that use radio transmissions might receive interference from other wireless systems, especially in areas where buildings are close together, and one transmitter can only support a limited number of users. Microwave transmissions can be blocked by solid objects and be subject to atmospheric conditions.

Certain communication cables, especially when used in conjunction with larger network-powered systems, are required by the *NEC* to be grounded. (See the Grounding and Circuit Interrupters section on page 311.) In addition, when communication cables are installed throughout a building, the codes typically require that they be kept separate from electrical cabling. In most cases communication cables cannot be placed in any raceway, compartment, conduit, outlet box, or junction box used for electric light or power. (There are exceptions for certain fiber optic and composite cables depending on how they are used.) When communication cables are run horizontally across a ceiling, they can usually remain exposed. However, the codes specify that the cables must be run in a "neat and workmanlike manner." This is accomplished by using hangers, straps, and clamps to keep the cables together. They are often secured at the ceiling using cable trays or J-hooks. Since the *NEC* allows many types of communication cables to be run together, the various communication vendors will typically share this common path until they reach their respective outlet locations.

Note

Although the *NEC* sets requirements for conduits, raceways, and wire ways, it does not regulate cable trays.

When communication cables are run down a wall to a particular outlet, many jurisdictions (especially in certain occupancies) require the low-voltage cable(s) to be run in a conduit. Conduit is also required in rated walls. Since the cable must be separate from the electrical cable/conduit, it will require a separate conduit. For example, in a typical office a computer and/or telephone outlet is often located next to an electrical outlet. Two conduits would be installed in the wall: one for the electrical wiring and one for the low-voltage wiring. The cutouts for the conduit and the box would be similar to those required for the electrical components. In addition, if the conduit or box penetrates a rated assembly or membrane, it must meet the same rating requirements as electrical boxes. (See the earlier section on Electrical Boxes.)

Note

The plastic sleeves covering communication cables can be very toxic if exposed to a fire. The *NEC* now requires old, abandoned cables that are accessible to be removed from a building.

It is not uncommon for communication systems to be rewired as new types of cabling become available. This is especially true for computer systems that may require a cable upgrade in order to increase the speed of the individual computers. These old cables create unnecessary fire loads and toxic gases should a fire occur and could restrict the airflow in a plenum space. As a result, the 2002 edition of the *NEC* has made it clear that when old low-voltage cables are abandoned, all accessible portions of the cabling must be removed.

Types of Communication Systems

Various types of communication systems are discussed below. The low-voltage cabling used for most of these systems must meet the requirements found in the *NEC* as discussed in the last section. Besides this, there are very few other electrical code requirements for communication systems. Instead, a few of the systems have other requirements that need to be met, such as building code or accessibility requirements. Others should meet industry standards that are available. You will also notice that the line between various communication systems is not always clear. For example, certain systems can share the same infrastructure as another system. In addition, more systems are using computers as their means of control. If they are connected to the main network computer, not only do they become more dependent on one another, but a particular system might also be required to meet additional requirements. (See inset titled *Building Automation Systems* on page 324.)

Telecommunication Systems

Telecommunications is a term that includes both voice and data communication. (Radio communication is sometimes included as well.) It is used here to include telephone and computer systems. As already discussed, the *NEC* has specific requirements for the main equipment room that houses the telecommunication system. It also includes specific requirements for the installation of cables. Most other requirements for telecommunication systems are found in standards developed by the NFPA or by the Telecommunications Industries Association (TIA), in conjunction with the Electronics Industries Alliance (EIA) and ANSI. The standards cover everything from the testing and fabrication of components to the design and installation of an entire system. The NFPA standards include *NFPA 75, Protection of Information Technology Equipment* and *NFPA 76, Fire Protection of Telecommunication Facilities.*

These standards provide specifications and guidance for the installation and maintenance of the telecommunication system. Some of the requirements will affect the design and location of the communication room, as well as the overall design of a space or building. For example, the standards typically limit the

Note

In addition to providing clear floor space at an accessible public telephone, you need to make sure the telephone is located on an accessible route within the building.

PUBLIC TELEPHONES

Public telephones are not regulated by the *NEC*. Instead, the Americans with Disabilities Act (ADA) sets a number of regulations. Title IV of the ADA deals specifically with telecommunication services and sets regulations for accessible public telephones. (Refer to Chapter 1 and Appendix A.) Specific requirements are included in the ADA guidelines. (Similar requirements are also in the *ICC/ANSI 117.1* accessibility standards.)

Public telephones can include public pay telephones, public closed-circuit telephones, or other telephones for public use. Although the installation of public phones is usually the responsibility of the telephone company, there are a variety of public phones, and not all are accessible. As the designer, you must be aware of the ADA and other accessibility requirements, and be able to specify the correct type of public phone. Whenever one or more public telephones are provided, at least one telephone must be accessible. When one or more banks of telephones are provided, additional phones may need to be accessible.

Accessible public telephones must allow either a forward or parallel approach with a required clear floor space of at least 30 inches by 48 inches (760 mm by 1220 mm) in each case. Bases, side enclosures, fixed seats, and other protruding objects cannot reduce this floor space. The actual height of the telephone depends on the type of access and the depth of any obstruction (e.g., a shelf). However, all operable parts must be within allowed reach ranges. Other accessible requirements include volume controls, text telephones, push-button controls, position of telephone directories, length of cords, and signage displays.

length of a copper cable run going from the communication room to a data outlet to about 300 feet (91.4 m). In addition, the standard *TIA/EIA-589-B* incorporates the concept of *zone cabling* (also called zone distribution) for open office areas. This consists of dividing the ceiling into sections or zones and then running communication cables to the center of each zone. An intermediate multi-user outlet or terminal is installed in the ceiling within each zone so that separate cables can be run from the terminal to the outlets in a wall or in a run of workstations. Then, when the layout of an area changes, the cabling only needs to be changed in that particular zone up to the point in the ceiling, not all the way back to the main panel. This avoids having to abandon and remove old cables every time there is a change. (The terminals installed in the ceiling must be of the same rating required of the ceiling cable.)

Note

Required text telephones are based on the number of interior and exterior telephones. See the ADA guidelines for additional information.

Low-voltage cables for telephone (voice) outlets and computer (data) outlets are often "terminated" together so that they run through the same conduit to one box. The number of outlets or jacks will determine the size of the box. It is not unusual to have an outlet with four jacks, two for voice and two for data, or even more. Neither the *NEC* nor the standards specify the location of these voice and data outlets. Instead, you will locate them based on the layout and function requirements of the space. However, when mounting voice and data outlets, you need to stay within the reach ranges of the ADA guidelines and the ICC/ANSI

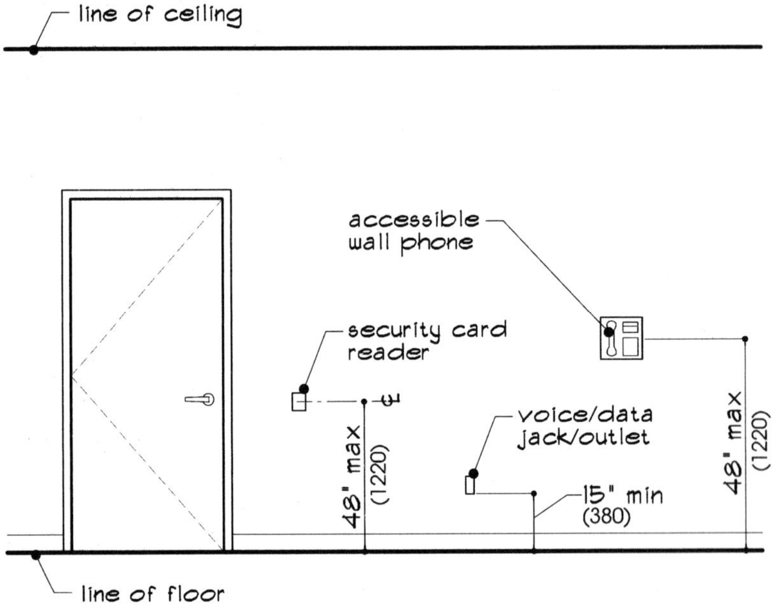

Figure 8.9 Typical Accessible Communication Device Locations

standards. This is shown in Figure 8.9. Outlets must be mounted on the wall at least 15 inches (380 mm) above the floor—similar to electrical outlets. Even if an area is not required to be accessible, this height is recommended in case the function of the space changes. (See section on Outlet Boxes on page 306 for more accessibility requirements.) If you are locating an accessible wall-mounted telephone, it must be within 48 inches (1220 mm) above the floor, as shown in Figure 8.9. (See also inset titled *Public Telephones* on page 329.)

Television and Radio Systems

The NEC includes some requirements for the installation of television and radio systems. Most of these requirements pertain to the exterior antennae usually located on top of the building to which the interior cabling is attached. Other requirements are geared toward the fire rating of the interior coaxial cable that connects the devices to the radio and television receiving equipment. (See the Low-Voltage Cabling section on page 325.) This equipment is used to operate such things as closed-circuit television, cable television, and security television cameras.

Alarm and Voice Communication Systems

Alarm and voice communication systems include such things as fire and smoke alarms, voice notification systems, intercom systems, and assistive listening systems. Some of these systems are used together or for multiple functions while others are stand-alone systems. For example, a fire alarm system might also include a voice notification system so that the occupants in the building can be given direction during an emergency. This is required by the building codes in some occupancies such as Factories. (See Chapter 6.) This notification system can also be used as the building's general public address system. For example, many schools have public address systems to make general announcements on a daily basis. This could also be used for emergency evacuations, as well.

The requirements for fire and smoke alarm systems are given in the building codes. The building codes will indicate when they are required and reference standards for additional information. Certain accessibility requirements may also apply. (See section on Alarm Systems in Chapter 6.) These systems typically use low-voltage wiring that must meet additional requirements in the *NEC*. When the alarm system is connected to a building automation system (BAS), the alarm system usually takes precedence over other connected systems because it is critical to the safety of the building occupants. That is why some jurisdictions do not allow its connection to a BAS. However, if it is connected to the other building systems, it can provide added features and often better response times. (See inset titled *Building Automation Systems* on page 324.)

Note

Unlike a standard public address system, a voice communication system is required by the codes and is tied to the fire alarm system.

Another type of voice communication system that is required by the building codes and the ADA guidelines is an assistive listening system. It is required in Assembly occupancies where audible communication is integral to the use of the space. Examples would include a movie theater, a performing arts center, and a courtroom; however, they may be required in other building types as well. The assistive listening system is installed in conjunction with the main sound system and consists of accessible receivers. These receivers amplify the sound and are made available to those with hearing disabilities. The building codes specify the quantities and types of receivers required within a space or building based on the capacity of seating in the assembly area. The ADA guidelines and the ICC/ANSI standard provide additional requirements.

Note

The new *ADA-ABA Accessibility Guidelines* and the 2003 ICC/ANSI standard include new assistive-listening performance standards not required in previous editions.

Audiovisual Systems

Audiovisual systems include everything from the basic stereo system used in a small conference room to a full production audiovisual (AV) or multimedia room. Although the codes do not require or regulate the use of an AV system, you should be aware that multiple types of low-voltage cables may need to be used when wiring the equipment in these systems. They may also require connection to one of the other regulated communication systems in the building. For example, the television in a conference center might include videoconferencing capabilities, which requires connection to the telecom system in order for it to operate, or a computer power-point presentation may need to be connected both to the projector and the computer network. In addition, more AV systems are starting to incorporate computers as part of the main control of the overall system. Although there are multiple standards for the components that make up an AV system, few if any are available for the overall design and installation. As these systems become more advanced, more design and installation related industry standards may be developed.

Security Systems

Security systems used inside a building typically concentrate on protecting the building from unauthorized entry. (Others may be used to contain the occupants.) Examples include intrusion detection and alarms, identification systems such as card readers and biometric identifiers (i.e., fingerprint scanners and voice recognition), closed-circuit television (CCTV), and locking systems. These security components can be used individually and in unlimited combinations. The goal is to keep occupants safe.

Although security systems are not required by the code, some aspects of their use and installation are controlled by the codes. In fact, some security components can be in conflict with fire protection requirements, which require occupants to exit a building quickly during an emergency. Because it is an issue of life safety, the *Life Safety Code* (*LSC*) and the building codes regulate security systems when they affect exiting. A number of standards must be followed including security related industry standards. Most door hardware and locking related standards are created by the Builders Hardware Manufacturers Association (BHMA), including newer standards geared to high-security doors.

One of the biggest concerns is that the locking of doors for security reasons cannot interfere with the required means of egress. However, whether part of a standard security system or special security system (i.e., psychiatric hospitals or prisons), certain doors within the means of egress may require locks. Various locking systems are available that will serve the security issues while not endangering the occupants. Typically, you first need to determine if the lock needs to be fail safe or fail secure. The lock is considered to be *fail safe* if the door automatically unlocks when power goes out, such as in the event of a fire. If the lock is *fail secure*, the door will remain locked even in the event of the loss of power. This type of lock may interfere with exiting if additional precautions are not provided, such as constant monitoring by personnel.

Three types of locks are typically used for security:

1. *Mechanical locks:* Mechanical locks are opened either with a key or by a code entered into a push-button mechanism. These types of locks are not usually allowed on an exit door unless there is constant supervision of the door. However, if it is an exterior door, a push bar or other type of panic hardware can be installed on the interior to allow exiting without a key.
2. *Electrical locks:* Electrical locks can be electromechanical or electromagnetic. Two of the more common types of *electromechanical* locks include delayed egress or alarmed doors. Since they can be fail safe or fail secure, you must specify the proper action if the door is required for exiting. Standards that apply to electromechanical locks include *ANSI/BHMA 156.5* and *ANSI/BHMA 156.25*, as well as *ANSI/UL 1034, Burglary-Resistant Electric Locking Mechanisms. Electromagnetic* locks, often referred to as *maglocks*, use a magnetic field to hold the metal plate on the door or jamb in place. (These locks are similar to electromagnetic door holders, which are used to hold open fire-rated doors and release them to close when the fire alarm is activated.) Since they have no mechanical parts and depend on electricity, they are considered fail safe and can be safely connected to the fire alarm system and the security system. Standards that apply to electromagnetic locks include *ANSI/BHMA A156.23* and *ANSI/BHMA A156.24*. Remember that since these doors do not rely on a mechanical latch for closure, additional hardware may be needed on a rated door to properly latch the door as required by the code.

Note

In the future, the *NFPA 72, National Fire Alarm Code* will include more security-related issues for emergency notification within a building.

Note

Other types of security systems are used to contain the occupants, such as at prisons and psychiatric wards. These systems may have different requirements for manual and automatic locks.

3. *Pneumatic locks:* Pneumatic locks use electromechanical devices and pneumatic air pressure. They are used largely in Institutional occupancies such as hospital and prison facilities. These locks can be locked and released electronically and manually.

The design of a security system should be considered when designing a means of egress. Each type of door should be reviewed both separately and as part of the whole exiting plan. In some cases, you may need to review the plan with a code official. In addition, when a security system is installed as part of a building automation system (BAS), it cannot disrupt other systems that affect life safety. (See the inset titled *Building Automation Systems* on page 324.) If the fire alarm is connected to the BAS, the BAS must be programmed to establish the proper relationship. The fire alarm typically must take precedence over the security issues. For instance, if a fire activated the fire alarm, certain security doors that are locked must be allowed to open for proper egress. If the power fails, the security doors will unlock as well (depending on the occupancy). This may be good in an emergency to help evacuate a building, but it can also leave a building exposed. It is always a good idea to include manual locks on security doors so that they can be locked after a building is evacuated.

If a space is required to be accessible, even a high-security area, the security devices that are used by the occupants (or visitors) must be accessible. The requirements are found in the ADA guidelines and the ICC/ANSI standard. Not only must door handles be accessible (see Chapter 4), but also all security devices must be within accessible reach ranges and must have controls or buttons that are easy to use. The acceptable range is shown at the security card reader in Figure 8.9; however, the actual location will depend on the type of device and how it is used. For example, a card reader will require someone to pass a security card in front of it, while a key pad will need to be viewed by the person punching in the numbers. You need to consider a standing person as well as someone in a wheelchair when deciding on a height. (In some cases, two devices may be needed—one high and one low.) In addition, the clear floor space in front of the device should be considered and might affect the location of the door. There should typically be at least a 30-inch by 48-inch (760 mm by 1220 mm) floor clearance in front of the device. If a turnstile is used you must provide a means for a person in a wheelchair to get though. (Refer to the ADA guidelines for specifics.)

CHECKLIST

The checklist in Figure 8.10 combines a number of code and standard requirements for electrical and communication systems. Although an engineer might

Electrical and Communication Checklist

Date:____________

Project Name:____ Space: ____________

Occupancy (new or existing):____

Electrical Requirements Engineer Required? ___ YES ___ NO

Types of Electrical Panels (check those that apply and note locations, sizes, etc.)

__ Switchboard: ____

__ Panel Board(s): ____

__ Branch Panel Board(s): ____

Special Cabling Conditions : ____________________ Conduit Required: __YES __NO

Location of Receptacle Outlets : ____

__ EXISTING __ NEW (Rating of wall(s): ____________)

Location of Switches : ____

__ EXISTING __ NEW (Rating of wall(s): ____________)

Special Types of Outlets and/or Circuits (check those that apply and note locations)

__ Dedicated Outlets: ____

__ Ground Fault Circuit Interrupters (GFCI): ____

__ Arc Fault Circuit Interrupters (AFCI): ____

__ Other: ____

Types of Required Equipment (check those that apply, list new and existing, specify if over 120V)

__ Light Fixtures: ____

__ Appliances: ____

__ Equipment: ____

Types of Electrical Systems (check those that apply, list new and existing, etc.)

__ Emergency Electrical System: ____

__ Required Standby System: ____

__ Optional Standby System: ____

__ Uninterrupted Power Supply System (UPS): ____

Communication Requirements Engineer Required? ___ YES ___ NO

Type of Communication Systems [3] (check those that apply and insert information)

SYSTEM	VENDOR OR CONSULTANT	CENTRAL LOCATION OF SYSTEM	TYPE OF CABLING OR SPECIAL NOTES
___ Building Telephone System			
___ Public Telephone System			
___ Computer System			
___ Cable TV Services			
___ Closed Circuit TV System			
___ Satellite TV System			
___ Voice Notification System			
___ Intercom System			
___ Assistive Listening System			
___ Audio/Visual System			
___ Security System			
___ Other ____________			

NOTES:

1. Refer to codes and standards for specifics. Also check the ADA guideline and ICC/ANSI standard for accessible mounting locations.
2. Be sure to note on floor plans the location of fire-rated walls for placement of required fire dampers and fire stops.
3. Also see checklist in Chapter 6 for information on various alarm and other notification type systems as required by the codes.

Figure 8.10 Electrical and Communication Checklist

determine specific requirements, you should at least note the items listed. The checklist begins by asking you the project and space name and its occupancy classification. (See Chapter 2 for more information on occupancy classifications.) When using this checklist, you might want to use a floor plan of the space to mark the locations rather than filling in the blanks. The floor plan can then be attached to the checklist as backup. It will also be useful for coordination with the engineer. For each project the checklist asks you if an engineer is required. This will depend on the size of the project, the amount of electrical or communication work, and the jurisdiction of the project. (See Chapter 10.)

The first part of the checklist concentrates on the electrical requirements. It notes the main electrical items you should determine in your project. You should know where the electrical panels are and their sizes, especially if you need to coordinate the size of a new electrical room or closet with the engineer. Use the "Special Cabling Conditions" to note such things as the use of a plenum mechanical system or types of rated walls that will affect the type of cabling used. Also note if conduit will be required.

The next several items pertain to the types of outlets located in the project. In some cases, you may be reusing all existing receptacles and/or switches. If you are adding new ones, be sure to determine if any will be located in a rated wall and note this in the space provided or on the floor plan. Indicate any special types of outlets as well. The last two electrical categories pertain to types of light fixtures, equipment, appliances, or special systems that may be included in the project. Check those that apply and include any specifics that are required. Use this checklist to remind you of the types of outlets and equipment that should be labeled or noted on your drawings. It is also a good idea to attach the cut sheets of any items that are specified. For example, you may specify the light fixtures and appliances, the client might specify certain equipment being used in the space, and the electrical engineer will specify other electrical devices.

The second half of the checklist pertains to communication systems. Check off the systems that apply to this project and write in additional ones as required. Since most of the details are determined by a consultant, the communication vendor, or an engineer, this part of the checklist is to help you keep these systems organized. Spaces are provided for you to fill in the names of the companies installing the system as well as where the main part of the system will be located. For example, certain items will be included in the communication room. Other items, such as the surveillance monitors for the security system, will be located in other spaces. Any other system considerations should also be noted, including any special cabling required. As the design of these systems develop, you can add the necessary information as well as equipment and outlet locations to your floor plans.

CHAPTER 9

FINISH AND FURNITURE SELECTION

Over the years there have been many fatal fires in the United States due to flammable finishes and upholstery. One of the most noted incidents is the 1942 fire in Boston's Coconut Grove nightclub, which claimed the lives of 492 people. In response to that deadly fire, Boston established regulations dealing with interior finishes, known today as the *Boston Fire Code*. Fatal fires continue to occur in which finishes and furniture are a contributing factor. In 2003 alone there were several nightclub and nursing home fires in the United States that claimed multiple lives. Whether or not the interior finishes or upholstered furniture are the *cause* of the fire, they are likely to contribute to the spread of the fire. A wallcovering, for example, that is *not* flame resistant can spread a fire down the length of an entire corridor in a matter of seconds, setting other flammable items, such as draperies and upholstery, on fire and creating deadly smoke, heat, and toxic fumes.

Building codes and standards give strict instructions on the selection and use of interior finishes and furnishings. Chapter 5 discussed fire prevention through the use of rated interior building materials and assemblies (e.g., wall, floor, and ceiling systems). This chapter concentrates on the products that are either placed on top of the building materials (e.g., finishes) or set within the compartments created by the building materials and structural elements (e.g., furniture). These items are considered part of the fuel load and can contribute to the ignition and spread of a fire. As a result, finishes and furniture must undergo testing as well.

The ratings given to finishes and furniture, however, are different from those given to building materials and assemblies. Finish and furniture ratings are usually obtained by smaller-scale flame tests rather than larger full-scale fire tests.

These smaller-scale finish tests typically test the finish on the substrate or top component of the construction assembly. On the other hand, the large-scale fire tests, as discussed in chapter 5, test the entire assembly including the substrate, supports, fasteners, and any other parts. (These larger fire tests may sometimes include a finish as part of the assembly, but they still supply only an assembly rating.)

This chapter describes the various finish and furniture standards and tests and their results. From this you can understand how to select products based on the ratings in conjunction with the requirements found in the codes. The building codes, the fire codes, and the *Life Safety Code (LSC)* each have a section or chapter dedicated to interior finishes and/or furnishings. Other related items are mentioned in the occupancy sections of the codes or other chapters in the code. These codes and standards as well as the accessibility requirements related to finishes and furniture are explained in this chapter. It also includes information on other requirements not specified in the codes that are your responsibility to know and use for both safety and liability reasons.

It is important to understand the codes and standards that affect interior finishes and furniture. Interpreting charts, understanding test requirements, and selecting materials and furnishings that meet the codes are critical. Remember, your client's safety is in your hands.

KEY TERMS

Note

The terminology used to describe products that are more resistant to fire has changed over the years. *Flameproof* is a common term that is usually incorrect, since very few products are totally unaffected by fire. The correct terms are *flame retardant* and *flame resistant.*

Below is a list of terms used when discussing finish and furniture requirements. They are defined and discussed in this chapter. They can also be found in the Glossary.

Backcoating
Expanded vinyl wallcovering
Fireblock
Flame resistance
Flame spread
Flammability
Fuel load
Heat barrier
Mock-up
Plastic
Smoldering

TYPES OF FINISHES AND FURNISHINGS

Interior finishes and furnishings covered by the codes and standards include a variety of materials and products and can be divided into seven categories. They are listed and defined as follows and are discussed throughout this chapter.

- *Ceiling finishes:* Exposed interior surfaces of a building, including suspended ceiling grids and coverings that can be applied to fixed and movable ceilings, soffits, beams, space frames, and other similar elements.
- *Wall finishes:* Exposed interior surfaces of a building, including coverings that may be applied over fixed or movable walls and partitions, columns, and other similar elements. Examples include paint, vinyl and paper wallcovering, wood paneling, and applied acoustical finishes.
- *Floor finishes:* Exposed interior surfaces of a building, including coverings that may be applied over a finished or unfinished floor, stair (including risers), ramp, and other similar elements. Examples include hardwood, ceramic tile, vinyl, linoleum, carpets, and rug.
- *Window treatments:* Decorative elements that control the amount of light from a window area. These can include draperies, liners, blinds, and shutters. Curtains used in a space for privacy may also be included. These elements can be made of textiles, wood, vinyl, and other similar materials.
- *Trim and decorative materials:* Exposed decorative elements or protective materials attached to the interior wall or ceiling. This includes decorative moldings, wainscoting, baseboards, chair rails, picture rails, handrails, and door and window moldings.
- *Furnishing finishes:* Exposed finishes found in case goods furniture, systems furniture, and soft seating, such as fabrics, wood veneers, and laminates. This category also includes nonexposed finishes, such as the foam in seating, liners in drapery, and other similar elements.
- *Furniture:* Whole pieces of furniture rather than separate parts and finishes. This category usually includes upholstered products, such as seating and panel systems. Also included are mattresses, which consist of the whole mattress composition, including fabric, padding, coils, and similar bedding assemblies.

Until recently, codes often regulated only the first four categories. However, this is changing as requirements are getting stricter and more standards are being developed for both finishes and furnishings. In addition, the various codes are referencing more of these standards. Since some states are also requiring the use of finish and/or furniture standards not yet mentioned in the codes, be sure to check

Note

Most interior finishes and furnishings are considered combustible. However, the codes typically require that they have some degree of flame spread and smoke development restrictions in order for them to be used in many building interiors.

Note

Movable partitions or panel systems are typically classified as furniture. However, if they exceed a certain height, a jurisdiction may consider them to be walls, in which case they would need to meet fire separation requirements. (See Chapter 5.)

with the jurisdiction of your project. It is your responsibility to check the requirements and select furnishings and their finishes wisely, using your knowledge of codes and standards.

COMPARING THE CODES

The two main sources for interior finish regulations are the building codes and the *Life Safety Code (LSC)*. The *International Building Code (IBC)*, the *NFPA 5000*, and the *LSC* each have a chapter dedicated to interior finishes and furnishings. Although the chapters in the codes are organized differently, much of the information is the same. Each chapter includes restrictions on wall and ceiling finishes, floor finishes, decorations and trim, and other special finishes, such as expanded wallcovering and cellular or foam plastics. The *LSC* chapter also includes requirements on furnishings.

In some cases, you will need to reference other sections of the codes. For example, the building codes include a chapter on glass and glazing that has information on the use of safety glass. Finishes for plumbing fixtures and restrooms are found in the plumbing codes as well as the environmental chapter of the *IBC*. (See Chapter 7 for more information.) In addition, each separate occupancy chapter in the NFPA codes and special occupancy sections in the I-Codes may list additional finish and/or furniture requirements. (See Using the Codes later in this chapter.)

You may also need to reference the fire codes if one is required in your jurisdiction. Both the *International Fire Code (IFC)* and the *Uniform Fire Code (UFC)* include information on finish and furnishing requirements. The *IFC* includes the information in one chapter. Although similar to the *IBC*, the *IFC* also includes information on furnishings for specific occupancies as well as a section on decorative vegetation (e.g., natural cut trees and artificial vegetation). The *UFC* includes finish information within various chapters; however, it mostly refers you to and duplicates the information in the *LSC*.

> **Note**
>
> Standard *NFPA 705* is a standard test that can be used in the field by a code official to assess finishes already installed. (This standard was originally an appendix of *NFPA 701*.)

Similar to codes for construction materials as discussed in Chapter 5, the requirements for interior finishes and furnishings often refer you to various standards. They include standards from the National Fire Protection Association (NFPA), Underwriters Laboratories (UL), and American Society for Testing and Materials International (ASTM). Figure 9.1 is an example of the finish and furniture related standards from NFPA. You need to be familiar with these various standards to use the codes and when specifying finishes and furniture. Understanding the standards may also help when using fire models for performance design. (See next section.) As you will see later in this chapter, in addition to the standards referenced in the codes, there are other industry standards that you

NFPA 253	Method of Test for Critical Radiant Flux of Floor Covering Systems Using Radiant Heat Energy Source
NFPA 255	Method of Test of Surface Burning Characteristics of Burning Materials
NFPA 258	Determining Smoke Generation of Solid Materials
NFPA 260	Methods of Tests and Classification System for Cigarette Ignition Resistance of Components of Upholstered Furniture
NFPA 261	Method of Test for Determining Resistance of Mock-Up Upholstered Furniture Material Assemblies to Ignition by Smoldering Cigarettes
NFPA 265	Method of Fire Tests for Evaluating Room Fire Growth Contribution of Textile Coverings on Full Height Panels and Walls
NFPA 266	Method of Test for Fire Characteristics of Upholstered Furniture Exposed to Flaming Ignition Source (NO LONGER IN PRINT - withdrawn by NFPA in 2003)
NFPA 267	Method of Test for Fire Characteristics of Mattresses and Bedding Assemblies Exposed to Flaming Ignition Source (NO LONGER IN PRINT - withdrawn by NFPA in 2003)
NFPA 269	Test Method for Developing Toxic Potency Data for Use in Fire Hazard Modeling
NFPA 270	Test Method for Measurement of Smoke Obscuration Using a Conical Radiant Source in a Single Closed Chamber
NFPA 271	Method of Test for Heat and Visible Smoke Release Rates for Materials and Products Using an Oxygen Consumption Calorimeter
NFPA 272	Method of Test for Heat and Visible Smoke Release Rates for Upholstered Furniture Components or Composites and Mattresses Using an Oxygen Consumption Calorimeter
NFPA 286	Methods of Fire Tests for Evaluating Contribution of Wall and Ceiling Interior Finish to Room Fire Growth
NFPA 701	Methods of Fire Test for Flame Propagation of Textiles and Films

NOTE: There are other standards organizations with standards similar to those shown above. These include ASTM and UL standards. See other figures in this chapter for more detail.

Figure 9.1 Common NFPA Standards for Finishes and Furnishings

STAGES OF FIRE DEVELOPMENT

To gain a better understanding of how a fire can harm a human being and why fire codes are necessary, it is important to review the different stages in the development of a fire. They can be divided into three stages:

Stage 1: Known as the time of ignition, this first stage is the *initial growth* of a fire. Smoke produced during this stage can travel many feet from the room of origin and pose a threat to humans.

Stage 2: This is the *growth stage,* when the fire begins to ignite material in the immediate area, including finishes and furniture. As a fire starts to consume a large part of a building, the heat generated may cause *flashover*. This is when all the combustible materials in an area or room become heated to their ignition temperature, causing the materials in that area to simultaneously ignite. This explosion usually occurs when a fire reaches the 1200-degree range and will cause the fire to spread rapidly. It also can greatly increase the rate of toxic smoke.

Stage 3: In this stage the fire is *fully developed*, causing the entire building to quickly become dangerous. Smoke, heat, toxic gases, and possible structural collapse can harm those who remain within range.

The rate at which these stages of fire development can progress varies tremendously with the construction of a building and the finishes and furniture used within. However, the first 5 to 10 minutes of a fire are the most critical. The materials and finishes you select can either contribute to the growth or prevent the spread of a fire—and can play a large role in the beginning stages of a fire. The goal is to lengthen the amount of time during which the occupants can safely evacuate a building.

Note

The state of California has developed some of its own finish and furniture standards through its California Bureau of Home Furnishings and Thermal Insulation Department. Known as *technical bulletins,* several are discussed in this chapter.

must follow as well. In addition, many individual cities and states also have their own finish and/or furniture regulations. Some of the most stringent ones include the city of Boston and the states of California, Florida, Massachusetts, New Jersey, and New York. Be sure to check the jurisdiction of your project to see if there are more stringent requirements.

The next section of this chapter will describe the various finish and furniture standards. How to use this information is described in more detail later in the chapter. (See section on Using the Codes, page 368.)

STANDARDS AND TESTING

Rather than listing all the specific requirements for finishes and furnishings, the codes reference a number of standards. However, remember that the codes set minimum requirements, and sometimes there may be a stricter standard available. In some cases, as the designer, it will be up to you to follow the strictest standards within the industry. (See the section on Documentation and Liability in Chapter 10, page 412.) This section describes the various standards and related tests referred to by the codes and/or required by certain jurisdictions.

Each finish and furniture test has a particular purpose. Certain tests may not be consistent with the use of the material in your design. For example, one of the more common tests, the *Steiner Tunnel Test*, is considered a small-scale test and is not appropriate for all finish applications. The *Radiant Panel Test*, on the other hand, is for finishes applied to floors and does not take into account flooring finishes used in other applications, such as on walls. In other situations, a certain test may better represent the actual or proposed use of a finish or furniture assembly. For example, although the *Steiner Tunnel Test* and the *Room Corner Test* both test wallcoverings, the *Room Corner Test* is a more realistic test. The *Room Corner Test* apparatus more closely simulates an actual room. For these reasons, you should be familiar with each test procedure and the acceptable outcomes. It is important to know the intent of the test and recognize the limitations of the test results.

Note

Finish and furniture testing is constantly changing. Older tests are being improved and new tests are being developed. It is critical to keep abreast of the changes to make sure you continue to specify finishes and furniture that pass the appropriate tests.

In addition, the results of the finish and furniture tests are given in several ways. Some of the tests are pass/fail, while others determine and assign a specific class or ranked rating. For example, the *CAL 133* and the *NFPA 701* tests are strictly pass/fail tests. If a finish passes, you are allowed to use it; if it fails, you cannot use it. Other tests, such as the *Steiner Tunnel Test* and the *Radiant Panel Test*, assign class ratings to the tested finishes. Still others, such as *LC-50*, provide you with a ranked number rating. In both of these cases, the manufacturer must supply you with the letter or number rating for these tests. For example, a tunnel test will result in an A, B, or C rating. You then compare these ratings to what is required by the codes. (The type of result for each test is described in this section.)

Other standard tests are also available or are being developed specifically for the use of performance codes. Many of these standards are geared toward computer modeling and the analysis of materials as fire hazards within a specific project. They are used to help substantiate the use of a performance code. These additional standards are not listed in the codes, but are available from the various standards organizations. They are not discussed in this book. If you need documentation to support the use of an unusual finish or furnishing, you will typically work with an engineer who will create the computer models using the appropriate standards.

The standard tests that are described below have been grouped by the common test name. Within each category, specific test names will be listed, depending on the standards organization that provides the test. In many cases the ASTM, NFPA, and UL will have their own written standard for the same test.

COMMON TEST NAMES	STANDARD NAME/NUMBER	TYPE OF RATING
STEINER TUNNEL TEST	ASTM E84 NFPA 255 UL 723 Chamber Test (UL 992) (withdrawn in 1999)	Class Rating
RADIANT PANEL TEST	ASTM E648 NFPA 253 (also formerly NBS IR75-950)	Class Rating
PILL TEST	DOC FF1-70 (CFR 1630) DOC FF2-70 (CFR 1631) ASTM D2859	Pass or Fail
VERTICAL FLAME TEST	NFPA 701 ASTM D6413 UL 214	Pass or Fail
ROOM CORNER TEST		
(textile materials)	NFPA 265 UL 1715	Pass or Fail
(non-textile materials)	NFPA 286 ASTM E2257 (similar)	Pass or Fail
SMOLDER RESISTANCE TEST		
(component)	NFPA 260 (formerly 260A) ASTM E1353 CAL 116	Class Rating
(mock-up)	NFPA 261 (formerly 260B) ASTM E1352 CAL 117	Pass or Fail
TOXICITY TEST	LC-50 (or Pitts Test) NFPA 269 ASTM E1678	Ranked
UPHOLSTERED SEATING TEST		
(full scale)	ASTM E1537 UL 1056 CAL 133 NFPA 266 (withdrawn in 2003)	Pass or Fail
(small scale)	NFPA 272 (formerly 264A) ASTM E1474	Ranked
MATTRESS TEST		
(commercial applications)	ASTM E1590 CAL 129 NFPA 267 (withdrawn in 2003) UL 1895 (withdrawn in 2002)	Pass or Fail
(all applications)	DOC FF4-72 (CFR 1632)	Pass or Fail

NOTE: Any number of the above tests may be required by a jurisdiction, depending on the occupancy and its location within a building. In addition, there may be other tests and/or test names not listed above that are more specific to a jurisdiction.

Figure 9.2 Summary of Tests for Finishes and Furnishings

These test names are each labeled with the organization's initials and test number. For example, *UL 723* is a standard test by Underwriters Laboratories numbered 723.

As you read through this section, refer to Figure 9.2. It summarizes the various finish and furniture tests discussed. Along the left-hand side of the chart are the common test names for the various tests that apply to finishes and furniture. The specific standard designations as published by the various standards organizations are listed in the next column according to the type of test. (Although some tests have been withdrawn and are no longer in print, they are listed in case a code or jurisdiction is still requiring the test.) The right-hand side of the chart lists whether the tests result in a pass/fail rating, a class rating, or a ranked rating.

Steiner Tunnel Test

The *Steiner Tunnel Test* is the principal test used to determine both the flame spread and smoke development ratings in the classification of interior finishes applied to walls, ceilings, and other structural elements, such as columns. As one of the first interior finish tests, its name comes from the fact that finishes are tested in a tunnel-like apparatus that is 25 feet (7.62 m) in length. Although the procedure of the test has been refined over the years, the overall test has not changed much since its inception. The same test is used by the ASTM, NFPA, and UL standards organizations under these names:

- *ASTM E84, Standard Test Method for Surface Burning Characteristics of Building Materials*
- *NFPA 255, Standard Method of Test of Surface Burning Characteristics of Building Materials*
- *UL 723, Test for Surface Burning Characteristics of Building Materials*

Note

The position of the finish sample in the *Steiner Tunnel Test* makes it difficult for some finishes (e.g., plastics) to be tested without a screen for support. Because of this, the codes sometimes recommend other standards.

Using the tunnel apparatus, a finish is tested in a horizontal position. In the test, a finish sample the length of the tunnel is attached to the ceiling, as shown in Figure 9.3. The sample consists of the finish and any required substrate and/or adhesive (or other securing method) that would be used in the actual installation of the finish. For example, if wallcovering is intended to be used on gypsum board, the sample will consist of the wallcovering applied to one layer of gypsum board using the adhesive recommended by the manufacturer. Once the sample is secured, a flame is started at one end and a regulated draft is applied through the tunnel. The actual time that it takes the flame to travel down the length of the tunnel is measured and is used to create the flame-spread index (FSI). A photoelectric cell located at the opposite end of the tunnel also measures the density of

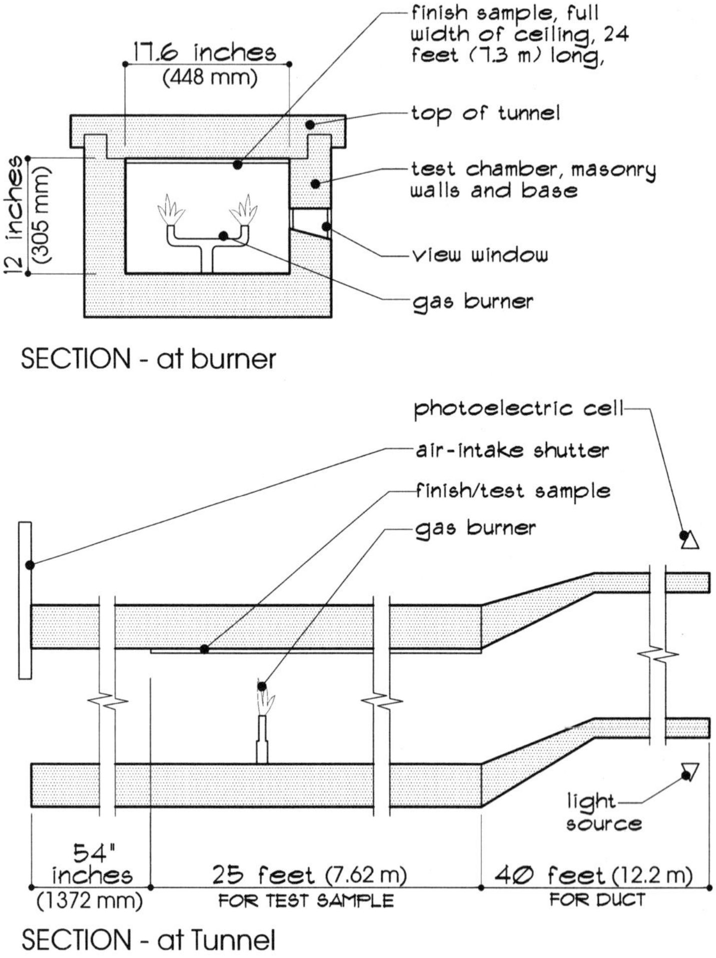

Figure 9.3 Steiner Tunnel Test Apparatus

the smoke in relation to a light source. This determines the smoke development index (SDI). These two indexes are used to assign a classification to the finish.

In the building codes, these classifications are grouped into three categories for interior wall and ceiling finishes, with Class A being the most restrictive and Class C being the least. (Floor finishes have a different test and rating system, as described next.) The classifications consist of the following:

> **Note**
>
> Some woods that have been treated with a fire retardant can qualify as a Class A interior finish. Most untreated wood will either have a Class C flame spread rating or no rating at all.

- *Class A:* Flame spread 0–25, smoke development 0–450. Includes any material classified at 25 or less on the flame spread test scale and 450 or less on the smoke test scale.

- *Class B:* Flame spread 26–75, smoke development 0–450. Includes any material classified at more than 25 but not more than 75 on the flame spread test scale and 450 or less on the smoke test scale.
- *Class C:* Flame spread 76–200, smoke development 0–450. Includes any material classified at more than 75 but not more than 200 on the flame spread test scale and 450 or less on the smoke test scale.

Note

Class A, B, and C designations for wall and ceiling finishes used by the ICC codes, the NFPA codes, and the *Standard Building Code (SBC)* correlate directly with the Class I, II, and III designations used by the *National Building Code (NBC)* and the *Uniform Building Code (UBC)*.

The *flame spread* index (FSI) indicates the speed at which a fire may spread across the surface of a material. The lower the number, the slower the fire will spread, which allows more time to evacuate the space or building. The index is determined by comparing the results of the test to the burning characteristics of two known materials, glass-reinforced cement board and red oak flooring. Arbitrarily, the cement board is given a flame spread of 0 and red oak flooring is assigned a flame spread of 100. All other materials are assigned FSI values based on their test results. Both interior finishes and building materials can be required by the codes to pass this test. Figure 9.4 shows the flame spread ratings for a variety of materials. This will give you an idea of the wide range of possible results depending on the type of material.

Note

The acoustical tiles used in suspended ceiling systems must also be tested using the *Steiner Tunnel Test*.

The *smoke development* index (SDI) determines how much visibility there is in a given access route when a material is on fire and creating smoke. The maximum SDI of 450 was determined by Underwriters Laboratories and is based solely on the level of visibility through the smoke created by the test. This would affect an occupant's ability to see exit signs while evacuating a building. Notice that the

Material	Flame spread
Glass-fiber sound-absorbing blanks	15 to 30
Mineral-fiber sound-absorbing panels	10 to 25
Shredded wood fiberboard (treated)	20 to 25
Sprayed cellulose fibers (treated)	20
Aluminum (with baked enamel finish on one side)	5 to 10
Asbestos-cement board	0
Brick or concrete block	0
Cork	175
Gypsum board (with paper surface on both sides)	10 to 25
Northern pine (treated)	20
Southern pine (untreated)	130 to 190
Plywood paneling (untreated)	75 to 275
Plywood paneling (treated)	100
Carpeting	10 to 600
Concrete	0

Figure 9.4 Typical Flame Spread of Common Materials (*International Building Code 2000 Commentary*. Copyright 2002. Falls Church, Virginia: International Code Council, Inc. Reproduced with permission. All rights reserved.)

smoke development rating remains the same in each classification. Any finish with an SDI over 450 would mean that it would create too much smoke and, therefore, would not be allowed by the codes.

Since the smoke development requirement does not change, it is the FSI number that distinguishes the difference in each class. Note, however, that there is no direct relationship between the FSI and the SDI. One finish could have low ratings on both while another may have a low flame spread but a high smoke development rating. Any tested finish that results in an FSI or SDI above what is allowed by the codes would be considered a nonrated finish.

Note

The *Chamber Test* or *UL 992* used to be an alternate test for wall and ceiling finishes, but this test was withdrawn by UL in 1999.

Radiant Panel Test

The *Radiant Panel Test* is used to rate interior floor finishes such as carpet, resilient flooring, and hardwood floor assemblies. It was originally created by the National Institute of Standards and Technology (NIST) and was known as *NBS IRS75-950*. (NIST was previously known as the National Bureau of Standards.) More currently, there are two standard tests available:

- ❑ *NFPA 253, Standard Method of Test for Critical Radiant Flux of Floor Covering Systems Using a Radiant Heat Energy Source*
- ❑ *ASTM E648, Standard Test Method for Critical Radiant Flux of Floor-Covering Systems Using a Radiant Heat Energy Source*

Originally developed to simulate the type of fire that develops in corridors and exitways, the test measures the floor covering's tendency to spread a fire. Although flooring is not considered a major cause of fire spread, the flooring material in exit access corridors can be of concern because it can add to fire growth when flame and hot gases radiate through the walls from a fire in an adjacent room.

The test determines the minimum energy required to sustain flame on a floor covering. In this test, a finish sample is secured to a substrate and then placed at the bottom of the test chamber, as shown in Figure 9.5. The finish sample consists of the entire floor-covering system, which includes the floor covering, any required padding, adhesive (or other securing method), and the substrate. The sample is preheated by a radiant heat source mounted at a 30-degree angle from the sample and then exposed to a gas burner. If the sample begins to burn, two things are measured as soon as the flame goes out: the length of the burn marks and the amount of radiant heat energy at the furthest part of the burned area. Both of these measurements are compared to existing data (e.g., a flux profile graph) in order to determine the *critical radiant flux* (CRF).

Note

The NFPA notes that most fire deaths due to smoke inhalation in the U.S. occur in areas other than the room of fire origin and are caused by fires that have spread beyond the room of origin.

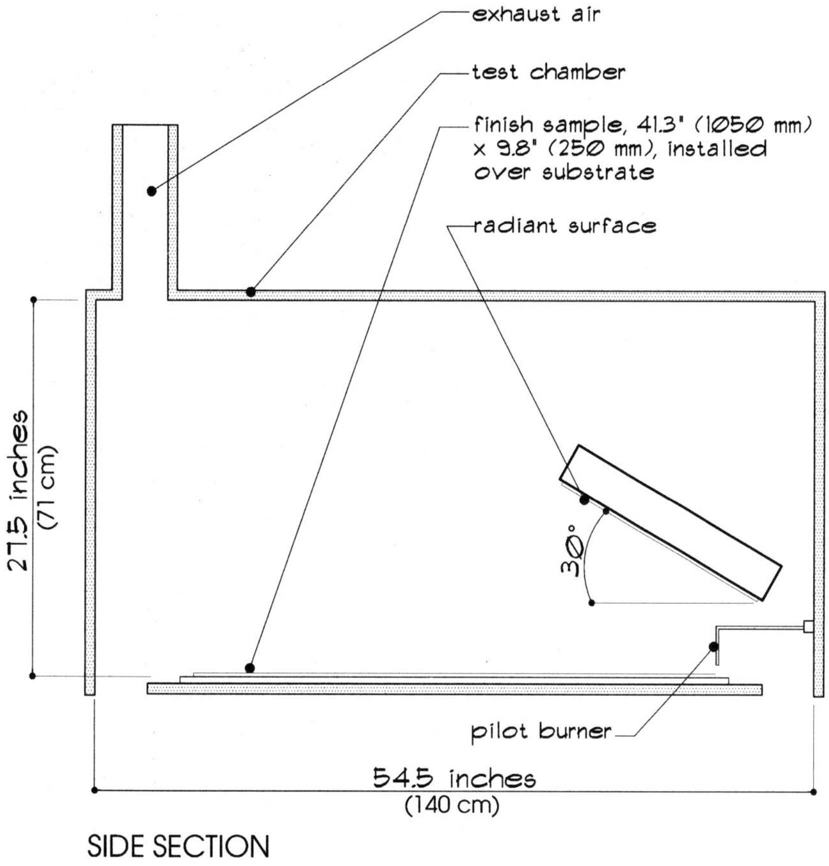

Figure 9.5 Radiant Panel Test Apparatus

The CRF is measured in watts per square centimeter. The higher the value, the more heat energy it takes to ignite the finish, making it more resistant to flame spread. Test results determine whether a floor finish will be considered a Class I or a Class II. Class I is more flame resistant. (Floor coverings that do not fall within one of these two categories are considered nonrated or nonclassed.) The CRF for each is shown below.

- *Class I:* Critical radiant flux, minimum of 0.45 watts per square centimeter.
- *Class II:* Critical radiant flux, minimum of 0.22 watts per square centimeter.

These two classes are referenced by the codes. Not all occupancies require a floor finish that has been tested by the *Radiant Panel Test*. If it is required, only exits and exit access corridors are typically regulated. (See the section titled Using the

Codes later in this chapter.) Although this test is often associated with the testing of carpet, these ratings will also apply to other floor finishes. This includes resilient floors such as VCT, as well as hardwood flooring installed over a combustible substrate such as plywood. (Hardwood floors applied directly to concrete are typically not required to be rated.) When furring strips are used under a floor covering, such as hardwood floors, other code restrictions may apply, as discussed later in this chapter. (See the section on Other Restrictions on page 386.)

Pill Test

In addition to the *Radiant Panel Test*, all carpets manufactured for sale in the United States have been required, since 1971, to meet a federal flammability standard. Also known as the *Pill Test*, it uses a methenamine tablet (or pill) to ignite the carpet during the test. This pill replicates a small ignition source such as a slow burning cigarette or a glowing ember from a fireplace.

Note

When carpet is used as a finish other than on a floor, more stringent tests are required.

The test consists of placing a carpet sample under a metal plate with an 8-inch (205 mm) diameter opening so that a circle surrounds the carpet sample as shown in Figure 9.6. A pill is placed in the center of the sample and ignited. Once the flame or glow has gone out, the distance the carpet has burned beyond the original ignition point is measured and recorded. If the burn extends to within one inch (2.5 cm) of the edge of the metal plate, the sample fails.

This pass/fail test indicates the ease of surface ignition and surface flammability of a material. There are two versions of this test produced by the

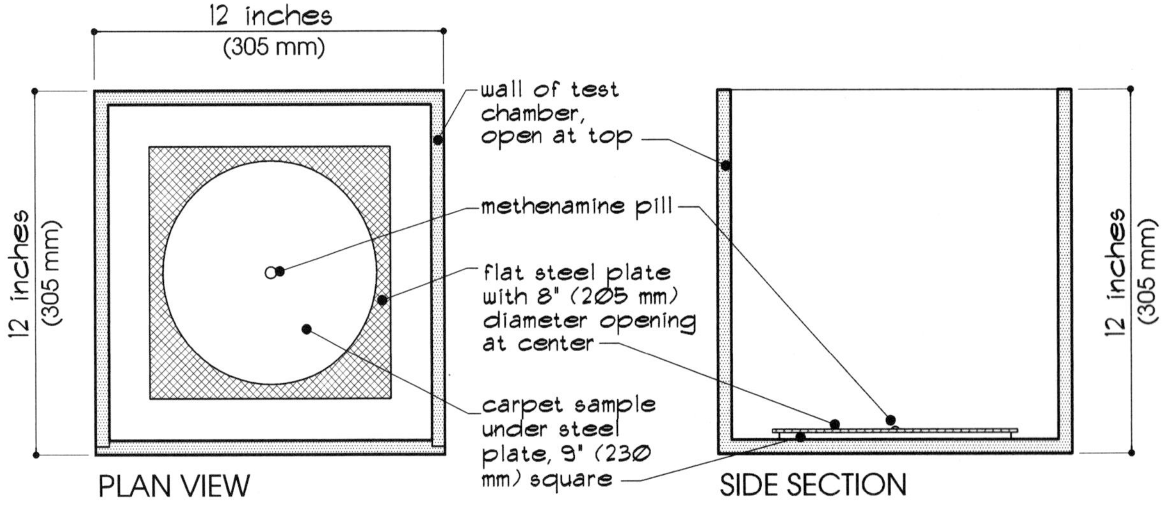

Figure 9.6 Pill Test Apparatus

federal government: one regulates large rugs and wall-to-wall carpeting and the other is for area rugs. ASTM has a standard for this test as well. The three tests are:

- *DOC FF1-70 (or CPCS 1630 CFR), Standard for the Surface Flammability of Carpets and Rugs*
- *DOC FF2-70 (or CPCS 1631 CFR), Standard for the Surface Flammability of Small Carpets and Rugs*
- *ASTM D2859, Standard Test Method for Ignition Characteristics of Finishes Textile Floor Covering Materials* (includes testing procedures for carpets and rugs)

The federal government requires that all carpets and rugs sold in the United States be tested using *DOC FF1-70* and *DOC FF2-70* except for small rugs, which are not required to pass the *Pill Test*. If a carpet or rug does not pass, it must be labeled as flammable. The building codes typically require all carpets and large rugs (e.g., those tested by *DOC FF1-70*) to pass this *Pill Test* no matter what occupancy they are used in. Smaller rugs are not covered by the building code, but their use should be limited, especially in commercial occupancies, if they have not passed the *Pill Test*. (You may need to confirm their use with a code official.) Although this test is considered standard protocol, other flooring finish regulations are required for occupancies that warrant more careful restrictions or where a codes official deems it necessary for a particular situation. (See *Radiant Panel Test*.)

Vertical Flame Test

Vertical flame tests are generally required for *vertical treatments* such as curtains, draperies, window shades, large wall hangings or tapestries, and plastic films used for decorative purposes. Any vertical finish that is exposed to air on both sides is considered a vertical treatment. This includes wall hangings because air can get between the wall and the hanging. Another example would be fabric installed in a track system over a wall or ceiling as an acoustical barrier. However, if a fabric or tapestry is fully secured to a wall using adhesive, it will usually need to meet the requirements of a *Steiner Tunnel Test*—or a *Room Corner Test*, as described next.

Note

In 1989, *NFPA 260A/B* was divided into two separate standards: *NFPA 260* and *NFPA 261*.

The vertical flame tests include the following:

- *NFPA 701, Standard Methods of Fire Tests for Flame Propagation of Textiles and Films*
- *ASTM D6413, Standard Test Method for Flame Resistance of Textiles (Vertical Test)*
- *UL 214, Test for Flame-Propagation of Fabrics and Films*

These tests are more realistic than the *Steiner Tunnel Test* because a flame source is used to create a vertical burning of the finish rather than the horizontal burning used in the tunnel test. *NFPA 701* is the oldest version of the test and has been modified and improved over time. The most current version is divided into two separate pass/fail tests known as Test Method 1 and Test Method 2.

In both test methods, the sample must be exposed to conditions similar to the way the fabric will be used. For example, fabrics for table linens must be laundered and drapery fabrics should be dry-cleaned. This gives the most realistic test results. It also indicates how important it is for clients to know how to clean and maintain the items you specify and install. If they do not follow the manufacturer's recommendations, the fabric's performance in a fire will be affected. (Note, however, that when the vertical treatments cover a large area, they may also be required to pass the *Steiner Tunnel Test* or the *Room Corner Test*.) The two test methods are described next.

Test Method 1

Test Method 1 is a small-scale test and is required for lighter-weight fabrics that are either single-layered or multilayered. These might include window curtains and drapes and other treatments such as swags, vertical folding shades, roll-type window shades, and fabric blinds (vertical and horizontal). It also includes stage or theater curtains, hospital privacy curtains, display booth separators, table skirts, and linens, as well as textile wall hangings. (The maximum weight of the fabric is typically set at 700 grams per square meter—or approximately 20.5 ounces per square yard.)

The test consists of hanging a fabric sample vertically on a bar located near the top rear of an open-face test cabinet as shown in Figure 9.7. A gas burner is applied to the lower edge of the sample. Once the flame source is removed, the sample is allowed to burn until it extinguishes itself. If any part of the sample falls to the floor, it must self-extinguish within 2 seconds. In addition, the weight of the sample after the test is compared to its original weight. It cannot lose more than 40 percent of its original weight. Both of these requirements must be met for the test to pass.

Test Method 2

Test Method 2 is a similar test done on a larger scale. It is used for heavier fabrics and fabrics that have vinyl coatings, such as blackout blinds and lined draperies using a vinyl-coated blackout lining. It also includes plastic films, awnings, tarps, and banners. In addition, this test might be used for larger drapery assemblies that have multiple layers and folds. This test takes into account the effect of air trapped between fabric layers.

Unlike Test Method 1, this test uses a four-sided cabinet. Whenever possible, the fabric sample is tested in a folded configuration (similar to a drape on a rod).

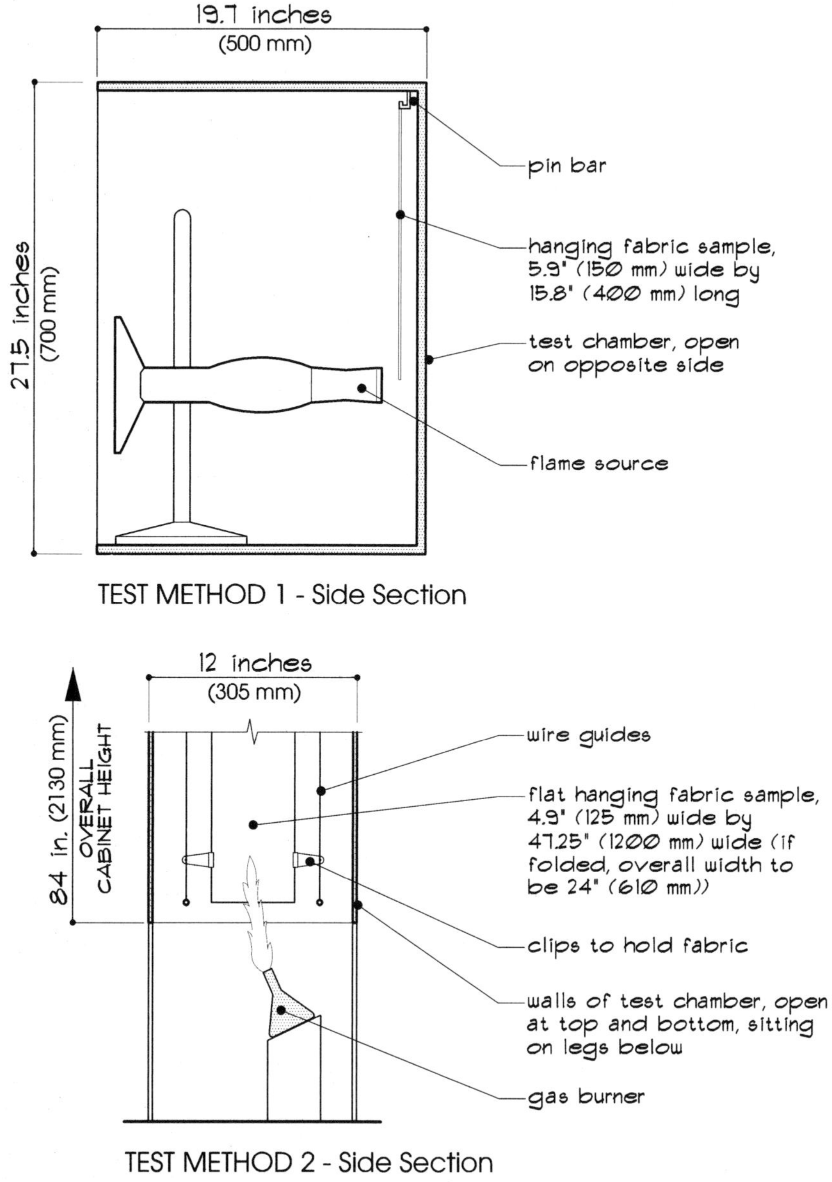

Figure 9.7 Vertical Flame Test Apparatus

However, certain heavier fabrics or multilayer assemblies that do not easily fold are tested in a flat configuration. In each case, the sample is hung from a rod at the top of the cabinet and exposed to a flame source at the bottom for two minutes. (Figure 9.7 shows an example of a flat configuration.) When the flame source is removed, the sample must self-extinguish within 2 seconds in order to pass the test. In addition, the burn marks left on the sample cannot exceed a certain length of char—17.1 inches (435 mm) for flat fabric samples and 41.3 inches (1050 mm) for folded fabrics. If the char remaining from the burn exceeds this, the fabric will fail even if it extinguished itself within 2 seconds.

Room Corner Test

Another standard test must be used when napped, tufted, or looped textiles are used as "wallcoverings" on walls and ceilings. This typically includes carpets and carpet-like textiles. Currently there are two versions of the test—one specifically for textile wallcoverings and the other for non-textile wall and ceiling finishes, such as expanded vinyl wallcovering. All of these tests are generally referred to as the *Room Corner Test*. As the name implies, an entire room is used in the test and the flame source is located in one corner of the room. (In the past, only a simulated corner of a room was constructed. However, the more current versions of the test use a full room.)

The *Room Corner Test* is a more accurate representation of actual building conditions because of the full room simulation. The test determines how an interior finish material will add to fire growth (including heat and smoke) and create combustion products such as gases. It also determines whether the finish will cause flashover or fire spread beyond the initial fire location. And, since it is considered a more stringent test than the *Steiner Tunnel Test*, the codes will usually allow this test in lieu of meeting the requirements of the tunnel test. (See building codes for specifics.) The two versions of the tests are described separately below.

Textile Wallcoverings

Note

If you add a backing to an approved textile during installation, you must have it retested. The backing makes the original test invalid.

In the past, some of the model code organizations had their own version of the *Room Corner Test*. However, the most current test standards for textile wallcoverings include:

- *NFPA 265, Standard Methods of Fire Tests for Evaluating Room Fire Growth Contribution of Textile Coverings on Full Height Panels and Walls*
- *UL 1715, Fire Test of Interior Finish Material*

These are pass/fail tests that simulate a fire within a full-size room, as shown in Figure 9.8. Finish samples are secured to the walls in the room using the

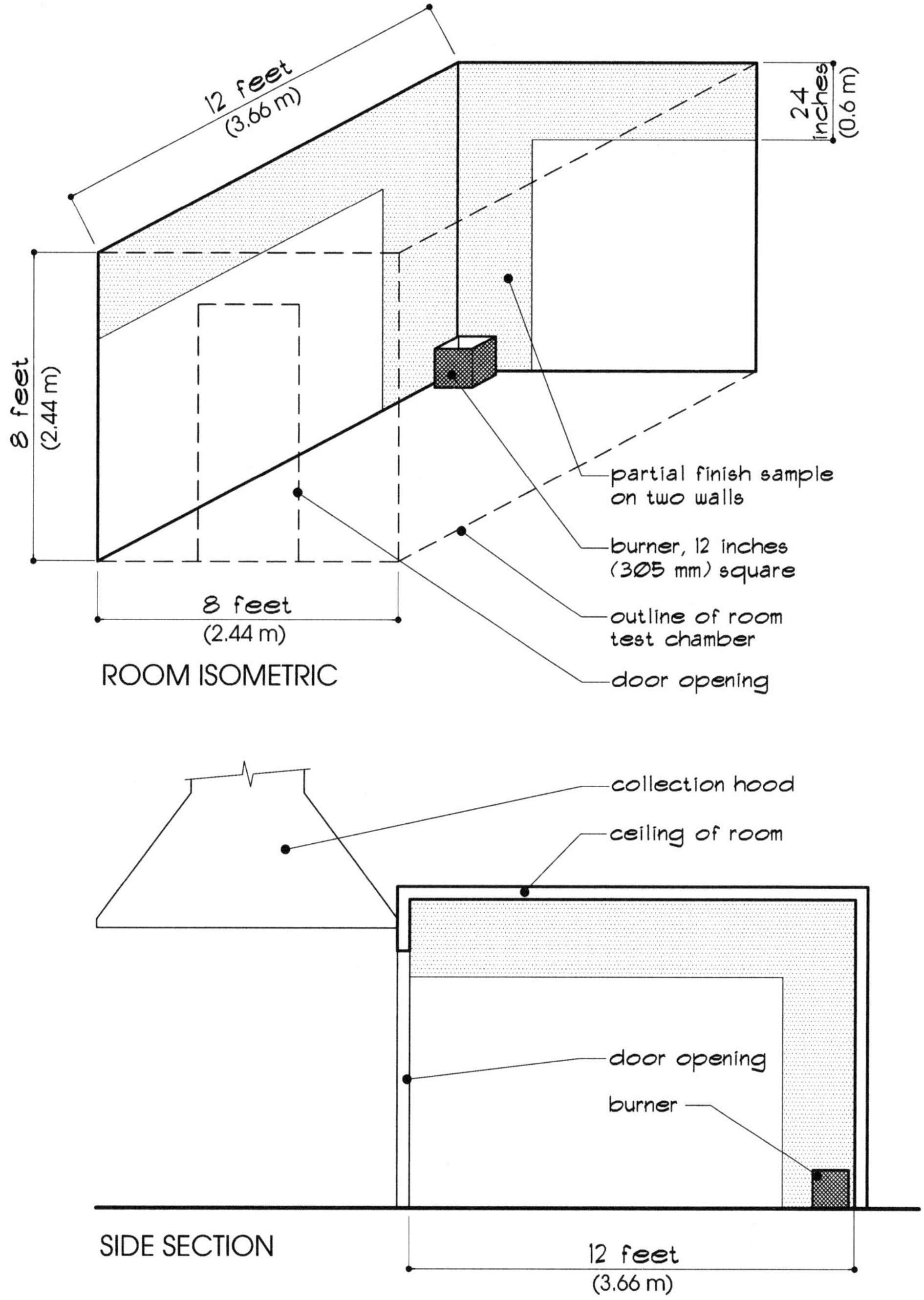

Figure 9.8 Room Corner Test Apparatus

adhesive intended for actual use. The test allows for two options. Method A requires the finish sample to be mounted partially on two walls of a compartment like that shown in Figure 9.8. Method B requires the finish sample to be mounted fully on the one rear and two long side walls.

Once the finish sample is secured to the walls, the rest of the test is the same. A fire source is started in the corner of the room. A square box located 2 inches (51 mm) from the back corner of the room is ignited. (See Figure 9.8.) It is first ignited at a heat level of approximately 40 kW for 5 minutes and then increased to approximately 150 kW for an additional 10 minutes. A duct system located outside the open doorway of the room collects the gases created by the fire and measures the gas velocity, temperature, and concentrations of gases. A finish passes the test if certain criteria as listed in the standard are met. For example, the flame cannot extend to the ceiling during the first heat exposure, and flashover cannot occur during the second heat exposure. Finishes tested using Method A must meet more criteria than Method B. Regardless if Method A or Method B is used, if all listed criteria are not met, the finish fails.

Nontextile Wallcoverings

There are two other standards that are also considered *Room Corner Tests.* However, they test nontextile type wallcoverings that can be used on walls and ceilings. The standards are similar:

- ❑ *NFPA 286, Standard Methods of Fire Tests for Evaluating Room Fire Growth Contribution of Textile Coverings on Full Height Panels and Walls*
- ❑ *ASTM E2257, Standard Test Method for Room Fire Test of Wall and Ceiling Materials and Assemblies*

The basis for these tests and the *Room Corner Tests* described above is similar. For example, the same simulated room, as shown in Figure 9.8, is used—same size, same instruments, same burning source, and so on. The finish samples are even applied to the room in the same way as Method B described above. However, for this test the finish sample must also be secured to the ceiling of the room as well as the walls. (If it is exclusively a ceiling finish, then the finish sample can be applied only on the ceiling.) Additionally, the flame source is placed closer to the corner of the room so that it is in direct contact with the walls. The first ignition heat level and exposure length is also the same as in the test for the textile wallcovering, but the second exposure increases to approximately 160 kW for 10 minutes. In addition to the criteria mentioned above, all newly tested finishes are also given a smoke release value. If the finish does not pass all the required criteria or exceed the smoke release value (which is similar to the 450 SDI set by the *Steiner Tunnel Test*), it will fail.

The *ASTM E2257* test is similar to the NFPA test, except that different heat levels and time frames are used during the test. At this time, most codes in the United States typically require the use of *NFPA 286* but not *ASTM E2257*.

Smolder Resistance Test

Smolder Resistance Tests are also known as *Cigarette Ignition Tests*. A cigarette ignition test analyzes the smoldering resistance of a finish. It is a nonflame test that uses an actual lit cigarette as the ignition source to see how a product will smolder before either flaming or extinguishing. The test consists of putting a lighted cigarette on a sample and then covering it with a layer of sheeting material. The cigarette is allowed to burn its full length unless ignition occurs. (If ignition occurs, the sample automatically fails.) Once the cigarette burns its full length, the char length is measured in all directions. If the char is longer than allowed by the test, the sample does not pass. The allowed char length depends on the version of the test used, but typically it must not exceed 1.5 to 2 inches (38 to 51 mm).

Note

The cigarettes used in smolder-resistance tests must meet certain standards of their own to make sure the testing remains consistent.

This test determines the performance of upholstered furniture and its components in relation to a smoldering cigarette. (Keep in mind that these items are not exposed to an open flame; therefore, it is not a good test for flame spread or severe fire exposure.) Although the methods used are virtually the same, there are two types of this test. One version of the test evaluates the individual components that make up a piece of furniture, while the other version evaluates a combination of components or a partial mock-up of the piece of furniture. Each is explained below.

Components

When a *Smolder Resistance Test* is used on an individual finish or textile, it is a pass/fail test. These tests include the following:

- *NFPA 260, Standard Methods of Tests and Classification System for Cigarette Ignition Resistance of Components of Upholstered Furniture*
- *ASTM E1353, Standard Test Methods for Cigarette Ignition Resistance of Components of Upholstered Furniture*
- *CAL 116, Requirements, Test Procedure and Apparatus for Testing the Flame Retardance of Upholstered Furniture*

Note

Some states, such as New York, have passed laws that require low-ignition strength cigarettes to be sold in an attempt to reduce the number of fires started by cigarettes.

This test applies to a wide variety of furniture components and includes cover fabrics, interior fabrics, welt cords, decking materials, and barrier materials, as well as filling or padding materials. These filling/batting materials can be natural or man-made fibers, foamed or cellular materials, resilient pads of natural or man-made fibers, or loose particulate filling materials such as shredded polyurethane or feathers and down.

Depending on the component, the finish sample could be tested on one of two types of test apparatus: a "decking material tester" or a "mini-mockup tester." Both of these are shown in Figure 9.9. For example, samples that consist of decking material are typically tested horizontally using the decking material tester. Other components, such as fabrics, welt cords, filling or padding, and barrier materials, are assembled individually or in combination to fit on the standard base unit of the mini-mockup tester. The mini-mockup allows these materials to be tested with the cigarette in a crevice. In each case, the lighted cigarette is covered with a sheeting material to ensure that it has direct contact with the sample.

As previously described, the test measures the char size left on the fabric or material. Although the test provides a cigarette resistance classification, Class I or Class II, it is essentially a pass/fail test. If the material resists ignition from the cigarette and does not exceed the maximum char length, it passes the test and is classified as Class I. Any material that does not pass the test is classified as Class II.

Mock-ups

Another *Smolder Resistance Test* was developed specifically for furniture mock-ups. The test is more realistic because the mock-up consists of multiple components used in realistic combinations. The most common of this type of tests include:

- *NFPA 261, Standard Method of Test for Determining Resistance of Mock-up Upholstered Furniture Material Assemblies to Ignition by Smoldering Cigarettes*
- *ASTM E1352, Standard Test Method for Cigarette Ignition Resistance of Mock-up Upholstered Furniture Assemblies*
- *CAL 117, Requirements, Test Procedures and Apparatus for Testing the Flame Retardance of Resilient Filling Materials Used in Upholstered Furniture*

Note

There are other standards available that test the smoke density of an entire construction assembly. (See Chapter 5.) These assemblies may include the interior finish. Examples include *NFPA 258* and *270* as well as *ASTM E662* and *E1995.*

All the materials that are to be used in the actual upholstered furniture are included in the mock-up, similar to the actual piece of furniture. The mock-up is shaped similarly to the mini-mockup in Figure 9.9 (i.e., the back and side armrest do not have to be shaped like the actual piece of furniture) except that two sides are required instead of one—one side represents the back and the other the arm of the upholstered piece. The overall size of the mock-up is also larger than the one in the previous test. It is 25.5 inches (648 mm) long by 21.25 inches (540 mm) deep with two sides perpendicular to each other that are 14.5 inches (368 mm) above the floor.

The test is essentially the same as the component mini-mockup test previously described, except that multiple cigarettes are lit at the same time during the

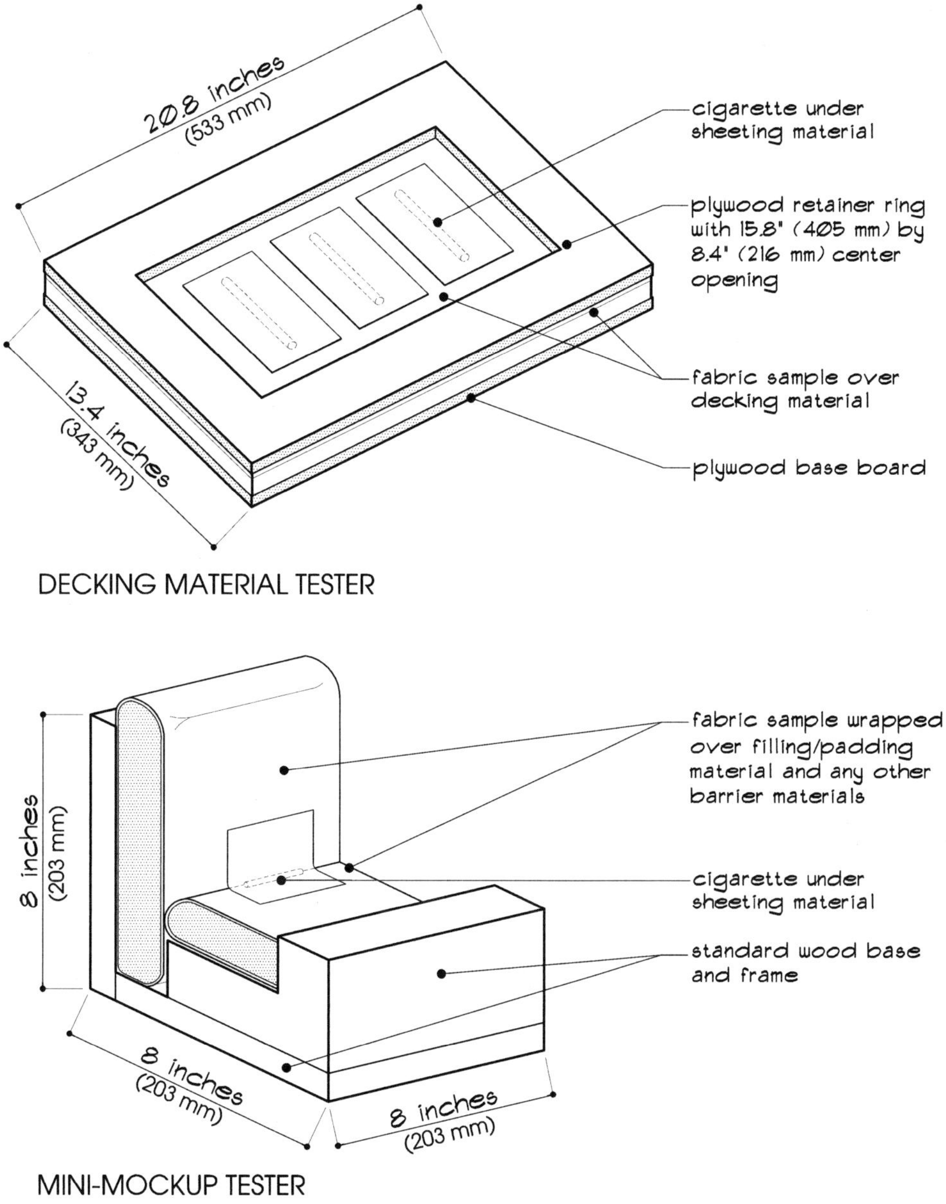

Figure 9.9 Smolder Resistance Test: Tester Options

test instead of just one. For example, cigarettes are put in the crevices of the seat cushion and armrest, on the cushion edge, in the center of the cushion, on top of armrests, and so on. As a result, the test gives a better indication of how a whole piece of furniture will react rather than just one layer. At the end of the test the char length is measured and the mock-up sample is given a pass or fail rating. It passes if ignition did not occur and the char falls within the designated length. (Note that the *CAL 117* test is slightly different than the others but may be updated and revised in the near future.)

Toxicity Test

Toxicity testing is one of the newer types of finish and furnishing tests. Originally developed by the University of Pittsburgh and known as the *Pitts Test* or *LC-50*, the same test is now also available from NFPA and ASTM. The various names include:

- *LC-50* or *Pitts Test*
- *NFPA 269, Standard Test Method for Developing Toxic Potency Data for Use in Fire Hazard Modeling*
- *ASTM E1678, Standard Test Method for Measuring Smoke Toxicity for Use in Fire Hazard Analysis*

Note

The *LSC* and the building codes do not necessarily mention or require every finish and furniture test discussed in this chapter. Some are required locally while others you should use as a matter of practice.

The test measures the amount of toxicity a material emits when it is burned. The testing covers a wide range of materials in addition to finishes and furniture. Included are wall, ceiling, and floor finishes, furniture upholstery, mattresses, and bed pads, as well as electrical wire and conduit, mechanical ductwork, thermal insulation, and plumbing pipes. The degree of toxicity is reported as a LC-50 value. (LC-50 or LC_{50} represents the measure of lethal toxic potency.)

The test consists of subjecting a small finish sample (or other material) to an ignition source and then exposing it to radiant heat lamps for 15 minutes. The smoke produced is collected through a connecting chimney for 30 minutes. (See Figure 9.10.) Various methods are used to monitor the concentration of gaseous toxicants. The data collected, along with the measured mass loss of the test sample, are used to predict a LC-50 rating of the test sample. The same procedure is then repeated using six live mice in order to confirm the predicted LC-50, and adjustments are made as required based on the reaction of the mice.

Ultimately, the test determines an LC-50 rating for the product. Although it is a rated test, at this time there are no set standard ratings. However, more manufacturers are testing their products and listing the LC-50 ratings on them. Therefore, when selecting a finish or furnishing with an LC-50 rating, you should compare two or more products. The higher the test score the better, since higher

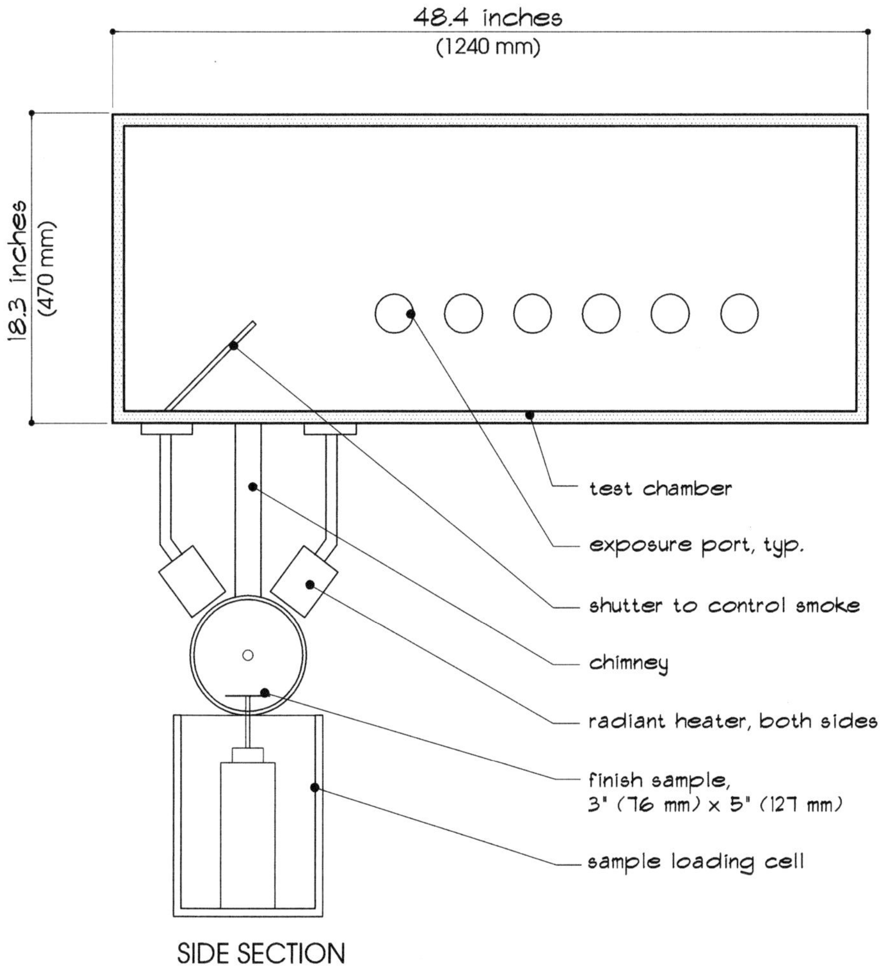

Figure 9.10 Toxicity Test Apparatus

ratings are less toxic. Some jurisdictions try to stay within or above the natural wood ratings of LC-16 through LC-25.

Although the tests are not currently required by the ICC or NFPA codes, this may change in the future. Some jurisdictions will require the test. For example, the state of New York was the first to enforce the test and keeps a database of all the finishes and products that have been tested. To sell products in New York, manufacturers are required to register the test results with New York's Department of State, Office of Fire Prevention and Control in Albany. If a project is

Note

In the future, some states, such as California, may ban certain fire retardants used in plastics, foam, and upholstered furniture due to the toxins they emit.

located in New York, you need to obtain the LC-50 rating and the appropriate testing information for a product from either the manufacturer or the state. Other jurisdictions may have a different procedure. (If you are not sure if it is required, check with your code official.)

Upholstered Seating Test

Most of the standard tests described so far tested individual finishes and components. Other tests are available for upholstered seating and mattresses. These test more of the full assembly. There are two basic types: full-scale tests and small-scale tests. A *full-scale test* can use an actual piece of furniture or a large mock-up of that piece of furniture, whereas a *small-scale test* uses smaller mock-ups that consist of multiple parts or components of a piece of furniture.

Full-Scale Tests

Note

Not all upholstered furniture will require *CAL 133* testing. Some may just require a *Smolder Resistance Test.* The results of both tests can be improved with the use of certain fabric backcoatings, interliners, fire blockers, and special rated foams.

The full-scale test is a pass/fail test of a *whole* piece of furniture rather than of an individual finish or material. It was first developed by the state of California and titled *California Technical Bulletin 133*, also referred to as either *CAL 133* or *TB 133*. Since then other standards organizations have developed similar tests. Tests that are considered full-scale furniture tests are shown below. (*NFPA 266* is no longer being published as of 2003, but may still be required by a jurisdiction.)

- ❑ *ASTM E1537, Standard Test Method for Fire Testing of Upholstered Furniture*
- ❑ *UL 1056, Standard for Safety for Fire Test of Upholstered Furniture*
- ❑ *CAL 133, Flammability Test Procedure for Seating Furniture for Use in Public Occupancies*
- ❑ *NFPA 266, Standard Method of Test for Fire Characteristics of Upholstered Furniture Exposed to Flaming Ignition Source* (withdrawn by NFPA in 2003)

Note

Many furniture manufacturers currently offer *CAL 133*–compliant products. It is required of all members of both the Business and Institutional Furniture Manufacturers Association (BIFMA) and the American Furniture Manufacturers Association (AFMA).

The aim of the test is to eliminate the flashover that occurs in the second phase of a fire. (See the inset titled *Stages of Fire Development* on page 342.) It is a flame resistance test that measures the carbon monoxide, heat generation, smoke, temperature, and weight loss of an entire piece of furniture. The test sample is either an actual upholstered piece of furniture or a full-scale mock-up that simulates the actual construction of the furniture item. As shown in Figure 9.11, a burner is held just above the upholstered seat, ignited for a total of 80 seconds, and then turned off. Combustion is allowed to continue for up to 30 minutes as the exhaust hood located above the test sample collects all the products of combustion. The furniture sample passes the test if the peak heat release and the

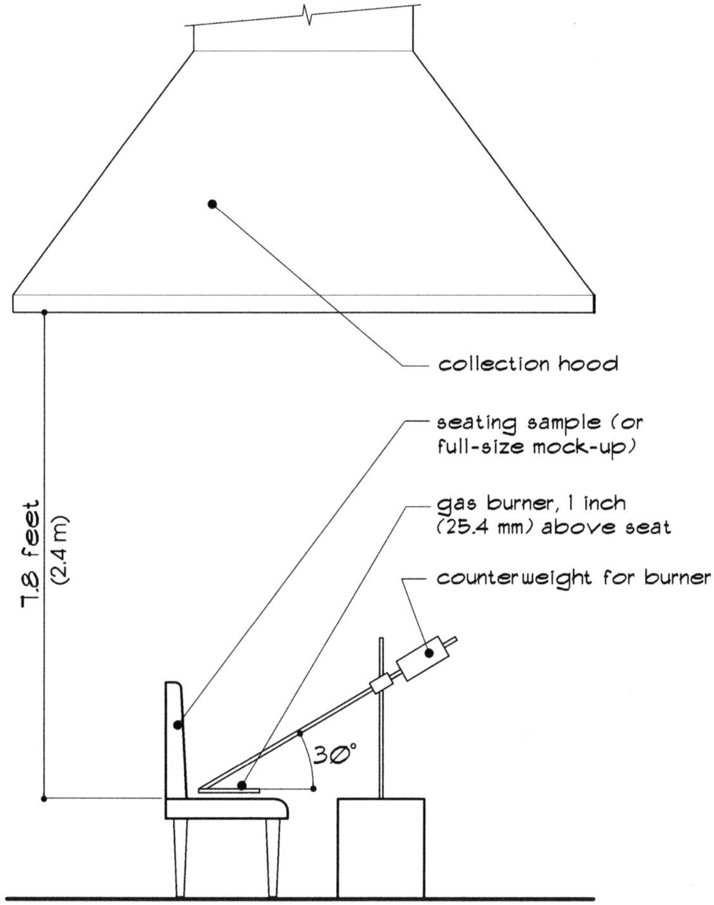

SIDE ELEVATION

Figure 9.11 Upholstered Seating Test Apparatus: Full-Scale

total energy release do not exceed a predetermined level. (Each test is essentially the same, although *CAL 133* uses an alternative size test room and as a few stricter requirements.)

The test was originally developed for furniture used in public spaces in the state of California. It is intended for furniture in public buildings in any area or room that contains 10 or more pieces of seating. This applies to prisons, health care facilities, nursing homes, day care facilities, stadiums, auditoriums, and public assembly areas in hotels and motels.

Since the test's conception, a number of cities and other states have followed California's lead and are also enforcing *CAL 133* or one of the other similar standards. In addition, the newer editions of the *Life Safety Code* reference the ASTM version of the test. Be sure to check with the jurisdiction of your project to determine if it is required. Even if it is not required, you may want to specify *CAL 133* products in certain projects to provide the best protection to the occupants.

With this test, the separate materials that make up the furniture cannot be approved for individual use. The entire piece of furniture must be tested and approved. (See inset titled *Using CAL 133* on page 368.)

Small-Scale Tests

The small-scale tests listed below typically apply to upholstered furniture and mattresses used in commercial, institutional, and high-risk occupancies. The tests measure how quickly upholstered furniture and mattresses will ignite. They also measure the rate of heat release.

- *NFPA 272, Standard Method of Test for Heat and Visible Smoke Release Rates for Upholstered Furniture Components or Composites and Mattresses Using and Oxygen Consumption Calorimeter* (formerly *NFPA 264A)*
- *ASTM E1474, Standard Test Method for Determining the Heat Release Rate of Upholstered Furniture and Mattress Components or Composites Using a Bench Scale Oxygen Consumption Calorimeter*

This test is based on the direct relationship between the heat of combustion and the amount of oxygen present. The NFPA standard gives specific instruction on the preparation of the test sample; however, it references another NFPA standard, *NFPA 271*, for both the type of test apparatus to be used and the specifics of the test procedure. The test sample consists of various components, including the fabric and padding material of the proposed upholstered item plus any layers in between such as liners, polyester fiber, and other fillers. These are assembled into a small finish sample in the shape of a small block. After it is placed in the test apparatus as shown in Figure 9.12, it is first exposed to a radiant heat source and then to a spark ignition source. After a sustained flame occurs, the igniter is turned off and the duct system above the sample collects data for a specified time period. The test assesses and ranks the ignitability, heat release, smoke obscuration, mass loss, and toxicity of the sample being tested.

Although this standard tests only a portion of a piece of furniture or mattress, the data can be useful in predicting the performance of a full piece of furniture. However, because the results can be greatly affected by the actual configuration of the upholstered piece of furniture, it is typically better to use a large-scale furniture test for the most reliable results.

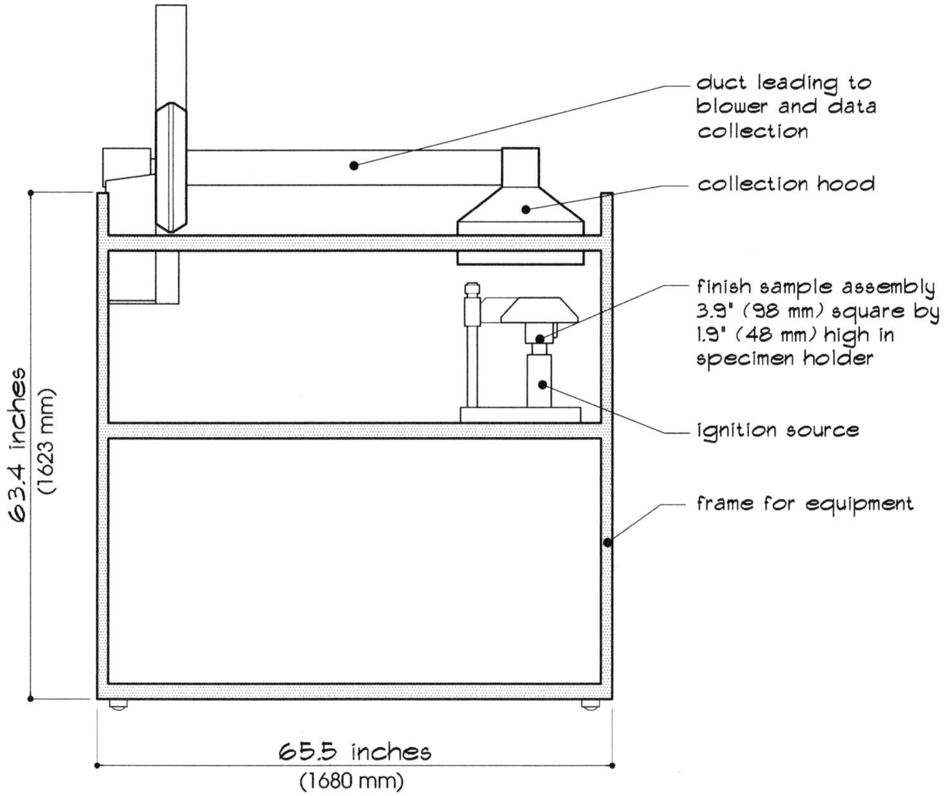

Figure 9.12 Upholstered Seating Test Apparatus: Small-Scale

Mattress Test

Although mattresses can be tested using the small-scale tests mentioned in the previous section, there are other tests that apply only to mattresses. These include the following. (Note that the last two tests were withdrawn in 2003 and are no longer being published; however, a jurisdiction may still require their use.)

- ❑ *ASTM E1590, Standard Test Method for Fire Testing of Mattresses*
- ❑ *CAL 129 (or California Technical Bulletin 129), Flammability Test Procedure for Mattresses Used in Public Buildings*
- ❑ *DOC FF4-72 (or CFR 1632), Standard for Flammability of Mattresses*
- ❑ *NFPA 267, Standard Method of Test for Fire Characteristics of Mattresses and Bedding Assemblies Exposed to Flaming Ignition Source* (withdrawn by NFPA in 2003)
- ❑ *UL 1895, Standard for Fire Test of Mattresses* (withdrawn by UL in 2003)

Note

All mattresses sold and used in the U.S. must pass the federal test *DOC FF4-72*. In addition, mattresses used in certain commercial facilities must also pass stricter tests.

The first two tests are used to determine the heat release, smoke density, generation of toxic gases (carbon monoxide), and weight loss that occur when an individual mattress or a mattress with its foundation (i.e., box spring) is exposed to a flame. This test method uses a full-scale mattress and applies specifically to bedding used in public occupancies, such as hotels, dormitories, hospitals, and jails. (It is not intended for use in the evaluation of residential mattresses.)

To conduct the test, the mattress or assembly is placed on a frame with an exhaust hood above, similar to Figure 9.11. However, instead of the gas burner being placed on top of the mattress, a T-shaped gas burner is positioned to the side and slightly below at the centerline of the test sample. The exhaust hood collects all the products of combustion during the test and for up to 30 minutes after the flame is removed. The result of the pass/fail test is based on the peak heat and energy release. (The *CAL 129* test has slightly different requirements.)

The third test listed, *DOC FF4-72*, is required by the federal government and is applicable to mattresses used in single-family dwellings as well as commercial projects. It is a pass/fail test that measures the char size created when exposed to a lit cigarette, similar to the *Smolder-Resistant Test* discussed earlier in this chapter. It is required for most types of mattresses, as well as mattress pads sold in the United States.

Note

In the future, California may require another mattress test titled *CAL TB 603,* which would be stricter than *NFPA 272* and *CAL TB 129.*

Now that you have a better understanding of the various finish and furniture standards, you can see why a variety of tests are required. The required test for a finish depends on the application of the finish. For example, the same fabric will need a different test or more than one test, depending on whether it is used as a drapery, an upholstery, or a wallcovering. Furniture items have their own tests. The type of test required is often dependent on where it will be used. For example, mattresses used in a hotel must pass a more stringent test than the *DOC FF4-72,* which is required for all mattresses. (See Figure 9.2.) A variety of finishes and furniture and the most common type of tests required for each are shown in Figure 9.13. However, a jurisdiction may require an additional test in some cases. If you are working with a new type of finish or using a finish in an unusual application, be sure to check with the local code official.

Certain jurisdictions may require other tests not discussed above for both finishes and furniture. Typically, they will be similar to one of the tests described but have a different standard number or name. It could be a newer test as well. For example, the state of California continues to develop its own state finish and furniture standards. In addition, industry standards continue to be developed as concerns for other safety issues are identified. The government, standards organizations, and industry representatives must consider if new regulations are warranted. Often their decisions are based on actual occurrences that cause unreasonable risk of death, injury, or significant property loss.

Note

Government regulations permit patients to bring their own furniture to a nursing home even though the codes require fire-tested furniture and mattresses when furnished as new by the nursing home in nonsprinklered buildings.

FINISH CATEGORY	FINISH EXAMPLES	TYPICAL TEST REQUIRED
CEILING TREATMENTS	Ceiling Tiles Fabric Coverings Vinyl Coverings Special Finishes	Steiner Tunnel Test Room Corner Test
WALL COVERINGS	Vinyl Wallcoverings Fabric Wallcoverings Expanded Vinyl Wallcoverings Wood Paneling Wood Veneers	Steiner Tunnel Test Room Corner Test
FLOOR COVERINGS [1]	Carpets Rugs Carpet Padding Hard Surface Flooring Resilient Flooring	Pill Test Radiant Panel Test
WINDOW TREATMENTS AND VERTICAL HANGINGS [1]	Draperies Liners Blinds Wood Shutters Wall Hangings Acoustical Fabrics Panel Fabrics	Vertical Flame Test
TRIM AND DECORATIVE MATERIALS [2]	Decorative Moldings Wainscoting Chair Rails Picture Rails Baseboards	Steiner Tunnel Test Room Corner Test
UPHOLSTERIES	Fabrics Vinyls Battings Welt Cords Foams Interliners Fillings	Steiner Tunnel Test Smolder Resistance Test Smoke Density Test
FURNITURE	Seating Panel Systems Mattresses	Smolder Resistance Test Upholstered Seating Test Mattress Test

NOTES:

1. Some finish applications may require an additional test as required by a jurisdiction.
2. If all or part of a finish consists of plastic, it might also need to pass UL 1975 for foam plastics or ASTM D2843 for light transmitting plastics.
3. Any of the finish or furniture applications listed above may also require a toxicity test.

Figure 9.13 Typical Regulated Finishes and Required Tests

USING CAL 133

Whether or not *CAL 133* or one of the other related standards is required in your jurisdiction, you may want to specify *CAL 133*-tested products whenever possible. Furniture testing is becoming more accepted and enforced throughout the country. As laws and standards are getting stricter, there are more areas of liability for the designer. (Refer to the section on Documentation and Liability in Chapter 10.) Here are some other issues to consider:

- ❑ Selecting a special fabric or "C.O.M." (customer's own material) will change the *CAL 133* test results for a piece of furniture. The cost of retesting by the manufacturer may be passed on to you. The lead time or length of production may also be extended.
- ❑ You may have the option of specifying a fire block liner to make a piece of furniture *CAL 133* compliant. Fire block liners are often used between the foam and upholstery instead of using a flame-retardant foam. Other items such as fire-retardant thread might also need to be considered. You must work with the manufacturer and with the requirements of the test standards.
- ❑ Buildings with sprinklers are not always required to have *CAL 133* tested furniture. However, should a fire occur, the lack of tested furniture can become an issue.
- ❑ Be aware that specifying custom furniture, as well as having furniture reupholstered, can be a problem. Unless you build a mock-up and have it tested, there is no way a one-of-a-kind piece of furniture can be tested under *CAL 133*. It ruins the piece being tested.
- ❑ As with all other tested finishes and furniture, how a piece of furniture is cleaned and maintained affects its rating. As the designer you should be giving the appropriate maintenance information to your clients so that furniture is maintained to the manufacturer's specifications.

USING THE CODES

Note

Except for a general note in Chapter 17 of the *ICCPC*, the performance codes do not discuss alternate options for finishes and furniture.

As mentioned earlier, each of the building codes, the fire codes, and the *Life Safety Code* (*LSC*) have a chapter or section on interior finishes. Many of the standards and tests described in the last section are required by one or more of the codes. These will be listed within the text of each code either in the finish chapters, the various occupancy chapters, or in other areas. For example, each building code also has chapters on glazing and plastics that you may need to reference. (Also see inset titled *Plastic Finishes* on page 388.) The NFPA codes will have additional requirements in their occupancy chapters. You may need to look in multiple locations to see which standard is required, based on the type of finish or furniture you are using and where it will be located in a building. Stricter requirements may also be required for certain occupancies or building types. If you are working in a jurisdiction that requires more than one of these code publications, you will need to compare the requirements to make sure you are using the most restrictive ones—especially since many jurisdictions use both a building code and the *LSC*.

Each finish chapter in the building code and the *LSC* also includes an interior finish table that specifies required finishes for certain means of egress and types of buildings. The table is described in more detail below and is followed by an example of how to use it.

The Table

The interior finish table in the building codes and the *LSC* provides the allowable ratings for various finishes. Figure 9.14 shows a copy of the *LSC* Table A.10.2.2, "Interior Finish Classification Limitations." It includes information on wall, ceiling, and floor finishes. (The *NFPA 5000* contains a similar table in its appendix, but it indicates only new occupancies.) The table in the *IBC* is Table 803.5, "Interior Wall and Ceiling Finish Requirements by Occupancy." Unlike the NFPA tables, the table in the *IBC* does not specify floor finishes, since this information is included within its text. In addition, the *IBC* divides the table into sprinklered and nonsprinklered buildings, while the NFPA tables are based on nonsprinklered buildings and use a footnote in the table to cover requirements for sprinklered buildings.

To use the finish tables correctly, you need to be familiar with the five different finish classes and know the occupancy classification or use of the space. There are three classes for wall and ceiling finishes (Classes A, B, and C), which are obtained using the *Steiner Tunnel Tests*, and two separate classes for interior floor finishes (Classes I and II), which are obtained using the *Radiant Panel Tests*. (Refer to section on Standards and Testing earlier in this chapter.) These different classes recognize that when escaping a fire within a building, people must move away from the flames while traveling through the means of egress toward an exit. It is important for the exits to be free of fire and smoke for safety and visibility. Therefore, the assigned classes become stricter as you move toward an exit and are strictest at the exit.

Before using the *LSC* table shown in Figure 9.14 you need to determine both the occupancy classification of the building and whether it is considered "new" or "existing." (This is described in Chapter 2.) Once you know the occupancy, the table lists the finish classes allowed in each area of the building. Each of the codes divides these areas similarly. They consist of exits, exit access corridors, and other rooms or spaces. (Refer to the section on Types of Means of Egress in Chapter 4 on page 115 for a description of each.) For clarification, the *IBC* lists the exit category as "vertical exits and exit passageways."

Note

If you are working on a building in one of the cities or states with its own code, you must check that jurisdiction for further requirements. (Other states are beginning to increase their standards as well.)

Table A.10.2.2 Interior Finish Classification Limitations

Occupancy	Exits	Exit Access Corridors	Other Spaces
Assembly — New			
>300 occupant load	A I or II	A or B I or II	A or B
≤300 occupant load	A I or II	A or B I or II	A, B, or C
Assembly — Existing			
>300 occupant load	A	A or B	A or B
≤300 occupant load	A	A or B	A, B, or C
Educational — New	A I or II	A or B I or II	A or B; C on low partitions†
Educational — Existing	A	A or B	A, B, or C
Day-Care Centers — New	A I or II	A I or II	A or B
Day-Care Centers — Existing	A or B	A or B	A or B
Day-Care Homes — New	A or B I or II	A or B	A, B, or C
Day-Care Homes — Existing	A or B	A, B, or C	A, B, or C
Health Care — New	A	A B on lower portion of corridor wall†	A B in small individual rooms†
Health Care — Existing	A or B	A or B	A or B
Detention and Correctional — New (sprinklers mandatory)	A or B I or II	A or B I or II	A, B, or C
Detention and Correctional — Existing	A or B I or II	A or B I or II	A, B, or C
1- and 2-Family Dwellings, Lodging or Rooming Houses	A, B, or C	A, B, or C	A, B, or C
Hotels and Dormitories — New	A I or II	A or B I or II	A, B, or C
Hotels and Dormitories — Existing	A or B I or II†	A or B I or II†	A, B, or C
Apartment Buildings — New	A I or II	A or B I or II	A, B, or C
Apartment Buildings — Existing	A or B I or II†	A or B I or II†	A, B, or C
Residential, Board and Care — *(See Chapter 32 and Chapter 33)*			
Mercantile — New	A or B I or II	A or B	A or B
Mercantile — Existing Class A or Class B Stores	A or B	A or B	Ceilings — A or B; walls — A, B, or C
Mercantile — Existing Class C Stores	A, B, or C	A, B, or C	A, B, or C
Business and Ambulatory Health Care — New	A or B I or II	A or B	A, B, or C
Business and Ambulatory Health Care — Existing	A or B	A or B	A, B, or C
Industrial	A or B I or II	A, B, or C I or II	A, B, or C
Storage	A or B I or II	A, B, or C I or II	A, B, or C

Notes:
1. Class A interior wall and ceiling finish — flame spread 0–25, (new) smoke developed 0–450.
2. Class B interior wall and ceiling finish — flame spread 26–75, (new) smoke developed 0–450.
3. Class C interior wall and ceiling finish — flame spread 76–200, (new) smoke developed 0–450.
4. Class I interior floor finish — critical radiant flux, not less than 0.45 W/cm^2.
5. Class II interior floor finish — critical radiant flux, not less than 0.22 W/cm^2 but less than 0.45 W/cm^2.
6. Automatic sprinklers — where a complete standard system of automatic sprinklers is installed, interior wall and ceiling finish with flame spread rating not exceeding Class C is permitted to be used in any location where Class B is required and with rating of Class B in any location where Class A is required; similarly, Class II interior floor finish is permitted to be used in any location where Class I is required, and no critical radiant flux rating is required where Class II is required. These provisions do not apply to new detention and correctional occupancies.
7. Exposed portions of structural members complying with the requirements for heavy timber construction are permitted.

†See corresponding chapters for details.

Figure 9.14 *Life Safety Code (LSC)* Table A.10.2.2 Interior Finish Classification Limitations (Reprinted with permission from *NFPA 101®*—2003, *Life Safety Code*, Copyright © 2003, National Fire Protection, Quincy, MA. This reprinted material is not the complete and official position of the NFPA on the referenced subject, which is represented only by the standard in its entirety.)

As you read across the table in Figure 9.14 for a particular occupancy, it will tell you which class of finishes is allowed in each of these areas. Generally, the closer you get to the exterior of a building or exit discharge, the stricter class rating and fire resistance the finish must have. Spaces that are not separated from a corridor, such as reception areas in Business occupancies and waiting areas in Health Care occupancies, would be considered part of the exit access corridor.

Notice in the table that some occupancies have a symbol or footnote following the recorded class. This indicates that the occupancy has further finish restrictions or requirements. Further research will be required in the *LSC* or the building codes under the specified occupancy. The fire codes may also have requirements specific to a certain occupancy. Occupancies and building types that most often have additional finish-related requirements follow, with examples for each.

- ❑ *Assembly:* Fabric of stage curtains, motion picture screens, stage scenery, specifics for assembly seating, storage of personal effects and clothing versus metal lockers, exhibit booths
- ❑ *Educational (and Day Care):* Percentage of artwork/teaching materials attached to walls, storage of personal effects and clothing versus metal lockers
- ❑ *Health Care:* Allowances for finishes below 48 inches (1.2 m) in corridors, fabrics for cubicle curtains, allowable wall decorations, rated upholstered furniture and mattresses, size of soiled linen receptacles
- ❑ *Detentional/Correctional:* Fabric of privacy curtains, allowable wall decorations, waste container specifications, rated upholstered furniture and mattresses (also with regard to vandalism)
- ❑ *Mercantile:* Plastic signage, temporary kiosks, display window allowances
- ❑ *Hotels and Dormitories:* Draperies, mattresses
- ❑ *Board and Care/Nursing Homes:* New upholstered furniture and mattresses
- ❑ *Unusual Structures:* Water-resistant finishes in buildings located in flood zones, finish restrictions in atriums
- ❑ *Hazardous:* Limited use of combustible finishes

The general rule of thumb is that stricter finishes are required in occupancies where the occupants are immobile or have security measures imposed on them that restrict freedom of movement, such as Health Care facilities and Detentional/Correctional facilities, or where occupants are provided with overnight accommodations, such as hotels and dormitories. In contrast, more relaxed requirements are found in Industrial and Storage occupancies where occupants are assumed to be

Note

The *LSC* and the building codes have different requirements for sprinklers and how they affect the use of interior finishes and furnishings. See Chapter 6 and the codes for more information.

Note

Decorative vegetation such as natural cut trees and artificial plants are also regulated by the codes. The *International Fire Code (IFC)* includes requirements for these in its Interior Finish chapter.

alert, mobile, and fewer in number. Certain buildings that have fewer stories and lower occupant loads may also allow fewer restrictions.

Note

Most finish and furniture standards do not apply to one- and two-family dwellings. The exceptions are the *Pill Test* for carpets and rugs and some mattress tests.

Note, also, at the bottom of the table that automatic sprinklers used throughout a building can change the required finish class ratings. The NFPA uses this note to allow a required finish class to be reduced by one rating if there is an approved automatic sprinkler system in a building. For example, if a space in an unsprinklered building normally requires a *Steiner Tunnel Test* Class B, the same space in a sprinklered building would require a Class C finish. As noted above, the *IBC* specifies this information more clearly within the table itself. Therefore, it is important to know if the building you are working on is sprinklered and where the sprinklers are located. (You must make sure the sprinkler system is up to date and meets all the code requirements for an automatic sprinkler system in that jurisdiction before you allow any reduction in a finish class.)

Example

Figure 9.15 is a floor plan of a grade school without a sprinkler system. If you were designing the interiors of this existing school, you would refer to a code table such as the table in Figure 9.14. Under "Educational—Existing" in the occupancy column of this table it tells you the following:

- ❑ Class A wall and ceiling finishes must be used in all exit areas, such as stairwells.
- ❑ Class A or B finishes are allowed in exit access areas, such as corridors.
- ❑ Any of the three classes (A, B, or C) is allowed in all the remaining spaces, such as classrooms, offices, and so on.

However, many grade schools are considered multiple occupancies by the codes because of the gymnasiums, auditoriums, and/or cafeterias typically built with them. If the auditorium in this grade school, for example, was designed for 325 people, the finish requirements for this area would be found in the occupancy column of the table under "Assembly—Existing" in the subcategory ">300 occupant load." The required finish classes are almost the same except, in this case, Class C finishes will not be allowed in the general areas of this assembly space.

If you were selecting wallcoverings, then for this grade school you would have to decide whether to (1) use a higher-rated wallcovering in the auditorium assembly and access areas and then use a Class C wallcovering in the remainder of the school, or (2) upgrade all general area wallcovering in the educational part of the school to a Class B so the wallcoverings in the school would match those of the auditorium. (Class A wall and ceiling finishes will still be required in

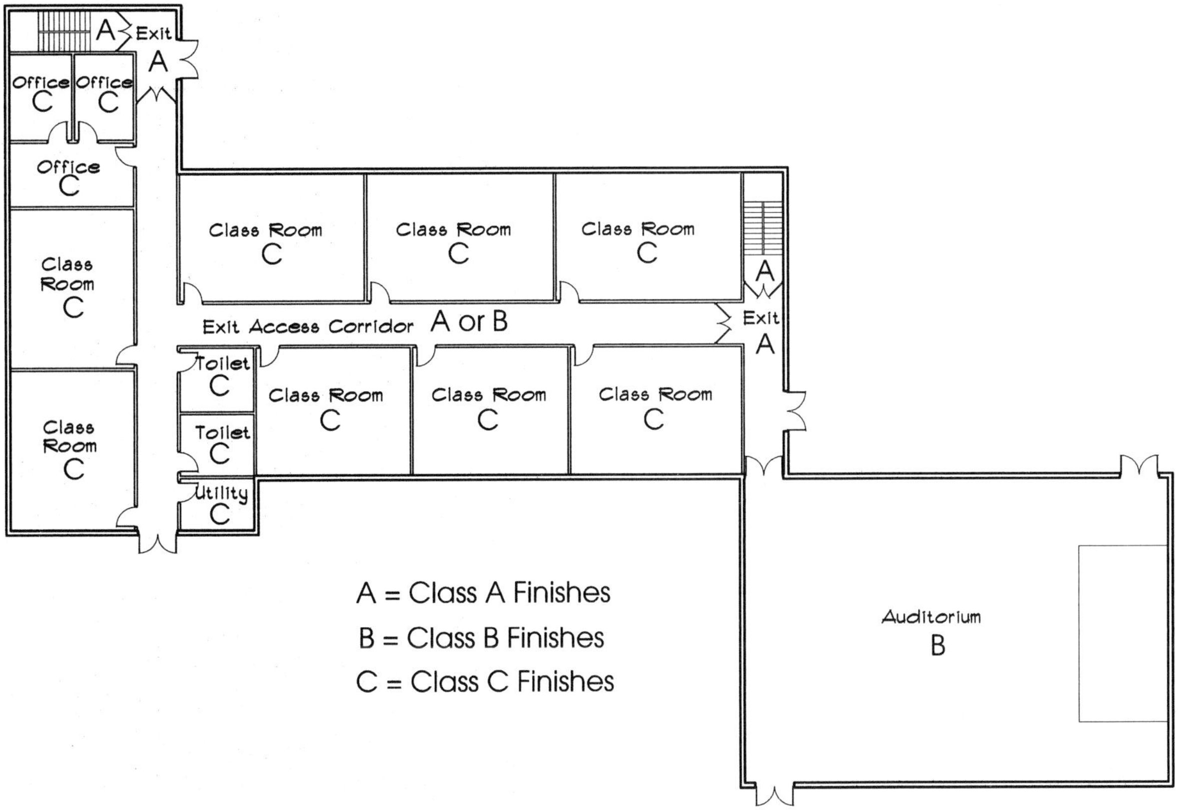

Figure 9.15 Finish Selection Example (High School) (nonsprinklered building)

the exit areas.) The final decision may be determined by cost or aesthetics, but in either case the code requirements must be met.

In the previous example, the table did not specify a particular class of floor finish anywhere in the school. However, let's say you are designing the interior of a new day care center. For this building type, the table indicates that a Type I or II floor finish is required in exits and exit access corridors. Therefore, you must use floor coverings that have been tested using one of the standard flooring *Radiant Panel Tests.* (See Figure 9.2.) When specifying finishes, you also need to be careful if one building or space is used for multiple functions. For example, it is common for day care centers to be located in buildings that share other functions, such as churches or residential homes. You need to make sure you are meeting the requirements of the most restrictive use.

Note

Since 1998, certain federal agencies have been directed to use Environmentally Friendly Products (EFP).

SUSTAINABILITY AND LEED

Sustainability and green design are used to make a space or building more environmentally friendly. Although the codes, standards, and federal regulations address some sustainable issues, such as energy/water efficiency and indoor air quality, they do not address sustainable buildings as a whole. The U.S. Green Building Council (USGBC) developed the Leadership in Energy and Environmental Design (LEED) program to meet this need. LEED provides a framework for assessing building performance and rates buildings on their overall environmental sustainability.

First launched in 2000, LEED was originally developed primarily for the construction of new buildings; there are now additional programs available. (Others are planned for the future.) The more current programs include the following:

- ❑ *LEED-NC:* LEED for New Construction and Major Renovations—overall, a combination of LEED-CS and LEED-CI.
- ❑ *LEED-CS:* LEED for Core and Shell—used for new construction of building core and shell for commercial buildings to include the structure, envelope, and building systems such as central HVAC
- ❑ *LEED-CI:* LEED for Commercial Interiors—addresses the specifics of tenant spaces and the systems within those spaces primarily for commercial and institutional buildings
- ❑ *LEED-EB:* LEED for Existing Buildings—used for the sustainable operation and upgrades of existing buildings that do not require major renovations

Depending on the program selected, buildings are awarded credits under different areas of design. For example, the interiors program (LEED-CI) addresses "areas" such as the selection of sustainable tenant spaces, efficiency of water, energy efficiency of lighting and lighting controls, resource utilization for interior building systems and furnishing, and indoor environmental quality. By surpassing the minimum standards in each category, points are earned, and the total is used to classify a building into one of four levels. Although the point breakdown is different for each program, the levels are the same: Certified, Silver, Gold, and Platinum. These classifications provide a building recognition within the green building sector and possible government incentives.

Specific requirements must be met when specifying energy and water efficient fixtures and equipment. Certain building finishes and furniture can also obtain LEED points for interior projects. The most common examples include:

- ❑ Finishes made with at least some recyclable content and/or rapidly renewable materials.
- ❑ Wood products that are from sustainably harvested forests.
- ❑ Materials and finishes that typically release odorous or potentially irritating contaminants must be specified as low-emitting materials. This includes adhesives, sealants, paints and coatings, carpet, composite wood, and agrifiber products.
- ❑ Furniture that meets low-emitting requirements.

LEED does not certify products. However, some of the credits in the rating system require the use of certified products. Several organizations that do this include Greenguard, Greenseal, and Scientific Certification Systems. Directories of sustainable products are also available to assist with selection and specification. As a designer you can take an USGBC exam to obtain LEED accreditation and obtain the knowledge necessary to initiate the rating system. However, you must be sure that the codes and standards required by a jurisdiction are being met as well.

OBTAINING TEST RESULTS

Some of the standards and tests described earlier in this chapter are specifically referenced and are therefore required by the code. Others are industry standards that you must be familiar with so that you know when to reference and use them. For each test standard used, you need to know if the test results in a pass/fail, a specific class rating, or a ranking. If you refer back to Figure 9.2, this information is shown for each type of test. For example, the *Radiant Panel Test* is a ranked test, and you found out earlier that it results in a Class I or a Class II. The manufacturer tests its products using these standards and provides the appropriate test results for each item. You then compare these ratings to what is required by the codes. (When selecting finishes and furniture, you need to request this information if it is not clearly provided by the manufacturer.)

Note

As the designer, it is important that you keep abreast of the most current testing and code requirements, even if a jurisdiction does not require them.

The important thing to remember is that most manufacturers typically test their products before putting them on the market. Manufacturers realize that their finishes and furnishings must meet code requirements if you are going to specify them. To use these products, it is crucial for you to know how to find and obtain the required test results.

Pretested Finishes and Furniture

Many manufacturers either list the test results on their samples and products or provide the information upon request. (See inset titled *Testing Agencies* in Chapter 1 on page 34.) Some examples are the written information on the back of carpet books and on cards attached to fabric samples. You can find similar labels and information on most wallcoverings, floor coverings, ceiling coverings, and other finishes. Even certain furniture must be labeled with the required tests.

Figure 9.16 shows labels from the back of two different fabric samples made by KnollTextiles. Along with other necessary information, each KnollTextiles label indicates the standard tests the fabric has passed. If you refer to Sample A in Figure 9.16, you are able to determine immediately which tests the fabric passed. Each test standard that this fabric meets is listed under "Flame Retardant Ratings." To determine the type of tests the fabric in Sample B has passed, you need some additional information. Note the five symbols near the bottom of the label. Each of the symbols indicates that the fabric has passed certain industry standards.

Note

Manufacturer representatives can be very helpful in determining technical and code information on their products. Remember, manufacturers need to comply with the industry standards to remain competitive.

These symbols were created by the Association for Contract Textiles (ACT). ACT was founded in 1985 to provide the design industry with information to help designers choose the right products for their projects. Concentrating on the contract interiors market, ACT sets standards for upholstery, wallcoverings, panels

Name	Quadrate
	Hazel Siegel Design ©1990
Style Number	K643/3
Color	Navy
Content	Cotton 52%, Rayon 48%
Width	52 inches
Repeat	3¼ inches horizontal, 3¼ inches vertical

Flame Retardant Rating: ASTM E-84. Class "A" flamespread rating. Passes. UL #723, NFPA #255, ANSI #2.5, California Bulletin #117.

Light Fastness: Meets 40 hour NAFM requirement. AATCC-16A test method.

Durability: Exceeds 70,000 double rubs. NAFM requirement 15,000 double rubs. Wyzenbeek Test Method.

KnollTextiles. A Division of Knoll International. P.O. Box 157
East Greenville, PA 18041 800 523.0346 / 800 343.KNOLL

SAMPLE A

Name	Calligraphy
Style Number	K369/9
Color	Iris
Content	Rayon 51%, Polyester 49%
Width	54 inches
Repeat	5 inches vertical, 6¾ inches horizontal
Primary Use	Upholstery

Flame Retardant Rating: California Technical Bulletin #117 - Section E.

Colorfastness: AATCC-8, Wet Crocking, Class 4.5. Dry Crocking, Class 5.

Lightfastness: AATCC-16E, Class 5 at 40 hours.

Physical Properties: Brush pill ASTM D3511. Breaking strength ASTM D3597-D1682-6. Seam slippage ASTM D3597-D434-75.

Durability: Exceeds 70,000 double rubs Wyzenbeek Method.

Cleaning Code: S

†Copyright: This style is a copyrighted textile design. ©Knoll 1998.
All rights reserved.

KnollTextiles. P.O. Box 157 East Greenville, PA 18041
Knoll 1 800 343-5665

SAMPLE B

Figure 9.16 Typical Labels for a Finish Sample (Reprinted with permission from *KnollTextiles.*)

and upholstered walls, and drapery. A total of five symbols are voluntarily used by a large number of textile manufacturers on their products. The symbols indicate a material's characteristics in flame resistance, colorfastness, physical properties (such as pilling, breaking, and seam slippage), and abrasion. For each symbol, ACT indicates the test(s) or standard(s) that the material must meet in order to bear the symbol.

Although all this information is important to you when specifying finishes, the main symbol that relates directly to the codes is the flame resistance symbol. This symbol is shown in Figure 9.17 along with the type of application for the interior finish and the standards that it meets. It indicates that a fabric has passed

Flame Resistance

Flammability testing determines a fabric's resistance to burning.

APPLICATION	PASSES
Upholstery	California 117 Section E
Direct Glue Wallcoverings	ASTM E 84 (adhered method)
Panels and Upholstered Walls	ASTM E 84 (unadhered method)
Drapery	N.F.P.A. 701 Small Scale

Figure 9.17 Flame Resistance Portion of ACT Textile Performance Guidelines (Reprinted with permission from the Association for Contract Textiles (ACT).)

the *Steiner Tunnel Test* (*ASTM E 84*), the *Vertical Flame Test* (*NFPA 701*), and the *Smolder Resistance Test* (*California 117*). So, if a material's specifications or tag indicates the flame symbol, you automatically know that the material passes those three tests. (Note, however, that it does not tell you which class rating of the *Steiner Tunnel Test* the finish received.)

Referring back to Sample B in Figure 9.16, since the label has a flame symbol, you are now able to tell which tests that fabric has passed. (Under the category "Flame Retardant Ratings," *CAL 117* is listed as well. This is redundant, because the flame symbol already indicates the same requirements.) Once you are familiar with the symbols, it will make selection of flame-resistant materials easier.

Note

Some finishes will list multiple test results on their sample information. This will allow you to use the same finish in more than one type of application.

Upholstered furniture also has an industry system for flammability labeling; however, it is geared more toward prefabricated furnishings typically used in smaller Residential occupancies. It is a voluntary industry standard that was originally created in 1978 by the Upholstered Furniture Action Council (UFAC) to increase the cigarette-ignition resistance of upholstered furniture. It consists of multiple tests for the various components such as the fabric, foam, barrier materials, welting, and decorative materials. (The tests are similar to the *Smolder Resistant Tests* described earlier in this chapter.) If an upholstered piece of furniture passes the required tests, the manufacturer is allowed to attach an approved UFAC hangtag. For many interior projects, especially nonresidential projects, you will typically specify and/or purchase upholstered furniture that is manufactured specifically for a project. In these cases, the UFAC label will not apply, since you will be specifying textiles and furniture that meet other code and industry standards. Still, you should be aware of it and know to look for it, especially when purchasing prefabricated furniture.

Nontested Finishes and Furniture

There will be situations when testing information is not available. For example, you may select a finish that is geared toward use in a private residence where codes are not as strict, or a finish from a smaller manufacturer that makes specialty items and cannot afford to test all of its finishes and/or furniture. In these cases, it is up to you to have the item tested or make sure it is properly treated.

Note

Certain finishes may be required in toilet and bathing facilities, but these are usually specified in the plumbing codes. (See Chapter 7 for more information.)

The standards organizations such as UL, ASTM, and NFPA can help you determine where to get your finishes tested. There are a number of *testing companies* throughout the country that will perform the tests necessary to classify a material. Figure 9.18 provides a list of some of these flame testing agencies. Others can be found by searching the Internet. (Note that some are treatment companies, as well.)

Applied Textiles Lab Services
Better Fabrics Testing Bureau
Building Technologies (Finland)
California Bureau of Home Furnishings and Thermal Insulation
CSTB (France)
Inchape Testing Services
Kiesling-Hess Fabric Service Company, Inc.
Schneider-Banks, Inc.
SGS U.S. Testing Company
Southwest Research Institute
United States Testing Company
VTEC Laboratories, Inc.
Warnock Hersey International, Inc.

Figure 9.18 Sample of Flame Testing Agencies

Note

Other testing agencies can be found by searching websites such as www.astm.org and www.findtesting.com.

However, these flame tests can be costly, because they need to be performed under conditions simulating actual installations. For example, a wallcovering should be tested on the appropriate wall surface with the adhesive that will be used to secure it to the wall, or a carpet with the padding that will be used underneath it. The alternative is to have the finish treated. This is often much more cost effective. Before doing so, though, it is suggested that you make sure the jurisdiction will allow an added fire-retardant coating as a way to meet finish code requirements.

Note

In addition to chemical treatments and applied coatings, some finishes, such as plastics and foam, can be impregnated with a flame retardant during fabrication.

There are several *treatment companies* that will add fire-retardant coatings, also known as flame-resistant finishes, to materials that have not initially passed the required tests. (Ask your local manufacturer representative for locations.) The retardant can be either a surface treatment or a fire-resistant coating applied as a backing. It will delay ignition of a material and slow flame spread, usually without changing the basic nature of the material. (See the inset titled *Flame-Retardant Treatments* on page 379.) It can also lower the smoke development value.

The typical procedure is for you to send your fabric (or any other finish) to the treatment company and tell them which tests your finish must comply with. The treatment company will add the appropriate fire-retardant coating. For example, if you know a fabric wallcovering needs to have a Class B rating, tell the company it must meet the *Steiner Tunnel Test*'s Class B rating. If you are working in one of the stricter jurisdictions, such as the city of Boston, you can tell the testing company that your fabric needs to pass the *Boston Fire Code* or any of the other required codes. In addition, if you are working with sustainable finishes, you need to make sure low-emission treatments are used. (See the inset titled *Sustainability and LEED* on page 374.)

When wood is used as an interior finish, it may need to be treated as well. For example, if you are using wood veneer as a wallcovering in a commercial space, it may need to meet the appropriate class rating of the *Steiner Tunnel Test* as required by the codes. Very few woods qualify as a Class A or B. Most are considered Class C or below. (Some wood species are shown in Figure 9.4.) It depends on the species of wood and the thickness of the wood being used. Typically, thinner woods and veneers have worse ratings than thicker ones. However, some new types of intumescent paints and coatings may be applied to the wood to improve its performance and obtain a better rating. Since this is usually done in the field, you need to be sure you are working with an expert who really knows the product and how to use it. You should also check with a code official to make sure they will accept this type of finish to meet code requirements.

The fire-retardant treatments and coatings can usually upgrade nonclassed finishes and can even improve the performance of some rated materials to a higher class. Upon completion of the work, a treatment company will send you a

Note

Whenever concentrated amounts of furniture are used in a project, be sure to check the design load of the building or space. (See the inset titled *Design Loads*, page 75.) Some examples include library areas, file rooms, and assembly seating.

FLAME-RETARDANT TREATMENTS

A flame-retardant treatment may be necessary for certain items in a project; however, you should be aware that the treatment can sometimes alter the finish or piece of furniture. Below are a number of problems that can occur when a fire retardant is added to a fabric.

- ❑ The fabric may shrink.
- ❑ The hand or feel of the fabric may change, perhaps resulting in stiffening of the fabric.
- ❑ The strength of the fabric may decrease, causing it to tear more easily.
- ❑ If a fabric has a texture, the texture may flatten or become distorted.
- ❑ The treated fabric may give off toxic fumes, especially in the presence of fire.
- ❑ A wet treatment may cause the dye in the fabric to bleed or possibly change or fade in the future.
- ❑ A treated fabric may no longer meet low-emitting standards as required for indoor air quality in sustainable buildings.

If you are concerned about any of these issues, consult the company treating the fabric and, when necessary, submit a sample for testing prior to purchasing or treating the entire amount. The results are often based on the content of the fabric and the type of treatment used. It is also better to have a fabric treated prior to applying it to a surface or piece of furniture in case there are any problems.

Certificate of Flame Resistance, indicating which tests the finish will pass. If this is done in the field, you will need to obtain the appropriate information from the manufacturer and the company that applied the coating.

Note

If a regulation defines a carpet as a floor covering only, do not specify it as a wallcovering without further clarification or testing. (See the discussion of the *Room Corner Test* in this chapter.)

Similar steps must be taken for any finish or furnishing when the necessary test results are not given by the manufacturer. This can include, but is not limited to, any of the finishes listed in Figure 9.13. Remember, however, that it can be very costly to have a piece of upholstered furniture tested. For example, the *CAL 133* test ruins an entire piece of furniture during the test. Therefore, it is only worthwhile to have this test done if you are planning to order a large quantity of the same item. On the other hand, more manufacturers are beginning to test their upholstered furniture with specific fabrics so that they are able to tell you if it will meet certain furniture code requirements. In addition, some manufacturers can modify their upholstered furniture to comply with *CAL 133* by adding or substituting certain materials during fabrication.

ACCESSIBILITY REQUIREMENTS

The accessibility chapter of the building codes, the ADA guidelines, and the ICC/ANSI standard put very few accessibility restrictions on finishes and furniture. The pertaining regulations can be broken down into three main categories: floor finishes, seating, and worksurfaces. However, you also need to consider any operable parts that are part of a finish or furnishing system. Each of these is described below. Be sure to check the codes, the ADA regulations, and any other required accessibility standards for the specifics and to determine the most stringent requirements. (Also see Accessibility Requirements in Chapter 2.)

Accessible Finishes

Note

Directly gluing a carpet to the floor instead of using a pad will help to eliminate thickness problems, as well as future warping or binding of the carpet during wheelchair use.

Currently, floor coverings are the main type of finish that must meet accessibility requirements. Both the ADA guidelines and the ICC/ANSI standard require that the floor surface along accessible routes and in accessible rooms be stable, firm and slip-resistant. Floor finishes, such as carpet and padding, cannot be too thick or too loose, and must be securely fastened at the edges. This is often accomplished in commercial projects by using carpet that is glued directly to the floor (without padding) or by using carpet tiles. Slip-resistant finishes are especially important at ramps and steps. They also become critical when using hard surface flooring such as polished marble and ceramic tile. Even highly polished VCT can be a problem. As a result, some manufacturers now have products that provide a rougher finish coat. Not only do you need to specify the correct finishes, but you may need to specify the correct way to clean or seal the finished product as well.

Accessible floor finish requirements also include beveled transitions or ramps for even slight changes in elevation that can occur between different floor surfaces. For example, as shown in Figure 9.19, there is usually a change in floor level where stone or marble butts up to another type of flooring. Floor changes can also occur at the threshold of a door. The goal is to make sure that wheelchairs have easy access. Typically, the change in vertical height cannot be more than 0.5 inch (13 mm). If the overall height is between 0.25 inch (6.4 mm) and 0.5 inch (13 mm), a bevel must be added with a slope not steeper than a ratio of 1 to 2. This is shown in Section A and Section B in Figure 9.19. If the distance is 0.25 inch (6.4 mm) or less, no bevel is required, as shown in Section C. When a change in elevation is more than 0.5 inch (13 mm), as shown in Section D, the requirements for an accessible ramp must be met. (See the section on Ramps in Chapter 4.)

Note

Since floors in accessible paths of travel must be slip-resistant, polished floor finishes such as marble and VCT can become a problem. Special slip-resistant sealers may need to be used.

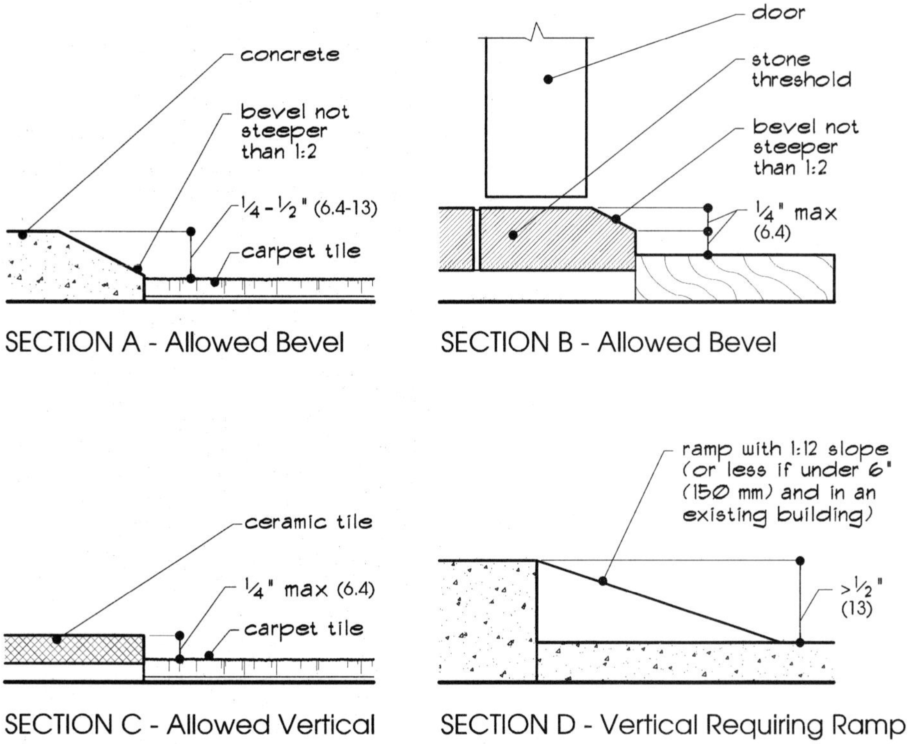

Figure 9.19 Accessible Floor Level Change Examples

Note

The original *ADAAG* temporarily suspended requirements for detectable warnings from 1994 to 2001. These requirements became enforceable again in July 2001 but have been revised once more in the new ADA guidelines.

Note

Although other finishes are not currently regulated by the ADA guidelines, you may want to do additional research on finishes that can be helpful, especially in public spaces. For example, darker baseboards may be helpful in corridors for those who are visually impaired.

Flooring surfaces that create detectable warnings may be required in certain occupancies, as well. A detectable warning consists of a change in floor finish to alert someone with poor vision of an approaching obstacle or change in level. The warnings typically consist of contrasting textures, such as alternate smooth and rough stone, grooved concrete, or rubber flooring with a raised pattern. Although they are mostly required at building exteriors and transportation platforms, they can apply to interiors as well—for example, at an entrance to a hazardous area or at the top of an escalator or exposed stairway. (The original *ADAAG* temporarily suspended its requirement for detectable warnings for several years; however, during this time the requirements were still required by the ICC/ANSI and other accessibility standards. The new ADA guidelines also limit the requirements for detectable warnings.)

Accessible reach ranges must be considered for certain finishes or furnishings when they are located in spaces required to be accessible. For example, the controls to a window blind or drape must be at accessible heights and easy to operate. They must be located between 15 inches and 48 inches (380 mm to 1220 mm) above the floor to allow either a front approach or a side approach. (Clear floor space in front of the controls should also be provided.)

Although other finishes are not regulated by the ADA guidelines or the ICC/ANSI standard, you should be aware of the benefits of using certain finishes for accessibility reasons. For example, using handrails along corridors in Health Care occupancies that contrast with the wall finish makes them easier for people with visual impairments to see. Contrasting baseboards also help. Using finishes this way can be especially helpful in public spaces and occupancies where a wide variety of people use the space.

Accessible Furniture

Accessibility regulations for furniture can be divided into seating and worksurface-related items. Requirements for these can be found in the accessibility chapter of the building codes, the ADA guidelines, and the ICC/ANSI standard, depending on the item used and the type of space. Often, the codes will tell you when an item is required to be accessible and then refer to the ICC/ANSI standard for the specifics. The code requirement is usually based on the building type or occupancy. For example, in a restaurant the building code typically requires that at least five percent of the dining tables be accessible. You would then need to refer to the ICC/ANSI standard to determine what makes a table accessible. Many of these same requirements are also found in the ADA guidelines.

In other projects, it may not always be clear when a piece of furniture needs to be accessible. Spaces designed specifically for public use must meet the requirements of the ADA guidelines, but other areas of a space, such as certain employee work areas, are not necessarily required to be accessible. For example, the furniture in every employee office or workstation is not required to be accessible. In some cases, these items only need to be adjustable and/or replaceable to meet changing needs. Yet, shared spaces in an employee work area (e.g., breakrooms and conference rooms) are usually designed to be accessible to allow for a variety of current and future employee needs.

In addition, when placing furniture you should consider any other required accessibility clearances. For example, a bookcase located across from a desk in an office should not block the clearance required at the door. (See Figure 4.4 in Chapter 4.) Any minimum paths of travel must also be maintained. This includes corridors, aisles, and aisle accessways. This is explained in more detail in Chapter 4. Seating and furniture requirements are discussed below.

Seating

It is not the type of seat that is regulated, but rather the number and location that are provided for wheelchairs. The ADA guidelines generally require seating to be accessible in all public and common use areas. This can be as simple as providing enough space among the other seating in a waiting area to allow a person in a wheelchair to wait. Other public-use areas like restaurants must provide wheelchair access to all their tables. (A few exceptions are allowed.) In addition, the placement of surrounding furniture must allow the required maneuvering areas, even though the furniture may seem movable. (Usually, only a certain percentage of the dining surfaces or tables are required to be accessible.)

When there are fixed seats, the building codes and the ADA guidelines also require a certain number of the seating spaces to be provided for wheelchairs. This is especially important in Assembly occupancies, where the number of wheelchair locations is based on the quantity of total seats provided. For example, a movie theater with fixed stadium seating must allow for special wheelchair locations that are equally dispersed with the other seating and meet a variety of requirements. (See Figure 2.12A in Chapter 2.) Even study carrels in libraries must meet certain accessibility percentage requirements. (Refer to the ADA guidelines, the building codes, and the ICC/ANSI standard for specifics.)

In nonpublic or employee work areas, the ADA guidelines require that accessible-type seating be provided when required for special needs. For example, a person may need a desk chair with special features. In these cases you should work closely with the client to determine what type of seating is required.

Worksurfaces

Accessible worksurface regulations refer to tables and desks as well as counters. Counters can include hotel reception desks, hospital check-in desks, security check desks, teller windows, ticketing counters, and check-out counters in retail stores. The building codes, the ADA guidelines, and the ICC/ANSI standard will specify when worksurfaces and counters in public spaces must be accessible. For example, the IBC requires a sales counter in a retail store to be accessible. If there is more than one, a percentage of the total must be accessible. Similarly, the ADA guidelines require reception desks in public areas (or at least one of them, if there is more than one) to be accessible to the public. In each case a portion of the counter at least 36 inches (915 mm) in length must be no higher than 36 inches (915 mm) above the floor with clear floor space in front so that the public can access the desk. An example is shown on the top of Figure 9.20.

Note, however, that the employee side of the desk does not necessarily need to meet accessible requirements such as reach ranges, clear access spaces, and location of equipment. That decision should be based on a variety of factors and is usually up to the owner of the building and/or space. For example, if there is only one reception desk in a space, you will typically want to make the entire desk accessible should an employee with special needs be hired in the future. You could also design the desk so that the employee side is adjustable. On the other hand, if there are multiple reception desks in the same space, not all of them are required to be fully accessible. The final decision is usually made by the client. Instead, they may need to be made accessible for employees in the future. (Be sure to document these decisions. See Responsibility for Compliance in Appendix A.)

To make the employee side of the desk accessible, you must follow additional requirements as found in the ADA guidelines and the ICC/ANSI standard. The same requirements would apply to other tables and desks that are required to be accessible. Typically, the top of the worksurface must be between 28 and 34 inches (710 and 865 mm) above the floor. There must also be at least a 27-inch (685 mm) high by 30-inch (760 mm) wide by 19-inch (485 mm) deep clear kneespace below the worksurface and a certain amount of clear floor space leading up to the worksurface. Other requirements can be seen in Figure 9.20. Examples are shown for a desk and table, but similar requirements would apply to other types of accessible furniture as well as shared worksurfaces, including items such as library study carrels, restaurant tables, and conference tables. (The same requirements also apply to breakroom and kitchen counters, as explained in Chapter 7.)

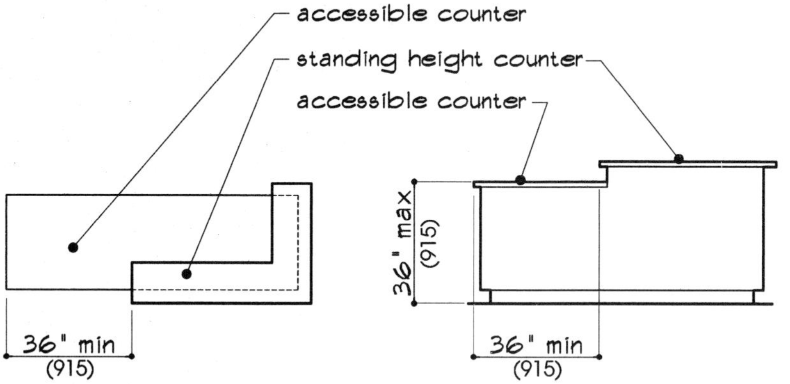

ACCESSIBLE SERVICE COUNTER - Plan View and Elevation

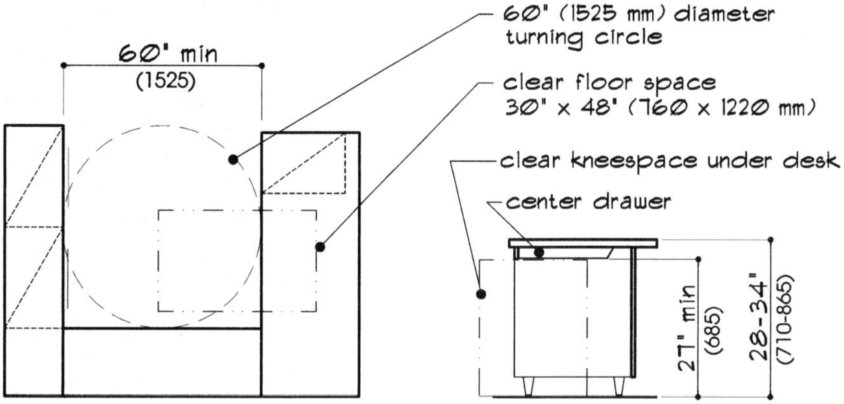

ACCESSIBLE DESK - Plan View and Section

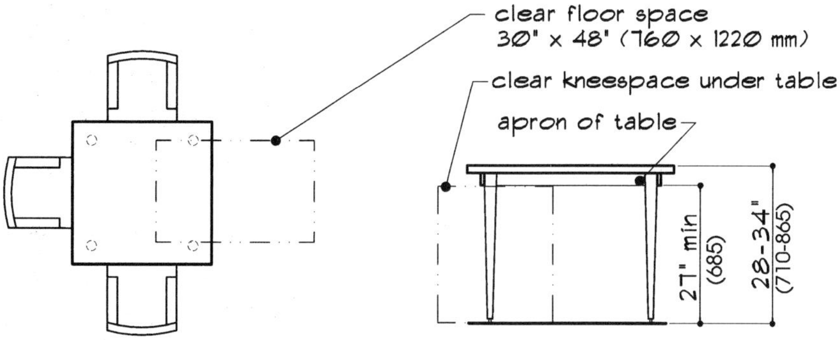

ACCESSIBLE TABLE - Plan View and Section

Figure 9.20 Accessible Furniture Examples

OTHER RESTRICTIONS

This section includes many common code restrictions used by most of the codes mentioned in this chapter as they relate to interior finishes and furnishings. However, you will always run into exceptions and unusual circumstances. For these you should consult the local code official. The importance of knowing what is expected and enforced by the officials in the jurisdiction of your project cannot be stressed enough.

Note

When considering specific code requirements, remember that some jurisdictions are still using older editions of the code publications. These editions are not always as strict as the newer ones.

1. *10 percent rule:* When trims and decorative finishes are kept to a maximum of 10 percent of the wall and ceiling areas of a space, they can usually have a lower rating than what is typically required. Typically, trim is required to meet or exceed Class C of the *Steiner Tunnel Test*; however, if it does not exceed 10 percent, combustible materials are typically allowed. These finishes must be evenly distributed, such as crown molding or wainscoting. If they are concentrated in a specific area, such as a paneled law office, this rule does not apply and additional testing and/or finish treatment is usually required. Noncombustible trims and decorative materials are not limited. (Some occupancies, such as certain Assembly types, may allow a higher percentage before this rule applies.)
2. *Thickness rule:* Any wall or ceiling covering that is more than 0.036 inch (0.90 mm) thick is to be treated as an interior finish. Therefore, thermally thin finishes such as paint and most wallpapers (not vinyl wallcoverings), when applied to noncombustible building materials, do not have to be rated. Various tests have proven that thermally thin finishes do not significantly contribute to the fuel of a fire when they are applied to noncombustible building materials such as gypsum board, brick, and concrete. (This rule does not apply when finishes are continually applied on top of each other.)

Note

Vinyl wallcovering is regulated in all thicknesses because of its burning characteristics. It has a high smoke density.

3. *Furring strips:* When interior finishes are applied to furring strips instead of directly to noncombustible building materials, the furring strips cannot exceed a thickness of 1.75 inches (44 mm). In addition, the intervening spaces between the strips must be filled with a fire-rated material or fire blocked at intervals of not more than 8 feet (2438 mm). Examples could include wood flooring or wall paneling installed over furring strips. These code requirements reduce the chance of fire spread between the finish and the construction assembly behind it. (Note that wood flooring cemented directly to a noncombustible floor assembly is also typically allowed.)
4. *Sprinkler rule:* When a building has an automatic sprinkler system, the codes may allow a lower finish class rating, and finishes without ratings may sometimes replace rated finishes. (Be sure to check with the jurisdiction of

your project. An existing sprinkler system may not meet the most current requirements for an automatic sprinkler system and thus would not allow you to use the lower-rated finishes.)

5. *Means of egress:* All exits and paths of travel to and from the exits must be clear of furnishings, decorations, or other objects. This includes no draperies on or obscuring exit doors and no mirrors on or adjacent to exit doors. In addition, attention must not be drawn away from the exit sign.
6. *Structural building elements:* Certain exposed building structural members are required to be enclosed. For example, steel beams typically are enclosed in gypsum board or sprayed with a fire-retardant coating. Other structural elements such as heavy timber columns, beams, and girders found in construction Type IV are typically allowed to remain exposed, since they occur on specific spacings and do not constitute a continuous surface to allow flame spread. (These architectural regulations are specified by the structural sections of the codes.)

Note

When renovating an existing space you should always remove existing finishes before installing new.

7. *Foam plastics:* Cellular or foam plastic materials typically cannot be used as wall or ceiling finishes unless they comply with the 10 percent rule. In addition, they must meet multiple tests as specified in both the finish chapter and the plastic chapter of the building codes. Typically, if foam plastics are used as a finish, they must not only meet the flame spread requirements of the *Steiner Tunnel Test*, but also meet a large-scale test such as the *Room Corner Test* and be of a certain thickness and density. In addition, the codes may specify that certain foam furnishing, or contents be tested using *UL 1975, Standard for Fire Test for Foamed Plastics Used for Decorative Purposes*. (Foam plastics that do not meet a large-scale test are typically allowed only when the foam plastic is covered by a noncombustible material that acts as a thermal barrier.)
8. *Light-transmitting plastics:* Light-transmitting plastic includes items such as Plexiglas and resin panels that can be used in a variety of applications, such as wall panels, light-diffusing panels, and signage. These are also available with fabrics sandwiched between two layers. Specific requirements for these plastics are found in the plastics chapter of the building codes and include large-scale test requirements as well as size, fastening, and sprinkler requirements. (Plastic veneers are to comply with the finish chapter in each code.) (Also see the inset titled *Plastic Finishes* on page 388.)
9. *Insulation:* Various types of insulation can be used on an interior project. Those used within an assembly, such as a wall assembly, for sound insulation must meet the requirements of the assembly especially as they apply to fire codes. (See Chapter 5.) Other types of insulations, such as those

used as an acoustical panel on the surface of a wall or ceiling, must meet minimum flame spread and smoke density ratings. Materials that meet Class A of the *Steiner Tunnel Test* are often required. Similar requirements apply to the insulation materials used to wrap pipes and ducts, including those used to cover plumbing pipes under accessible sinks. (See Chapter 7.)

10. *Safety glass:* The requirements for glass are covered by the "Glass and Glazing" chapter in the building codes. In addition to fire-rated glazing, glass can be used in a number of other interior applications. Examples include a glass panel in a stair railing, a shower enclosure, a decorative glass sign or feature, and a table top. Based on the location and the thickness and size of the glass, the codes will require the glazing to pass certain tests to meet

PLASTIC FINISHES

In the past, plastic-related codes were geared toward plastics (e.g., insulation) used on the exterior of a building. However, it has become more common for plastics to be used as decorative elements in interior projects, and some code requirements apply to these as well. Essentially, there are two main types of plastics. The first is *thermosetting plastic* that cannot be softened again after having been cured. This includes materials such as polyurethane, melamine, epoxy, and silicone. When exposed to fire, they typically decompose rather than burn and have the potential for creating toxic gases. The second is the type of plastic that can be recycled. It is called *thermoplastic* and is capable of being repeatedly softened by heating and hardened by cooling. It consists of acrylics (Lucite and Plexiglas), acetates, polycarbonate (Lexan), polyester (Mylar), polyurethane, and certain resins, as well as nylon. During a building fire, these typically melt.

The codes divide these various plastics into several different categories for the purpose of providing restrictions:

- ❑ Foam or cellular plastics—such as those used for trim and moldings
- ❑ Pyroxylin plastics (consisting of imitation leather or other materials coated with pyroxylin)—such as those used as upholstery on furniture or wall panels
- ❑ Light-transmitting plastics—such as those used as panels with back lighting for light diffusion
- ❑ Plastic veneers—such as those used on millwork or as decorative panels
- ❑ Plastic signage—especially larger signs such as those used in covered malls

The building codes provide requirements for these plastics in both the finish chapter and the plastic chapter. When using plastics, you will need to reference both chapters—as well as the occupancy chapters and the fire codes, in some cases. The use of plastics may also affect the location of sprinkler heads. For example, additional sprinkler heads are often required where large light-transmitting plastic panels are used.

safety glass requirements. For example, tempered glass is often required. (See section on Glazing in Chapter 5.)

Interior finishes may be further restricted by the occupancy classification of a building. Certain building occupancies require stricter codes and more specific requirements. For example, pyroxylin plastic such as imitation leather is not allowed in Assembly occupancies. These additional requirements are addressed by the building codes, the fire codes, the *LSC*, the ADA guidelines, and the ICC/ANSI standard in specific occupancy sections. (Also see list in Using the Codes section earlier in this chapter.)

Generally, occupancies where the occupants have mobility difficulties have stricter requirements than occupancies with fully mobile occupants. The occupancies that allow overnight provision for multiple occupants are usually the strictest. These include Health Care facilities, Detentional/Correctional facilities, and most Residential occupancies (except single-family homes). For example, hotels must use additionally rated finishes and furnishings such as bedding and draperies.

Note

Although codes for interior finishes are much stricter on commercial projects, they should be considered *equally critical* in residential projects. Deaths occur more often in residential fires.

CHECKLIST

The checklist in Figure 9.21 has been designed to help you with any project that requires finish and/or furniture selection. It can be used for one particular project, or a separate checklist can be used for each space or room within the project. This is helpful if you have a variety of rooms or spaces, each with its own finishes and furnishings. It is also helpful when some rooms or areas have stricter requirements than others. For example, requirements for public areas are often stricter, and typically require finishes and furniture that are different from those of other areas within the project.

The top of the checklist asks you for the project and space name, the occupancy classification of the project (and whether it is new or existing), and the building type. It is important to determine the occupancy and the building type in the beginning, since both are needed to determine which tests are required by the codes. (See Chapter 2 for more information on occupancy classifications.)

The rest of the checklist assists you with finish selection and testing research. The first column lists the most common wall finishes, ceiling finishes, floor coverings, window treatments, and furnishings/furniture. Check the ones that will be used in the space or project so you can narrow down the amount of finishes and furnishings that must be researched, tested, or treated. Blank spaces have been left to fill in items not listed on the checklist.

Finishes and Furniture Checklist

Date:____________

Project Name:____ Space: ____________________

Occupancy (new or existing):____

Type of Space (check one): ______ Exit ______ Exit Access ______ Other Space

REGULATED FINISHES AND FURNISHINGS (check those that apply)	**TEST METHOD REQUIRED** (fill in test name)	**MANUFACTURER AND CATALOG #**	**MANUFACTURER TESTED** (yes or no)	**FINISH TREATMENT** (yes or no)	**DATE COMPLETED**
Wallcoverings __ Vinyl Wallcovering __ Textile Wallcovering __ Expanded Vinyl Wallcovering __ Carpet Wallcovering __ Light-Transmitting Plastics __ Wood Paneling __ Wood Veneers __ Decorative Molding/Trim __ Other:____________					
Ceiling Finishes __ Ceiling Tile __ Textile Ceiling Finish __ Plastic Light Diffusing Panels __ Decorative Ceiling __ Decorative Molding/Trim __ Other:____________					
Floor Coverings __ Carpet (Broadloom) __ Carpet Tile __ Rugs __ Carpet Padding __ Resilient Flooring __ Hardwood Flooring __ Other:____________					
Window Treatments __ Draperies __ Liners __ Blinds __ Wood Shutters __ Other:____________					
Furnishings/Furniture __ Fabric __ Vinyl/Leather __ Batting __ Welt Cord __ Interliners __ Filling __ Seating __ Mattresses __ Plastic Laminates/Veneers __ Other:____________					

NOTES:

1. Refer to codes and standards for specific information. Also check the ADA guidelines and ICC/ANSI standard for accessibility related finish and furniture requirements.
2. Attach all testing verification including copies of manufacturer labels and treatment certificates.

Figure 9.21 Finishes and Furniture Checklist

Once you know the types of finishes and furnishings you will need to specify, use the charts in Figures 9.2 and 9.13 and refer to the codes to determine which tests are required. For example, if you are using direct-glue carpet on the floor, you may need only to verify that it passes the *Pill Test*. In other types of spaces it may require a Class I or Class II rating; if it is being used as a wall finish, the *Room Corner Test* must be verified as well. Use the second column to write down the name of the test required for each finish and furnishing you checked off in the first column. If it is a rated test, include the rating required by the code. (See Figure 9.2 for test names and specific standard numbers.)

Note

Remember that if a manufacturer cannot verify that a furnishing passes the *CAL 133*, there is no way to have it treated. (Refer to inset titled *Using CAL 133*, p. 368, and the discussion preceding it.) You must find furniture that is built according to the *CAL 133* requirements.

You should not start selecting finishes or furniture until you have determined the tests required for each area. Then, as you select and research each finish or piece of furniture, you can compare the product information and labels to the checklist to see if they meet the testing requirements. Indicate the manufacturer and the catalog number of the finish or piece of furniture you select in the third column of the checklist. Use the remaining part of the checklist to indicate either the test results verified by the manufacturer or the name of the treatment company that will treat the finish.

For each finish or furnishing listed, be sure any necessary tests are completed. If required tests are listed on the manufacturer's label or finish book, make a copy of the information. If the manufacturer cannot verify that a finish has passed a required test, you will need to have the finish treated (if allowed by the jurisdiction) and make sure the treatment company sends you a certificate verifying its compliance with the test.

After you have gathered all the testing information and have the required documentation, you should attach it to the checklist and file it with your project files in case this information is required in the future. In addition, check the ADA guidelines and any other required accessibility codes or standards to determine if any special regulations must be met, and document these as well.

CHAPTER 10

CODE OFFICIALS AND THE CODE PROCESS

Each chapter in this book deals with a specific step in the code process, beginning in Chapter 1 with determining the publications required by a code jurisdiction and ending in Chapter 9 with finish and furniture requirements. Throughout each chapter, references are made to code officials, jurisdictions, and the code approval process. This chapter concentrates on the code process as a whole. It introduces you to the different types of code officials and various steps that should be undertaken for a smooth approval of your design. How to properly document the code information is discussed, as well.

As you read this chapter, the important thing to remember is that as the designer it is your responsibility to design the interior of a building in conjunction with the codes, standards, and federal regulations required in that jurisdiction. You must make sure your research of these regulations is thorough and properly recorded in your project drawings and specifications. It is your responsibility to make sure your design meets the intent of the codes. It is the codes official's job to review your drawings and verify their code compliance. Although the code official is there to guide you and answer your questions, it is not the official's responsibility to design the space or to do the research for you. You must learn to apply the various code requirements properly and work in conjunction with the code officials.

Note

There are various types of code consultants who can be used to provide added expertise during code research, especially on large projects.

THE AUTHORITY HAVING JURISDICTION

As you become familiar with the codes, you will notice that the codes often refer to the *Authority Having Jurisdiction*, or *AHJ*. This term is used to indicate the entity that has the authority or right to decide whether a design and construction is compliant with the required codes and to enforce code compliance. In general, it can mean a legally defined area, a specific code department, or an individual code official who has the right to review and approve construction. Together, these entities decide which codes are being enforced, manage the review and approval of the design and construction, and monitor construction within their area to assure that buildings are safe. As the designer, it is important for you to know the roles and responsibilities of the AHJ and know how and when to work with them to assure that a project meets the code requirements. Each type of AHJ is described in more detail in this section.

Code Jurisdictions

The code jurisdiction of a project is determined by the location of the building. A jurisdiction is defined as a geographical area that uses the same codes, standards, and regulations. The specific authority that enforces the code can vary from state to state. Most often they are regulated on a local level, such as a county or city municipality. When a local jurisdiction chooses a code, the code becomes a local law and is enforced by the local code department. (See the section on Code Enforcement on page 397.)

In other cases the state mandates a statewide code that must be followed by each jurisdiction within the state. Sometimes this state code is used in conjunction with other locally adopted codes, or it might apply to buildings in more rural areas that do not have a local code. Typically, the state will at least enforce regulations on state-owned buildings.

Just as each jurisdiction decides which codes are being enforced, it also decides when to change or update the codes. The newest edition of the code may not be the one being enforced. Each jurisdiction can also make amendments to a code that can change the standard code requirements. These modifications may call for more stringent or just different requirements.

It is important to check with the jurisdiction of a project to determine which edition of the codes and standards is being enforced and if there are any addendums you need to follow. In addition, you should confirm which jurisdiction governs your project. You may find that one project falls under the authority of more than one jurisdiction. For example, a building within the city limits may need to follow the requirements of both the city and the state. On the other hand, a rural project might not have a local governing code, so you would need to meet the requirements of the state.

Code Departments

The code department is the local government agency that administers and enforces the codes within a jurisdiction. Some small jurisdictions may have a codes department that consists of only one person or code official, while larger jurisdictions may consist of many different agencies and departments. The administration chapters in the building codes and the *LSC* give basic requirements for the code review and administrative process. However, each code department can modify these requirements to suit the organization of their own department. For example, large code departments may require multiple sets of drawings to be submitted, whereas a small code department may require only one set. These modifications are often included in the local amendments to the enforced code. (See inset titled *The Administration Chapter* on page 397.)

It is important for you to contact the code department that will be reviewing your project to understand how their department works. You will also want to know the roles of the code officials who will be working with you to make sure a project complies with the codes during design and construction. Remember, when the codes use the term AHJ, this will include the code department.

Code Officials

A code official, also known as a building official, is someone who has the authority to administer, interpret, and enforce the provisions of the adopted and/or amended code within a particular jurisdiction. The code official, then, would also be included when the codes refer to the AHJ. However, the term "code official" has been used throughout this book as a general term to describe a broad number of different people and functions.

In reality, the role of a code official can be filled by a variety of people, each with a different job title. The number of code officials will vary by jurisdiction. In smaller jurisdictions one person may have several responsibilities. For example, there may be one person who does multiple types of inspections. In larger jurisdictions there may be several people with the same title grouped into a department, each with his or her area of expertise. Some jurisdictions may also hire a private agency to handle some of the responsibilities. The most common types of code officials are described as follows:

> **Note**
>
> The *Authority Having Jurisdiction,* or AHJ, can be a legally defined area, an organization, a code department, or an individual code official.

- ❑ *Plans Examiner:* A code official who checks the floor plans and construction drawings both in the preliminary stages and the final permit review stage of a project. The plans examiner checks for code and standards compliance. As the designer, you will be working most closely with the plans examiner.
- ❑ *Building Inspector:* A code official who visits the project job site after a permit is issued to make sure all construction complies with the codes as specified in the construction drawings and in the code publications. (See section on Construction and Inspection Process later in this chapter.)

- *Fire Marshal:* A code official who typically represents the local fire department. A fire marshal checks the drawings in conjunction with the plans examiner during both the preliminary stages and the final permit plan review, checking the drawings for fire code and means of egress compliance. The fire marshal also typically reviews the project job site upon completion of construction.

With the growing complexity of the building industry, the role of the code official has increased in scope. Most jurisdictions require code officials to have specific levels of experience in the design or construction industry. The administration chapter in each building code sets experience standards, but each jurisdiction can modify this based on the qualifications they think are important. Code officials must understand how the building's structural system, means of egress, detection and suppression systems, and similar aspects work together to conform to the code requirements to protect the occupants of the space or building. They must also understand the actual building process. (See inset titled *The Administration Chapter* on page 397.)

Like the model codes, the International Code Council (ICC) has developed a certification process for code officials. This process requires knowledge of specific areas of construction and code compliance in order to qualify for assigned titles. A "Certified Building Official" (CBO) has passed examinations on technology, legal issues, and code enforcement management. To allow specialization in code enforcement, the ICC has also developed separate certifications, such as "Code Officials" for building, electrical, plumbing, mechanical, housing, and accessibility areas of construction. This certification requires a CBO to be experienced with inspections in their specific area of expertise, such as electrical, for both residential and commercial buildings. CBOs must also have experience doing plan reviews for various types of projects. NFPA has set up similar certification programs to coordinate with their codes. In some jurisdictions, this type of certification has become mandatory to be employed as a code official.

With the introduction of new materials and new types of integrated systems, the job of the building official is requiring a new level of design knowledge. Like other professionals involved with the design and construction industry, building officials attend continuing-education seminars to keep up with changes in the codes and technology. It is becoming more and more important for the code official to be involved early in the design process in order to develop the best design. This will become increasingly true with the use of performance codes, since the code official will have to agree that the design satisfies the performance description. There will be situations in which neither the designer nor the code official will be able to rely on the straightforward approach of the prescriptive code for a particular design solution. (See inset titled *Using Performance Codes* on page 19.)

THE ADMINISTRATION CHAPTER

The first chapter in the building codes is the "Administration" chapter. This chapter discusses the qualifications and responsibilities of the code official and the code process. It also includes requirements you need to meet as the designer. Here is a list of typical requirements included in the administrative chapter:

- ❑ Scope of work requiring code compliance
- ❑ Duties and powers of the code official and the code department
- ❑ Fees and permits
- ❑ Construction documents requirements
- ❑ Inspections
- ❑ Certificate of occupancy
- ❑ Service utilities
- ❑ Means of appeals
- ❑ Violations
- ❑ Stop work order

The "Administration" chapter of the building codes is the one that is most often modified by the local jurisdictions.

CODE ENFORCEMENT

As discussed in the previous section, each jurisdiction adopts its own set of codes. In addition to the codes required by the local jurisdiction, a single project can be under the authority of several local agencies. These agencies develop and enforce their own regulations on certain project types. Examples include schools, day cares, restaurants, and hospitals. These regulations may be enforced on a state, county, or city level. For example, the local health department will usually have specific requirements that must be met for restaurants. Other building types, such as hospitals, may need to comply with other state and local regulations. Some zoning and historical ordinances can also affect an interior project. Depending on the project, you may need to incorporate the requirements of these agencies in addition to the codes and standards. It may be helpful to have a review with a representative from the required agencies before finalizing a design. And in some cases, a site visit after construction is required for approval.

Note

To locate the proper jurisdiction, you may have to call the nearest city hall with the exact location of the project.

The enforcement of federal laws and regulations such as the ADA is a little more complicated. Each federal agency enforces its regulations in federal buildings. However, for other types of projects that are not federally owned or funded, there is no clear enforcement procedure. Although these federal laws are mandatory, individual federal agencies do not have the manpower to enforce the laws in every jurisdiction. And, unless they are adopted as part of the local code (and so become enforceable locally), the code jurisdictions do not review or enforce them either. Therefore, many state and local jurisdictions formally adopt the federal regulations or create laws that are stricter than the federal requirements so that they can legally enforce them. For example, many states have created their own energy-efficiency laws that meet or exceed federal requirements. In other instances, the federal government will certify a comparable document. For example, a jurisdiction can create a modified version of the ADA guidelines and have it certified by the Department of Justice (DOJ). This creates a document that they can use for local enforcement. (Because this is a long and complicated process, not many jurisdictions have done it.) This means that in most cases, there is no review or enforcement process at the local level for the ADA. Even though a local jurisdiction does not enforce the ADA or other federal laws, it is still your responsibility as the designer to know what the laws are and to incorporate them into your projects. (See Appendix A for more information on the ADA.)

Note

Code officials review and inspect projects using all codes and standards required by that jurisdiction. However, they do not review or inspect projects according to federal regulations such as the ADA guidelines.

THE CODE PROCESS

Although the process for code approval may change slightly, depending on the type of project and the jurisdiction in which you are working, the ultimate goal is to meet all the code requirements so that a building permit can be obtained. Most interior projects, unless they consist of minor repairs or minimal finish or furniture selection, cannot be constructed without a permit.

To obtain a permit with the least amount of delay or difficulty, you should use the process encouraged by the code officials in the jurisdiction of the project. Learn to work with the code officials as you move through the code process explained in this section. Several steps are done directly by the designer, which include the initial project research, preliminary review, and any appeals that may be necessary. The other steps in the process directly affect the construction contractor and include the permit approval, the inspection process, and the final approval, which allows the space to be occupied. Each step is shown in Figure 10.1. Refer to the figure as the various items are explained.

Note

A jurisdiction may allow some interior projects to be built without stamped and sealed drawings. The decision is usually based on a building's total area and number of stories.

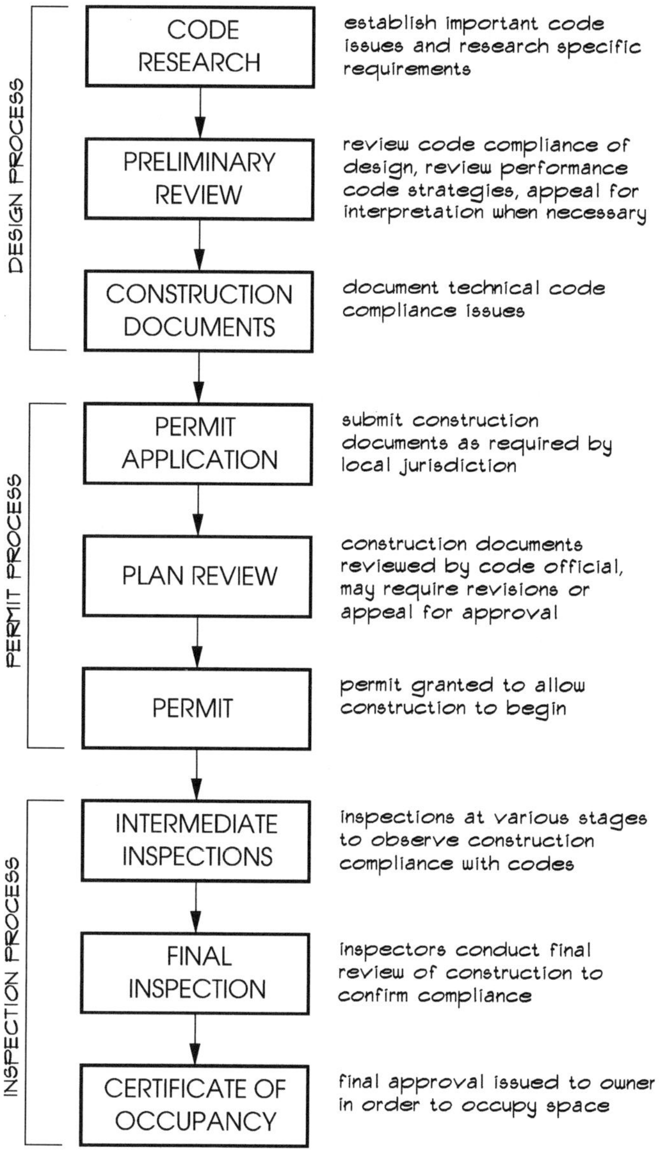

Figure 10.1 Typical Steps in the Code Process

Code Research

In order to do your research, you must determine the jurisdiction of the project. Remember, the jurisdiction may be a township, city, county, or state. And, in some cases, state and local codes may both apply. (See sections on Code Jurisdictions and Code Enforcement earlier in this chapter.) You will need to call or visit the local codes department and ask them which codes and standards are enforced. Since each jurisdiction can make amendments, deletions, and additions that alter the original code publication, you need to know what these changes are. For example, a jurisdiction that adopts the *International Building Code (IBC)* may have some local ordinances that override specific *IBC* requirements. You should also ask if any other local agency regulations or ordinances will affect the project. For example, local health codes usually apply to projects that include food preparation. You are also responsible for knowing which federal regulations apply to a project. (See section on Federal Regulations in Chapter 1.)

Note

Some projects may require the code official(s) to walk through the existing building at the beginning of a project to determine code compliance. This is especially important in older buildings that require updating. (See Appendix C.)

In addition, you will need to know which edition of the codes is being used and how often new editions are adopted. As described in Chapter 1, most codes and standards have major updates every two or three years and minor changes on a yearly basis. However, jurisdictions are not required to use the updates. Since each jurisdiction adopts these changes on a different schedule, it is important to know when any changes occur. (Some jurisdictions have mailing lists and provide notices when updates occur.)

As you are determining the code publications and the editions required, you should also determine what is required by the jurisdiction to obtain a final project approval. For example, depending on the size and the scope of a project, specific floor plans and specifications may be required. For interior projects, the required construction documents typically include stamped construction drawings indicating demolition plans, partition plans, reflected ceiling plans, and power and communication plans, as well as required elevations, details, and schedules. The specifications can be part of the drawings or included as a separate document. On certain projects, specific details, stamped engineering drawings, and engineering calculations may be required as well. (See section on Construction Documents later in this chapter.)

Note

Many code departments sell copies of the code publications they have adopted. These copies should indicate all required amendments. (See Appendix E for additional sources.)

Most jurisdictions have strict requirements as to who can design a project and what types of drawings are required for an interior project. For example, many drawings must be stamped by a licensed architect and/or engineer registered within the state of the project. In some jurisdictions, registered interior designers are allowed to stamp drawings as well. Other projects may not require a professional stamp. Projects that require a professional stamp are usually determined by the use, size, and scope of the work being done. If a professional stamp is required, the design and documentation must be done under the direct supervision of the registered professional. To meet these various requirements, many firms employ a variety of design professionals. As an individual you may have to collaborate with others to complete a project.

After you have determined which codes and standards apply to your project, you should research the specific requirements that will apply, beginning with the occupancy classification. For example, if you are renovating an existing elementary school, you would concentrate on the code requirements for Educational occupancies. But, if the project includes renovation of the cafeteria, you may need to review the requirements for Assembly as well. You should do this before you start designing the project. A majority of the research should be done in the programming stage of the design process at the same time that you are collecting client and building information. The code requirements can then be incorporated into the design from the beginning, which avoids having to redesign to meet the code requirements later. It may be helpful to write down or copy the main sections of the codes that apply to the project and keep them with the project files. (Refer to the section on Documentation and Liability later in this chapter.) This documentation, along with the use of the checklists provided in this book, will help you remember the code issues that affect the design of the project. This can be especially useful if questions arise later.

Later in the design process you may be required to do additional research as well. For example, once you begin laying out office furniture systems, you may need to do additional research for minimum aisle widths and accessible clearances. As you become more familiar with the codes, you may not have to check every specific requirement; however, keep in mind that codes change and the requirements for different project types can be different. For example, the minimum corridor width is typically 44 inches (1118 mm), but for Educational uses the minimum corridor is 72 inches (1829 mm) wide. Doing proper research and knowing the codes that apply to a project during design is an important part of getting a project approved by the code official.

Preliminary Review

Most code jurisdictions have some form of preliminary plan review procedure that can occur in the early stages of a project. Although you might not require a preliminary review on all projects, for some projects this might be crucial. It may be as informal as faxing a floor plan indicating the pertinent code issues or as formal as a meeting with a number of code officials. When arranging a preliminary review meeting, you should request the plans examiner, the fire marshal, and any other necessary official to be present so all code concerns can be addressed at once.

Note

If two required codes have conflicting requirements, usually the most restrictive requirement applies. However, the code official has the authority to make the final decision.

As shown in Figure 10.1, the plan review should occur in the preliminary stages of the design process, typically during the schematic design phase. You should have completed a majority of your code research and be prepared to discuss and clarify specific code issues. The preliminary floor plans should be to scale and have enough detail to discuss the major code topics. For example, the overall size of the building or space should be provided and the division of occupancies and the arrangement of exits should be indicated. If you are designing only a portion of a building, be sure to have a location plan that indicates the layout of the remaining portions of the floor or building.

The purpose of the preliminary review meeting is to review the major code issues and to determine if the conclusions drawn from your research are valid. For example, discuss any code conflicts you may have found in your research. Also ask the code officials if they have any concerns with your design and if they foresee any potential problems. Likewise, if you know there is a situation that cannot easily meet the code requirements, be prepared with your own alternative solutions. It is not wise to rely on code officials to solve the problem, because they may come up with a solution that meets the intention of the code but that does not fit with your design intentions.

Note

Having an approval signature from a code review meeting may become important during the permit approval process as well as the inspection process.

During the meeting, take notes so that you can make the necessary changes to the design. It is also important to prepare a summary of the meeting for your records. After the meeting you should send a copy of the summary to each attending code official and ask him or her either to sign off on the summary, indicating acceptance, or to send you a written confirmation of the summary. On smaller projects you may be able to make the necessary corrections and notations directly on the preliminary floor plan and ask the code officials to sign their approval on it. In either case, it is important to get all approvals and permissions in writing, since each code official can have a different interpretation of the same code, as discussed in the following section on the appeals process.

In some cases, you may have to obtain a review by sending a project to the actual code organization that publishes the code being enforced in that jurisdiction. The ICC, for example, will review specific issues of a project—such as fire protection, sprinklers and standpipes, means of egress, lighting and ventilation, and other similar issues. The project is reviewed to see if it is in compliance with each of the codes published by that code organization, including building, mechanical, electrical, and plumbing. This type of service is offered to design professionals and the state and local jurisdictions enforcing the codes. There is usually a fee for this type of review, although if you are a member of a code organization, your membership may include an interpretation of a requirement. Most of the time a review is best handled through the local code officials, but a more formal review service may help identify particular design problem areas. (Jurisdictions may use these services when workloads cause a delay in the permitting process.) Third-party code consultants who specialize in code review are also available.

Note

Most code officials are more than happy to meet with you, but not every jurisdiction endorses the pre-approval process described in this section. You should request a meeting whenever you find it necessary to clarify code issues after doing your own code research.

If a design requires the use of a performance code instead of certain prescriptive requirements, then a preliminary review with the code official is necessary and not optional. In fact, a concept report may need to be submitted before you begin the design, because the code official must agree to the use of the performance criteria in the particular building or space. When using performance codes, the code official must also agree that the design satisfies the code intent before the completion of the construction documents. If this process is not done correctly and the code official rejects the design, a lot of time, money, and energy will be wasted.

Formal reviews for compliance with federal regulations are not normally done for most projects. Although the DOJ will review projects for compliance, it is a lengthy process and usually considered only for very large or public projects. Some federal agencies, such as the ADA Access Board, may provide an interpretation when requested. However, these interpretations are not an official approval. In most cases, you must use your best judgment as to whether a design complies with the federal regulation.

Note

If you are a member of a code organization, your membership often allows you to get an interpretation of a specific code requirement from the organization's technical department.

As the designer it is your responsibility to know the codes, standards, and federal regulations and to plan your design accordingly. However, it is important to clarify all issues at the beginning of a project, especially code issues. The preliminary code review helps you to do this. In addition, it typically results in a smoother permit approval. (See the section on the Permit Process later in this chapter.) Not only will you have incorporated the necessary requirements into your drawings, but also the code officials will be familiar with the project before the plans are brought in for review for the construction permit.

Appeals Process

All codes, standards, and regulations are written for the safety and protection of the occupant. However, they are not always as specific as you would like them to be. Often a code provision can have more than one interpretation. Usually these discrepancies can be settled with the help of a code official. Code officials undergo training and attend code review classes and, therefore, can usually provide additional insight to a specific code provision. They also have access to the expertise of other officials.

Note

Interpretations of the codes, standards, or federal regulations can usually be obtained from the organizations that publish them. However, this can be time-consuming, and there is no guarantee that the local code official will agree with the interpretation.

However, you may not always agree with the code official's interpretation. For example, there may be an alternative method of achieving the same code compliance. This will be even truer as more performance codes are adopted. (See inset titled *Using Performance Codes* on page 19.) In addition, no code will be able to address every design situation. You may be working in an older building where making changes can be cost-prohibitive, or you may want to use a new building material or finish material that is not covered by the code. In most cases it is to your benefit to try to work out a solution with the code official. If a mutual solution cannot be reached or an allowed performance criteria cannot be found, you may decide to use the appeals process.

Note

Often a good source for justifying an appeal is a code publication used by another jurisdiction. For example, you may be able to find an alternative code or method in the *Life Safety Code (LSC)*.

The appeals process is a formal request made in writing either through a code official or directly to a Board of Appeals. Generally, each of the codes designates specific reasons why an appeal can be made. The codes also regulate who can make the appeal: usually the owner or a representative of the owner. As the designer, you can typically represent the owner and make the appeal to the board. The Board of Appeals consists of a variety of professionals that meet to review conflicts in how a code is interpreted or applied to a specific situation. The board does not have the authority to waive a code requirement. Rather, it is the board's responsibility to review the appeal, listen to both sides, and decide whether the appeal follows the intent of the code. This process can occur in the early review process or could occur when a project fails to be approved for a permit. (This is why an early review can be very important.)

Note

The words *variance* and *appeal* are sometimes used interchangeably. However, variances usually apply to local zoning laws and appeals apply to the codes.

Figure 10.2 is a building code appeals form indicating the typical information required. (Usually separate appeal requests must be made for building, plumbing, mechanical, and electrical codes.) Once the Board of Appeals receives your appeal, both the designer and the code official are scheduled to present their side of the issue. As the designer, you must be prepared to explain the current code interpretation and how you specifically plan to comply with the code within the design project. If your appeal is accepted, the board grants a variance for that particular project. This variance applies only to the situation at hand; for other projects and even future projects in the same space, you must go through a similar process.

Permit Process

A permit is typically required for any interior project that requires construction. This includes but is not limited to any of the following:

- ❑ New construction or additions to an existing building
- ❑ Alterations made to a building
- ❑ Change in occupancy
- ❑ Installation of regulated equipment
- ❑ Certain types of repairs or building maintenance

The permit is issued based on the construction documents consisting of drawings, specifications, and any other documentation that may be required. (See Documentation and Liability section later in the chapter.) In most cases a licensed contractor obtains the permit for the project. However, some jurisdictions (especially in larger cities) require a third party, known as a code expeditor,

METROPOLITAN GOVERNMENT OF NASHVILLE AND DAVIDSON COUNTY, TENNESSEE
DEPARTMENT OF CODES ADMINISTRATION

APPEAL UNDER THE FIRE AND BUILDING CODES

APPEAL CASE NO.: ____________ MAP & PARCEL NO.: ____.____.____
COUNCIL DISTRICT: ____________

TO THE METROPOLITAN BOARD OF FIRE AND BUILDING CODE APPEALS:

The undersigned hereby appeals the decision of the Director of the Department of Codes Administration, Metropolitan Government of Nashville and Davidson County, Tennessee, wherein a Building Permit and/or a Certificate of Occupancy are refused for: ____
____
____

located at ____

Said Building Permit and/or Certificate of Occupancy was denied for the reason of:
____
____
____
____
____
____
____

Based on the powers and duties generally of the Metropolitan Board of Fire and Building Code Appeals, as set out in the Code of the Metropolitan Government of Nashville and Davidson County, Tennessee, Section § 2.80.080, a variance, interpretation or exception is hereby requested in the above requirement as applied to this property.

Date Submitted: ____________________ Appeal Taken By: ____________________

APPELLANT: ____________________ SIGNATURE OF APPELLANT: ____________________

Appellant Address: ____

City, State, ZIP: ____________________ Telephone: (____) ____________________

Person Representing Appellant: ____

Owner of Property: ____________________ Appeal Fee Amount Received: $____________

Lessee of Property: ____________________ Check Number or Cash: ____________

Individual Who Should Receive Notice:____
(Name, Address, City, State, Zip and Telephone Number)

Board Of Fire and Buidling Code Appeals meets on the Second (2nd) Tuesday of every month at 9:00 A.M. on the First (1st) Floor of the Howard Office Building – Howard Auditorium, 700 2nd Avenue, South, Nashville, Tennessee. This Appeal form must be completed and the Appeal Fee of Fifty ($50.00) Dollars received one (1) week prior to the Board Meeting to be placed on the next scheduled meeting Agenda. A representative must be present at the meeting to provide reasons why the Board should grant the request and answer any questions relevant to the request.

Figure 10.2 Sample Fire and Building Code Appeal Form

Note

In some jurisdictions it is almost imperative that an expeditor be used as a go-between between the contractor and the codes department in order to obtain a permit.

Note

Many jurisdictions have computerized the permit process. Instead of filling out a form, the code department either enters your project information directly into a computer or allows you to file over the Internet.

to obtain the permit. In some cases, the building owner or a registered design professional can also get the permit. Figure 10.3 is an example of a building permit. Each jurisdiction requires slightly different information. Most jurisdictions also require separate permits for plumbing, electrical, and mechanical work. These are usually obtained by the appropriate subcontractors, since these permits make each subcontractor legally responsible for the specified work.

To obtain the permit the contractor must submit a permit application and a permit fee. (Some jurisdictions now have electronic permit applications that allow them to be filed over the Internet.) A specific number of construction documents must also be submitted. It is at this stage that the code officials fully review the drawings and specifications. Therefore, it is important that all relevant code correspondence made during the preliminary review and any granted appeals be attached to the application or noted directly on the construction drawings. This is especially helpful if the same code officials are not checking the plans in both the preliminary review and the permit plan review.

The whole process can take one day or several weeks, depending on the size of the project, the number of code officials who must check the project, and the workload of the code department. The set of documents is typically checked by both a plans examiner and a fire marshal. Some jurisdictions will have more than one examiner check the drawings. For example, there may be separate building, mechanical, plumbing, and electrical code examiners, as well as other local and/or state code examiners.

If there are any code discrepancies on the drawings or in the specifications, the building official will require corrections to be made before the permit is issued. This will necessitate making the appropriate changes and submitting the updated documentation. Upon approval, the code official(s) will stamp or write *approved* on the drawings. The code department keeps one set of drawings, and at least one set must be kept on the job site at all times. Some jurisdictions will issue a plans approval letter, which should be kept in your files. In addition, the permit itself must be clearly posted at the job site during construction.

Construction and Inspection Process

The code process does not stop with the issue of a permit. During the construction of a project, a code official must make several inspections of the job site. This is done to guarantee that the work matches what is required by the construction documents and that the work continues to comply with the codes. Inspections must be made at certain intervals during the construction, usually before the work is concealed or covered up by the next phase of construction.

City of Anywhere USA

Application for a Building Permit

City of Anywhere
Building Department
123 Main Street
Anywhere, USA 32134
201-345-8532

Application is hereby made for a building permit to accomplish the work described below. Necessary compliance shall be observed and all requirements of the Codes shall be complied with.

Date:______________

Property Information:

Project Address: ______________________________ **Suite #:**__________
Project Name: ____
Subdivision: ______________________ **Lot:**__________ **Block:**__________
Section:__________ **Township:**__________ **Range:**__________ **Map#:**__________
Parcel ID #:____
Zoning Use:______________ **Fire Zone: Y/N Flood Zone: Y/N Landslide Zone: Y/N**
Water System:______________ **Sewer System:**______________
Proposed Use:____

Owners Information:

Name: ____

Address:____

City: ______________________ **State:**______________ **Zip:**______________

Phone:______________ **Fax:**______________ **Email:**______________

Contractor Information:

Company Name:______________________ **City Tax ID:**______________
Principle Agent:______________________ **License Number:**______________
Phone:______________ **Fax:**______________ **Email:**______________

Permit Information:

Work Class:______________ **Master Permit Number:**______________
Description of Work:____
____

Valuation of Work:$______________ **ContructionType: IA, IB, IIA,IIB,IIIA,IIIB,IV, VA,VB**
Occupancy Type:
A1,A2,A3,A4,A5,B,E,F1,F2,H1,H2,H3,H4,H5,I1,I2,I3,I4,R1,R2,R3,R4,M,S1,S2,U
Total Building Sq. Footage:______________ **Total Building Height:**______________
Sprinkler System: Y/N Permit Area Sq Footage:______________ **Floor Number:**______
Soil Erosion Permit #:______________________ **Sewer Impact #:**______________
Report Code:__________ **Notes:**______________________________________
____

I hereby certify that I have read this application and that all information contained herein is true.

Date:______________ **Signature:**______________________________________
Check:_______ **Cash:**______ **Permit Cost:**______________

Figure 10.3 Sample Application for Building Permit (Reproduced with permission from the International Code Council.)

It is typically the responsibility of the contractor to notify the codes department when it is time to make an inspection. Depending on the type of interior project, these intervals usually include the following:

> **Note**
>
> As the designer, you should also be periodically checking the construction of your project to ensure that it is following your design and code instructions. This should be part of every construction administration.

1. *Framing inspection:* The walls, ceiling, and floors are usually framed and completed on one side. Gypsum board may be attached to one side of the walls, but all framing must be exposed. The side that is open allows the inspector to check the construction materials and framing.
2. *Systems inspection:* Separate inspections are made for the plumbing, mechanical, and electrical installations. This includes automatic sprinkler systems as well. Certain jurisdictions may also require an inspection of some communication systems. These inspections can be made at the same time as the framing inspection if these systems are complete. There is usually a preliminary rough-in inspection before the walls are closed and then a final inspection at the end of construction as part of the final inspection.

> **Note**
>
> Unfortunately, there is no guarantee that preapproved plans or even plans that receive a permit will be approved in the field. An inspector may see a code noncompliance in the field that was missed on the construction drawings. If this occurs, either the designer must work out the discrepancy with the appropriate code official or the contractor must make the changes necessary to comply to the code.

3. *Gypsum board/lath inspection:* When all the gypsum board or lathing is in place but before any taping or plaster is done, the inspector will check to make sure all wall and ceiling assemblies are built to code. Rated assemblies such as fire and smoke-rated assemblies may require additional inspections.
4. *Fire-resistant assemblies and penetration inspection:* After the rated assemblies, including walls and floor/ceiling assemblies, are taped and plastered, they are inspected again. For example, the joints and intersections of rated assemblies with other rated assemblies and exterior walls are inspected. Penetrations in rated assemblies are inspected for proper installation and sealing as well.
5. *Energy efficiency inspection:* The insulation of mechanical ducts, the water heating equipment, and the HVAC system is inspected for compliance with energy standards.
6. *Special inspection:* Certain inspections occur after the construction or installation of a specific design element is complete, such as an elevator, swimming pool, or other special element. In addition, the codes specify when certain products and systems require a separate inspection. These include special wall panels, sprayed fire-resistant material, and smoke control systems. Special inspections may also be required when materials or systems are used as alternative materials or systems as part of a performance approach to the code. And, a special inspection may be required for materials used in unusual or creative ways. The code official will let you know when a special inspection is required for an individual situation.

7. *Final inspection:* Once the project is complete, the inspector will do one final walk-through to confirm compliance of all remaining codes and to make sure the space is ready to be occupied. In some jurisdictions a separate inspection may need to be done by a fire marshal as well.

At each intermediate inspection, the construction can continue only if the inspector grants an approval. If the inspector finds that the project is not acceptable, a correction notice is issued and another inspection is scheduled. If the inspector feels that a condition is unsafe or that the construction is not being carried out in an acceptable manner, a stop work order will be issued. This means that no other work on the site can occur until the specific problem is addressed.

An inspection may not always be done by a code official. Some jurisdictions allow or even require the owner to have the construction process inspected by a separate inspection agency. This is sometimes referred to as a self-inspection. In this case, a third party performs the site inspections and documents the process. The inspection information is submitted to the local code official to verify that inspections are being done. This process must be approved by the local code jurisdiction. The code official often still performs the final inspection necessary for the Certificate of Occupancy.

Note

Special inspections might be required when using performance codes or unusual construction materials. It may be necessary for the installation to be observed by the inspector.

Sometimes changes must be made to the construction documents after construction begins. For example, a change may be necessary because of a stop work order or to clarify an item on the construction drawings. In other cases, the owner may request a design change. These changes should be submitted to the codes department as well as to the construction site. In some cases, the code official will issue a plans approval letter for each revision. The code officials will review the project according to the set they have approved. If there is a conflict between their approved set and what is being built, it can delay inspections and approvals.

Final Approval

The inspection process is the way that the code officials verify that the project is being built according to the most current drawings and that the actual construction meets the applicable codes. When the final inspections are completed, the construction of the project is typically considered finished. However, before the occupants can move into the space or building, additional approvals are necessary. These may include a Certificate of Completion, Certificate of Occupancy, Temporary Certificate of Occupancy, or Phased Certificate of Occupancy. One or more of these certificates may be issued by the code official to indicate that public services can be connected to the building or that it is safe for people to occupy the space or building. The various certificates are described next.

Certificate of Completion

A certificate of Completion is issued when the structure or systems are complete within a space or building. This type of certificate is usually necessary to connect to local utilities, especially in new construction. However, it does not give the right to occupy the space or building. A Certificate of Occupancy must still be issued to occupy the space or building.

Certificate of Occupancy

A Certificate of Occupancy (C of O) is issued after the final inspection has been completed. The person who obtained the building permit typically requests the C of O from the code official. This is usually the contractor. If during the final inspection the code inspector, including the fire marshal, is satisfied that the building or space complies with the code and the construction is complete, a certificate is issued. In some jurisdictions, the Certificate of Occupancy is also referred to as a Use and Occupancy (U and O) letter. The certificate is typically required before the tenant can occupy the building or space, and it must be posted in a conspicuous location in the building. Once the Certificate of Occupancy is issued, the code process is complete.

Temporary Certificate of Occupancy

The client might not want to wait until all portions of the overall project are completed before occupying the facility. Or, a certain aspect of the project cannot be completed because of delay in the arrival of material or equipment, for example, custom granite countertops or water fountains. In those cases, some jurisdictions will issue a Temporary Certificate of Occupancy. This will allow the project or portions of the project to be occupied as long as the code official feels that the occupants will not be in any danger because the entire project is not complete. The uncompleted work must eventually be inspected before a final Certificate of Occupancy is issued. The Temporary Certificate of Occupancy is also known as a Partial Certificate of Occupancy or a Partial Use and Occupancy Permit. It is usually issued with a time limit, such as 90 days, giving the contractor the time to complete the work.

Note

A temporary certificate of occupancy may be issued on projects when part of a building can be safely occupied before the completion of the remainder of the project.

Some jurisdictions will not issue a temporary certificate because often owners or contractors never request final inspections once they have occupied the space. And because building official may lose track of a project, they do not know if the final work was ever done correctly.

Phased Certificate of Occupancy

For a larger project, construction may be done in phases. Often these phases are determined during the design process and incorporated into the construction documents. This Phased Certificate of Occupancy allows the client to occupy the portions of the project that are complete. For example, in the renovation of several floors of a hospital, it may be important to allow the renovated emergency room to be occupied as soon as it is completed without waiting for the renovation of the cafeteria on the floor above to be completed. It also allows code officials to do final inspections on the completed areas. In other cases, each part of a large project could be permitted separately, and then each part would have its own review and inspection process and receive a separate Certificate of Occupancy.

Note

To accommodate tight construction schedules, some jurisdictions allow building permits to be issued in phases. This becomes especially important in new buildings, where construction can begin while designers complete the interior details.

ECONOMIC OPTIONS IN CODES

Thorough code research is imperative for the safety of building occupants, but a number of options are allowed by the code that can affect the cost of the project. These options are frequently overlooked, resulting in needless construction costs. In his book *Building and Safety Codes for Industrial Facilities,* Joseph N. Sabatini lists a number of reasons for overlooked cost savings in industrial buildings. They can be generalized to include all design projects.

1. *Options are not clear in the codes.* Sometimes options, alternatives, or exceptions are scattered throughout the chapters, and finding them requires familiarity and expertise.
2. *Nonfamiliarity and infrequent use of codes lead to poor enforcement.* Many designers merely spot-check the codes on an intermittent basis, and therefore miss important details because they do not have the time to review them thoroughly.
3. *Some trade-offs are interdisciplinary.* Since some designers are scheduled to participate in planning on a staggered basis, poor communication and coordination result.
4. *Preliminary meetings do not involve all disciplines.* Sound economic decisions can be made only if all disciplines are involved in the early planning stages.
5. *Design time is too short.* Because of committed investments, interest payments, and the income that a facility will bring as soon as it is in operation, design time is often abbreviated, and therefore comprehensive code reviews are often not done.
6. *Overkill.* Because of item 5, conscientious professionals use overkill and include items in the design that are not always mandated by the building codes, regulations, and enforced standards.

DOCUMENTATION AND LIABILITY

Building codes and the standards they reference are continually being updated, especially those that pertain to interiors. For example, some of the testing requirements for interior finishes and furniture are fairly recent, and more tests are constantly being developed. Newer federal regulations may also be developed, such as accessibility and energy related issues. Even if not yet required, they may benefit the project and its occupants.

Note

Some code departments will not issue a permit if you incorporate more stringent codes not currently enforced by that jurisdiction. If that is the case, be sure to document all correspondence.

It is crucial when designing interior projects to keep current with the codes and regulations. Even if the jurisdiction of a project does not yet require some of the stricter codes or standards, you should know what they are and use them. Not only are people's lives at stake, but also you may be held liable should an incident occur. You need to prove that you used the most advanced test or strictest requirement available at the time you designed the project.

It is important to reference specific code sections and standard numbers and note which edition of the publication you are using. When conducting a code review, it is a good idea to make copies of all chapters and/or paragraphs that apply to the project. On larger projects you may want to summarize these sections on cover sheets. In addition, collect written evidence of any materials that must meet certain regulations. For example, when you are requesting the results of a performance test from a manufacturer or an outside source, it is your responsibility to obtain the results in writing. Equally important is to have the documentation organized to show the research you have done for each code issue.

Note

When using performance codes, documentation is very important. All documentation must be clear and designated separately from prescriptive code requirements.

The development of a checklist or a standard evaluation form is very useful, since the ease of establishing compliance with standards is in direct proportion to the quantity and quality of your documentation. You should also have a general checklist, such as the one in Figure 10.4, to make sure each code topic has been covered in every project.

Use this checklist in conjunction with the more specific checklists introduced in each chapter of this book. You may want to add to these checklists or develop your own. It is impossible to put every code requirement on a checklist, since the requirements will be different on every project. Instead, the purpose of the checklist is to remind you of the code and standard requirements that must be researched and documented on the drawings and specifications. When necessary, you should always attach the appropriate backup. The backup could consist of a copy of the manufacturer's warranty or specifications, a product label listing the codes and standards with which the product complies, or a copy of a certificate from a testing agency. Attaching reduced floor plans with additional notes might also be helpful. (Also see Responsibility for Compliance in Appendix A.)

Note

Properly and consistently prepared code documentation is imperative should any liability issues occur after a project is completed.

Summary Interior Project Checklist

Date:____________

Project Name:____ Space: ________________________________

1 DETERMINE WHICH CODES ARE REQUIRED (Chapter 1)
- ___ Building Code
- ___ Fire Code
- ___ Performance Code
- ___ Other Code Publications
- ___ Local Codes and Ordinances
- ___ Government Regulations
- ___ Standards and Tests

2 OCCUPANCY REQUIREMENTS (Chapter 2)
- ___ Determine Building Types(s)
- ___ Determine Occupancy Classification(s)
- ___ Calculate Occupant Load(s)
- ___ Adjustments to Occupant Load(s)
- ___ Review Specific Occupancy Requirements
- ___ Compare Code and Accessibility Requirements

3 MINIMUM TYPES OF CONSTRUCTION (Chapter 3)
- ___ Determine Construction Type
- ___ Determine Ratings of Building Elements
- ___ Calculate Maximum Floor Area (as required)
- ___ Calculate Building Height (as required)
- ___ Review Construction Type Limitations

4 MEANS OF EGRESS REQUIREMENTS (Chapter 4)
- ___ Determine Quantity and Types of Means of Egress
- ___ Calculate Minimum Widths
- ___ Determine Arrangement of Exits
- ___ Calculate Travel Distance
- ___ Determine Required Signage
- ___ Compare Code and Accessibility Requirements
- ___ Review Emergency Light Requirements

5 FIRE RESISTANCE REQUIREMENTS (Chapter 5)
- ___ Determine Use of Fire Walls
- ___ Determine Fire Barriers and Partitions
- ___ Determine Smoke Barriers and Partitions
- ___ Determine Location of Opening Protectives
- ___ Determine Location of Through Penetration Protectives
- ___ Review Types of Fire Tests and Ratings Required
- ___ Compare Code and Standard Requirements
- ___ Review Requirements During Assembly Specification
- ___ Check All Enforced Standards

6 FIRE PROTECTION REQUIREMENTS (Chapter 6)
- ___ Determine Fire and Smoke Detection Systems
- ___ Determine Required Alarm Systems
- ___ Determine Types of Extinguishing Systems
- ___ Review for Possible Sprinkler Tradeoffs
- ___ Compare Code and Accessibility Requirements
- ___ Coordinate with Engineer (as required)

7 PLUMBING REQUIREMENTS (Chapter 7)
- ___ Determine Types of Fixtures Required
- ___ Calculate Number of Each Fixture Required
- ___ Determine Required Toilet/Bathing Facilities
- ___ Review for Finishes, Accessories and Signage
- ___ Compare Code and Accessibility Requirements
- ___ Coordinate with Engineer (as required)

8 MECHANICAL REQUIREMENTS (Chapter 7)
- ___ Determine Type of Air Distribution System(s)
- ___ Determine Items Affecting Cooling Loads
- ___ Determine Access and Clearance Requirements
- ___ Figure Zoning and Thermostat Locations
- ___ Check for Accessibility and Energy Efficiency Compliance
- ___ Coordinate with Engineer (as required)

9 ELECTRICAL REQUIREMENTS (Chapter 8)
- ___ Determine Types/Locations of Outlets, Switches, Fixtures
- ___ Determine Emergency Power and Lighting Requirements
- ___ Check for Accessibility and Energy Efficiency Compliance
- ___ Compare Requirements During Selection/Specification
- ___ Coordinate with Engineer (as required)

10 COMMUNICATION REQUIREMENTS (Chapter 8)
- ___ Determine Systems Required by Client
- ___ Compare Needs versus Code/Standard Requirements
- ___ Check for Accessibility Compliance
- ___ Coordinate with Engineer/Consultant (as required)

11 FINISH AND FURNITURE REQUIREMENTS (Chapter 9)
- ___ Review Tests and Types of Ratings Required
- ___ Determine Special Finish Requirements
- ___ Determine Special Furniture Requirements
- ___ Compare Code and Accessibility Requirements
- ___ Compare Requirements During Selection/Specification
- ___ Check All Enforced Standards

NOTE: Be sure to review all codes and standards required in the jurisdiction as well as required federal regulations. Consult the jurisdiction having authority at any step in question.

Figure 10.4 Summary Interior Project Checklist

Documentation to clients is a critical part of a project as well. They need to know how to maintain a building so that it continues to meet codes. For example, if finishes are not cleaned appropriately, they might not retain their fire retardancy or slip resistance. Other maintenance might affect the indoor air quality of the mechanical system, energy efficiency of an electrical system, or water conservation of plumbing fixtures. Depending on the size and type of the project, you might supply some or all of this information. On larger projects, the project specifications should specify that the contractor supply the client with record drawings (as-builts) of each system installed, as well as operation and maintenance (O & M) manuals that explain how to use and maintain each system and/or material. Client training may also be required.

Note

The length of time to keep project records and code documentation is highly debatable. However, according to *Guidelines,* published by Victor O. Schinnerer & Co., Inc., many states have a *statue of repose*, which sets a time limitation on how long after a project is completed a suit can be brought against a designer or design company.

The importance of documenting every project in construction drawings, specification books, and project files cannot be stressed enough. Although it has been mentioned throughout this book that the use of performance codes requires additional research and documentation for approval, all projects must be well documented concerning codes. Even if you follow all the codes throughout an entire project, if you cannot prove it when asked, the research was useless. Be sure to keep all your research, correspondence with the code officials, and other documentation on file with the project records.

Construction Documents

Construction documents include drawings, specifications, and any additional documentation required by a code jurisdiction. Having certain information documented on the drawings makes the review by code officials easier. They automatically know which code issues were considered in the development of the design. It is especially important that in all documentation you use the proper terminology. For example, a corridor is an enclosed passageway but an aisle is not enclosed. The code requirements for these two are very different.

Note

Although it is rarely done, a permit can be revoked after construction begins if it is discovered that information used to grant the permit was in error, even if the error was made by a code official.

Some codes actually require certain information to be included in the construction documents. Other information is required by the jurisdiction. This section lists the typical code information that should be included in the construction documents, either on the drawings or in the written specifications. Note, however, that this list is not all-inclusive.

Cover Sheet

- ❑ Applicable code publication(s) and edition(s) (recognize local or state amendments)
- ❑ Applicable standards and regulations

- ❑ Name of the design professional responsible for the design of each aspect (plan, electrical, mechanical, etc.)
- ❑ Construction type(s)
- ❑ Area of space designed (square footages or square meters)
- ❑ Building area limitations
- ❑ Occupancy classification(s)
- ❑ Sprinkler status of building or space (i.e., sprinklered or unsprinklered)
- ❑ Occupant load per floor (or area if necessary)
- ❑ Identification of any appeals or equivalencies granted

Drawings

- ❑ Location plan (when designing a portion of a floor or building)
- ❑ Identification of use of rooms and spaces
- ❑ Compartmentation of the fire areas
- ❑ Location of rated walls and floor/ceiling assemblies
- ❑ Location of rated doors, windows, and other through-penetrations
- ❑ Exit access and exit doors (size, location, swing, hardware, security, etc.)
- ❑ Egress routes (location, size, and components)
- ❑ Details of stairs and ramps which are part of the means of egress
- ❑ Location and heights of electrical devices
- ❑ Location of exit signs
- ❑ Details of emergency lighting and/or systems
- ❑ Location and placement of furnishings and finishes
- ❑ Accessibility clearances and critical dimensions
- ❑ Sections of rated assemblies (walls, ceilings, etc.)
- ❑ Details for penetrations (electrical, plumbing, environmental and communication conduits, pipes, and systems)
- ❑ Elevations (indicating mounting heights and locations of equipment and accessories)

Specifications, Schedules, and Legends

- ❑ Types of rated wall and floor/ceiling assemblies
- ❑ Types of rated doors, frames, and hardware
- ❑ Types of rated windows and through-penetrations
- ❑ Types of electrical outlets, including GFCIs and AFCIs
- ❑ Types of light fixtures, including emergency lights and exit signs

Note

Certain sections in each code indicate specific information that must be included in the construction document prior to code review. A jurisdiction may have additional requirements.

- ❑ Types and locations of regulated finishes and furniture
- ❑ List of required standards and tests

Additional information may be required for review by the code official for approval of the design. Because this documentation is usually developed by an engineer or consulting professional, the information may not be located in your drawings or specifications. This may include the following:

- ❑ Sprinkler riser diagram
- ❑ Sprinkler coverage calculations
- ❑ Mechanical load calculations
- ❑ Plumbing fixture calculations

Performance Design Documentation

Note

If performance-related codes are used on a project, typically only a certain portion of the project will be designed using performance criteria. The prescriptive codes will be used on the rest of the project.

When a performance requirement has been used as part of the design, it should be clearly shown in the construction documents. The performance documentation must be delineated from the rest of the documentation, because it often will require a separate review process. The design and review of the performance portions of a design is composed more like a team than when using prescriptive codes. The team should include design professionals, special experts, and code officials who are all qualified to evaluate the proposed design. In most cases, an architect or engineer will be required. In some cases, the code official may choose to have the design reviewed by another consultant who may be more knowledgeable in the review of performance designs or a specific area of design. This is often referred to as contract review. In all cases, the documentation of the design must be acceptable to the code official having jurisdiction.

The documentation of a performance design may include some or all of the following information:

- ❑ Performance criteria
- ❑ Technical references and resources
- ❑ Plans, specifications, and details of the building design
- ❑ Design assumptions, limitations, and factors of safety used
- ❑ Description of the design hazards
- ❑ Input information for calculations and computer modeling
- ❑ Calculations
- ❑ Computer modeling
- ❑ Scope of inspection and testing required to demonstrate compliance
- ❑ Prescriptive requirements used

- ❑ Maintenance requirements
- ❑ Reliability of the method of research and process

Depending on which aspect of the building has been designed to meet the performance criteria, the documentation may include drawings, specifications, and additional reports. It might be clearly indicated in the main set of construction documents or be separately documented and cross-referenced to the main set. Additional media, such as computer modeling, may also be part of the documentation.

Once it has been approved, anyone involved with the ownership or management of the building has to be notified that the building was approved based on a performance code. A performance design option is designed for the actual situation. If any aspect of the building is changed during design or after the client occupies the space, it may require reapproval by the local code official. Even the maintenance done by the client after move-in can affect the safety of the building.

FUTURE TECHNOLOGY

Computers are quickly becoming a powerful force in code enforcement. Each of the code organizations sells computerized versions of its code publications. Software packages are also available to assist you in your code research by providing you with search capabilities. For example, you can do a word search for a particular code topic or a specific code reference number or table.

In addition, a variety of new computer programs are available to model how different aspects of a building will act in a fire, earthquake, and other emergency situations. Many of the computer modeling programs are already accessible to the design industry. By using these programs, alternatives to typical existing code solutions can be developed and incorporated into buildings.

The use of this type of technology requires training in the software and an advanced knowledge of the applicable prescriptive and performance code requirements and criteria. In most cases, it will require a specialist in the field to develop this type of performance data. However, this type of technology will become increasingly common with the continued use of performance codes. For example, computer models can be used to investigate possible fire scenarios so that you can design the most effective way to address the fire in that specific building and configuration. These computer models then become part of the documentation to support your design.

Other technologies are affecting the construction of the building as well. Increasingly, building systems are being run by computers and integrated together. (See inset titled *Building Automation Systems* in Chapter 8 on page 324.) As the building industry becomes more complex with new products and construction techniques, both designers and code officials have to continue to keep up with these new technologies. Although this will ultimately affect the development and enforcement of codes, the code publications and requirements may not always be able to stay current with the changes in technology.

In addition, changes in the way we think about buildings, such as sustainable design and better indoor air quality, will also need to be addressed within the codes in the future. Currently, the use of "green" products or sustainable building design is not addressed in the typical codes. Instead, designers are following industry standards. (See inset titled *Sustainability and LEED* in Chapter 9 on page 374.) For now, the use of new technology, new products, and sustainable design are incorporated into a project through the use of alternate methods or performance aspects of the codes. This will require additional research and documentation and may require additional reviews with the code official before your project can be approved.

Codes, standards, and federal regulations will remain an important part of the design process as we move into the future. An early and comprehensive code research at the beginning of each interior project is crucial to the smooth development of a project, not to mention the safety of the building occupants. In addition, thorough documentation of your research is a must.

Remember, code officials have the same goal as designers—the health, safety, and welfare of the building occupants. It is important to build a good relationship with the code officials. Since not every jurisdiction is the same, you need to learn the local system. Learn how to work within the system and with the various personalities. Code officials are a valuable resource. Working together, you can usually determine design solutions that comply with the required codes, standards, and federal regulations.

APPENDIX A

ABOUT THE ADA

As mentioned in Chapter 1, the Americans with Disability Act (ADA) is a federal civil law that prohibits discrimination against people with disabilities. Since it is a federal law, the code officials in a jurisdiction cannot decide whether or not it applies in their area; ADA is enforceable in the entire United States. The better question may be: Does the project have to conform to the ADA guidelines? And, to what extent must the project meet the requirements in the ADA guidelines?

Note

Both places of public accommodation and commercial facilities have requirements for compliance with the ADA.

PLACES REQUIRING ACCESSIBILITY

Title III is the segment of the law that requires compliance in places of public accommodation and commercial facilities. The levels of compliance for public accommodations and commercial facilities are slightly different. A place of *public accommodation* is defined by ADA as any facility that is owned, leased, leased to, or operated by a private entity whose operation affects commerce and falls within one of the 12 categories listed below. Some examples are provided in each category, although other types of facilities may apply as well.

- *Place of lodging:* A hotel, assisted living facility, or dormitory (except for owner-occupied establishments renting fewer than six rooms)
- *Establishment serving food:* A restaurant, bar, or cafeteria
- *Place of exhibition or entertainment:* A sports arena, theater, or concert hall
- *Place of public gathering:* An auditorium, convention center, or city hall
- *Sale or rental establishment:* A grocery store, clothing store, or shopping center
- *Service establishment:* A doctor's office, beauty shop, funeral parlor, pharmacy, or hospital
- *Station for public transportation:* An airport, train station, or bus stop
- *Place of public display:* A museum, library, or art gallery
- *Educational facility:* An elementary school, college classroom, or preschool

Note

Federally funded buildings are covered by the Architectural Barriers Act (ABA) and must comply with the requirements of the *UFAS* or the new *ADA-ABA Accessibility Guidelines.*

❑ *Recreation areas:* An amusement park, nature park, or zoo

❑ *Place of exercise:* A gym, health spa, or bowling alley

❑ *Social service center:* A homeless shelter, adoption agency, or day care

A public accommodation must comply with requirements for new construction or altered buildings as defined by the ADA. As a facility that provides services and goods to the public, it must also comply with the ADA requirements that apply to policies, practices, and procedures that affect the ability of a disabled individual to use their services. For example, in a restaurant, the tables would be required to be accessible and the servers would be required to read a menu to a person who had a sight disability.

Note

Certain Residential occupancies may also need to meet the requirements of the *Federal Housing Accessibility Guidelines (FHAG).*

Commercial facilities include nonresidential facilities whose operations affect commerce but are not generally open to the public. Examples would include factories and warehouses as well as other businesses that do not typically receive clients or guests, such as a telemarketing office. These facilities must be compliant with the ADA for use by employees. Commercial facilities must meet the requirements for new construction and are not allowed to use some of the alternative requirements for alterations. (The different levels of compliance are discussed below). Some facilities could be considered both a commercial facility and a place of public accommodation. For example, if a commercial facility such as a car factory allows the public to tour its facilities, the path of the tour would then be a place of public accommodation. In addition, the way that the tour was conducted (by guided tour or written instructions, for example) would have to be accessible to persons with disabilities. The employee areas of the facility, however, would need to meet the requirements for commercial facilities. Because the requirements for public accommodation include procedures and policies, it is considered a slightly higher level of overall compliance than commercial facilities. However, the requirements in the ADA guidelines that affect the actual spaces are similar.

Note

The ADA covers other aspects of accessibility that can affect a project, including employment, communication, and equipment.

Although almost all places of public activity are included in the definition of a place of public accommodation, there are some types of facilities that are not required to be compliant with the ADA. These include facilities that are owned and operated by religious entities, one- and two-family dwellings, private clubs, and certain government facilities. Those entities or facilities may not be completely exempt from compliance, however, if part of their facility is utilized as a place of public accommodation. For example, if a church rents part of its facility to a day care during the week and the day care is not operated by the church, the area that the day care leases would be required to meet ADA requirements. (Although compliance is technically the day care's responsibility, this may have to be resolved in the landlord-tenant agreement. See Responsibility and Compliance later in this appendix.) Similarly, if part of a private residence is used for a business and it is usual for clients to come there for the operation of the business, that part of the residence that is used for the business would be required to meet the requirements even though private residences are exempt from the ADA.

Conversely, an educational facility that is operated by a synagogue, for example, may not be required to conform to the ADA guidelines, because of the exemption for religious entities. In some cases, it may be clear whether your project needs to comply with ADA, whereas in other cases, you may need to discuss this further with your client to determine if the space would be considered a public accommodation and/or commercial facility. It may be wise to seek an opinion from the Access Board for projects that are not clear. (See Resources in Appendix E.)

State and local government facilities are also required to be compliant with the ADA under Title II. They must meet the standards of new construction and alterations as well as provide access to all programs that are offered as part of their services. However, currently state and local governments have the choice of following either the ADA guidelines or the *Uniform Federal Accessibility Standards (UFAS)* in order to meet these requirements.

Federal buildings are not required to be compliant with the ADA. Instead, federal buildings must comply with the Architectural Barriers Act (ABA) for accessibility. The Access board is working to make these requirements more consistent, but slight differences may remain. If you are working on a space for a federal agency or a federally funded project, you may need to research the specific guidelines. In addition, some residential building types may need to comply with the requirements of the Federal Housing Act (FHA). (See inset titled *Accessibility Requirements—ANSI, ADAAG, UFAS, and FHAG* in Chapter 1 on page 32.)

Note

Differences in the technical and scoping requirements of the new *ADA-ABA Accessibility Guidelines*, the 2004 ICC/ANSI standard and the newest editions of the *IBC* are minimized because of collaboration between the Access Board, the ICC, and ANSI.

ORIGINAL *ADAAG*

The ADA references guidelines that give designers specific design criteria for accessibility in all aspects of interior and architectural design. The original document is known as the *ADA Accessibility Guidelines (ADAAG)*. These guidelines apply to construction and alterations of places of public accommodation and commercial facilities. It is not within the scope of this book to include all the requirements of the ADA guidelines. However, it is important to understand that the requirements found in the guidelines are presented as either scoping requirements or technical requirements. Scoping requirements tell you how many accessible toilets, water fountains, doors, and so on you must provide. Technical requirements give you specific requirements or dimensions that have to be met for the door, sink, millwork, and so on to be accessible.

The original *ADAAG* also covers special occupancy sections including restaurants and cafeterias, medical care facilities, business and mercantile, libraries, transient lodging, and transportation facilities. These include both scoping and technical provisions that are specific to the building use. (See Chapter 2 for more information.) The appendix section of the *ADAAG* includes additional information to clarify the requirements and increase accessibility. This information is not mandatory. In addition, designers must keep in mind that other accessibility standards as well as those required in the building code will typically apply to a project. The highest level of accessibility should always be provided.

NEW ADA GUIDELINES

As mentioned in Chapter 1, the Access Board is responsible for revisions to the ADA guidelines. The Access Board continues to do research as to how to provide for accessibility to the disabled. Once a proposed change is developed, it goes through a thorough process of review by governmental agencies and the public. In finalizing the proposed change, the Access Board also considers public and industry related comments that have been submitted and the potential future cost implications of new technical requirements. Even after a change or addition has been finalized and issued by the Access Board, it is still not enforceable as part of the ADA until the DOJ (or other federal agency) approves it and incorporates it into the ADA guidelines.

Note

Revisions to the ADA guidelines made by the Access Board are enforceable only when approved by the Department of Justice (DOJ).

Since the first publication of the *ADAAG*, there have been several proposed changes. However, only a few have actually been approved and officially added to the document. For example, revisions to the reach ranges for ATMs and fare vending machines have been made and requirements for transportation facilities have been added. The DOJ can also decide to suspend a requirement for a period of time if the requirement is not providing safety and accessibility as intended. For example, the detectable warning requirements at curb ramps and other areas were suspended for several years but are now in effect again.

The Access Board is constantly developing revisions to the ADA guidelines. More recently, they have been working in conjunction with the International Code Council (ICC) and the American National Standards Institute (ANSI), as well as other individuals and organizations, to create a totally new document. The new guidelines update technical requirements, share technical criteria for both the ADA and the ABA, and are intended to be more consistent with the requirements of the building codes, such as the *International Building Code (IBC)*, and the ICC/ANSI accessibility standard *ICC/ANSI 117.1*. This revision includes a reorganized format, graphics, and numbering system. Many of the requirements remain the same as in the original *ADAAG*, but there are some differences. In addition, new topics and accessibility categories have been added. (Refer to Figure 1.4

in Chapter 1.) The Access Board has completed and released the new *ADA-ABA Accessibility Guidelines* and even has it available on their Web site. However, it will not be enforceable until the appropriate federal agencies approve it.

As a designer, it is your responsibility to understand and keep abreast of the most current ADA guidelines. Once a change occurs to the guidelines and it becomes law, it may be immediately applicable to a project. The most current information can be found on the Web sites of the Access Board and the DOJ. (See Appendix E.) It is important to note that some of the more current printings of the guidelines, including the ones available on line, may consist of sections that are not yet enforceable. You can also request that the Access Board notify you of updates and request their quarterly magazine, which includes ongoing information about proposed changes to the ADA guidelines.

LEVEL OF COMPLIANCE

Depending on whether your project involves new construction, an alteration of an existing space, or minor cosmetic changes to an existing facility, the ADA law provides for different levels of required compliance with the ADA guidelines. Generally, the requirements for new construction are most stringent. When an existing building is being altered for renovation or for accessibility, some alternative solutions are allowed. Below is a general overview of the varying levels of compliance for each type of construction project.

New Construction

In most cases in new construction, all aspects of your design will have to comply with the ADA guidelines. A project being built from the ground up or a completely new tenant space within an existing building, for example, would both be considered new construction, according to the ADA.

Note

New construction must comply with the *new construction* requirements of the ADA almost without exception.

However, even in new construction there are some aspects of a space that may not have to meet the ADA guidelines, such as areas used only by employees. For example, the shelves and storage cabinets in a teacher's workroom in an elementary school (used only by teachers) would not all have to be within the reach ranges described by the guidelines. According to the employment sections of the ADA, however, if a disabled teacher was hired, then areas used by that teacher would need to be modified. Other miscellaneous rooms, such as an electrical closet or mechanical room, typically do not apply, either.

For areas accessible to the public, the minimum requirement is that everyone must be able to "approach, enter, and exit" each room. For example, even hotel rooms that are not required to be accessible should provide the clearances at the door to allow a visitor in a wheelchair to open the door from the hall and from inside the room. In areas that will be *used* by the general public and employees, such as exhibits in a museum, full accessibility must be provided. And in most projects, it is appropriate to make most spaces, even shared work areas, completely accessible according to the ADA guidelines. The level of accessibility that your project must meet should be established early in the design process.

Alterations

In the case of an alteration or renovation to an existing building, rules for compliance are more complex. Changes made to the area must conform to the ADA guidelines unless existing conditions make compliance impossible. In addition, alterations to one area may require additional changes in adjacent areas. For example, if a "primary function" space, such as a small auditorium in a high school, is altered and made to be more accessible, the ADA may require that the path to the primary function area and certain support areas, such as the corridors to the auditorium and to the bathrooms, drinking fountains, and telephones, be altered to provide a similar level of accessibility.

Note

An alteration to an exiting building must comply with the ADA guidelines to the maximum extent possible. In some cases, an alteration will not have to meet the guideline requirements (e.g., if the change is structurally unfeasible or would cause an unsafe condition).

However, the ADA does provide some options. If it can be proven that the cost of alterations to support areas and the path of travel to them exceeds 20 percent of the cost of the alteration of the primary function area, those changes would not be required. The 20 percent rule may allow alterations for accessibility to be done in increments, but it is not intended to allow building owners to make a series of small alterations to an existing building in order to avoid a more costly accessibility update. To prevent this, the law specifies that the total cost of alterations in a three-year period may be accessed to determine if an appropriate allotment of cost has been spent on accessibility updates.

Existing Facilities

Unlike building codes, the ADA also applies to existing buildings even if no alterations or renovations are planned. Owners may seek the advice of a design professional concerning how ADA applies to them. When the ADA law was passed, it allowed for a two-year period for the removal of "architectural barriers" from existing buildings. The intent was to allow building owners to begin to make changes to their existing buildings, such as adding ramps, widening doors, adding power-assisted doors, and fixing other existing barriers, to bring their buildings into compliance with the law and make them accessible.

Since the initial two-year period has ended, owners are now expected to have evaluated their facilities and to have removed the "architectural barriers" that could keep persons with disabilities from using their buildings. Now, legal suits can be brought against the owner of a facility that is not compliant. Legal suits are typically filed by persons with disabilities who feel that the building conditions prevent them from gaining services.

> **Note**
>
> Existing facilities must be modified as *readily achievable* to meet the requirements of the ADA.

There are some options for accommodating the needs of persons with disabilities without making physical changes. However, conforming to ADA regulations should be pursued to the extent of "readily achievable." An accessible path to the building from the exterior, an accessible entrance into the building, an accessible path to the goods or services, accessible toilet facilities, and then direct access to the actual goods and services is the order of priority that ADA sets for making changes to an existing building. For commercial facilities, those areas that are required to be accessible should meet the same level of accessibility as "readily achievable." (Additional exceptions are allowed for existing buildings that are deemed historic. See Existing and Historic Buildings in Appendix B for more information.)

To the Maximum Extent Feasible

For all project types, the law requires that an attempt to meet the ADA guidelines be "to the maximum extent feasible." If the alterations needed to meet the requirements are not "readily achievable," both structurally and financially, the law allows for exceptions when the alteration could be considered an "undue burden." One example might be that, during the renovation of an auditorium, it is determined that an assistive listening system, although required by ADA guidelines, exceeds the budget for this phase of the project and is disproportionate to the profit that the owner receives from the auditorium.

Many times these burdens are hard to determine. They are usually decided on a case-by-case basis by the regulating authority or the courts. (Review some of the resources in the Bibliography for additional information.) When determining whether the cost of renovation is not "readily achievable," the financial resources of the facility, the number of employees, and the type of facility are taken into account. The decision to limit the scope of accessibility should be determined by the owner and should be primarily a financial decision, not a design decision. It is typically the owner's responsibility to provide the legal documentation to support this decision.

Another way that the government encourages building owners to make their existing facilities accessible is through tax incentives. Small businesses, in particular, may receive tax credits for architectural and system modifications for accessibility purposes. Other provisions allow expenditures to be treated as a tax deduction instead of as a capital expenditure. Although not within the scope of this book or within the scope of typical design services, designers should be aware that these incentives are available.

REGULATION AND ENFORCEMENT

Note

Regulation and enforcement of the ADA guidelines in design projects works differently than the enforcement of code requirements.

Often projects must also meet state accessibility requirements and accessibility requirements included in the building codes. This may result in conflicts between the different requirements. As mentioned in Chapter 1, the Access Board, the American National Standards Institute (ANSI), and the International Code Council (ICC) continue to work to coordinate the requirements to minimize differences. However, slight differences still exist. In addition, a jurisdiction may be using a different edition of a code or ICC/ANSI standard. The NFPA codes also include accessibility requirements. In all cases, the highest level of accessibility should be provided. For accessibility requirements included in various codes and standards, what is needed for compliance can be clarified as part of the code review process, but the ADA process is different.

Because the ADA is a civil rights law, it is enforced through the judicial system. Currently enforcement occurs through a private suit by an individual or by legal action taken by a federal agency in support of a discrimination claim. In most cases, there is not a local agency that will review a project for compliance with the ADA guidelines. States can develop individual accessibility standards and submit them for review by the Department of Justice (DOJ) for certification. If the standard is found to sufficiently address accessibility issues consistent with the guidelines, the new standard is considered *certified.* Projects can then be reviewed by local building officials for accessibility compliance. For example, Texas, Washington, Maine, and Florida currently have accessibility standards certified by the DOJ to be consistent with the original *ADAAG.* This process, however, still does not guarantee that the project is in complete compliance with the ADA and its guidelines. Should legal action be taken, the certified standard may not be enough to prove compliance.

In many cases, compliance with the ADA guidelines will be clearly defined. If not, you can request clarification of specific issues of concern from the Access Board. In addition, each state now has a central contact to assist with technical questions. A list of these state code contacts can be found on the Access Board's Web site. (See Appendix E.) Projects can also be sent to the Department of Justice or the Access Board for review; but this process may not be practical except for significantly large projects.

RESPONSIBILITY FOR COMPLIANCE

It makes sense that your client, as the owner or tenant of a building, is responsible for compliance with the ADA in their space or building. Even in the design process they can make decisions about issues that affect the level of accessibility. For example, the client sometimes limits the scope of work because of budget: they decide what will be changed within an existing building or how much will be constructed. The owner or tenant also maintains the space after construction. All of this affects the accessibility of the building or space.

Typically, the owner of a building and a tenant within a building are responsible for the accessibility of the parts of a space that are under their individual control. For example, an accessible entrance into a building would be the owner's responsibility, but the accessibility of a work area within the tenant space would be the tenant's responsibility. The specific responsibilities between owner and tenant can sometimes be allocated by the lease. For example, the lease may state that the owner is responsible for using accessible hardware on tenant corridor doors. However, if a part of the facility is noncompliant, both may be held responsible by the law. (But remember, owners or tenants that are a religious entity or a private club would not be required to comply with the ADA.)

Note

Often, additional accessibility requirements, as found in the building codes and the ICC/ANSI standard, will apply to your project. It will depend on the code jurisdiction.

In addition, as designer, you should be aware of recent legal cases between the DOJ and design firms that suggest that the design professional and potentially others in the construction process may hold some legal responsibility for compliance with ADA. It may be reasonable to assume that the designer is familiar with the requirements in the ADA guidelines in order to apply them to the design. However, the issue of responsibility under the law is sometimes unclear. There have been legal actions that have named the designer as the responsible party for compliance with the ADA. What is clear is that you should seek a complete understanding of the need for compliance as a joint effort between the client and your design efforts in the development of the project. Documenting your decisions in drawings and other written documents is important. The clarity of the ADA is still being discovered through the judicial system and the subsequent modifications to the ADA and its guidelines.

If your project can be considered a public accommodation or a commercial facility, then the requirements in the ADA guidelines will apply to your project. (See the exceptions mentioned earlier.) In addition, state and local code jurisdictions may have other accessibility requirements that need to be considered. In cases where the requirements seem to conflict, the requirement that provides for the greater degree of accessibility should be used. If necessary, an opinion from the proper jurisdiction or agency is advisable.

APPENDIX B

FAMILY RESIDENCES

Note

The NFPA does not have a separate code for family residences. Instead, the *NFPA 5000* and the *Life Safety Code* each contain a chapter specific to this building type.

Single-family residences and duplexes are considered Residential occupancies by the building codes. However, there is a separate code publication available specifically for these building types that may be required in the jurisdiction of your project. Prior to the development of the International Codes, the code that applied to these types of residences was called the *One and Two Family Dwelling Code (OTFDC)*. It was published by the Council of American Building Officials (CABO). However, it is now part of the I-Codes as published by the International Code Council (ICC) and is called the *International Residential Code (IRC)*. The first publication of the *IRC* was in 2000. Similar to the other I-Codes, the *IRC* is updated on a three-year cycle. The current edition is 2003 and the next edition will be 2006. The *IRC* is the main code used for single-family homes, two-family homes, duplexes, and townhouses that have their own means of egress. (Other Residential occupancies would be covered by the building code.)

One of the main differences between the *IRC* and the other codes that have been discussed in this book is that all the code requirements are contained in one publication. Unlike codes for other types of projects, which may require using separate code publications for building, fire protection, plumbing, mechanical, and electrical code requirements, these are all included in the *IRC* for family residences. Like the other codes, however, the *IRC* also refers to a variety of standards and other publications. Although family residences do not have as many interior related regulations as other buildings, a number of interior codes and standards are still required. Brief descriptions of the most common interior regulations are given in this appendix. (They are listed in the same order as in the rest of the book.)

Note

In some projects, a code official may require the use of additional codes and standards, especially for plumbing, mechanical, and electrical requirements.

CONSTRUCTION TYPES AND BUILDING SIZE

Unlike the building codes, the *IRC* does not specify different construction types. Family residences are typically wood structures. In some areas, metal framing is also frequently used or required, especially where seismic codes are enforced. However, most houses today still consist of wood framing. Concrete and concrete block are typically used to create the foundation of the structure. Because there are fewer variations in how a residence is built, the *IRC* specifies both the types of material that can be used and the requirements for proper construction. This includes the foundation, floors, walls, ceilings, and the roof of a residence. Even requirements for exterior materials, such as brick, stucco, and wood siding that are used for aesthetic reasons, are included in the *IRC*. The *IRC* also provides requirements for the construction of interior walls, which generally consist of wood studs with gypsum board, or lathe and plaster in older homes.

Note

The *IRC* specifies many aspects of *habitable* residential spaces, including mimimum room sizes and proper lighting, ventilation, and heating requirements.

Performance-like provisions for the use of alternate construction methods and engineered designs are included in the *IRC*. There are additional requirements for residences that are constructed in areas of the country that are affected by high winds, seismic forces, and other unique conditions. A code official must approve any alternative materials and construction methods.

Although the total area of a residence is generally not regulated, to be considered a family residence covered by the *IRC*, the structure typically cannot be more than three stories high. If it has more than three stories, the building codes will apply. (See section on Building Heights and Areas in Chapter 3.) However, the *IRC* does place minimum square footage requirements and minimum ceiling heights in each habitable room within the residence. For example, the minimum area of a habitable room, except for a kitchen, is 70 square feet (6.5 sm) and the ceiling height in a habitable room must typically be a minimum of 7 feet (2134 mm) above the finished floor.

MEANS OF EGRESS

Because the normal number of occupants in a residence is much less than in a similarly sized nonresidential space, determining a safe level of means of egress is not as complicated for residences as it is for nonresidential spaces. The *IRC* requires a minimum of one regulated exterior exit door in each residence. It must be at least 3 feet (914 mm) wide by 80 inches (2032 mm) high and have a specific type of landing on each side. Other doors to the exterior are allowed to have smaller widths. The width of interior doors is not regulated, but the code does set a minimum width for all hallways and exit accesses. The minimum corridor width, for example, is typically 3 feet (914 mm). (A larger width may be required by the accessibility standards for accessible houses.)

Note

Most homes rely on exterior windows as a means of egress during an emergency. The codes set minimum requirements for the size, height, and operation of these windows.

For all sleeping areas (i.e., bedrooms) within a residence, the *IRC* requires an emergency means of egress from these areas. The code typically allows this exit to be an operable window. The bottom of the window cannot be more than 44 inches (1118 mm) above the floor, and the window must have a clear opening of a certain dimension that allows a person to exit through the window in case of a fire.

Note
Townhouses require stricter separation requirements than two-family dwellings.

Stairs and ramps within a residence are regulated as well. However, the dimensions are not as strict as the building codes. For example, tread sizes are allowed to be smaller and riser sizes are allowed to be higher than stairs in nonresidential spaces, and only one handrail is usually required. Similar to other codes, the *IRC* specifies other handrail requirements, such as the mounting height and the handrail grip size. Guards are also required at changes of elevations over a certain height in locations such as porches, balconies, and raised floor areas.

FIRE RESISTANCE

Note
As more people turn toward home health care, additional fire hazards are being created that may not be covered by the codes. Added precautions must be taken.

Fire and smoke separation is required between two or more family dwellings, such as a duplex or a townhouse. Depending on whether they are side by side or above each other, they must be separated by either a fire-resistance-rated wall or a rated floor assembly. Wall assemblies must typically extend to the underside of the roof, and floor assemblies must be continuous to each exterior wall. Any required through-penetrations must be firestopped. Draftstops in attic spaces may be required, as well. (See Chapter 5.)

In single-family residences, the main separation requirement pertains to attached garages. A one-hour assembly must separate any part of the garage that connects to the house, including walls and ceilings. Other fire code requirements are specified for items such as fireplaces and wood-burning stoves.

FIRE PROTECTION

Note
Although the installation of sprinkler systems in private residences is not required by the codes, some jurisdictions have begun to require them.

Fire and smoke detection in family residences mainly consists of smoke detectors. The *IRC* requires that all new homes have smoke detectors that are interconnected and tied into the electrical system with battery backup. Typically, they must be installed in each sleeping room, outside each sleeping area, and on all inhabitable floors. These detectors are required to be interconnected so that if a detector indicates smoke in one area, all of the detectors will sound. The *IRC* also references the household fire-warning equipment provision of the *National Electrical Code (NEC)* for the installation of these systems. If a significant renovation or addition is being made to an existing residence or if a bedroom is added to an existing residence, the code requires that an interconnected smoke-detecting system be added. In some cases, the code official may allow a non-interconnected system to be installed instead. Older homes require at least battery-operated detectors. Although not a component of fire protection, carbon monoxide detectors may be required by some jurisdictions as well. (See inset titled *Carbon Monoxide Detection* on page 228.)

Manual fire extinguishers are the main means of fire suppression in residences. The *IRC* does not require automatic sprinkler systems within family residences. However, some jurisdictions are beginning to require sprinkler systems in family residences as well as in multi-tenant residential units such as townhouses. The voluntary use of sprinkler systems within residences is also growing. In some jurisdictions, trade-offs may be available to developers that will allow them to build more houses on less land when automatic sprinkler systems are installed. These incentives, as well as a desire for more personal protection from fire damage, may cause others to choose to incorporate sprinkler systems within family dwellings or duplexes. When sprinkler systems are installed, the *IRC* refers you to the National Fire Protection Association (NFPA) standard *NFPA 13D, Installation of Sprinkler Systems in One and Two Family Dwellings and Manufactured Homes* for installation standards. (Also see Sprinkler Systems in Chapter 6.)

Note

The installation of carbon monoxide detectors/alarms may be required in some jurisdictions.

PLUMBING

The minimum requirements for plumbing fixtures in family residences typically include one kitchen sink, one water closet, one lavatory, one bathtub or shower unit, and one washing machine hookup. (In a duplex residence, one washing machine hookup may be adequate if it is available to both units.) In addition, each water closet and bathtub or shower must also be installed in a room with privacy. Some jurisdictions may require additional plumbing fixtures, based on the number of bedrooms.

Note

Plastic plumbing pipes are not allowed in some jurisdictions.

The *IRC* generally specifies the size, clearances, installation requirements, and finishes for most fixture types. For example, a shower must have a minimum area of 900 square inches (0.581 s m), have a minimum dimension of 30 inches (762 mm) in one direction and a minimum height of 70 inches (1778 mm), and be surrounded by nonabsorbent materials. Usually these dimensions are less that those required by the plumbing codes for other buildings. For each type of fixture, additional standards are referenced as well. This includes faucets that regulate the maximum temperature of water. In most cases, the manufacturer will have produced the fixture to meet the applicable standards for its use, or the contractor will be aware of its proper installation; however, you must check the standards for each type of fixture, especially in custom design. If accessibility standards are required, you must refer to the appropriate accessibility standard, as well.

MECHANICAL

> **Note**
>
> Limits on the length of certain ventilation and exhaust pipes may dictate the location of an appliance, such as a clothes dryer or vented stove top.

Ventilation in a family residence is directly tied into the size and quantity of exterior windows and how much natural ventilation they supply. For example, the *IRC* specifies that a bathroom should have an operable window of a certain size. If it does not have a window, an exhaust fan with a duct leading directly to the exterior of the building is required. Another important ventilation requirement has to do with the venting of certain common appliances such as dryers, range hoods, fireplace stoves, and HVAC equipment. For example, a dryer exhaust must be ducted to the outside, yet the code sets maximum length limitations that may restrict the location of a laundry room within the house. You should check the ventilation requirements for new or relocated appliances.

The heating system of a house must be able to maintain a specific room temperature in all habitable rooms. Because of the size of a house can vary greatly, a wide variety of systems can be used. Some examples include air units, heat pumps, and baseboard heating. In addition, all heating, ventilating, and air conditioning (HVAC) equipment and appliances must meet certain standards and have a factory-applied label. They must also be located where they are easy to access and maintain.

ELECTRICAL

> **Note**
>
> Although often seen in older homes, exposed lamps such as pull chain and keyless fixtures are typically not allowed in new residential construction.

> **Note**
>
> Newer installations do not allow electrical outlets directly above baseboard heating units.

Although the *IRC* has several chapters dedicated to electrical requirements, including energy-efficiency related items, it also refers to the NFPA's *National Electrical Code (NEC)*. Some of these requirements were discussed in Chapter 8, such as that all electrical outlets must be certain distances apart and that GFCI outlets must be used in wet areas. Other requirements are more specific to residential homes. For example, all inhabitable rooms require a wall switch to control lighting. Certain light fixtures are limited by the code as well.

One of the newest electrical requirements for residences is called the arc-fault circuit interrupter (AFCI). It is a device that protects a circuit and/or outlet from an electrical arc (or bright flash of electrical discharge), which is a cause of many electrical fires. All outlets within sleeping rooms must be on an AFCI protected circuit. This includes the receptacles as well as all other outlets, such as those required for light fixtures and smoke detectors. (See Chapter 8.)

A number of interior appliances also have specific electrical code and/or standards requirements. These include ranges and ovens, open-top gas broiler units, clothes dryers, and water heaters.

FINISHES

Requirements for finishes in private residences are not nearly as strict as those required in other occupancies. The *IRC* requires that all wall and ceiling finishes, except for trims (i.e., baseboards and chair rails) and materials that are less than 0.036 inch (0.90 mm) thick, meet specific *ASTM E84* testing requirements as issued by the American Society for Testing and Materials (ASTM). (*ASTM E84*, also known as the *Steiner Tunnel Test*, is discussed in Chapter 9.) An alternate test *NFPA 286* is also allowed. The most popular residential finishes, wallpaper and paint, are both exempt from these requirements. Some finishes, such as wood veneer and hardboard paneling, must conform to other standards as well. Finishes in shower and bath areas are also regulated. These areas must be finished with a smooth, hard, and nonabsorbent surface (i.e., ceramic tile, marble, or vinyl tile). If glass is used, safety issues must be addressed.

ACCESSIBILITY

The Americans with Disabilities Act (ADA) does not apply to private residences. Instead, the Fair Housing Act (FHA) sets most of the accessibility standards for residences, yet it pertains mostly to multi-unit housing. (See Chapter 1.) Should you want to make a residence accessible, the ICC/ANSI accessibility standard, *ICC/ANSI 117.1*, also has a section dedicated to dwelling units.

Most private residences are not required to be accessible. However, housing built with government funds may require partial or full accessibility. Other interior projects may require a house to be "adaptable." This means that the house could easily be converted to be accessible. An adaptable house may include such things as adjustable counters, movable cabinetry, structurally reinforced walls for future grab bars, and specific fixtures and equipment, such as wall-mounted water closets and a stove with front controls. The additional maneuvering space would also have to be designed into the layout of the dwelling. When a private residence is *required* to be accessible, you must meet the requirements of the *FHA Accessibility Guidelines (FHAG)*.

Note

In the future the *IRC* will have an appendix containing provisions for home day cares operating within a dwelling.

Note

The new *ADA-ABA Accessibility Guidelines* includes requirements for dwelling units throughout its text. Although not required for private residences, they can be referenced when designing an accessible home.

This appendix provides a general overview of residential codes, standards, and accessibility regulations. You must refer to the *IRC* for any specific information. If a jurisdiction does not require the use of the *IRC*, you may need to use the accepted building code instead. (You may also be required to refer to the One- and Two-Family Dwelling chapter in the *Life Safety Code*.) In addition, the *IRC* covers many topics in one publication and may not give enough information for every type of project. In some cases, the code official may refer you to other codes or standards, especially for plumbing, mechanical, and electrical requirements. At the very least, residential codes set the minimum requirements to assure that the occupants' health, safety, and welfare are addressed.

APPENDIX C

EXISTING AND HISTORIC BUILDINGS

The way codes apply to interior projects in existing buildings and historical buildings is slightly different from the way they apply to a new building. In some cases even a different code may apply. A building can be considered an *existing* building if it falls into one of four categories:

1. A building or structure erected and occupied prior to the adoption of the most current building code.
2. A permit has been pulled for the construction of the building.
3. A building is currently under construction.
4. The shell of the building is completed but unoccupied, and individual tenant spaces are being constructed.

You can see that eventually every building is considered an existing building. Whether an existing building is *historical* depends on two things. It must be either listed in the *National Register of Historical Places* or designated as historical under a specific state or local law. Both types of buildings are briefly described in this appendix.

When you are working on projects in existing and historical buildings, many of the codes, standards, and federal regulations described throughout this book must still be referenced. The building codes each have a short chapter geared toward existing buildings. For example, the *International Building Code (IBC)* has a chapter called "Existing Structures" and the *NFPA 5000* has a chapter called "Building Rehabilitation." Each of these chapters also includes requirements for historic structures. The *Life Safety Code (LSC)* has separate requirements for existing occupancies within each of its occupancy chapters.

Note

The requirements found in the *IEBC* are sometimes less restrictive than those found in the *IBC*.

Alternate means and methods requirements found in the building codes and performance criteria found in the performance codes may also be useful. These requirements and criteria set goals instead of exact requirements so that alternative solutions can be developed that address the unique conditions found in older buildings. If the use of performance codes is allowed by the jurisdiction, and you decide to use performance criteria, be sure to work closely with a code official.

Note

The first I-Code specifically for existing buildings became available in 2003, called the *International Existing Building Code (IEBC)*.

In addition to requirements within the building codes, other publications may apply as well. For example, in the past, the Southern Building Code Congress International (SBCCI) published the *Standard Existing Building Code*, and the International Conference of Building Officials (ICBO) published the *Uniform Code for Building Conservation*. These are now available from the International Code Council (ICC) as part of their legacy codes. In some jurisdictions, these existing building codes may still be referenced. However, in 2003, the ICC developed the first *International Existing Building Code (IEBC)*. This code establishes regulations specifically for repairs, alterations, and work performed because of changes in occupancy in existing buildings and historic buildings. It also includes requirements for additions and relocated buildings. The *IEBC* includes both prescriptive and performance-based code requirements, as well as accessibility requirements. In general, it is meant to encourage the reuse of existing buildings by setting realistic standards while still providing for reasonable life safety within an existing building. When working in an existing or historic building, you must confirm with the jurisdiction if one of the existing building codes will apply.

As with most projects, some federal guidelines may also apply. For example, many of the ADA guidelines discussed throughout this book will still apply to certain existing and historic buildings. (See Appendix A.) In addition, depending on the use of the project, other federal guidelines may include the Department of Housing and Urban Development's (HUD) *Rehabilitation Guidelines* and the U.S. Department of Interior's (DOI) *Secretary of the Interior's Standards for Rehabilitation*, written specifically for historic buildings on the *National Register*. (Refer to the Bibliography on the companion Web site for additional sources.)

EXISTING BUILDINGS

Note

The USGBC now has a LEED rating for existing buildings, known as *LEED-EB*.

Because codes change over time, there are almost always parts of any existing building that do not comply with the most current codes. When a repair, alteration, or addition is made to a portion of an existing building, the codes do not normally require the whole building to comply with the most current building codes. So when changes occur, it has to be decided to what extent the new work within the existing building and the other areas will need to meet the current codes. If the *IEBC* or a similar existing building code is not used in your jurisdiction, it will be up to the code official to decide. However, the *IEBC* can be used to clarify what requirements must be met. The *IEBC* (if allowed by the jurisdiction) refers to the *IBC* to set certain code requirements and includes alternate code requirements when meeting *IBC* requirements may not be reasonable.

Both the *IBC* and the *IEBC* classify the extent of work occurring within an existing building as repairs, alterations, changes in occupancy, and additions. These levels of work are specifically defined in the chapter on "Classification of Work" within the *IEBC*. These same types of work are also addressed in a separate chapter for historic buildings in the *IBC*. In addition, in the *IEBC*, alterations are further divided into three separate levels. In general, the more work that is being done, the more improvements within an existing building will be required by the code. The different levels of work as found in the *IEBC* are discussed next. The NFPA codes use similar categories; however, some of the details may vary. If you are working in a jurisdiction that requires the *LSC* in addition to the *IBC* or the *IEBC*, be sure to review each publication. Since the *IEBC* is sometimes more lenient, you may need to consult a code official.

Repairs

According to the *IEBC*, *repairs* include patching or restoration of materials, elements, components, equipment, or fixtures of a building. It is considered the lowest level of change within a building, because in most cases the work is done for maintenance reasons only.

> **Note**
>
> When using the *IEBC*, work is designated by repairs, alterations, change in occupancy, or additions.

Usually when repairs are made to an existing building, the *IEBC* allows the current conditions to be maintained and does not require the area or materials to be brought up to current code. For example, fire protection, accessibility, and means of egress are allowed to be repaired so that the same level of safety is maintained. However, there are exceptions. For example, hazardous materials or conditions such as asbestos and lead-based paint cannot be reused. Or, for example, glazing located in hazardous locations that is being replaced must meet the current requirements for safety glazing. In addition, some system requirements call for an increased level of safety but not to the level of what would be required for new construction. This typically applies to the structural, electrical, mechanical, and plumbing systems. You will need to check the specific requirements for each type of system.

Alterations

Typically, work done to a building that is not a repair or an addition is considered an alteration. For *alterations* made to an existing building, the codes typically require only the new work to comply as long as it does not cause other portions of the building to be in violation of the code. For example, the new work cannot demolish an existing fire wall or block an existing exit. However, the *IEBC* creates three separate levels of alterations. Each represents a different level of work that is being performed within the building. The more work that is done, the higher the level of compliance with the *IBC* or with the *IEBC* is required. Level 1 represents the least amount of work and Level 3 represents the most amount of work. For example, the significant difference between a Level 2 alteration and a Level 3 alteration is the proportionate amount of the building being altered. Below is a brief description of the three levels.

Note

There are three levels of alterations according to the *IEBC*. Each requires a different level of code compliance with the *IEBC* and the *IBC*.

- *Level 1:* A Level 1 alteration includes the removal and replacement or covering of existing materials, elements, or equipment, using new materials, elements, or equipment. This would include replacing tile in a restroom or a handrail on a stair.
- *Level 2:* This level of alteration includes the modification to the layout of a space, to doors or windows, or to a building system, or the installation of new equipment. Alterations considered to be Level 2 may require additional work to that area or other areas of the building other than what was originally intended.
- *Level 3:* This level of alteration applies when the work area exceeds more than 50 percent of the building area.

Whether or not the *IEBC* is being used in your jurisdiction, if the design calls for a significant change, the code official can require that more of the building be brought up to code. For example, in the renovation of an older building where a large amount of electrical work is being done, the code official can require that the entire electrical service and wiring be updated, especially if more than 50 percent of the system is being changed. In the past, this has been referred to as the *50 percent rule.* In all cases, if you are doing an extensive renovation, you should work closely with a code official to determine what level of compliance will be required for your project and building.

Change in Occupancy

When the purpose or level of activity within a building changes, it is considered a *change in occupancy.* This can occur if a new tenant moves into the building or an existing tenant changes its use or classification. (See New versus Existing Occupancies in Chapter 2.) The space must typically meet the most current code requirements for that occupancy. However, other spaces within the building can usually be left alone. The *IEBC* chapter on "Change of Occupancy" discusses to what extent the codes must be met. In most cases, the requirements are based on if the new occupancy is considered more or less hazardous than the original occupancy.

The *IEBC* also includes minimum accessibility requirements for a change in occupancy. These include (1) one accessible entrance, (2) one accessible route from the entrance to the primary function area, and (3) the use of accessible signage. However, changes to an existing building must still meet certain ADA guidelines which may be more stringent than the *IEBC*. (Requirements in the ADA guidelines might also affect areas outside the space of the occupancy. See Appendix A.)

Additions

According to the codes, an addition is an increase in the floor area, number of stories, or height of a building. In most cases, new additions to an existing building must comply with the current building code. In the *IEBC*, most of the requirements focus on how the increase in area or height will affect the structural components of the existing building. Additions to Residential occupancies also require an increase in fire protection.

Whether you are doing minimal work such as a repair, a small alteration, or a large renovation for reuse of an existing building, you must establish which level of the *IEBC* applies to your project. In some jurisdictions, when working on an interior project in an existing building, you may be required to have the building evaluated by a code official to determine if any additional changes are required. In other jurisdictions, you may be directed to use the *IEBC* or a similar document to determine the required codes for any work performed in an existing building. What is required generally depends on the size of the alteration, the type of occupancy, and the condition of the existing building. On the other hand, if you are working on a project in an older building, you may want to have a code official walk the building with you even if it is not required. This is especially helpful when you are changing the occupancy of the entire building. An initial walk-through can give both of you a better understanding of your options as you proceed.

You must also refer to the ADA (or the FHA in certain Residential occupancies). Although the ADA specifically states that existing buildings must fully comply with the accessibility requirements as stated in the ADA guidelines, there are some alternate solutions for existing buildings and for alterations to existing buildings. For example, the ADA does allow exceptions where compliance with the ADA guidelines is either structurally infeasible, too costly, or would cause an unsafe situation. These exceptions must be fully analyzed. Refer to the ADA and other experts when necessary. (See Appendix A for more information.)

HISTORICAL BUILDINGS

When working on a project in a historical building, there is an obvious need to balance protecting the historical character of a building or interior space and providing an acceptable level of life safety. It is important to research the codes that apply and to be aware of alternative requirements. As previously mentioned, the *IBC*, the *NFPA 5000*, and the *IEBC* all have special provisions for historical buildings. (The *IEBC* has a separate chapter titled "Historic Buildings.") Many jurisdictions have state or local regulations for historical buildings, as well. It is important to check for the correct local procedures before starting a project. For example, some historical regulations control only the preservation of the exterior of a building; however, this may include any interior work that is visible from the exterior of the building.

The key to historical projects is to determine which codes must be met and what approval procedures must be followed. Communication with your code department and historic preservation organizations is imperative. Some historical organizations have the power to grant alternatives or waivers to code provisions. For example, some jurisdictions may allow safety equivalencies. In addition, many of the codes include alternative requirements that can be used if approved by the code official. It may also be necessary to apply to the appeals or variance boards for special circumstances. (See Chapter 10.)

In most cases, a historic structure will be required to be accessible if used by the public. In some cases, a limited level of accessibility may be allowed by the building codes and the accessibility standards. In each of the building codes, there are provisions for accessibility for historic structures. These codes provide minimum requirements and specify alternate solutions when compliance with their accessibility chapters is not feasible. Typically these alternate solutions and reduced level of accessibility must be approved by the local code official.

The ADA allows exceptions or alternative solutions for historical buildings when a requirement threatens a building's historical significance—for example, where the required change or addition would destroy a historical detail of the building or space. Some of these alternative solutions are stated in the ADA guidelines. Others may need to be discussed with your state or local historical preservation official or directly with the ADA Access Board. Remember, though, that approval of an alternative solution for one space or area does not exempt the whole building from meeting other requirements.

The ADA does specifically state minimum requirements that all historical buildings must meet. These include (1) at least one accessible route into the building, (2) at least one accessible toilet when toilet facilities are provided, (3) access to all public areas on the main floor, and (4) accessible displays and written information. There are a number of requirements in the ADA guidelines that can typically be met without major disruption. Examples include installing compatible offset hinges to widen doorways, adding full-length mirrors and raised toilet seats in restrooms, and replacing door and faucet handles with lever controls. However, all ADA regulations must be followed whenever possible.

Remember that an old or historic building still must be safe. In addition to the codes and documents already mentioned, there are some NFPA standards that may help you develop alternatives for safety and accessibility as well:

- *NFPA 909, Protection of Cultural Resources,* which includes Appendix L, "*Guideline on Fire Ratings of Archaic Materials and Assemblies*"
- *NFPA 914, Fire Protection in Historic Structures*

When existing conditions seem to make meeting the codes and accessibility requirements difficult, the exemptions allowed for existing and/or historic buildings should be considered. It may be necessary to discuss alternatives with the local officials or federal officials. In other cases, a code variance may be required. However, whether the building is existing or historical, the overall goal when making interior changes is to make the building as safe as possible—and in the process, as accessible as possible.

APPENDIX D

ABBREVIATIONS

The companion Web site, www.wiley.com/harmon, contains a comprehensive list of abbreviations for organizations, associations, agencies, and institutions that are often used when reading code publications or talking to code officials and other professionals. Included are standards organizations, code organizations, professional associations, and government agencies. When available, Web sites have been included in parentheses. The most common code and standards publications and federal regulation acronyms have also been included and are highlighted with italics. (Older model code publications no longer being updated are included on the list, but they have been noted with an asterisk to distinguish them from the more current ones.) The list is in alphabetical order by abbreviation.

APPENDIX E

CODE RESOURCES

Eventually you will want to start your own codes library, or you may need to find a specific book for a project you are working on. This appendix includes the names, addresses, phone numbers, and Web sites of the many codes, standards, national organizations, and government regulatory agencies. A list of professional bookstores in the United States can be found on the Web site for this book at www.wiley.com/harmon.

All of the codes and standards organizations carry their own publications. Some of these sources are listed in the Bibliography of this book on the accompanying Web site. Many of these organizations also sell literature and forms to complement these publications. The national organizations can provide supportive data on the codes and standards. Each of the federal regulatory agencies supplies a copy of its own regulations and provides other literature upon request.

Professional bookstores carry a variety of the code publications and many other useful reference books. Many of them now have on-line catalogs and ordering. Most will also mail you a free book listing or catalog upon request. The bookstores have been listed by state with a number of on-line bookstores included on this book's Web site at www.wiley.com/harmon.

CODES ORGANIZATIONS

International Code Council (ICC)
5203 Leesburg Pike, Suite 600
Falls Church, VA 22041
(800) 786-4452
www.iccsafe.org

National Fire Protection Association (NFPA)
1 Batterymarch Park
Quincy, MA 02169-7471
(617) 770-3000
www.nfpa.org

FEDERAL REGULATORY AGENCIES

Architectural and Transportation Barriers Compliance Board
(ATBCB, also known as The Access Board)
1331 F Street NW
Suite 1000
Washington, DC 20004-1111
(800) 872-2253
(800) 993-2822 (TTY)
www.access-board.gov

National Institute of Standards and Technology (NIST)
100 Bureau Drive
Gaithersburg, MD 20899-8600
(301) 975-6478
(301) 975-8295 (TTY)
www.nist.gov

National Park Service (NPS)
1849 C Street NW
Washington, DC 20240
(202) 208-6843
www.nps.gov

Occupational Safety and Health Administration (OSHA)
200 Constitution Avenue NW
Washington, DC 20210
(202) 523-8148
www.osha.gov

U.S. Department of Energy (DOE)
1000 Independence Avenue SW
Washington, DC 20585
(800) dial-DOE
www.doe.gov

U.S. Department of Housing and Urban Development (HUD)
451 Seventh Street SW
Washington, DC 20410
(202) 708-1455
www.hud.gov

U.S. Department of the Interior (DOI)
1849 C Street NW
Washington, DC 20240
(202) 208-3100
www.doi.gov

U.S. Department of Justice (DOJ)
Office of Americans with Disabilities Act
Civil Rights Division—Disability Rights Section
950 Pennsylvania Avenue NW
Washington, DC 20530-0001
(202) 514-0301 (Voice)
(202) 514-0383 (TTY)
www.usdoj.gov

U.S. Department of Labor (DOL)
Frances Perkins Building
200 Constitution Avenue NW
Washington, DC 20210
(866) 4-USA-DOL
(877) 889-5627 (TTY)
www.dol.gov

U.S. Department of Transportation (DOT)
400 7th Street, SW
Washington, DC 20590
(202) 366-4000
www.dot.gov

U.S. Environmental Protection Agency (EPA)
Ariel Rios Building
1200 Pennsylvania Avenue NW
Washington, DC 20460
(202) 272-0167
www.epa.gov

U.S. Federal Communications Commission (FCC)
1919 M Street NW
Washington, DC 20554
(202) 632-7260 (Voice)
(202) 632-6999 (TDD)
www.fcc.gov

U.S. Federal Emergency Management Agency (FEMA)
500 C Street SW
Washington, DC 20472
(202) 566-1600
www.fema.gov

STANDARDS ORGANIZATIONS

American National Standards Institute (ANSI)
1819 L Street NW
6th Floor
Washington, DC 20036
(202) 293-8020
www.ansi.org

American Society of Heating, Refrigeration, and Air Conditioning Engineers (ASHRAE)
1791 Tullie Circle NE
Atlanta, GA 30329
(404) 636-8400
www.ashrae.org

American Society for Testing and Materials (ASTM)
100 Barr Harbor Drive
West Conshoshocken, PA 19428-2959
(610) 832-9585
www.astm.org

National Fire Protection Association (NFPA)
1 Batterymarch Park
Quincy, MA 02169-7471
(617) 770-3000
www.nfpa.org

Underwriters Laboratories (UL)
333 Pfingsten Road
Northbrook, IL 60062-2096
(877) 854-3577
www.ul.com

NATIONAL ORGANIZATIONS

National Conference of States on Building Codes and Standards (NCSBCS)
505 Huntmar Park Drive
Suite 210
Herndon, VA 20170
(703) 437-0100
www.ncsbcs.org

National Institute of Building Sciences (NIBS)
1090 Vermont Avenue NW
Suite 700
Washington, DC 20005-4905
(202) 289-7800
www.nibs.org

PROFESSIONAL BOOKSTORES

A list of professional bookstores and on-line bookstores can be found on this book's companion Web site: www.wiley.com/harmon.

BIBLIOGRAPHY (BY TOPIC)

The bibliography for this book is organized by the following topics, and can be found on the companion Web site at www.wiley.com/harmon.

ACCESSIBILITY

CODE INFORMATION AND CODE OFFICIALS

COMMUNICATION REQUIREMENTS

CONSTRUCTION TYPES AND BUILDING SIZES

ELECTRICAL CODES

EXISTING AND HISTORIC BUILDINGS

FINISHES AND FURNISHINGS

FIRE PROTECTION

FIRE RESISTANT MATERIALS AND ASSEMBLIES

MEANS OF EGRESS

MECHANICAL CODES

OCCUPANCY CLASSIFICATION

PLUMBING CODES

RESIDENTIAL—ONE AND TWO FAMILY

SUSTAINABILITY

GLOSSARY

ACCEPTABLE METHODS When using performance codes, these are the design, analysis and testing methods that have been approved for use in developing design solutions for compliance with a code requirement.

ACCESSIBLE As it applies to accessibility, a building, room, or space that can be approached, entered, and used by persons with disabilities. Also generally applies to equipment that is easy to approach without locked doors or change in elevation or to wiring that is exposed and capable of being removed.

ACCESSIBLE MEANS OF EGRESS See Means of Egress, Accessible.

ACCESSIBLE ROUTE A continuous and unobstructed path connecting all accessible elements and spaces of a building including corridors, floors, ramps, elevators, lifts, and clear floor spaces at fixtures.

ACCESSIBLE UNIT A dwelling unit or sleeping unit that meets all the requirements for accessibility.

ADDITION An expansion, extension, or increase in the gross floor area of a building, the number of stories, or the height of a building.

AFTER FLAME When an item continues to hold a flame after the source of ignition is removed.

AISLE An unenclosed path of travel that forms part of a exit access or the space between elements such as furniture and equipment that provides clearance to pass by and/or use the elements.

AISLE ACCESSWAY The initial portion of an exit access that leads to an aisle.

ALARM NOTIFICATION APPLIANCE A part of the fire alarm system which notifies occupants that a fire has been detected; can include audible, tactile, visible and/or voice instruction.

ALARM SYSTEM See Emergency Alarm System and Fire Alarm System.

ALARM VERIFICATION A feature of a fire alarm system that delays notification of occupants in order to confirm the accuracy of the smoke or fire detection.

ALLEY See Public Way.

ALTERATION Any construction or modification to an existing building or facility other than a repair or addition.

ALTERNATE METHODS Refers to methods, materials, and systems used other than those specifically mentioned in the codes; use of these alternates requires prior approved from the authority having jurisdiction. (See also Equivalency.)

ANNULAR SPACE The opening around a penetrating item.

ANNUNCIATOR A device with one or more types of indicators, such as lamps and alphanumeric displays, that provide status information about a circuit, condition, or location.

APPROVED Acceptable to the code official or Authority Having Jurisdiction (AHJ).

ARC FAULT CIRCUIT INTERRUPTER A device that disconnects the electrical power to the circuit when it detects an unexpected electrical surge (or arc); typically required in sleeping rooms; commonly known as AFCI.

AREA, FIRE The aggregate floor area enclosed and bounded by fire walls, fire barriers, exterior walls, and/or fire-rated horizontal assemblies of a building.

AREA, GROSS FLOOR The area within the inside perimeter of a building's exterior walls, exclusive of vent shafts and interior courts, with no deduction for corridors, stairs, closets, thickness of interior walls, columns, toilet rooms, mechanical rooms, or other unoccupiable areas.

AREA, GROSS LEASABLE The total floor area designated for tenant occupancy and exclusive use measured from the centerlines of joint partitions to the outside of the tenant walls; includes all tenant areas as well as those used for storage.

AREA, NET FLOOR The area actually occupied within a building *not* including accessory unoccupied areas such as corridors, stairs, closets, thickness of interior walls, columns, toilet rooms, and mechanical rooms.

AREA OF REFUGE A space or area providing protection from fire and/or smoke where persons who are unable to use the stairways can remain temporarily to await instruction or assistance during an emergency evacuation; protection can be created by rated enclosures and/or an approved fire protection system. (Code term.)

AREA OF RESCUE ASSISTANCE An area that has a direct access to an exit where people who are unable to use stairs may remain temporarily in safety to await further instructions or assistance during emergency evacuations. (Accessibility term.)

AREA, WORK The portion of a building affected by renovation or modification based on work indicated on construction documents. In some jurisdictions the work area may also include incidental areas not included in the permit but that are affected by the work.

AS-BUILT DRAWINGS See Record Drawings.

ASSEMBLY, CONSTRUCTION Building materials used together to create a structure or building element.

ASSEMBLY, FIRE DOOR Any combination of a door, frame, hardware, and other accessories that together provide a specific degree of fire protection to the opening in a rated wall.

ASSEMBLY, FIRE-RATED A combination of parts (including all required construction materials, hardware, anchorage, frames, sills, etc.) that when used together make up a structural or building element that has passed various fire tests and has been assigned a fire rating; includes fire resistant assemblies and fire protection assemblies. (See also Rating, Fire Resistance and Rating, Fire Protection.)

ASSEMBLY, FIRE WINDOW Any combination of glazing or glass block, frame, hardware, and other accessories that together give protection against the passage of fire.

ASSEMBLY, FLOOR FIRE DOOR Any combination of a fire door, frame, hardware, and other accessories installed in a horizontal plane which together provide a specific degree of fire protection to a through opening in a fire rate floor.

ATRIUM A roofed, multistory open space contained within a building that is intended for occupancy.

ATTIC The space between the ceiling joists of the top story and the roof rafters above.

AUTHORITY HAVING JURISDICTION (or AHJ) Used by the codes to indicate organizations, offices, or individuals that administer and enforce the codes. See also Jurisdiction, Code Department, and Code Official.

AUTOMATIC That which provides a function without human intervention.

AUTOMATIC CLOSING An opening protective (e.g., door, window) that has a closure that is activated by smoke or heat, causing it to close in an emergency to prevent the spread of fire and smoke.

AUTOMATIC FIRE-EXTINGUISHING SYSTEM An approved system that is designed and installed to automatically detect a fire and discharge an extinguishing agent without human intervention to suppress and/or extinguish a fire; can consists of carbon dioxide, foam, wet or dry chemical, a halogenated extinguishing agent, or an automatic sprinkler system.

AUTOMATIC SPRINKLER SYSTEM A system using water to suppress or extinguish a fire when its heat-activated element is heated to a specific temperature or above.

BACKCOATING The process of coating the underside of a fabric or finish to improve its durability and/or serve as a heat barrier.

BACKDRAFT See Flashover.

BALLAST A magnetic coil that adjusts current through a fluorescent tube, providing the current surge to start the lamp.

BANDWIDTH Refers to the capacity for communication cabling to move information; for telephone cabling it is measured in cycles per second (Hertz) and for data cabling it is measured in bits per second (bps).

BARRIER Any building element, equipment, or object that restricts or prevents the intended use of a space and/or protects one building material or finish from another.

BARRIER, FIRE A continuous fire resistance-rated vertical or horizontal assembly of materials designed to resist the spread of fire in which openings are protected; used to protect an enclosure and can consist of wall, floor, and ceiling assemblies. (See also Partition, Fire.)

BARRIER, SMOKE A continuous vertical or horizontal membrane, such as a wall, floor, or ceiling assembly (with or without protected openings) that is designed and constructed to restrict the movement and passage of smoke. (See also Partition, Smoke.)

BASEMENT Any story of a building that is partially or completely below grade level, located so that the vertical distance from the grade to the floor below is greater than the grade to the floor above.

BATHING FACILITY A room containing a bathtub, shower, spa, or similar bathing fixture either separately or in conjunction with a watercloset and lavatory. Also sometimes called a bathroom.

BORROWED LIGHT An interior stationary window that allows passage of light from one area to the next.

BOX, ELECTRICAL A wiring device that is used to contain wire terminations where they connect to other wires, switches, or outlets.

BOX, JUNCTION An electrical box where several wires are joined together.

BRANCH A horizontal pipe that leads from a main, riser, or stack pipe to the plumbing fixture or sprinkler head.

BUILDING Any structure usually enclosed by walls and a roof used or intended for supporting, sheltering, enclosing, or housing any use or occupancy including persons, animals, and property of any kind.

Includes private buildings (not open to the public) and public buildings.

BUILDING CODE Regulations that stress the construction of a building and the hazardous materials or equipment used inside.

BUILDING CORE A building element that is vertically continuous through one or more floors of a building, consisting of shafts for the vertical distribution of building services. (See also Shaft.)

BUILDING ELEMENT Any building component that makes up a building, such as walls, columns, floors, and beams, and can include load-bearing and nonload-bearing elements; known as structure elements in some older codes. (See also Structural Elements.)

BUILDING ENVELOPE Term used by energy codes to refer to the element of a building which encloses condition spaces through which thermal energy is capable of being transferred to or from the exterior or other spaces not inside the shell of the building envelope.

BUILDING, EXISTING Any structure erected and occupied prior to the adoption of the most current appropriate code, or a structure for which a construction permit has been issued.

BUILDING HEIGHT See Height, Building.

BUILDING, HISTORIC A building or facility that is either listed in or eligible for listing in the *National Register of Historic Places*, or that is designated as historic under a state or local law.

BUILDING OFFICIAL See Code Official.

BUILDING TYPE A specific class or category within an occupancy classification.

CABLE A conductor, consisting of two or more wires combined in the same protective sheathing and insulated to keep the wires from touching.

CEILING HEIGHT See Height, Ceiling.

CEILING RADIATION DAMPER See Damper, Ceiling Radiation.

CHANGE IN USE or OCCUPANCY See Occupancy, Change in Use.

CHILDREN As defined by the codes, people 12 years old and younger (i.e., elementary school age and younger).

CIRCUIT The path of electrical current that circles from the electrical source to the electrical box or fixture and back to the source.

CIRCUIT, BRANCH A circuit that supplies electricity to a number of outlets or fixtures.

CIRCUIT BREAKER A safety device that opens or disconnects a circuit to stop the flow of electricity when an overload or fault occurs.

CIRCULATION PATH An interior or exterior way of passage from one place to another such as walks, corridors, courtyards, stairways, ramps.

CLEAN OUT An access opening in the drainage system used to remove obstructions.

CLEAR FLOOR SPACE The minimum unobstructed floor or ground space required to accommodate a single stationary wheelchair and its occupant.

CLOSED-CIRCUIT TELEPHONE A telephone with a dedicated line, such as a house phone, courtesy phone, or phone that must be used to gain entrance to a facility.

CODE DEPARTMENT A local government agency that administers and enforces the codes and standards within a jurisdiction; also sometimes referred to by the codes as *Authority Having Jurisdiction*, or AHJ.

CODE OFFICIAL An officer or other designated authority charged with the administration and enforcement of the codes, standards, and regulations with a jurisdiction; also known as a building official and sometimes referred to by the codes as *Authority Having Jurisdiction*, or AHJ.

CODE, PERFORMANCE A code that is generally described and gives you an objective but not the specifics of how to achieve it. The focus is on the desired outcome, not a single solution, and compliance is based on meeting the criteria established by the performance code; engineering tools, methodologies, and performance criteria must be used to substantiate the use of the code requirement.

CODE, PRESCRIPTIVE A code that provides a specific requirement that must be met for the design, construction, and maintenance of a building. The focus is on a specific solution to achieve an objective or outcome based on historical experience and established engineering.

CODE VIOLATION Not complying with a code as stated in a code book or required by a jurisdiction, whether the noncompliance is deliberate or unintentional.

C.O.M. An acronym for "customer's own material"; refers to fabrics that are ordered separately from the furniture that they will cover.

COMBINATION FIRE/SMOKE DAMPER See Damper, Combination Fire/Smoke.

COMBUSTIBLE Refers to materials, such as building materials or finishes, that are capable of being ignited or affected by excessive heat or gas in a relatively short amount of time.

COMMON PATH OF TRAVEL That portion of an exit access along which occupants are required to travel before two separate and distinct paths of egress travel to separate exits are available. Paths that merge are also considered common paths of travel.

COMMON USE See Use, Common.

COMPARTMENTATION The process of creating confined spaces or areas within a building for the purpose of containing the spread of fire or smoke.

COMPARTMENT, FIRE A space within a building enclosed by fire barriers on all sides, including the top and bottom.

COMPARTMENT, SMOKE A space within a building enclosed by smoke barriers on all sides, including the top and bottom.

CONCEALED Items in a building rendered inaccessible by the structure or finish of the building.

CONDITIONED SPACE An area, room, or space being heated and/or cooled by any equipment or appliance.

CONDUCTOR A cable or wire that carries and distributes electricity.

CONDUIT, ELECTRICAL A raceway or pipe used to house and protect electrical wires and cables.

CONDUIT, PLUMBING A pipe or channel for transporting water.

CONSULTANT An individual who provides specialized services to an owner, designer, code official, or contractor.

CONSTRUCTION ASSEMBLY See Assembly, Construction.

CONSTRUCTION DOCUMENTS Written, graphic, electronic, and pictorial documents prepared or assembled for describing the design, location, and physical characteristics of the elements of the project necessary for obtaining a building permit; includes construction drawings, specifications, and any other required code information.

CONSTRUCTION DRAWINGS The floor plans, elevations, notes, schedules, legends, and other drawing details used to convey what is being built and included as part of the construction documents.

CONSTRUCTION TYPE The combination of materials and assemblies used in the construction of a building based on the varying degrees of fire resistance and combustibility.

CONTRACT REVIEW Similar to a plan review but performed by a consultant who is retained by the code department for that purpose. (See also Plan Review.)

CONTROL AREA A building or portion of a building where hazardous materials are allowed to be stored, dispensed, used, or handled in maximum allowable quantities.

CORRIDOR A passageway that creates a path of travel that is enclosed by walls, a ceiling, and doors that lead to other rooms or areas or provides a path of egress travel to an exit.

COURT See Egress Court.

DAMPER, CEILING RADIATION A listed device installed in a ceiling membrane of a fire-resistance rated floor/ceiling or roof/ceiling assembly to automatically limit the radiative heat transfer through an air inlet/outlet opening.

DAMPER, COMBINATION FIRE/SMOKE A listed device that meets the requirements of both a fire damper and a smoke damper.

DAMPER, FIRE A listed device installed in ducts or air transfer openings that automatically closes upon detection of heat to interrupt migratory airflow and restrict the passage of flame.

DAMPER, SMOKE A listed device installed in ducts and air transfer openings that is designed to resist the passage of air and smoke during an emergency.

DEAD-END CORRIDOR A hallway in which a person is able to travel in only one direction to reach an exit.

DEAD LOAD The weight of permanent construction such as walls, partitions, framing, floors, ceilings, roofs, and all other stationary building elements and the fixed service equipment of a building. (See also Live Load.)

DELUGE SYSTEM An automatic sprinkler system connected to a water source that delivers a large amount of water to an area upon detection of fire by a separate automatic detection system.

DEMARK The point in a communication room or other location in a building where the wiring from the utility company enters the building and is connected to the building wiring.

DESIGN DOCUMENTS See Construction Documents.

DETECTABLE WARNING A standardized surface texture applied to or built into a walking surface to warn visually impaired people of hazards in the path of travel.

DETECTOR, FIRE A device that detects one of the signatures of a fire and initiates action.

DETECTOR, HEAT A fire detector that senses heat produced by burning substances and initiates action.

DETECTOR, SMOKE A device that detects the visible or invisible particles of combustion and initiates action.

DEVICE: A unit of an electrical system that is intended to carry but not utilize electric energy.

DISABLED A person who has a condition that limits a major life activity. This can include the inability to walk and difficulty in walking, reliance on walking aids, blindness and visual impairment, deafness and hearing impairment, uncoordination, reaching and manipulation disabilities, lack of stamina, difficulty in interpreting and reacting to sensory information, and extremes in physical size. (See also Severe Mobility Impairment.)

DRAFT STOP A continuous membrane used to subdivide a concealed space within a building (such as an attic space) to restrict the passage of smoke, heat, and flames.

DRAIN PIPE Any pipe that carries wastewater in a building. (See also Soil Pipe.)

DUCT An enclosed rectangular or circular tube used to transfer hot and cold air to different parts of a building; can be rigid or flexible.

DWELLING Any building that contains one or two dwelling units to be built, used, rented, leased, or hired out and intended for living purposes. (See also Living Space.)

DWELLING UNIT A single unit providing complete independent living facilities for one or more persons, including permanent provisions for living, sleeping, eating, cooking, and sanitation.

EGRESS A way out or exit.

EGRESS COURT An outside space with building walls on at least three sides and open to the sky that provides access to a public way.

ELEVATOR A hoistway and lowering mechanism equipped with a car or platform that moves on glides in a vertical direction through successive floors or levels. (See also Hoistway.)

ELEVATOR LOBBY A space directly connected to the doors of an elevator.

EMERGENCY ALARM SYSTEM A system that provides indication and warning of emergency situations involving hazardous materials and summons appropriate aid. A signal may be audible, visual, or voice instruction.

EMPLOYEE WORK AREA As used for accessibility purposes, any or all portions of a space used only by employees and only for work; excludes corridors, toilet facilities, breakrooms, etc.

ENERGIZED Electrically connected to a source of voltage.

ENERGY The capacity for doing work in various forms which is capable of being transformed from one into another, such as thermal, mechanical, electrical, and chemical.

ENERGY ANALYSIS A method for determining the annual (8,760 hours) energy use of the proposed design and standard design based on hour-by-hour estimates of energy use.

ENERGY, RENEWABLE Includes energy derived from natural daylighting and photosynthetic processes and other solar radiation sources such as wind, waves, tides, and lake or pond thermal differences, as well as from the internal heat of the earth, such as nocturnal thermal exchanges.

ENERGY, SOLAR Source of natural daylighting and thermal, chemical, or electrical energy derived directly from the conversion of solar radiation.

ENTRANCE Any access point into a building or portions of a building used for the purpose of entering.

ENTRANCE, PUBLIC An entrance that is not a service entrance or a restricted entrance.

ENTRANCE, RESTRICTED An entrance that is made available for common use on a controlled basis, but not public use, and that is not a service entrance.

ENTRANCE, SERVICE An entrance intended primarily for the delivery of goods and services.

EQUIVALENCY Term used by the codes to indicate alternate systems, methods, and/or devices that are allowed because they have been determined by a code official to meet or exceed a specific code requirement.

ESSENTIAL FACILITIES See Facilities, Essential.

EXHAUST AIR Air removed from a conditioned space through openings, ducts, plenums, or concealed spaces to the exterior of the building and not reused.

EXISTING BUILDING OR STRUCTURE See Building, Existing.

EXIT The portion of a means of egress that leads from an exit access to an exit discharge and is separated from other interior spaces by fire-rated construction and assemblies as required to provide a protected path of travel.

EXIT ACCESS The portion of a means of egress that leads from an occupied portion of a building to an exit.

EXIT DISCHARGE The portion of a means of egress between the termination of an exit and the public way.

EXIT ENCLOSURE Similar to an exit passageway but can be in a vertical or horizontal direction.

EXIT, HORIZONTAL A fire-rated passage that leads to an area of refuge on the same floor within a building or on the same level of an adjacent building.

EXIT PASSAGEWAY A fire-rated portion of a means of egress that provides a protected path of egress in a horizontal direction to the exit discharge or public way.

EXIT, SECONDARY An alternative exit, not necessarily required by codes.

EXPANDED VINYL WALLCOVERING A wallcovering that consists of a woven textile backing, an expanded vinyl base coat layer, and a nonexpanded vinyl skin coat distinguishing it from standard vinyl wallcovering; typically requires a more stringent finish test.

FACILITY All or any portion of buildings, structures, site improvements, elements, and pedestrian or vehicular routes located on a site.

FACILITIES, ESSENTIAL Buildings or other structures that are intended to remain operational in the event of extreme environmental loading from flood, wind, snow, or earthquake.

FAMILY TOILET FACILITY A single-toilet facility that provides additional space to allow for someone to assist in the room.

FAUCET A fitting that controls the flow of water at the end of a water supply line.

FEEDER A conductor that supplies electricity between the service equipment and the branch circuits.

FENESTRATION Term used by energy codes to include skylights, roof windows, vertical windows (fixed and operable), opaque doors, glazed doors, glass block, and combination opaque/glazed doors. (See also Opaque Areas.)

FIRE ALARM SYSTEM A system that is activated by the detection of fire or smoke or by a manual *pull* station which sends a signal to the occupants of a controlled area that a fire has been detected; it may also be activated by an extinguishing system.

FIRE AREA See Area, Fire.

FIRE BARRIER See Barrier, Fire.

FIRE BLOCKER Fire-rated material used to protect materials that are not fire rated.

FIRE BLOCKING A building material (such as caulk or expandable foam) installed to resist the free passage of flame to other areas of the building through concealed spaces.

FIRE COMMAND CENTER The principal location where the status of various detection, alarm, and other control systems are displayed and can be manually controlled.

FIRE COMPARTMENT A space within a building enclosed by fire barriers on all sides, including the top and bottom.

FIRE DAMPER See Damper, Smoke.

FIRE DEPARTMENT CONNECTION A hose connection at grade or street level for use by the fire department for the purpose of supplying water to a building's standpipe and/or sprinkler system.

FIRE DETECTOR See Detector, Fire.

FIRE DOOR ASSEMBLY See Assembly, Fire Door.

FIRE EXIT HARDWARE Similar to panic hardware but additionally provides fire protection, since it is tested with and included as part of a fire door assembly.

FIRE EXTINGUISHING SYSTEM See Automatic Fire Extinguishing System.

FIRE LOAD See Fuel Load.

FIRE MODEL A structured approach using engineering analysis and quantitative assessments to predict one or more effects of a fire.

FIRE PARTITION See Partition, Fire. (See also Fire Wall.)

FIRE PROTECTION Refers to assemblies and opening protectives that have been chemically treated, covered, or protected so that they prevent or retard the spread of fire and smoke.

FIRE PROTECTION RATNG See Rating, Fire Protection.

FIRE PROTECTION SYSTEM Approved devices, equipment, and systems or combinations of systems which are intended to protect the life safety of the occupants and the structural integrity of the building in the event of a fire; includes fire and smoke detectors, fire alarms, and extinguishing systems.

FIRE RATING The time in minutes or hours that materials or assemblies have withstood a fire exposure as established by a standard testing procedure; includes fire resistance and fire protection ratings.

FIRE RESISTANCE RATING See Rating, Fire Resistant.

FIRE RESISTANT Refers to construction materials, assemblies, and textiles that prevent or retard the passage of excessive heat, hot gases, or flame.

FIRE RISK The probability that a fire will occur with the accompanying potential for harm to human life and property damage.

FIRESTOP An assembly or material used to prevent the spread of fire and smoke through openings in fire resistive assemblies.

FIRE SUPPRESSION SYSTEM See Fire Extinguishing System.

FIRE WALL A fire-rated wall having protected openings, which restricts the spread of fire and extends continuously from the foundation to or through the roof with sufficient structural stability under fire conditions to allow collapse of construction on either side without collapse of the wall.

FIRE WINDOW ASSEMBLY See Assembly, Fire Window.

FLAME RESISTANT Refers to finishes or furniture that prevent, terminate, or inhibit the spread of a flame upon application of a flame or nonflaming ignition source with or without removal of the ignition source.

FLAME RETARDANT A chemical or other treatment used to render a material flame resistant.

FLAME RETARDANT TREATMENT A process for incorporating or adding flame retardants to a finish or other material.

FLAME SPREAD The propagation of flame over a surface or the rate at which flame travels along the surface of a finish.

FLAMMABILITY The relative ease with which an item ignites and burns.

FLAMMABLE Capable of being ignited.

FLASHOVER A stage in the development of a contained fire in which all exposed surfaces reach ignition temperatures more or less simultaneously and fire spreads rapidly throughout the space.

FLOOR AREA The amount of floor surface included within the exterior walls. (See also Area, Net Floor and Area, Gross Floor.)

FLOOR FIRE DOOR ASSEMBLY See Assembly, Floor Fire Door.

FLUE A passageway within a chimney or vent through which gaseous combustion products pass.

FUEL LOAD Amount of combustible material present in a building or space that can feed a fire, such as combustible construction materials, paper, books, computers, and furniture.

FULL-SCALE TEST The simulation of an actual fire condition, such as for a full-size room or a full-size piece of furniture with all its contents.

FUSE A safety device that contains metal that will melt or break when the electrical current exceeds a specific value for a specific time period, causing the flow of electricity to stop.

FUSIBLE LINK A connecting link of a low-melting alloy that melts at a predetermined temperature, causing separation.

GLAZING The process of installing glass into frames; sometimes refers to the glass itself.

GRADE The average of finished ground level where it adjoins the building at the exterior wall.

GROUNDED As it relates to electrical work, connected to the earth or to some conducting body that serves in place of the earth.

GROUND FAULT CIRCUIT INTERRUPTER A device that detects small current leaks and disconnects the electrical power to the circuit or appliance should a current lead occur, for the protection of the user; often required in areas with water; commonly known as GFCI or GFI.

GUARD or **GUARDRAIL** A system of rails or other building components located near open sides of elevated walking surfaces that minimizes the possibility of a fall.

HABITABLE SPACE A room or enclosed space in a building used for living, sleeping, eating, or cooking but excluding bathrooms, toilet rooms, closets, halls, storage or utility spaces, and similar areas.

HANDICAPPED See Disabled.

HANDRAIL A horizontal or sloping rail intended for grasping by the hand for guidance or support.

HAZARDOUS MATERIAL A chemical or other substance that is a physical or health hazard, whether the material is in usable or waste condition; includes combustible or flammable materials, toxic, noxious or corrosive items, or heat-producing appliances. (See also Toxic Material.)

HEAT BARRIER A liner or backcoating used between upholstery and the filling underneath to prevent the spread of flame or smoldering heat.

HEAT DETECTOR See Detector, Heat.

HEIGHT, BUILDING The vertical distance from the grade plane to the average height of the highest roof surface.

HEIGHT, CEILING The clear vertical distance from finished floor to finished ceiling directly above.

HEIGHT, STORY The clear vertical distance from finished floor to the finished floor above or finished floor to the top of the joists supporting the roof structure above.

HIGH-RISE BUILDING A structure with a floor used for human occupancy exceeding 75 feet above the lowest level of access by a fire department vehicle.

HISTORIC BUILDING See Building, Historic.

HOISTWAY A vertical shaft for an elevator or dumbwaiter.

HOME RUN Refers to wiring that is continuous from a device directly back to a main electrical panel or communication equipment without any interruptions or intermediate connections.

HORIZONTAL EXIT See Exit, Horizontal.

HORIZONTAL PASSAGE Allows movement between rooms or areas on the same floor or story—for example, a door, archway, or cased opening.

INCIDENTAL USE An small area, space, or room that exists within another larger occupancy or building type that is considered more hazardous than the rest of the occupancy or building. (See also Occupancy, Accessory.)

INGRESS An entrance or the act of entering.

INITIATING DEVICE A component of the fire protection system that is the initial notification of fire, such as a smoke detector or a manual fire alarm box.

INSANITARY A condition which is contrary to sanitary principles or injurious to health.

INTERIOR FINISH Any exposed interior surface of a building, including finished ceilings, floors, walls, window treatments, and decorative trim, as well as other furniture and furnishings.

INTERIOR ROOM Any enclosed space or room within the exterior walls of a building.

JURISDICTION A legally constituted governmental unit, such as a state, city, or municipality, that adopts the same codes, standards, and regulations; often referred to by the codes as *Authority Having Jurisdiction*, or AHJ.

LABELED Refers to any equipment or building material and assemblies that include a label, seal, symbol, or other identification mark of a nationally recognized testing laboratory, inspection agency, or other organization acceptable to the jurisdiction concerned with product evaluation, which attests to the compliance with applicable nationally recognized standards. (See also Listed.)

LANDING, DOOR A level floor surface immediately adjacent to a doorway or threshold.

LANDING, INTERMEDIATE A level floor surface between two flights of stairs or ramps.

LIGHT-DIFFUSING SYSTEM When light-transmitting plastic is positioned below independently mounted electrical light sources (or natural light sources) to create a light feature, not including similar plastic lenses, panels, grids, or baffles used as part of the electrical or light fixture.

LIGHT FIXTURE A complete lighting unit consisting of at least one lamp (and ballast when applicable) and the parts required to distribute the light, to position and protect the lamp, and to connect the lamp to the power supply (with a ballast when required). Also referred to as a luminaire.

LIMITED COMBUSTIBLE Refers to material that is not considered noncombustible, yet that still has some fire-resistive qualities; a term used by the National Fire Protection Association.

LINTEL The member that is placed over an opening in a wall to support the wall construction above.

LISTED Refers to equipment or building materials and assemblies included in a list published by a nationally recognized testing laboratory, inspection agency, or other organization acceptable to the jurisdiction concerned with product evaluation which periodically tests the items to confirm they meet nationally recognized standards and/or have been found suitable to be used in a specified manner. (See also Labeled.)

LIVE LOAD Any dynamic weight within a building, including the people, furniture, and equipment, and not including dead load, earthquake load, snow load, or wind load. (See also Dead Load.)

LIVING AREA See Dwelling Unit.

LIVING SPACE A normally occupied space within a dwelling unit other than sleeping rooms utilized for things such as living, eating, cooking, bathing, washing, and sanitation purposes.

LOAD BEARING ELEMENT Any column, girder, beam, joist, truss, rafter, wall, floor, or roof that supports any vertical structural element in addition to its own weight; also known as a bearing element.

LOW-VOLTAGE LIGHTING Lighting equipment that is powered through a transformer such as cable conductor, rail conductor, or track lighting.

LUMINAIRE See Light Fixture.

MAIN The principal artery of any continuous piping or duct system to which branch pipes or ducts may be connected.

MAKEUP AIR Air that is provided to replace air being exhausted.

MANUAL FIRE ALARM A manual device used to signal a fire; usually used by an occupant.

MARK An identification applied to a product by a manufacturer indicating the name of the manufacturer and the function of the product or material. (See also Labeled.)

MASONRY The form of construction composed of stone, brick, concrete block, hollow clay tile, glass block, or other similar building units that are laid up unit by unit and set in mortar.

MEANS OF EGRESS A continuous and unobstructed way of exit travel, both horizontally and vertically, from any point in a building to a public way; it consists of the exit access, the exit, and the exit discharge.

MEANS OF EGRESS, ACCESSIBLE A continuous and unobstructed way of exit travel from any point in a building that provides an accessible route to an area of refuge, a horizontal exit, or a public way.

MEANS OF ESCAPE A way out of a building that does not conform to the strict definition of a means of egress but does provide an alternate way out.

MEMBRANE PENETRATION An opening created in a portion of a construction assembly that pierces only one side (or membrane) of the assembly.

MEZZANINE An intermediate floor level placed between a floor and the ceiling above in which the floor area is not more than one-third of the room in which it is located.

MOCK-UP, FURNITURE A full or partial representation of a finished piece of furniture that utilizes the same frame, filling, and upholstery as the finished piece.

NATURAL PATH OF TRAVEL The most direct route a person can take while following an imaginary line on the floor, avoiding obstacles such as walls, equipment, and furniture to arrive at the final destination.

NOMINAL DIMENSION Not the actual size, it is the commercial size by which an item is known. For example, the nominal size of a stud is 2×4 and the actual size is $1\frac{1}{2} \times 3\frac{1}{2}$ inches.

NONCOMBUSTIBLE Refers to material, such as building materials and finishes, that will not ignite, burn, support combustion, or release flammable vapors when subject to fire or heat.

NONLOAD-BEARING ELEMENT Any column, girder, beam, joist, truss, rafter, wall, floor, or roof that supports only its own weight; also known as a nonbearing element.

NONPOTABLE WATER Water that is not safe for drinking, cooking, or personal use.

NOSING The leading edge of the tread on a stair and of the landing within a stairwell.

NUISANCE ALARM An alarm indicating a problem with a building system due to mechanical failure, malfunction, improper installation, or lack of proper maintenance; an alarm activated by an unknown cause.

OCCUPANCY The use or intended use of a building, floor, or other part of a building.

OCCUPANCY, ACCESSORY An occupancy that exists with another occupancy in the same space or building but is much smaller than the main occupancy. (See also Incidental Use.)

OCCUPANCY, CHANGE IN USE A change in the purpose or level of activity within a building that involves a change in application of code requirements.

OCCUPANCY, MIXED A building or space that contains more than one occupancy; in some cases parts of the common egress paths are shared by the occupancies.

OCCUPANCY, MULTIPLE A more general term that includes any building used for two or more occupancy classifications.

OCCUPANCY, SEPARATED A multiple occupancy where the occupancies are separated by fire resistance-rated assemblies.

OCCUPANT The person or persons using a space, whether they are tenants, employees, customers, or other.

OCCUPANT CONTENT A term used by some of the older codes, it is the actual number of total occupants for which exiting has been provided. This is the maximum number of people that can occupy the space.

OCCUPANT LOAD Refers to the number of people or occupants for which the means of egress of a building or space is designed; total number of persons that may occupy a building or space at any one time.

OCCUPIABLE SPACE Refers to a room or enclosed space designed for human occupancy that is equipped with means of egress, light, and ventilation as required by the codes.

OPAQUE AREA Term used by energy codes to consist of all exposed areas of a building envelope which enclose conditioned space except openings for windows, skylights, doors, and building service systems. (See also Fenestration.)

OPENING PROTECTIVE Refers to a rated assembly placed in an opening in a rated wall assembly (such as a fire door or window) or rated ceiling assembly (such as a floor fire door) designed to maintain the fire resistance or the wall assembly.

OUTLET, FIXTURE An electrical box in which electrical wiring is connected to a light or the light switch; can also be called a lighting outlet.

OUTLET, RECEPTACLE An electrical box in which the electrical wiring allows the connection of a plug-in appliance or other equipment.

OWNER Any person, agent, firm, or corporation having a legal or equitable interest in the property.

PANIC HARDWARE A door latching assembly that has a device to release the latch when force is applied in the direction of exit travel. (See also Fire Exit Hardware.)

PARAPET The part of a wall entirely above the roof line of a building.

PARTITION A nonstructural interior space divider that can span horizontally or vertically, such as a wall or suspended ceiling.

PARTITION, FIRE A continuous fire-resistance-rated vertical assembly of materials designed to restrict the spread of fire, in which openings are protected; typically used to separate areas on the same floor of a building but not between floors; usually less restrictive than a fire barrier. (See also Barrier, Fire.)

PARTITION, PARTIAL A wall that does not extend fully to the ceiling and is usually limited by the codes to a maximum height of 72 inches (1830 mm).

PARTITION, SMOKE A continuous membrane that is designed to form a barrier to limit the transfer of smoke; usually less restrictive than a smoke barrier. (See also Barrier, Smoke.)

PASSAGEWAY An enclosed path or corridor.

PATH OF TRAVEL A continuous, unobstructed route that connects the primary area of a building with the entrance and other parts of the facility.

PENETRATION FIRE STOP A through-penetration fire stop or a membrane-penetration fire stop.

PERFORMANCE CODE See Code, Performance.

PERFORMANCE TEST The check of a component for conformity to a performance criteria or standard, performed during manufacturing, at the site during or after installation, or at a certified testing agency.

PERMANENT SEATING Any multiple seating that remains at a location for more than 90 days.

PERMIT An official document issued by the code jurisdiction (or AHJ) that authorizes performance of a specified activity.

PHYSICALLY DISABLED or **CHALLENGED** See Disabled.

PICTOGRAM As it relates to accessibility, a pictorial symbol that represents activities, facilities, or concepts.

PLAN REVIEW The review of construction documents by code official(s) to verify conformance to applicable prescriptive and performance code requirements.

PLASTIC See Thermoplastic and Thermoset Plastic.

PLATFORM The raised area within a building used for worship or the presentation of music, plays, or other entertainment; considered temporary if installed for not more than 30 days.

PLATFORM LIFT A type of elevator, typically used when a ramp is not possible, to transport people short vertical distances.

PLENUM SPACE A chamber that forms part of an air circulation system other than the occupied space being conditioned; includes the open space above the ceiling, below the floor, or in a vertical shaft.

PLUMBING CHASE An extra-thick wall consisting of studs with a space between them to create a wall cavity allowing for wide plumbing pipes.

PLUMBING FIXTURE Any receptacle, device, or appliance that is connected to a water distribution system to receive water and discharge water or waste.

POTABLE WATER Water that is satisfactory for drinking, cooking, and cleaning and that meets the requirements of the local health authority.

PRESCRIPTIVE CODE See Code, Prescriptive.

PROTECTED Refers to a building or structural element that has been covered (or protected) by a noncombustible material so that it obtains a fire resistance rating.

PUBLIC ENTRANCE See Entrance, Public.

PUBLIC USE See Use, Public.

PUBLIC WAY Any street, alley, or other parcel of land open to the outside air leading to a street, permanently appropriated to the public for public use, and having a clear and unobstructed width and height of no less than 10 feet (3048 mm).

RACEWAY An enclosed channel designed to hold wires and cables.

RADIANT HEAT The heat that is transmitted through an object to the other side.

RAMP A walking surface that has a continuous slope steeper than 1 in 20 (5 percent slope).

RAMP, CURB A short ramp cutting through a curb or built up to it; usually used on the exterior of a building.

RATING, FIRE PROTECTION The period of time a fire opening protective assembly (e.g., fire door, fire damper, etc.) will maintain the ability to confine a fire when exposed to a fire as determined by a test method.

RATING, FIRE RESISTANCE The period of time that a building element, component, or assembly (i.e., wall, floor, ceiling, etc.) will withstand exposure to fire in order to confine a fire or maintain its structural function as determined by a test method.

READILY ACHIEVEABLE A term used by the Americans with Disabilities Act (ADA) to indicate a change or modification that can be done without difficulty or large expense.

RECEPTACLE As it applies to electrical work, a contact device installed at the outlet for the connection of an attachment plug.

RECORD DRAWINGS Drawings that document the location of all devices, appliances, wiring, ducts, or other parts of various building systems; often referred to as *as-built* drawings.

REFLASH The reignition of a flammable item by a hot object after the flames have been extinguished.

REFRIGERANT A substance utilized to produce refrigeration by its expansion or vaporization.

REHABILITATION Any work undertaken to modify an existing building.

RENEWABLE ENERGY See Energy, Renewable.

REPAIR The reconstruction or renewal of any part of an existing building to good and sound condition for the purpose of its maintenance.

RESTRICTED ENTRANCE See Entrance, Restricted.

RETURN AIR The air removed from a conditioned space through openings, ducts, plenums, or concealed spaces to the heat exchanger of a heating, cooling, or ventilation system; either recirculated or exhausted.

RISER, PLUMBING A water pipe that runs vertically one full story or more within a building to supply water to branch pipes or fixtures.

RISER, STAIR The vertical portion of a stair system that connects each tread.

ROUGH-IN The installation of all parts of a system that can be completed before the installation of fixtures such as running pipes, ducts, conduit, cables, etc.

SALLY PORT See Security Vestibule.

SECURITY BOLLARD Any device used to prevent the removal of products and/or shopping carts from store premises.

SECURITY GRILLE A metal grating or a gate that slides open and closed, either vertically or horizontally, for security and protection.

SECURITY VESTIBULE An enclosed compartment with two or more doors where only one door is released at a time to prevent continuous passage for security reasons.

SEISMIC Refers to that which is a result of an earthquake.

SELF-CLOSING As applied to a fire door or other opening, equipped with an approved device (e.g., closer) that will ensure closing after having been opened. (See also Automatic Closing.)

SELF-LUMINOUS A fixture illuminated by a self-contained power source and operating independently of an external power source.

SERVICE ENTRANCE See Entrance, Service.

SEVERE MOBILITY IMPAIRMENT The ability to move to stairs without the ability to use the stairs.

SHAFT An enclosed vertical opening or space extending through one or more stories of a building connecting vertical openings in successive floors or floors and the roof. (See also Building Core.)

SIDE LIGHT A frame filled with glass or a solid panel that is attached to the side of a door frame.

SIGN or SIGNAGE A displayed element consisting of text or numbers or verbal, symbolic, tactile, and pictorial information.

SILL The horizontal member forming the base of a window or the foot of a door.

SITE A parcel of land bounded by a property line or a designated portion of a public right-of-way.

SMOKE ALARM An alarm that responds to smoke and is not connected to another system; can be a single-station or multiple-station alarm.

SMOKE BARRIER See Barrier, Smoke.

SMOKE COMPARTMENT A space within a building enclosed by smoke barriers on all sides, including the top and bottom.

SMOKE DAMPER See Damper, Smoke.

SMOKE DETECTOR See Detector, Smoke.

SMOKE PARTITION See Partition, Smoke.

SMOKEPROOF ENCLOSURE An exit consisting of a vestibule and/or continuous stairway that is fully enclosed and ventilated to limit the presence of smoke and/or other products of combustion during a fire.

SMOLDERING Combustion that occurs without a flame but that results in smoke, toxic gases, and heat, usually resulting in a charred area.

SOIL PIPE A pipe that carries sewage containing solids. (See also Drain Pipe.)

SOLAR ENERGY See Energy, Solar.

SPACE A definable area such as a room, corridor, entrance, assembly area, lobby, or alcove.

SPECIFICATIONS Written information that is a part of or an addition to construction drawings that logically communicate the requirements of the construction and installation as part of the overall construction documents.

SPRINKLERED Refers to an area or building that is equipped with an automatic sprinkler system.

SPRINKLER HEAD The part of a sprinkler system that controls the release of the water and breaks the water into a spray or mist.

STACK PIPE A vertical main that can be used as a soil, waste, or venting pipe.

STAIR A change in elevation, consisting of one or more risers.

STAIRWAY One or more flights of stairs with the required landings and platforms necessary to form a continuous and uninterrupted vertical passage from one level to another.

STANDPIPE SYSTEM A fixed, manual extinguishing system, including wet and dry systems, with outlets to allow water to be discharged through hose and nozzles for the purpose of extinguishing a fire.

STORY See Height, Story.

STORY, NUMBER OF Typically counted starting with the primary level of exit discharge and ending with the highest occupiable level.

STRUCTURAL ELEMENT Any building component such as columns, beams, joists, walls, and other framing members that are considered load bearing and are essential to the stability of the building or structure.

STRUCTURE See Building.

STRUCTURE ELEMENTS See Building Elements.

SUPPLY AIR The air delivered to a conditioned space through openings, ducts, plenums, or concealed spaces by the air distribution system, which is provided for ventilation, heating, cooling, humidification, dehumidification, and other similar purposes.

TACTILE Describes an object that can be perceived by the sense of touch.

TECHNICALLY INFEASIBLE A change or alteration to a building that has little likelihood of being accomplished due to existing structural conditions that would affect an essential load-bearing element or because other existing physical constraints prohibit modification or addition of items that are in full and strict compliance with applicable codes and/or accessibility requirements.

TELEPHONE BANK Two or more adjacent public telephones, often installed as one unit.

TENANT A person or group of people that uses or occupies a portion of a building through a lease and/or payment of rent.

TENANT SEPARATION A wall or floor/ceiling assembly between tenants.

TEXT TELEPHONE Similar to computers with modems, a type of keyboard input and visual display output that provides telephone communications for persons with hearing or speech impairments; also known as a TDD or TTY.

THERMOPLASTIC Plastic material that is capable of being repeatedly softened by heating and hardened by cooling and in the softened state can be repeatedly shaped for molding and forming.

THERMOSET PLASTIC Plastic material that after having been cured cannot be softened again.

THERMOSTAT An automatic control device triggered by temperature and designed to be responsive to temperature.

THROUGH-PENETRATION An opening created in a portion of a horizontal or vertical construction assembly that fully passes through both sides of the assembly.

THROUGH-PENETRATION PROTECTIVE A system or assembly installed in or around a through-penetration to resist the passage of flame, heat, and hot gases for a specified period of time; includes firestops, draftstops, and dampers.

TOILET FACILITY A room containing a water closet and usually a lavatory but not a bathtub, shower, spa, or similar bathing fixture. Also known as a single-toilet facility. A room with multiple waterclosets is known as a multiple-toilet facility.

TOWNHOUSE A single-family dwelling constructed in attached groups of three or more units in which each unit extends from foundation to roof and is open space on at least two sides.

TOXIC MATERIAL A material that produces a lethal dose or lethal concentration as defined by the codes and standards.

TRANSIENT LODGING Facilities other than medical care and long-term care facilities that provide sleeping accommodations.

TRANSOM An opening above a door that is filled with glass or solid material.

TRAP A fitting or device that creates a liquid seal at a plumbing fixture to prevent the passage of odors, gases, and insects back into the fixture.

TREAD, STAIR The horizontal portion of a stair system that connects each riser.

TRIM Picture molds, chair rails, baseboard, handrails, door and window frames, and similar decorative or protective materials used in fixed applications.

TURNSTILE A device used to control passage from one area to another, consisting of revolving arms projecting from a central post.

UNDUE HARDSHIP A term used by the Americans with Disabilities Act (ADA) to mean "significantly difficult or expensive"; also known as undue burden.

UNISEX TOILET FACILITY A single-toilet facility that is intended for use by both males and females.

UNPROTECTED Refers to materials in their natural state that have not been specially treated.

UNSANITARY See insanitary.

USE, COMMON As it refers to accessibility, the interior or exterior circulation paths, rooms, spaces, or elements that are not for public use but are instead made available for use by a restricted group of people.

USE GROUP or TYPE Sometimes referred to as building type, use group usually gets more specific and can be a subclassification within a building type. (See also Building Type.)

USE, PUBLIC Interior or exterior rooms, spaces, or elements that are made available to the general public.

VALVE A device used to start, stop, or regulate the flow of liquid or gas into piping, through piping, or from piping.

VARIANCE A grant of relief from certain requirements of the code which permits construction in a manner otherwise prohibited by the code where specific enforcement would require hardship.

VENEER A facing attached to a wall or other structural element for the purpose of providing ornamentation, protection, or insulation, but not for the purpose of adding strength to the element.

VENTILATION The process of supplying or removing conditioned or unconditioned air by natural or mechanical means to or from a space.

VENTILATION AIR The portion of supply air that comes from outside the building plus any recirculated air that has been treated to maintain the desired quality of air within a space.

VENT, MECHANICAL The part of the air distribution system that dispenses and collects the air in a space, including supply diffusers and return grilles.

VENT PIPE (also called a flue) A pipe that provides a flow of air to the drainage system and allows the discharge of harmful gases to prevent siphonage or backpressure.

VERTICAL OPENING An opening through a floor or roof.

VERTICAL PASSAGE Allows movement from floor to floor—for example, a stairway or an elevator.

WALL, CAVITY A wall, typically built of masonry or concrete, arranged to provide a continuous air space within the wall. (See also Plumbing Chase.)

WALL, DEMISING A wall that separates two tenant spaces in the same building, typically requiring a fire rating. (See also Tenant Separation.)

WALL, EXTERIOR A bearing or nonbearing wall that is used as an enclosing wall for a building other than a party wall or fire wall.

WALL, FIRE A fire-rated wall that extends continuously from the foundation of a building to or through the roof with sufficient structural stability to allow collapse of one side while leaving the other side intact, typically requiring a 3-hour to 4-hour fire rating.

WALL, PARAPET The part of any wall that extends above the roof line.

WALL, PARTY See Fire Wall.

WASTE The discharge from any plumbing fixture that does not contain solids.

WHEELCHAIR LIFT See Platform Lift.

WHEELCHAIR SPACE A space for a single wheelchair and its occupant. (See also Area of Refuge.)

WIRELESS SYSTEM A system or part of a system that can transmit and receive signals without the aid of a wire.

WORK AREA See Area, Work.

WORKSTATION An individual work area created by the arrangement of furniture and/or equipment for use by occupants or employees.

ZONE CABLING A ceiling distribution method for communication cables in which ceiling spaces are divided into sections or zones so that cables can be run to the center of each zone, allowing for flexible, changeable cabling of open office areas; also called zone distribution.

ZONE, FIRE A protected enclosure within a building created by rated walls or a contained fire suppression system that can be controlled separately from other areas of the same building.

ZONE, HVAC A space or group of spaces within a building with heating or cooling requirements that are similar and are regulated by one heating or cooling device/system.

INDEX